CANADIAN CRIMINAL JUSTICE

A PRIMER / SIXTH EDITION

CANADIAN CRIMINAL JUSTICE

A PRIMER / SIXTH EDITION

CURT T. GRIFFITHS
SIMON FRASER UNIVERSITY

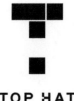

TOP HAT   **NELSON**

TOP HAT

Canadian Criminal Justice, Sixth Edition
by Curt T. Griffiths

VP, Product Solutions:
Claudine O'Donnell

Publisher, Digital and Print Content:
Leanna MacLean

Marketing Manager:
Claire Varley

Content Manager:
Suzanne Simpson Millar

Photo and Permissions Researcher:
Jessie Coffey

Senior Production Project Manager:
Imoinda Romain

Production Service:
Manoj Kumar, MPS Limited

Copy Editor:
Michael Kelly

Proofreader:
MPS Limited

Indexer:
MPS Limited

Design Director:
Ken Phipps

Higher Education Design Project Manager:
Pamela Johnston

Interior Design Modifications:
Ken Cadinouche

Cover Design:
deboraH brock

Cover Image:
The Good People Series, "Mid Summer Night Gathering," figurative palette knife painting. © G.O.D. Laurie Justus Pace. Graphics One Design, 2014

Compositor:
MPS Limited

Library and Archives Canada Cataloguing in Publication

Griffiths, Curt T. (Curt Taylor), 1948–, author
   Canadian criminal justice: a primer/Curt T. Griffiths,

Simon Fraser University.—Sixth edition.

First edition written by Alison J. Cunningham. Includes bibliographical references and index. Issued in print and electronic formats.
ISBN 978-0-17-672440-5 (softcover).—ISBN 978-0-17-685383-9 (PDF)

   1. Criminal justice, Administration of—Canada—Textbooks.
2. Textbooks. I. Cunningham, Alison J., 1959– . Canadian criminal.
II. Title.

HV9960.C2G75 2018   364.971
C2018-900512-2
C2018-900513-0

ISBN-13: 978-0-17-672440-5
ISBN-10: 0-17-672440-0

To Sandra, my partner on the journey of radical amazement,

and

to the Bradys and their adventures,
past, present, and future.

About the **Author**

Curt Taylor Griffiths (Ph.D., Sociology, University of Montana) is a Professor in the School of Criminology and Coordinator of the Police Studies Program at Simon Fraser University in Vancouver. Among his primary areas of teaching and research are policing, corrections, comparative criminal justice, legal reform and capacity-building, enhancing the effectiveness of international development initiatives, and the dynamics of community justice.

Professor Griffiths has been a Visiting Expert at the United Nations Far East Institute for the Prevention of Crime and Treatment of Offenders (UNAFEI), Tokyo, Japan, and a Visiting Fellow at the American University in Cairo and at Tokiwa University, Mito, Ibaraki, Japan. He has conducted research and evaluations and worked with justice agencies and community organizations in a variety of jurisdictions, including Egypt, Japan, Dominica, the Netherlands, and Latvia, as well as in the remote Canadian north.

Professor Griffiths is the author or co-author of more than 100 research reports and articles and of several college/university-level texts, including *Canadian Criminal Justice: A Primer, Canadian Police Work,* and *Canadian Corrections* (with Danielle Murdoch). He is a member of the editorial boards of *The International Review of Victimology, International Criminal Justice Review,* and *Police Practice and Research: An International Journal.*

Courtesy of Sandra Snow

Brief **Contents**

Table of **Contents**

Preface

THE GOAL OF THIS TEXT

The Canadian criminal justice system is a complex, dynamic, and ever-changing enterprise. How the various components of the system operate and the extent to which they succeed in preventing and responding to crime and criminal offenders affect not only the general public but also criminal justice personnel and offenders. This edition of *Canadian Criminal Justice: A Primer*, Sixth Edition, is designed with the same basic objectives as the previous editions: to present in a clear and concise fashion materials on the criminal justice system in Canada and to highlight the key issues surrounding this country's responses to crime and offenders. This book is not an exhaustive examination of all facets of the criminal justice process. Rather, its intent is to present, with broad brush strokes, information on the structure and operations of the criminal justice system, at the same time identifying some of the more significant challenges and controversies that arise at each stage of the justice process.

ORGANIZATION OF THE TEXT

This edition of the text is organized into six parts. Part I is designed to set the framework for the study of Canadian criminal justice. Chapter 1 sets out the foundations of the criminal justice system, Chapter 2 highlights key features of the dynamics of the criminal justice process, and Chapter 3 discusses inequality, racism and discrimination, and the lived experiences of Indigenous peoples, racialized groups, and persons in visible/cultural/religious minorities as a backdrop for the study of Canadian criminal justice.

Part II contains three chapters that focus on various dimensions of Canadian policing. Chapter 4 discusses the structure and roles of the police; Chapter 5 examines police powers and decision-making; and Chapter 6 considers police strategies, operations, and engagement.

Part III presents materials on the criminal courts. Chapter 7 examines the structure and operation of the criminal courts; Chapter 8 looks at the prosecution of criminal cases; and Chapter 9 discusses sentencing in the criminal courts.

Part IV contains three chapters that focus on Canadian corrections. Chapter 10 discusses correctional alternatives to confinement; Chapter 11 reviews correctional institutions; and Chapter 12 examines the release, re-entry, and reintegration of offenders into the community.

Part V contains Chapter 13, which examines the youth justice system.

Part VI is titled "Reconsidering Criminal Justice," and in Chapter 14, the final chapter of the text, the challenges to and opportunities for criminal justice reform are discussed.

Part Openers provide a concise introduction for students and highlight key trends in the criminal justice system that will be discussed in the chapters following.

Learning Objectives are set out at the beginning of each chapter. They identify the purpose of the materials that are presented and serve to orient the reader to the chapter.

Tables, graphs, charts, and photographs are interspersed throughout the book, and provide visual representations of data, current events, or key people and places in the criminal justice system.

A running glossary proceeds throughout the text, with key terms defined in the margins, for easy retrieval from students.

Each chapter ends with a **Summary**, to help students reflect on what they have just learned. **Key Points Review** and **Key Term Questions** have been retained and updated from the fifth edition, to test knowledge of specific topics.

New to the Sixth Edition, **Critical Thinking** and **Class/Group Discussion Exercises** at the end of the chapter further engage the student in considering and discussing critical issues in the justice system. Many of the exercises centre on actual cases and events.

Lastly, **Media Links** have been carefully selected to provide students with access to persons who are involved in some way with the criminal justice system, as well as to provide a more in-depth examination of issues that were raised in the chapter.

CHANGES TO THE SIXTH EDITION

In addition to updating legislation, inserting new court rulings, and including new materials on all facets of the justice system, there are a number of significant changes in this edition. These include the following:

FEATURE BOXES

There are several formats that are used to present materials and to engage the student reader. The **Perspective** feature provides first-hand accounts that capture the dynamics of the criminal justice system; boxes strategically placed throughout the chapters highlight case studies, innovative programs, and important court decisions. **At Issue** boxes are centred on topics that are the subject of debate, and challenge students to consider various perspectives and to answer questions that will assist them in formulating their thoughts on the topic. **Research File** boxes appear throughout the book, and summarize the research literature on criminal justice policies and programs. And general boxes (no title) provide stories generally in the news or engaging for students, and delve into a topic more deeply.

FILE BOXES

In each chapter, there are a number of file boxes that are designed to highlight important events, research studies, and cases. **Police File** boxes appear in Part II; **Court File** boxes are included in Part III; **Legal File** boxes are included in Parts II and III; **Criminal Justice Files** appear in Part I; **Corrections Files** in Part IV; and **Youth Justice Files** in Part IV.

NOTABLE CHAPTER-SPECIFIC CHANGES

Chapter 1: This chapter has been re-written and examines how crimes are "created," Canadian law, the Canadian legal system, and the criminal law in a diverse society. A new section in Chapter 1, "Thinking Critically about the Criminal Justice System," provides students with suggestions on how to be a critical thinker and how to consider the materials presented in the text.

Chapter 2: This chapter introduces students to the purpose of the criminal justice system, and the role and responsibilities of governments in the administration of justice. The competing models of criminal administration are discussed, as are the flow of cases through the system and several of the features of the criminal justice process. Restorative justice is introduced, and it is noted that this alternative approach to justice will be considered throughout the text, rather than having its own dedicated chapter as in the previous edition.

Chapter 3: This is a new chapter that focuses on considerations in the study of criminal justice. It includes a discussion of the issues surrounding racism, discrimination, and inequality, and the experiences of Indigenous and racialized persons and members of visible/cultural/religious minority groups in Canada. The chapter is designed to provide the reader with exposure to the lived experiences of persons who may be subjected to racism and discrimination, which, in turn, will contribute to an understanding of issues such as racial profiling and biased policing and the overrepresentation of Indigenous persons and Blacks in the criminal justice system. The issues of racism and discrimination are key themes in the text.

Additional considerations in the study of criminal justice are also presented in this chapter, again to provide background context for the materials presented in subsequent chapters.

Chapter 13: This is another new chapter in the text, and it examines the youth justice system. Many adults who come into conflict with the law first became involved in the youth justice system. This fact compels an understanding of the approach to youth in conflict, the legislation and programs designed to address their issues, and their experiences in the youth justice system, both under supervision in the community and in youth correctional facilities.

INSTRUCTOR RESOURCES

The **Nelson Education Teaching Advantage (NETA)** program delivers research-based instructor resources that promote student engagement and higher-order thinking to enable the success of Canadian students and educators.

The following instructor resources have been created for *Canadian Criminal Justice: A Primer*, Sixth Edition. Access these ultimate tools for customizing lectures and presentations at retail.tophat.com.

NETA TEST BANK

This resource includes more than 350 multiple-choice questions written according to NETA guidelines for effective construction and development of higher-order questions. Also included are more than 250 true/false questions, 150 short-answer questions, and 140 essay questions.

NETA POWERPOINT

Microsoft® PowerPoint® lecture slides have been created for every chapter. There is an average of 25 slides per chapter, many featuring key figures, tables, and photographs from *Canadian Criminal Justice: A Primer*, Sixth Edition. NETA principles of clear design and engaging content have been incorporated throughout, making it simple for instructors to customize the deck for their courses.

IMAGE LIBRARY

This resource consists of digital copies of figures, tables, and photographs used in the book. Instructors may use these jpegs to customize the NETA PowerPoint or create their own PowerPoint presentations. An Image Library Key describes the images and lists the codes under which the jpegs are saved. Codes normally reflect the chapter number (e.g., C01 for Chapter 1), the figure or photo number (e.g., F15 for Figure 15), and the page in the textbook. For example, C01-F15-pg26 would correspond to Figure 1-15 on page 26.

NETA INSTRUCTOR'S MANUAL

This resource is organized according to the textbook chapters and addresses key educational concerns, such as typical stumbling blocks student face and how to address them. Other features include common student misconceptions, in-class activities, online activities, suggested answers to questions in the text, and links to video clips with questions for discussion or homework submission.

STUDENT ANCILLARIES

Bring course concepts to life with interactive learning and exam preparation tools that integrate with the printed textbook. Students activate their knowledge using engaging online resources. Visit retail.tophat.com for access.

A Unique Learning **FRAMEWORK**

Part Openers provide a concise introduction for students and highlight key trends in the criminal justice system that will be discussed in the chapters following.

Learning Objectives identify the purpose of the materials that are presented and serve to orient the reader to the chapter.

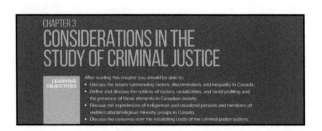

Perspective boxes provide first-hand accounts that capture the dynamics of the criminal justice system.

PERSPECTIVE

A Physician's Perspective on the Burdens and Ethics of Assisted Death

If you ask the public, what you're really asking them is, "Do you want to have a right to access these interventions if you come to the end of your life and you're suffering?" That's a very different question than if you ask a medical professional, "Do you want to kill your patients? Or do you want to assist in the death of your patients?" One is a right, the other is an obligation. Those are intricately related. If someone in society has a right to something, it means someone else has an obligation to provide that. So basically the Supreme Court that has told Canadian physicians, after

AT ISSUE 7.1

SHOULD THERE BE INDEPENDENT OVERSIGHT OF THE JUDICIARY?

Earlier in this book, it has been noted that the police are the only criminal justice agency that is subjected to outside civilian oversight. The legal profession, including the judiciary, is self-regulated; that is, the only structures of accountability exist within the legal profession. Concerns have been raised about the ability of provincial and territorial law societies to both represent and regulate the profession and the effectiveness of the Canadian Judicial Council as oversight bodies.[a] As well, it is noted that most complaints that are made to the Canadian Judicial Council are not made public but rather are kept private between the complainant,

not subject to the direction or control of the executive branch of government."[c]

A review of the record indicates that few complaints ultimately result in the removal of a judge from the bench. As well, since the disciplinary procedure was established in 1971, there have been very few public inquiries by the council into the behaviour of a federal judge. Most complaints (which average less than 200 per year) are handled by the chairperson of the council and are not publicized but kept between the complainant, the judge, and the CJC. It might be argued that this practice limits the transparency of the council's work.

At Issue boxes challenge students to consider the various perspectives of a topic and answer questions that will assist them in formulating their thoughts on the topic.

General boxes provide stories generally in the news or engaging for students, and delve into a topic more deeply.

BOX 1.1

THE FUNCTIONS OF THE CRIMINAL LAW

In Canadian society, the criminal law provides the following functions:

- acts as a mechanism of social control
- maintains order
- defines the parameters of acceptable behaviour
- reduces the risk of personal retaliation (vigilantism, or people taking the law into their own hands)

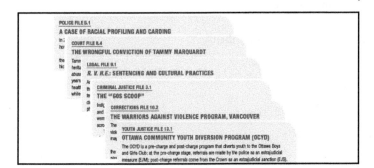

POLICE FILE 6.1
A CASE OF RACIAL PROFILING AND CARDING

COURT FILE 8.4
THE WRONGFUL CONVICTION OF TAMMY MARQUARDT

LEGAL FILE 9.1
R. V. H.E.: SENTENCING AND CULTURAL PRACTICES

CRIMINAL JUSTICE FILE 3.1
THE "60S SCOOP"

CORRECTIONS FILE 10.2
THE WARRIORS AGAINST VIOLENCE PROGRAM, VANCOUVER

YOUTH JUSTICE FILE 13.1
OTTAWA COMMUNITY YOUTH DIVERSION PROGRAM (OCYD)

The OCYD is a pre-charge and post-charge program that diverts youth to the Ottawa Boys and Girls Club: at the pre-charge stage, referrals are made by the police as an extrajudicial measure (EJM); post-charge referrals come from the Crown as an extrajudicial sanction (EJS).

File boxes highlight important events, research studies, and cases. Police File boxes appear in Part II; Court File boxes are included in Part III; Legal File boxes are included in Parts II and III; Criminal Justice Files appear in Part I; Corrections Files in Part IV; and Youth Justice Files in Part IV.

RESEARCH FILE 13.1
A PROFILE OF INDIGENOUS YOUNG WOMEN IN CUSTODY

A study ($N = 500$) of youth in custody in British Columbia found that, among the Indigenous young women

- 97 percent had left home early to live on their own, on the streets, or in foster care;
- 82 percent had been in foster care at some point;
- 80 percent reported childhood trauma, including physical abuse (80 percent), sexual abuse (65 percent), and mental health issues in the family (30 percent);
- 80 percent had been introduced to hard drug use at an early age; and
- Compared to non-Indigenous young women in custody, had spent more time in their lives in custody.

Research File boxes appear throughout the book, and summarize the research literature on criminal justice policies and programs.

SUMMARY

This chapter was designed to provide background context to the study of the Canadian criminal justice system. Inequality, racism, prejudice, and discrimination were introduced as features of Canadian society. These are often manifested in racial profiling and the racialization of groups and individuals. Women, Indigenous persons, Muslims, and sexual minorities have lived experiences that affect their quality of life and may place them at risk of being victimized or of coming into conflict with the law.

Summaries encourage students to reflect on what they have just learned.

CRITICAL THINKING EXERCISE

Critical Thinking Exercise 3.1

Indigenous Experiences

The study of the involvement of Indigenous persons in the criminal justice system requires an understanding of their historical and contemporary circumstances. Watch the film *We Will Be Free* at

CLASS/GROUP DISCUSSION EXERCISE

Class/Group Discussion 3.1

The "Colonized Mind" of Indigenous Persons

Jana-Rae Yerxa is Anishinaabe from Little Eagle and Couchiching First Nation and belongs to the Sturgeon clan. She uses the concept of the "colonized mind" of Indigenous persons to explain the experiences of Indigenous peoples and their perspectives and perceptions.

Critical Thinking Exercises and Class/ Group Discussion Exercises at the end of the chapter further engage the student in considering and discussing critical issues in the justice system. Many of the exercises focus on actual cases and events.

MEDIA LINKS

"Warriors Against Violence," *CBC News*, July 6, 2015, http://www.cbc.ca/news/indigenous/warriors-against-violence-tries-to-heal-aboriginal-men-1.3136168

"Who's Watching? 4,500 Outstanding Warrants for Alleged Probation and Conditional Sentence Violations in Ontario," *Global News*, May 10, 2017. Follow the links in this article for a several part media series on probation in Ontario, http://globalnews.ca/news/3430313/4500-outstanding-warrants-for-alleged-probation-and-conditional-sentence-violations-in-ontario.

"Who's Watching? Ontario's Probation System 'a Joke,' Say Offenders" (Part 1), *Global*

Media Links have been carefully selected to provide students with access to persons who are involved in some way with the criminal justice system, as well as to provide a more in-depth examination of issues that were raised in the chapter.

Acknowledgements

I would like to acknowledge the many people throughout the criminal justice system who have contributed to the ideas and information that have been incorporated into this book. My love and thanks to my life partner, Sandra Snow, for her unwavering support and encouragement.

I would also like to thank the reviewers of the previous edition of the text for their invaluable comments, criticisms, and suggestions:

Stephen Schneider, Saint Mary's University

Eva Wilmot, Camosun College

Nathan Innocente, University of Toronto at Mississauga

Cat Baron, Algonquin College

Vicki Ryckman, Loyalist College

As always, it has been a pleasure to work with the professionals at Nelson: Leanna MacLean, Suzanne Simpson Millar, and Imoinda Romain.

A Note to **Instructors**

SEMI-ANNUAL UPDATES

The dynamic nature of the Canadian criminal justice system presents challenges in ensuring that the materials in the text are accurate and up-to-date. Throughout the system, there are high-profile issues being debated, court decisions that are impacting every facet of the system, and a veritable explosion of criminal justice research. With editions of the text on a four-year publication cycle, the materials can become dated, often by the time the print dries on a new edition.

To address this, updates for each of the chapters will be provided to course instructors semi-annually—in the spring and fall of each calendar year. The updates will include significant legal cases and impactful court rulings, new research findings, and major changes in legislation, policy, and operations of the various components of the justice system. New Critical Thinking Exercises and Class/Group Discussion Exercises will also be provided to accompany the new materials.

These updates will be designed to provide instructors and students with current materials that will enhance the study of the Canadian criminal justice system. The first update will be available in spring 2019.

As always, I encourage feedback on the book generally and on any specific materials in it, errors of fact, and omissions. Feel free to contact me at griffith@sfu.ca with any comments, questions, or suggestions for future editions of the book.

Thanks.
Curt Taylor Griffiths, Ph.D.
Vancouver, British Columbia
April 2018

© Laurie Justus Pace. Graphics One Design, 2014

PART I

CANADIAN CRIMINAL JUSTICE:
SETTING THE FRAMEWORK

Chapter 1: The Foundations of Criminal Justice
Chapter 2: Understanding the Criminal Justice System
Chapter 3: Considerations in the Study of Criminal Justice

- A 10-year-old girl disappeared while walking home from a friend's house in Toronto in 2013. Her body parts were later found in bags floating in Lake Ontario. Police canvassed about 300 homes in her neighbourhood and asked men to provide DNA. One man who refused was arrested and subsequently convicted. He later pleaded guilty to first-degree murder. **At Issue:** To what extent, if any, should the police be allowed to conduct a "DNA sweep" (or "blooding") in order to attempt to solve a crime? (see Chapter 5).
- In 2012, N.S., a Muslim woman living in Ontario, wanted to wear her niqab (full face veil revealing only the eyes) while testifying in a preliminary hearing involving charges against her uncle and cousin for sexual assault. **At issue:** Should a Muslim woman who wears a niqab be permitted by the judge to testify in court against her alleged perpetrator? (see Chapter 8).
- In April 2013, a 16-year-old boy shot his 15-year-old cousin with a hunting rifle at a playground, paralyzing him. Both boys were African Nova Scotians. The boy was subsequently found guilty of attempted murder. **At Issue:** Should cultural assessments play a role in the sentencing of young offenders? (see Chapter 13).

These cases all occurred in the past few years and provide a snapshot of the dynamic nature of the criminal justice system and the complex issues that surround its operation. The three chapters in this part are designed to set the framework for the study of the Canadian criminal justice system. Chapter 1 sets out the foundation of the legal system and discusses the origins and application of the criminal law. It is noted that who and what are defined as criminal is ever-changing and that, in a democratic society, tensions often exist between the criminal law and the rights of individuals. Chapter 2 provides information to understand the criminal justice system, including its purpose, the competing models of criminal justice administration, the flow of cases through the system, and a discussion of the effectiveness of the system.

The materials in Chapter 3 are presented to provide a backdrop for the study of Canadian criminal justice. There is a discussion of inequality, racism and discrimination, and the lived experiences of Indigenous peoples, racialized groups, and persons in visible/cultural/religious minorities. A number of additional issues that surround the criminal justice system are also identified and discussed.

© Laurie Justus Pace, Graphics One Design, 2014

CHAPTER 1
THE FOUNDATIONS OF CRIMINAL JUSTICE

After reading this chapter, you should be able to

- Describe what is meant by *critical thinking*.
- Define *crime* and discuss how crime is constructed.
- Discuss the differing perspectives on the origins and application of the criminal law.
- Identify the types of Canadian law and the functions of the criminal law.
- Discuss the key principles of Canadian law.
- Describe the origins and importance of the rule of law.
- Discuss the importance of the *Canadian Charter of Rights and Freedoms*.
- Describe the main provisions of the *Canadian Charter of Rights and Freedoms*.
- Discuss the Canadian *Criminal Code*.
- Discuss the issues surrounding the application of criminal law in a diverse society.

The criminal justice system is an integral, and high-profile, component of Canadian society. It is also very dynamic, often controversial, and either very effective in achieving "justice" or not, depending upon one's perspective and experience. The controversies that surround the criminal justice system, such as whether certain groups or individuals are treated differently than others, are often a reflection of issues in the larger Canadian society. And, as in Canadian society, politics often plays a role in defining what behaviour is a crime and what the response will be.

On a daily basis, there is a continual stream of events, persons, and issues related to criminal justice, as well as ongoing debates as to whether the justice system is fair; provides "justice" for victims, offenders, and communities; and is capable of addressing its challenges.

The major components of the criminal justice system are the police, the courts, and corrections. However, the victims of crime, offenders, and the community are also important considerations and will be discussed throughout the following chapters. All of these groups have a stake in the criminal justice process and may be impacted by the events and decisions that occur during it. Certain groups of offenders, including Indigenous and racialized persons and others, may face particular challenges. This text is designed to stimulate a research-informed discussion that also includes the "voices" of persons in conflict with the law, crime victims, and justice system personnel.

THINKING CRITICALLY ABOUT THE CRIMINAL JUSTICE SYSTEM

The criminal justice system is a complex enterprise and there are often no "right" or "wrong" answers to the issues that arise. Rather, there are different perspectives on the justice system, its operation, and what action is required to address the issues that are identified. Assuming the role of a *critical thinker* will be very beneficial in reading and reflecting on the materials.

WHAT IS CRITICAL THINKING?

It has been said, "Critical thinkers distinguish between fact and opinion; ask questions; make detailed observations; uncover assumptions and define their terms; and make assertions based on sound logic and sound evidence." Call it "healthy skepticism." A critical thinker considers multiple points of view and is fair and open-minded to all ideas. Conclusions are reached based on a thoughtful consideration of the issues. **Critical thinking** has also been called *thorough thinking*.[1]

To become a critical thinker, one must engage in the following:

- Ask questions: Engage curiosity and question statements and assertions.
- Consider multiple points of view: Be fair and open-minded to all ideas.
- Draw conclusions: Examine the outcome of your inquiry in a more demanding and critical way.

In reading and thinking about the materials in this text, it is important to maintain a "critical eye"—that is, to be a critical thinker and to ask the questions that critical thinkers ask. The At Issue boxes that are embedded in the chapters of this book and the Critical Thinking Exercises at the end of each chapter are designed to stimulate you and your fellow students' thinking about critical issues in criminal justice, to help you consider various perspectives on these issues, and to assist you in reaching your own conclusions.

Critical thinking (thorough thinking)

In examining an issue, distinguishing between fact and opinion, considering multiple points of view, and being open-minded to all ideas.

The physician's comments on assisted death in the nearby Perspective box highlight that there are often issues of ethics that arise in the law.

WHAT IS A CRIME AND WHY?

The obvious answer to this question is, "a crime is whatever is against the law." However, it's much more complex than this. Beyond the very serious traditional types of crime, such as murder, what is or is not a crime is not set in stone but has changed over the course of Canadian history.

WHAT IS A CRIME?

Needless to say, without crime there would be no criminal justice system. A **crime** is generally defined as an act or omission that is prohibited by criminal law. Every jurisdiction sets out a limited series of acts (crimes) that are prohibited and punishes the commission of these acts by a fine or imprisonment or some other type of sanction. In exceptional cases, an omission to act can constitute a crime—for example, failing to give assistance to a person in peril or failing to report a case of child abuse.

Two critical ingredients of a crime are the commission of an act (*actus reus*) and the mental intent to commit the act (*mens rea*). A crime occurs when a person

- commits an act or fails to commit an act when under a legal responsibility to do so;
- has the intent, or *mens rea*, to commit the act;
- does not have a legal defence or justification for committing the act; *and*
- violates a provision in criminal law.

Crime

An act or omission that is prohibited by criminal law.

THE SOCIAL CONSTRUCTION OF CRIME

Have you ever thought about why, up until 2018, marijuana use (except for medicinal purposes) was illegal, but drinking alcohol has been legal for decades? And why only marijuana but not cocaine? To say the least, there is not always agreement about what should be against the law. Murder? Yes. Impaired driving? Yes. Bank robbery? Sure. Assisted suicide? Somewhat more contentious, even though it is legal (see At Issue 1.1).

It is also important to distinguish between behaviours that may be considered *deviant* by a large portion of society, and crimes. While crime is behaviour that breaks the law, deviance is behaviour that is contrary to the norms and values of the larger society. Dressing Goth is not against the law, but may be viewed as deviant by the average passer-by as may be cross-dressing. Deviance includes criminal behaviour and

---

AT ISSUE 1.1

MEDICAL ASSISTANCE IN DYING:[a] THE TENSION BETWEEN THE LAW, RELIGION, AND PROFESSIONAL PRACTICE

In 2015, in the case of *Carter v. Canada (Attorney General)* (2015 SCC 5), the SCC ruled that section 14 and paragraph 241(b) of the *Criminal Code* were unconstitutional because they prohibited physicians from assisting in the consensual death of another person. In June 2016, Bill C-14, *An Act to amend the Criminal Code and to make related amendments to other Acts (medical assistance in dying)*, received Royal Assent and made assisted dying legal for terminally ill patients. The provinces and territories were responsible for developing the appropriate procedures for medically assisted death.

Medically assisted death continues to be surrounded by controversy. Proponents argue that the new provisions give the control over life to patients where it belongs and that patients should be able to end their pain and suffering. A survey of Canadians (*N* = 2,271) in 2016 found that nearly 72 percent of respondents were strongly in support of physician-assisted death, and 74 percent supported allowing persons to request suicide before they became too ill to do so.[b]

Opponents, which include physicians, have argued that assisted dying violates their oath to care for patients.[c] The Christian Medical and Dental Society of Canada initiated court proceedings against the College of Physicians and Surgeons of Ontario, arguing that the policy which states that physicians who are opposed to medically assisted death on moral, religious, or other grounds must refer the patient to another physician who will carry out the practice, makes them ethically responsible for the patient's death. This puts physicians who opposed medically assisted death in the position of being between their legal responsibilities and their rights under the Charter. Physicians who do not refer could be disciplined by the College of Physicians and Surgeons.

On the other hand, the BC Civil Liberties Association challenged the constitutionality of the law because it excludes people with long-term disabilities, and those with "curable" medical conditions whose only treatment options are those that some people may find unacceptable.

Given the various perspectives on the practice, the debate over assisted death is likely to continue.

QUESTIONS

1. How does one balance the legal and ethical issues surrounding assisted dying?

2. In your view, should this be a legal issue?

3. Should all physicians be required to abide by the law?

4. What position would you take regarding the refusal of some physicians to assist a patient in dying or refusing to refer a patient to another physician who would assist the patient to die?

5. What does this issue illustrate about the interplay between the law, religious views, and professional ethics?

---

[a] Medical assistance in dying in Canada includes both assisted suicide and voluntary euthanasia. Assisted suicide is the act of intentionally killing oneself with the assistance of another who provides the knowledge, means, or both (Health Law Institute, Dalhousie University, n.d.). In cases of assisted suicide, a physician provides drugs to a terminally ill patient who then takes the drug to end his or her life. In cases of euthanasia, a physician administers a lethal drug to relieve suffering, which ends the person's life.

[b] A. Csanady. 2016, June 10. "Strong Majority of Canadians Want Assisted Suicide Bill to Allow for 'Advance Consent': Poll," *National Post.* http://nationalpost.com/news/politics/strong-majority-of-canadians-want-assisted-suicide-bill-to-allow-for-advanced-consent-poll/wcm/edc245f6-68ce-40f0-9ca7-a96da827bff6.

[c] A. Jerome. 2017, April 7. "Physicians Opposed to Assisted Dying Say Their Charter Rights Are Being Violated," *The Lawyer's Daily.* https://www.thelawyersdaily.ca/articles/2856/physicians-opposed-to-assisted-dying-say-their-charter-rights-are-being-violated.

Additional sources: Department of Justice Canada. 2016. "Medically Assisted Dying: Supreme Court of Canada Ruling." http://www.justice.gc.ca/eng/cj-jp/ad-am/scc-csc.html; R. Gallagher. 2016. "Physician-Assisted Suicide and Euthanasia: The Issues," *Canadian Virtual Hospice.* http://www.virtualhospice.ca/en_US/Main + Site + Navigation/Home/Topics/Topics/Decisions/Physician_Assisted + Suicide + and + Euthanasia_ + The + Issues.aspx; S. Fine. 2016, June 22. "Christian Doctors Challenge Ontario's Assisted-Death Referral Requirement," *Globe and Mail.* https://www.theglobeandmail.com/news/national/christian-doctors-challenge-ontarios-assisted-death-referral-policy/article30552327; Health Law Institute, Dalhousie University. n.d. "Assisted Suicide." http://eol.law.dal.ca/?page_id=236.

a wide range of other behaviours that are not against the law, but may be frowned upon by the larger society. What is viewed as deviant changes over time: until recent years, tattoos and piercings would have been considered as deviant, but today are not generally viewed as unusual.

The criminal law is not static, however, and, almost overnight, legislative enactments or judicial decisions can render behaviours that were previously illegal merely deviant. In 2013, for example, the Supreme Court of Canada (SCC) struck down Canada's prostitution laws as unconstitutional (*Canada (Attorney General) v. Bedford*, 2013 SCC 72).

A key concept that assists in understanding what is, or is not, a crime is the **social construction of crime**. This is the process by which the "same behaviour may be considered criminal in one society and an act of honour in another society or in the same society at a different time."[2] Whether a behaviour is defined as a "crime" is not a consequence of the behaviour itself, but is the result of the *social response* to the behaviour or to the persons or groups who are engaged in it.[3]

Criminologists often conduct historical analyses in an attempt to understand (1) the factors involved in the definition of behaviours as criminal, (2) an increase or decrease in the severity of the criminal law, (3) the response of the criminal justice system, and (4) the factors that influenced the repeal of a criminal law, resulting in the decriminalization of certain behaviours. The Canadian criminologist Neil Boyd has pointed out, "Law can be fully comprehended only by documenting and analyzing the social, political, and economic contexts that give it life and continue to influence its existence."[4]

Researchers have conducted historical studies of criminal law reform in an attempt to understand how the social, economic, and political environment may influence legislation. For example, laws against opium use first passed in the early 1900s have been linked to anti-Asian prejudice among Euro-Canadians of the day. Similarly, a review of how marijuana came to be illegal in Canada reveals the prominent role of one Emily Murphy, an Alberta magistrate who was also an anti-drug crusader. Writing under the pen name of Janey Canuck, she wrote a series of articles that were later made into a book titled *The Black Candle*. In the book, Murphy "raged against 'Negro' drug dealers and Chinese opium peddlers 'of fishy blood' out to control and debase the white race."[5]

The shifts in the definition of behaviours as illegal or deviant provide fascinating insights into the dynamic nature of criminal law and the behaviours that are defined as criminal. There may be, for example, massive violation of the criminal law, and yet the behaviour of the individuals involved may not be viewed as criminal.

A historical example is the massive violation of the prohibition laws against drinking alcoholic beverages by Canadians during and after World War I. An erosion in public support for anti-drinking laws, however, ultimately resulted in the repeal of prohibition. Similarly, the widespread recreational and medicinal use of marijuana by many Canadians, accompanied by changing attitudes toward the drug and the high costs of enforcement, culminated in its legalization by the federal Liberal government in 2018.

A key role in criminalizing certain activities is often played by **moral entrepreneurs**—individuals, groups, or organizations who seek action against certain groups of people or certain behaviours and bring pressure on legislators to enact criminal statutes. Historically, and recently, moral entrepreneurs have tended to be most active in the area of victimless crimes, such as drug and alcohol use and prostitution. Examples of moral entrepreneurs include Mothers Against Drunk Driving (M.A.D.D.) and pro-choice and pro-life groups.

The issues that surround medical assistance in dying can be used to illustrate the challenges and controversy that often surrounds the application of the criminal law in Canadian society (At Issue 1.1).

Social construction of crime

The notion that the legal status of behaviours is not determined by the behaviour itself, but is the result of the social response to the behaviour.

Moral entrepreneurs

Individuals, groups, or organizations who seek action against certain groups of people or certain behaviours and bring pressure on legislators to enact criminal statutes.

As society changes, certain behaviours may be criminalized. The pervasiveness of computer technology led to a number of additions to the *Criminal Code* (R.S.C. 1985, c. C-46), including destroying or altering computer data (s. 430[1.1]), using the Internet to distribute child pornography (s. 163.1), and communicating with a child for the purposes of facilitating the commission of certain sexual offences (s. 172.1). The pervasiveness of cellphones has led to provincial and territorial legislation related to distracted driving.

Conversely, some activities have been decriminalized over the years; that is, the laws against them have been repealed or struck down. Laws that were applied against homosexuals and Chinese immigrants no longer exist. Other laws have been in the *Criminal Code* for decades but have not been enforced. In 2017, the federal government introduced legislation deleting so-called "Zombie laws" from the *Criminal Code*, laws that had been on the books for decades and were no longer enforced and many of which had been struck down by the courts but remained in the *Criminal Code*. These included laws against "spreading false news" (somehow very relevant again in the early 21st century), "water-skiing at night," "duelling," "possessing crime comics," and "feigning marriage," as well as section 365, which made it an offence to fraudulently "pretend to exercise any kind of witchcraft, sorcery, enchantment or conjuration."[6] At times, the SCC has used the *Charter of Rights and Freedoms* to strike down laws that are inconsistent with the Charter's provisions and protections.

THE ORIGINS AND APPLICATION OF THE CRIMINAL LAW

A key component of the study of the criminal justice system is understanding the origins and application of the criminal law. The differing perspectives on where criminal laws come from and how they are applied via the criminal justice system are reflected in two models. The first, the **value consensus model**, views crime and punishment as reflecting society's commonly held values as well as its limits of tolerance. This view assumes that there is a consensus on what should be against the law.

Value consensus model

The view that what behaviours are defined as criminal and the punishment imposed on offenders reflect commonly held opinions and limits of tolerance.

Through the application of laws, a society reaffirms the acceptable boundaries of behaviour and maintains social cohesion. Indeed, there probably *is* consensus that murder should be against the law. Incest is another act that is widely condemned. Such offences, called *mala in se* (wrong in themselves), are perceived as so inherently evil as to constitute a violation of "natural law."

The **conflict model**, the second theory of the origins and application of criminal law, draws our attention to the fact that some groups are better able than others to influence which behaviours and persons are criminalized. In particular, conflict theorists see the rich and privileged as having an advantage in influencing law reform and in what happens to persons who become involved in the criminal justice system.

Conflict model

The view that crime and punishment reflect the power some groups have to influence the formulation and application of criminal law.

Scholars who conduct research using a conflict perspective might ask the following questions:

- Why does a person who steals less than $100 from a convenience store often receive a much more severe sentence than a stockbroker who defrauds investors of millions of dollars of investors' money?

- Why are crimes committed by corporations (such as banks that engage in money laundering, companies that fail to create and maintain healthy and safe working environments, and companies that illegally dispose of hazardous wastes) most often dealt with through civil court and often involve paying fines rather than being prosecuted under the criminal law and its sanctions?

- Why are Canadian correctional institutions populated by large numbers of Indigenous persons, Blacks, and at-risk and vulnerable persons with low education and skill levels, high rates of alcohol and drug addiction, and dysfunctional family backgrounds? Are these groups actually more criminal than other groups in society?
- What role do interest groups play in influencing the enactment of criminal legislation or in decriminalizing certain behaviour?

Conflict theorists highlight some of the inequities and paradoxes in the system. If someone takes money from a bank at gunpoint, it is called robbery. A business decision that causes a bank collapse, thus depriving thousands of account holders of their money, is called a bad day on the stock market. Conflict theorists believe that our attention is wrongly focused on street crime when the greater risk to most people lies in the actions of elites, including corporations that dump toxic waste, fix prices, condone unsafe workplaces, and evade taxes.

THE TYPES OF CANADIAN LAW

The two basic types of law in Canada are **substantive law** and **procedural law**. Substantive law sets out the rights and obligations of each person in society. This includes the *Criminal Code* and other legislation that defines criminal offences and the penalties for persons found guilty of committing criminal offences. Procedural laws are the legal process that protect and enforce the rights set out in substantive law. Examples of procedural law are the procedures for arresting a person or selecting a jury in a criminal trial.[7] See Figure 1.1.

Substantive law

Law that sets out the rights and obligations of each person in society; includes the *Criminal Code*.

Procedural law

The legal processes that protect and enforce the rights set out in substantive law.

THE CANADIAN LEGAL SYSTEM

The Canadian legal system is a **common law** system, with the exception of Quebec, which has a civil law system. Judges in a common law system are guided by past decisions. The common law system originated in Europe and was imported to Canada in the 17th and 18th centuries. The common law emerged from decisions made

Common law

Law that is based on custom, tradition, and practice and is generally unwritten.

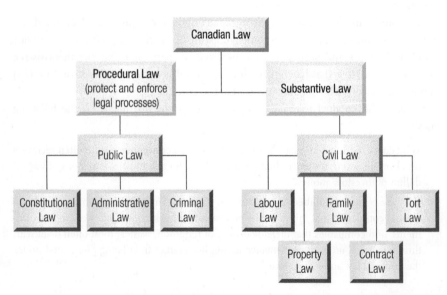

◄ FIGURE 1.1

The Divisions of Law

Precedent

A judicial decision that may be used as a standard in subsequent similar cases.

Stare decisis

The principle by which the higher courts set precedents that the lower courts must follow.

Statute law

Written laws that have been enacted by a legislative body such as the Parliament of Canada.

Case law

Law that is established by previous court decisions and is based upon the rule of precedent.

Criminal law

That body of law that deals with conduct considered so harmful to society as a whole that it is prohibited by statute, prosecuted and punished by the government.

by judges in the royal courts and was based on the notion of **precedent**: "Whenever a judge makes a decision that is said to be legally enforced, this decision becomes a precedent: a rule that will guide judges in making subsequent decisions in similar cases."[8] A unique feature of the common law is that it exists in past decisions of judges rather than being embodied in legal codes or legislation.

In contrast, the civil law system in Quebec is based on the French *Code Napoléon*. It is composed of civil codes, which are comprehensive statement of rules to be followed by judges. Judges first refer to the codes and then to previous court decisions.[9]

Canadian courts are organized in a hierarchy, with the Supreme Court of Canada at the top (see Chapter 7). The principle whereby higher courts set precedents that lower courts must follow is known as *stare decisis* (Latin for "to stand by what was decided"). Underlying this principle is the idea that like cases should be treated alike. Especially when the law is not precise, judicial interpretation can add clarification so that all courts are playing by the same rule book, so to speak. Once the SCC rules on a thorny legal issue, all courts below it are bound to apply that ruling in subsequent cases.

As a consequence, our **statute law**—both civil (except in Quebec) and criminal—is found both in statutes and in judicial precedents (the latter referred to as **case law**). In other words, many laws—such as those in the *Criminal Code*—are written down or codified. But through their decisions in cases, judges can interpret, modify, extend, restrict, or strike down statutory laws.

THE CRIMINAL LAW

The criminal law is one type of public law, the others being constitutional law, administrative law, and taxation law. **Criminal law** can be defined as "that body of law that deals with conduct considered so harmful to society as a whole that it is prohibited by statute, prosecuted and punished by the government."[10] The criminal law defines which acts (or omissions) are against the law and sets out the available penalties. It also sets out the rules that police and judges must follow in criminal matters, including procedures for making arrests, gathering evidence, and presenting evidence in court. Private law, by contrast, regulates relationships between individuals other than the state and is used to resolve disputes between private citizens.

The functions of the criminal law are set out in Box 1.1.

THE SOURCES OF CRIMINAL LAW

In Canada, there are two primary sources of criminal law: legislation and judicial decisions. Merely denoting the sources of criminal law, however, tells us very little about

---

BOX 1.1

THE FUNCTIONS OF THE CRIMINAL LAW

In Canadian society, the criminal law provides the following functions:

- acts as a mechanism of social control
- maintains order
- defines the parameters of acceptable behaviour
- reduces the risk of personal retaliation (vigilantism, or people taking the law into their own hands)
- assists in general and specific deterrence
- prosecutes criminalized behaviour
- protects group interests

---

the *process* of law-making or the factors that influence the creation of criminal law. A variety of explanations have been used by scholars studying the phenomena of crime and the societal response to it.

Historically, researchers focused on the individual offender and attempted to determine what factors distinguish criminals from non-criminals. The nearly exclusive focus on the criminal offender overshadowed the process through which behaviours and individuals came to be defined as criminal. In recent years, however, attention has increasingly focused on the process through which laws are formulated and applied and to the activities of legislators, special-interest groups, and criminal justice decision-makers. Throughout the text, the activities of criminal justice decision-makers, including police officers, judges, and parole board members, will be discussed.

THE PRINCIPLES OF CANADIAN LAW

There are a number of principles that provide the foundation for Canadian law. These are set out in Table 1.1.

THE RULE OF LAW

A key component of the foundation of the criminal justice system is the **rule of law**. The rule of law can be traced back to the English *Magna Carta*, which was originally issued by King John near Windsor Castle in England in June 1215. A number of passages in the document spoke to judicial procedure, including the creation of a permanent court at Westminster and the imposition of fines on commoners and peers alike "only

Rule of law

The requirement that governments, as well as individuals, be subjected to and abide by the law.

TABLE 1.1

THE PRINCIPLES OF CANADIAN LAW

Principle	Meaning
actus non facit reum nisi mens sit rea (an act does not make a person guilty unless he or she has a guilty mind).	Each crime has two components. The first is *actus reus*, or the act of doing something. The second is *mens rea*, or the guilty intent. To be convicted of most crimes (but not all), a person must have done something criminal, and usually (but not always) must have intended to do it. Children under the age of 12 and persons with some severe mental disorders who are deemed unable to form *mens rea* are not held criminally responsible for their actions.
nullum crimen sine lege, nulla poena sine lege (no crime without a law, no punishment without a law).	The rules cannot be changed in the middle of the game. Laws cannot be applied retroactively.
ignorantia juris non excusat (ignorance of the law is no excuse).	There is an expectation that every citizen be familiar with all the laws and therefore able to distinguish between legal and illegal behaviour. This expectation is a fiction because the law is constantly changing and, at any given point in time, is subject to debate and differing interpretations. However, the legal system would grind to a halt if defendants were able to claim that they had no idea their alleged offences were illegal.
nemo tenetur seipsum accusare (no one is compelled to incriminate himself).	Criminal suspects and defendants have the right to remain silent during the police investigation. If they are forced or threatened to make a confession, that statement will be inadmissible in court. In addition, a criminal defendant may choose not to testify in his or her defence. This principle is enshrined in the Charter.
nemo debet bis vexari pro eadem causa (no one should be twice troubled by the same cause).	This principle is more commonly known as "double jeopardy." An alleged offender cannot, under most circumstances, be tried twice for the same offence. In contrast to the American criminal justice system, however, an alleged offender in Canada can be retried after being acquitted if the Crown successfully appeals the decision by claiming problems with the correct application of the law at the trial.

► King John signs the *Magna Carta* at Runnymede, near London, in June 1215

according to the degree of the offense." Perhaps the most famous, and enduring, was this statement:

> No Free-man shall be taken, or imprisoned, or dispossessed, of his free tenement, or liberties, or free customs, or be outlawed, or exiled, or in any way destroyed; nor will we condemn him, nor will we commit him to prison, excepting by the legal judgment of his peers, or by the law of the land. To none will we sell, to none will we deny, to none will we delay right or justice.[11]

The key principles of the rule of law are set out in Criminal Justice File 1.1.

The *Magna Carta* and other documents provided the basis for the emergence of the rule of law, which became the foundation of English Law and, subsequently, the Canadian (English-speaking) legal system.

The essence of the rule of law is that no one person is above the law, all persons are bound by the law and are entitled to protection by the law, and the law should

---

CRIMINAL JUSTICE FILE 1.1

KEY PRINCIPLES OF THE RULE OF LAW

- The government and its officials and agents, as well as individuals and private entities, are accountable under the law.
- The laws are clear, publicized, stable, and just; are applied evenly; and protect fundamental rights, including the security of persons and property.
- The process by which the laws are enacted, administered, and enforced is accessible, fair, and efficient.
- Justice is delivered timely by competent, ethical, and independent representatives and neutrals who are of sufficient number, have adequate resources, and reflect the makeup of the communities they serve.

Source: Excerpted from The World Justice Project, "What Is the Rule of Law?" http://www.worldjusticeproject/org/whatrule-law. Reprinted with permission of The World Justice Project.

be observed and enforced equally. The rule of law provides the standard to which criminal justice officials must adhere and will be held accountable. While an admirable principle, the materials presented in the following chapters will reveal that this ideal is often not achieved.

THE *CANADIAN CHARTER OF RIGHTS AND FREEDOMS*

The principles of the rule of law and the influence of the *Magna Carta* can be seen in the ***Canadian Charter of Rights and Freedoms***, which is the primary law of the land and guarantees fundamental freedoms, legal rights and quality rights for all citizens of Canada, including those accused of crimes, "subject only to such reasonable limits prescribed by law as can be demonstrably justified in a free and democratic society." Among the "fundamental freedoms" given to all Canadian citizens are the following:

- freedom of conscience and religion
- freedom of thought, belief, opinion, and expression, including freedom of the press and other media of communication
- freedom of peaceful assembly
- freedom of association

With respect to "legal rights," the Charter states, "Everyone has the right to life, liberty and security of the person and the right not to be deprived thereof except in accordance with the principles of fundamental justice" (s. 7). More specific rights granted to Canadians have implications for the powers of the police (see Chapter 5) and the prosecution of criminal cases (see Chapter 8) and are discussed in those chapters.

The Charter provides a number "equality rights" for citizens (s. 15):

(1) Every individual is equal before and under the law and has the right to the equal protection and equal benefit of the law without discrimination and, in particular, without discrimination based on race, national or ethnic origin, colour, religion, sex, age or mental or physical disability.

(2) Subsection (1) does not preclude any law, program or activity that has as its object the amelioration of conditions of disadvantaged individuals or groups including those that are disadvantaged because of race, national or ethnic origin, colour, religion, sex, age or mental or physical disability.

With respect to "enforcement," the Charter states (s. 24):

(1) Anyone whose rights or freedoms, as guaranteed by this Charter, have been infringed or denied may apply to a court of competent jurisdiction to obtain such remedy as the court considers appropriate and just in the circumstances.

(2) Where, in proceedings under subsection (1), a court concludes that evidence was obtained in a manner that infringed or denied any rights or freedoms guaranteed by this Charter, the evidence shall be excluded if it is established that, having regard to all the circumstances, the admission of it in the proceedings would bring the administration of justice into disrepute.[12]

The *Charter of Rights and Freedoms* provides protection for individuals and ensures fairness during legal proceedings. All of the components of the criminal justice system must operate in such a way as not to violate the rights guaranteed to Canadians in the Charter. Canadian courts have restricted, extended, or better defined the Charter rights of citizens. Unfortunately, as we'll see throughout the text, the criminal justice system does not always act in a manner that respects and protects the Charter rights of Canadian citizens.

THE *CRIMINAL CODE* OF CANADA (1892)

Canadian criminal law is enshrined in the **Criminal Code** of Canada. In the early days of Canada, each province had its own criminal law. This was a result of British influence, Canada being part of the dominion. Attempts to create a unified criminal law in England in 1878 had failed. At Confederation in Canada in 1867, then Prime Minister Sir John A. Macdonald insisted that Canada should have a single criminal law for the entire country and not replicate the English model.[13]

The first complete *Criminal Code* was produced in 1892 under the leadership of Sir John Thompson who was minister of justice at the time and would later become prime minister (1892–1894). Among the provisions in Canada's first *Criminal Code* were the following:

- If a sentence of death is passed upon any woman, she may move in arrest of execution on the ground that she is pregnant. If upon the report of (medical practitioners), it appears to the court that she is so with child, execution shall be arrested until she is delivered of a child, or until it is no longer possible in the course of nature that she be so delivered.

- Whenever whipping may be awarded for any offence ... the number of strokes shall be specified in the sentence and the instrument to be used for whipping shall be a cat-o'-nine-tails unless some instrument is specified in the sentence. Whipping shall not be inflicted on any female.

- In all cases where an offender is sentenced to death, the sentence shall be that he be hanged by the neck until he is dead.[14]

The *Criminal Code* is federal legislation that sets out criminal laws, procedures for prosecuting federal offences, and sentences and procedures for the administration of justice. The original version of the *Criminal Code* dates from 1869. The *Criminal Code* is a "living" document in that it has been revised many times since 1892 to reflect changes in what behaviours are viewed as criminal and in philosophies of punishment. The current version of the code is three times longer than the original version.

CRIMINAL LAW AND CIVIL LAW: WHAT'S THE DIFFERENCE?

As one among several legal systems that exist in Canada, the criminal justice system concerns itself only with offenders who are criminally liable for wrongdoing. The government assumes the responsibility for prosecuting the alleged offender who, on conviction, is placed under the supervision of corrections authorities. In contrast, civil law cases are disputes between individuals. The person who feels wronged brings the legal action, and the "loser" may be required to pay damages. In contrast to criminal cases, there is no potential for loss of liberty in a civil suit.

A key difference between criminal law and civil law relates to the standard of proof required to convict a person of wrongdoing. In a criminal trial, the prosecutor must prove that the defendant is guilty "beyond a reasonable doubt." In a civil trial, liability is determined by using the standard of "the balance of probabilities." The standard is one of reasonable probability or reasonable belief rather than proof beyond a reasonable doubt. Because this reasonable probability is a much lower standard of proof, a defendant might be found not guilty in criminal court but liable in a civil suit.

Paul Fearn/Alamy Stock Photo

▲ Sir John Thompson

Criminal Code

Federal legislation that sets out criminal laws, procedures for prosecuting federal offences, and sentences and procedures for the administration of justice.

▼ The Canadian *Criminal Code*, continually under construction

Courtesy of Paul Lachine/Illustrator

THE CRIMINAL LAW IN A DIVERSE SOCIETY

The application of the criminal law is challenging in a diverse society such as Canada. The tension between cultural practices in persons' countries of origin and accepted behaviour in Canadian society are often acute.

A key issue is the extent to which the criminal law can be effective in modifying cultural practices that are viewed as contravening the values of Canadian society. A related issue is whether there are limits to the use of the criminal law and to what extent it should, or can, be applied in a diverse society. This issue is highlighted in At Issue 1.2.

The crime of honour killings illustrates the challenges of diversity. Honour killings are most commonly defined as the premeditated killing of a family member, most often a woman, who has engaged in certain behaviour, such as pre-marital or extra-marital relationships, that are believed to have brought shame and dishonour to the family.[15] These killings are often planned and may involve a number of family members.[16] The Human Rights Commission of the UN General Assembly and the Council of Europe's Committee of Ministers and other international organizations

---

AT ISSUE 1.2

SHOULD THE CRIMINAL LAW BE APPLIED TO RELIGIOUS PRACTICES?

In 2017, the Quebec National Assembly passed Bill 62 (2017, c. 19), *An Act to foster adherence to State religious neutrality and, in particular, to provide a framework for religious accommodation requests in certain bodies*. This legislation requires citizens to uncover their faces while giving and receiving government services.[a] The "religious neutrality law" requires a woman to have her face uncovered to check out a book from the library, while riding on transit, when accessing health services, or when working in a daycare centre, among other scenarios. The law does provide for a person to ask for religious accommodation on a case-by-case basis, and the final decision is left with front-line public employees. A poll conducted in Quebec (*N* = 609) found that 87 percent of Quebecers supported the legislation.[b]

The provincial justice minister stated that this requirement was not directed toward any one religious group: "Having your face uncovered is a legitimate question of communication, identification and security."[c]

A representative of a women's rights group warned that the law would "have a discriminatory effect on religious groups who are targeted, in particular women."[d]

Legal experts said that the law would most likely be challenged in court, one lawyer stating, "I have never seen a more flagrantly unconstitutional law."[e] The executive director of the National Council of Canadian Muslims stated, "It's not the business of the state to be in the wardrobes of the nation."[f] In his initial response to the legislation, the prime minister stated, "I think we have to respect that this is a debate that's ongoing in society and we respect that the National Assembly in Quebec has taken a position on this."[g] Among the online comments in response to the legislation were the following two distinct opinions:

Ban the burka in public, period. Believe it or not, we are entitled to be offended by something that represents the subjugation and oppression of women and is a barbaric throwback to the 8th century.

Governments should not legislate how people dress or worship. The ban won't stand against the Charter's enshrined freedom of religion.[h]

QUESTIONS

1. What is your view of this legislation?

2. In your view, does the legislation violate the fundamental rights of citizens as guaranteed by the *Charter of Rights and Freedoms*?

3. In your view, is this an instance in which the law is being used as an instrument of social policy? If yes, should it be?

---

[a] I. Peritz. 2017, October 18. "Quebec Bans Face Covering in Public Services, Raising Worries among Muslims," Globe and Mail. https://www.theglobeandmail.com/news/national/quebec-bans-face-covering-in-public-services-raising-worries-among-muslims/article36638544.

[b] Ibid.

[c] G. Hamilton. 2017, October 18. "Quebec Passes Bill Banning Niqab, Burka while Receiving Public Services," National Post. http://nationalpost.com/news/politics/quebec-passes-bill-62.

[d] Ibid.

[e] Peritz, "Quebec Bans Face Covering in Public Services."

[f] Ibid.

[g] J. Bryden. 2017, October 20. "Mr. Charter Trudeau Offers Only Veiled Criticism of Quebec Bill 62 Banning Face Coverings," *Toronto Sun*. http://www.torontosun.com/2017/10/20/mr-charter-trudeau-wont-condemn-bill-62-quebec-veil-ban.

[h] Hamilton, "Quebec Passes Bill Banning Niqab."

THE SHAFIA HONOUR KILLINGS: CULTURE CLASH AND THE LAW

In January 2012, a father, mother, and brother were convicted in the deaths of four female family members in what was described as "honour killings." Mohammad and Tooba Mohammad Yahya and their son Hamed had pled not guilty in the deaths of four family members who were found in the family's vehicle submerged in a lock on the Rideau Canal in June 2009. The victims were Hamed's three sisters and their father's previous wife from a polygamous marriage. They were subsequently convicted of first-degree murder and given automatic life sentences with no chance of parole for 25 years. The Shafias had moved to Canada from Afghanistan 15 years earlier, and there was evidence of abuse in the family as the father attempted to control his daughters' social lives and exercise his patriarchal authority. He was particularly upset that one of the daughters was dating and wanted to move out of the family home.

This case ignited an ongoing debate as to whether there should be a separate section in the *Criminal Code* for honour killings to highlight their inappropriateness and to deter this practice in Canada. A research study found that honour killings are on the rise in Canada, with 12 victims since 1999.[a] Opponents to this contend that existing provisions in the *Criminal Code* are sufficient and that persons perpetuating honour killings have always received the maximum allowable sentence under law.[b] The federal government appears to have no plan to amend the *Criminal Code* to insert a provision on honour killings.

The Shafia case raises a larger issue as to whether there are limits on the ability of the criminal law to change behaviour. See the Media Link, "The House of Shafia," at the end of this chapter.

Tooba Mohammad Yahya, her husband, Mohammad Shafia, and their son, Hamed Mohammed Shafia, are escorted by police officers into the Frontenac County Court on the first day of trial in Kingston, Ontario, on October 20, 2011.

[a] M.P. Robert. 2011. "Les crimes d'honneur ou le deshonneur du crime: etude des cas canadiens," *Canadian Criminal Law Review*, 16(1), 49–87.

[b] Ibid.

Additional sources: Canadian Press. 2017, March 27. "Mohammad Shafia, Convicted in So-Called Honour Killings, Ordered to Pay Wife's Legal Fees," *CBC News*. http://www .cbc.ca/news/canada/montreal/mohammad-shafia-legal-fees-1.4043176; Postmedia News. 2015, October 13. "Shafia Parents and Son, Convicted in Honour Killing of Four Family Members, Seek New Trial," *National Post*. http://nationalpost.com/news/canada/shafia-parents-and-son-convicted-in-honour-killing-of-four-family-members-seek -new-trial.

have taken a stance against honour killings and have urged countries to take action against this practice.

There is no official record of the number of honour killings in Canada. One of the more high-profile cases is presented in Criminal Justice File 1.2.

SUMMARY

The discussion in this chapter has set out the foundations of the legal system. *Crime* was defined, and it was noted that there is a social construction of crime, a reflection of changing times and mores. It was noted that the criminal law is not static and that what behaviour is legislatively defined as criminal can change overnight. There are instances in which controversy arises when the criminal law is applied to issues of ethics, morality, and religiousity. The criminal law was identified as one type of public law and the functions of the criminal law were set out. The rule of law and the *Charter of Rights and Freedoms* are two key parts of the foundation of the criminal justice system. There are several principles that also provide the foundation for Canadian law. The role, principles, origins, and application of the criminal law were examined, and a number of case studies were presented to illustrate the dynamic nature of the criminal law as well as the challenges of applying the criminal law in a diverse society.

KEY POINTS REVIEW

1. A critical thinker considers multiple points of view and is fair and open-minded to all ideas.

2. It can be said that crime is a social construction in that what is considered criminal behaviour changes based on the social response to the behaviour rather than the behaviour itself.

3. There are differing views on the origins and application of the criminal law, one that considers the law and its application as reflection of societal consensus and the other that emphasizes the role of the criminal law as an instrument of the powerful.

4. The criminal law is one type of public law.

5. The two primary sources of the criminal law are legislation and judicial decisions.

6. The Canadian legal system is a common law system with the exception of Quebec, which has a civil law system (although the *Criminal Code* applies to the entire country).

7. The criminal law has a number of functions, including maintaining order, defining the parameters of acceptable behaviour, and assisting in general and specific deterrence, among others.

8. There are a number of principles that provide the foundation for Canadian law, including the two components of a crime: *actus reus* (the act of doing something) and *mens rea* (guilty intent).

9. A key component of the criminal justice system is the rule of law, which was first established in the *Magna Carta* in England in 1215 and is composed of a number of key principles, including that the government, individuals, and private entities are accountable under the law and that laws must be evenly applied and must protect the fundamental rights of citizens.

10. Another key component of the foundation of the criminal justice system is the *Charter of Rights and Freedoms*.

11. Canadian criminal law is enshrined in the *Criminal Code*.

12. There are key differences between the criminal law and civil law.

13. The application of the criminal law is challenging in a diverse society such as Canada.

KEY TERM QUESTIONS

1. What is **critical thinking (thorough thinking)** and how can it assist in the study of the criminal justice system?

2. What is a **crime** and what are the two essential requirements for a behaviour to be considered criminal?

3. What is meant by the **social construction of crime**?

4. Who are **moral entrepreneurs** and what role do they play in relation to the criminal law?

5. Contrast the **value consensus model** and the **conflict model** as explanations for the origins and application of criminal law.

6. How do **substantive law** and **procedural law** differ?

7. What is meant by Canada as having a **common law** legal system?

8. What role do the following play in the Canadian system of criminal law: (a) **precedent**, (b) *stare decisis*, (c) **statute law**, and (d) **case law**.

9. Define **criminal law** and note its functions.

10. What are the origins and key principles of the **rule of law**?

11. Describe the fundamental freedoms, equality rights, and enforcement provisions of the *Canadian Charter of Rights and Freedoms*.

12. Describe the origins and content of the *Criminal Code*.

CRITICAL THINKING EXERCISE

Critical Thinking Exercise 1.1

The Ever-Changing *Criminal Code*

The discussion in this chapter has revealed that what behaviour is a crime has changed over time, and continues to change.

Your Thoughts?

1. Can you think of a behaviour that is currently against the law that may become legal in the future?

2. If so, what factors might come into play that contribute to the change?

3. In your view, should a particular drug that is currently illegal be legalized if it is used widely?

CLASS/GROUP DISCUSSION EXERCISE

Class/Group Discussion Exercise 1.1

Mass Law Violating and the De Facto Legalization of Criminal Behaviour

Throughout Canadian history, there are examples of behaviours that, while against the law, were nevertheless engaged in by a substantial number of persons. This is illustrated by the path to legalization that was followed by alcohol and marijuana. These substances, although illegal at the time, were widely used. In both cases, and particularly in the case of marijuana, people convicted of marijuana possession were given criminal records and even sent to jail. This continued up through 2017, prior to the federal government legalizing the substance. For both alcohol and marijuana, there were *tipping points* that ultimately led to their legalization. One contributor was mass violation of the law.

Your Thoughts?

1. Should mass violation of the law play a role in changing the law? Or should this be the responsibility of governments?

2. If so, should mass violation be the only determinant?

MEDIA LINK

"The House of Shafia," *The Fifth Estate*, CBC News. http://www.cbc.ca/fifth/episodes/2011-2012/the-house-of-shafia.

REFERENCES

1. D. Ellis. 2006. *Becoming a Master Student* (11th ed.). New York: Houghton Mifflin Company, p. 218.

2. R. Rosenfeld. 2009, December 14. "The Social Construction of Crime," *Oxford Bibliographies*. http://www.oxfordbibliographies.com/view/document/obo-9780195396607/obo-9780195396607-0050.xml.

3. Ibid.

4. N. Boyd. 2007. *Canadian Law. An Introduction* (4th ed.). Toronto: Thomson Nelson, p. 49.

5. K. MacQueen. 2013, June 10. "Why It's Time to Legalize Marijuana," *MacLean's*. http://www.macleans.ca/news/canada/why-its-time-to-legalize-marijuana.

6. K. Harris. 2017, March 7. "Federal Government to Axe 'Zombie Laws' from Canada's Criminal Code," *CBC News*. http://www.cbc.ca/news/politics/criminal-code-reform-zombie-laws-1.4013869.

7. Department of Justice Canada. n.d. "What Is the Law?" http://www.justice.gc.ca/eng/csj-sjc/just/02.html.

8. Department of Justice Canada. n.d. "Canada's System of Justice." http://www.justice.gc.ca/eng/dept-min/pub/just/03.html.

9. Department of Justice Canada. n.d. "Where Our Legal System Comes From." http://www.justice.gc.ca/eng/csj-sjc/just/03.html.

10. "Criminal Law." n.d. *Duhaime's Law Dictionary*. http://www.duhaime.org/LegalDictionary/C-Page5.aspx.

11. J.R. Stoner. 2009. "First Principles—The Timeliness and Timelessness of Magna Carta." http://www.firstprinciplesjournal.com/articles.aspx?article=1307.

12. Department of Canadian Heritage. 2017. Excerpts from *Canadian Charter of Rights and Freedoms*. Reproduced with the permission of the Minister of Canadian Heritage and the Minister of Public Works and Government Services. The Charter is available online at http://laws-lois.justice.gc.ca/eng/Const/page-15.html.

13. L. Duhaime. 2014. "1892, Canada's Criminal Code," *Canadian Legal History*. http://www.duhaime.org/LegalResources/CriminalLaw/LawArticle-94/1892-Canadas-Criminal-Code.aspx.

14. Ibid.

15. A.A. Muhammad. 2010. *Preliminary Examination of So-Called "Honour Killings" in Canada*. Ottawa: Department of Justice Canada, p. 2. http://www.justice.gc.ca/eng/rp-pr/cj-jp/fv-vf/hk-ch/hk_eng.pdf

16. Ibid.

© Laurie Justus Pace, Graphics One Design, 2014

CHAPTER 2
UNDERSTANDING THE CRIMINAL JUSTICE SYSTEM

LEARNING OBJECTIVES

After reading this chapter, you should be able to

• Discuss the purpose of the criminal justice system.
• Discuss the roles and responsibilities of the federal government and provincial/territorial governments, as related to criminal justice.
• Compare and contrast the two models of criminal justice administration.
• Describe the flow of cases through the criminal justice system, including the criminal justice "funnel."
• Discuss the role of discretion in the criminal justice system.
• Describe the task environments of the criminal justice system.
• Discuss the issue of ethics in criminal justice.
• Compare the levels of accountability of criminal justice system personnel.
• Discuss the factors that are associated with public confidence in the criminal justice system.
• Describe what is meant by the "politics of criminal justice."
• Discuss the deterrent value of the criminal justice system.
• Describe the restorative justice approach as an alternative response to persons in conflict with the law.

THE CRIMINAL JUSTICE SYSTEM

The **criminal justice system** is generally considered to contain all of the agencies, organizations, and personnel that are involved in the prevention of, and response to, crime; persons charged with criminal offences; and persons convicted of crimes. It includes not only criminal justice professionals but also thousands of volunteers who work in criminal justice agencies and in NGOs (non-governmental organizations) and other not-for-profit groups that deliver programs and services on a contract basis. For example, these agencies and organizations supervise offenders on bail, assist victims, provide community-based and institutional programming, and supervise parolees. Generally speaking, the provinces and territories are responsible for the administration of justice.

The criminal justice system includes crime prevention and crime reduction, the arrest and prosecution of suspects, the hearing of criminal cases by the courts, sentencing and the administration and enforcement of court orders, parole and other forms of conditional release, and supervision and assistance for ex-offenders released into the community. These groups include, among others, the John Howard Society, the Elizabeth Fry Society, the St. Leonard's Society, and various Indigenous organizations. Provincial governments often contract organizations like these to deliver such services. In recent years, restorative justice approaches (discussed later in the chapter) have become part of the criminal justice process as well.

THE PURPOSE OF THE CRIMINAL JUSTICE SYSTEM

There is no one commonly used statement of purpose of the criminal justice system. Components of such a statement would include the notions of "justice" for all persons, including victims and offenders and the community; respecting the rights of victims and offenders; and ensuring the safety and security of communities. A survey of Canadians ($N = 4,200$) found that 72 percent felt that a primary goal of the criminal justice system should be separating persons who commit serious crimes from the rest of society.[1] However, this same survey revealed that a similar percentage of those surveyed identified as a primary goal of the justice system the successful rehabilitation and reintegration of offenders back into the community.[2] And there was strong support (69 percent of those surveyed) for the notion that offenders should be incarcerated only if alternatives to confinement were not appropriate.[3]

While historically the criminal justice system has been focused on reacting to criminal behaviour, in recent years there has been an increasing emphasis on prevention of crime and problem-solving, be it the police addressing the issues surrounding problem premises, or the activities of problem-solving courts for specialized groups of offenders.

A statement of purpose that includes these components and will be used for this text is: *The purpose of the criminal justice system is to prevent and respond to criminal behaviour while ensuring that rights of victims and offenders are respected, that justice is achieved, and that communities are safe and secure.*

THE ROLE AND RESPONSIBILITIES OF GOVERNMENTS IN CRIMINAL JUSTICE

Each level of government in Canada—federal, provincial/territorial, and municipal—plays a role in the justice system. The division of responsibilities between the federal and provincial governments was spelled out in the ***Constitution Act, 1867***.

The basic division is that the federal government decides which behaviours constitute criminal offences, while the provincial/territorial governments are responsible for law enforcement and for administering the justice system.

Criminal justice system

All of the agencies, organizations, and personnel that are involved in the prevention of, and response to, crime; persons charged with criminal offences; and persons convicted of crimes.

Constitution Act, 1867

The legislation setting out the division of responsibilities between the federal and provincial governments.

Note that there are a number of unique features of the criminal justice system that would not be apparent in the *Constitution Act*. The RCMP, for example, are involved as a federal, provincial, and municipal police service (see Chapter 4).

The federal government is responsible for the *Criminal Code*. There is also federal legislation that targets specific types of criminal behaviour and offenders. The *Anti-terrorism Act* (S.C. 2001, c. 41), for example, gives the justice system broad powers to identify, prosecute, convict, and punish terrorist groups and individuals, while the *Sex Offender Information Registration Act* (S.C. 2004, c. 10) established a national sex offender database containing information on convicted sex offenders.

IS THE CRIMINAL JUSTICE SYSTEM A "SYSTEM"?

In certain scholarly quarters, there is an ongoing debate as to whether the criminal justice system really is a "system." (Yes, some scholars spend sunny days in July thinking about these things.) A number of observers have argued that the criminal justice system is best described as a "loosely coupled system" within which there are checks and balances. For example, the courts can provide a check on the use of force by police.[4]

There are a number of factors that work against the criminal justice system being a "system" in the true sense of the word: (1) the different mandates of criminal justice agencies; and (2) a lack of interoperability, that is the inability of hardware and software from multiple data bases from multiple agencies to "communicate" with one another.

The failure of agencies to share information can have significant consequences for victims, offenders, and the community. Incomplete materials in an offender's file, such as risk assessments and in-depth examinations of release plans, can hinder the ability of a parole board to make an informed decision on an inmate's application for conditional release. Similarly, the failure of a halfway house to notify parole supervision authorizations in a timely manner of an offender being AWOL can jeopardize the safety of crime victims and the community. With these caveats in mind, the discussion in this text will refer often to the criminal justice system.

MODELS OF CRIMINAL JUSTICE ADMINISTRATION: DUE PROCESS VERSUS CRIME CONTROL

Just as there are competing views of the origins and application of the criminal law (discussed in Chapter 1), there are two competing perspectives on the value systems underlying the administration of criminal justice—the **crime control** model and the **due process** model. These were first set out over 50 years ago by the late Herbert L. Packer, a law professor at Stanford University.[5] In their pure form, the models conflict with one another. In practice, the criminal justice system reflects elements of both models. And which model is emphasized at any point in time will depend upon a variety of factors, not the least of which is the perspective of the government of the day. See Table 2.1.

There is a fine balance to be struck between (1) giving criminal justice agencies such as the police and prosecutors the unfettered power to apprehend and prosecute offenders (crime control), and (2) protecting citizens from the potential abuses of that power (due process). At various points in time, the political climate of a jurisdiction may determine which model is predominant (see the section "The Politics of Criminal Justice").

AN ADVERSARIAL SYSTEM OF CRIMINAL JUSTICE

The Canadian criminal justice system is an **adversarial system**. This means that the advocates for each party—in criminal cases, the defence lawyer and prosecutor—present their cases before a neutral judge or a jury. The standard that must be met by

Crime control (model of criminal justice)

An orientation to criminal justice in which the protection of the community and the apprehension of offenders are paramount.

Due process (model of criminal justice)

An orientation to criminal justice in which the legal rights of individual citizens, including crime suspects, are paramount.

Adversarial system

A system of justice that is based on two opposing sides—the prosecution and the defence—arguing the guilt or innocence of a person before a judge or jury.

TABLE 2.1

THE CRIME CONTROL AND DUE PROCESS MODELS OF CRIMINAL JUSTICE ADMINISTRATION

Crime Control Model	Due Process Model
Primary purpose of the criminal justice system is protection of the public through deterrence and incapacitation of offenders.	Primary purpose of the criminal justice system is to ensure that there is equal justice for all citizens, regardless of wealth, social status, or political connections.
Criminal offenders are responsible for their behaviour.	Criminal offenders are responsible for their behaviour.
The administration of justice should be swift, certain, and efficient.	The administration of justice must be deliberate and ensure procedural fairness.
Criminal justice system should focus on the rights of victims rather than protecting the rights of criminal defendants.	The criminal justice system should focus on ensuring that the rights of criminal defendants are protected and that the powers and discretion of criminal justice decision-makers are structured and confined.
There is a strong presumption of guilt.	There is a presumption of innocence and the onus is on the criminal justice system to prove guilt. The possibility exists that a defendant may be factually guilty but legally innocent if proper procedures and rights of the accused have been violated.
Model reflects conservative values.	Model reflects liberal values.

the prosecution is proof **beyond a reasonable doubt**; that is, "doubt based on reason and common sense, which must be logically based upon the evidence or lack of evidence" and which upholds the presumption in law that a person is innocent until they are proven guilty.[6] This is a much higher burden of proof than is required in civil cases. In an adversarial system, there is a presumption of innocence. The burden is on the prosecution to prove that the accused is guilty, not the responsibility of the accused to prove their innocence.

This system is in contrast to the inquisitorial system of justice that operates in many jurisdictions in continental Europe. In this system, a judge, or panel of judges, assumes the role of investigating the crime. Our adversarial system has many rules of procedure and evidence governing criminal prosecutions. Some of these common-law rules have been enshrined in the *Charter of Rights and Freedoms*.

A basic premise of the adversarial system is that the truth will emerge from the materials presented by the defence and Crown. Another premise is that the judge or jury will be a neutral third party and will make decisions solely on the evidence, not subject to any other influence.

Critics of the adversarial system contend that the process encourages the parties to present a distorted version of events. There are also concerns with the quality of legal representation for many defendants and the ability of the criminal justice system to *solve problems* rather than merely react to them. This latter concern has provided the impetus for the development of specialized courts, which focus the approach of therapeutic jurisprudence in a problem-solving framework in which court personnel collaborate with the police, social services, and mental health professionals (see Chapter 7). The attempt to improve the problem-solving of the justice system has also led to the development of various restorative justice approaches, which are discussed later in the chapter.

The overrepresentation of Indigenous persons and others in sentenced populations raises questions as to whether an adversarial system of justice provides a level playing field and suggests that certain accused persons may be at a disadvantage in the criminal justice system.

Beyond a reasonable doubt

The standard that must be met to convict a defendant in a criminal case, which requires that the facts presented provide the only logical explanation for the crime.

THE FLOW OF CASES THROUGH THE CRIMINAL JUSTICE SYSTEM

Figure 2.1 illustrates how cases proceed through the criminal justice system. You will want to refer to this figure often as you read the following chapters. The figure is useful in telling us who is where in the system at any given point in the process; however, it provides little insight into the actual *dynamics* of criminal justice—that is, how decisions are made by justice personnel, the challenges they face in preventing and responding to crime, the role of crime victims, and the effectiveness of efforts to prevent and respond to crime, and address the needs of victims, offenders, and the community. These and other issues will be addressed in later chapters.

The criminal justice system responds to law breaking with investigation, prosecution, and (when appropriate) punishment. It does not, however, respond to every breach of the law. Only a portion of the criminal acts committed come to the attention of the police, and a much smaller percentage of these are heard in the courts or lead to a sentence of incarceration. In reality, as the discussion in Chapter 8 will reveal, most cases are resolved with a guilty plea (often through plea negotiation) and few cases go to trial. So dramatic is the attrition of cases in Canadian criminal justice that it is

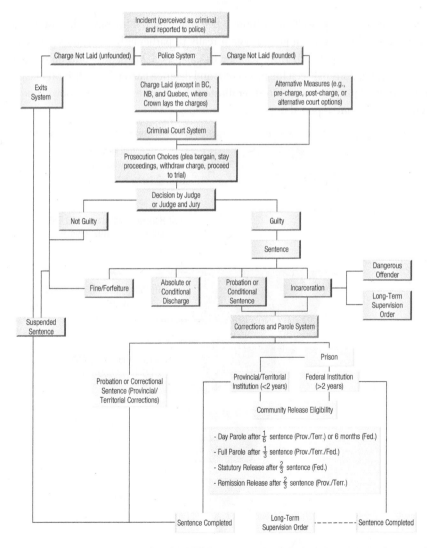

FIGURE 2.1 ▶

Flow of Cases through the Criminal Justice System

Source: From Roberts/Grossman. *Criminal Justice in Canada*, 3E. © 2008 Nelson Education Ltd. Reproduced by permission. www.cengage.com/permissions.

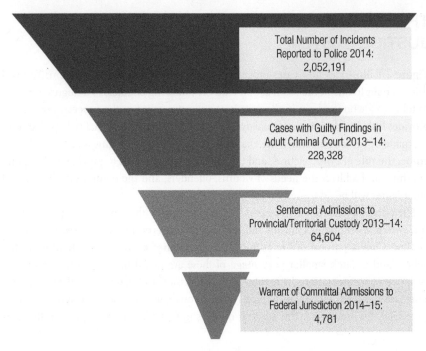

◀ FIGURE 2.2

The Criminal Justice Funnel

Source: Criminal Justice Funnel. 2017. *Corrections and Conditional Release: Statistical Overview*, p. 13. Public Safety Canada. http://www.publicsafety .gc.ca/cnt/rsrcs/pblctns/2012-ccrs/2012-ccrs-eng .pdf. This information was reproduced with the permission of the Minister of Public Safety and Emergency Preparedness Canada, 2017.

often represented graphically by a funnel. See Figure 2.2. This raises the issue as to how adversarial the criminal justice system really is, particularly when most cases are decided without a trial and, as we will see in Chapter 8, are settled outside of court through negotiations between the prosecutor and defence lawyer. The attrition of cases in the criminal justice process is further illustrated in Figure 2.3, which shows spousal assault cases that are reported by victims.

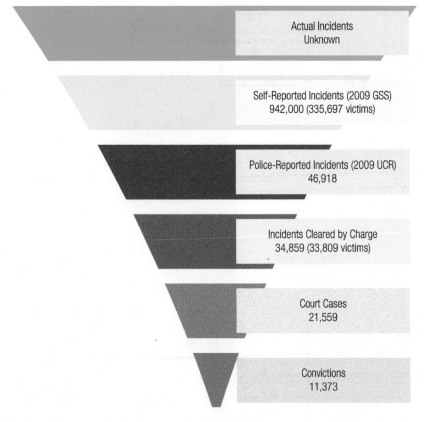

◀ FIGURE 2.3

The Attrition of Reported Spousal Assault Incidents, 2009

Note: GSS stands for the General Social Survey. UCR stands for Uniform Crime Reporting Survey.

Source: *An Estimation of the Economic Impact of Spousal Violence in Canada, 2009*, Figure 3.1. Spousal Violence Attrition Pyramid, http:// www.justice.gc.ca/eng/rp-pr/cj-jp/fv-vf/rr12_7/ rr12_7.pdf, Department of Justice Canada, 2012. Reproduced with the permission of the Department of Justice Canada, 2014.

THE DYNAMICS OF CRIMINAL JUSTICE

A key feature of criminal justice research is documenting the *dynamics* of the criminal justice process. This involves exploring how the system works in practice—that is, how police officers exercise discretion, how judges make sentencing decisions, and the factors that influence the release decisions of parole boards.

The materials in this text are designed to highlight the activities of individual justice personnel as well as how justice system organizations and agencies carry out their mandates. In a democratic society, there will always be tension between the efforts of the State to maintain order and to ensure the rights of citizens. This tension is reflected in the crime control and due process models of justice discussed in the previous section. The actions and decisions of individual criminal justice personnel and of their agencies are discussed in the following chapters.

To understand the criminal justice system requires a perspective that extends beyond organizational charts and legislative frameworks. A number of observers have pointed out that there has been little progress in developing theories of criminal justice due in part to the complexity, diversity, and scope of the criminal justice system.[7,8] Traditionally, scholars have studied the three components of the justice system—the police, courts, and corrections—and have not focused on the development of unifying theories.

In studying the operation of the criminal justice system, there are a number of different facets that can be examined, including: (1) the behavior of criminal justice personnel, such as police officers; (2) the activities of criminal justice organizations, such as correctional institutions services; and (3) the aggregate characteristics of the criminal justice system and its components in the context of larger societal issues, such as racism and inequality.[9]

THE ROLE OF DISCRETION IN THE CRIMINAL JUSTICE SYSTEM

Discretion

The power or right to decide or act according to one's own judgment.

A key factor in understanding how cases flow through the criminal justice system is **discretion**. Criminal justice personnel respond to a wide variety of events in a wide variety of settings in conditions that often are not ideal. They carry out their tasks within the framework of written laws and policies, but they also exercise considerable discretion when making decisions. This can lead to inconsistencies in how laws are applied, how cases are processed in the courts, and what decisions are made about offenders by police officers, judges, and correctional authorities.

Historically, the justice process has been structured in a way that criminal justice professionals have a considerable amount of discretion in carrying out their roles. However, this appears to be changing. The increasing focus on risk management and risk assessment in corrections, for example, has diminished the discretion exercised by probation officers in supervising persons on probation.[10] This is discussed in Chapter 9.

Many factors influence criminal justice personnel when they make discretionary decisions. At the centre of all these influences is the decision-maker, a human being who brings to his or her work a unique combination of education, training, personal experiences, and perhaps religious beliefs. It would be naive to think that life experiences and community pressure do not sometimes influence the decisions made by criminal justice personnel. For example, the decision-making of parole boards has come under intense scrutiny in recent years, due in large part to several high-profile cases in which offenders released by parole boards committed heinous crimes.

Even if discretion were not a factor, different justice system personnel would often make different decisions in a given situation. This is referred to as *disparity*

Vancouver's poverty-ridden Downtown Eastside   Chinatown in Montréal   Qikiqtarjuaq, Nunavut, population 520

THE CANADIAN PRESS/Jonathan Hayward

Photononstop / Alamy Stock Photo

Ansgar Walk, Wikipedia Commons

▲ What do each of the photos suggest to you about the task environment and the demands on and challenges for the criminal justice system?

in decision-making and is due, in large measure, to the considerable professional autonomy of criminal justice personnel. For example, a sentencing judge may order probation, even though another judge would have sent the same offender to prison. Similarly, a parole applicant's chances for release may depend on the composition of the parole board panel that particular day.

THE TASK ENVIRONMENTS OF CRIMINAL JUSTICE

Another concept that is helpful in understanding the dynamics of the criminal justice system is the **task environment**. A task environment is the cultural, geographic, and community setting in which the criminal justice system operates and in which criminal justice personnel make decisions. These environments range from small Inuit villages in Nunavut to inner-city neighbourhoods in major urban centres, such as Toronto.

The characteristics of a particular task environment influence the types of crime that justice system personnel are confronted with, the decision-making options that are available, the effectiveness of justice policies and programs, and the potential for developing community-based programs and services. In addition, the same urban area may contain a variety of task environments, ranging from neighbourhoods with a high concentration of shelters for the homeless, to neighbourhoods with large populations of recently arrived immigrants, to exclusive, high-income neighbourhoods. Unique challenges are faced by criminal justice personnel in remote and northern areas of the country, where there are few resources and community-based programs for victims and offenders.

Crime manifests itself differently in remote Arctic villages than in Vancouver's skid row or in a wealthy suburban Montreal neighbourhood (the highest rates of violent crime are in Canada's North). As these factors vary, so too may community expectations of the justice system and the relations between the justice system and the citizens it serves.

Task environment

The cultural, geographic, and community setting in which the criminal justice system operates and justice personnel make decisions.

ETHICS IN CRIMINAL JUSTICE

Closely related to the discretion and decision-making of personnel in the criminal justice system is the issue of **ethics**. Ethics can be defined as "the foundation of knowledge that describes right/wrong or better/worse … and applies to issues of harm/care and fairness/reciprocity" (www.ethicsdefined.org). There are many factors that enter into judging ethical acts, as events and situations rarely present a right/wrong scenario. Most situations fall into a "grey" area—"the space between black and white" (www.ethicsdefined.org).

The focus on ethics highlights the presence of moral issues in the criminal justice system. Recall the characterization earlier in the discussion that the criminal justice system is, first and foremost, a human (rather than scientific) enterprise. The foundation

Ethics

The foundation of knowledge that describes right/wrong or better/worse and applies to harm/care and fairness/reciprocity.

of the system is the criminal law, enacted by legislators; criminal justice agencies are staffed by personnel with a range of professional qualifications; and persons who become involved in the justice system present a broad range of issues, including mental illness and addiction.

The criminal justice system is first and foremost a human enterprise; that is, the decisions of police officers, judges, probation/parole officers, and parole boards are often based not on scientific formulas but on professional judgment, experience, and intuition. These personnel may find themselves in *ethical dilemmas*, which are situations in which criminal justice personnel are presented with difficult choices in carrying out their responsibilities.[11] Combined with the discretion that is given to criminal justice personnel, including police officers, judges, probation and parole officers, and others who work in the justice system, it is not surprising that ethical considerations are ever-present.[12]

ACCOUNTABILITY IN THE CRIMINAL JUSTICE SYSTEM

A key to an effective criminal justice system is accountability of criminal justice officials and agencies. Officials must adhere to the rule of law and the law generally. Justice system personnel may be subject to criminal and/or civil prosecution as well as to both internal and external review bodies, although, as the materials in Table 2.2 illustrate, some officials in the justice system are subjected to more oversight than others.

Criminal justice agencies may also be held accountable by crime victims and offenders through the civil courts. Crime victims may sue to recover damages from justice agencies that did not fulfill their mandate to protect, and offenders and suspects may sue to recover damages for actions taken by criminal justice personnel. Examples of such actions include excessive force by police, wrongful convictions by the criminal courts, and the failure of systems of corrections to manage the risk posed by offenders in the community who subsequently inflicted harm on victim(s).

A landmark case with respect to the civil liability of a criminal justice agency was the case of *Jane Doe v. Toronto (Metropolitan) Commissioners of Police* (1998 CanLII 14826 (ON SC)). In this case, Ms. Doe sued the Police Services Board, arguing that her victimization by a serial rapist was due to the negligence of the police in informing her that a rapist was active in her neighbourhood. The presiding judge in the Ontario Court (General Division) agreed that the police were negligent in failing to warn Jane

TABLE 2.2

ACCOUNTABILITY OF CRIMINAL JUSTICE PERSONNEL: A COMPARISON

Position	Internal and External Oversight
Police officer	Internal and external accountability; civilian oversight; subject to criminal charges and civil suits
Crown counsel	Subject to internal review; no independent oversight; generally immune from prosecution and being required to testify in court
Defence lawyer	Subject to review/sanction by professional association; no independent oversight
Judge	Provincial/territorial judges subject to internal review; federal judges subject to review/sanctioning/dismissal by the Canadian Judicial Council; eight public inquiries into the behaviour of judges from 1971 to 2009; removal rare; no external independent oversight for any judges
Probation officer	Subject to internal review; generally immune from prosecution; no external independent oversight
Parole board member	Subject to internal review; generally immune from prosecution; no external independent oversight
Parole officer	Subject to internal review; generally immune from prosecution; no external independent oversight

Doe and other women in the area. The Toronto Police were ordered to pay $220,000 to Ms. Doe for pain and suffering and medical interventions.[13] Subsequent cases over the years have used this precedent in finding the criminal justice system negligent in fulfilling its responsibilities to the public.

The issue of accountability and oversight is a key theme in the text and is discussed throughout the text.

PUBLIC CONFIDENCE AND TRUST IN THE CRIMINAL JUSTICE SYSTEM

For the criminal justice system to be effective requires that the public have confidence and trust in it. Research suggests that Canadians may have only a "moderate" level of confidence in the criminal law and that many persons have a general lack of trust in the system.[14] This is due, in part, to the fact that most Canadians have very little under-standing of the criminal justice system and how it works.[15] They also tend to overesti-mate the amount of crime and the levels of violent crime. One study (N = 4,200) found that those surveyed believed that almost 50 percent of all crime involved violence, despite the fact that the actual figure is much lower.[16] A report of the Canadian Bar Association found widespread distrust of the justice system, which was viewed as being only "for people with money, arbitrary, difficult to navigate and inaccessible to ordinary people … and even unfair."[17]

Public confidence and trust are increased if the criminal justice system is considered to be legitimate, that is, "the belief that authorities, institutions, and social arrangements are appropriate, proper, and just."[18] The justice system must be viewed as ensuring the security of the community while at the same time protecting the rights of citizens. Research indicates that Canadians place a high value on the criminal justice system "getting it right" (not convicting innocent persons; see Chapter 8) and on the system having clear rules and guidelines.[19]

The extent to which the general public views the justice system as legitimate will affect the levels of confidence in the system and the extent to which the public will sup-port specific initiatives and participate in partnerships. When persons or communities lose confidence in the ability of the justice system to protect them, this may result in vigilantism. This is discussed in Chapter 6.

For example, legitimacy allows the police to effectively respond to crime and dis-order and to rely upon public cooperation in their efforts.[20] Persons who do not view the police as legitimate are less likely to comply with the directives of police officers and to obey the law generally.[21] They may also be less likely to become involved in collaborative efforts to improve relationships between the police and the community.[22] Similarly, in corrections, if the persons in conflict with the law perceive that they are being treated in a fair and just manner, the effectiveness of correctional interventions may be improved. The discussion in this text will reveal that, for a variety of reasons, certain groups have not viewed the justice system as legitimate.

Figure 2.4 identifies some of the negative consequences when communities depend on the justice system to respond to and solve a variety of problems. The vicious circle that results from unmet expectations is depicted in Figure 2.5.

In the words of one observer, the hidden message in Figure 2.5 is that "paid profes-sionals are seen as care providers and problem solvers, inferring that community groups do not need to bother…[P]rofessionals compound this sense by operating on assump-tions about their own capacity for defining problems and coming up with remedies, rejecting citizens as problem definers and solvers."[23]

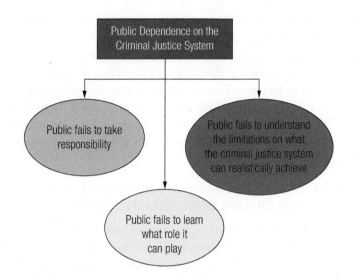

FIGURE 2.4 ►

Consequences of Overdependence
on the Criminal Justice System

Source: C.G. Nicholl. 1999. *Community Policing,
Community Justice, and Restorative Justice:
Exploring the Links for the Delivery of a Balanced
Approach to Public Safety.* Washington, DC: U.S.
Department of Justice, Office of Community
Oriented Policing Services.

THE MEDIA AND PUBLIC ATTITUDES TOWARD THE CRIMINAL JUSTICE SYSTEM

For most Canadians, news media stories are the primary source of information about the criminal justice system, although there are other sources, including personal experience, movies, and shows accessed on television or the Internet.[24,25] The public seems to have an insatiable appetite for crime and chaos; witness the success of the television drama *CSI* and its various spin-offs. Crime and police shows produced in Canada and the United States consistently attract the largest viewing audiences. These shows, however, may oversimplify complex issues of crime and criminal justice. The media tend to be biased toward sensational crimes and to simplify crime and justice issues, and the public for its part tends to generalize from specific events.

The tendency of the media to focus on sensational cases, combined with the failure of criminal justice agencies to educate the populace, contributes to an uninformed and misinformed public. For example, the public overestimates the number of offenders who are released on parole, their revocation rates, and the recidivism rate generally.[26]

Community sentiment about offenders and the justice system are often expressed through interest groups that lobby for more severe sanctions for criminal offenders, longer periods of incarceration, and more stringent requirements for release. Community residents, for example, are often very vocal in opposing offenders who have been released from prison taking up resident in their neighbourhood. This is discussed in Chapter 12.

FIGURE 2.5 ►

Consequences of Unmet
Expectations

Source: C.G. Nicholl. 1999. *Community Policing,
Community Justice, and Restorative Justice:
Exploring the Links for the Delivery of a Balanced
Approach to Public Safety.* Washington, DC: U.S.
Department of Justice, Office of Community
Oriented Policing Services.

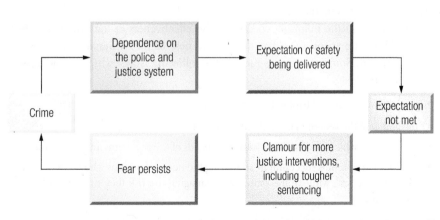

Findings from studies that have examined efforts to involve and educate the public about the criminal justice system have been mixed. An evaluation of the effectiveness of the federal government initiatives designed to engage and educate the general public on issues related to corrections was unable to determine whether these initiatives improved public confidence in the criminal justice system.[27] Other studies have found that programs and materials designed to provide community residents with factual information in crime and the criminal justice system resulted in higher levels of confidence in the system.[28] This suggests that public confidence in the criminal justice system is a complex, multi-faceted notion.

THE POLITICS OF CRIMINAL JUSTICE: THE AGENDA OF THE FEDERAL CONSERVATIVE GOVERNMENT (2006–15)

Politics can have a significant impact on the criminal justice system. An excellent case example of this is provided by the legislative agenda of federal Conservative government (2006–15). When in power, the Conservatives adopted an American-style, "get tough," crime control approach to offenders.[29] This approach was a radical departure from the more liberal model of corrections practice that had prevailed in Canada for many decades under successive Liberal governments. The liberal model was centred on treatment and rehabilitation and a view that the criminal justice system could address the underlying reasons why persons came into conflict with the law.

In fall 2015, the Liberal party won the federal election and has since indicated it would review many of the above-noted initiatives. In late 2016, the federal government announced that it was exploring the possibility of introducing exceptions to mandatory minimum sentences and reinvesting in judges the discretion in sentencing.[30] As of 2017, there had been more than 100 constitutional challenges to mandatory minimum penalties, and the courts had overturned several of them.[31]

In the words of one legal observer, the shift from the position of the federal Conservative government to that of the Liberal government served to "swing the balance away from the Conservative view that crime is a moral problem to a more modern and realistic view that crime relates to poverty and mental illness and marginalization."[32]

IS THE CRIMINAL JUSTICE SYSTEM EFFECTIVE?

> In its present state, by every measure that matters, the criminal justice system is failing to deliver what can fairly be expected of it.[33]

In 2016, a study examined the performance of the criminal justice system in all of the provinces and territories on five major objectives: (1) public safety, (2) support for victims of crime, (3) cost and resources, (4) fairness and access to justice, and (5) efficiency. The results are presented in Table 2.3.

A key theme in the following chapters is the effectiveness of the criminal justice system. There are many ways that the effectiveness of the criminal justice system can be assessed. Some of the ways include the following issues, which are addressed throughout the text:

- public confidence and trust in the system
- the ability of the system to prevent and respond to crime
- the extent to which the system addresses the needs of crime victims and their families
- whether the system is successful in addressing the needs of persons who come into conflict with the law, while at the same time managing the risk they may present to the community

TABLE 2.3

PERFORMANCE OF THE CRIMINAL JUSTICE SYSTEMS IN THE PROVINCES AND TERRITORIES: OVERALL RANKING AND GRADES

Province	Rank	Public Safety	Support for Victims	Cost and Resources	Fairness and Access	Efficiency	Overall
PE	1	B+	B+	B+	B	A	B+
NL	2	B	B+	C+	B+	B	B
NB	3	B+	C+	B+	B	B	B
PQ	4	B	C+	B	B+	C+	B
NS	5	B	B	C+	B+	C+	B
AB	6	C+	B	B+	C	C+	C+
ON	7	B	B	B	C+	C	C+
BC	8	C+	C	B	C+	B	C+
SK	9	C	C+	C	C+	B	C+
NU	10	C	F	F	A+	A	C+
NW	11	C+	F	F	B+	A	C
MN	12	C+	C	D	C+	C	C
YK	13	C	F	F	B+	B+	C

QUESTIONS

1. What is the report card for your jurisdiction?
2. What current incidents and issues in your jurisdiction might reflect the grades that were received for the various performance measures?

Source: B. Perrin and R. Audas. 2016. *Report Card on the Criminal Justice System: Evaluating Canada's Justice Deficit.* Toronto: MacDonald-Laurier Institute, p. 4. Reprinted by permission of the Macdonald-Laurier Institute.

- the effectiveness of specific policies and programs, as measured by evaluation studies
- adherence of the system to the rule of law and the *Charter of Rights and Freedoms*
- the extent to which the system treats all persons fairly under the law, without prejudice or discrimination

These are only a few of the possible measures of effectiveness. See Critical Thinking Exercise 2.1 at the end of the chapter.

ARE THE CRIMINAL LAW AND THE CRIMINAL JUSTICE SYSTEM A DETERRENT?

An important question is whether the criminal law and the criminal justice system serve as a deterrent to criminal behaviour. Studies of the deterrent effect of the criminal law suggest that the law can serve as a deterrent only when certain conditions are present: (1) People must be aware that there are legal sanctions that will be applied if they engage in certain behaviours; (2) there must be certainty of punishment; and (3) the sanction must be applied swiftly when a crime is committed.[34] Most Canadians are not involved in criminal offending, but there are a variety of reasons why people choose not to violate the law. These include pressures to conformity—that is, from family, employment, and peers. The criminal would not be ranked among the top reasons, if it were ranked at all.

For those who are intent on committing crime, it is likely that the criminal law and the criminal justice system offer little in the way of deterrence. There is neither certainty nor swiftness of punishment. The clearance, or "catch," rate for many types of crime is quite low. The imposition of punishment is often far from swift. The criminal justice system is based on an adversarial model that incorporates many elements of due process. Summing up a review of the research on deterrence, one scholar concluded, "The empirical evidence leads to the conclusion that there is a marginal deterrent effect for legal sanctions … it is very difficult to state with any precision how strong a deterrent effect the criminal justice system provides.…"[35]

It is also unlikely that the criminal law and the criminal justice system are a deterrent to persons with mental illness, addiction issues, or other impairments or disabilities. Still others are caught in situations of poverty and are marginal to mainstream society. A smaller percentage are driven by the prospect of financial gain, such as persons involved in organized crime.

Historically, the response of the system has often been slow and deliberate. Months, or even years, would pass before a determination of guilt or innocence was made and the appeal process was exhausted. This has likely changed with the decision of the Supreme Court of Canada (SCC) in 2016 in the case of *R. v. Jordan* (2016 SCC 27). This case set specific time limits on the disposition of cases after charges are filed. The implications of this case are discussed in Chapter 7.

EVIDENCE-BASED POLICIES AND PROGRAMS

The effectiveness of the criminal justice system also turns on the extent to which legislation, policies, and programs are **evidence-based**—that is, have been shown by research to be effective in achieving specified objectives. Unfortunately, as the discussion in this text reveals, too often legislation, such as the imposition of mandatory minimum sentences, and policies and operations of the police, courts, and corrections fall far short of evidence-based practice.

Evidence-based practices

Policies, strategies, and programs that have been shown by research to be effective in achieving specified objectives.

RESTORATIVE JUSTICE: AN ALTERNATIVE APPROACH TO CRIMINAL JUSTICE

Concerns about the effectiveness of the traditional adversarial system of criminal justice and a variety of other influences have led to the search for alternative ways to respond to people in conflict with the law. **Restorative justice** provides an alternative framework for responding to criminal offenders. It focuses on problem-solving, addressing the needs of victims and offenders, involving the community on a proactive basis, and fashioning sanctions that reduce the likelihood of reoffending. It is based on the principle that criminal behaviour injures not only victims but also communities and offenders, and that efforts to address and resolve the problems created by criminal behaviour should involve all of these parties.

Restorative justice

A problem-solving approach to responding to offenders based on the principle that criminal behavior injures victims, communities, and offenders, and that all of these parties should be involved in efforts to address the causes of the behaviour and its consequences.

Restorative justice takes a problem-solving approach that seeks to address the underlying causes of criminal behaviour, the harm done, and to reduce the likelihood of reoffending. Offenders are required to acknowledge and assume responsibility for their behaviour, and there is an effort to create a "community" of support and assistance for the victim and the offender, as well as for the long-term interests of the community.

Restorative justice is not a specific practice, but rather a set of principles that provides the basis for a community and the justice system to respond to crime. Key notions in restorative justice are healing, reparation and reintegration, and the prevention of future harm.[36] The use of restorative justice is not confined to the criminal justice system. It is used in schools, workplaces, and a variety of other settings. Check out the

FIGURE 2.6 ▶

The Relationships of
Restorative Justice

Source: T.F. Marshall. 1999. *Restorative Justice:
An Overview*. Home Office Occasional
Paper 48. London: Home Office. Reprinted by
permission of the Home Office under the terms of
the Open Government Licence (OGL). http:
//www.nationalarchives.gov.uk/doc
/open-government-licence/version/2/.

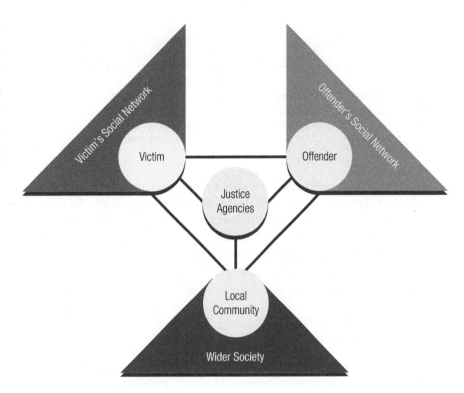

YouTube video "Restorative Resources: Restorative Justice in Schools" (www.youtube
.com/watch?v=9pYuA3o6WuU). Figure 2.6 depicts the relationships among the various
parties that may be involved in a restorative justice approach.

The concept of restorative justice is best illustrated by comparing it with the principles of retributive justice, upon which the adversarial system of criminal justice is
based. The key differences are listed in Table 2.4.

TABLE 2.4

THE PRINCIPLES OF RETRIBUTIVE JUSTICE AND RESTORATIVE JUSTICE

	Retributive Justice	Restorative Justice
Focus	Focus on establishing blame and guilt	Focus on problem-solving, obligations, and the future
Stigma	Stigma of crime permanent	Stigma of crime removable
Redemption	No encouragement for repentance and forgiveness	Possibilities for repentance and forgiveness
People	Dependence upon professionals; experts; non-residents	Direct involvement by participants; local participants
Process	Adversarial; State versus offender; victim ignored, offender passive	Consensus; community versus problem; victim's and offender's roles recognized in both problem and solution: victim rights/needs recognized; offender encouraged to take responsibility
Issues	Laws broken	Relationships broken
Accountability	Offender accountability defined as taking punishment	Offender accountability defined as understanding impact of action and helping decide how to make things right
Community	Community represented abstractly by the State	Community as facilitator
Tools	Punishment/control	Healing/support
Procedure	Fixed rules	Flexible

Source: Adapted from Canadian Resource Centre for Victims of Crime. 2011. *Restorative Justice in Canada: What Victims Should Know.* http://www.rjlillooet.ca/documents/restjust.pdf,
p. 3. Reprinted with permission from the Canadian Resource Centre for Victims of Crime.

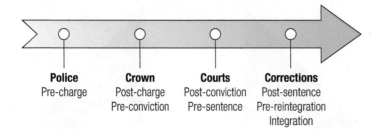

Police
Pre-charge

Crown
Post-charge
Pre-conviction

Courts
Post-conviction
Pre-sentence

Corrections
Post-sentence
Pre-reintegration
Integration

◀ FIGURE 2.7

Restorative Justice: Entry Points in the Criminal Justice System

Source: *The Effects of Restorative Justice Programming: A Review of the Empirical, 2000,* Figure 2.1, p. 7. Entry Points in the Criminal Justice System, http://www.justice.gc.ca/eng/rp-pr/csj-sjc/jsp-sjp/rr00_16/rr00_16.pdf. Department of Justice Canada, 2000. Reproduced with the permission of the Department of Justice Canada, 2017.

The primary objectives of restorative justice are to fully address the needs of victims of crime and to prevent reoffending by reintegrating offenders back into the community. Regardless of the specific restorative justice approach, the process ends with an agreement on how the offender will address the harm caused by the crime. This may include a written or verbal apology, the payment of restitution to the victim, provisions to assist the offender in changing his or her behaviour (e.g., attending a drug treatment program), and/or performing service to the community.[37]

ENTRY POINTS FOR RESTORATIVE JUSTICE IN THE CRIMINAL JUSTICE SYSTEM

There are a number of entry points in the criminal justice system where restorative justice approaches can be used: police (pre-charge), Crown (post-charge), court (post-convictions/pre-sentence), corrections (post-sentence), and following sentence expiry. Circles of Support and Accountability (COSAs), for example, involve community residents and justice and social service personnel working with high-risk sex offenders who have completed their sentence but are still in need of assistance. See Figure 2.7.

Restorative justice initiatives are discussed throughout the text. These include victim–offender mediation, circle sentencing, community holistic healing programs, and family group conferences. There are examples of restorative justice programs operating in rural, suburban, and urban communities. There are critical differences among the various models of restorative, including their mandate and relationship to the formal adversarial system, the role of the crime victim and other participants, and the procedures for preparation for the event and for monitoring and enforcing the agreement.[38,39]

SUMMARY

This chapter has highlighted a number of important considerations in the study of the criminal justice system. The purpose of the criminal justice system was discussed, along with the two competing models of criminal justice administration. The flow of cases through the justice system was illustrated by a "funnel," reflecting the fact that there is significant attrition in cases through the criminal justice process. The role of discretion as exercised by criminal justice system personnel was discussed, as were the associated issues of ethics and accountability. Criminal justice personnel work in a variety of task environments that affect the challenges they face. Ethics and accountability were discussed as important considerations in criminal justice, and it was noted that there is variation in the oversight and accountability of criminal justice personnel. There was a discussion of the various task environments in which the criminal justice system operates and a consideration of the effectiveness of the justice system.

It is important that the public have confidence in the criminal justice system, and the extent to which the general public views the system as legitimate will impact the levels of support for justice system policies and practice. It was noted that, for most Canadians, the media is the primary source of information about the criminal justice system, and the pervasiveness of social media has resulted in near-instantaneous sharing of information on justice-related issues. The legislative agenda of the former federal Conservative government was used as an example of how politics can affect the criminal justice system. Restorative justice has a number of features that distinguishes it from the adversarial system of justice, and it presents an alternative response to persons in conflict with the law.

KEY POINTS REVIEW

1. There is no one commonly used statement of purpose of the criminal justice system.
2. The federal and provincial/territorial governments have specific roles in the criminal justice system.
3. In certain scholarly quarters, there is an ongoing debate as to whether the criminal justice system is a "system."
4. There are competing models used to explain criminal justice administration.
5. The Canadian criminal justice system is an adversarial system, which may place certain persons at a disadvantage.
6. The flow of cases through the criminal justice system can be depicted by a funnel.
7. A key feature of the criminal justice system is the exercise of discretion.
8. Criminal justice personnel carry out their responsibilities in variety of task environments.
9. It is important that criminal justice personnel be held to ethical standards and are accountable, although some officials in the criminal justice system are subject to more oversight than others.
10. It is essential that the public have confidence in the criminal justice system.
11. The criminal justice system can be significantly impacted by politics.
12. There is some question as to whether the criminal justice system is effective in meetings its objectives.
13. Restorative justice presents an alternative framework for responding to persons in conflict with the law.

KEY TERM QUESTIONS

1. Identify the components of the **criminal justice system**.
2. Why is the **Constitution Act, 1867** important in the study of Canadian criminal justice, and what responsibilities does it assign for criminal justice?
3. Compare and contrast the **crime control** and **due process** models of criminal justice administration.
4. What is meant by the criminal justice system as an **adversarial system**?
5. Define the concept of **beyond a reasonable doubt**.
6. What is **discretion**, and what role does it play in the criminal justice system?
7. What is a **task environment** in criminal justice, and why is this concept important in the study of criminal justice?

8. Define **ethics** and note its role in the criminal justice system.

9. What is meant by **evidence-based practices** in the criminal justice system?

10. Define the concept of **restorative justice** and then compare its principles with those of the adversarial system of criminal justice.

CRITICAL THINKING EXERCISE

Critical Thinking Exercise 2.1

Measuring the Effectiveness of the Criminal Justice System

The discussion in this chapter identified a number of metrics that could be used to determine the effectiveness of the criminal justice system.

Your Thoughts?

1. Can you think of others?

2. What challenges might be encountered in determining the effectiveness of the criminal justice system?

CLASS/GROUP DISCUSSION EXERCISE

Class/Group Discussion Exercise 2.1

The Goals and Values of the Criminal Justice System

There can be a variety of views on the goals and values that should be reflected in the criminal justice system. Rate each of the following potential goals and values on a scale of 1 to 7, with 1 being "Not Important" and 7 being "Important."

The criminal justice system should:

Promote respect for the law

1   2   3   4   5   6   7

Be timely

1   2   3   4   5   6   7

Consider the circumstances of those who are vulnerable and marginalized

1   2   3   4   5   6   7

Place as much focus on addressing underlying social factors

1   2   3   4   5   6   7

Reduce the chances of convicting an innocent person

1   2   3   4   5   6   7

Prevent crime

1   2   3   4   5   6   7

Treat everyone fairly

1   2   3   4   5   6   7

Promote a sense of trust or confidence in the criminal justice system

1   2   3   4   5   6   7

Provide information accounting for tax dollars spent

1   2   3   4   5   6   7

Be transparent or clear about rules and guidelines

1   2   3   4   5   6   7

Once you've completed the ranking, discuss your results with classmates. Then compare your and your classmates' rankings with the results of a survey ($N = 4{,}200$) of Canadians, presented in Figure 2.8.

Your Thoughts?

1. How did your ranking compare to those of your classmates?

2. Was there any consensus on the primary goals and values of the justice system?

3. How did your and your classmates' rankings compare to those of 4,200 Canadians that were presented in Figure 2.8?

4. What might be the source of differences between you and your classmates' rankings and those of the respondents in the Canada-wide survey?

Source: Ekos Research Associates. 2017. *National Justice Survey: Canada's Criminal Justice System*. Ottawa: Department of Justice Canada, p. 29. http://epe.lac-bac.gc.ca/100/200/301/pwgsc-tpsgc/por-ef/justice_canada/2017/015-16-e/report.pdf.

FIGURE 2.8 ▶

Important Aspects of Criminal Justice System

Source: Ekos Research Associates. 2017. *National Justice Survey: Canada's Criminal Justice System*. Ottawa: Department of Justice, p. 29. http://epe.lac-bac.gc.ca /100/200/301/pwgsc-tpsgc/por-ef/justice _canada/2017/015-16-e/report.pdf.

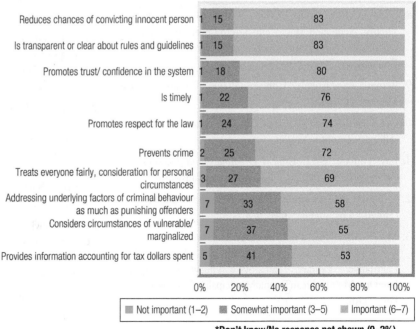

"How important is it that the criminal justice system...?"

	Not important (1–2)	Somewhat important (3–5)	Important (6–7)
Reduces chances of convicting innocent person	1	15	83
Is transparent or clear about rules and guidelines	1	15	83
Promotes trust/ confidence in the system	1	18	80
Is timely	1	22	76
Promotes respect for the law	1	24	74
Prevents crime	2	25	72
Treats everyone fairly, consideration for personal circumstances	3	27	69
Addressing underlying factors of criminal behaviour as much as punishing offenders	7	33	58
Considers circumstances of vulnerable/ marginalized	7	37	55
Provides information accounting for tax dollars spent	5	41	53

*Don't know/No response not shown (0–2%)

EKOS Research Associates Inc.

$N = 4{,}200$

National Justice Survey 2016

MEDIA LINKS

"Restorative Justice in the Criminal Justice System" (a police officer speaks about restorative justice), http://www.youtube.com/watch?v=R9tl4YmYYnI

"Restorative Justice Is the Law," http://www.heartspeakproductions.ca

"Restorative Practices to Resolve Conflict/Build Relationships: Katy Hutchinson at TEDx/West VancouverED," https://www.youtube.com/watch?v=wcLuVeHlrSs

REFERENCES

1. Ekos Research Associates. 2017. *National Justice Survey: Canada's Criminal Justice System*. Ottawa: Department of Justice, p. 24. http://epe.lac-bac.gc.ca/100/200/301/pwgsc-tpsgc/por-ef/justice_canada/2017/015-16-e/report.

2. Ibid., p. 25.

3. Ibid.

4. J.B. Snipes and E.R. Maguire. 2007. "Foundations of Criminal Justice Theory," in *Criminal Justice Theory: Explaining the Nature and Behavior of Criminal Justice*, edited by D.E. Duffee and E.R. Maguire, 27–50. New York: Routledge, at p. 29.

5. H. Packer. 1964. "Two Models of the Criminal Process," *University of Pennsylvania Law Review, 113*, 1–68.

6. *R. v. Lifchus* (1997) 3 S.C.R. 320 at para. 30, 1997 SCC CanLII 319.

7. T.J. Bernard and R.S. Engel. 2001. "Conceptualizing Criminal Justice Theory," *Justice Quarterly, 18*(1), 1–30.

8. J. Hagan. 1989. "Why Is There So Little Criminal Justice Theory? Neglected Macro- and Micro-Level Links between Organization and Power," *Journal of Research in Crime and Delinquency, 26*(2), 116–135.

9. Bernard and Engel, "Conceptualizing Criminal Justice Theory," pp. 5, 18.

10. C.T. Griffiths and D. Murdoch. 2018. *Canadian Corrections* (5th ed.). Toronto: Nelson.

11. J.M. Pollock. 2012. *Ethical Dilemmas and Decisions in Criminal Justice* (8th ed.). Belmont, CA: Wadsworth.

12. C. Banks. 2013. *Criminal Justice Ethics: Theory and Practice* (3rd ed.). Los Angeles: Sage, p. 3.

13. M. Drent. 1998. "The Jane Doe Decision: Implications for Police Liability," *Backgrounder 26*. Toronto: The Legislative Library. http://www.sgmlaw.com/en/about/JaneDoevMetropolitcanTorontoMunicipalityCommissionersofPolice.cfm.

14. Ekos Research Associates, *National Justice Survey*, p. 21.

15. Ibid., p. 10.

16. Ibid., p. 16.

17. Canadian Bar Association. 2013. *Reaching Equal Justice: An Invitation to Envision and Act*. Ottawa: Author, p. 6. http://www.lsuc.on.ca/uploadedFiles/For_the_Public/About_the_Law_Society/Convocation_Decisions/2014/CBA_equal_justice.pdf.

18. T. Tyler. 2006. "Psychological Perspectives on Legitimacy and Legitimation," *Annual Review of Psychology, 57*, 375–400 at p. 376.

19. Ekos Research Associates, *National Justice Survey*, p. 29.

20. T. Tyler. 2004. "Enhancing Police Legitimacy," *The Annals of the American Academy of Political and Social Science, 593*, 84–99 at p. 85.

21. T.R. Tyler and Y.J. Huo. 2002. *Trust in the Law: Encouraging Public Cooperation with the Police and Courts*. New York: Russell-Sage.

22. C.T. Griffiths and P. Clark. 2017. "Building Police Legitimacy in a High Demand Environment: The Case of Yukon, Canada," *Policing: An International Journal of Police Strategies and Management, 40*(3), 560–573.

23. C.G. Nicholl. 1999. *Community Policing, Community Justice, and Restorative Justice: Exploring the Links for the Delivery of a Balanced Approach to Public Safety*. Washington, DC: U.S. Department of Justice, Office of Community-Oriented Policing, at pp. 57–58. http://www.cops.usdoj.gov/Publications/e09990014_web.pdf.

24. K. Dowler, T. Fleming, and S.L. Muzzatti. 2006. "Constructing Crime: Media, Crime, and Popular Culture," *Canadian Journal of Criminology & Criminal Justice, 48*(6), 837–850.

25. Ekos Research Associates, *National Justice Survey*, p. 8.

26. Parole Board of Canada. 2012. *Performance Monitoring Report 2011/2012*. Ottawa: Author. http://pbc-clcc.gc.ca/rprts/pmr/pmr_2011_2012/pmr_2011_2012-eng.pdf.

27. Public Safety Canada. 2013. *Public Safety Canada 2010–2011 Evaluation of the Effective Corrections and Citizen Engagement Initiatives*. Ottawa: Author. http://www.publicsafety.gc.ca/cnt/rsrcs/pblctns/vltn-ffctv-crrctns-2010-11/index-eng.aspx.

28. N. Boyd. 2012. *The Rule of Law, the Charter of Rights and Confidence in the Legal System: Lessons from Canada*. Vancouver: International Centre for Criminal Law Reform and Criminal Justice Policy.

29. A.N. Doob and C.M. Webster. 2015, May 4. "The Harper Revolution in Criminal Justice Policy. . . and What Comes Next," *Policy Options*. http://policyoptions.irpp.org/magazines/is-it-the-best-of-times-or-the-worst/doob-webster.

30. S. Fine. 2016, November 1. "Federal Government Plans to Reduce the Use of Mandatory Minimum Prison Sentences," *Globe and Mail*. https://www.theglobeandmail.com/news/national/ottawa-plans-to-reduce-use-of-mandatory-prison-sentences/article32609570.

31. J. Bronskill. 2016, December 13. "Justice Tracking Over 100 Court Challenges to Mandatory Minimum Penalties," *Canadian Press*. http://www.cbc.ca/news/politics/mandatory-minimums-constitutional-challenges-1.3893961.

32. Cited in Fine, "Federal Government Plans to Reduce the Use of Mandatory Minimum Prison Sentences."

33. C. Klingele, M.S. Scott, and W.J. Dickey. 2010. "Reimaging Criminal Justice," *Wisconsin Law Review*, 4, 953–998.

34. M.A. Jackson and C.T. Griffiths. 1995. *Canadian Criminology*. Toronto: Harcourt, Brace, Jovanovich.

35. R. Paternoster. 2010. "How Much Do We Really Know about Criminal Deterrence?" *The Journal of Criminal Law & Criminology*, 100(3), 765–824 at p. 765.

36. R.B. Cormier. 2002. *Restorative Justice: Directions and Principles—Developments in Canada* [User report 2002-02]. Ottawa: Department of the Solicitor General Canada. http://publications.gc.ca/collections/Collection/JS42-107-2002E.pdf.

37. Prison Fellowship International. 2008. "What Is Restorative Justice?" Washington, DC: Centre for Justice & Reconciliation. http://www.pfi.org/cjr/restorative-justice.

38. Y. Dandurand and C.T. Griffiths. 2006. *Handbook on Restorative Justice Programmes*. Vienna, Austria: United Nations Office on Drugs and Crime. http://www.unodc.org/pdf/criminal_justice/06-56290_Ebook.pdf.

39. G. Johnstone and D.W. Van Ness. 2006. *Handbook of Restorative Justice*. Portland, OR: Willan Publishing.

© Laurie Justus Pace, Graphics One Design, 2014

CHAPTER 3
CONSIDERATIONS IN THE STUDY OF CRIMINAL JUSTICE

LEARNING OBJECTIVES

After reading this chapter, you should be able to

- Discuss and define the concepts of racism, discrimination, and inequality in Canada.
- Define and discuss the concepts of racialized persons, racialization, and racial profiling.
- Discuss the experiences of Indigenous and racialized persons and members of visible/cultural/religious minority groups in Canada.
- Discuss the concerns over the escalating costs of the criminal justice system.
- Describe the changing boundaries of criminal justice agencies.
- Discuss the issues that surround victims in the criminal justice system.
- Discuss the health and wellness issues of offenders and criminal justice system personnel.
- Discuss the concerns regarding the lack of diversity among criminal justice system personnel.

One theme in this text is how racism, discrimination, and inequality are manifested in the criminal justice system and the impact of these on the experiences of the community, offenders, victims, and criminal justice system personnel. The discussion in this chapter highlights the importance of considering the historical and contemporary experience of certain groups in Canadian society that may affect their views of and experiences in the criminal justice system. These materials can also inform policies and programs designed to address the specific needs of persons in these groups.

The materials presented in the text will reveal that the criminal justice system is populated by a disproportionate number of Indigenous persons, racialized persons, and those who are vulnerable and marginalized in Canadian society. This includes persons with addictions, mental illness, and intellectual disabilities (i.e., limitations in intellectual functioning), and persons in living in poverty. These persons are at high risk of victimization and of being in conflict with the law, and they present challenges for the criminal justice system.[1]

MULTICULTURALISM AND DIVERSITY IN CANADA

Canada prides itself on being a diverse, multicultural society. A poll conducted in 2016 ($N = 2,001$) found that 43 percent of respondents identified multiculturalism and diversity as the attribute that made Canada unique.[2] Canada's visible minority population has grown steadily between 1981 and 2006, in large part due to increasing immigration from countries other than Europe.[3] The visible minority population has grown faster than the total population.[4]

However, observers have cautioned that, while there are strengths associated with multiculturalism, including the promotion of greater tolerance, there are weaknesses, including the creation of fault lines between groups and the view that multiculturalism is incompatible with liberal Western values.[5]

INEQUALITY

A key feature of Canadian society is inequality. Research, for example, has found that there has been increasing income inequality.[6] This increase was most pronounced for those persons in the top 1 percent of the population, who earn 39.1 percent of income in the country.[7] In contrast, more than 1 million children are living in low-income households.[8] Low income and poverty are associated with poor health, a lack of access to services, and a higher risk of becoming involved in the criminal justice system. Poverty, for example, has been found to be related to child anxiety/depression and anti-social behaviour.[9]

Inequality is also reflected in the gap in workplace wages between men and women. It is estimated that gender inequality in the workplace costs Canada $150 billion a year.[10] Data indicate that women working full-time earn 74.2 cents for every dollar that full-time male workers make.[11] This disparity is due, in part, to gender differences in industry and occupation.[12] Surveys have found that, while a majority of Canadians feel that gender equality has progressed, the wage gap is viewed as a major obstacle to professionals in this area.[13] Although the wage gap has decreased in recent years, there are still discrepancies that have a significant impact on women, their families, and the economy.[14]

RACISM, PREJUDICE, AND DISCRIMINATION

Racism, **prejudice**, and **discrimination** have been long-standing features of Canadian society and these may be manifested at times in the criminal justice system. Racism is *prejudice, discrimination, or antagonism directed against someone of a different race based on the belief that one's race is superior.*[15]

Prejudice is *the unsubstantiated, negative pre-judgment of individuals or groups, generally on the basis of ethnicity, religion, or race.*[16] Discrimination is *an action or a decision that treats a person or a group negatively for reasons such as their race, age, or disability.*[17]

These dynamics may exist at any one point in the criminal justice system, including in the decision-making of police officers, in the courts at sentencing, and in institutional and community-based corrections. The presence of prejudice, discrimination, and racism is not always overt, but may be subconscious on the part of justice system personnel or may be subtle and not readily identifiable. Also, persons in conflict with the law may perceive that they are the victims of prejudice, discrimination, and racism even in instances where there is no substantial proof that it has occurred. Nevertheless, it is important to understand the basis of these perceptions.

The United Nations has raised questions about Canada's record on anti-racism, citing the continuing challenges facing Indigenous peoples.[18,19] There is evidence that racism and discrimination exist in Canada, particularly with respect to women, Indigenous persons, persons in racialized groups, and others. This is reflected in the increase in police-reported hate crimes related to religion or race and ethnicity.[20] Hate crimes against the Muslim population, for example, increased 61 percent in 2015. Hate crimes involving violence related to sexual orientation increased 59 percent in 2015. In 2017, controversy over Canada's immigration policy spilled over into street-level conflicts between anti-racist and anti-fascist groups and far-right groups who oppose Canada's admission of refugees.

Canadian scholars and policy-makers have generally given little attention to the relationships between race, crime, and criminal justice.[21] It has been over two decades since a commission of inquiry on systemic racism in the Ontario criminal justice system found that there were decisions in the criminal justice system that reflected a bias against racialized persons.[22] Recall from Chapter 1 the conflict model of the origins and application of the criminal law wherein the law is formulated and applied by the powerful and used against those who are vulnerable.

The Canadian public appears to be aware of this issue. A survey (N = 1,000) of Canadians found that 69 percent of respondents felt that there was racism in Canada, and nearly half had heard persons make racist remarks.[23] An online survey (N = 1,000)

Racism

Prejudice, discrimination, or antagonism directed against someone of a different race based on the belief that one's race is superior.

Prejudice

The unsubstantiated, negative pre-judgment of individuals or groups, generally on the basis of ethnicity, religion, or race.

Discrimination

An action or a decision that treats a person or a group negatively for reasons such as their race, age, or disability.

IS IT POSSIBLE TO END RACISM IN THE CRIMINAL JUSTICE SYSTEM?

The issue of racism in the criminal justice system was first highlighted in 1995 in the *Report of the Commission on Systemic Racism in the Ontario Criminal Justice System*. Over two decades later, the issues of racism, prejudice, and discrimination in the justice system are even more pronounced. A recent high-profile effort by the Ontario provincial government is centred on public education and awareness and anti-racism strategies. Given the inability to successfully address these issues to date, it could be argued that these strategies will have little effect.

QUESTIONS

1. In your view, why have racism, prejudice, and discrimination continued to exist in Canadian society? In the criminal justice system?
2. From your lived experience, what do you think would be the most effective ways to address these issues?
3. How optimistic are you that these issues can be successfully addressed? What is the basis for your optimism/pessimism?

in Vancouver found that 82 percent of visible minorities indicated they had been subjected to prejudice or other forms of discrimination.[24]

To address these issues, in 2017, the province of Ontario announced a three-year strategic plan.[25] This comprehensive plan has a number of components, including legislation, targeted public education and awareness, an anti-Black racism strategy, and an Indigenous-focused anti-racism strategy, among others. See At Issue 3.1.

RACIALIZED PERSONS, RACIALIZATION, AND RACIAL PROFILING

Three key concepts in the discussion of racism, prejudice, and discrimination are **racialized persons, racialization,** and **racial profiling.** Canada's National Council of Welfare defines racialized persons as *persons, other than Indigenous people, who are non-Caucasian in race or non-white in colour.*[26] Racialization is the process by which societies construct races as real, different, and unequal in ways that matter to economic, political, and social life.[27] Racial profiling has been defined as "any action undertaken for reasons of safety, security or public protection that relies on stereotypes about race, colour, ethnicity, ancestry, religion, or place of origin rather than on reasonable suspicion, to single out an individual for greater scrutiny or different treatment."[28]

A report on racial profiling by the Ontario Human Rights Commission in 2017 cautioned that there is often no independent verification in cases where a person's or group's perception is that they have been racially profiled.[29]

Profiling can also occur in the larger community. A survey of a sample of Ontarians ($N = 1,503$) found that being racially profiled by a private business or retail service (46.6 percent) was mentioned more frequently than being profiled by the police (37.9 percent).[30]

A survey of a non-random sample of persons in Ontario ($N = 1,503$) found that four in 10 reported having been racially profiled.[31] See Figure 3.1.

The same survey found that the majority of Blacks (93 percent) in the sample felt they were profiled due to their "race or colour," while the majority of Muslim respondents (79 percent) identified their religion as the reason they were profiled.[32]

Racial profiling has a profound effect on the individual who is profiled, including loss of self-esteem, dignity, and sense of safety and security, both on families and on the social fabric of communities. See Figure 3.2.

Racialized persons

Persons, other than Indigenous people, who are non-Caucasian in race or non-white in colour.

Racialization

The process by which societies construct races as real, different, and unequal in ways that matter to economic, political and social life

Racial profiling

Any action undertaken for reasons of safety, security or public protection that relies on stereotypes about race, colour, ethnicity, ancestry, religion, or place of origin rather than on reasonable suspicion, to single out an individual for greater scrutiny or different treatment.

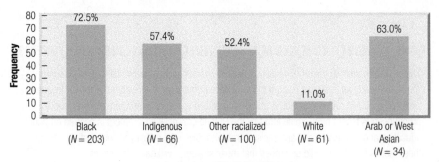

◄ FIGURE 3.1

Reported Incidence of Racial Profiling among Survey Respondents by Racial or Ethnic Background (*N* = 1,503)

Source: Ontario Human Rights Commission. 2017. *Under Suspicion. Research and Consultation Report on Racial Profiling in Ontario.* Toronto: Author, p. 20. http://ohrc.on.ca/sites/default/files/Under%20suspicion_research%20and%20consultation%20report%20on%20racial%20profiling%20in%20Ontario_2017.pdf. © Queen's Printer for Ontario, 2017. Reproduced with permission.

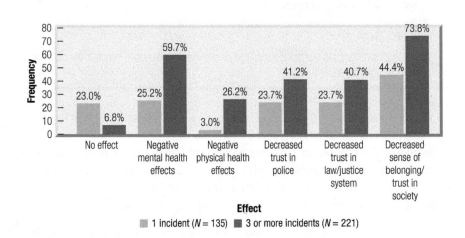

◄ FIGURE 3.2

Reported Effects of Racial Profiling by Number of Reported Incidents in the Last 12 Months

Source: Ontario Human Rights Commission. 2017. *Under Suspicion. Research and Consultation Report on Racial Profiling in Ontario.* Toronto: Author, p. 26. http://ohrc.on.ca/sites/default/files/Under%20suspicion_research%20and%20consultation%20report%20on%20racial%20profiling%20in%20Ontario_2017.pdf. © Queen's Printer for Ontario, 2017. Reproduced with permission.

Although most frequently discussed in the context of policing (see Chapter 4), racial profiling can occur at any stage of the criminal justice system and in society in general. Black accused persons, for example, may be more likely to be denied bail due to an assumed higher level of risk (Chapter 7) and are disproportionately placed in segregation in correctional institutions (Chapter 11).

Perceptions are important in the discussion of racial profiling; although there may not be intent on the part of criminal justice personnel to profile, if members of a racialized group *perceive* they are being profiled, the impact may be the same as if the intent were present.

Persons who are racialized often face challenges in accessing justice.[33] Criminal legal aid programs, funded by the federal government and the provincial and territorial governments, are designed to facilitate access to justice for poor and marginalized persons.[34] Racial profiling not only results in the alienation of communities and individuals, but also has been found to be ineffective as a strategy for ensuring community safety and security.[35,36]

Caution should be exercised in assuming that all members of these groups share the same experiences and perspectives. For example, one participant in a group session conducted as part of the Black Experience Project stated, "I'm born in Montreal and I'm of Haitian descent, I have … nothing in common with you all like nothing, except that I'm Black and I'm here…."[37] Similarly, a survey of Muslims found considerable diversity of opinion on a wide range of topics, including whether Muslim women should be allowed to wear a niqab when participating in a citizenship ceremony.[38]

THE EXPERIENCES OF WOMEN

> The exclusion of women from all public offices is a relic of days more barbarous than ours. And to those who would ask why the word "person" should include females, the obvious answer is, why should it not?[39]

This statement was made by Lord Sankey, Lord Chancellor of Great Britain, as part of the unanimous decision of England's Privy Council (which at that time ran Canada's legal affairs) in October 1929. It established that Canadian women were to have the legal status of "persons." Women had been given the right to vote in the four Western provinces in 1916, in Ontario in 1917, in Nova Scotia in 1918, in New Brunswick in 1919, in PEI in 1922, but not until 1940 in Quebec. (Indigenous persons were not granted the right to vote until 1960.) However, prior to this decision in 1929, they were not allowed to participate in politics.[40]

There have been significant improvements in the education levels of women in Canada.[41] Women are more likely than men to have a high school diploma, and women account for the majority of enrolments in college and university programs.[42]

The level of income and socio-economic status of women is strongly linked to their level of life satisfaction, health, and mental health.[43,44] For example, women who report that they have very good or excellent health are those with higher levels of income and education.[45] Conversely, those women with the lowest incomes report considerably lower levels of good health and more health problems.[46]

The experience of women as victims of crime and in the justice system is illustrated in crime statistics. The rates of self-report violent victimization are higher among women (85 per 100,000 versus 67 per 100,000 for men).[47]

The most common crime committed against women is assault,[48] and women represent nearly 90 percent of all sexual assault victims.[49] The rate of violent victimization is highest among women aged 15 to 24, and the risk of being the victim of violence is higher among those women with mental health issues.[50]

Bias may occur in how the criminal justice system responds to women who have been victimized. In the discussion of police operations in Chapter 6, it is noted that there are high rates of dismissals of allegations of sexual assault made by women, while at the sentencing stage of the criminal justice process, discussed in Chapter 9, there are criminal court judges who blame the victim in their court rulings.

THE EXPERIENCES OF INDIGENOUS PERSONS

In this text, the term *Indigenous* will be used to denote status and non-status Indians, Métis, and Inuit, although another commonly used term is *Aboriginal*. Indigenous persons are disproportionately represented as both victims and offenders at all stages of the criminal justice system.[51]

The rate at which Indigenous persons report experiencing violent victimization is more than double that of non-Indigenous persons (160 incidents per 1,000 population compared with 74 incidents per 1,000 population).[52] While Indigenous people represented about 4 percent of the total Canadian population in 2006 (the most recent population count available), 27 percent of homicide victims in 2009 were Indigenous.[53]

The issues surrounding the overrepresentation of Indigenous persons in Canada's criminal justice system are discussed throughout the text. At this juncture, it is important to comment, albeit briefly, on the events that may contribute to this overrepresentation.

INDIGENOUS PERSONS IN CANADIAN SOCIETY: THE LEGACY OF COLONIZATION

Many Indigenous people live on the margins of Canadian society. This is reflected in pervasive poverty, high rates of unemployment, low levels of formal education, and high death rates from accidents and violence. On nearly every measure of health and well-being, Indigenous persons are much worse off than non-Indigenous persons.[54]

More than half of Indigenous students fail to graduate from high school, and the unemployment rate among Indigenous persons is twice that of non-Indigenous persons. Indigenous youth may be prime targets for gang recruitment, which may result in involvement in the criminal justice and corrections systems.[55] In the province of Manitoba, for example, Indigenous youth make up 23 percent of the general population but 84 percent of the youth in sentenced custody.[56]

The subordinate political and economic condition of Indigenous peoples is a consequence of their colonization by Europeans and of Canadian government policies that have exerted control over virtually every aspect of Indigenous life. These policies have had a devastating impact on the social, political, and economic fabric of Indigenous communities.[57] As one Indigenous youth stated:

> The history that's so commonly accepted is just one side of the story. No one wants to acknowledge all the historical trauma that we face today by losing the land, and the reserves systems, and colonization—how that even affects us today. It needs to be acknowledged if we want to heal. To understand how deep this trauma goes and how it's still happening.[58]

A significant contributor to these conditions was the residential school system that was operated by the federal government from the late 1880s until the 1990s. In the residential school system, Indigenous children were forcibly removed from their families, often for many years. During this time, 150,000 Indigenous children were sent to residential schools. At its peak in 1930, 80 residential schools were in operation across the country (except in Newfoundland, New Brunswick, and Prince Edward Island).[59] The intergenerational impact of residential schools was identified by the Truth and Reconciliation Commission (TRC) as a major factor in Indigenous persons' conflict with the law.

In the residential schools, many operated by religious orders including the Catholic and Anglican churches, Indigenous children were subjected to physical, sexual, and psychological abuse. Children were punished for practising their own cultures and for using their own language, resulting in feelings of shame about one's identity and a loss of cultural practices and language acquisition across generations.[60]

The residential school system fractured Indigenous families, helped destroy traditional cultures and values, and shredded the fabric of many Indigenous communities.[61] A poll of Canadians in 2015 (N = 1,511) found that 70 percent of those surveyed agreed with the finding of the Truth and Reconciliation Commission that the residential school system was "cultural genocide."[62]

While most Canadians are aware of the residential schools and their impact, so did the "'60s Scoop," profiled in Criminal Justice File 3.1, also had a devastating impact on Indigenous children, their families, and communities.

Less well known, but equally as impactful for some Indigenous persons, their families, and communities, was the system of tuberculosis (TB) sanitoriums that operated across the country from the late 1800s until the mid-1900s. TB, a bacterial infection that primarily affects the lungs, was the leading cause of death in Canada in 1867, and hospitals were designed to isolate those persons with the disease, often for periods of

▶ Cree students attending the Anglican-run Lac la Ronge Mission School in La Ronge, Saskatchewan, 1949

Bud Glunz/National Film Board of Canada. Photothèque/PA-134110

up to two years. This was prior to the development of drug therapy that is used today for the disease.

Indigenous persons, including Inuit, were sent thousands of kilometres from their home communities in the North to sanitoriums in the south—Inuit from the western Arctic to a hospital in Edmonton and those from the eastern Arctic to a hospital in Hamilton, Ontario.[63] This fractured families and often resulted in the loss of language.

CRIMINAL JUSTICE FILE 3.1

THE "'60S SCOOP"

Indigenous families and communities were further fractured during the years between the 1960s and 1980s. In what became known as the "'60s Scoop," as many as 16,000 Indigenous children were removed from their families by child welfare workers and placed in non-Indigenous families across Canada, the U.S., and the U.K. This was done without the consent of their parents.

The impact of this on the culture and identity of Indigenous children was significant and has often been referred to as "cultural genocide" and as contributing to the high numbers of Indigenous youth in care. In the words of one survivor:

> I lost everything, including my name. I lost my family. I lost my language. I lost everything about my culture. This should have never happened. It was wrong.[a]

In 2017, an Ontario court judge ruled that the federal government had breached its duty of care to the thousands of Indigenous children who were removed from their families. In the view of the court, the loss of identify contributed to addiction, mental health issues, and fractured lives experienced by many of the children in their adult lives.[b] That same year, the federal government reached an $800 million settlement with those who had been removed from their birth families.

[a] A. Russell. 2016, August 23. "What Was the ''60s Scoop'? Aboriginal Children Taken from Homes a Dark Chapter in Canada's History," *Global News*. http://globalnews.ca/news/2898190/what-was-the-60s-scoop-aboriginal-children-taken-from-homes-a-dark-chapter-in-canadas-history.

[b] J. Gallant. 2017, February 14. "Judge Rules in Favour of '60s Scoop Victims" *Toronto Star*. https://www.thestar.com/news/gta/2017/02/14/judge-rules-in-favour-of-sixties-scoop-victims.html.

As one Indigenous man who was sent to a TB sanitorium as a child recalled:

> When I was there, I had a good grasp of the English language and I spoke English fluently. When I came back into my community, I spoke not one word of my own language and I couldn't remember how to speak it. I haven't spoken it for many years and it's only now just coming back to me.[64]

THE EXPERIENCES OF INDIGENOUS WOMEN

Indigenous women face a number of unique challenges that may place them at risk. A contributor is the stereotypes held of Indigenous women by Canadian society. (For example, view the film, "Shit Canadians Say to Aboriginal Women," listed in the Media Links section at the end of this chapter.) Also, although the gap in life expectancy between Indigenous and non-Indigenous women has been narrowing, it persists.[65]

The living arrangements of Indigenous women also play a role in the challenges they face. Household crowding, for example, is associated with health and social issues, including mental health problem and family violence. In 2006, 31 percent of Inuit women and girls were living in crowded homes, compared to 3 percent of non-Indigenous women, and 14 percent of First Nations women and girls were living in crowded dwellings, over three times higher than the proportion of non-Indigenous women (3 percent).[66]

Indigenous women are generally less likely than their non-Indigenous counterparts to be part of the paid workforce, and the rates of unemployment among Indigenous women are twice as high than for non-Indigenous women (13.5 percent versus 6.4 percent).[67] Indigenous women are much more likely to live in households with incomes under the poverty line.[68]

These factors, and histories of trauma in their personal lives, contribute to placing Indigenous women at high risk of victimization, as reflected in the following:

- Indigenous women are more likely to be affected by all types of violent victimization.[69]
- The homicide rate for Indigenous women is nearly six times higher than that for non-Indigenous women—4.82 per 100,000 population versus 0.82 per 100,000 population.[70]
- Indigenous women experience higher rates of spousal violence; they are three times more likely than non-Indigenous women to report being the victim of spousal violence (10 percent versus 3 percent, respectively).[71,72]
- Young Indigenous women may be particularly at risk of sexual assault, particularly if they had parents who attended residential schools and had experienced childhood sexual abuse.[73]

For an account of the historical and contemporary context of violence against Indigenous women, see the work by Anne McGillivray and Brenda Comaskey entitled *Black Eyes All of the Time*.[74] These issues are reflected in the tragedy of missing and murdered Indigenous women and girls, which is discussed later in the text.

SEXUAL MINORITIES

Persons with various sexual orientations may encounter prejudice and discrimination and may be at risk of victimization. Research on the victimization of minority groups shows that individuals who self-identify as homosexual or bisexual are much more likely than individuals who self-identify as heterosexual to experience victimization.[75] Gay and bisexual women, for example, are more likely to be victimized than heterosexual women.[76]

LGBTQ YOUTH

An example of the challenges faced by sexual minorities is illustrated by the experiences of LGBTQ youth. A study of homeless youth in Toronto ($N = 100$ youth who were poly-substance abusers, then five focus groups with 27 youth) found greater use of methamphetamines and opioids among homeless LGBTQ youth than their heterosexual peers.[77] These circumstances and behaviours place LGBTQ at a high risk of victimization, contact with the police, and involvement in the criminal justice system.

Transgender youth have reported barriers to accessing supportive and knowledgeable health care.[78] These youth are most likely to encounter discrimination than their peers in the shelter system.[79] In a survey ($N = 762$, 54 percent of whom were Indigenous youth) of street-involved and marginalized youth in British Columbia, participants reported a lack of both culturally relevant services and LGBTQ-related services, in addition to being discriminated against based on their race and/or skin colour.[80] One observer noted, "The threat of violence and harassment on the streets is exacerbated for LGBTQ youth due to frequent encounters with homophobia and transphobia."[81]

Attention is also being given to the experience of Indigenous Two-Spirit/LGBTQ persons.[82] An exploratory study of this group ($N = 50$) in Winnipeg and Vancouver found that they faced challenges in being accepted for their identities—for example, as male, gay, Indigenous youth both in their home Indigenous communities and in the urban centres to which they had migrated.[83] These struggles had a significant impact on their health and well-being, and often led them to become involved in substance abuse and to be at increased risk of physical and sexual assault.[84]

THE EXPERIENCES OF MUSLIMS

Groups may also be discriminated against and be victimized by violence due to their religious beliefs. This has been experienced by Muslims in Canada.

A poll of Canadians in 2017 ($N = 2,513$; 1,024 in Quebec and 1,489 elsewhere in Canada) focusing on attitudes toward minority and immigrant groups found that only 12 percent of the respondents felt that Muslims were integrated in Canadian society, and that one in three Quebecers and one in four of other Canadians were in favour of banning Muslim immigration to Canada.[85]

A survey of Muslims ($N = 600$) found that one-third (35 percent) of those surveyed indicated they had experienced discrimination or unfair treatment by others in Canada in the past five years because of their religion (22 percent), ethnic or cultural background (22 percent), language (13 percent), or sex (6 percent). (Note: Individual percentages exceed total because some individuals have experienced discrimination for more than one of these reasons.) The combined total for discrimination due to religion and/or ethnicity/culture was 30 percent.[86]

Concerns have been expressed about the rise of Islamophobia ("fear of Muslims") across Canada, but particularly in Quebec.[87] Anti-Muslim graffiti has appeared across the country, including on schools in Calgary and on the cars of Muslim families. In 2017, Parliament passed Motion 103, which stated that the House of Commons called on the federal government to condemn Islamophobia and "all forms of systemic racism and religious discrimination." Note that motions are not legislation, but recommend a certain course of action by government.

MUSLIM EXPERIENCES IN QUEBEC

Although Muslims often face challenges in all regions of the country, these have been particularly acute in the province of Quebec. Recall from Chapter 1 that provincial legislation (Bill 62) was passed in October 2017 requiring women to uncover their faces when providing, or receiving, government services. Although this legislation will likely be challenged in court and perhaps found to be unconstitutional, its passage suggests there are divisions between the Muslim community and the larger Canadian society.

This legislation was passed against the backdrop of a number of critical incidents that significantly affected the Muslim community. More recently, on January 29, 2017, a mass shooting occurred at the Islamic Cultural Centre of Quebec City. Six persons were killed and 19 more wounded by a lone gunman at this mosque in the suburb of Sainte-Foy. On August 6, 2017, the vehicle of the president of the Islamic Cultural Centre of Quebec City was torched at his home in an arson attack.

Other incidents in the province included a pig's head being left at the front door of a mosque (Muslims do not eat pork) in 2016 and a referendum in June 2017 in which the residents of the community of Saint-Apollinaire (population 6,400) voted to deny a zoning change that would have allowed the Islamic Cultural Centre to open a Muslim cemetery. The far-right group La Meute ("Wolf Pack") was identified as having mobilized community opposition to the cemetery.[88,89] The municipal government in Quebec City subsequently sold land to the Centre culturel Islamique de Québec to be used for a Muslim cemetery.[90]

▲ Graffiti on a Quebec City mosque in 2014

THE CANADIAN PRESS/Sean Kilpatrick

THE EXPERIENCES OF BLACKS

Blacks in Canada have experienced racism, prejudice, and discrimination historically and in contemporary times. For purposes of this text, the term "Black" includes persons who self-identify as "Black," "African," "African-Canadian," "Caribbean," "Afro-Canadian," and others. Observers have argued that, historically, Blacks in Canada have been subjected to "structural violence" perpetrated by state-funded institutions, including the criminal justice system and, most notably the police.[91]

Support for this view is provided by the historical record, which indicates that, far from being a promised land for escaping slavery in the U.S., in Canada, Blacks were subjected to segregated and inferior schools, excluded from employment opportunities, and subjected to racial stereotyping and discrimination.[92] They were also held as slaves in some parts of the country. An advertisement placed by one Peter Russell of York on February 10, 1806, read:

> To be sold. A Black Woman named Peggy, aged 40 years, and a boy, her son, named Jupiter, aged about 15 years, both of them the property of the Subscriber.[93]

In Nova Scotia, the Council of Parties of the Nova Scotia Home for Colored Children Restorative Inquiry (RI) (https://restorativeinquiry.ca) has reported on systemic racism in the province and its impact on Black families and communities. The inquiry, ongoing as of the end of 2017, has proceeded within a restorative framework that will develop strategies to address the issues that are identified. Among the findings of the RI has been the need for strong role models for African Nova Scotian youth.[94]

Black children and youth are disproportionately represented in child welfare, child protection, and youth justice systems; in the numbers living in poverty; and among those at high risk of sexual exploitation and violence. In Toronto, Black children comprise 41 percent of the youth in care of the Children's Aid Society, a number that is five times their representation in the general population.[95]

Black children drop out of school at a higher rate than other children, and the rates of unemployment of Black youth in Ontario is nearly two times the provincial rate.[96]

There are concerns that the experiences of Black women, which include racism, have not received sufficient attention in the feminist movement.[97] As one observer noted, "In Canada, black women and other women of colour find themselves missing not only from movements for gender diversity, but also from seats of power. Bank boards, newsrooms, hospital boards and executive positions are all spaces where white women see themselves better represented."[98]

The history of oppression of Blacks is the basis for the arguments being made by defence counsel for Blacks accused of crimes—that is, that the history of Black oppression and racism should be considered at sentencing, much as those of Indigenous persons are. This issue is discussed in Chapter 9. Similar to their counterparts in the U.S., Black adults are overrepresented in correctional institutions in Canada.[99] This is discussed in Chapter 11.

THE BLACK EXPERIENCE PROJECT

The Black Experience Project in the Greater Toronto Area is an example of one initiative that is facilitating dialogue on the issues that are important to the Black community. In recognition of the importance of "giving voice" to groups in a diverse society and to understand their "lived experience," the Environics Institute, in partnership with Ryerson University's Diversity Institute, the United Way of Greater Toronto, the YMCA of Greater Toronto, and other organizations, have created The Black Experience Project (www.theblackexperienceproject.ca).

The initiative, which involves extensive community consultation and dialogue, focuses on the challenges and opportunities in the Black community in the Greater Toronto Area. Among the issues being addressed are education, physical and mental health, employment, and community safety. The community safety issues that have been identified are perceptions of bias toward Blacks by police and the stigmatization and criminalization of young Black men. The dialogue has noted the importance of relationships of trust between the police and the Black community, as well as the need for police outreach and community engagement. View "The Black Experience Project" video listed in the Media Links section at the end of this chapter.

ADDITIONAL CONSIDERATIONS

There are a number of additional issues that surround the criminal justice system in the early 21st century and that provide the backdrop for the discussions in the following chapters.

THE ESCALATING COSTS OF THE CRIMINAL JUSTICE SYSTEM

The criminal justice system is a very expensive enterprise. Over the past decade, criminal justice expenditures have increased both in real terms and as a percentage of GDP (gross domestic product), despite the overall decline in crime rates across the country.[100] See Figure 3.3; also, a breakdown of expenditures is presented in Figure 3.4.

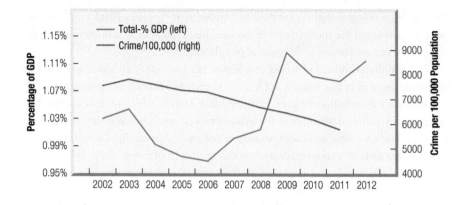

◄ FIGURE 3.3

Canadian Crime Rate and Criminal Justice Expenditures as a Percentage of GDP

Source: R. Story and T.K. Yalkin. 2013. *Expenditure Analysis of Criminal Justice in Canada.* Ottawa: Office of the Parliamentary Budget Officer, p. 2. http://www.pbo-dpb.gc.ca/web/default/files/files/files/Crime_Cost_EN.pdf. Reprinted with permission of the Office of the Parliamentary Budget Officer.

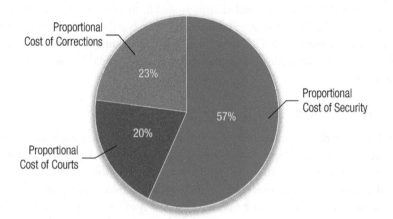

◄ FIGURE 3.4

Criminal Justice Expenditure Proportion, 2012

Source: R. Story and T.K. Yalkin. 2013. *Expenditure Analysis of Criminal Justice in Canada.* Ottawa: Office of the Parliamentary Budget Officer, p. 18. http://www.pbo-dpb.gc.ca/web/default/files/files/files/Crime_Cost_EN.pdf. Reproduced with the permission of the Parliamentary Budget Officer.

The high cost of crime and the criminal justice response is also illustrated by the figures in Figure 3.5, which set out the costs for selected offences. The "cost" for each type of crime includes victim costs, such as direct economic losses to property and wages, and medical costs due to injury; expenditures for police, courts, and corrections; "opportunity costs" resulting from the decision of a person to engage in crime rather than a legitimate activity; and intangible costs, such as pain and suffering of victims.[101,102]

A key question is whether the Canadian public is getting "value for money"; that is, do the expenditures on the police, the courts, and corrections and related programs and services make communities safe from crime, address the needs of crime victims, and intervene in such a way so as to reduce the likelihood that offenders will continue their criminal behaviour? Unfortunately, the answer to these questions is often, "We're not certain."

THE CHANGING BOUNDARIES OF CRIMINAL JUSTICE AGENCIES

Historically, there have been very clear boundaries between the various components of the criminal justice system. The police focused on the apprehension of offenders, the courts on prosecuting and sentencing, and corrections on implementing the sentences of the courts. This often resulted in agencies operating in "silos," focused only on their specific mandate and not considering the larger context of a problem of crime and disorder, specific patterns of criminal behaviour, or the needs of offenders, which are often multifaceted (such as those with addictions or mental illness).

The siloed approach is slowly changing, and criminal justice agencies are partnering with social services, health, and other agencies and community resources to address the

FIGURE 3.5 ▶

Costs of Crime and the Criminal Justice System for Selected Offences, 2014

Source: T. Gabor. 2015. Costs of Crime and Criminal Justice Responses [Research report 2015-R022]. Ottawa: Public Safety Canada, p. 6. https://www.publicsafety.gc.ca/cnt/rsrcs/pblctns/2015-r022/2015-r022-en.pdf. This information was reproduced with the permission of the Minister of Public Safety and Emergency Preparedness Canada, 2017.

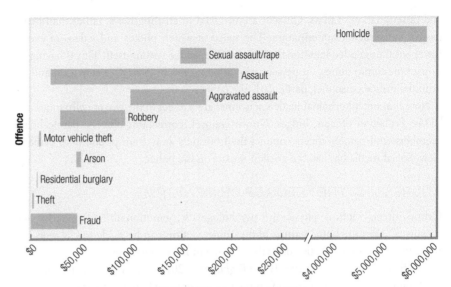

needs of persons in conflict with the law. Multi-agency teams, such as the police working with social workers and mental health professionals, are common. These teams may focus on a specific neighbourhood or on groups of offenders. This is a more holistic approach to problem-solving and has the potential to effectively address the underlying issues that contribute to crime and disorder, rather than merely respond to the symptoms of these issues.

Although agencies can benefit from moving outside of their traditional sphere of activities, there are concerns that collaboration may blur the mandates of individual components of the justice system; for example, when parole officers work in teams with police officers, it may create an inordinate focus on surveillance and control to the detriment of the helping and assistance role of parole officers.[103]

THE RISE OF THE SURVEILLANCE SOCIETY

A key feature of life in the early 21st century is the pervasiveness of technology and, more specifically, surveillance technology. Most citizens do not realize that, every day, their activities are recorded by video cameras—while shopping, when standing at a bus stop, even while driving. Ostensibly, the application of surveillance technology is to ensure the safety and security of the general public. A major challenge is defining the parameters within which technology can be used and how the privacy and other rights of citizens can be protected. A challenge is ensuring that the rights of citizens are protected.

The use of high technology in the criminal justice system is in its infancy, although concerns are already being raised. In some instances, technology has obvious benefits; for example, allowing prison inmates to conduct video chats with their loved ones who may be unable to travel to the institution for visits, or realizing a reduction in reoffending by sex offenders who are monitored via GPS.[104] On the other hand, the use of GPS tracking devices raise privacy issues and the question of whether there should be limits on the intrusion of technology in the lives of offenders.

Technology now allows any citizen with a cellphone or PDA to record, photograph, transmit, and receive information instantaneously, without filters and outside mainstream media, which has traditionally dominated the production

and dissemination of news. Citizens are involved in creating news, rather than being passive consumers of information. The speed at which photos and videos of events travel has transcended traditional media and the justice system itself. This is having an impact on communities, on persons who are engaged in disruptive activities, and on criminal justice personnel, particularly the police.

Note that not all criminal justice personnel are subject to the eye of cellphones and PDAs: Probation officers, judges, Crown counsel, corrections officers, parole board members, and parole officers conduct their business away from public (and camera) view. Social media has had the greatest impact on the police.

ADDRESSING THE NEEDS OF CRIME VICTIMS

Crime affects victims physically, psychologically, emotionally, financially, and socially.[105] After the initial trauma of the crime, victims can be made to feel worse by the actions of criminal justice officials, resulting in **re-victimization**.

The federal *Canadian Victims Bill of Rights* (S.C. 2015, c. 13, s. 2) sets out a number of statutory rights for the victims of crime, including the right to information, participation, protection, and restitution. These rights include being provided with information on victim programs and services, and on offenders' progress through the system. There is also provincial and territorial legislation designed to ensure that crime victims have rights in the criminal justice process.

Despite this, many crime victims find the justice system to be complex and confusing, and they have difficulty understanding the decisions that are made and the sanctions that are imposed on their perpetrators. Although victims are a heterogeneous group with diverse needs and perceptions, there are common themes in their complaints and concerns. In the adversarial system of justice, crime victims are often an afterthought. Criticisms that may be voiced by victims include not receiving sufficient information about developments in the case and being excluded from key decisions that are made throughout the criminal justice process.

This has been compounded by criminal justice system personnel who are not trained to be sensitive to the needs of crime victims. A study of the survivors of sexual violence in three Canadian cities ($N = 114$) found that just over 50 percent of the women had no confidence in the police, and two-thirds indicated that they did not have confidence in the criminal justice system or the criminal court process.[106]

THE HEALTH AND WELLNESS OF OFFENDERS AND CRIMINAL JUSTICE PROFESSIONALS

There is an increasing recognition that the adversarial system of justice, with its sole focus on the alleged criminal behaviour of the accused, has obscured larger health and wellness issues that may have played a role in the behaviour and that must be addressed if intervention efforts are to be successful. Studies have discovered that many offenders are suffering from trauma due to their experiences as children and adults.

There is also attention being given to the health and wellness of criminal justice professionals. This has resulted in the development of assessment protocols as well as a number of intervention and assistance programs. The health and wellness issue is discussed throughout the text.

Of particular concern is the experience of women professionals in the criminal justice system. The materials presented in this text reveal that women who work in policing, the legal system, and corrections are subject to harassment and discriminatory treatment. This may have a significant impact on their health and well-being.

Re-victimization

The negative impact on victims of crime caused by the decisions and actions of criminal justice personnel.

THE LACK OF THE DIVERSITY AMONG CRIMINAL JUSTICE PROFESSIONALS

Ideally, the profile of criminal justice professionals should reflect the diversity of Canadian society. Historically, the police services, courts, and systems of corrections have been staffed primarily by Caucasian males. There has been some progress. Statistics indicate, for example, that there have been significant increases in the numbers of women working in justice-related occupations. Women now comprise the following percentage of these occupations: judges, 36 percent versus 14 percent in 1991; lawyers and notaries, 42 percent; probation and parole officers, 65 percent; correctional service officers, 32 percent; and sworn police officers, 20 percent versus 7 percent in 1991.[107] Although trending in the right direction, there is still insufficient gender diversity in the criminal justice professions.

The absence of Canada-wide data precludes a determination of the numbers of Indigenous persons, persons from racialized groups, and others from visible/cultural/religious minority groups who work in the criminal justice system. Some information is available from police services (discussed in Chapter 4), and a number of reports have identified the lack of diversity in the judiciary as a major issue (discussed in Chapter 7).

SUMMARY

This chapter was designed to provide background context to the study of the Canadian criminal justice system. Inequality, racism, prejudice, and discrimination were introduced as features of Canadian society. These are often manifested in racial profiling and the racialization of groups and individuals. Women, Indigenous persons, Muslims, and sexual minorities have lived experiences that affect their quality of life and may place them at risk of being victimized or of coming into conflict with the law.

Additional considerations in the study of the criminal justice system are the escalating costs of criminal justice and the question as to whether the Canadian public is getting "value for money"; the changing boundaries of criminal justice agencies as reflected in the development of multi-agency partnerships; the challenges posed by the rise of the surveillance society due to the pervasiveness of technology; the challenges faced by crime victims; concerns with the health and wellness of offenders and criminal justice professionals; and the lack of diversity among criminal justice professionals.

KEY POINTS REVIEW

1. Although Canada prides itself on being a diverse, multicultural society, there are fault lines between groups.

2. A key feature of Canadian society is inequality, as reflected in the gap in workplace earnings between men and women.

3. Racism, prejudice, and discrimination have been long-standing features of Canadian society and are manifested in the criminal justice system.

4. Canadian scholars have given relatively little attention to the relationships between race, crime, and criminal justice.

5. Key concepts in the discussion of racism, prejudice, and discrimination are racialized persons, racialization, and racial profiling.

6. Racial profiling can occur in society and in the criminal justice system and can have a profound effect on the individual who is profiled.

7. The level of income and the socio-economic status of women is closely linked to their level of life satisfaction, health, and mental health, which are, in turn, associated with their risk of victimization.

8. The subordinate political and economic condition of Indigenous persons is a consequence of their colonization by Europeans and government policies, including the residential school system.

9. Indigenous persons are overrepresented at all stages of the criminal justice system as both victims and offenders.

10. Indigenous women face unique challenges that place them at risk of victimization.

11. Persons with various sexual orientations may encounter prejudice and discrimination, which place them at risk of victimization and involvement in the justice system.

12. Muslims in Canada have experienced prejudice and discrimination, as reflected in recent events in the province of Quebec.

13. The historical record reveals that Blacks in Canada have been subjected to racism and discrimination historically and in contemporary times.

14. Additional issues surrounding the criminal justice system include the escalating costs of the criminal justice system, the changing boundaries of criminal justice agencies, the rise of the surveillance society, the needs of crime victims, the health and wellness of offenders and criminal justice professionals, and the absence of diversity in the criminal justice system workforce.

KEY TERM QUESTIONS

1. Define and describe **racism**, **prejudice**, and **discrimination** and their role in Canadian society.

2. Define **racialized persons**, **racialization**, and **racial profiling** and describe why these concepts are important in any study of the criminal justice system.

3. What concerns surround the potential **re-victimization** of crime victims by the criminal justice system?

CRITICAL THINKING EXERCISE

Critical Thinking Exercise 3.1

Indigenous Experiences

The study of the involvement of Indigenous persons in the criminal justice system requires an understanding of their historical and contemporary circumstances. Watch the film *We Will Be Free* at https://www.youtube.com/watch?v=OXT2JXe8mnA.

Your Thoughts?

1. What are your five take-aways from the film?

2. In what way does the film assist you in understanding the involvement of Indigenous peoples in the criminal justice system and how this may be best addressed?

CLASS/GROUP DISCUSSION EXERCISE

Class/Group Discussion 3.1

The "Colonized Mind" of Indigenous Persons

Jana-Rae Yerxa is Anishinaabe from Little Eagle and Couchiching First Nation and belongs to the Sturgeon clan. She uses the concept of the "colonized mind" of Indigenous persons to explain the experiences of Indigenous peoples and their perspectives and perceptions. Access "The Unravelling of a Colonized Mind" at VAW Legal Information Resource, at http://vawlawinfo.ca/understanding-the-first-nation-metis-and-inuit-context/placing-violence -against-first-nation-metis-and-inuit-women-in-historical-context.

Your Thoughts?

1. How might the notion of the "colonized mind" assist in understanding the experience of Indigenous peoples with the criminal justice system?

2. Why would it be important for persons who work in the criminal justice system to understand the notion of the "colonized mind" among Indigenous peoples?

MEDIA LINKS

Racism and Discrimination

"History of Racism in Canada," *British Columbia Teachers' Federation*, March 27, 2012. https://www.youtube.com/watch?v=dvqXh83IJgM

"Racial Profiling by Stores, Landlords and Companies: Are We Racist?" *CBC Marketplace*, February 26, 2016, https://www.youtube.com/watch?v=WjmDwWUhEpg&list =PLeyJPHbRnGaZmzkCwy3-8ykUZm_8B9kKM

"Is Winnipeg Really the Most Racist City in Canada?" *Winnipeg Alternative Media*, January 26, 2015, https://www.youtube.com/watch?v=svOxBkbOHXY

Women

"Did You Know? The Famous Five and the Persons Case," CPAC, March 17, 2014, https://www.youtube.com/watch?v=if_pyx5dm9Y

Indigenous Persons

"Stolen Children: Residential School Survivors Speak Out," *The National*, June 2, 2015, https://www.youtube.com/watch?v=vdR9HcmiXLA

"Canadian History and the Indian Residential School System," *School District 27 Residential Schools and Reconciliation*, July 17, 2014, https://www.youtube.com/watch?v=6-28Z93hCOI

"Full Story: Failing Canada's First Nations Children," *16×9 on Global*, March 5, 2016, https://www.youtube.com/watch?v=xhEh-D7IRQc

"Our Home and Native Land—Wikwemikong," *CPAC*, April 13, 2010, https://www.youtube .com/watch?v=ell3X6Afn3U

"Shit Canadians Say to Aboriginal Women," March 2, 2012, https://www.youtube.com/ watch?v=7mKZ7PBfCXA

Finding Dawn, National Film Board, 2006, https://www.nfb.ca/film/finding_dawn

"Highway of Tears," *CBS News*, December 21, 2013, https://www.cbsnews.com/videos/highway-of-tears-2

Blacks

"Deeply Rooted," *CBC Short Docs*, http://www.cbc.ca/shortdocs/shorts/deeply-rooted

Journey to Justice, National Film Board of Canada, 2000, https://www.nfb.ca/playlists/nfb_celebrates_black_history_month/playback/#16

"Being Black in Canada," *CBC News*, March 14, 2014, https://www.youtube.com/watch?v=EIe1WQe2Cx0

"Stolen from Africville," *Stolen from Africa*, May 14, 2014, https://www.youtube.com/watch?v=_gSrNH5_nk0

"The Black Experience Project," July 21, 2017, https://vimeo.com/226503372

REFERENCES

1. V. Marinos, D. Griffiths, J. Robinson, L. Gosse, C. Fergus, S. Stromski, and K. Rondeau. 2017. "Persons with Intellectual Disabilities and the Criminal Justice System: A View from Criminal Justice Professionals in Ontario," *Criminal Law Quarterly*, 64(102), 83–107.

2. Environics Institute for Survey Research. 2016. *Survey of Muslims in Canada 2016*. Toronto: Author, p. 9. http://www.environicsinstitute.org/uploads/institute-projects/survey%20of%20muslims%20in%20canada%202016%20-%20final%20report.pdf.

3. T. Chui and H. Maheux. 2011. "Visible Minority Women," in *Women in Canada: A Gender-Based Statistical Report* (6th ed.). Statistics Canada Catalogue no. 89-503-X. Ottawa: Minister of Industry, p. 5. http://www.statcan.gc.ca/pub/89-503-x/2010001/article/11527-eng.pdf.

4. Ibid.

5. E.S. Ng and I. Bloemraad. 2015. "A SWOT Analysis of Multiculturalism in Canada, Europe, Mauritius, and South Korea," *American Behavioral Scientist*, 59(6), 619–636.

6. A. Heisz. 2016. "Trends in Income Inequality in Canada and Elsewhere," in *Income Inequality: The Canadian Story* (vol. V), edited by D.A. Green, W. C. Riddell, and F. St-Hilaire, 77–102. Montreal: Institute for Research on Public Policy. http://irpp.org/wp-content/uploads/2016/01/aots5-heisz.pdf.

7. Conference Board of Canada. 2013. "Income Inequality." http://www.conferenceboard.ca/hcp/details/society/income-inequality.aspx.

8. L. Young. 2017, September 13. "1.2 Million Canadian Children Living in Poverty: Census," *Global News*. https://globalnews.ca/news/3739960/canadian-census-children-poverty.

9. L. Strohschein and A.H. Gauthier. 2017. "Poverty Dynamics, Parenting, and Child Mental Health in Canada," *Society and Mental Health*. Advance online publication. doi:10.1177/2156869317731603

10. S. Devillard, T. Vogel, A. Pickersgill, A. Madgavkar, T. Nowski, M. Krishnan, T. Pan, and D. Kechrid. 2017. *The Power of Parity: Advancing Women's Equality in Canada. Report*. Toronto: McKinsey & Company. www.mckinsey.com/global-themes/gender-equality/the-power-of-parity-advancing-womens-equality-in-canada.

11. T. Grant. 2017, March 6. "Who Is Minding the Gap?" *Globe and Mail*. https://www.theglobeandmail.com/news/national/gender-pay-gap-a-persistent-issue-in-canada/article34210790.

12. T. Schirle. 2015. "The Gender Wage Gap in the Canadian Provinces, 1997–2014," *Canadian Public Policy*, 41(4), 309–319.

13. M. Racco. 2017, July 5. "Gender Equality in Canada: Where Do We Stand Today?" *Global News*. https://globalnews.ca/news/3574060/gender-equality-in-canada-where-do-we-stand-today.

14. C. Williams. 2010. "Economic Well-Being," in *Women in Canada: A Gender-Based Statistical Report* (6th ed.). Statistics Canada Catalogue no. 89-503-X. Ottawa: Minister of Industry. http://www.statcan.gc.ca/pub/89-503-x/2010001/article/11388-eng.pdf.

15. OXFORD LIVING DICTIONARIES: Definition of "racism" as seen online at https://en.oxforddictionaries.com/definition/racism. By permission of Oxford University Press.

16. *The Canadian Encyclopedia*. n.d. "Prejudice and Discrimination in Canada." http://www.thecanadianencyclopedia.ca/en/article/prejudice-and-discrimination.

17. Canadian Human Rights Commission. n.d. "What Is Discrimination?" https://www.chrc-ccdp.gc.ca/eng/content/what-discrimination-1.

18. Chinese & Southeast Asian Legal Clinic. 2017, August 15. "UN Committee Questions Canada's Record on Anti-Racism" [news release]. https://globenewswire.com/news-release/2017/08/15/1084905/0/en/UN-Committee-Questions-Canada-s-Record-on-Anti-Racism.html.

19. S. Paradkar. 2017, August 14. "NGOs Tell UN Panel Canada Is Failing on Ending Racism: Paradkar," *Toronto Star*. https://www.thestar.com/news/gta/2017/08/14/ngos-tell-un-panel-canada-is-failing-on-racism-paradkar.html.

20. B. Leber. 2017. *Police-Reported Hate Crime in Canada, 2015*. Statistics Canada Catalogue no. 85-002-X. Ottawa: Minister of Industry, p. 3. http://www.statcan.gc.ca/pub/85-002-x/2017001/article/14832-eng.pdf.

21. A. Owusu-Bempah and S. Wortley. 2014. "Race, Crime, and Criminal Justice in Canada," in *The Oxford Handbook of Ethnicity, Crime, and Immigration*, edited by S. Buerius and M. Tonry, 281–320. New York: Oxford.

22. M. Gittens and D. Cole (Co-Chairs). 1995. *Report of the Commission on Systemic Racism in the Ontario Criminal Justice System*. Toronto: Queen's Printer for Ontario, p. 56. http://www.ontla.on.ca/library/repository/mon/25005/185733.pdf.

23. *The Globe and Mail* and Nanos Research. 2016, May. "Views on Racism in Canada." http://www.nanosresearch.com/sites/default/files/POLNAT-S15-T682.pdf.

24. F. Merali. 2017, March 6. "New Survey Finds Racism Is 'Alive and Well' in B.C.," *CBC News*. http://www.cbc.ca/beta/news/canada/british-columbia/vancity-poll-on-racism-1.4011796.

25. Province of Ontario. 2017. *A Better Way Forward: Ontario's 3-Year Anti-Racism Strategic Plan*. Toronto: Queen's Printer for Ontario. https://files.ontario.ca/ar-2001_ard_report_tagged_final-s.pdf.

26. National Council on Welfare. 2012. *Poverty Profile: Special Edition*. Ottawa: Author, p. 1. https://www.canada.ca/content/dam/esdc-edsc/migration/documents/eng/communities/reports/poverty_profile/snapshot.pdf.

27. Ontario Human Rights Commission. n.d. "Racial Discrimination, Race and Racism" [fact sheet]. http://www.ohrc.on.ca/en/racial-discrimination-race-and-racism-fact-sheet.

28. Ontario Human Rights Commission. *Under Suspicion*, p. 94.

29. Ibid., p. 19.

30. Ibid., p. 29.

31. Ibid., p. 19.

32. Ibid., p. 21.

33. A. Go. 2014, July 14. "The Access to Justice Challenges of Chinese Canadians," *Legal Aid Ontario Blog*. http://blog.legalaid.on.ca/2014/07/14/the-access-to-justice-challenges-of-chinese-canadians.

34. Department of Justice Canada. 2014. *Report of the Deputy Minister Advisory Panel on Criminal Legal Aid*. Ottawa: Author. http://www.justice.gc.ca/eng/rp-pr/csj-sjc/esc-cde/rr14/index.html.

35. Commission des droits de la personne et des droits de la jeunesse (Commission on Human Rights and Youth Rights). 2011. *Racial Profiling and Systemic Discrimination of Racialized Youth*. Quebec: Author, p. 49. http://www.cdpdj.qc.ca/publications/Profiling_final_EN.pdf.

36. Ontario Human Rights Commission. 2003. *Paying the Price: The Human Cost of Racial Profiling*. Toronto: Author. http://www.ohrc.on.ca/sites/default/files/attachments/Paying_the_price%3A_The_human_cost_of_racial_profiling.pdf.

37. K. Connely, W. Cukier, C. Grant, K. Neuman, K. Newman-Bremang, and M. Wisdom. 2014. *The Black Experience Project: A Greater Toronto Area Study Capturing the Lived Experience of a Diverse Community. Phase 1—Community Engagement. Final Report*. Toronto: Environics Institute, p. 10. http://www.environicsinstitute.org/uploads/institute-projects/black%20experience%20project%20gta%20-%20phase%201%20final%20report.pdf.

38. Environics Institute for Survey Research, *Survey of Muslims in Canada 2016*, p. 30.

39. Status of Women Canada. n.d. "The History of the Persons Case." http://www.swc-cfc.gc.ca/commemoration/pd-jp/history-histoire-en.html.

40. Ibid.

41. M. Turcotte. 2011. "Women and Education," in *Women in Canada: A Gender-Based Statistical Report* (6th ed.). Statistics Canada Catalogue no. 89-503-X. Ottawa: Ministry of Industry, p. 6. http://www.statcan.gc.ca/pub/89-503-x/2010001/article/11542-eng.pdf.

42. Ibid., p. 17.

43. T.H. Mahony. 2011. "Women and the Criminal Justice System," in *Women in Canada: A Gender-Based Statistical Report* (6th ed.). Statistics Canada Catalogue no. 89-503-X. Ottawa: Ministry of Industry, p. 12. http://www.statcan.gc.ca/pub/89-503-x/2010001/article/11416-eng.pdf.

44. M. Turcotte. 2011. "Women and Health," in *Women in Canada: A Gender-Based Statistical Report* (6th ed.). Statistics Canada Catalogue no. 89-503-X. Ottawa: Ministry of Industry, pp. 6–7. http://www.statcan.gc.ca/pub/89-503-x/2010001/article/11543-eng.pdf.

45. Ibid., p. 7.

46. Ibid., p. 21.

47. T.H. Mahony, J. Jacob, and H. Hobson. 2017. "Women and the Criminal Justice System," in *Women in Canada: A Gender-Based Statistical Report* (7th ed.). Statistics Canada Catalogue no. 89-503-X. Ottawa: Minister of Industry, p. 4. http://www.statcan.gc.ca/pub/89-503-x/2015001/article/14785-eng.pdf.

48. Ibid., p. 5.

49. Ibid., p. 5.

50. Ibid., p. 12.

51. Department of Justice Canada. 2017. "JustFacts: Indigenous Overrepresentation in the Criminal Justice System." http://www.justice.gc.ca/eng/rp-pr/jr/jf-pf/2017/jan02.html.

52. Mahony, Jacob, and Hobson, "Women and the Criminal Justice System," p. 7.

53. V. O'Donnell and S. Wallace. 2011. "First Nations, Métis and Inuit Women," in *Women in Canada: A Gender-Based Statistical Report* (6th ed.). Statistics Canada Catalogue no. 89-503-X. Ottawa: Minister of Industry, p. 42. http://www.statcan.gc.ca/pub/89-503-x/2010001/article/11442-eng.pdf.

54. M. McNally and D. Martin. 2017. "First Nations, Inuit and Métis Health: Considerations for Canadian Health Leaders in the Wake of the Truth and Reconciliation Commission of Canada Report," *Healthcare Management Forum*, 30(2), 117–122.

55. Native Women's Association of Canada. 2007, June. *Aboriginal Women and Gangs: An Issue Paper*. Paper presented at the National Aboriginal Women's Summit, Corner Brook, NL. https://www.nwac.ca/wp-content/uploads/2015/05/2009-Aboriginal-Women-and-Gangs-an-Issue-Paper.pdf.

56. Canadian Council of Provincial Child and Youth Advocates. 2010, June 23. *Aboriginal Children and Youth in Canada: Canada Must Do Better* [position paper]. http://www.cyanb.ca/images/positionpaper-e.pdf.

57. M.B. Castellano, L. Archibald, and M. Degagne. 2008. *From Truth to Reconciliation: Transforming the Legacy of Residential Schools*. Ottawa: Aboriginal Healing Foundation. http://www.ahf.ca/downloads/from-truth-to-reconciliation-transforming-the-legacy-of-residential-schools.pdf.

58. A.R. Hatala, T. Pearl, K. Bird-Naytowhow, A. Judge, E. Sjoblom, and L. Liebenberg. 2017. "'I Have Strong Hopes for the Future': Time Orientations and Resilience among Canadian Indigenous Youth," *Qualitative Health Research*, 27(9), 1330–1344 at p. 1334.

59. Truth and Reconciliation Commission of Canada. 2015. *Honouring the Truth, Reconciling for the Future: Summary of the Final Report of the Truth and Reconciliation Commission of Canada*. Winnipeg: Author. http://www.trc.ca/websites/trcinstitution/File/2015/Honouring_the_Truth_Reconciling_for_the_Future_July_23_2015.pdf.

60. D. Chansonneuve. 2007. "Addictive Behaviours Among Aboriginal People in Canada," Ottawa: Aboriginal Healing Foundation. http://www.ahf.ca/downloads/addictive-behaviours.pdf.

61. Castellano, Archibald, and Degagne, *From Truth to Reconciliation: Transforming the Legacy of Residential Schools*.

62. L. Hensley. 2015, July 9. "Residential School System Was 'Cultural Genocide,' Most Canadians Believe According to Poll," *National Post*. http://nationalpost.com/news/canada/residential-school-system-was-cultural-genocide-most-canadians-believe-according-to-poll/wcm/0f5cb01d-3716-434a-a4a1-dc77465c8e0b.

63. K. Bennett. 2016, November 9. "Telling the Story of Hundreds of Inuit, Sick with TB, Who Were Shipped to Hamilton," *CBC News*. http://www.cbc.ca/news/canada/hamilton/telling-the-story-of-hundreds-of-inuit-sick-with-tb-who-were-shipped-to-hamilton-1.3842103.

64. J. Moffatt, M. Mayan, and R. Long. 2013. "Sanitoriums and the Canadian Colonial Legacy: The Untold Experiences of Tuberculosis Treatment," *Qualitative Health Research*, 23(12), 1591–1599.

65. O'Donnell and Wallace, "First Nations, Métis and Inuit Women," p. 17.

66. Ibid., pp. 22–23.

67. Ibid., p. 26.

68. Ibid., p. 40.

69. Mahony, Jacob, and Hobson, "Women and the Criminal Justice System," p. 7.

70. Ibid., p. 22.

71. D.A. Brownridge. 2008. "Understanding the Elevated Risk of Partner Violence Against Aboriginal Women: A Comparison of Two Nationally Representative Surveys of Canada," *Journal of Family Violence*, 23(5), 353–367.

72. Mahony, Jacob, and Hobson, "Women and the Criminal Justice System," p.16.

73. M.E. Pearce, A.H. Blair, M. Teegee, S.W. Pan, V. Thomas, H. Zhang, M.T. Schechter, and P.M. Spittal. 2015. "The Cedar

Project: Historical Trauma and Vulnerability to Sexual Assault Among Young Aboriginal Women Who Use Illicit Drugs in Two Canadian Cities," *Violence Against Women*, 21(3), 313–329. http://refugeeresearch.net/wp-content/uploads/2017/05/Pearce-et-al-2015-Sexual-assault-against-young-Aboriginal-women.pdf.

74. A. McGillivray and B. Comaskey. 1999. *Black Eyes All of the Time: Intimate Violence, Aboriginal Women, and the Justice System*. Toronto: University of Toronto Press.

75. Mahony, Jacob, and Hobson, "Women and the Criminal Justice System," p. 10.

76. Ibid.

77. L. Barnaby, R. Penn, and P.G. Erickson. 2010. *Drugs, Homelessness & Health: Homeless Youth Speak Out About Harm Reduction*. Toronto: Wellesley Institute. http://homelesshub.ca/sites/default/files/homelessyouthspeakout_shoutclinic2010_v2.pdf.

78. N.S. Quintana, J. Rosenthal, and J. Krehely. 2010. *On the Streets: The Federal Response to Gay and Transgender Homeless Youth*. Washington, DC: Center for American Progress. https://cdn.americanprogress.org/wp-content/uploads/issues/2010/06/pdf/lgbtyouthhomelessness.pdf.

79. Ibid.

80. E. Saewyc, A. Smith, B. Dixon-Bingham, D. Brunanski, S. Hunt, S. Simon, M. Northcott, and The McCreary Centre Society. 2008. *Moving Upstream: Aboriginal Marginalized and Street Involved Youth in B.C.* Vancouver: McCreary Centre Society. http://www.mcs.bc.ca/pdf/Moving_Upstream_Websmall.pdf.

81. I.A. Abramovich. 2012. "No Safe Place to Go: LGBTQ Youth Homelessness in Canada: Reviewing the Literature," *Canadian Journal of Family and Youth*, 4(1), 29–51 at p. 33.

82. J. Ristock, A. Zoccole, L. Passante, and J. Potskin. 2017. "Impacts of Colonization on Indigenous Two-Spirit/LGBTQ Canadians' Experiences of Migration, Mobility, and Relationship Violence," *Sexualities*. Advance online publication. doi:10.1177/1363460716681474

83. Ibid., p. 8.

84. Ibid., p. 8.

85. T. Kheiriddin. 2017, March 13. "Guess What Canada: We're Kinda Racists, Too," *iPolitics Insights*. http://ipolitics.ca/2017/03/13/guess-what-canada-were-racists.

86. Environics Institute for Survey Research, *Survey of Muslims in Canada 2016*, p. 38.

87. M. Scotti. 2017, January 31. "Quebec City Shooting: Is Islamophobia 'More Manifested' in Quebec?" *Global News*. http://globalnews.ca/news/3216525/quebec-city-shooting-is-islamophobia-more-manifested-in-quebec.

88. J. Montpetit. 2016, December 4. "Inside Quebec's Far Right: A Secretive Online Group Steps into the Real World," *CBC News*. http://www.cbc.ca/news/canada/montreal/quebec-far-right-la-meute-1.3876225.

89. J. Montpetit. 2017, July 18. "Quebec City Mayor Worried about Far-Right Group Linked to Cemetery Referendum," *CBC News*. http://www.cbc.ca/news/canada/montreal/la-meute-far-right-saint-apollinaire-cemetery-1.4210975.

90. T.T. Ha. 2017, July 19. "Muslim Cemetery Fallout Deepens as Quebec Mosque Reveals It Received Hate Package," *Globe and Mail*. https://www.theglobeandmail.com/news/national/hateful-package-sent-to-quebec-city-mosque-before-muslim-cemetery-vote/article35729286.

91. R. Maynard. 2017. *Policing Black Lives: State Violence in Canada from Slavery to the Present*. Halifax and Winnipeg: Fernwood Press.

92. E.M.A. Thornhill. 2008. "So Seldom for Us, So Often Against Us: Blacks and Law in Canada," *Journal of Black Studies*, 38(3), 321–337 at p. 326.

93. Ibid.

94. Council of Parties of the Nova Scotia Home for Colored Children Restorative Inquiry. 2017. *Council of Parties Report: Winter 2016/17*. Halifax: Author, p. 12. https://restorativeinquiry.ca/sites/default/files/inline/documents/Council_of_Parties_Report_WEB.pdf.

95. Ministry of Children and Youth Services. 2017, July 26. "Helping Black Youth Succeed Through Mentorship" [news release]. https://news.ontario.ca/mcys/en/2017/07/helping-black-youth-succeed-through-mentorship.html?_ga=2.223764955.192494557.1509145107-1987501095.1509145107.

96. S. Contenta, L. Monsebraaten, and J. Rankin. 2016, June 23. "CAS Study Reveals Stark Racial Disparities for Blacks, Aboriginals," *Toronto Star*. https://www.thestar.com/news/canada/2016/06/23/cas-study-reveals-stark-racial-disparities-for-blacks-aboriginals.html.

97. S. Anderson. 2016, March 9. "Today's Feminist Problem? Black Women Are Still Invisible," *Globe and Mail*. https://www.theglobeandmail.com/opinion/todays-feminist-problem-black-women-are-still-invisible/article29082375.

98. Ibid.

99. Owusu-Bempah and Wortley, "Race, Crime, and Criminal Justice in Canada," p. 282.

100. B. Runciman and G. Baker. 2017. *Delaying Justice Is Denying Justice. An Urgent Need to Address Lengthy Court Delays in Canada*. Ottawa: Standing Senate Committee on Legal and Constitutional Affairs, p. 7. https://sencanada.ca/content/sen/committee/421/LCJC/reports/Court_Delays_Final_Report_e.pdf.

101. T. Gabor. 2015. "Costs of Crime and Criminal Justice Responses" [Research summary 2015-S022]. https://www.publicsafety.gc.ca/cnt/rsrcs/pblctns/2015-s022/2015-s022-en.pdf.

102. T. Gabor. 2015. *Costs of Crime and Criminal Justice Responses* [Research report 2015-R022]. Ottawa: Public Safety Canada. https://www.publicsafety.gc.ca/cnt/rsrcs/pblctns/2015-r022/2015-r022-en.pdf.

103. C.T. Griffiths and D. Murdoch. 2018. *Canadian Corrections* (5th ed.). Toronto: Nelson.

104. P. Bulman. 2013. "Sex Offenders Monitored by GPS Found to Commit Fewer Crimes." *NIJ Journal*, 271, 22–25. http://www.nij.gov/journals/271/gps-monitoring.htm.

105. M. Lindsay. 2014. *A Survey of Survivors of Sexual Violence in Three Canadian Cities*. Ottawa: Department of Justice Canada, pp. 14–15. http://www.justice.gc.ca/eng/rp-pr/cj-jp/victim/rr13_19/rr13_19.pdf.

106. Ibid., p. 7.

107. Mahony, Jacob, and Hobson, "Women and the Criminal Justice System," p. 41.

© Laurie Justus Pace. Graphics One Design, 2014

PART II

THE POLICE

Chapter 4: The Structure and Roles of the Police
Chapter 5: Police Powers and Decision-Making
Chapter 6: Police Strategies, Operations, and Engagement

Policing is perhaps the most high-profile, dynamic, and oftentimes controversial component of the Canadian criminal justice system. Police officers are required to play a multifaceted role: counsellor, psychologist, enforcer, mediator, and listener. They must be able to understand and empathize with the feelings and frustrations of crime victims; at the same time, they must develop strategies to cope with the dark side of human behaviour, which they encounter every day. Officers must walk a fine line between carrying out their enforcement role and ensuring that the rights of law-abiding citizens and suspects are protected.

How police services and police officers respond to the multifaceted demands that are placed on them affects individual citizens and their neighbourhoods and communities, as well as officers and the police services within which they work. Police are the only agents of the criminal justice system with whom most Canadians ever have contact. This contact often gives rise to concerns with the powers and decision-making of the police.

In contrast to personnel in other components of the justice system, police officers work in environments that are always changing. Technological developments, most notably the prevalence of mobile phone cameras, Internet-based platforms such as YouTube, and social networking sites such as Facebook, have significantly increased the visibility of police actions.[1] Concurrent with this has been an expansion in the structures of oversight and accountability of the police.

The chapters in this section focus on the various facets of Canadian policing. Chapter 4 describes the structure and operation of police services in this country.

Chapter 5 focuses on police powers and decision-making, and Chapter 6 examines the strategies that the police employ to prevent and respond to crime.

© Laurie Justus Pace, Graphics One Design, 2014

CHAPTER 4
THE STRUCTURE AND ROLES OF THE POLICE

LEARNING OBJECTIVES

After reading this chapter, you should be able to

- Discuss the evolution of policing in Canada.
- Discuss the current structure of policing in Canada.
- Define police work and describe the issues that surround police work in a democratic society.
- Discuss the various roles of the police.
- Discuss what is meant by *political policing*.
- Describe the structures of police governance.
- Describe the recruitment and training of police officers.
- Describe what is meant by the *working personality* of police officers and the issues that surround this concept.
- Discuss the challenges of police work, including occupational stress injuries and the experience of women police officers with sexual harassment and discrimination.

A Day in the Life of a Toronto Police Officer

The old floorboard creaks as a tall, burly man with a scruffy beard comes barging out of the painted green door. The hallway is stuffy in the old apartment building near Parkdale neighbourhood. It's just after 10 p.m. on Saturday night and many of the neighbours poke their heads out to eavesdrop while others flee from the scene and wait outside for the incident to be over.

An ambulance waits outside the apartment with its lights on. A woman without socks or shoes waits, a chunk of flesh exposed on her head after her black hair was ripped out. Her boyfriend came home late after a night at the bar and she found messages to another woman on his phone. When she approached him about it, he attacked her.

Aged, brown walls surround the police officers in the hallway, the only exit is now 50 feet behind them. Abruptly the man comes closer and raises his arms while simultaneously yelling at the officers.

"Ha—three against one, let's go," he bellows.

The situation is too tight for the officers to use a Taser, and pepper spray would only leave the officers struggling in a mist that burns like hot sauce in your eyes. It would impact the officers more than the man who had been drinking.

In the blink of an eye, everyone is pinned against the floor, wrestling against each other in the cramped hallway. The man slammed into the female officer during the commotion and it is hard to determine who is who in the brawl.

"Give us the knife," yells one of the officers. "Stop resisting."

The brawl lasts only a few seconds, but the eerily silent hallway makes the situation even more uncomfortable to those watching from their apartment doors. More uniformed officers have arrived in the hallway now. One of the original officers gets the man in handcuffs and says he is "HBD"—has been drinking. A paramedic assesses the man for injuries and then places him into a police vehicle.

Inside the ambulance the woman is providing her side of the story to one of the younger police officers. His demeanour is calm and collected; he speaks just above a whisper. The woman agrees to give a video statement back at the station, the best form of evidence in court. Unfortunately, it is common for the victims to refuse pressing charges even after they call police.

As the woman exits the ambulance and walks barefoot toward the apartment to gather her things, her boyfriend can be heard viciously banging on the door inside the court vehicle as it pulls away down the narrow street.

The two street lights act as a spotlight on top of the officers as they discuss the incidents that unfolded. They plan their next moves and actions. One will ride with the victim to the station, two will ride in the larger vehicle with the suspect, and 14 Division Sergeant Nelson Barreira will continue doing loops of the neighbourhood going over and over in his head what happened, just like he does every day on the job, for every call.

Source: Excerpted from A. Kelly. 2016, June 11. "What It's Really Like: Being a Toronto Police Officer," *Toronto City News.* http://toronto.citynews.ca/2016/06/11/what-its-really-like-being-a-toronto-police-officer. Used with permission of Rogers Media Inc. All rights reserved.

DEFINING POLICE WORK

Policing

The activities of any individual or organization acting legally on behalf of public or private organizations or persons to maintain security or social order.

A definition of **policing** must include both public and private police and is the *activities of any individual or organization acting legally on behalf of public or private organizations or persons to maintain security or social order while empowered by either public or private contract, regulations or policies, written or verbal.*[2]

The above quote is an acknowledgement that the public police no longer have a monopoly on policing, although with a few exceptions, they retain a monopoly on the use of force. An increasing role in safety and security in the community is being played by private security services and parapolice officers—that is, community constables that have limited powers of enforcement. Police scholars have referred to the new reality as the **pluralization of policing**.

THE LEGISLATIVE FRAMEWORK OF POLICE WORK

Police officers carry out their tasks within a number of legislative frameworks that define their roles, powers, and responsibilities. The *Canadian Charter of Rights and Freedoms* is perhaps the most impactful on the powers and activities of the police, particularly the "Legal Rights" section (see Chapter 1). There is also provincial and municipal legislation, which includes a wide range of statutes such as motor vehicle administration acts, highway traffic acts, liquor acts, and provincial/municipal police acts. All of these provide the framework within which police services are structured and delivered. As well, the various police acts set out the principles of policing, providing for and defining the activities of police commissions and municipal police boards, and setting out the processes for filing complaints against and the disciplinary procedures for police officers.

PERSPECTIVES ON THE ROLE OF THE POLICE

There are two competing perspectives on the role of the police, the **social contract perspective** and the **radical perspective**. These perspectives are similar in orientation to the value consensus and conflict models of the origins and application of the criminal law discussed in Chapter 1.

THE SOCIAL CONTRACT PERSPECTIVE

The social contract perspective views the police as a politically neutral force that acts primarily to enforce the law and protect the public. The power of police and their mandate to use force against citizens is justified under the social contract vision of society. The police use of force as necessary to maintain order and maximize collective good by maintaining a safe and workable society. Citizens are understood to voluntarily surrender some of their power and rights and delegate them to the state and to the police force. The police are viewed as a politically neutral force that uses its powers to enforce the laws within the confines of a defined set of rules. The social contract perspective informs mainstream views of policing, which see police as a protective force against crime and social disorder.

THE RADICAL PERSPECTIVE

While the social contract perspective depicts the police as a neutral agent of the State providing for the safety and security of citizens, the proponents of the radical perspective point out that since the police support the government, which, in turn, supports the interests of the ruling class, the police are never politically neutral.[3]

The radical perspective on the police is captured in the following narrative:

> Policing is part of the complex technologies, or methods of control (such as corrections institutions, public health administration, public education administration and corporate management) whose primary function in history has been to consolidate the social power of the capitalist class and administer the working class and poor. . . . [T]he police are integral to the manner in which the state controls and contains civil society in general and people in particular.[4]

Pluralization of policing

The expansion of policing beyond the public police to include parapolice and private security.

Social contract perspective (on the role of the police)

A perspective that considers the police to be a politically neutral force that acts primarily to enforce the law and protect the public.

Radical perspective (of the role of the police)

A perspective that views the police as an instrument used by governments and powerful interests to suppress dissent, stifle protest, and help maintain the status quo.

The radical perspective considers police as a repressive force that is instrumental in the maintenance of an unjust social system: "The police are primarily utilized by the government to maintain the status quo and to protect the powerful against any perceived threats" (ActivistRights.org.au). This includes conducting surveillance on individuals and groups who are deemed to be a threat to national security and suppressing public protests. For a radical perspective on the role of police in Canada, view the documentary film *Into the Fire (Canada Is a Police State)*, listed in Media Links section at the end of this chapter.

Proponents of this perspective of the police and of Canadian society as a "police state" cite as evidence the historical record. There are numerous historical and contemporary examples wherein the police were used by the government to "pacify" the Canadian west, so that it could be settled and developed; to break strikes and suppress citizen protests; and to monitor the activities of Canadians who were/are deemed to be a threat to the State. The persons most often the subject of government and police interest have been those involved in various political activities and/or who had beliefs or engaged in behaviour (including sexual) that were viewed as a threat to the stability and status quo of the State. Continuing to the present, the police have spied on citizens and have engaged in activities that violated citizens' rights. Police services, particularly the Royal Canadian Mounted Police (RCMP) and the Canadian Security Intelligence Service (CSIS), have maintained extensive secret data files on citizens and engaged in activities that have often been determined to be illegal.

Canadian scholars Reg Whitaker, Gregory Kealey, and Andrew Parnaby have labelled this phenomenon **political policing**.[5] There are numerous examples of this in Canadian history and in contemporary times.

Throughout the 20th century, the RCMP carried out extensive surveillance of politicians, university students, and faculty, and it maintained confidential files on hundreds of thousands of Canadians. Covert surveillance on university campuses began during the First World War and continued into the late 1990s.[6,7] The force was especially interested in left-wing student organizations and faculty during the 1960s, and it used student informants as well as undercover police to gather information. In the 1980s, a Royal Commission that was investigating alleged illegal activities of the RCMP reported that the RCMP Security Service (since disbanded and replaced by the civilian Canadian Security Intelligence Service) maintained hundreds of thousands of files on Canadians. Police surveillance and its impact on citizens' rights continues to be the source of controversy and this is discussed in Chapter 5.

The terrorist attacks of 9/11 in the U.S. accelerated police surveillance on groups and persons identified as posing a terrorist threat. In Canada, increasing concerns with "homegrown terrorists" have led to an expansion of police powers and ongoing proposals for legislation that would give the police even greater authority to conduct surveillance of persons and groups deemed to pose a threat. "Extremist travellers," persons intent on leaving Canada to join conflicts in other parts of the world and those returning from conflict zones with terrorist training and combat experience, have become a major focus of police services.

Whatever framework you bring to the understanding of the role of police in society, there is no doubt that they are a powerful force. On the one hand, the police enjoy high levels of public support; on the other, the police (along with the military) have a virtual monopoly on legitimate force combined with an array of weapons and tactics that provide the potential for coercion and repression. As the front line of the criminal justice

Political policing

Secretive police investigative activities and surveillance of persons and groups deemed to be a threat to the stability and status quo of the State.

system, the police have always been drawn into situations involving social disorder and public protests, including demonstrations against global capitalism.

POLICE WORK IN A DEMOCRATIC SOCIETY

The separation of powers between the police and government is considered an important tenet of liberal democracy. The separation of powers assists in ensuring that the police are not used in a partisan political way to harass and punish political opponents and dissidents. There is also a separation of roles and powers between the courts and the police. It is the police role to bring suspected offenders before the courts and the courts' role to decide on guilt or innocence and, in the case of conviction, decide on punishment. Among all of the institutions and organizations in society, it is the police that can have a direct impact on the rights and freedoms of individual citizens. This is due to the powers that police officers are given under the law. All police services operate in a political environment since the police are mandated to enforce the criminal law, which reflects political values and political ends.[8]

The Law Commission of Canada has identified four key values that form the framework within which to understand police work in Canadian society:

- *Justice*: The police maintain peace and security in the community while ensuring that individuals are treated fairly and human rights are respected.
- *Equality*: All citizens are entitled to policing services that contribute to their feelings of safety and security.
- *Accountability*: The actions of police services, and police officers, are subject to review.
- *Efficiency*: Policing services must be cost-effective.[9]

Ideally, policing in a democratic society is focused on the safety and security of citizens while ensuring that the rights of citizens (and suspects) are protected. The police are to be apolitical, fair, and impartial. It is in attempting to reconcile these values—protecting public order and individual rights—that the inherent tensions of policing in a democratic society are revealed. There are natural tensions between the power and authority of the police and their legal mandate to maintain order on the one hand, and the values and processes that exist in a democratic society on the other. This tension is inevitable and, generally, irreconcilable.[10]

These tensions may also result in conflicts between the police and other components of the criminal justice system, notably the courts. Police officers often complain that the rights of offenders are given more attention than those of victims and law-abiding citizens, and officers are often frustrated when offenders are released on technicalities or receive court sentences that they deem to be lenient. There is little doubt that the Charter and court decisions have had a major impact on the powers and procedures of the police, and this is considered in Chapter 5. The increasing use of technology in police work has also raised concerns, in particular about the privacy of citizens, and this topic is also addressed in Chapter 5. Concerns have also been raised about what is perceived to be the increasing *militarization* of police services in Canada. See At Issue 4.1.

The governments and the public rely on the police to prevent and respond to crime and to apprehend offenders; yet at the same time, these governments are committed to the principles of democracy and due process. It is not surprising, then, that police officers often experience conflict in carrying out their duties and that the police are often "caught in the middle." Police services often find themselves caught between the directives of governments and persons involved in civil disobedience.

OFFICER FRIENDLY BECOMES GI JOE: SHOULD THE CANADIAN POLICE BE PREVENTED FROM BECOMING MILITARIZED?

There are increasing concerns that police services in Canada are becoming militarized, reflecting a trend that has occurred in the United States. In the U.S., a study by the American Civil Liberties Union found that "the militarization of American policing is evident in the training that police officers receive, which encourages them to adopt a 'warrior' mentality and think of the people they are supposed to serve as enemies, as well as in the equipment they use, such as battering rams, flashbang grenades, and APCs [armoured personnel carriers]."[a]

There are concerns that the militarization of the police is occurring in Canada as well. The New Glasgow (Nova Scotia) Regional Police Service, which serves the two communities of New Glasgow and Trenton (combined population of approximately 12,500, according to the 2016 Census), received a light-armoured vehicle from the Department of National Defence (DND) to be used in a variety of situations. By 2017, the police service's emergency response team (ERT) had been disbanded and the police service was attempting to regift the vehicle to another police service for free.[b]

In 2010, the Ottawa Police Service spent $340,000 to purchase an armoured vehicle equipped with steel bodywork, machine-gun-proof glass, gun ports, and a roof turret.[c] Records indicate that, in addition to armoured vehicles (with the armaments removed), the DND has donated night-vision goggles and military apparel to police services.[d]

A major concern is that, rather than making communities safer and more secure, militarization drives a wedge between the police and the community and undermines the original principles of Sir Robert Peel (see Police File 4.2).

QUESTIONS

1. What is your view of police services acquiring military equipment?
2. If you were on a municipal council, would you support the police service acquiring an armoured personnel carrier?
3. How would you respond to the argument that this type of hardware is required to counter terrorist threats?

---

[a] American Civil Liberties Union. 2014. *War Comes Home: The Excessive Militarization of American Policing.* New York: Author, p. 3. https://www.aclu.org/sites/default/files/assets/jus14-warcomeshome-report-web-rel1.pdf.

[b] P. Mulligan. 2017, May 30. "Nova Scotia Town Trying to Regift Light Armoured Vehicle It Doesn't Use," *CBC News.* http://www.cbc.ca/news/canada/nova-scotia/new-glasgow-police-cougar-light-armoured-vehicle-gift-halifax-1.4138028.

[c] M. Spratt. 2014, August 15. "The Creeping Militarization of the Police," *iPolitics.* http://www.ipolitics.ca/2014/08/15/the-creeping-militarization-of-the-police.

[d] D. Quan. 2014, August 29. "Canadian Forces Donate Surplus Military Hardware to Police Agencies," *Canada.com.* http://o.canada.com/news/national/rcmp-defends-acquisition-of-surplus-military-hardware.

GOVERNANCE AND OVERSIGHT OF THE POLICE

While it is important that the police be free from political interference, there must be governmental and judicial oversight of police activities. As one police scholar has noted:

> No other criminal justice professional comes under as much constant and public scrutiny—but no other criminal justice professional wields so much discretion in so many circumstances. The scrutiny is understandable when one realizes that the police are power personified.[11]

A key issue in any discussion of police work is how the police are to be governed. On the one hand, the police require a degree of operational autonomy to effectively and efficiently carry out their mandated tasks. Given the nature of their mandated role, the police need to be free from government interference and influence. It is important that the police not become an instrument for implementing government policy or supporting specific political agendas. Historically, this has been unavoidable.

On the other hand, the principles of due process and of a democratic society require that there be mechanisms in place to govern the police, to ensure that police services do not exceed their mandate and compromise the rights of citizens. However, as several observers have noted, the precise nature and extent of the independence required by the police has remained unclear.[12]

Figure 4.1 sets out the structures of police governance. Note that there are differences in how federal, provincial, regional, and municipal police services are governed. There are separate agencies for investigating complaints against the police, and these

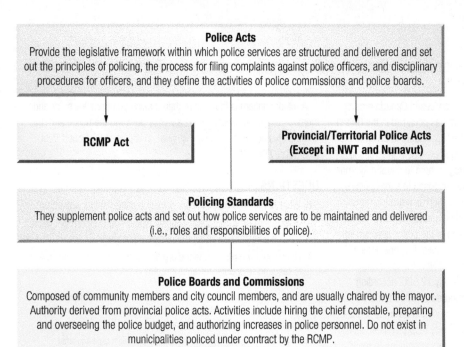

are discussed in Chapter 5. Important to the discussion are the explanations of **police acts**, **policing standards**, and **police boards and police commissions**.

DEFINING FEATURES OF THE POLICE ROLE

Two defining features of the police role are the authority of the police and the authority to use force. The police can use their authority to deprive citizens of their freedom as well as to use physical force and, in extreme circumstances, lethal force. Canadian police officers derive their authority from the *Criminal Code* (R.S.C. 1985, c. C-46) and various provincial statutes. The legal authority of police officers, however, does not automatically translate into *moral* authority. The latter requires officers to establish their legitimacy in the community.[13] The importance of police legitimacy is discussed in Chapter 6.

Police observers have pointed out, however, that police officers are generally quite subtle in their exercise of authority. They often project it merely by being a uniformed presence in public settings and by soliciting information from citizens.

Police officers also have the authority to use force. With the exception of correctional officers, no other personnel in the criminal justice system are invested with this authority. This authority is integral to all facets of the police role, from selection and training to operational patrol and high-risk policing situations. And while most incidents are resolved without the use of force, the potential for its use is always present. In recent years there have been several high-profile cases involving police officers who used force in encounter situations. The police use of force and its consequences for police services, officers, suspects, and the community is considered in Chapter 5.

THE EVER-EXPANDING POLICE ROLE

The primary activities of the police have traditionally been viewed as centring on three major categories:

- *Crime control* involves responding to and investigating crimes, and patrolling the streets to prevent offences from occurring.

Police acts

The legislative framework for police service.

Policing standards

Provisions that set out how police services are to be maintained and delivered.

Police boards and police commissions

Bodies that provide oversight of police.

- *Order maintenance* is designed to prevent and control behaviour that disturbs the public peace, including quieting loud parties, policing protests, responding to (and often mediating) domestic and neighbourhood disputes, and intervening in conflicts that arise between citizens. It is this role of the police that is most often the subject of criticism and investigation.

- *Crime prevention and service* requires collaborating with community partners to prevent crime and providing a wide range of services to the community, often as a consequence of the 24-hour availability of the police.

A large portion of police work involves officers restoring order in situations of conflict without resorting to the criminal law.[14] In carrying out these functions the police have a broad discretion. This is discussed in Chapter 6.

These categories, however, may no longer accurately capture the diversity and complexity of the police role in a highly technological, globalized community. The police role has become much more multifaceted in recent years, often referred to as *diversification*. Increasingly, police services are being asked to address non–law enforcement issues. This is partly a consequence of *downloading*, wherein the police are required to fill gaps in service that are the mandated responsibility of other agencies and organizations. For example, police services across the country are spending an increasing portion of their time and resources responding to high-risk and vulnerable populations, including the mentally ill. When governments cut the numbers of social workers and mental health workers, as well as funding for shelter beds and for specialized facilities for the mentally ill, there is a direct impact on the demands placed on the police resources.

In 2012, the chief of the London, Ontario, police service estimated that the police response to the mentally ill cost $12 million, monies that the chief acknowledged would have been better spent developing programs and services for this high-needs population.[15] A study providing services, including policing, to persons who were homeless and mentally ill in Toronto, Montreal, and Vancouver found the average cost to be $50,000 per person per year.[16] The challenges surrounding the police and persons with mental illness are discussed in Chapter 6.

In addition, most police services have developed an extensive network of collaborative partnerships with agencies and community organizations to address issues related to crime and disorder.[17] This is also discussed in Chapter 6.

In considering the myriad roles of the police in Canadian society, the following questions can be posed: What does the community expect of the police? How do the police view their role? How are the police used by governments to monitor and control groups that are deemed to be threats to social stability?

THE IMPACT OF LEGISLATION AND COURT DECISIONS

New laws and amendments to existing legislation can have a sharp impact on police powers (discussed in Chapter 5), on the demands placed on police services, and on how police services set, and attempt to achieve, their operational priorities. Literally overnight, behaviour that was once criminal can become legal, as occurred with the legalization of marijuana in 2018. On the other hand, the *Anti-terrorism Act* (S.C. 2001, c. 41), enacted by Parliament following the terrorist attacks in the United States in September 2001, gave new powers to the police and created a new crime—*terrorist activity*. This is an example of the social construction of crime, discussed in Chapter 1.

The police are also spending an increasing amount of time documenting their activities and fulfilling procedural requirements. The decision of the Supreme Court of

Canada in *R. v. Stinchcombe* ([1991] 3 SCR 326), which held that accused persons had a constitutional right to full disclosure of materials related to the police investigation, requires the police to prepare detailed reports, and case investigators may spend as much time on this "disclosure" as on the initial investigation. In a major case investigation, the disclosure package can run into the thousands of pages. The expectation is that police services have the capacity to fulfill these requirements. The role of legislation and court decisions in defining the powers of the police is discussed in Chapter 5.

CORE POLICING IN THE EARLY 21ST CENTURY

Core policing in the early 21st century is most accurately characterized as quality-of-life policing, which promotes healthy communities. It is the type of policing that requires officers to have a multifaceted skill set and to respond to a variety of order maintenance, service demands, and community expectations. Its other attributes include the following:

- developing and sustaining partnerships with the community
- taking initiatives to improve the quality of life in communities and neighborhoods
- providing reassurance to community residents and reducing the fear of crime
- conducting outreach to newcomer groups, Indigenous peoples, and vulnerable groups
- engaging in collaborative partnerships with agencies and organizations, including operating specialized patrol units
- increasing the use of statistical analysis to ensure that resources are deployed effectively and efficiently[18]

The extent to which any one police service is able to fulfill all of these functions will depend upon the leadership of the organization, the resources that the police service is provided by municipal and provincial governments, and the quality of the relationships and partnerships that exist between the police and the community. The various roles of the police are illustrated in Police File 4.1.

POLICING A DIVERSE SOCIETY

As noted in Chapter 3, a key feature of Canada is diversity. And this diversity is increasing. Two-thirds of newcomers to Canada settle in the urban centres of Vancouver, Toronto, and Montreal. Many of them have had negative experiences with, or hold less than favourable attitudes toward, the police in their countries of origin. Urban centres are also attracting increasing numbers of Indigenous persons from rural and remote areas. A study conducted in 2016 found that Toronto was the world's most diverse city. Fifty-one percent of the city's population is foreign-born, and there are 230 nationalities among its residents.[19]

This diversity has significant implications for police work. Section 15(1) of the *Charter of Rights and Freedoms* guarantees equality rights: "Every individual is equal before and under the law and has the right to the equal protection and equal benefit of the law without discrimination and, in particular, without discrimination based on race, national or ethnic origin, colour, religion, sex, age or mental or physical disability." Section 3(e) of the *Canadian Multicultural Act* (R.S.C. 1985, c. 24 (4th Supp.)) states that it is the policy of the Government of Canada to "ensure that all individuals receive equal treatment and equal protection under the law, while respecting and valuing their diversity."

The *Canadian Human Rights Act* (R.S.C. 1985, c. H-6) prohibits discrimination on the grounds of "race, national or ethnic origin, colour, religion, age, sex, sexual

THE MULTIFACETED ROLE OF THE POLICE

What does each of the following images suggest about the role of the police?

THE CANADIAN PRESS/Darryl Dyck

Police and RCMP officers force protesters from a road on Burnaby Mountain as Kinder Morgan contractor vehicles arrive at the site where a borehole is being drilled in preparation for the Trans Mountain Pipeline expansion in Burnaby, British Columbia, on November 21, 2014.

THE CANADIAN PRESS/Kevin Van Paassen

A police officer is sprayed by parade goers during the WorldPride Parade in Toronto, Ontario, on June 29, 2014. The parade, which was the culmination of WorldPride 2014, attracted over a million people.

THE CANADIAN PRESS/Paul Chiasson

RCMP officers arrest an asylum claimant and her two daughters who crossed the border into Canada from the United States on March 17, 2017, near Hemmingford, Quebec.

THE CANADIAN PRESS/Michael Hudson

A Toronto police officer helps a homeless man who has been injured after falling into the curb on Yonge Street outside the Toronto Eaton Centre on December 22, 2009.

THE CANADIAN PRESS/Darren Calabrese

G20 summit protesters clash with riot police in downtown Toronto on June 26, 2010.

Aurora Photos/Alamy Stock Photo

The SPEAR (Special Patrol Enforcement and Awareness) Team of the RCMP in Fort McMurray, Alberta

orientation, gender identity or expression, marital status, genetic characteristics, family status, disability and conviction for an offence for which a pardon has been granted or in respect of which a record suspension has been ordered" (s. 3(1)). Many provinces, including Ontario, British Columbia, Alberta, and Manitoba, have human rights codes that mirror the federal human rights code and contain sections creating human rights tribunals and proclaiming the right of residents to be free from discrimination. The debate over racial profiling by the police, discussed in Chapter 5, is illustrative of the human rights issues that surround policing a diverse community.

Police services must strive to reflect the diversity of the communities they police, and officers must have the training to interact with a diverse population that may have English or French as a second language. Diversity also creates opportunities for the police to engage in innovative partnerships with the community and to collaborate in addressing problems of crime and social disorder. Community policing provides a framework for this and is discussed in Chapter 6.

A BRIEF HISTORY OF POLICING

The first full-time police force was created in London in 1829 by Sir Robert Peel in response to increasing fear of crime and disorder associated with the Industrial Revolution. Prior to this, policing was a community responsibility based on the notion that every individual was responsible to their neighbours. Peel faced opposition from the public and politicians who were concerned about the power that would be vested in a formal police force, and when Peel finally won acceptance of his police plan for London, he was denounced as a potential dictator.

Peel attempted to legitimize the new police force by arguing that the police would serve the interests of all citizens, that the police would include the prevention of crime as part of their mandate, and that the force's officers would be recruited from the working class. In a determined effort to create a professional police force and to reduce public suspicion and distrust of the police, he established high standards of recruitment and training and selected constables from the community. Peel also introduced the concept of community police stations. In contrast to the local watchmen who preceded them, the new police were to be proactive rather than reactive and were to engage in crime prevention activities.

Peel formulated several principles for law enforcement, which even today are viewed as the basis for policing. See Police File 4.2.

THE EVOLUTION OF POLICING IN CANADA

In the early days, before Canada existed as the country it is today, laws were enforced on an informal basis by community residents. In Halifax, for example, tavern owners were charged with maintaining order. For many years, policing remained closely tied to local communities. As settlements grew and the demands of law and order increased, however, this arrangement lost its effectiveness. The first police constables appeared on the streets of Quebec City in the mid-1600s and in Upper Canada (now the province of Ontario) in the early 1800s.

The early municipal police forces generally had a three-part mandate: (1) to police conflicts between ethnic groups, and between labourers and their employers; (2) to maintain moral standards by enforcing laws against drunkenness, prostitution, and gambling; and (3) to apprehend criminals.[20] The historical record indicates that early municipal police forces were heavily influenced by politics and patronage.

Many of the jurisdictions that ultimately became provinces after Confederation in 1867 originally had their own police forces. Most often, these were established in response to the disorder associated with gold strikes (for example, in British Columbia and Ontario). The earliest police force of this type was founded in 1858 in British Columbia (then a colony); that force continued to police the province until 1950, when policing services were contracted out to the RCMP. The police forces that had been established in Alberta, Saskatchewan, and Manitoba suffered from poor leadership and a lack of qualified officers. Between 1917 and 1950, the RCMP assumed provincial policing responsibilities in all provinces except Ontario, Quebec, and parts of Newfoundland and Labrador. To this day, those are the only three provinces with provincial police services.

▼ North-West Mounted Police officers, Dawson, Yukon, July 1900

The North-West Mounted Police (now the RCMP) was founded in 1873 to maintain law and order in, and to ensure the orderly settlement of, the previously unpoliced and sparsely settled North-West Territories (in rough terms, present-day Alberta and Saskatchewan). During its early years, the force was beset by internal difficulties and resented by both settlers and federal legislators. The historical record points to high rates of desertion, resignation, and improper conduct, due in part to the harsh conditions of the frontier.

Attempts during the 1920s to phase out the force were driven by resistance in many regions to its expansion into provincial policing. It was anticipated that as these areas became more populated, the responsibility for policing would shift to local communities; for a variety of reasons, this did not happen. The emergence of the RCMP as a national police force involved in policing provinces and municipalities was, in fact, more an accident of history than part of a master plan.[21]

CANADIAN POLICING: A PROFILE

The following list provides a snapshot of policing today in Canada:

- Policing is the largest component of the criminal justice system and receives the biggest slice of the funding pie (approximately 60 percent).
- The number of police officers (199 per 100,000 population) is lower than in other international jurisdictions, including Scotland (337), England and Wales (244), and the U.S. (238).
- The numbers of police officers in Canada have declined in recent years, due to retirements and cutbacks in funding.
- Diversity in police services is increasing, albeit slowly.
- The number of women police officers continues to increase, and they now represent one in five officers.
- The number of civilians working in police services, particularly at the managerial level, continues to increase.[22,23]

Illustrative of the point about declining numbers of police officers is the situation in Winnipeg, a community that has historically had one of highest crime rates in Canada.[24] Despite increases in several categories of serious crime during 2015 to 2016—for example, homicide (+13 percent), attempted murder (+56 percent), and sexual assault with a weapon (+78 percent)—the number of police officers in the Winnipeg Police Service has been declining, and the number of residents per police officer increased. See Figures 4.2 and 4.3.

THE STRUCTURE OF CONTEMPORARY CANADIAN POLICING

Public policing in Canada is carried out at four levels: federal, provincial, municipal, and Indigenous. In addition, there are private security services and parapolice services. The latter are generally staffed by officers with special constable status. These include the Canadian Pacific Railway Police Service and the Canadian National Railway Police Service (which carry out policing roles for their respective organizations), as well as transit police forces, which provide security and protection for property and passengers in major urban centres such as Montreal, Toronto, and Vancouver.

There are also other law enforcement and security agencies, including the Canada Border Services Agency (CBSA), whose officers are armed; the Canadian Security Intelligence Service (CSIS); and the Communications Security Establishment (CSE), which focuses on collecting foreign signals intelligence, protecting computer networks, and providing assistance to federal law enforcement and security agencies.[25]

The arrangements for delivering police services across Canada are quite complex. In Ontario, for example, the London Police Service—an independent municipal police service—is responsible for policing within the city boundaries, while the London detachment of the Ontario Provincial Police (OPP) has jurisdiction in the rural areas

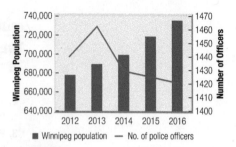

▲ FIGURE 4.2

Winnipeg Population versus Number of Police Officers

Source: Adapted from Winnipeg Police Service. 2017. *Annual Report, 2016.* Winnipeg: Author, p 3. http://www.winnipeg.ca/police/AnnualReports/2016/2016_wps_annual_report_english.pdf. Reprinted by permission of the Winnipeg Police Service.

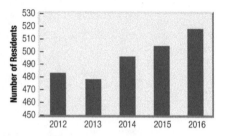

▲ FIGURE 4.3

Winnipeg Residents per Police Officer

Source: Adapted from Winnipeg Police Service. 2017. *Annual Report, 2016.* Winnipeg: Author, p 3. http://www.winnipeg.ca/police/AnnualReports/2016/2016_wps_annual_report_english.pdf. Reprinted by permission of the Winnipeg Police Service.

outside the city. The RCMP has its provincial headquarters in London and operates as a federal police force in the areas policed by the London Police Service and the OPP.

The Royal Newfoundland Constabulary—a provincial police force—is responsible for providing policing services to three areas of Newfoundland and Labrador: St. John's, Mount Pearl, and the surrounding communities referred to as Northeast Avalon; Corner Brook; and Labrador West, which includes Labrador City, Wabush, and Churchill Falls. The rest of the province is policed, under contract, by the RCMP.

In the Greater Vancouver Region, some municipalities are policed by municipal police services, while others are policed under contract by the RCMP. Concerns about the extent to which the municipal and RCMP detachments in the area effectively communicate with one another and address the challenges of organized crime and gang violence, among other issues, have led to calls for a regional police service.

Five Canadian police services—the RCMP, the Toronto Police Service, the Ontario Provincial Police (OPP), the Sûreté du Québec (SQ), and the Service de police de la Ville de Montréal (SPVM)—account for just over 60 percent of all police officers in Canada.

Canadian police services vary greatly in size and in terms of the areas for which they are responsible. At one end of the scale, there are three-officer RCMP detachments in many remote northern communities, such as the community of Igloolik in Nunavut; at the other, there are thousands of officers in the urban centres of Toronto and Montreal.

FEDERAL POLICE: THE ROYAL CANADIAN MOUNTED POLICE

Royal Canadian Mounted Police Act

Federal legislation that provides the framework for the operation of the RCMP.

The RCMP is organized into 15 divisions, plus RCMP headquarters in Ottawa. Each division is headed by a commanding officer. The ***Royal Canadian Mounted Police Act*** (R.S.C. 1985, c. R-10) provides the framework for the force's operations. As the federal police force in all provinces and territories, the RCMP enforces most federal statutes and the provisions of various legislative acts.

There are a number of features that distinguish the RCMP from other Canadian police services. All RCMP recruits are trained at its training academy in Regina, Saskatchewan. The officers are then deployed across the country in detachments.

Contract policing

An arrangement whereby the RCMP and provincial police forces provide provincial and municipal policing services.

The RCMP is a federal police force, yet about 60 percent of its personnel are involved in **contract policing**; that is, they serve as provincial and municipal police officers under agreements between the RCMP and the provinces/territories. (Note again that Ontario and Quebec have their own provincial police forces and that the Royal Newfoundland Constabulary serves parts of Newfoundland and Labrador.) This makes the RCMP a truly national force.

Until recently, RCMP officers, unlike their municipal and provincial police counterparts, were not allowed to form a union. A decision of the Supreme Court of Canada (*Mounted Police Association of Ontario v. Canada*, 2015 SCC 1) held that the ban on RCMP officers having a union was unconstitutional and gave officers the right to collective bargaining. As of late 2018, the National Police Federation had applied for certification to represent the 18,000 members of the RCMP.

The RCMP is involved in a broad range of policing activities, including federal policing, contract policing at the provincial and municipal levels, and international peacekeeping. One result of the broad range of policing activities of the RCMP is that its resources and capacities are often overextended, and observers have questioned whether the RCMP has sufficient resources to deliver policing services effectively on all of these fronts.[26]

There are also increasing concerns in municipalities policed under contract by the RCMP about fiscal accountability: While municipal police services are subject to local police boards and municipal councils, in those municipalities where the RCMP polices under contract, there are no police boards, and the local mayor and council have no mandate to oversee their work. Some observers thus argue that the RCMP is "in" but not "of" the communities they police, and that it is often difficult to ensure that RCMP detachments are responsive to the community's priorities and requirements.

PROVINCIAL POLICE

There are three provincial police forces in Canada: the Ontario Provincial Police (OPP; www.opp.ca), the Sûreté du Québec (SQ; www.sq.gouv.qc.ca), and the Royal Newfoundland Constabulary (RNC; www.justice.gov.nl.ca/rnc). Provincial police forces are responsible for policing rural areas and the areas outside municipalities and cities. They enforce provincial laws as well as the *Criminal Code*. Some municipalities in Ontario are policed under contract by the OPP. Outside Ontario and Quebec and certain parts of Newfoundland and Labrador, the RCMP provides provincial policing under contract with provincial governments. When the RCMP acts as a provincial police force, it has full jurisdiction over the *Criminal Code* as well as provincial laws.

REGIONAL POLICE SERVICES

Regional police services have been a feature of policing in Canada for many years, particularly in the eastern parts of the country.

Today, a number of regional police services, including the Peel Regional Police (the largest regional police force in Canada) and the Halton Regional Police, provide policing services to more than 50 percent of Ontarians. In Quebec, the Service de police de la Ville de Montréal (SPVM) provides policing services to the city of Montreal as well as several surrounding municipalities. There are only two regional police forces west of Ontario: the Dakota Ojibway Police Service, in Manitoba, and the Lakeshore Regional Police Service, an Indigenous police force that provides services to five First Nations in northern Alberta.

Proponents of regional policing contend that it is more effective at providing a full range of policing services to communities and is less expensive than having a number of independent municipal departments. Critics of regional policing argue that, with the exception of Indigenous regional police services, this arrangement is too centralized and does not offer the opportunity for effective community policing.

MUNICIPAL POLICE

As the name suggests, municipal police services have jurisdiction within a city's boundaries. Municipal police officers enforce the *Criminal Code*, provincial statutes, and municipal bylaws, as well as certain federal statutes such as the *Controlled Drugs and Substances Act* (S.C. 1996, c. 19). Most police work is performed by services operating at this level.

A municipality can provide police services in one of three ways: by creating its own independent police service; by joining with another municipality's existing police force, which often means involving itself with a regional police force; or by contracting with a provincial police force—the OPP in Ontario, the RCMP in the rest of Canada (except Quebec).

Municipal police officers constitute the largest body of police personnel in the country, if you include both police employed by municipal departments and those who have been contracted through the RCMP or the OPP. There is no provision under Quebec provincial law for the Sûreté du Québec to contract out municipal policing services. The Toronto Police Service has more than 5,000 officers; at the other end of the spectrum, some remote communities are policed by detachments of only one or two officers.

Municipalities with their own policing services generally assume the costs of those services, which are sometimes underwritten by the provincial government. A notable trend in Ontario has been a decline in the number of independent municipal police services in favour of contracting with the OPP, although in recent years, a number of municipalities have explored the potential of re-establishing municipal police services in order to reduce costs.

INDIGENOUS POLICE

Indigenous peoples are becoming increasingly involved in the creation and control of justice programs. It is in the area of policing that they have assumed the greatest control over the delivery of justice services. One objective is to provide police services that are more integrated into Indigenous communities.

Within the framework of the federal First Nations Policing Program (FNPP), established in 1992, the federal government and provincial/territorial governments and Indigenous communities can negotiate agreements for police services that best meet their needs. These communities have the option of developing an autonomous, reserve-based police force or using Indigenous officers from the RCMP or the OPP in Ontario. Funding for Indigenous police forces is split between the province and the federal government. The activities of autonomous Indigenous police forces are overseen by reserve-based police commissions or by the local band council. Indigenous police forces often work closely with the OPP, the SQ, and the RCMP.

Among the larger autonomous Indigenous police forces—which are involved in policing multiple reserve communities—are the Ontario First Nations Constable Program, the Six Nations Police Service in Ontario, the Amerindian Police in Quebec, and the Dakota Ojibway Police Service in Manitoba. There are smaller Indigenous police forces in other provinces. Indigenous police officers generally have full powers to enforce on reserve lands the *Criminal Code*, federal and provincial statutes, and band bylaws. The Supreme Court has held that Indigenous police constables in Ontario have "territorial jurisdiction" that is not confined to the territorial boundaries of the reserve (*R. v. DeCorte*, [2005] 1 SCR 133).

Officers in Indigenous police services may play an even more multifaceted role than police officers in more populated areas of the country. Commenting on this, and on the social issues facing many Indigenous communities, the police chief in an Indigenous police service in Quebec noted, "Being a police officer in the north, you're the ambulance driver, the undertaker, the social worker. You name it, we've done it. I've even been a Dr. Phil at times."[27] In 2015 in this chief's community of 650 residents, officers responded to 64 suicide attempts in the previous 12 months, a rate of about one attempt per every 12 residents.

Canadian police scholars have argued that the FNPP, under which Indigenous police services operate, was "set up to fail."[28] These police services have been challenged by a lack of funding, often struggle to respond effectively to the high rates of crime and disorder that exist in some Indigenous communities, and often do not provide culturally appropriate services.

▼ An officer with the Tyendinaga Police Service in Ontario. Since 1992, governments and Indigenous communities have negotiated agreements for police services that best meet their needs.

THE CANADIAN PRESS/Lars Hagberg

POLICE ORGANIZATIONS

The major urban police services have similar divisions, or sections. These include the following:

- *Operational patrol*: Patrol division, dog or canine unit, identification squad, traffic, reserve/auxiliary
- *Investigative*: General investigation, major crimes, special crimes (e.g., sexual offences)
- *Support services*: Information, report, or filing; communications centre; victim services; community services/crime prevention
- *Administrative*: Finance and payroll, property office
- *Human resources*: Staff development, recruiting, training
- *Research and planning*: Strategic planning, crime analysis, audit

Canadian police services, like their counterparts worldwide, have a rank structure that reflects their paramilitary organization. Most police services have a chief constable, one or more deputy chief constables, superintendents, and inspectors (often referred to as commissioned officers, although they are not actually commissioned), and non-commissioned officers, including staff sergeants, sergeants, corporals, detectives, and constables.

PRIVATE SECURITY SERVICES

Recent years have seen exponential growth in private security, which is now providing services previously performed by provincial and municipal police services. There are two main types of private security: security firms that sell their services to businesses, industries, private residences, and neighbourhoods; and alternatively, companies that employ their own in-house security officers. Across Canada, a number of communities have hired private security firms to provide 24-hour security patrols.

Generally, private security personnel have no more legal authority than ordinary citizens to enforce the law or protect property. However, private security officers can arrest and detain people who commit crimes on private property. Recent court cases suggest that private security personnel must adhere to the provisions in the *Charter of Rights and Freedoms* only when making an arrest.

Private security officers outnumber police officers by four to one in Canada and are engaged in a wide range of activities, including crowd control, protecting businesses and property (including shopping malls and college and university campuses), and conducting investigations for individuals and businesses. In some venues, such as sporting events and concerts, private security officers and police officers may work in collaboration.

In recent years, the total number of police officers in Canada has declined, while the number of private security officers has continued to increase. For example, private security licences issued in British Columbia increased from 7,743 to 21,878 between 2004 and 2015 (+182.5 percent). During that time period, the number of police officers in the province increased at a much slower rate, from 7,072 to 8,754 (+23.8 percent).[29] Although historically characterized by a degree of distrust, the relationships between the public police and private security in Canada seem to be improving.[30]

There are many instances in which public police work in collaboration with private security. At the West Edmonton Mall, for example, there is both private

▼ One of the many duties undertaken by private security officers includes working sporting events, such as this Toronto Raptors game at the Air Canada Centre in Toronto.

security and a police sub-station, and in Waterloo, Ontario, the police work closely with bank and insurance company investigators to share information on cases. It is likely that there will be increasing integration of public police and private security in the future.[31]

The rapid growth of the private security industry has led to concerns with the transformation of private security officers into *parapolice* through the extension of their activities beyond loss prevention and the protection of property to encompass order maintenance and enforcement.[32,33] Other observers have expressed the concern that although public police are accountable to oversight commissions and—in the case of municipal and provincial police forces—to elected community officials, no similar systems of governance are in place for private security officers.[34]

POLICE PEACEKEEPING

RCMP officers, along with their provincial and municipal counterparts, are involved in a variety of international peacekeeping activities. This has included Sierra Leone, Afghanistan, Sudan, and Haiti. The officers function mainly as technical advisers and instruct local police forces in new policing strategies.

There has been considerable debate around the effectiveness of these deployments, with some observers arguing that the impact of the officers is minimal and that the missions are mounted in order to "show the flag"—that is, to raise the profile of the Canadian government overseas. Among the difficulties that have been identified are the lack of pre-deployment training for officers being sent on peacekeeping missions and the fact that Canadian officers are often part of a multinational force of police officers, among whom there is wide disparity in both skills and level of professionalism.[35] The deployment of police officers overseas is one example where police officers may be being used for political purposes.

THE POLICE RESPONSE

The police respond to a wide variety of demands and situations—many unrelated to crime and to the maintenance of public order—and carry out their duties in settings ranging from megacities (such as Montreal, Toronto, and Vancouver) to rural communities and hamlets in the remote North. The rates of crime and the types of calls to which the police respond depend on the specific community environment in which police officers carry out their work. Some communities present more demands and challenges than others.[36] The rates of violent crime in Canada are highest in remote, northern Indigenous and Inuit communities, areas where there are the fewest resources.[37]

Citizen calls for service received by the Waterloo Regional Police Service are presented in Police File 4.3.

More serious calls for service may require patrol officers to remain at the scene for longer periods of time. Although priority 1 calls (the most serious) are often less than 10 percent of the calls received by a police service, the time spent by officers on-scene and in the subsequent investigation may be very time- and resource-intensive.

The complexity of crime has also continued to increase. Many forms of criminal activity are highly sophisticated and involve international criminal syndicates that require costly and time-consuming investigations. These syndicates engage in such transnational criminal activities as human trafficking, money laundering, and drug smuggling. The emergence of cybercrime has also challenged police services to develop new capacities for surveillance.

POLICE FILE 4.3

CITIZEN CALLS FOR SERVICE, WATERLOO REGIONAL POLICE SERVICE, 2016

2016 Top Ten Citizen-Generated Calls	Frequency	New Call Every...
1. Compassionate to locate	11,738	45 minutes
2. Bylaw complaint	9,077	58 minutes
3. Unwanted person	6,838	1 hour, 17 minutes
4. Theft under $5,000	6,009	1 hour, 28 minutes
5. Domestic dispute	5,712	1 hour, 32 minutes
6. Motor vehicle collision/property damage	5,010	1 hour, 45 minutes
7. Driving complaint	4,851	1 hour, 49 minutes
8. Injured/sick person	3,878	2 hours, 16 minutes
9. Dispute	3,496	2 hours, 31 minutes
10. Alarm	3,470	2 hours, 32 minutes

Source: Waterloo Regional Police Service. 2017. *Waterloo Regional Police Service Annual Report*, 2016. http://www.atyourservice2016.ca/citizen-calls.html. Reprinted with permission of the Waterloo Regional Police Service.

THE RECRUITMENT AND TRAINING OF POLICE OFFICERS

POLICE RECRUITMENT

The increasing complexity of the police role requires that only highly qualified persons are recruited and trained. Even with the cutbacks in policing budgets, police services are competing for qualified candidates.

People who are interested in a career in policing must have both **basic qualifications** and **preferred qualifications**. The basic qualifications include Canadian citizenship (although some departments consider permanent residents), a minimum age of 19 (the average age of police recruits in many departments is over 25), physical fitness, and a grade 12 education. Also, the applicant cannot have any prior criminal convictions or pending charges, and must exhibit common sense and good judgment.

Preferred qualifications—which are highly prized by police services—include any (or ideally, a combination of) the following: knowledge of a second language or culture, related volunteer experience, postsecondary education, and work/life experience. Ontario has standardized the criteria for assessing prospective applicants through its Constable Selection System, which is used by most of the province's police services. Prospective recruits file one application, which is then vetted through this system. This system has done away with multiple applications to several police services and consequent duplication of the assessment effort.

A challenge is to develop measures to assess the validity of the criteria used to select and train police recruits, and to determine whether the attributes of police recruits have an impact on their performance during their policing careers.[38] It has been noted that police recruits are not "blank slates" when they arrive at the training academy; they bring with them attitudes and beliefs that may influence their views of persons and situations as police officers. A key issue is how these are either enhanced or modified by their experience in the training academy.[39] While all major police services in Canada

Basic qualifications (for police candidates)

The minimum requirements for candidates applying for employment in policing.

Preferred qualifications (for police candidates)

Requirements that increase the competitiveness of applicants seeking employment in policing.

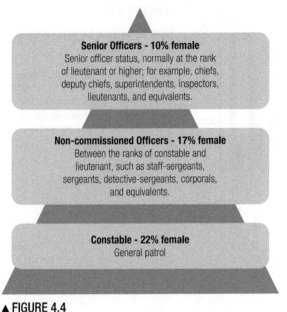

▲ FIGURE 4.4

Women in Police Officer Ranks in Canada, 2014

Source: Manitoba Status of Women. 2014. *Women and Policing in Canada: A Status Brief and Discussion Paper*. Winnipeg: Author, p. 2. https://www.gov .mb.ca/msw/publications/pdf/2014_women_in_policing_brief.pdf. Reprinted by permission of Copyright, Manitoba Government.

administer psychological tests to applicants, the application process in Quebec includes testing designed to measure the applicant's emotional intelligence and to determine whether the person will encounter problems if hired in the police service.

INCREASING OFFICER DIVERSITY IN POLICE SERVICES

Canadian police services are making efforts to increase the diversity in their ranks. There has been, for example, a steady increase in the number of women officers, although in 2016, women still comprised only 21 percent of all sworn police officers. There has also been a significant increase nationally in the number of women at the higher ranks of police services: 13 percent in 2016, as compared to 6 percent in 2006.[40] See Figure 4.4, which outlines the distribution of women in police officer ranks in Canada. In 2016, a graduating recruit class in the Toronto Police Service was 48 percent women, one in three of the recruits were visible minorities, and among them, dozens of languages were spoken.[41]

Over the past decade, police recruiting has undergone significant changes because of the increasing pressure on police services to reflect the gender and cultural and ethnic diversity of the communities they police.

Many police services have developed special initiatives and programs to attract qualified visible minority and Indigenous recruits. The OPP, for example, operates *PEACE* (Police Ethnic and Cultural Exchange), wherein visible minority students participate in a police-sponsored summer employment program. Also, the Edmonton Police Service operates a mentorship academy to encourage women, Indigenous people, and members of visible minority and diverse communities to apply to the force. The 12-session academy is taught by members of the police service and includes such topics as leadership, interpersonal skills, and public speaking.[42]

Another diversity initiative has been the development of uniforms that include a hijab (a scarf that covers the head and chest) that would be worn by women Muslim police officers.

Although the number of women police officers and visible minority officers in Canadian police services has gradually increased, both groups are underrepresented

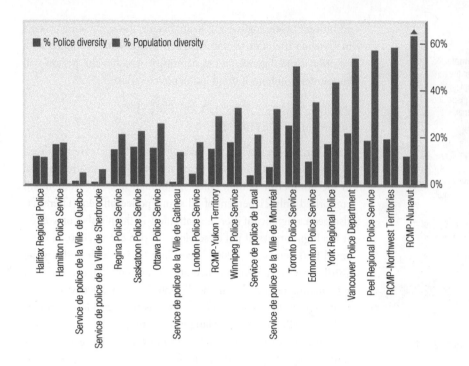

■ % Police diversity   ■ % Population diversity

◄ FIGURE 4.5

How Well Police Services Reflect Their Communities

Source: J. Marcoux, K. Nicholson, V.-L. Kubinec, and H. Moore. 2016, July 14. "Police Diversity Fails to Keep Pace with Canadian Populations," *CBC News.* http://www.cbc.ca/news/canada/police -diversity-canada-1.3677952. Reprinted by permission of CBC.

in police services, particularly at the higher ranks. A study conducted in 2016 found that only in Halifax was the diversity in the police service reflective of that in the community: 11.6 percent of the community is non-white, while 12.1 percent of the officers are either Indigenous or visible minorities.[43] In Toronto, where just over 50 percent of community residents are non-white, only 25 percent of the police service is. The underrepresentation of Indigenous and minority group persons is most pronounced in Quebec: Montreal is four times more diverse than the SPVM, and in Sherbrooke, Quebec City, and Gatineau, fewer than 1 percent of police officers are Indigenous or from a minority group.[44] See Figure 4.5.

Some observers have argued that, while increasing the diversity of police services is important, it is equally important to focus on changing the culture of the police. Sandy Hudson, the co-founder of Black Lives Matter in Toronto, states, "I don't know whether or not more racialized faces on the police force is going to [bring about change]. . . . There has to be a real commitment to changing policy, to changing structure, and to changing the institution as a whole, otherwise these issues don't really get solved."[45]

POLICE TRAINING

Just as important as recruiting qualified people to become police officers is training them well. There are several different models of police training in Canada. Municipal police recruits may be trained "in house," at a residential or non-residential training academy, or at a combination of both. Recruits in the Calgary Police Service (CPS), for example, are trained at the Chief Crowfoot Learning Centre, which is operated by the CPS, while municipal officers in Ontario receive a portion of their training in-house prior to being sent to the Ontario Police College in Alymer, Ontario. In British Columbia, recruits in municipal police services are sent to the Justice Institute of British Columbia, a non-residential facility, where they complete a three-block training course. Blocks I and III are in the academy, and Block II is completed in the field under the supervision of a field training officer in their home department.

In contrast, RCMP cadets are sent to the RCMP training depot in Regina for six months of training prior to being sent to a detachment for six months of field training. Unlike their provincial and municipal counterparts, the cadets are not hired by the RCMP prior to being sent to training and are generally offered employment as a regular member after successfully completing training at the depot.

Police recruits generally receive instruction in the law, community relations, methods of patrol and investigation, and firearms handling. They are also provided with driver training and physical training. Having completed this training, the recruits are usually assigned to general patrol duties for three to five years. Thereafter, they are eligible to apply to specialty units.

Besides providing knowledge and skills, training academies provide a mechanism for socializing new recruits into the occupation of policing. Far too little attention has been paid by police scholars to the experiences of police recruits in training programs as they are transformed into police constables, and to how these experiences shape their attitudes, expectations, and behaviour.

Most police recruits are motivated, at least initially, by a desire to help people and serve the community. The training experience can have a strong impact on this, however. Research studies have found that, for many recruits, the police academy experience makes them more cynical, more suspicious of people, and, generally, more vigilant.[46] The extent to which recruits exhibit these attitudinal and behavioural traits, however, depends upon the personalities and values of the individual.

There are attributes of the police academy that do not fit well with the principles of community policing, including a hierarchical, paramilitary structure that encourages an "us versus them" mentality, deference to authority, and the development of strong bonds and in-group loyalty among recruits. The extent to which these features of the police academy experience have hindered the implementation of community policing has yet to be researched in Canada.[47]

Despite the critical role that recruit training plays in policing careers, very little is known about how new recruits feel about the training they receive. As well, little is known about the relevance and impact of academy training once recruits are assigned to operational patrol.

THE FIELD TRAINING EXPERIENCE

Operational field training

Instructing the recruit how to apply principles from the training academy in the community.

During this second component of the training/learning process, known as **operational field training**, the recruit learns to apply the basic principles taught at the training centre. Under the guidance and assistance of a field training officer (FTO), the recruit is exposed to a wide variety of general police work.

During this critical phase, the specially trained senior officer (often referred to as the field trainer or mentor) makes sure that the recruit is able to meet the demands and challenges of police work.

Police services are paying increasing attention to ensuring continuity between the training a recruit receives in the academy and the supervision provided once the new recruit is involved in operational policing. FTOs play a significant role in the training process and have a strong influence on the attitude and policing style that the new recruit develops. A key objective of the FTO is to enhance the skills and knowledge the recruit has gained at the academy in a way that lessens the "disconnect" between the training academy and the street. This will reduce the likelihood that the new officer will become cynical and discard the skill sets and attitudes learned in recruit training.

As the former director of a police training academy stated, "Some outstanding book-smart recruits struggle on the street, and others that struggle in the academy do well on the street. Until you actually get new officers out on the street, it's difficult to tell how they are going do to, how they are going to interact and handle encounter situations."[48]

THE POLICE OCCUPATION

Largely as a consequence of the unique and multifaceted role that the police play in society, there are some distinctive features of the occupation.

THE WORKING PERSONALITY OF POLICE OFFICERS

The various pressures and demands placed on police officers contribute to what researchers have called the **working personality of the police**. This concept is used to explain how the police view their role and the world around them. It was first identified and defined by the criminologist Jerome Skolnick, who wrote, "The police, as a result of the combined features of their social situation, tend to develop ways of looking at the world distinctive to themselves, cognitive lenses through which to see situations and events."[49]

Among the features of the working personality are a preoccupation with danger, excessive suspiciousness of people and activities, a protective cynicism, and difficulties exercising authority in a manner that balances the rights of citizens with the need to maintain order. It is argued that, as a consequence of these personality attributes, many police officers tend to view policing as a career and a way of life, rather than merely a nine-to-five job; value secrecy and practise a code of silence to protect fellow officers; and exhibit strong in-group solidarity—often referred to as *the blue wall*— owing to job-related stresses, shift work, and an "us versus them" division between police and non-police. As well, police officers may exhibit attitudes, often referred to as the *blue light syndrome*, that emphasize the high-risk, high-action component of police work.[50]

In the over 50 years since Skolnick first proposed the notion of a working personality, there have been many changes in the activities and strategies of police officers, as well as in the diversity of police officers themselves. One of the most significant developments has been the emergence of community policing, a model of policing centred on police–community partnerships that bring officers into close contact with community residents in a wide range of crime prevention and response activities. Various community policing strategies can succeed in reducing the distance (and distrust) between the police and the communities they serve.

These and other changes in the activities of the police have led to the suggestion that the "us [police] versus them [public]" dichotomy is much too general and that it fails to account for the wide variety of relationships that exist between the public and the police, as well as the differences among police officers themselves with respect to how the police role is carried out.[51,52]

That a police subculture exists has many positive implications. For example, it encourages camaraderie and trust among police officers, helps individual officers cope with the more stressful aspects of police work, and is a source of general support. A more negative view of the police subculture is warranted, however, if and when the group solidarity it generates comes at the expense of positive police–community relations, an openness to new strategies and models of policing, and/or a cover-up of police wrongdoing. The *blue wall of silence* may also be an obstacle to addressing the health and wellness of police officers, discussed below.[53]

Working personality of the police

A set of attitudinal and behavioural attributes that develops as a consequence of the unique role and activities of police officers.

CHALLENGES IN POLICE WORK

Police officers often encounter challenges related to their profession that may have an impact on their health and well-being. Stressors include shiftwork, which can lead to fatigue; being an Indigenous, visible/cultural minority, or LGBTQ officer; and attempting to maintain a work/life balance.[54,55,56] In addition, police officers posted to rural and remote communities may be at particular risk of fatigue, given the absence of support resources and the need to be continually on duty.

The challenges of police work are illustrated by the prevalence of occupational stress injuries and the issues surrounding the sexual harassment of women officers.

OCCUPATIONAL STRESS INJURIES

There is an increasing focus on the health and wellness of the police and other first responders and the extent to which these personnel suffer from **occupational stress injuries**. These are injuries that may be physical and/or mental and are a consequence of their organizational and operational experiences on the job.

Although police work can be satisfying and challenging, it can also be stressful. The effects of stress experienced by police officers range from minor annoyances (which can be managed) to alcohol or drug addiction and suicide.[57,58] Occupational stress injuries can affect the officer, his or her family, and the officer's performance on the job. Studies have also found that officers with high stress levels are more susceptible to engaging in misconduct.[59]

A study of work life and employee well-being among a large sample (N = 4,500) of Canadian police officers found that 75 percent of the officers worked more than 45 hours per week and 64 percent were not able to get everything done during work hours and took home work to complete outside of their regular hours on evenings and weekends.[60] An officer in Ontario spoke about the impact of his mental health issues on his family:

> My family took a lot of the brunt of my anger and of my sicknesses. . . . Any of my anger or discomfort, I would yell at them, I would blame my wife for everything. . . . The mental stress I had downloaded on my family. They had to carry me and they took the brunt of all my behaviors [at home] and then I would go to work, I put the uniform on and put on a show and made it look like I was okay and continue and make sure no one knew.[61]

It has also been found that the police organization itself may be the greater source of stress for officers.[62] Poor leadership, a lack of transparency in the promotion process, and a perceived lack of support from supervising officers may exacerbate the stressors in a police officer's operational environment.[63]

In Canada, police officers in remote areas, assigned to small detachments, may experience high stress levels because of the challenging environments in which they work. Remote and rural communities often have much higher rates of crime—especially violent crime—than urban centres. Policing in these high-demand environments, where backup may not be readily available, can take a toll on officers. In recognition of this, officers are generally posted to these isolated locations for no more than two or three years.

A study (N = 4,957) of U.S. and Canadian police officers found that just over 40 percent of the officers suffered from at least one sleep disorder.[64] The results of a national study of Canadian first responders are presented in Research File 4.1.

Officers who are involved in critical incidents, such as a shooting, or who are exposed to extreme violence, individual suffering, and death may develop **post-traumatic stress disorder (PTSD)**, an extreme form of critical incident stress that includes nightmares, hypervigilance, intrusive thoughts, and other forms of psychological distress.[65]

Occupational stress injuries

Physical and/or mental conditions in police officers caused by their organizational and operational experiences on the job.

Post-traumatic stress disorder (PTSD)

An extreme form of critical incident stress that includes nightmares, hypervigilance, intrusive thoughts, and other forms of psychological distress.

MENTAL DISORDERS AMONG CANADIAN FIRST RESPONDERS

In the first study of its kind, a 2016 nationwide online survey ($N = 5{,}813$) designed to assess the health and wellness of first respondents was administered to municipal, provincial, and RCMP officers, paramedics, 911 dispatchers, correctional workers, and firefighters. The study found the following:

- Among respondents, 44.5 percent reported symptoms consistent with one or more mental disorders, as compared to 10 percent of the general population.

- The responses of women first responders were more likely than men to indicate mental disorder, particularly among women firefighters.

- The symptoms of occupational stress injuries were more prevalent among first responders with more years of service and more exposure to traumatic events.

- Municipal and provincial police officers have more access to support services than their RCMP counterparts, who are transferred frequently and may work in rural and northern communities where such services are not available.

Source: R.N. Carleton, T.O. Afifi, S. Turner, T. Taillieu, S. Duranceau, D.M. LeBouthillier, . . . G.J.G. Asmundson. 2017. "Mental Disorder Symptoms among Public Safety Personnel in Canada," *The Canadian Journal of Psychiatry*, 1–11. Advance online publication. doi:10.1177/0706743717723825

Traumatic events such as homicides, suicides, the deaths of children, and multi-victim accidents can take a toll on officers and lead to burnout.[66] These experiences may be compounded by shiftwork, which results in officers working all hours of the day and night with a significant impact on sleep patterns. The experience of one Ontario Provincial Police officer is described in Police File 4.4.

A study of the health and wellness of officers in a large urban police service found that the officers employed a variety of coping strategies to deal with the stressors in their work. These included constructive self-help coping strategies, such as speaking with loved ones, exercising, and bringing humour to otherwise difficult situations; destructive self-help coping strategies, including excessive use of alcohol; and seeking professional help.[67] Although the economic costs associated with PTSD, including short- and long-term health costs, the costs of treatment, and the impact on police officers and their families, have not been calculated in Canada, they can be presumed to be substantial.[68]

Canadian police services have developed a range of in-house programs and collaborations with mental health professionals to address occupational stress injuries of officers.

OFFICER "DAVID"

Officer David has been with the OPP for more than 20 years, but one event overshadows his career. Years ago, he shot and killed a man who attempted to murder two fellow officers. The incident left him with nightmares and hypervigilance symptoms. He also had to face the internal and external investigations that accompany such incidents, as well as a civil lawsuit by the deceased's family. Fortunately, he had a supportive detachment commander who made the necessary arrangements for him and his wife to see the OPP Staff Psychologist, afforded him time away from work, and encouraged him to file a WSIB claim. Soon after the shooting, Officer David was referred to a community psychologist who diagnosed him with post-traumatic stress disorder. However, his treatment was short-lived, and he once again found himself back at work in "suck it up" mode. Memories of the shooting and uncontrollable bouts of crying continued to plague him. But this time, he responded by avoiding his family, burying himself in work, and drinking alcohol to numb the pain and sleep at night. After years of struggling for control, he became suicidal and was hospitalized. He went on a long-term leave from work, obtained WSIB benefits, and underwent treatment. Like others in his position who have been steeped in the police culture, he was embarrassed to find himself suffering from mental illness. While many of those we spoke to expressed frustration with the return-to-work process and the lack of meaningful work available to individuals recovering from operational stress injury, Officer David was able to return to work successfully, in a rewarding position.

Source: A. Marin. 2012. *In the Line of Duty*. Toronto: Ombudsman of Ontario, p. 19. https://www.ombudsman.on.ca/Files/sitemedia/Documents/Investigations/SORT%20 Investigations/OPP-final-EN.pdf. Reprinted by permission of the Office of the Ombudsman of Ontario.

These include critical incident stress intervention teams and peer-support programs, which are based on the principle that officers who have experienced similar challenges and overcome mental health issues are best suited to support their colleagues who are facing similar situations.[69]

One challenge to the effectiveness of these initiatives is that officers often feel there is stigma associated with seeking help. As one officer stated, "There is still very much an attitude of 'If you can't handle it you should quit.'"[70] An Ontario Provincial Police officer recalled how, historically, the culture of policing deterred officers from seeking assistance:

> When I started in policing over 32 years ago, the profession had a culture that often viewed any expression of emotional or psychological pain as a weakness. Cops were to be tough. If they dared go to a supervisor or colleague with such a problem, they may have been told to "suck it up." Sadly, an environment of a reluctance to self-identify was alive and well. Thankfully, that's no longer the case. We have learned much about posttraumatic stress disorder (PTSD) during the last three decades and policing has come to terms with how it affects our profession.[71]

The development and expansion of health and wellness programs in police services have served to change the attitudes towards occupational stress injuries. Evidence that the stigma associated with seeking help may be decreasing is reflected in the doubling of the number of officers in the Toronto Police Service seeking assistance for psychological issues during the years 2014 to 2016.[72]

In recognition of the pervasiveness of PTSD in police and other first responders, a number of provinces have passed legislation designating it as an occupational disease in order to facilitate access to treatment services as a component of benefit plans.[73]

THE EXPERIENCE OF WOMEN POLICE OFFICERS

A major source of stress for women police officers may be sexual harassment and discrimination in the workplace.[74] This often involves unwanted sexual advances by another officer and/or obscene comments, which often thrive due to there being an "old boys' club" in the police service.[75] Police mothers in particular may face challenges of negative workplace responses to their pregnancy and in re-establishing their credibility upon returning to work.[76]

In 2017, a class action suit for more than $165 million was launched by past and present members of the Waterloo Regional Police Service, alleging unwanted sexual advances, career sabotage, and personal attacks.[77]

In 2016, the RCMP settled a class action harassment suit brought by over 500 former and current women RCMP officers who alleged they had been the subject of harassment while on the job. It is estimated that payments to the former and current officers could exceed $100 million.[78] The suit had alleged that women experienced gender-based discrimination and harassment, including name-calling, sexist pranks, and verbal propositions for sexual favours.

A 2017 report by the Civilian Review and Complaints Commission (CRCC) for the RCMP found that bullying and harassment of both male and women officers, including intimidation of officers by their supervisors, continued to be serious issues within the RCMP.[79]

Women officers may have little faith in the police organization to deal appropriately with complaints of harassment.[80] Women may also be hesitant to report being harassed due to fears of career suicide—that is, the fear they will be ostracized and shunned in the department and have limited opportunities for career advancement.[81]

THE INDIVIDUAL EXPERIENCES OF WOMEN POLICE OFFICERS

SERGEANT, BC MUNICIPAL POLICE SERVICE

I have never been made to feel any different as a police officer because I'm a female in this department. Yes, there may have been a boys' club mentality back in the day, but I have never experienced it. I've had nothing but positive experiences here. [On] my first patrol watch, I was the only female on that watch, and again they made me feel totally welcome, totally supported. In terms of if I was treated any differently by anybody, I think I would see more of the sensitive calls that were dispatched. Perhaps, if somebody came in and they wanted to speak with a female, I was the default female. . . . Right off the bat it gave me a lot of experience dealing with sensitive calls and victims who have variant levels of distress that maybe they may not be overly comfortable talking about.

In terms of the guys on my squad, they were fantastic, they were great, they welcomed me. I always felt like they had my back, always, and not just because I was a female but because I was part of the squad.[a]

CONSTABLE, TORONTO POLICE SERVICE

A Toronto police officer says she suffered "repeated and systematic" sexual harassment by her supervisors in a "poisoned work environment" that eventually pushed her to take medical leave, the Human Rights Tribunal of Ontario has heard.

Heather McWilliam alleges she was "humiliated and segregated" over nearly eight years as a constable at 23 Division, including being called "degrading names" such as "c--t, bitch and dyke."

McWilliam, a former RCMP officer, says a superior officer once made a sexual joke about wanting her to "ride his horse." Const. Heather McWilliam says she heard sexual or sexist comments every single shift during her seven years in the Toronto Police Service.

There were other jokes about masturbation and oral sex, McWilliam alleges, and she says a superior officer once passed around photos, taken from Facebook, of her and other female officers in bikinis. [...]

McWilliam's lawyer, Kate Hughes, says the application is not about a few "bad apples" but rather a "poisoned workplace environment" within Toronto police that condones and accepts harassment against female officers.

"They are the object of jokes, the object of sexual objectification, talking about how they look, and the size of women's breasts," Hughes said on Thursday.

Female officers who come forward with complaints are considered "rats" and not "team players," Hughes said, which is particularly concerning for police officers who rely on each other for protection on the job.

"They may have to save your life one day," Hughes told the tribunal.

Filing complaints is a "career ender" for female officers, Hughes argued, and many who do are pushed to settle outside court, which keeps the allegations private.[b]

[a] C. Dobie. 2014, August 14. "Women: A Growing Force in the City," *New Westminster Record*. http://www.newwestrecord.ca/news/women-a-growing-force-in-the-city-1.1313416. Reprinted by permission of the publisher

[b] Trevor Dunn, 2016. "Toronto police officer alleges 'repeated and systemic' sexual harassment on the job," *CBC News*, November 3, http://www.cbc.ca/news/canada/toronto/toronto-police-officer-alleges-repeated-and-systemic-sexual-harassment-on-the-job-1.3835390. Reprinted by permission of CBC.

As one officer told the CCRC inquiry:

I am afraid that I will be unjustly disciplined by being suspended without pay, of being charged with a Code of Conduct violation, or being disciplined by the Force and losing my employment and my career–all because I came forward with what I have endured.[82]

Among the conclusions of the CCRC report was that the RCMP had resisted making the necessary organizational reforms to address the issues surrounding harassment in the workplace.

The extent to which harassment is an issue in police services may depend in large measure on the culture of the individual police service, which, in turn, is highly influenced by the senior leadership. This is reflected in the experiences of the women officers presented in Police File 4.5.

SUMMARY

The discussion in this chapter has examined the structure and roles of the police in Canada. Modern policing developed in England in the early 1800s, and a number of key principles of policing were identified that provide the basis for policing in contemporary times. Community self-policing in early Canada gradually gave way to organized police services, and today policing is carried out at the federal, provincial, municipal, and Indigenous levels.

It was noted that there has been a pluralization of policing, wherein the public and private police share responsibility for the safety and security of communities. The challenges of policing in a democratic society, which centre on maintaining order while ensuring individual rights, were discussed as was the police role in contemporary society and the efforts of police services to more accurately reflect the diversity of the communities they police. There has been an increasing focus on the health and wellness of police officers and on the experiences of women police officers who may experience sexual harassment and discrimination in the workplace.

KEY POINTS REVIEW

1. The first full-time police force was created in London in 1829 by Sir Robert Peel who set out a number of principles that still apply to policing.

2. Early municipal police forces in Canada had a mandate to police conflicts between groups, to maintain moral standards, and to apprehend criminals.

3. It is by historical accident that the RCMP is today involved in federal, provincial, and municipal policing.

4. The four levels of policing in Canada are federal, provincial, municipal, and Indigenous communities.

5. The RCMP has a number of distinct features, including training all of its recruits in a central location prior to their deployment across the country.

6. There has been a rapid growth in private security services.

7. In a democratic society, there are natural tensions between the power and authority of the police and the values and processes that exist in a democratic society.

8. The structures of police governance include police acts, policing standards, and police boards and commissions.

9. Traditionally, the police role has been categorized into crime control, order maintenance, and service, although in current times this may not capture the complexity of the police role.

10. Police services have developed a number of programs to increase their diversity.

11. There are a variety of models across the country for training police recruits.

12. The various pressures and demands placed on police officers contribute to what researchers have called the working personality of the police, although there is some evidence to suggest that there has been some erosion in the "us versus them" mentality of the police.

13. Police officers encounter challenges related to their profession, as illustrated by the prevalence of occupational stress injuries and the experiences of women police officers in the workplace.

KEY TERM QUESTIONS

1. Define **policing**.

2. What is meant by the **pluralization of policing**?

3. Define and contrast the **social contract perspective** and the **radical perspective** on the role of the police.

4. What is meant by **political policing**?

5. Discuss the role of **police acts**, **policing standards**, and **police boards and commissions** in police governance.

6. Describe the components of **core policing**.

7. What is the *Royal Canadian Mounted Police Act*?

8. Define **contract policing**.

9. Identify the **basic qualifications** and **preferred qualifications** for police candidates required by police services in the recruitment process.

10. Why is **operational field training** considered to be an important part of the training/learning process for new police officers?

11. Define the **working personality of the police** and identify its components.

12. Discuss **operational stress injuries** and how they may be manifested in police officers.

13. What is **post-traumatic stress disorder** and what are some of its symptoms?

CRITICAL THINKING EXERCISE

Critical Thinking Exercise 4.1

A Police Service Recruiting Video: A Closer Look

Watch the video, "Becoming a Police Officer: Kingston Police Force," at https://www.youtube.com/watch?v=_9RVuDlrVao.

Your Thoughts?

1. What is your assessment of this recruiting video?

2. In your view, does it accurately reflect what the police do?

3. What topics, if any, are missing from the video?

CLASS/GROUP DISCUSSION EXERCISE

Class/Group Discussion Exercise 4.1

Should the Role and Numbers of Private Security Officers Be Expanded?

The number of private security officers in Canada continues to increase. Proponents of private security contend that increasing and expanding the role of private security provides a way to control policing costs, while at the same time ensuring public safety and security. A key argument that is offered in support of the expansion of private security is economic: that subcontracting services to private security firms provides an opportunity to save money. For example, the total compensation of a police officer with the Service de police de la Ville de Montréal (SPVM) is approximately $120,000, compared to $40,000 for a private security agent.[a]

Opponents of expanding the role and use of private security counter that these organizations are not subject to the same level of oversight as the public police; for example, they are not accountable to provincial police acts or to oversight by police complaint agencies; private security officers do not receive sufficient training (in most provinces/territories, it averages

40 hours); and that the first allegiance of private security officers is to private business, rather than to the public.

Your Thoughts?

1. What is your view on private security?

2. Should there be limits on what private security officers can do?

3. Where do you most frequently see private security officers?

4. Should cost be the primary consideration as to whether the role of private security should be expanded?

[a] M. Bédard and J. Guénette. 2015, January 29. "Private Reinforcement for Public Police Forces?" *MEI*. http://www.iedm.org/52244-private-reinforcements-for-public-police-forces.

MEDIA LINKS

Into the Fire (Canada Is a Police State), Press for Truth, April 21, 2011. https://www.youtube.com/watch?v5zejD0UkMGGY

"Behind the Line," *The Fifth Estate*, CBC, December 9, 2011. http://www.cbc.ca/player/play/2245698171

"Whistleblowers: Victoria Cliffe—Sexual Harassment in the RCMP," *The Fifth Estate*, CBC, September 1, 2016. https://www.youtube.com/watch?v=1E5t_pAXyu0

"Peter's Story," Royal Canadian Mounted Police," December 10, 2014. https://www.youtube.com/watch?v=Bs7sub82RNM

REFERENCES

1. A. Goldsmith. 2010. "Policing's New Visibility," *British Journal of Criminology*, 50(5), 914–934.

2. C. Clarke and C. Murphy. 2002. *In Search of Security: The Roles of Public Police and Private Agencies* [discussion paper]. Ottawa: Law Commission of Canada, p. 8. https://dalspace.library.dal.ca/bitstream/handle/10222/10292/In%20Search%20of%20Security%20Discussion%20Paper%20EN.pdf?sequence=1.

3. *Polite Ire*. 2012. "The Police: The Case Against," p. 5. https://libcom.org/library/police-case-against.

4. R. Jochelson, K. Kramer, and M. Doerksen. 2014. *The Disappearance of Criminal Law: Police Powers and the Supreme Court*. Black Point, NS: Fernwood Publishing, p. 10.

5. R. Whitaker, G.S. Kealey, and A. Parnaby. 2012. *Secret Service: Political Policing in Canada from the Fenians to Fortress America*. Toronto: University of Toronto Press.

6. S. Hewitt. 2000. "'Information Believed True': RCMP Security Intelligence Activities on Canadian University Campuses and the Controversy Surrounding Them, 1961–1971," *Canadian Historical Review*, 81(2), 191–228.

7. S. Hewitt. 2002. *Spying 101: The RCMP's Secret Activities at Canadian Universities, 1917–1997*. Toronto: University of Toronto Press.

8. P.K. Manning. 2005. "The Police: Mandate, Strategies, and Appearances," in *Policing: Key Readings*, edited by T. Newburn, 191–214. Portland, OR: Willan Publishing.

9. Law Commission of Canada. 2006. *In Search of Security: The Future of Policing in Canada*. Ottawa: Minister of Public Works and Government Services, pp. 120–121. https://dalspace.library.dal.ca/bitstream/handle/10222/10293/In%20Search%20of%20Security%20Report%20EN.pdf?sequence=1&isAllowed=y.

10. S. Miller and J. Blackler. 2005. *Ethical Issues in Policing*. Aldershot, UK: Ashgate Publishing Limited.

11. J.M. Pollock. 2010. *Ethical Dilemmas and Decisions in Criminal Justice*. Belmont, CA: Wadsworth/Cengage Learning, p. 182.

12. Miller and Blackler, *Ethical Issues in Policing*.

13. Ibid.

14. D.H. Bayley. 2005. "What Do the Police Do?" in *Policing: Key Readings*, edited by T. Newburn, 141–149. Portland, OR: Willan Publishing.

15. S. Meyer. 2013, January 23. "$12M in Policing Costs Spent on Mental Health Calls," *Our London*. https://www.ourlondon.ca/news-story/1492346--12m-in-policing-costs-spent-on-mental-health-calls.

16. E.A. Latimer, D. Rabouin, Z. Cao, A. Ly, G. Powell, T. Aubry, . . . P.M. Goering, for the At Home/Chez Soi Investigators. 2017. "Costs of Services for Homeless People with Mental Illness in 5 Canadian Cities: A Large Prospective Follow-up Study," *CMAJ Open*, 5(3). http://cmajopen.ca/content/5/3/E576.full.pdf+html?sid=d0a46cc2-8a19-46e7-80d1-62d26955b9a0.

17. C. Murphy. 2012. "Canadian Police and Policing Policy, Post-9/11," in *Canadian Criminal Justice Policy: Contemporary Perspectives*, edited by K. Ismaili, UJ. Sprott, and K. Varma, 1–20, Toronto: Oxford University Press, p. 15.

18. C.T. Griffiths. 2016. *Canadian Police Work* (4th ed.). Toronto: Nelson.

19. G. Ngabo. 2016, May 16. "Toronto the Diverse: BBC Study Declares City Most Diverse in the World," *Metro News*. http://www.metronews.ca/news/toronto/2016/05/16/toronto-the-diverse.html.

20. T.J. Juliani, C.K. Talbot, and C.H.S. Jayewardene. 1984. "Municipal Policing in Canada: A Developmental Perspective," *Canadian Police College Journal*, 8(3), 315–385.

21. Griffiths, *Canadian Police Work*.

22. M. Burczycka. 2013. *Police Resources in Canada 2012*. Statistics Canada Catalogue no. 85-225-X. Ottawa: Minister of Industry. http://www.statcan.gc.ca/pub/85-225-x/85-225-x2012000-eng.pdf.

23. J. Greenland and S. Alam. 2017. "Police Resources in Canada, 2016," *Juristat*, 37(1). Statistics Canada Catalogue no. 85-002-X. Ottawa: Minister of Industry. http://www.statcan.gc.ca/pub/85-002-x/2017001/article/14777-eng.pdf.

24. C.T. Griffiths and N. Pollard. 2013. *Policing in Winnipeg: An Operational Review*. Ottawa: Canadian Police Association. http://curtgriffiths.com/wp-content/uploads/2014/09/WPS-operational-review.pdf.

25. "What We Do and Why We Do It." n.d. Communications Security Establishment. https://www.cse-cst.gc.ca/en/inside-interieur/what-nos.

26. P. Palango. 1998. *The Last Guardians – The Crisis in the RCMP*. Toronto: McClelland and Stewart.

27. C. Curtis. 2016, May 22. "Special Report: For Quebec's Aboriginal Police, Critics Say Pay Is No Match for the Danger," *Montreal Gazette*. http://montrealgazette.com/storyline/for-quebecs-aboriginal-police-critics-say-pay-is-no-match-for-the-danger.

28. J. Kiedrowski, N. Jones, and R. Ruddell. 2017. "'Set Up to Fail': An Analysis of Self-Administered Indigenous Police Services in Canada," *Police Practice and Research*, 18(6), 584–598.

29. R. Montgomery and C.T. Griffiths. 2015. *The Use of Private Security Services for Policing* [Research report 2015-R041]. Ottawa: Public Safety Canada, p. 7. https://www.publicsafety.gc.ca/cnt/rsrcs/pblctns/archive-2015-r041/2015-r041-en.pdf.

30. G. Kitteringham. 2009, December 21. "Relationship between Public Police and Private Security Is Improving," *Canadian Security*. https://www.canadiansecuritymag.com/Education/Editorial/Relationship-between-public-police-and-private-security-is-improving.html.

31. Montgomery and Griffiths, *The Use of Private Security Services for Policing*.

32. R. McLeod. 2002. *Parapolice: A Revolution in the Business of Law Enforcement*. Toronto: Boheme Press.

33. G.S. Rigakos. 2003. *The New Parapolice: Risk Markets and Commodified Social Control*. Toronto: University of Toronto Press.

34. Montgomery and Griffiths, *The Use of Private Security Services for Policing*, p. 7.

35. B. Dupont and S. Tanner. 2009. "Not Always a Happy Ending: The Organisational Challenges of Deploying and Integrating Civilian Peacekeepers (A Canadian Perspective)," *Policing & Society*, 19(2), 134–146.

36. K. Keighley. 2017. "Police-Reported Crime Statistics in Canada, 2016," *Juristat*, 37(1). Statistics Canada Catalogue no. 85-002-X. Ottawa: Minister of Industry. http://www.statcan.gc.ca/pub/85-002-x/2017001/article/54842-eng.pdf.

37. M. Allen and S. Perrault. 2015. "Police-Reported Crime in Canada's Provincial North and Territories, 2013," *Juristat*, 35(1). Statistics Canada Catalogue no. 85-002-X. Ottawa: Minister of Industry. http://www.statcan.gc.ca/pub/85-002-x/2015001/article/14165-eng.pdf.

38. B. Henson, B.W. Reyns, C.F. Klahm, and J. Frank. 2010. "Do Good Recruits Make Good Cops? Problems Predicting and Measuring Academy and Street-Level Success," *Police Quarterly*, 13(1), 5–26.

39. D.P. Rosenbaum, A.M. Schuck, and G. Cordner. 2011. *The National Police Research Platform: The Life Course of New Officers. Research Review*. Washington, DC: National Institute of Justice. https://www.nationallawenforcementplatform.org/wp-content/uploads/2017/05/RecruitsLifeCourse.pdf.

40. Greenland and Alam, "Police Resources in Canada, 2016," p. 3.

41. S.-J. Battersby. 2016, February 12. "Meet the Newest Members of the Toronto Police," *Toronto Star*. https://www.thestar.com/news/gta/2016/02/12/meet-the-newest-members-of-the-toronto-police.html.

42. N. Keeler. 2017, June 25. "'A Diverse Group': Edmonton Police Launch Canada's First Mentorship Academy," *CBC News*. http://www.cbc.ca/news/canada/edmonton/edmonton-police-mentorship-academy-1.4175177.

43. J. Marcoux, K. Nicholson, V.-L. Kubinec, and H. Moore. 2016, July 14. "Police Diversity Fails to Keep Pace with Canadian Populations," *CBC News*. http://www.cbc.ca/news/canada/police-diversity-canada-1.3677952.

44. Ibid.

45. Ibid.

46. J.B.L. Chan. 2003. *Fair Cop: Learning the Art of Policing*. Toronto: University of Toronto Press.

47. A.T. Chappell and L. Lanza-Kaduce. 2009. "Police Academy Socialization: Understanding the Lessons Learned in a Paramilitary-Bureaucratic Organization," *Journal of Contemporary Ethnography*, 39(2), 131–158.

48. Personal communication, September 2013.

49. J.K. Skolnick. 1966. *Justice without Trial: Law Enforcement in Democratic Society*. New York: John Wiley and Sons, p. 4.

50. A. Goldsmith. 1990. "Taking Police Culture Seriously: Discretion and the Limits of the Law," *Policing and Society*, 1(2), 91–114.

51. S. Herbert. 1998. "Police Subculture Revisited," *Criminology*, 36(2), 343–369.

52. E.A. Paoline. 2004. "Shedding Light on Police Culture: An Examination of Officers' Occupational Attitudes," *Police Quarterly*, 7(2), 205–237.

53. A. Marin. 2012. *In the Line of Duty*. Toronto: Ombudsman of Ontario, p. 83. https://www.ombudsman.on.ca/Files/sitemedia/Documents/Investigations/SORT%20Investigations/OPP-final-EN.pdf.

54. K. Dowler and B. Arai. 2008. "Stress, Gender and Policing: The Impact of Perceived Gender Discrimination on Symptoms of Stress," *International Journal of Police Science & Management*, 10(2), 123–135.

55. K.D. Hassell and S.G. Brandl. 2009. "An Examination of the Workplace Experiences of Police Patrol Officers: The Role of Race, Sex, and Sexual Orientation," *Police Quarterly*, 12(4), 408–430.

56. C. Ma, M.E. Andrew, D. Fekedulegn, J.K. Gu, T.A. Hartley, L.E. Charles, J.M. Violanti, and C.M. Burchfiel. 2015. "Shift Work and Occupational Stress in Police Officers," *Safety and Health at Work*, 6(1), 25–29. https://www.ncbi.nlm.nih.gov/pmc/articles/PMC4372186.

57. M. Morash, R. Haarr, and D.-H. Kwak. 2006. "Multilevel Influences on Police Stress," *Journal of Contemporary Criminal Justice*, 22(1), 26–43.

58. J.R.L. Parsons. 2004. "Occupational Health and Safety Issue of Police Officers in Canada, the United States, and Europe: A Review Essay." https://www.mun.ca/safetynet/library/OHandS/OccupationalHS.pdf.

59. M.L. Arter. 2008. "Stress and Deviance in Policing," *Deviant Behavior*, 29(1), 43–69.

60. L. Duxbury and C. Higgins. 2012. *Caring About Those Who Serve: Work-Life Conflict and Employee Well-Being Within Canada's Police Departments*. Ottawa and London, ON: Carleton University and the University of Western Ontario. http://sprott.carleton.ca/wp-content/files/Duxbury-Higgins-Police2012_fullreport.pdf.

61. Marin, *In the Line of Duty*, p. 20.

62. J.M. Shane. 2010. "Organizational Stressors and Police Performance," *Journal of Criminal Justice*, 38(4), 807–818.

63. K.D. Hassell, C.A. Archbold, and A.J. Stichman. 2011. "Comparing the Workplace Experiences of Male and Female Police Officers: Examining Workplace Problems, Stress, Job Satisfaction and Consideration of Career Change," *International Journal of Police Sciences and Management*, 13(1), 37–53.

64. B. Pearsall. 2012, June. "Sleep Disorders, Work Shifts and Officer Wellness," *NIJ Journal*, 270. https://www.ncjrs.gov/pdffiles1/nij/238487.pdf.

65. K.M. Gilmartin. 2002. *Emotional Survival for Law Enforcement: A Guide for Officers and Their Families*. Tucson, AZ: E-S Press.

66. W.P. McCarty and W.G. Skogan. 2013. "Job-Related Burnout Among Civilian and Sworn Police Personnel," *Police Quarterly*, 16(1), 66–84.

67. Griffiths and Pollard, *Policing in Winnipeg: An Operational Review*.

68. S. Wilson, H. Guliani, and G. Boichev. 2016. "On the Economics of Post-Traumatic Stress Disorders Among First Responders in Canada," *Journal of Community Safety and Well-Being*, 1(2), 26–31.

69. Marin, *In the Line of Duty*, p. 43.

70. Griffiths and Pollard, *Policing in Winnipeg: An Operational Review*.

71. Marin, *In the Line of Duty*, p. 79. Reprinted by permission of the Office of the Ombudsman of Ontario.

72. M. Smee. 2016, August 18. "More Toronto Police Officers Than Ever Seeking Help, TPS Psychologist Says," *CBC News*. http://www.cbc.ca/news/canada/toronto/more-toronto-police-officers-than-ever-seeking-help-tps-psychologist-says-1.3727301.

73. *CBC News*. 2015, December 22. "PTSD to Be Recognized as Work-Related Disease in Manitoba Starting Jan. 1." http://www.cbc.ca/news/canada/manitoba/ptsd-to-be-recognized-as-work-related-disease-in-manitoba-starting-jan-1-1.3376872.

74. K. Dowler and B. Arai. 2008. "Stress, Gender and Policing: The Impact of Perceived Gender Discrimination on Symptoms of Stress," *International Journal of Police Science & Management*, 10(2), 123–135.

75. J. O'Brien. 2016, August 30. "Growing Number of Women on Canadian Police Forces No Match for 'Old Boys' Club,' Researcher Finds," *National Post*. http://nationalpost.com/news/canada/growing-number-of-women-on-canadian-police-forces-no-match-for-old-boys-club-researcher-finds.

76. D. Langan, C.B. Sanders, and T. Agocs. 2017. "Canadian Police Mothers and the Boys' Club: Pregnancy, Maternity Leave, and Returning to Work," *Women & Criminal Justice*, 17(4), 235–249.

77. M. McQuigge. 2017, June 1. "Former Officers Suing Ont. Police Service Alleging Gender-Based Discrimination," *CTV News*. http://www.ctvnews.ca/canada/former-officers-suing-ont-police-service-alleging-gender-based-discrimination-1.3439329.

78. K. Harris. 2016, October 6. "Mounties Offer Apology and $100M Compensation for Harassment, Sexual Abuse Against Female Members," *CBC News*. http://www.cbc.ca/news/politics/rcmp-paulson-compensation-harassment-1.3793785.

79. Civilian Review and Complaints Commission for the RCMP. 2017. *Report into Workplace Harassment in the RCMP*. Ottawa: Author, pp. 2–3. https://www.crcc-ccetp.gc.ca/pdf/harassmentFinR-eng.pdf.

80. D. LeBlanc. 2012, September 17. "Female Mounties Fear Backlash Over Reporting Harassment, Report Shows," *Globe and Mail*. https://www.theglobeandmail.com/news/national/female-mounties-fear-backlash-over-reporting-harassment-report-shows/article4550565.

81. A. Lupton. 2016, November 18. "Female Police Officers Risk 'Career Suicide" with Harassment Complaints, Lawyer Says," *CBC News*. http://www.cbc.ca/news/canada/toronto/programs/metromorning/kate-hughes-heather-mcwilliam-human-rights-complaint-police-1.3856752.

82. Civilian Review and Complaints Commission, *Report into Workplace Harassment in the RCMP*, p. 16.

© Laurie Justus Pace, Graphics One Design, 2014

CHAPTER 5
POLICE POWERS AND DECISION-MAKING

LEARNING OBJECTIVES

After reading this chapter, you should be able to
- Discuss the impact of the *Charter of Rights and Freedoms* on police powers.
- Describe how the police are held accountable for their actions.
- Discuss the role of discretion in police decision-making and the factors that can influence the decisions of police officers.
- Describe the issues that surround biased policing and racial profiling.
- Discuss the police practice of street checks/carding and the relationship of this practice to biased policing and racial profiling.
- Discuss the police use of force, less-lethal force options, and the use of lethal force.
- Describe the powers of the police with respect to search and seizure, detention and arrest, the interrogation of crime suspects, and entrapment as a limitation on police powers.
- Describe the various types of police misconduct and the challenges that surround the complaint process.

This incident highlights the controversial topic of racial profiling, which is one of the issues that surrounds police powers and decision-making.

In the opening pages of the text, it was noted that, in a democratic society, there will always be tension between the need to maintain order and the rights of citizens. This tension is evident in the discussion of the powers and decision-making of the police. How can society extend the police sufficient authority to ensure order and pursue criminals, while at the same time protect the rights of citizens? To imagine what life would be like in a "police state," you need only look to countries where the police have no limits on their power. A police force with unlimited power might be more effective, but it would also interfere with the freedoms Canadians enjoy.

A key question is: How can Canadian society balance the rights of citizens with the police authority to ensure order and to pursue criminal offenders? Some in Canada feel that the police have too much power as reflected in the radical perspective of the police discussed in Chapter 4. Defining the limits of police power is an ongoing process.

One of the difficulties is that persons who have contact with the police may not know what powers the police have nor their individual rights. This may be particularly problematic for persons newly arrived in Canada but may also be the case for many Canadian citizens, including the elderly and the mentally disabled. The situation is made even more complex by the fact that the powers of the police, and the limitations placed on the police by legislation and court decisions, are constantly evolving. The website http://scc.lexum.org is a good resource for following Supreme Court of Canada (SCC) decisions related to police powers.

THE *CHARTER OF RIGHTS AND FREEDOMS* AND POLICE POWERS

The *Canadian Charter of Rights and Freedoms* has had a significant impact in defining the powers of the police. The Charter entrenched the constitutional rights of those accused of crimes, who have the right to challenge the actions of the police if those rights have been violated.[1]

Several sections of the Charter set out the rights of citizens, including the following:

Section 7: Everyone has the right to life, liberty and security of the person and the right not to be deprived thereof except in accordance with the principles of fundamental justice.

Section 8: Everyone has the right to be secure against unreasonable search or seizure.

Section 9: Everyone has the right not to be arbitrarily detained or imprisoned.

Section 10. Everyone has the right on arrest or detention

(a) to be informed promptly of the reasons therefor;

(b) to retain and instruct counsel without delay and to be informed of that right; and

(c) to have the validity of the detention determined by way of *habeas corpus* and to be released if the detention is not lawful.

Section 11: Any person charged with an offence has the right

(a) to be informed without unreasonable delay of the specific offence …

Charter rights, combined with pre-existing legal rules, are designed to provide legal safeguards against the unlimited use of police power.

Besides entrenching constitutional rights for persons accused of crimes, the Charter gave those accused the right to challenge the actions of the police in situations where those rights might have been violated. These safeguards include the following:

- The police must have a search warrant to get information from Internet services about the identity of subscribers who are under investigation (*R. v. Spencer*, 2014 SCC 43).

- There are limits on the use of "Mr. Big" stings (see below), whereby suspects are placed in the position where they have "confessed" to committing a crime (*R. v. Hart*, 2014 SCC 52).

- Severe restrictions have been placed on the investigative strategy of placing an undercover officer in a jail cell to elicit evidence from a criminal suspect (*R. v. Hurley*, 2010 SCC 18).

- All relevant information gathered during a case investigation must be disclosed to the defence counsel (*R. v. Stinchcombe*, [1991] 3 SCR 326). (See Chapter 8.)

- In crafting policies for strip searches, the police must consider that Indigenous women and other minorities may have a fear of strip searches and, due to their life experiences, may experience a strip search as a sexual assault (*R. v. Golden*, 2001 SCC 83).

However, in its rulings, the SCC has also given the police significant powers:

- The SCC has ruled in favour of the police practice of using thermal-imaging technology deployed for aircraft to detect high levels of "heat" from homes, a key indicator of marijuana grow-ops (*R. v. Tessling*, 2004 SCC 67).

- The court reaffirmed the principle that the police can continue to question a suspect at length, even if the suspect repeatedly tries to invoke his or her right to silence (*R. v. Singh*, 2007 SCC 48).

- The SCC held that the Charter does not require the presence, upon request, of defence counsel during a custodial interrogation (*R. v. McCrimmon*, 2010 SCC 36; *R. v. Sinclair*, 2010 SCC 35).

- The court has given police the authority to use a warrant to obtain DNA from a suspect, by force if necessary (*R. v. Saeed*, 2016 SCC 24).

In addition, legislation may extend the powers of the police. The *Anti-terrorism Act* (S.C. 2001, c. 41) gives the police the authority to arrest a person without a warrant and have that person detained in custody if the officer suspects, on reasonable grounds, that the person's detention is necessary in order to prevent a specific terrorist activity.

The courts will continue to be involved in defining the powers of the police. The increasing use of high-tech surveillance devices by police will give rise to allegations that the police are abusing their authority and violating the rights of citizens. These issues surround the police practice of using a surveillance device known as an IMSI catcher (also commonly referred to as "Stingray"). These devices act as fake cellphone towers and force every cellphone within its range to connect and communicate essential identification information, including the cellphone's id, the id of the cellphone's SIM card, the cellphone carrier, and its country of origin.[2] A challenge is that the device not only records this information from the cellphone of a suspect but also from everyone else who is in range. Lawyers have argued that the use of these devices is illegal, and there no doubt will be legal challenges to their use in the future.[3]

POLICE ACCOUNTABILITY

The considerable powers of the police, including the authority to use lethal force and the ability to exercise discretion, require that there be structures of accountability and oversight. For Canadian criminologists Curtis Clarke and Chris Murphy, the **principle of accountability** means that "the actions of policing individuals/agencies are subject to review [and] there are formal channels that individuals can use to lodge complaints against policing bodies."[4]

Historically, the police investigated themselves. However, the increasing visibility of the police and a number of high-profile incidents have increased media and public scrutiny of the police. This provided the catalyst for the rise of civilian oversight and the emergence of models of accountability that include civilian involvement in investigations and, in several jurisdictions, independent civilian investigations and oversight.

Police officers can be held accountable for their actions under the *Criminal Code* (R.S.C. 1985, c. C-46), civil law, provincial statutes, and freedom of information acts. As well, various police boards, complaint commissions, and investigative units both within and outside police services have the authority to oversee and review the actions and decisions of police officers.

There are two external boards of review that oversee the activities of RCMP officers: the External Review Committee (ERC) and the Civilian Review and Complaints Committee for the RCMP (CRCC). The ERC hears appeals from RCMP members who have been disciplined for an infraction of force regulations (see http://www.erc-cee.gc.ca/index-en.aspx). The CRCC is an independent federal agency that receives and reviews complaints made by citizens about the conduct of RCMP officers who are policing under contract—that is, who are serving as provincial or municipal police officers (see https://www.crcc-ccetp.gc.ca). It may also initiate investigations into serious incidents involving the RCMP police or issues involving RCMP officers if the CCRC determines it is in the interests of the public to do so.

Governments may call commissions of inquiry or appoint task forces to enquire into specific incidents involving the police. In certain cases of a police-involved death, a coroner's inquest will be held. The objective of the inquest will be to determine the identity of the deceased, the me°dical cause of the death, and when, where, and how the death occurred. The inquest will also issue a number of (non-binding) recommendations designed to prevent deaths of a similar nature in the future.[5]

Principle of accountability

The actions of police officers and police services are subject to review and there are formal channels that individuals can use to lodge complaints against the police.

SHOULD THE POLICE PAY OFFENDERS FOR INFORMATION ON THE CRIME THEY HAVE COMMITTED?

Clifford Robert Olson was a serial child killer who terrorized the Greater Vancouver Region during 1980–81. He stalked and killed at least 11 children and sexually abused many others. Once apprehended, he blackmailed authorities in a cash-for-corpses agreement whereby his family was paid $100,000 in exchange for him leading police to the bodies of his victims. The families of the deceased children supported this decision in order to learn the circumstances of the deaths and to reach closure. The decision on the part of the police was highly controversial, and the ethics of the police decision were debated for many years.[a]

A similar case occurred in Winnipeg, wherein the Winnipeg Police Service paid a serial killer $1,500 for information on missing and murdered women in Manitoba. Arrested on a sexual assault charge unrelated to homicides, Shawn Lamb subsequently made a deal with the police to provide information on two women he confessed to killing if money were deposited into his canteen account in the jail. He subsequently agreed to a plea bargain and was sentenced to 20 years in prison with no possibility of parole for 10 years.[b]

More common is for the police to pay offenders for information. As an example, the RCMP in Kamloops, British Columbia, paid a low-level drug dealer $200,000 to assist them in apprehending the biggest drug dealers in the city.[c] Also in British Columbia, the RCMP paid an ex-gangster $400,000 to assist in an investigation.[d]

QUESTIONS

1. In your view, what ethical issues are raised by the practice of paying offenders for information?

2. Do you agree with the decisions of the police in the Olson case and the Lamb case to pay for information?

3. Are there any ethical issues raised by paying informants who may be involved in a criminal lifestyle for information?

4. Should there be guidelines on when and how much offenders should be paid for information?

5. Should the police consider the wishes of the victims' families when deciding whether to pay an offender for information about their crimes?

[a] I. Mulgrew. 2013, October 3. "Clifford Olson–Canada's National Monster–Dead at 71," *Vancouver Sun*. http://www.vancouversun.com/news/Clifford+Olson+Canada+national+monster+dead/5484826/story.html.

[b] M. McIntyre. 2013, November 15. "Cops Pay Serial Killer Lamb $1,500 for Information on Killings," *Winnipeg Free Press*. https://www.winnipegfreepress.com/local/Police-admit-paying-serial-killer-Lamb-for-information-on-killings-232090561.html.

[c] R. Koopmans. 2009, November 24. "Police Paid Informant $200,000," *Kamloops Daily News*. http://www.kamloopsnews.ca/news/city-region/police-paid-informant-200-000-1.1237152.

[d] K. Bolan. 2017, May 16. "Ex-UN Gangster Worked 20 Days for $400,000 in Deal with Mounties," *Vancouver Sun*. http://vancouversun.com/news/crime/ex-un-gangster-worked-20-days-for-400000-in-deal-with-mounties.

POLICE ETHICS

In carrying out their tasks, Canadian police officers are required to adhere to codes of conduct and ethics. These are contained in the various provincial police acts across the country, in provincial policy documents, and in the manuals of individual police services. The British Columbia Police Code of Ethics, for example, contains the statement of fundamental principles of policing, guiding values (i.e., citizenship, fairness, integrity, and respect), a statement of the primary responsibilities of police officers, and questions that should guide the ethical decision-making of officers.[6]

Among the questions that are designed to assist police officers in avoiding ethical difficulties are the following: "Is the activity or decision consistent with organizational or agency policy and the law?" "Do the outcomes or consequences generate more harm than good?" "What are the outcomes or consequences resulting from the activity or decision and whom do they affect?" and "Can the activity or decision be justified legally and ethically?" The code of conduct for Ontario police officers is set out in the Ontario *Police Services Act* (R.S.O. 1990, c. P. 15).

One example of the ethical dilemmas that the police face is the practice of paying offenders. See At Issue 5.1.

POLICE DISCRETION AND DECISION-MAKING

The majority of the thousands of decisions that police officers make in the course of their duties are routine. So too may the decisions of police officers be controversial, such as in the case of alleged biased policing and racial profiling, discussed below.

THE EXERCISE OF DISCRETION

A patrol officer who is faced with the need to make a decision and who chooses between different options is exercising **discretion**.

Discretion is an essential component of policing because no set of laws or regulations can prescribe what a police officer must do in each and every circumstance. Because it is impossible for officers to enforce all laws all of the time, they practise *selective* or *situational enforcement*. As the seriousness of the incident increases, however, the amount of discretion an officer can exercise decreases. The pervasiveness of cellphone cameras has also increased the visibility of police decision-making and the scrutiny of officer discretion and decision-making.

For police personnel, the authority to use discretion is set out in statutes such as the *Criminal Code*. For example, if an individual is found committing an offence, he or she *may* be arrested. Arrest, then, is not a strict obligation on the part of the police. The decisions a police officer makes may ultimately be scrutinized by the courts or the public, particularly when it is alleged that the officer abused discretionary powers and in doing so violated a person's legal rights. In the case of *R. v. Beaudry* (2007 SCC 5), for example, the SCC held that a police officer's discretion is not absolute and its use must be justified on both subjective and objective grounds. Officer Beaudry was convicted of obstruction of justice for having failed to gather evidence in an incident involving another police officer who was suspected of impaired driving.

There are situations in which a police officer's discretion is constrained. In cases of domestic violence, there are "mandatory charge" or "zero tolerance" policies that require police officers to arrest the suspect in cases where there is evidence that an assault has occurred, even if the alleged victim does not want an arrest to be made.

TYPIFICATIONS AND RECIPES FOR ACTION

Patrol officers bring to their work a set of cognitive lenses through which they make determinations about the people and events they encounter. They use a conceptual shorthand consisting of **typifications** and **recipes for action** to tailor their decision-making to the particular area and population being policed.[7] A visual cue such as a poorly dressed individual in an upscale neighbourhood would attract the attention of officers on patrol, as would a behaviour or activity considered out of place in a particular area. The risk is that racial profiling may result. Note that there may be among officers considerable variability in their policing "styles," and this will affect how they assess situations and the actions taken.

Officers who are assigned to a fixed geographical area for an extended period of time develop an intimate knowledge of its persons and places as well as extensive contacts with community groups, agencies, and organizations that are facilitative of police–community partnerships and the identification of and response to problems. How a situation or a person is "typified" may play a significant role in the recipes for action. This determination may involve judgments by police officers as to who they regard as "good" and "bad" people.[8] This may, in turn, affect how the officers exercise their discretion. A concern is that these cognitive processes may result in biased policing and the racial profiling of certain persons and groups.

BIASED POLICING AND RACIAL PROFILING

In carrying out their tasks, police officers must be aware of the Charter provisions that require the equal treatment of citizens (see Chapter 4). This applies to a wide range

Discretion

The power or right to decide or act according to one's own judgment.

Typifications

Constructs based on a patrol officer's experience that denote what is typical about people and events routinely encountered.

Recipes for action

The actions typically taken by patrol officers in various kinds of encounter situations.

of persons and groups in society. In recent years, a flashpoint between the police and communities has been racial profiling.

Police officers are expected to engage in **bias-free policing**, which requires that their decisions are "based on reasonable suspicion or probable grounds rather than stereotypes about race, religion, ethnicity, gender or other prohibited grounds."[9] Bias-free policing requires the equitable treatment of all persons of diversity.

One manifestation of biased policing is *racial profiling*, defined in Chapter 3. To refresh your memory, it is defined as "any action undertaken for reasons of safety, security, or public protection that relies on stereotypes about race, colour, ethnicity, ancestry, religion, or place of origin rather than on reasonable suspicion, to single out an individual for greater scrutiny or different treatment."[10] In *R. v. Brown* ([2003] OJ No. 1251), the Ontario Court of Appeal defined racial profiling as involving "the targeting of individual members of a particular racial group, on the basis of the supposed criminal propensity of the entire group." It has been noted that racial profiling "may result from police officers' internal implicit bias, which stems from unconscious stereotypes, or explicit bias, which arises from conscious stereotypes. Courts and tribunals have recognized that racial stereotyping will usually be the result of subtle unconscious beliefs, biases and prejudices."[11]

At issue is whether certain persons and groups, because of their attributes, are singled out for attention by the police based on who they are rather than what they have allegedly done. Racial profiling may be a consequence of **over-policing** and **pretext policing**. Over-policing occurs when the police focus disproportionately on a racialized population or neighbourhood. Over-policing often results in disproportionate police contacts with members of racialized groups and other visible/cultural/religious minority persons.

Pretext policing is most commonly associated with police stops or searches and may occur for a minor reason, such as a traffic violation, which then leads to a more intrusive intervention, such as a vehicle search.

RACIAL PROFILING VERSUS CRIMINAL PROFILING

Part of the difficulty in determining whether a police service and its officers engage in racial profiling is distinguishing between racial profiling and criminal profiling. As discussed in Chapter 4, a defining attribute of the police culture is suspiciousness of people and circumstances. While critics of the police argue that racial profiling is endemic to police work, police officers contend that they profile criminals, with particular attention to "signals and 'unusual fits.'"[12]

A visible-minority officer in the Hamilton Police Service offered the following perspectives on racial profiling, criminal profiling, and the importance of the context in which a person is identified for a police stop:

> When we're out on the street, we rely on our instincts. We are trained investigators in the sense that we need to do profiling. And what kind of profiling is that? Criminal profiling. It has nothing to do with racial profiling.... We profile criminals.[13]

This is the process of *typification* discussed earlier. The Ontario Human Rights Commission has made the distinction between racial profiling and criminal profiling by noting that criminal profiling is based on objective evidence of wrongdoing by an individual, while racial profiling is based on stereotypical assumptions about persons or groups of persons who are deemed more likely to engage in criminal behaviour.[14]

Bias-free policing

The requirement that police officers make decisions on the basis of reasonable suspicion and probable grounds rather than based on stereotypes about race, religion, ethnicity, gender, or other prohibited grounds.

Over-policing

A disproportionate police focus on a racialized population or neighbourhood.

Pretext policing

Police stops or searches for a minor reason that are used for more intrusive intervention.

PERCEPTIONS OF AND EXPERIENCES WITH BIASED POLICING AND RACIAL PROFILING

In examining the issues of biased policing and racial profiling, it is important to consider the lived experiences of racialized and other minority groups. A project focusing on youth in the Jane-Finch community in Toronto gathered the perceptions of young persons (N = 50).[15] One youth commented on the negative stereotypes that are often held of young Black men:

> People automatically see you as a black young person and they feel that you being black, you would never amount to nothing. Especially coming from the Jane-Finch community, automatically number one that they think is that you being black, you're never going to be nothing good. But that's not always true.[16]

Similarly, an Indigenous man offered this observation:

> The reservation I live on is located next to a town of 9,000 people. The police often sit on the road between the town and our reserve waiting for people who may violate the rules of the road. What the police will say is that they are conducting normal traffic monitoring. Yet if you drive out toward the west of the town where there is a non-native community the police presence is nearly non-existent. For all I know maybe it is a good place to issue tickets but to me it looks bad and looks like racial profiling (First Nations male, age 55 and over).[17]

The personal experiences with the police of a sample (N = 1,504) of Black residents in the city of Toronto or the Greater Toronto Area are presented in Figure 5.1. The responses reveal that there are issues surrounding police–Black encounters. However, the survey also revealed that a high percentage (64 percent) of Black men between the ages of 25 and 44 had personal experiences socializing with police, and 39 percent had been helped by the police.[18] These findings suggest that not all of the encounters between police and persons in the survey sample were negative.

STREET CHECKS AND CARDING

The issues surrounding racial profiling are illustrated by the ongoing controversy over the police practice of street checks, also referred to in some jurisdictions as *carding*. The terms will be used interchangeably in this discussion. Street checks/carding is an intelligence-gathering technique used by the police in which persons who have

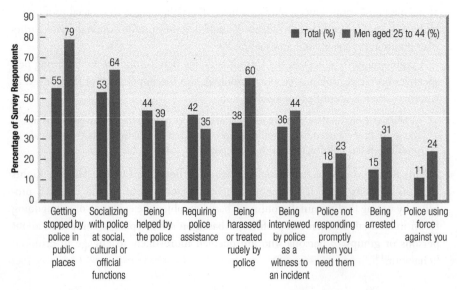

◀ FIGURE 5.1

Personal Experience with Police in Community or GTA, 2017

Sources: Paradkar, S. 2017. "Black Experience Project a Heart-Rending Snapshot of Black Lives in Toronto: Paradkar," thestar.com, July 20. https://www.thestar.com/news/gta/2017/07/20/black-experience-project-a-heart-rending-snapshot-of-black-lives-in-toronto-paradkar.html; https://www.theblackexperienceproject.ca/wp-content/uploads/2017/07/Black-Experience-Project-GTA-OVERVIEW-REPORT-4.pdf, pages 2786–2848; https://www.theblackexperienceproject.ca/wp-content/uploads/2017/04/Blace-Experience-Project-GTA-Detailed-Data-Tables.pdf

not committed an offence are stopped and questioned. Information gathered by the officer is then entered into a police database.[19] There are a variety of reasons why a police officer may stop an individual: it could be in response to a call from a community resident, to check on the well-being of a person, or in response to a report of a missing person.

Generally, however, the discussion about street checks/carding has centred on the findings from studies that a disproportionate number of Blacks and members of other racialized groups are stopped by the police. Analyses of police data suggest that Indigenous persons and members of racialized groups are more likely to be subjected to street checks.

For further insights into the impact of carding on police–community relations in Toronto, watch the video "Crisis of Distrust: Police and Community in Toronto," listed in the Media Links section at the end of the chapter.

STUDIES OF BIASED POLICING AND RACIAL PROFILING

The perceptions and experience of members of certain minority groups, particularly Blacks, have been validated by a number of studies. Keeping in mind that there are issues with how the data were gathered and analyzed in these studies, they nevertheless suggest that there are issues related to biased policing and racial profiling that need to be addressed.

A study in Kingston, Ontario, for example, found that Blacks were overrepresented in both traffic stops (2.7 times their proportion of the city's population) and pedestrian stops (3.7 times their proportion of the city's population).[20] In Halifax, a review of police records found that, during the period 2005 to 2016, Blacks were three times more likely to be stopped than Whites. The study also found that persons identified as Arab or West Asian were 1.9 times more likely to be stopped by police than Whites.[21] See Figure 5.2.

In Montreal, where it is estimated that Blacks are responsible for between 10 and 20 percent of crime, depending upon the type of offence, it has been found that they represent approximately 40 percent of those stopped and questioned.[22]

The results of a study of marijuana arrests in Toronto suggest that the police may over-police and racially profile Blacks. While surveys indicate that there is little difference in the rates of marijuana use between Blacks and other groups, an analysis of Toronto Police Service arrest data for 2003 to 2013 (N = 11,299) revealed that Blacks with no history of criminal convictions were three times more likely to be arrested by

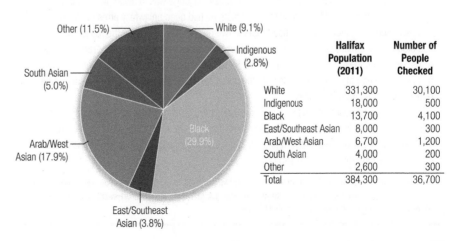

FIGURE 5.2 ▶

Chance of Receiving a Street Check in Halifax, by Population Group, 2005–16

Source: P. McGregor and A. MacIvor, 2017, January 9. "Black People 3 Times More Likely to Be Street Checked in Halifax, Police Say," *CBC News.* http://www.cbc.ca/news/canada/nova -scotia/halifax-black-street-checks-police-race -profiling-1.3925251. Reprinted by permission of CBC.

Other (11.5%) — White (9.1%) — Indigenous (2.8%) — South Asian (5.0%) — Arab/West Asian (17.9%) — Black (29.9%) — East/Southeast Asian (3.8%)

	Halifax Population (2011)	Number of People Checked
White	331,300	30,100
Indigenous	18,000	500
Black	13,700	4,100
East/Southeast Asian	8,000	300
Arab/West Asian	6,700	1,200
South Asian	4,000	200
Other	2,600	300
Total	384,300	36,700

officers for the possession of small amounts of marijuana than Caucasians with similar backgrounds.[23] More specifically, while Blacks comprise 8.4 percent of the city's population and Whites 53.1 percent, Blacks accounted for a disproportionate percentage of arrests. Note that this study did not examine whether the person who was arrested for possession of marijuana was also arrested for other offences.

A case in which an Ontario court determined that the police had engaged in racial profiling is presented in Police File 5.1. Note that the testimony of the police officers was that they were engaged in criminal profiling rather than racial profiling.

POLICE POLICIES ON RACIAL PROFILING AND STREET CHECKS/CARDING

A number of Canadian police services have taken measures to address the issue of racial profiling and the practice of street checks/carding. This includes upgrading training for officers, identifying officers at risk of engaging in racial profiling, and improving community relations.[24] Police services have operational policies that explicitly prohibit racial profiling by their officers. The Edmonton Police Service and the Calgary Police Service both have street check audits conducted by civilians designed to ensure that police stops are lawful and unbiased.[25]

The policy of the Ontario Provincial Police (OPP), for example, states, "Illegal profiling is not permitted and shall not be tolerated in any respect. Illegal profiling means taking law-enforcement actions, such as stopping/questioning/searching/detaining/arresting a person, based solely on the person's: race; sex; ancestry; age; sexual orientation; family status; place of origin; marital status; disability; creed; colour; citizenship; ethnic origin; [and/or] safe-sex partnership status."[26]

POLICE FILE 5.1

A CASE OF RACIAL PROFILING AND CARDING

In 2011, two Toronto police constables on patrol saw Mutaz Elmardy, a Black man, alone, walking home at night from the mosque.

The officers stopped Mr. Elmardy and questioned him. One of the officers later testified that they believed that he was in violation of his bail conditions and had also looked at their police vehicle as they had driven by, while the other officer was concerned that Mr. Elmardy had a weapon since he had his hands in his pockets. During the encounter, Mr. Elmardy was punched in the face, knocked to the ground, and handcuffed. He was not advised of his rights to contact a lawyer. A card was filled out indicating his skin colour (Black) and his birthplace (Sudan).

The case went to trial and the decision of the presiding judge was to award Mr. Elmardy $27,000. The judge found that during the encounter, he had been unlawfully arrested, searched, and assaulted. The judge also concluded that the two officers had lied about the reason why they had stopped Mr. Elmardy in the first place and that their decisions were based on "racial stereotypes." However, the judge did not find that Mr. Elmardy had been racially profiled, noting that he had been uncooperative and hostile toward the police and had not followed their request that he remove his hands from his pockets.

Mr. Elmardy appealed the ruling to the Divisional Court. Writing for the three-judge panel, one of the judges wrote in the decision: "Racial profiling has a serious impact on the credibility and effectiveness of our police services. It has led to distrust and injustice. It must stop." The court increased Mr. Elmardy's award to $80,000.

Source: Adapted from J. Gallant. 2017, April 8. "Ontario Court Awards $80,000 to Man Who Was Punched, Cuffed in Case of Racial Profiling," *Toronto Star.* https://www.thestar.com/news/gta/2017/04/08/ontario-court-awards-80000-to-man-who-was-punched-cuffed-in-case-of-racial-profiling.html.

In Ontario, concerns about street checks and racial profiling resulted in the provincial government setting province-wide guidelines for police services.[27] The policy includes the requirements that police officers inform citizens who voluntarily stop for them on the street why identifying information is being requested, that the citizen has the right to not provide any identifying information, and to provide to the citizen their name, badge number, and instructions on how to contact the provincial office of the Independent Police Review Director should they have any concerns about the encounter with the officer.[28]

The Ontario policy also requires police services to keep statistics on the age, race, and gender of persons in all attempted and completed street checks, and this information will be reviewed by an independent audit.[29]

Research has found that the extent to which policies on racial profiling are implemented and effective depends in large measure on the police organizational itself, the strength of its leadership, and the quality of training that officers receive.[30,31]

The issues surrounding over-policing, biased policing, racial profiling, and street checks/carding are complex. There is a need for more research that uses both analytics and the lived experiences of persons who have contact with the police, and of the police officers who are involved in encounters with community residents.

POLICE TREATMENT OF INDIGENOUS PERSONS

A key feature of Canadian criminal justice is the overrepresentation of Indigenous people at all stages of the justice system. The high rates of Indigenous arrests in many regions of the country have raised the question as to whether police officers discriminate against Indigenous people. Although there is no evidence that Indigenous people are systemically discriminated against by the police, there have been serious incidents in a number of jurisdictions that have subsequently been found to be the result of discriminatory actions on the part of police officers. These incidents have often overshadowed the positive relationships that have been established between many Indigenous communities and the police.

One example is the incidents that occurred in Saskatoon, where observers eventually coined the term "starlight tour" to describe the police practice of picking up impaired Indigenous people in the city, transporting them to outlying areas, and dumping them. In at least one case, these actions were directly responsible for the unlawful confinement of an Indigenous person. See Police File 5.2.

THE POLICE USE OF FORCE

The legal authority for the police to use force is found in the *Criminal Code*, which sets out the following principles: (1) Officers exercising force must be performing a duty they are required or authorized to do; (2) they must act on reasonable grounds; (3) they may use only so much force as is necessary under the circumstances; and (4) they are responsible for any excessive use of force. Provisions governing the use of force are also contained in provincial police statutes.

The use of force is intended to gain control and compliance—for example, during an arrest or while breaking up an altercation. Degrees of force can be placed on a continuum from officer presence and verbal commands through to lethal force. Police are trained to match the degree of force to the immediate requirements of the situation. The use of force in excess of what is necessary can leave the officer criminally or civilly liable for assault or, in rare cases, murder.

POLICE FILE 5.2

"STARLIGHT TOURS"

In January 2000, two Saskatoon police officers picked up an Indigenous man, Darrell Night, drove him to an industrial park on the outskirts of the city, and abandoned him in extreme winter weather. Luckily, Night was assisted by a security guard. He made his way back to the city, where he subsequently filed a complaint with the police. On the basis of his testimony, two city police officers were convicted at trial of unlawful confinement, fired from their positions, and sentenced to eight months in jail. The court rejected a request by the two officers that they be sentenced by an Indigenous sentencing circle. In 2003, the Saskatchewan Court of Appeal upheld the convictions and the officers began serving their sentences.

The *Night* case raised suspicions that the Saskatoon police had transported and dumped other Indigenous people outside the city, some of whom had frozen to death. Similar incidents included the discovery of the frozen bodies of Rodney Naistus on January 29, 2000 (a day after Night had been dumped), in the same industrial area, and of Lawrence Wegner, found frozen to death on February 3, 2000, in a field outside the city. Naistus was naked from the waist up; Wegner was not wearing shoes and had no jacket, even though it was winter. Subsequent investigations by the RCMP were not able to determine the circumstances surrounding the deaths of the two men.

The cases, however, focused attention on the death of an Indigenous teenager, Neil Stonechild, whose frozen body had been found in a field on the outskirts of Saskatoon 10 years earlier, on November 29, 1990. Stonechild was last seen alive by his friend Jason Roy; at the time, Stonechild was struggling with two Saskatoon police officers, who forced him into the back of a police cruiser. The temperature on the night Stonechild disappeared was −28°C. In February 2003, the province's justice minister announced a commission of inquiry into Stonechild's death. In its final report (available online at http://www .cbc.ca/news2/background/stonechild/stonechild_report.pdf), the commissioner, the Hon. Mr. Justice D.H. Wright, found that Stonechild was in the custody of the police on the night he disappeared and that the injuries that were on his body were caused by handcuffs.[a] However,

there was no evidence presented that the two police constables actually dropped Stonechild off outside the city, and therefore, the circumstances surrounding his death remain undetermined. Wright, however, was severely critical of the initial investigation conducted by the Saskatoon police, and rejected the version of events offered by the police. Despite this, the absence of evidence precluded criminal charges being laid against the officers who were last seen with Stonechild. For an account of the Stonechild case, see *Starlight Tour: The Last, Lonely Night of Neil Stonechild*.[b] The two officers were subsequently dismissed by the police service and in 2008, the Supreme Court denied an appeal by the two officers to have the findings of the Wright inquiry quashed.

These cases heightened tensions between Indigenous people (particularly Indigenous youths) and the police and seriously undermined earlier efforts by the Saskatoon police to improve police–Indigenous relations.

There are more recent examples of starlight tours, with Indigenous women in Val-d'-Or, Quebec, alleging they were subjected to this practice, and a Montreal police officer who was cited for ethics violations for driving a racialized person around the city in the back of a patrol car and dropping him off far from his residence.[c]

[a] Mr. Justice D.H. Wright (Commissioner). 2004. *Commission of Inquiry into Matters Relating to the Death of Neil Stonechild*. Regina: Department of Justice, Province of Saskatchewan. http://www.cbc.ca/news2/background/stonechild/stonechild_report.pdf.

[b] S. Reber and R. Renaud. 2005. *Starlight Tour: The Last, Lonely Night of Neil Stonechild*. Toronto: Random House Canada.

[c] The Canadian Press. 2017, October 10. "Former Montreal Cop Known as Agent 728 Cited for Ethics Violation," *Toronto Star*. https://www.thestar.com/news/canada/2017/10/10/former-montreal-cop-known-as-agent-728-cited-for-ethics-violations.html.

Additional sources: *CBC News*. 2003, April 14. "Wegner Death Remains a Mystery to Family." http://www.cbc.ca/news/canada/saskatchewan/wegner-death-remains-a-mystery-to-family-1.397142; G. Smith. 2004, October 27. "The Death of Neil Stonechild: Judge Rejects Police Version of Events One Cold Night in Saskatoon," *Globe and Mail*. https://www.theglobeandmail.com/news/national/the-death-of-neil-stonechild-judge-rejects-police-version-of-events-one-cold-night-in-saskatoon/article1006303.

THE FORCE OPTIONS FRAMEWORK

The *force options* approach to the use of force by police is the foundation of most police training in Canada. The approach is positive and professional in explaining how and why police use force in their day-to-day activities. It also provides police administrators and judicial review personnel with an objective framework in which to analyze use-of-force situations. It also allows police officers to explain, within an accepted format, how and why force was applied at the time of the altercation.

Although police officers often have no control over the types of encounter situations they become involved in, they can achieve a measure of control by exercising an appropriate level of response. These responses include five distinct force options that are available to police officers:

1. *Officer presence*: The mere presence of a police officer may alter the behaviour of the participants at an altercation, thereby enabling control of the situation.

2. *Dialogue*: Verbal and non-verbal communication skills may resolve the conflict and result in voluntary compliance.

3. *Empty hands*: Physical force is used to gain control.

4. *Compliance tools*: Equipment or weapons are used to gain control.

5. *Lethal force*: The situation requires complete incapacitation of the subject in order to gain control, and lethal force is the only option available to reduce the lethal threat.

DECISION-MAKING AND FORCE OPTIONS

Standard police procedures require that officers responding to an incident engage in a continual risk assessment of the situation in determining the appropriate level of intervention. In conducting this assessment, the responding officers must gather as much information as possible when the call is first received, while in route, during entry into the immediate area where the subject is located, and as the incident unfolds.

From an analysis of all of the available information surrounding an incident, the officer will attempt to select the most appropriate use-of-force response. The goal is to use the least violent option available that will safely gain control of the situation. The generally accepted use-of-force standard is *one plus one*, meaning that police officers have the authority to use one higher level of force than that with which they are confronted. The use of force in excess of what is necessary can leave the officer criminally or civilly liable for assault. There are a number of Canadian police officers who have been charged with murder or manslaughter following a use-of-force incident.[32]

Each encounter situation in which a police officer becomes involved has a unique set of circumstances and there is always the potential that the situation will escalate very rapidly, requiring the officer to make a split-second decision. Incidents involving persons who are mentally ill or drug-impaired are often characterized by a high level of unpredictability. This may make it difficult for police officers to develop, and effect, a prescribed plan of action.

The absence of national use-of-force statistics in Canada precludes a determination of the frequency with which the various force options are used.[33] Research studies have found that young, inexperienced male officers are more likely to use force improperly and that officers with four-year university degrees and with more years of policing experience are less likely to use physical force.[34,35] (Note: This has particular implications in contemporary police services—an increasing number of officers have fewer years on the job.) Research also suggests that male officers are more likely to shoot than women officers, and officers with a college education are less likely to be involved in shootings than officers with lower levels of education. Police officers with a history of involvement in shootings appear to be more likely to be involved in additional shooting incidents.[36]

LESS-LETHAL FORCE OPTIONS

A less-lethal force option can be described as a force option that is *highly unlikely* to cause death or serious injury to an individual when *properly applied* by a police officer. However, it is possible that death or serious injury may occur, hence the term *less-lethal* rather than *less-than-lethal*. Less-lethal weapons include pepper spray, tear gas, and conducted energy weapons (CEWs; most commonly referred to as Tasers). Police services have made efforts to train and equip officers with less-lethal force options.[37]

This possibility of serious harm is especially great if the force option is improperly applied by the police officer. In these instances, the less-lethal options may contribute to or even cause serious injury or death. This is illustrated by the ongoing controversy surrounding the use of the Taser by police officers in encounter situations.

THE TASER: LESS-THAN-LETHAL OR LETHAL WEAPON?

Tasers were adopted by Canadian police services as a force option beginning in the late 1990s. The Taser "gun" fires two metal darts that are attached to wires and enter the subject's skin, providing a shock of up to 50,000 volts of electricity. The expanded use of the Taser by police services is credited with reducing both the number of deaths of persons as a result of the police use of lethal force and, as well, the number of officers injured in the course of carrying out their duties.[38]

There has been widespread concern with the use of the Taser on persons who are in a state of "excited delirium," which may be the result of severe drug use (often cocaine or crystal meth), mental illness, or other causes, results in the person being incoherent, violent, and non-compliant. The concern is that the use of electric shocks on these persons can cause a heart attack, although the most recent research has been unable to establish a causal relationship between the use of Tasers and sudden in-custody deaths.[39] While Tasers have made the police safer, the costs have been a number of deaths in incidents where they were used.[40]

The issues surrounding the use of Tasers and the extent to which the use of Tasers may cause death are highlighted in the case of Robert Dziekanski, a Polish immigrant who died after being Tasered at Vancouver International Airport. See Police File 5.3.

DEADLY ENCOUNTERS: THE POLICE USE OF LETHAL FORCE

The decision to use lethal force is the most critical one any police officer can take. The decision is often made in a split second in circumstances involving fear, confusion, and cognitive distortion.[41] Generally, officers are permitted to use guns only to protect themselves or others from serious injury or to stop a fleeing felon whose escape is likely

---

POLICE FILE 5.3

THE DEATH OF ROBERT DZIEKANSKI

The most high-profile incident involving the police use of Tasers to date was the death of Robert Dziekanski at the Vancouver International Airport. At 2:50 p.m. on October 13, 2007, Mr. Dziekanski, an immigrant from Poland, arrived at the airport following a long flight from Poland. He was fatigued from the flight and spoke no English. For reasons that have still not been adequately explained, Mr. Dziekanski spent nearly 12 hours wandering around the international arrivals area without securing the assistance that would have led him to his waiting mother. At 1:20 a.m., he became agitated and confused, his situation made more difficult due to his limited English. The airport operations centre received calls that a man was acting strangely, and security personnel and RCMP officers were called. Four RCMP officers arrived on the scene and, within minutes, had Tasered Mr. Dziekanski a total of five times. He was restrained by the officers and died shortly thereafter of a heart attack. An autopsy revealed that there were no drugs or alcohol in Dziekanski's system.

The encounter was captured on a cellphone camera by a passenger in the terminal. See the video, "Vancouver Airport – Robert Dziekanski's Taser Death," in Media Links section at the end of the chapter. The RCMP originally stated that Dziekanski had been Tasered twice, although the video indicated that he had been Tasered a total of five times. The provincial government subsequently launched a public inquiry headed by a retired judge, Thomas Braidwood. The inquiry focused on how police use Tasers and, in the second phase of the inquiry, examined all of the circumstances surrounding the death of Mr. Dziekanski. On numerous occasions during the hearing, the four RCMP officers involved in the incident, and their superior officers, provided conflicting testimony.

Among the findings of the inquiry were that the responding officers did not make any reasonable attempt to de-escalate the situation, that the use of the Taser against Mr. Dziekanski had been premature and inappropriate, and that the four officers involved in the incident had given conflicting testimony to the inquiry that was not credible.[a] The officers were subsequently charged with perjury for lying to the commission and two of the officers were convicted. In 2017, one of the officers filed an appeal of his perjury conviction with the Supreme Court of Canada.

[a] T.R. Braidwood (Commissioner). 2010. *WHY? The Robert Dziekanski Tragedy. Braidwood Commission on the Death of Robert Dziekanski.* Victoria: Attorney General of British Columbia. https://www2.gov.bc.ca/assets/gov/law-crime-and-justice/about-bc-justice-system/inquiries/braidwoodphase2report.pdf.

---

to result in serious injury or death. The police use of lethal force is a rare occurrence within Canada, averaging less than 10 cases per year nationwide, as compared to the approximately 300 persons who are shot and killed by U.S. police officers every year.[42]

In the majority of police shootings that result in fatalities, the deceased had just committed a serious criminal offence. In some incidents, the deceased was wanted by the police for a serious criminal offence such as murder, attempted murder, robbery, aggravated assault, or drug trafficking.

There are also shooting incidents that are victim-precipitated homicides, or *suicide by cop* wherein the victim is the precipitator of the incident. Often these incidents involve despondent individuals who are suffering from suicidal tendencies, mental illness, or extreme substance abuse, and act in a manner calculated to force police to use lethal force.[43]

THE USE OF FORCE AND PERSONS WITH MENTAL ILLNESS (PWMI)

As noted in Chapter 6, police officers are increasingly being called to incidents involving persons with mental illness (PwMI). While the number of police-involved shootings per capita in Canada has remained fairly constant over the past decade, the percentage of cases involving PwMI has increased and now account for approximately 40 percent of the persons killed by police officers.[44] View the documentary film, "Hold Your Fire," listed in the Media Links section at the end of the chapter. For accounts of the impact of the death of a mentally ill relative in an encounter with the police, see the video link, "When Police Kill," in the Media Links section at the end of the chapter.

The shooting death of Sammy Yatim in an encounter with Toronto police in 2013 was a high-profile incident in which lethal force was used against a mentally ill man. See Police File 5.4.

POLICE FILE 5.4

THE TORONTO STREETCAR SHOOTING: THE DEATH OF SAMMY YATIM

THE CANADIAN PRESS/Galit Rodan

Torontonians protest the fatal shooting of Sammy Yatim and set up a memorial on the spot where he was killed in a streetcar.

On July 27, 2013, Toronto police responded to a call about a disruptive passenger on a streetcar. The man had wielded a knife and ordered everyone off of the streetcar. Witnesses would later say that he appeared to be unstable. Police officers surrounded the streetcar. Sammy Yatim, an 18-year-old with a history of mental illness, was subsequently shot nine times by Constable James Forcillo, a six-year member of the Toronto Police Service. A total of 22 police officers were present at the scene. He was then Tasered prior to being taken to hospital

where he was pronounced dead. The Ontario Special Investigations Unit assumed control of the investigation and subsequently charged Constable Forcillo with murder.[a]

In 2016, Forcillo was convicted of attempted murder and sentenced to six years in prison.[b] Read the decision of the court in *Her Majesty the Queen v. James Forcillo* at https://www.scribd.com /document/319558302/Forcillo-decision#from_embed. Note that the judge sentenced Forcillo to a year longer than the mandatory minimum of five years, holding the constable to a higher standard than regular citizens due to his position of trust.

The shooting sparked outrage in the community and a review of police use-of-force practice. This incident prompted an external review of the police use of force in the Toronto Police Service, with a specific focus on police encounters with the mentally ill.

---

[a] K.B. Carlson. 2013, August 19. "Toronto Police Officer Charged in Sammy Yatim Shooting to Turn Himself in Tuesday," *Globe and Mail*. https://www.theglobeandmail.com/news /toronto/ontario-police-watchdog-lays-second-degree-murder-charge-in-sammy-yatim -shooting/article13837354.

[b] A. Hasham. 2016, July 28. "Const. James Forcillo Sentenced to 6 Years in Sammy Yatim Shooting," *Toronto Star*. https://www.thestar.com/news/crime/2016/07/28/ const-james-forcillo-sammy-yatim-shooting-sentence.html.

Despite tragedies such as the shooting death of Sammy Yatim, in an overwhelming number of cases, police officers successfully resolve incidents involving PwMI. Nor does it appear that PwMI are subject to any higher levels of use of force than mentally stable suspects.[45] However, this incident and several others accelerated the debate over equipping police officers with body-worn video cameras. See At Issue 5.2.

SHOULD ALL POLICE OFFICERS BE EQUIPPED WITH BODY-WORN CAMERAS?

Andrew Francis Wallace/Toronto Star via Getty Images

Toronto Police Service officer with body-worn camera

A number of Canadian police services have equipped their officers with body-worn cameras (BWC). This technology has the potential to capture what the police officer is seeing, doing, and saying during an encounter. Proponents of BWCs argue that, among other potential benefits of BMCs, they increase the transparency of police operations and the accountability of police officers; provide an accurate record of police–citizen encounters, which can, in turn, reduce complaints against the police (and associated civil suits); reduce false accusations; and provide a more complete recording of police–citizen encounters than those recorded in the officer's court notebook.[a] It is also pointed out that BWCs can provide a more complete record of an encounter than smartphones used by bystanders. In this way, BWCs may serve to counter the selective recordings by citizens.

Among the concerns that have been expressed about BWCs are 1) the impact of BWCs on officer decision-making in encounter situations; 2) how the presence of BWCs will affect the willingness of victims and witnesses to speak with the police; 3) the impact of BWCs in police–citizen encounters in diverse communities, including Indigenous communities; 4) the response of the general public; 5) issues related to privacy legislation and the Charter; and 6) the costs of equipping officers with BWCs and maintaining the technology. As well, this technology does not record how the officer *perceives* what they are seeing as they enter an encounter situation and how this information is being cognitively processed. View the documentary film, "Police Shootings: Caught on Camera," listed in the Media Links section at the end of the chapter.

The findings from studies of BWCs have been mixed and observers have cautioned that BWCs are not a "fix-all."[b] Some have found that the presence of BWCs reduces assaults on police officers and the number of complaints filed against the police, while other studies have found no such impact. Public opinion on BWCs and the views of officers about BWCs has been found to be varied.[c] Although the public is generally familiar with BWCs, some studies have found that their presence may not improve police–community relationships, particularly between police and minority groups.[d] Officers participating in the study of BWCs in the Edmonton Police Service expressed concerns that BWCs would make them more "robotic" and "less effective in creating rapport."[e] There were also concerns that BWCs would cause officers to "hesitate to use appropriate levels of force."[f] A study in the U.K. found that rates of assault against the police who were wearing body-worn cameras increased, an outcome that was ascribed to officers being less assertive and being more vulnerable to assault.[g] From their study, one group of researchers concluded, "BWCs are not a simple 'plug and play' policy solution; significant variations across officers and circumstances affect the potential benefits of BWCs."[h]

Acquiring and equipping officers with BWCs and storing and retrieving video footage is expensive and a primary reason why many Canadian police services have not adopted this technology. The Calgary Police Service, for example, one of the early adopters of BWCs, has abandoned their use.

QUESTIONS

1. In your view, should all police officers be equipped with BWCs?
2. What arguments in support of them—and what concerns—do you have?

[a] National Institute of Justice. 2012. *A Primer on Body-Worn Cameras for Law Enforcement*, Washington, DC: U.S. Department of Justice. https://www.justnet.org/pdf/00-Body-Worn-Cameras-508.pdf.

[b] A. Bawany. 2015. "Survey: Police Body Cameras Aren't a Fix-All" [news release], University of Nevada, Las Vegas. https://www.unlv.edu/news/release/unlv-criminal-justice-survey-gauges-public-opinion-body-cameras-police-officers.

[c] T.I.C. Cubitt, R. Lesic, G.L. Myers, and R. Corry. 2017. "Body-Worn Video: A Systematic Review of the Literature," *Australian and New Zealand Journal of Criminology, 50*(3), 379–396.

[d] D. McClure, N. La Vigne, M. Lynch, and L. Golian. 2017. *How Body Cameras Affect Community Members' Perceptions of Police: Results from a Randomized Controlled Trial of One Agency's Pilot.* New York: Urban Institute. https://www.urban.org/sites/default/files/publication/91331/2001307-how-body-cameras-affect-community-members-perceptions-of-police_1.pdf.

[e] Edmonton Police Service. 2015. *Body Worn Video: Considering the Evidence. Final Report of the Edmonton Police Service Body Worn Video Project.* Edmonton: Author, p. 7. http://www.bwvsg.com/wp-content/uploads/2015/06/Edmonton-Police-BWV-Final-Report.pdf.

[f] Ibid.

[g] RAND. 2016, May 17. "Body-Worn Cameras Associated with Increased Assaults Against Police, and Increase Use-of-Force If Officers Choose When to Turn on Body-Worn Cameras" [news release]. https://www.rand.org/news/press/2016/05/17.html.

[h] McClure, La Vigne, Lynch, and Golian, *How Body Cameras Affect Community Members' Perceptions of Police*, p. 9.

POLICE POWERS IN INVESTIGATIONS

Police powers in investigations are continually being defined, and re-defined, by the courts. The following discussion provides an overview of several of the areas where police conduct in case investigations has been called into question by the courts. Illustrative of the issues that surround police powers in case investigations is the issue of the right of suspects to remain silent when interrogated by the police, the controversy that surrounds the use of the Mr. Big strategy, the investigative practice known as blood-letting, and the use of high-tech surveillance devices.

ENTRAPMENT: A MISUSE OF POLICE POWERS

Entrapment means just what it sounds like: A person ends up committing an offence that he or she would not otherwise have committed, largely as a result of pressure or cunning on the part of the police. In these situations, the police are most often operating undercover. The following are controversial examples of police practice:

- An expensive car is left with the keys in the ignition, observed by concealed officers waiting to arrest anyone who steals it.
- A police officer poses as a young girl while trolling websites frequented by pedophiles.
- An undercover officer poses as an intoxicated subway passenger, wearing expensive jewellery and a Rolex watch. Anyone who mugs him is arrested.
- An undercover officer poses as a potential client to arrest a prostitute who offers sexual services.

Proactive techniques like these can be an effective and cost-efficient use of personnel. They can help prevent crime in "victimless" offences (such as prostitution and drug possession) of the sort that are unlikely to generate citizen complaints. The controversy stems from the fact that there is a line between catching those habitually involved in lawbreaking and creating situational criminals. The concern is that in some situations, typically law-abiding people could be enticed into committing a crime.

The courts have determined that the line is crossed when a person is persistently harassed into committing an offence that he or she would not have committed had it not been for the actions of the police. People cannot be targeted at random. Rather, there should be a reasonable suspicion that the person is already engaged in criminal activity. For example, in the prostitution example above, the actions of the police do not constitute entrapment because such a reasonable suspicion exists. One of the landmark cases on entrapment is *R. v. Mack* ([1988] 2 SCR 903), presented in Legal File 5.1.

Canadian courts have generally not allowed the defence of entrapment, which requires there to have been a clear abuse of process. In *R. v. Pearson* ([1998] 3 SCR 620), the SCC made a clear distinction between the issue of entrapment and innocence: "Entrapment is completely separate from the issue of guilt or innocence. It is concerned with the conduct of the police and is dealt with at a separate proceeding from the trial on the merits" (see also *R. v. Campbell*, [1998] 3 SCR 533).

THE "MR. BIG" TECHNIQUE: A CONTROVERSIAL INVESTIGATIVE STRATEGY

A particularly controversial police investigation technique that has also raised issues about police powers is known as the **Mr. Big technique**. This involves police undercover officers making contact with crime suspects who are subsequently introduced to "Mr. Big," a purported organized crime boss. The target(s) are then invited to join the

Mr. Big technique

An investigative strategy designed to secure confessions from crime suspects through the creation of an elaborate scenario.

R. V. MACK: THE CASE OF THE RELUCTANT DRUG TRAFFICKER

The defendant was charged with drug trafficking. At the close of his defence, he brought an application for a stay of proceedings on the basis of entrapment. His testimony indicated that he had persistently refused the approaches of a police informer over the course of six months and that he was only persuaded to sell him drugs because of the informer's persistence, his use of threats, and the inducement of a large amount of money. He also testified that he had previously been addicted to drugs but that he had given up his use of narcotics. The application for a stay of proceedings was refused, and he was convicted of drug trafficking. The Court of Appeal dismissed an appeal from that conviction.

The central issue for the Supreme Court of Canada was whether the defendant had been entrapped into committing the offence of drug trafficking. The court held that the police in this case were not interrupting an ongoing criminal enterprise; the offence was clearly brought about by their conduct and would not have occurred without their involvement. The court stated that the persistence of the police requests and the equally persistent refusals, and the length of time needed to secure the defendant's participation in the offence, indicated that the police had tried to make the appellant take up his former lifestyle and had gone further than merely providing him with the opportunity.

For the court, the most important and determinative factor was that the defendant had been threatened and had been told to get his act together when he did not provide the requested drugs. This conduct was unacceptable and went beyond providing the appellant with an opportunity. The court found that the average person in the appellant's position might also have committed the offence, if only to finally satisfy this threatening informer and end all further contact. The court ruled that the trial judge should have entered a stay of proceedings.

Source: *R. v. Mack*, [1988] 2 SCR 903. Canadian Legal Information Institute. http://www.canlii.org/ca/cas/scc/1988/1988scc100.html.

crime group, but only if they admit to having committed a major crime. The strategy is prohibited in the U.S. and Europe, where it is considered to be entrapment, although Canadian courts have ruled that the police may engage in deception to catch criminals.

Proponents of the technique cite figures indicating that the technique has a 75 percent confession rate and a 95 percent conviction rate and has proven to be very effective in apprehending offenders who would have otherwise not been charged and convicted. Critics argue, however, that the practice raises legal, moral, and ethical issues.[46] Suspects who are questioned about crimes in a Mr. Big scenario enjoy none of the legal safeguards of those who are interrogated in a "custodial" setting.[47] There are concerns that Mr. Big stings are really dirty tricks that lead to false confessions and the conviction of innocent persons who have confessed to police in a Mr. Big operation and were later exonerated by DNA evidence.[48]

Historically, the courts had ruled that the police could engage in deception to apprehend criminals, and this included the Mr. Big strategy. However, in a ruling in 2014 (R. v. Hart, 2014 SCC 52), the SCC placed restrictions on the admissibility of evidence, including suspect confessions, garnered through the use of the Mr. Big technique. See Legal File 5.2.

SEARCH AND SEIZURE

The power of the police to search people and places and to seize evidence also illustrates the fine balance that must be maintained between protecting public order and ensuring the rights of citizens. Historically, under the common law, the manner in which evidence was gathered did not affect its admissibility in a criminal trial. That all

R. V. HART: LIMITING THE USE OF THE MR. BIG TECHNIQUE

Mr. Hart, who has a Grade 5 level of education and was on social assistance, was the prime suspect in the drowning deaths of his twin daughters in Newfoundland in 2002. In 2005, the RCMP spent over $400,000 to construct an elaborate Mr. Big operation, wherein officers posed as gangsters and recruited Hart to join their crime network. Mr. Hart participated in activities, including moving what he thought was stolen property. In addition to being wined and dined at restaurants and casinos, he was paid nearly $16,000. To remain part of the gang, Mr. Hart was required to "confess" to any previous crimes. The court concluded that the scenario required Mr. Hart to confess to a crime.

On the basis of his "confession," Hart was found guilty of first-degree murder and received a life sentence with no possibility of parole for 25 years. In 2012, the Newfoundland Court of Appeal overturned the conviction, finding that the lengths to which the RCMP went in the Mr. Big operation violated Mr. Hart's rights and that the tactics were excessive and unjust. The SCC agreed, noting that

Mr. Hart had been subjected to physical and psychological harm. At the time of the SCC decision, Hart had served nine years in prison.

In its decision, the SCC ruled that confessions obtained via the Mr. Big strategy rely on coercion, threats, and financial inducements and should be presumed to be inadmissible in court. However, the court left open the possibility that evidence gathered from Mr. Big stings could be admitted in court if the prosecutors are able to convince the presiding judge that the reliability of the evidence outweighs any prejudicial effects of the strategy. This will require the police and prosecutors to gather corroborating evidence to support the suspect's confession.[a] The courts continue to examine the use of the Mr. Big strategy in criminal investigations. See Critical Thinking Exercise 5.1 at the end of the chapter.

[a] T. Riddell and K. Puddister. 2014, August 6. "Who's in Charge of Mr. Big?" *National Post.* http://nationalpost.com/opinion/riddell-puddister-whos-in-charge-of-mr-big.

Additional sources: S. Woods. 2014, September 18. "A New Standard for 'Mr. Big' Confessions: R v Hart," *TheCourt.ca.* http://www.thecourt.ca/a-new-standard-for-mr-big-confessions-r-v-hart; *R. v. Hart*, 2014 SCC 52.

changed with the Charter, Section 8 of which protects all citizens against "unreasonable" search or seizure. Evidence obtained during an illegal search may be excluded from trial if, as indicated in Section 24 of the Charter, its use would bring the justice system into disrepute.

The Supreme Court of Canada has held in *R. v. S.A.B.* (2003 SCC 60) that for a search to be reasonable, (a) it must be authorized by law, (b) the law itself must be reasonable, and (c) the manner in which the search was carried out must be reasonable. This is illustrated in the case of R. v. Harrison (2009 SCC 34), presented in Legal File 5.3.

R. V. HARRISON: A CASE OF AN ILLEGAL SEARCH

On October 24, 2004, an Ontario Provincial Police officer pulled over a vehicle van near Kirkland, Ontario. The vehicle had been rented two days earlier at Vancouver International Airport. The officer had stopped the vehicle because it was missing the front licence plate, but quickly realized that it was registered in Alberta and was not required to have one. The officer then asked Mr. Harrison for his driver's licence, and Mr. Harrison indicated that he couldn't find it. The officer conducted a computer search and discovered that Mr. Harrison's licence had been suspended. Mr. Harrison was arrested for driving while his licence was suspended.

At trial, the officer stated to the court that he then searched the vehicle in the hope of finding the lost licence, although Mr. Harrison had already been arrested for driving while suspended. During the search of the vehicle, the officer found $4 million worth of cocaine. At trial, Mr. Harrison was found guilty, even though the trial judge stated that there had been a "brazen and flagrant" disregard for his rights

not to be subjected to arbitrary detention and unreasonable search and seizure. The appeal court agreed that the tactics, while violating Mr. Harrison's rights, were mitigated by the value of the evidence obtained by the officer in the search. The SCC disagreed with both of these courts and acquitted Mr. Harrison, the chief justice of the SCC noting in the decision that the violations of Mr. Harrison's rights were far from being technical or trivial.

QUESTIONS

1. Do you agree with the decision of the Supreme Court in this case?
2. Does this decision place too many restrictions on the powers of the police?
3. What if the officers had found a handgun rather than cocaine?

Sources: Canadian Press. 2009, July 17. "Top Court Throws Out $4M Seizure after Illegal Search," *CTV News.* http://www.ctvnews.ca/top-court-throws-out-4m-seizure-after-illegal-search-1.417622; *R. v. Harrison*, 2009 SCC 34.

There is considerable room for interpretation by the courts as to what constitutes an unreasonable search in any particular case and when admission of evidence would bring the administration of justice into disrepute. Since the passage of the Charter in 1982, there have been hundreds of court cases and numerous books and legal articles dealing with this issue; the same two decades have seen an ongoing debate about what constitutes a reasonable search. As a result, conditions and requirements have emerged regarding prior authorization for a search.

Generally, for a search by the police to be lawful, a **search warrant** must be issued. The Supreme Court of Canada has decided that warrants are required in the following situations:

- where there is to be secret recording of conversations by state agents
- in cases involving video surveillance
- for perimeter searches of residential premises
- before the installation of tracking devices to monitor people's movements

Search warrants are generally issued by a justice of the peace (JP). Before a warrant can be issued, an information must be sworn under oath before a JP to convince him or her that there are reasonable and probable grounds that there is, in a building or place, (1) evidence relating to an act in violation of the *Criminal Code* or other federal statute, (2) evidence that might exist in relation to such a violation, or (3) evidence intended to be used to commit an offence against a person for which an individual may be arrested without a warrant.

The following scenario illustrates the principle of reasonable and probable grounds. Your neighbours feel that you match the description of a crime suspect in a bank robbery re-enacted on a televised Crime Stopper program. They telephone the police and anonymously provide your name and address. Can this tip be used to establish reasonable and probable grounds for a search of your home? The answer is no. Although a possible starting point for a police investigation, anonymous tips do not provide reasonable and probable grounds. A concern in establishing reasonable and probable grounds is the source of the information, the credibility of which is likely to be questioned if it is anonymous.

A search *without* a warrant will generally be illegal, except in two types of situations:

1. While arresting a person, the officer may search the person and the immediate surroundings for self-protection (that is, to seize weapons), to prevent the destruction of evidence (for example, to stop the person from swallowing drugs), or for means of escape.
2. In an emergency situation where an officer believes that an offence is being, or is likely to be, committed, or that someone in the premises is in danger of injury, a premise may be entered. In *R. v. Godoy* ([1999] 1 SCR 311), for example, the Supreme Court of Canada held that the forced entry of police officers into a residence from which a disconnected 911 call had been made, and the subsequent arrest of a suspect who had physically abused his common-law partner, was justifiable.

Ultimately it is the courts that decide whether a search warrant has been properly obtained and executed or whether a warrantless search was legal.

The passage in 2001 of Bill C-36, the *Anti-terrorism Act*, expanded the authority of the police to search property associated with terrorist groups and/or activity.

THE POWER TO DETAIN AND ARREST

When most people think of police powers, they think automatically of arrest. Over the years, considerable confusion has surrounded the process of arrest. Many citizens do

▲ Police officers use force to make an arrest.

not know when the police have the right to make an arrest, nor do they know what their rights are in an arrest situation.

The power to arrest is provided by the *Criminal Code* and other federal statutes as well as by provincial legislation such as motor vehicle statutes. An arrest can be made to prevent a crime from being committed, to terminate a breach of the peace, or to compel an accused person to attend trial.

A portion of the Charter-based warning read by police officers in independent municipal police services in British Columbia is reproduced in Police File 5.4. Note that the specific wording of this communication of Charter rights may vary from police service to police service depending on the jurisdiction.

A formal "arrest" triggers certain requirements on the part of the police—for example to advise the suspect of the reason for the arrest, of the right to counsel, of the right to remain silent, and so on. That said, most persons are released shortly thereafter on an Appearance Notice, an Undertaking to Appear, or a Summons to appear in court at a future date. These notices are issued because the person meets the "public interest" requirements of the *Bail Reform Act*—that is, the seriousness of the offence; identity is established; there is no concern of a continuation of the offence, of a failure to appear in court, or for destruction of evidence. A criminal suspect who is placed into custody will generally be released as soon as possible, on the authority of the arresting officer, the officer in charge of the police lockup, or a JP.

If an arrest is warranted, and if there is time to do so, a police officer can seek an **arrest warrant** by swearing an **information** in front of a JP. If the JP agrees that there are "reasonable grounds to believe that it is necessary in the public interest," a warrant will be issued directing the local police to arrest the person. Accessing a JP can pose difficulties in rural areas. Several provinces (including British Columbia, Ontario, Manitoba, and Alberta) have developed telewarrant programs that provide 24-hour access to JPs.

Arrest warrant

A document that permits a police officer to arrest a specific person for a specified reason.

Information

A written statement sworn by an informant, normally a police officer, alleging that a person has committed a specific criminal offence.

POLICE FILE 5.4

COMMUNICATING CHARTER RIGHTS UPON ARREST OR DETENTION

Sec. 10(a) I am arresting/detaining you for _____ (State reason for arrest/detention, including the offence and provide known information about the offence, including date and place.)

Sec. 10(b) It is my duty to inform you that you have the right to retain and instruct counsel in private without delay. You may call any lawyer you want.

There is a 24-hour telephone service available which provides a legal aid duty lawyer who can give you legal advice in private. This advice is given without charge and the lawyer can explain the legal aid plan to you.

If you wish to contact a legal aid lawyer I can provide you with a telephone number.

Do you understand?

Do you want to call a lawyer?

Supplementary Charter Warning: (If an arrested or detained person initially indicated that he or she wished to contact legal counsel and then subsequently indicates that he or she no longer wishes to exercise the right to counsel, read the following additional charter warning.)

You have the right to a reasonable opportunity to contact counsel. I am not obliged to take a statement from you or ask you to participate in any process which could provide incriminating evidence until you are certain about whether you want to exercise this right.

Do you understand?

What do you wish to do?

Secondary Warning: (Name), you are detained with respect to (reason for detainment). If you have spoken to any police officer (including myself) with respect to this matter, who has offered to you any hope of advantage or suggested any fear of prejudice should you speak or refuse to speak with me (us) at this time, it is my duty to warn you that no such offer or suggestion can be of any effect and must not influence you or make you feel compelled to say anything to me (us) for any reason, but anything you do say may be used in evidence.

Police officers can apply for and receive warrants by fax or telephone instead of having to appear in person before a JP.

In Ontario, for example, the Telewarrant Centre is located in the Central East Region and operates 24 hours per day, 7 days per week. A justice of the peace assigned to the centre will consider search warrants and other emergency applications by law enforcement agencies around the province.

Sometimes the police must act quickly and have no time to secure a warrant from a JP. Police officers can arrest a suspect *without* an arrest warrant in the following circumstances:

- They have caught a person in the act of committing an offence.
- They believe, on reasonable grounds, that a person has committed an indictable offence.
- They believe, on reasonable grounds, that a person is about to commit an indictable offence.

Two additional conditions apply to making an arrest. First, the officer must not make an arrest if he or she has "no reasonable grounds" to believe that the person will fail to appear in court. Second, the officer must believe on "reasonable grounds" that an arrest is "necessary in the public interest." This is defined specifically as the need to

- establish the identity of the person;
- secure or preserve evidence of or relating to the offence; and/or
- prevent the continuation or repetition of the offence or the commission of another offence.

However, provisions in the *Anti-terrorism Act* give the police the power of preventative arrest. This allows them to arrest persons without a warrant on "reasonable suspicion" (rather than the standard "reasonable grounds") if it is believed that the arrest will prevent a terrorist activity. The person need not have committed any crime and can be detained for up to 72 hours.

In practice, arrests are usually made only in the case of indictable offences. For minor crimes (summary conviction offences), an arrest is legal only if the police find someone actually committing the offence or if there is an outstanding arrest warrant or *warrant of committal* (a document issued by a judge directing prison authorities to accept a person into custody upon sentencing, a *bench warrant* for failure to appear at a court process, or a document issued by a parole board to revoke an offender's conditional release).

An officer who makes an arrest without reasonable grounds risks being sued civilly for assault or false imprisonment. Moreover, a person who resists an unlawful arrest is not guilty of resisting a police officer in the execution of their duty.

There is a distinction between arrest and detention. The SCC has held that a detention occurs when a police officer "assumes control over the movement of a person by a demand or direction that may have significant legal consequence and that prevents or impedes access to [legal] counsel" (*R. v. Schmautz*, [1990] 1 SCR 398). In contrast, the primary purpose of an arrest is to compel an accused to appear at trial.

Whether the person has been arrested or detained, an important threshold in the criminal process has been crossed. According to section 10 of the Charter, anyone who has been arrested or detained has the right to be informed promptly of the reason for the arrest or detention. That person also has the right to retain and instruct counsel without delay, and furthermore, must be told about that right without delay. However, the suspect can choose to exercise that right or not. Also, a suspect who is interviewed by Canadian police officers in the United States must be informed of the right to counsel (*R. v. Cook*, [1998] 2 SCR 597).

Suspects have a right to retain counsel but do not have an absolute right to have that counsel paid for by the state. Moreover, section 10 of the Charter does not impose a duty on provincial governments to provide free legal representation to everyone who cannot afford it. In many provinces, free preliminary legal advice is available through a toll-free number on a 24-hour basis. When an arrested or detained person does not have or know a lawyer, police must inform that person of this number and hold off on further questioning to give the suspect an opportunity to access this advice. After that, however, to get free legal representation, the suspect must qualify for legal aid (see Chapter 7). The failure of police to advise a person in a timely manner of the right to counsel upon arrest is an infringement of their Charter rights.

THE RIGHT OF SUSPECTS TO REMAIN SILENT

Under Canadian law, police officers have no formal powers to compel crime suspects to answer their questions. Suspects have a right to remain silent, and police officers must inform them of that right. They must also inform suspects that any statements they do make may be used against them in a criminal trial.

There are some exceptions to this. The right to remain silent does not extend to situations where it would permit a citizen to obstruct a police officer from carrying out his or her duties. For example, if you ride your bike through a red light and a police officer wants to issue you a traffic citation, you must produce identification. (And, in practice, remaining silent may only make things worse: A person who refuses to answer some general questions asked by the officer may raise suspicions that result in an arrest.)

The courts have also taken a dim view of the use of trickery by police to obtain confessions. The classic case is when an undercover police officer is placed in a cell with a crime suspect and then attempts to encourage the suspect to make incriminating statements. The Supreme Court of Canada has held that there are strict limits on the extent to which police can use this tactic to obtain a confession from a suspect who has refused to make a formal statement to the police. Voluntary statements made by a suspect to a cellmate (who may be an undercover police officer) may not violate the suspect's right to remain silent and may be admissible at trial if such admission does not bring the administration of justice into disrepute. Suspects who have low levels of intelligence or other impairment may not understand their right to silence and its implications.

False confessions may also be made by persons who are mentally ill, stressed and fatigued, and who are experiencing withdrawal symptoms from drugs or alcohol.[49] In addition, it has been recognized that Indigenous suspects may be particularly vulnerable to provide misleading information, to acquiesce to police suggestions, or to falsely confess.[50] This is due to a number of factors, including their background and circumstance, a lack of understanding of their legal rights, and challenges in language and comprehension, among others.[51] This imposes on the police the obligation to take special precautions in interviewing Indigenous suspects, including ensuring that they understand their rights and communicating in a clear and unambiguous manner with suspects.

Although false confessions are rare, investigating officers must always carefully assess the reliability of a suspect's statement or confession against all other known facts. This, in turn, may lead to a person being wrongfully convicted, discussed in Chapter 8.

POLICE OFFICER MISCONDUCT

Although Canadians generally hold positive attitudes toward the police, incidents do occur as a result of which citizens take issue with police attitudes and behaviour or their failure to take action and exercise their discretion appropriately. Canadian courts have established that police officers are held to a higher standard of conduct than ordinary citizens.

Police misconduct ranges from unprofessional conduct to murder. Police officers may be held liable for violating the policies and procedures of the police service in which they work and are also liable, civilly and criminally, for their conduct. A review of RCMP complaints made between January 1, 2010, and October 9, 2015, found a range of alleged misconduct, from cheating on a scorecard in a charity golf tournament, to lying under oath, to engaging in a high-speed chase that resulted in the death of a pedestrian.[52]

The sanctions imposed on officers can range from a verbal or written reprimand, forfeiture of pay, suspension from the police service with or without pay, recommendations for counselling, or a directive that the officer resign. Officers may also resign voluntarily at any point prior to or during the proceedings. This is in addition to any charges that may be filed in civil or criminal court.

Historically, people in the community who had complaints about the behaviour of police officers were required to file their grievances with the officers' department, which then conducted an investigation. This was an intimidating process and probably deterred many potential complainants.

Today, police activities are overseen by a number of commissions, boards, and agencies established under provisions in provincial police acts. In Ontario, the Office of the Independent Police Review Director (OIPRD) is an agency staffed with civilians that receives and investigates complaints against police officers. In addition, there are units within police services that investigate alleged misconduct by officers. The Special Investigations Unit (SIU) in Ontario, the Alberta Serious Incident Response Team (ASIRT), and the Independent Investigations Office (IIO) in British Columbia are examples of outside civilian agencies that investigate cases involving serious injury, sexual assault, or death that may have been the result of criminal offences committed by police officers.

A review of the OIPRD, the Special Investigations Unit that investigates police–citizen incidents that result in serious injury or death, and the Ontario Civilian Police Commission, which is involved in the adjudication of appeals from police disciplinary hearings, found a number of deficiencies with respect to the transparency and accountability of these bodies. As well, the report expressed concerns about the exclusion of officers in autonomous Indigenous police services from civilian oversight and the experience of Indigenous persons with police oversight. Among the barriers to accessing the oversight bodies were a lack of knowledge of their existence and mandate, a fear of retaliation from officers should a complaint be filed, and the view that filing a complaint would be pointless.[53]

COMPLAINTS AGAINST THE POLICE

The most frequent complaints against police officers involve abuses of authority, the attitudes of officers, and the quality of service provided. Less frequent are complaints for very serious charges, including excessive use of force and death. The vast majority of complaints are resolved informally at the department or detachment level and are not forwarded to a complaints commissions. See Figure 5.3.

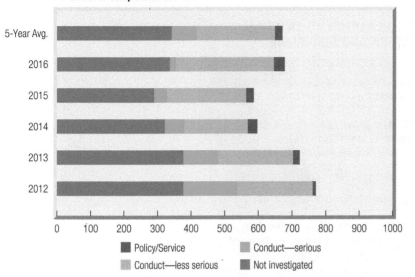

a. Number of Complaints Received

Legend:
- Policy/Service
- Conduct—less serious
- Conduct—serious
- Not investigated

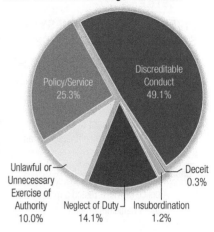

b. Sub-classification of Alleged Misconduct

- Discreditable Conduct 49.1%
- Policy/Service 25.3%
- Unlawful or Unnecessary Exercise of Authority 10.0%
- Neglect of Duty 14.1%
- Insubordination 1.2%
- Deceit 0.3%

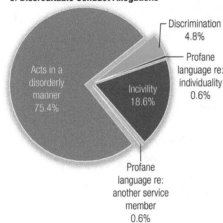

c. Discreditable Conduct Allegations

- Acts in a disorderly manner 75.4%
- Incivility 18.6%
- Discrimination 4.8%
- Profane language re: individuality 0.6%
- Profane language re: another service member 0.6%

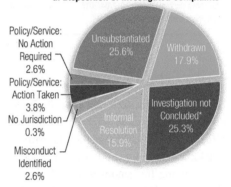

d. Disposition of Investigated Complaints

- Unsubstantiated 25.6%
- Withdrawn 17.9%
- Investigation not Concluded* 25.3%
- Informal Resolution 15.9%
- Policy/Service: No Action Required 2.6%
- Policy/Service: Action Taken 3.8%
- No Jurisdiction 0.3%
- Misconduct Identified 2.6%

FIGURE 5.3 ▲

Misconduct among Toronto Police Officers, 2016

Question: What do the statistics in the figures suggest about public complaints against the police in a large urban police service?

Source: Toronto Police Service. 2016. *Corporate Risk Management Annual Report, 2016.* Toronto: Author, pp. 24–26, 29. http://www.torontopolice.on.ca/publications/files/reports/crm2016annualreport.pdf. Reprinted by permission of the Toronto Police Service.

A review of Figure 5.3 indicates that "Discreditable Conduct" is the most frequent complaint, with the most common behaviour being "Acts in a Disorderly Manner." Complaints are most often made against officers with less than one to five years' experience. Note that 4.8 percent of the complaints were for alleged "Discrimination." Police constables accounted for the majority (81.2 percent) of the complaints, which is understandable given that these officers have the highest level of contact with community residents.[54]

Up to 50 percent of the formal complaints filed against the police are later determined, upon investigation, to be unsubstantiated. Many more are resolved informally, often by mediation between the officers involved and the complainant. In 2015–16, for example, the Office of the Public Complaint Commissioner (OPPC) in British Columbia concluded 777 complaint files. The files were concluded in the following manner: Withdrawn (13 percent); Discontinued (11 percent); Informally Resolved/Mediated (19 percent); Substantiated (6 percent); and Unsubstantiated (52 percent).[55]

Police File 5.5 presents a brief summary of two cases in which police services in British Columbia asked the OPPC to investigate the behaviour of officers. The charges against the officers are noted, as well as the discipline received by the officers.

POLICE FILE 5.5

INVESTIGATIONS REQUESTED BY THE DEPARTMENT: TWO CASE STUDIES OF POLICE OFFICER BEHAVIOUR AND DISCIPLINE

Case 1 Outcome	
The police officer, while off-duty, was removed from a nightclub for being intoxicated. In an attempt to regain entry, the officer identified himself/herself as an "undercover officer."	**Misconduct:** *Discreditable Conduct* **Discipline:** Written reprimand; one-day suspension; further training to assist the member in assessing his/her behaviours.
Case 2 Outcome	
1. A police officer arrested a male without sufficient grounds. 2. The officer used excessive force during the course of the arrest.	**Misconduct 1:** *Abuse of Authority* (×2) **Discipline:** Two-day suspension; retraining in the powers of arrest and detention, the *Controlled Drugs and Substances Act*, and use of force; directed to issue a letter of apology to the subject male and the officer's police partner.

Source: BC Office of the Police Complaint Commissioner. 2016. *Annual Report, 2015–2016*. Vancouver: Author, pp. 38, 40. https://opcc.bc.ca/wp-content/uploads/2017/04/2015-2016_OPCC_Annual_Report.pdf. Reprinted by permission of the BC Office of the Police Complaints Commissioner.

THE RELUCTANCE TO FILE A COMPLAINT

Despite the procedures that are in place for citizens to file complaints against the police, many may be reluctant to do so. This may be due to a lack of trust in the police and/or fear of retaliation. These sentiments may be particularly prevalent among Indigenous persons, Blacks, and persons in other racialized and minority groups. This was found to be the case among Indigenous women and girls in Saskatchewan, particularly in small communities.[56] These concerns are reflected in the comments of two Indigenous women in Saskatchewan:

> Why won't I file a complaint? I think it would make it to the shredder. And I've heard of people doing that and then getting picked on. All of a sudden, you've got all of them coming after you.
>
> Karen D. described the fear that she felt after she filed a complaint against the police, "I was scared shitless when I made the complaint. [I] feared for my life. After what happened to Neil Stonechild, how do I know they're not going to take me out."[57]

A review of policing in Yukon found similar challenges that prevented Indigenous persons using the complaint process. In citing the need for a more accessible complaint process, the study noted that many residents were apprehensive about filing a complaint due to fear of police reprisal, and that there was also a lack of knowledge about the process for filing a complaint.[58]

SUMMARY

The discussion in this chapter has focused on police powers and decision-making. The *Charter of Rights and Freedoms* has had a significant impact on police powers, which are continually being defined and redefined by the courts. There are structures of oversight and accountability for the police. Police officers have considerable discretion in carrying out their tasks, and they abuse their powers when they engage in biased policing and racial profiling. Indigenous persons, racialized persons, and members of other visible/cultural/religious minority groups are particularly susceptible to being profiled and subjected to street checks/carding by police.

Police officers have various less-lethal and lethal force options available to them, and there are cases in which both types of options have resulted in deaths. Officers can be held criminally and civilly liable for the misuse of force. The police have specific powers with respect to search and seizure, detention, and arrest, while suspects have certain rights to remain silent when being interrogated by the police. Entrapment is best viewed as an abuse of police powers. The Mr. Big investigative strategy is controversial, and the SCC has placed limits on its use.

Police misconduct spans a wide range of behaviour, and there are a variety of commissions, boards, and agencies that are responsible for overseeing and investigating alleged misbehaviour by police.

KEY POINTS REVIEW

1. The Canadian *Charter of Rights and Freedoms* has had a significant impact in defining the powers of the police.

2. Discretion is an essential component of policing, and the authority to use discretion is set out in statutes such as the *Criminal Code*.

3. Biased policing and racial profiling occur when police officers abuse their discretionary authority.

4. The study of biased policing and racial profiling requires a consideration of the lived experiences of persons in minority groups.

5. The issues surrounding racial profiling are illustrated by the ongoing controversy over street checks/carding.

6. Research studies and the courts have found that biased policing and racial profiling occur in some jurisdictions.

7. Starlight tours are illustrative of police discrimination toward Indigenous persons.

8. The legal authority for police to use force is found in the *Criminal Code*, although the absence of national use-of-force statistics precludes a determination of the frequency with which the various force options are used by police.

9. Police officers have less-lethal and lethal force options that can be used within the force options framework.

10. Illustrative of the issues that surround police powers is the police practice of entrapment and the Mr. Big investigative strategy.

11. Citizens have rights when it comes to the search and seizure authority of the police and police powers of detention and arrest.

12. Under Canadian law, the police have no formal powers to compel crime suspects to answer their questions.

13. In their rulings, Canadian courts have established that police officers are held to a higher standard of conduct than ordinary citizens.

14. Persons may be reluctant to file complaints against the police for fear of reprisal or a feeling that their complaint will not be taken seriously.

KEY TERM QUESTIONS

1. What is the **principle of accountability**?

2. Define **discretion** and note its role in police decision-making.

3. What are **typifications** and **recipes for action**? How do these concepts contribute to our understanding of the decision-making of the police?

4. Define **bias-free policing**, **over-policing**, and **pretext policing**, and then discuss why these concepts are important in the study of policing.

5. What is the **Mr. Big technique** used in police investigations, and why is it controversial?

6. Describe the use of **search warrants** and **arrest warrants** in policing.

7. What role does an **information** play in police response to accused persons?

CRITICAL THINKING EXERCISE

Critical Thinking Exercise 5.1

Limitations on the Use of the Mr. Big Strategy: A Case from the Appeal Court of Nova Scotia

As part of their investigation into a murder, police officers dressed up as gang members in order to elicit a confession from a woman that she was an accessory to the murder. The officers were searching for her friend, a former MMA fighter, who was suspected of being the killer. Posing as outlaw motorcycle gang members, the two officers confronted the woman in the underground parking garage of her apartment building. They told the woman they had been sent "by higher-ups from out west to clean up the mess" left behind by her friend, the killer. The officers called her a "rat," swore at her, blocked her from leaving the garage, prevented her from using her cellphone, and then drove her to another city two hours away. The woman confessed to the officers that she had helped her friend destroy evidence and escape. He was later arrested on a beach in Venezuela.

The woman was charged with being an accessory to murder. At trial, her defence lawyers argued that the police had violated her right to silence. The trial judge agreed, and the woman was acquitted. The Crown appealed and the appeal court, citing the decision of the SCC in *R. v. Hart*, denied the appeal in a unanimous decision. Writing for the court, one of the judges stated, "It is the unacceptable use of police tactics to coerce confessions that is problematic."

Your Thoughts?

1. What does this case illustrate about the potential problems with the Mr. Big investigative strategy?

2. Do you agree with the decision of the appeal court?

3. If so, what could the officers have done differently in an attempt to gather information from the woman, who they suspected of assisting the killer?

Source: R. Roberts. 2016, September 14. "Appeal Court Upholds Acquittal of Nova Scotia Woman Caught in 'Mr. Big' Sting," *Toronto Star*. https://www.thestar.com/news/canada/2016/09/14/appeal-court-upholds-acquittal-of-nova-scotia-woman-caught-in-mr-big-sting.html.

MEDIA LINKS

"Mr. Big Stings: Cops, Criminals and Confessions," *Fifth Estate*, January 16, 2015, http://www.cbc.ca/fifth/episodes/2014-2015/mrbig

"Honest Cops," December 11, 2013, www.youtube.com/watch?v=f23CPcTdY2M

"Crisis of Distrust: Police and Community in Toronto," *PLIToronto*, April 26, 2014, https://www.youtube.com/watch?v=u627BsqA5BM

"Vancouver Airport—Robert Dziekanski's Taser Death," November 14, 2007, https://www.youtube.com/watch?v=1CR_k-dTnDU

"When Police Kill," *Toronto Star*, August 2, 2017, https://www.thestar.com/news/gta/when-police-kill.html

"Inquest Hears 911 Call That Preceded Fatal Police Shooting," *CBC News*, October 21, 2013, http://www.cbc.ca/news/canada/toronto/inquest-hears-911-call-that-preceded-fatal-police-shooting-1.2129651

"Hold Your Fire," *CBC Firsthand*, August 25, 2016, http://www.cbc.ca/firsthand/episodes/hold-your-fire

"Enhanced Video of Shooting of Sammy Yatim by Toronto Police," July 28, 2013, https://www.youtube.com/watch?v=lG6OTyjzAgg

"Watch: Former Police Officer Analyzes Streetcar Shooting Video," *Global News*, July 30, 2013, https://globalnews.ca/news/751568/watch-former-police-officer-analyzes-streetcar-shooting-video

"Police Shootings: Caught on Camera," *Fifth Estate*, November 4, 2016, http://www.cbc.ca/fifth/episodes/2016-2017/police-shootings-caught-on-camera

REFERENCES

1. J. Cameron and J. Stribopolous. 2008. *The Charter and Criminal Justice Twenty-Five Years Later*. Markham, ON: LexisNexis.

2. J. Pearson. 2016, June 10. "The RCMP Surveilled Thousands of Innocent Canadians for a Decade," *Motherboard*. https://motherboard.vice.com/en_us/article/kb73an/the-rcmp-surveilled-thousands-of-innocent-canadians-for-a-decade.

3. C. Freeze. 2016, May 17. "Police Use of Surveillance Devices Against the Law: Lawyers," *Globe and Mail*. https://www.theglobeandmail.com/news/national/police-use-of-surveillance-devices-against-the-law-lawyers/article30073013.

4. C. Clarke and C. Murphy. 2002. *In Search of Security: The Roles of Public Police and Private Agencies* [discussion paper]. Ottawa: Law Reform Commission of Canada. https://dalspace.library.dal.ca/bitstream/handle/10222/10292/In%20Search%20of%20Security%20Discussion%20Paper%20EN.pdf?sequence=1&isAllowed=y.

5. Office of the Chief Coroner. 2011. *Report for 2009–2011*. Toronto: Author. https://www.mcscs.jus.gov.on.ca/sites/default/files/content/mcscs/docs/ec161620.pdf.

6. Justice Institute of British Columbia. 2005. "British Columbia Police Code of Ethics." http://www.jibc.ca/programs-courses/schools-departments/school-criminal-justice-security/police-academy/resources/bc-police-code-ethics.

7. R.J. Lundman. 1980. *Police and Policing—An Introduction*. New York: Holt, Rinehard, and Winston, pp. 110–111.

8. L. Westmarland. 2013. "'Snitches Get Stitches': US Homicide Detectives' Ethics and Morals in Action," *Policing & Society*, 23(3), 311–327 at p. 312.

9. Canadian Association of Chiefs of Police. 2004, August. "Bias-Free Policing," in *Resolutions Adopted at the 99th Annual Conference*. Vancouver: Author, p. 7. https://cacp.ca/resolution.html?asst_id=318.

10. Ontario Human Rights Commission. 2017. *Under Suspicion: Research and Consultation Report on Racial Profiling in Ontario*. Toronto: Author, p. 16. http://ohrc.on.ca/sites/default/files/Under%20suspicion_research%20and%20consultation%20report%20on%20racial%20profiling%20in%20Ontario_2017.pdf.

11. Ontario Human Rights Commission. 2016, November 28. "Response to the Race Data and Traffic Stops in Ottawa Report." http://www.ohrc.on.ca/en/ohrc-response-race-data-and-traffic-stops-ottawa-report

12. V. Satzewich and W. Shaffir. 2009. *Racism versus Professionalism: Claims and Counter Claims about Racial Profiling*. Hamilton: McMaster University, p. 209. http://www.queensu.ca/csd/publications/wps/6-EShaffirSatzewichpaper.pdf.

13. Ibid., p. 210.

14. Ontario Human Rights Commission. 2003. *Paying the Price: The Human Cost of Racial Profiling*. Toronto: Author, p. 10. http://www.ohrc.on.ca/en/paying-price-human -cost-racial-profiling.

15. Assets Coming Together Youth Project. 2010. *Jane-Finch Youth Speak Out: Turf, Violence, Well-Being*. Toronto: York University. http://www.yorku.ca/act/reports/Jane -FinchYouthSpeakOut.pdf.

16. Ibid., p. 5.

17. Ontario Human Rights Commission, *Under Suspicion*, pp. 35–36. © Queen's Printer for Ontario, 2017. Reproduced with permission.

18. S. Paradkar. 2017, July 20. "Black Experience Project a Heart -Rending Snapshot of Black Lives in Toronto: Paradkar," *Toronto Star*. https://www.thestar.com/news/gta/2017/07/20/ black-experience-project-a-heart-rending-snapshot-of-black -lives-in-toronto-paradkar.html.

19. O. Ha-Redeye. 2017, February 12. "Systemic Racism as a Basis for Excluding Evidence," *Slaw*. http://www .slaw.ca/2017/02/12/systemic-racism-as-a-basis-for -excluding-evidence.

20. T. Appleby. 2005, May 27. "Kingston Police More Likely to Stop Blacks, Study Finds," *Globe and Mail*. https://www .theglobeandmail.com/news/national/kingston-police -more-likely-to-stop-blacks-study-finds/article18228211.

21. P. McGregor and A. MacIvor. 2017, January 9. "Black People 3 Times More Likely to be Street Checked in Halifax, Police Say," *CBC News*. http://www.cbc.ca/news/ canada/nova-scotia/halifax-black-street-checks-police -race-profiling-1.3925251.

22. Commission des droits de la personne et des droits de la jeu- nesse. (Commission on Human Rights and Youth Rights). 2011. *Racial Profiling and Systemic Discrimination of Racialized Youth*. Quebec: Author, p. 27. http://www.cdpdj .qc.ca/publications/Profiling_final_EN.pdf.

23. J. Rankin and S. Contenta. 2017, July 6. "Toronto Marijuana Arrests Reveal 'Startling' Racial Divide," *Toronto Star*. https://www.thestar.com/news/insight/2017/07/06/toronto -marijuana-arrests-reveal-startling-racial-divide.html.

24. Ontario Human Rights Commission, *Paying the Price: The Human Cost of Racial Profiling*.

25. A. Huncar. 2017, August 24. "Alberta Government Launches Provincewide Consultation on Street Checks," *CBC News*. http://www.cbc.ca/news/canada/edmonton/alberta-street -check-consultations-1.4260272.

26. Ontario Provincial Police. 2011. *Destination Diversity. The Ontario Provincial Police Diversity Journey*. Orillia, ON: Author, p. 10. https://www.publicsafety.gc.ca/lbrr/archives/ cnmcs-plcng/cn31049-eng.pdf.

27. M. Draaisma. 2017, January 1. "New Ontario Rule Banning Carding by Police Takes Effect," *CBC News*. http://www.cbc.ca/news/canada/toronto/carding-ontario -police-government-ban-1.3918134.

28. R. Ferguson. 2016, March 22. "Ontario Updates Carding Regulations for Police," *Toronto Star*. https://www.thestar .com/news/queenspark/2016/03/22/province-updates-carding -regulations-for-police.html.

29. Ibid.

30. W.J. Kloss and P.F. McKenna. 2006. "Profiling a Problem in Canadian Police Leadership: The Kingston Police Data Collection Project," *Canadian Public Administration*, 49(2), 143–160.

31. K. Miller. 2009. "The Institutionalization of Racial Profiling Policy," *Crime & Delinquency*, 59(1), 32–58.

32. Canadian Press. 2016, July 28. "Some Canadian Police Officers Who Have Faced Murder or Manslaughter Charges," *Chronicle Herald*. http://thechronicleherald.ca/ canada/1383997-some-canadian-police-officers-who-have -faced-murder-or-manslaughter-charges.

33. E. Laming. 2017, July 18. "Canada Needs a National Database to Track Deadly Force by Police," *Huffington Post Canada*. http://www.huffingtonpost.ca/erick-laming/ deadly-force-by-police_a_23034831.

34. C.J. Harris. 2009. "Police Use of Improper Force: A Systematic Review of the Literature," *Victims and Offenders*, 4(1), 25–41. https://christopher-harris.wiki.uml.edu/file/ view/harris_police+UOF.pdf.

35. E.A. Paoline and W. Terrill. 2007. "Police Education, Experience, and the Use of Force," *Criminal Justice and Behavior*, 34(2), 179–196.

36. J.P. McElvain and A.J. Kposowa. 2008. "Police Officers Characteristics and the Likelihood of Using Deadly Force," *Criminal Justice and Behavior*, 35(4), 505–521.

37. Toronto Police Service. 2017. *Achieving Zero Harm/Death: An Examination of Less-Lethal Force Options, Including the Possible Expansion of Conducted Energy Weapons (C.E.W.s)*. Toronto: Author. http://www.tpsb.ca/images/ TPSBCEWConsultation_Agenda_DisPaper.pdf.

38. P. Bulman. 2010. "Police Use of Force: The Impact of Less-Lethal Weapons and Tactics," *NIJ Journal*, 267, 4–10. https://www.ncjrs.gov/pdffiles1/nij/233280.pdf.

39. Council of Canadian Academies and Canadian Academy of Health Sciences. 2013. *The Health Effects of Conducted Energy Weapons. The Expert Panel on the Medical and Physiological Impacts of Conducted Energy Weapons*. Ottawa: Author. http://www.scienceadvice.ca/uploads/eng/ assessments%20and%20publications%20and%20news%20 releases/cew/cew_fullreporten.pdf.

40. R. Karrass. 2017, February 24. "The Deadly Side of Tasers," *Lawyers Weekly*. http://karrasslaw.com/deadly-side-tasers.

41. G.P. Alpert. 2009. "Interpreting Police Use of Force and the Construction of Reality," *Criminology and Public Policy*, 8(1), 111–115.

42. R.B. Parent. 2006. "The Police Use of Deadly Force: International Comparisons," *The Police Journal: Theory, Practice, and Principles*, 79(3), 230–237.

43. V.B. Lord. 2012. "Factors Influencing Subjects' Observed Level of Suicide by Cop Intent," *Criminal Justice and Behavior*, 39(12), 1633–1646.

44. *CBC Radio*. 2016, January 21. "Close to 40 Per Cent of Civilians Killed by Police Are in Mental Crisis." http://www.cbc.ca/radio/thecurrent/the-current-for-january-21-2016-1.3413153/close-to-40-per-cent-of-civilians-killed-by-police-are-in-mental-crisis-1.3413219.

45. R.R. Johnson. 2011. "Suspect Mental Disorder and Police Use of Force," *Criminal Justice and Behavior*, 38(2), 127–145.

46. J. Brockman and K.T. Keenan. 2010. *Mr. Big: Exposing Undercover Investigations in Canada*. Halifax and Winnipeg: Fernwood Books.

47. Ibid.

48. K.W. Roach, M.S. Estabrooks, M. Shaffer, and G. Renaud. 2016. "The Hart of the (Mr. Big) Problem," *Criminal Law Quarterly*, 63(1/2), 151–178.

49. C. Sherrin. 2005. "False Confessions and Admissions in Canadian Law," *Queen's Law Journal*, 30(2), 601–659.

50. K. Watkins. 2016. "The Vulnerability of Aboriginal Suspects When Questioned by Police: Mitigating Risk and Maximizing the Reliability of Statement Evidence," *Criminal Law Quarterly*, 63(4), 474–503.

51. Ibid.

52. A. Crawford. 2016, November 17. "Half of Complaints against the RCMP Lead to Discipline, Data Suggests," *CBC News*. http://www.cbc.ca/news/politics/rcmp-disciplinary-database-1.3854365.

53. M.H. Tulloch (The Honourable). 2017. *Report of the Independent Police Oversight Review*. Toronto: Attorney General of Ontario. https://www.attorneygeneral.jus.gov.on.ca/english/about/pubs/police_oversight_review.

54. Toronto Police Service. 2016. *Corporate Risk Management Annual Report, 2016*. Toronto: Author, p. 27. http://www.torontopolice.on.ca/publications/files/reports/crm2016annualreport.pdf.

55. B.C. Office of the Police Complaints Commissioner. 2016. *Annual Report, 2015-2016*. Vancouver: Author, p. 57. https://opcc.bc.ca/wp-content/uploads/2017/04/2015-2016_OPCC_Annual_Report.pdf.

56. Human Rights Watch. 2017. *Submission to the Government of Canada. Police Abuse of Indigenous Women in Saskatchewan and Failures to Protect Indigenous Women from Violence*. New York: Author, p. 18. https://www.hrw.org/sites/default/files/supporting_resources/canada_saskatchewan_submission_june_2017.pdf.

57. Ibid.

58. S. Arnold, P. Clark, and D. Cooley. 2011. *Sharing Common Ground. Review of Yukon's Police Force. Final Report*. Whitehorse: Government of Yukon. http://www.policereview2010.gov.yk.ca/pdf/Sharing_Common_Ground_Final_Report.pdf.

© Laurie Justus Pace, Graphics One Design, 2014

CHAPTER 6
POLICE STRATEGIES, OPERATIONS, AND ENGAGEMENT

After reading this chapter, you should be able to

- Describe the issues that surround measuring the effectiveness of police strategies and operations.
- Compare and contrast the professional model of policing, community policing, and community-based strategic policing.
- Discuss the various techniques that are used in community-based strategic policing.
- Describe what is known about public attitudes toward and confidence in the police.
- Discuss the challenges of developing and sustaining police–community partnerships.
- Discuss the debate over the role and activities of groups such as Anonymous and Creep Catchers.
- Describe primary and secondary crime prevention programs and note their effectiveness.
- Discuss crime response strategies and crime attack strategies and their effectiveness.
- Discuss the issues that surround the increasing use of high technology in responding to and attacking crime.
- Discuss the relationship between the police and vulnerable/at-risk groups.

A Citizen's View of the Police and Cultural Communities, Saskatoon

I think police officers should be interacting with local cultural communities and they should participate in these occasions out of uniform. I find that the police uniform gives them a sense of authoritative figure [sic], which is the purpose, but sometimes these uniforms get to their head and sometimes cops mistreat people because they think they're better than others or have the power to treat people badly.

If police officers had the chance to communicate with cultural communities on a personal level without the labels of "an intimidating cop in uniform" and "minority," then I think they could appreciate one another better. This isn't restricted to cultural/religious communities, but also local projects like Friendship Inn, Egads, etc., for instance, places where there are high crime rates and where unfortunate people hangout. This would allow people to respect each other on another level and hopefully build some trust and understanding for one another.

Source: M. Lashley, G. Hassan, S. Rahimi, S. Thompson, M. Chartrand, S. Touzin, . . . A. Akhtar. 2014. *Cultural Competency and Canada's Security*. Montreal: McGill University, p. 101. http://www.environicsinstitute.org/uploads/news/cultural% 20competence%20and%20canada's%20security%20-%20final%20report%20april%202014.pdf.

Canadian police officers carry out their tasks in social, cultural, and political environments considerably more diverse than those faced by their predecessors. This has required police services to develop a wide range of strategies for preventing and responding to crime. There have also been major shifts in police practice, from more traditional approaches to multifaceted strategies that rely on sophisticated analyses. In this chapter, we trace this evolution and explore the strategies that police services are using to prevent and respond to crime and social disorder.

MEASURING THE EFFECTIVENESS OF POLICE STRATEGIES AND OPERATIONS

Most police services in Canada remain wedded to two traditional measures of police performance that are hold-overs from the professional model of policing: crime rates and clearance rates. Even in those police services that have adopted a community policing approach, the performance assessments of individual police officers are still heavily oriented toward enforcement activities.[1]

CRIME RATES AND CLEARANCE RATES

Strategic plans of police services generally contain percentage targets for crime reduction, and annual reports highlight achievements in reducing specific types of criminal activity in the community. **Clearance rates** are the proportion of the actual incidents known to the police that result in the identification of a suspect, whether or not that suspect is ultimately charged and convicted. Using these measures is problematic on a number of counts.

For crime rates, there can be problems of interpretation. For example, does an increase in official crime rates mean the police are ineffective? Or does it mean they are catching more criminals? Another problem with using official crime rates to assess police effectiveness is that the focus is on "crime fighting" to the exclusion of other measures of police performance. In addition, much of what the police are asked to do by governments and communities—and, in some instances, are required by legislation and policy to do—has little to do with crime rates.

Clearance rates

The proportion of the actual incidents known to the police that result in the identification of a suspect, whether or not that suspect is ultimately charged and convicted.

In most jurisdictions, police officers do not spend most of their time pursuing criminals. It is also important to note that the police may be unable to have an impact on the reasons why crime and disorder occur, including poverty, addiction, and family dysfunction.[2]

Further, not all police officers work in the same types of communities; some communities are more crime-ridden than others. Research in Quebec has found, for example, that police services in small communities are more likely to clear crimes than in large urban areas and in areas with high poverty levels.[3] And police officers do not all engage in the same type of police work; some are involved in patrol, others in investigative units, and so on.

With respect to the effectiveness of specialized law enforcement initiatives, the Canadian criminologist Thomas Gabor has noted that there have been few Canadian evaluations of law enforcement efforts to target organized crime, cybercrime, and white-collar criminals. Gabor argues that it is important to gather information on other factors, including enforcement costs, the number of investigations that lead to convictions, and the degree to which specific policing initiatives are effective in disrupting organized crime.[4]

CRIME DISPLACEMENT

In attempting to determine the effectiveness of police strategies, there is the slippery issue of **crime displacement**—"the relocation of crime from one place, time, target, offense, or tactic to another as a result of some form of crime initiative."[5] The implementation of a crime prevention program in one neighbourhood, for example, may cause criminals to move to an area that does not have the program. Instead of reducing crime, the program has just moved it. One way to reduce crime displacement is to implement crime prevention programs on a community-wide basis rather than only in specific areas. Also, it may be necessary to target a wide range of criminal activity instead of focusing only on specific types of crime.

Crime displacement

The relocation—due to effective crime prevention and crime response initiatives—of criminal activity from one locale to another.

ADDITIONAL MEASURES OF POLICE EFFECTIVENESS

Improving the quality of life in a community, having positive relationships with at-risk and vulnerable groups, and engaging in collaborative partnerships with other agencies and community organizations are important roles for the police, yet these activities are generally not measured. There are a number of additional measures of performance that capture the multifaceted role of the police, including levels of community and victim satisfaction with the police and feelings of safety, as measured by surveys; the success of the police in achieving effective target-hardening and problem-solving with respect to specific types of crime in identified problem areas in the community; and the extent to which the police are involved in developing innovative programs to address issues related to community diversity—for example, issues relating to the LGBTQ+ communities, the Indigenous, Blacks, and other racialized groups.

The ability of the police to be effective in carrying out their roles is dependent to a large extent on the model of policing that is adopted, and these are discussed below.

THE PROFESSIONAL MODEL OF POLICING

Even after the creation of formal police services in Canada (discussed in Chapter 4), policing remained closely tied to communities; police officers patrolled communities on foot and were responsible for a variety of tasks. With the introduction of mobile

A model of police work that is reactive,
incident-driven, and centred on random
patrol.

patrol cars in the 1920s and 1930s, a **professional model of policing** emerged that was
based on the three Rs: random patrol, rapid response, and reactive investigation.

The central premise of random patrol, also known as the *watch system*, is that the
mere presence and visibility of patrol cars serves as a deterrent to crime and, at the same
time, makes citizens feel safer. During a typical shift, patrol officers respond to calls and
spend the rest of their time patrolling randomly, waiting for the next call for service. In
this model of policing, any information that is gathered by the police is limited to specific situations and does not include an analysis of the problems that precipitate crime
and social disorder. Little attention is given to proactive police interventions designed
to prevent crime and to address the underlying causes of crime in communities. In
this model of policing, there is no, or limited, use of analytics to inform police policy
and operations.

Research studies have found, however, that, with the exception of specific targeted
strategies, levels of crime are generally unaffected by increases in the number of patrol
cars, quicker response times by patrol officers, or the number of arrests made by patrol
officers.[6] This lack of impact is due in part to the fact that many of the incidents to
which the police respond are only symptoms of larger problems in the community. In
fact, it is *how* police resources are allocated and deployed that makes a difference. If
the police respond only when they are called and deal only with the incident at hand,
the reasons *why* the incident occurred in the first place remain unaddressed, and this
increases the likelihood that similar incidents will happen again.

The emergence of community policing was precipitated in part by the recognition
that the police cannot prevent and respond to crime on their own; they require the
assistance of a variety of agencies and organizations as well as community residents.

COMMUNITY POLICING

The 1980s witnessed the re-emergence of an approach to policing that focused on
the community. In a back-to-the-future move, the tenets of community reflect Peel's
Principles that were set out in the early 1800s (see Police File 4.2). These highlighted
the importance of the police being connected to, rather than apart from, the community and accountable to the community.

DEFINING COMMUNITY POLICING

A philosophy of policing centred on
police–community partnerships and
problem-solving.

Community policing is based on the idea that the police and the community must
work together as equal partners to identify, prioritize, and solve problems such as crime,
drugs, fear of crime, social and physical disorder, and general neighbourhood decay,
with the goal of improving the overall quality of life in the area. Community policing
is based on the three Ps: prevention, problem-solving, and partnership with the community. Community policing can thus be defined as a philosophy, a management style,
and an organizational strategy centred on police–community partnerships and problem-solving to address problems of crime and social disorder in communities.

The police assume a proactive role in addressing issues in the community. This
requires that patrol officers be given the autonomy and opportunity to identify and
address issues in their areas.

The adoption of the community policing model resulted in the expansion of the
police mandate and activities. No longer were police officers solely focused on law
enforcement but rather they were required to become involved in a variety of activities
related to the quality of life in the community and to working with community residents

on a proactive basis to reduce victimization and the fear of crime, as well as to identify and address community problems. As community policing has evolved, it has also come to include a variety of operational strategies such that are focused on crime control and suppression, although the fundamental premise that the police must work closely with the community has not changed. This new model is known as *community-based strategic policing*.

Community policing is about much more than the introduction of new programs to a community; it involves substantial changes in the organization and delivery of police services, as well as an expansion of the roles and responsibilities of line-level police officers. Organizationally, patrol officers are given the autonomy and resources to identify issues in the areas they police and develop problem-solving strategies, often in partnership with the community or neighbourhood.

COMMUNITY-BASED STRATEGIC POLICING

Beginning in the late 1990s and accelerating with the terrorist attacks on the United States on September 11, 2001, police services have been facing increasing pressure to focus on public safety and security and to be more proactive in addressing specific threats. At the same time, they are expected to continue strengthening ties with other agencies and with the communities they serve. It appears that a new model of policing is emerging in the early 21st century—a post-community policing model that incorporates the key principles of community policing while at the same time includes crime response and crime attack strategies and a continuing emphasis on crime prevention. All of these approaches are discussed below.

This model has been labelled **community-based strategic policing**, the title capturing the importance of community engagement and of police services being strategic in their policies and operations.[7]

See Table 6.1 for a comparison of the professional and the community-based strategic models of police work.

A number of techniques are used by police services to "drive" community-based strategic policing. Many of these are based on analytics.

Community-based strategic policing

A model of police work that incorporates the key principles of community policing with crime prevention, crime response, and crime attack approaches.

TABLE 6.1

COMPARISON OF THE PROFESSIONAL AND COMMUNITY-BASED STRATEGIC MODELS OF POLICE WORK

Dimension	Professional Model	Community-Based Strategic Model
Administrative approach (locus of control)	Centralized/hierarchical	Decentralized with strong management and organizational support
Authority	Statute	Community/statute
Community role	Report violations of the law; passive; no involvement in identification and response to crime and disorder	Strategic partnerships, formalized by protocols and agreements, which integrate into police operations
Operational focus	Crime and disorder	Crime and disorder; national security; quality of life; fear of crime and disorder
Operational strategies	Random patrol; reactive investigations; rapid response	Targeted/directed patrol focused on hot spots; strategic partnerships: integrated service delivery; intelligence-led policing; ongoing evaluation; problem-based deployment of personnel

Source: Adapted from C.T. Griffiths. 2016. *Canadian Police Work* (4th ed.). Toronto: Nelson Education Ltd., pp. 220–221. Reproduced by permission. www.cengage.com/permissions.

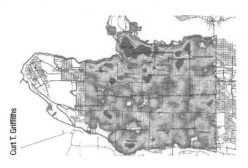

▲ A crime map of Vancouver showing crime hot spots in 2015

Intelligence-led policing

Policing that is guided by the collection and analysis of information that is used to inform police decision-making at both the tactical and strategic levels.

Compstat

A strategy designed to increase the effectiveness and efficiency of police services while holding police personnel accountable for achieving crime reduction objectives.

Predictive policing

The use of statistical analysis to identify the time and location where criminal activity is likely to occur.

CRIME ANALYTICS

Police services are increasingly adopting new technologies to improve their effectiveness and efficiency. Crime analysts use sophisticated statistical programs to create crime maps and to provide intelligence to police officers in patrol and investigative units. Crime analysts, many of them civilians, use sophisticated statistical tools to not only "mine" data gathered by the police service but also inform decision making and strategic planning.[8]

A key issue is how this technology will be managed to ensure that the rights of citizens are protected, another example of the ongoing tension between the efforts to ensure public safety and security while protecting citizens' rights.

INTELLIGENCE-LED POLICING

The strategy of **intelligence-led policing** is one example of how police services use technology to generate information and to deploy departmental resources more effectively. Key to intelligence-led policing are *crime maps*—that is, computer-generated maps of specific geographic areas that illustrate the incidence and patterns of specific types of criminal activity. This information can then be used to identify crime hot spots, to which patrol and investigative units can then be deployed.

COMPSTAT

Derived from the words "computer statistics," **Compstat** is designed to increase the effectiveness and efficiency of police services while also holding supervisors accountable for achieving objectives in crime reduction. Crime data are analyzed in order to provide intelligence to officers on where crimes are being committed and who is committing the crimes. Supervisors are held accountable for addressing the identified crime and disorder issues in their areas, often in a general meeting of senior police leadership and supervisors.[9]

As one staff sergeant stated, "Whether it's giving an area special attention, deploying undercover surveillance teams, or having teams develop their own projects, it's almost always driven by Compstat" (personal communication with C.T. Griffiths, September 2015).

There is considerable debate as to the effectiveness of Compstat and how it interfaces with the principles of community policing. There is concern that Compstat places too heavy an emphasis on crime fighting and generally does not include measures of other strategies within the community policing model.[10] Compstat is a good example of how community policing has been transformed by the increasing use of analytics.

PREDICTIVE POLICING

Perhaps the most sophisticated analytical approach, though still in its early stages of development, is **predictive policing**. Predictive policing uses statistical analysis to identify the time and location when criminal activity is likely to occur.

Using analytics, patrol units are directed to specific places where it is predicted a crime will occur. This increases the likelihood that an offender will be apprehended. Predictive policing has the potential to fundamentally alter how police resources are deployed and to increase the effectiveness and efficiency of patrol units.[11] Watch the video, "How Predictive Policing Software Works," listed in the Media Links section at the end of this chapter.

Predictive policing may have the greatest potential for reducing property-related crimes, which in many municipalities comprise the majority of serious offences. A pilot study of the use of predictive policing in the Vancouver Police Department, completed in 2017, found a 21 to 27 percent drop in property crime in neighbourhoods where the predictive policing model was applied. These decreases occurred at a time when property crime rates were rising in other parts of the city.[12,13]

Concerns have been raised that biased policing may contribute to certain areas, and persons, being identified as important for police attention in the predictive policing model.[14] Biased policing is discussed in Chapter 5.

Despite its importance, many police services have only a limited analytical capacity and are not able to provide their officers with real-time information on a crime, its location, and who the perpetrators might be. There is considerable evidence that crime analysis can assist in crime reduction and can increase the effectiveness and efficiency of police service delivery.[15]

THE POLICE AND THE COMMUNITY

In Chapter 3, it was noted that the relationships between the police and Indigenous, racialized, and other minority groups have often been fractured due to historical and contemporary events and circumstances. Effective policing requires that efforts be made to address the concerns of these groups. The discussion in Chapter 4 identified community consultation and collaboration as one of the features of core policing, the notion being that for the police to be effective, residents must be involved in identifying problems of crime and disorder and in generating solutions to those problems. This requires police services to develop strategies for community engagement, including outreach efforts to address the suspicion and distrust that may exist among Indigenous peoples, Blacks and other racialized persons, visible/cultural minorities, and newcomer groups.

PUBLIC ATTITUDES TOWARD AND CONFIDENCE IN THE POLICE

The discussion in Chapter 2 highlighted the importance of public trust and confidence in the criminal justice system. Research File 6.1 summarizes several of the key points about what is known about the community and community policing. Note that these

---

RESEARCH FILE 6.1

CITIZEN PERCEPTIONS AND LEVELS OF SATISFACTION

Public-opinion surveys and field research studies have found the following:

- There is strong support for increased visibility and accessibility of the police.
- Foot patrols are favoured by community residents.
- Residents who have informal contacts with the police hold more favourable opinions of the police than those who have formal contact with the police, although there is no evidence that informal contacts with the police reduce the number of complaints against the police.
- Residents who feel safe in their neighbourhoods and who have a positive feeling toward their community hold a higher opinion of the police.
- Community policing increases police legitimacy.

- Community policing has the potential to reduce fear of crime in communities.

Levels of Knowledge and Participation

- Community residents, even those who have been the victims of crime, tend not to become involved in community policing initiatives.
- Many citizens have little knowledge or understanding of the role and activities of community policing initiatives such as community police stations.
- Community residents have positive views of community police stations, but rarely use them.
- Police services have experienced considerable difficulty in generating and sustaining community interest and involvement in community policing initiatives.

---

are general findings and may vary between communities or even within communities, among Indigenous and racialized persons, and among other members of visible/cultural/religious minority groups.

The strategies used by police services in the community-based strategic policing model include recruitment and deployment of volunteers in community police stations and storefronts, foot and bike patrols, community police stations and storefronts, and team policing. Team policing—also referred to as *zone policing* or *turf policing*—involves permanently assigning teams of police to small neighbourhoods in an effort to maximize interaction and communication with the community. It also extends to the view that traditional police work, with its focus on enforcement, is not always the most effective way to deal with situations in the field. As one veteran officer noted:

> What I've come to see over my years is a lot of times, people don't need police officers. They just need people who care. So when I have recruits, I always tell them: it takes the first year to figure out how to wear a uniform and be that presence, and you spend the rest of your career trying to make people forget you're wearing one.[16]

The Ottawa Police Service, for example, sponsors a Somali Youth Basketball League (SYBL), a volunteer, not-for-profit basketball league that provides a safe environment for Somali youth. It develops life and leadership skills among the participants and also provides positive role models (http://www.ottawapolice.ca).

Police services and officers across the country involve themselves in a wide range of charitable events that not only raise money for important causes but also provide opportunities for officers to contribute to the community and to encounter community residents in a non–law enforcement capacity. One high-profile initiative is Cops for Cancer, which involves a wide range of fundraising activities; for example, some officers have their heads shaved for donations, and others cycle cross-country raising awareness and collecting donations.

THE POLICE AND RESTORATIVE JUSTICE APPROACHES

Restorative justice was introduced in Chapter 2 as an alternative for addressing and resolving crime, and the needs of victims, offenders, and the community. Among the more common restorative justice initiatives are victim–offender mediation, circle sentencing, community holistic healing programs, and family group conferences. These programs vary in the types of offences and offenders processed; the procedures for hearing cases, reaching dispositions, and imposing sanctions; and the extent to which justice system professionals, including police officers, are involved.

Among the better-known restorative justice programs in which police officers play a key role are circle sentencing and community and family group conferencing. Circle sentencing was first used in Yukon; family group conferencing originated in New Zealand and has been exported to Australia, Canada, and the United States. Circle sentencing is discussed in Chapter 9.

The nature and extent of participation of police officers in restorative justice initiatives across the country is unknown. Much depends on the types of collaborative partnerships that police services have established with the community and whether there are restorative programs. What is known is that, in their daily work, police officers use their discretion to informally resolve situations in which they become involved.

THE CHALLENGES IN DEVELOPING AND SUSTAINING POLICE–COMMUNITY PARTNERSHIPS

Efforts of the police to develop collaborative partnerships with the community may face a number of challenges. Community surveys have consistently found high (albeit declining) levels of public support for the police (much higher than any other component of the criminal justice system) and an expectation that police services will engage in proactive, preventive policing as well as reactive, enforcement-related activities. Police services often struggle to meet the expectations of the public.

In addition, certain segments of the community may hold less positive views of the police. This may be due in part to unrealistic expectations. Research studies show that citizens and communities that are in disorder tend to express lower levels of confidence in the police, reflecting the perception that the police are at least partially responsible for the disorder and crime.[17] Of all of the agencies in the criminal justice system, community residents tend to hold the police most responsible for neighbourhood disorder.[18] Across Canada, there are certain hot spots of police–community conflict, much of it centred in Indigenous, Black, other racialized, and visible/cultural minority communities.

Research studies indicate that police strategies that are most effective in improving public confidence in the police are those that increase community engagement.[19] Canadian police services have applied a number of other strategies to connect with community organizations and residents. Many police services in urban centres deploy community mobilization teams to develop and strengthen relationships with communities. In addition, police services are making extensive use of social media to disseminate information and to communicate with community residents. This includes Twitter, Facebook pages, departmental websites, and other forms of multi-media. Peel Regional Police, for example, have a YouTube channel and a Livestream page. A challenge is to design communication strategies that are effective in assisting the development of partnerships with all communities in a jurisdiction, including communities of diversity.

ANONYMOUS AND CREEP CATCHERS: GUARDIANS OF JUSTICE OR VIGILANTES?

A new feature of the criminal justice landscape has been the rise of groups attempting to address what are perceived to be the shortcomings of the justice system with respect to the prevention and response to crime. This has presented challenges for policing: On the one hand, these groups often have public support for targeting persons who may pose a risk to the community; on the other hand, there are dangers in these groups usurping the authority of the police and, potentially, violating the rights of citizens who are targeted.

ANONYMOUS

One group, Anonymous, has used the Internet as a platform in an attempt to hold alleged offenders and the criminal justice system accountable. The group, of unknown size, is distinguished by its Guy Fawkes masks, which are worn to protect members' identity. In 1605, Fawkes was part of a Roman Catholic group that plotted to blow up the English House of Lords during the state opening of Parliament. The "Gunpowder plot" was intended to kill King

▼ Research studies indicate that the most effective strategies for improving public confidence are ones that engage with the community.

Chris So/Toronto Star via Getty Images

▲ Groups such as Anonymous attempt to address perceived shortcomings of the justice system and are on the rise.

James I, a Protestant, and install his nine-year-old daughter on the throne to rule as a Roman Catholic monarch. The plot was discovered, and Fawkes was tortured and killed in 1606. A current member of Anonymous stated that the mask is a "convenient placard to use in protest against tyranny."[20]

The group has been involved in a number of high-profile crime cases in Canada and the U.S. It identifies persons through a process called "doxing"—an online "treasure hunt" searching for clues in online sources, including Facebook and comment boards. Information on one site is linked to information from other sites.[21]

The Death of Amanda Todd On October 10, 2012, 16-year-old Amanda Todd committed suicide by hanging at her home in British Columbia. Prior to her death, she had posted a video on YouTube that described, via flash cards, her experience of being blackmailed, bullied, and physically assaulted. See the video in the Media Links section at the end of the chapter.

In Grade 7, Amanda had been convinced by a stranger on the Internet to bare her breasts. The image was subsequently posted online and resulted in her being teased and bullied in school. A new term was coined to describe this action: "sextortion." Anonymous became involved in the case and alleged in a recorded statement on YouTube that they had identified the man who had blackmailed her. The group published his name and address, and he subsequently received death threats on Facebook and in e-mails. The police investigated and found that Anonymous had identified the wrong person. Anonymous did not issue an apology, stating that "it didn't care" if it was a case of mistaken identity since the man has been accused of similar crimes.[22] In 2017, a man from the Netherlands was sentenced by a Dutch court to 11 years in prison for the crime.

The Death of Rehtaeh Parsons Rehtaeh Parsons, a 17-year-old Nova Scotia woman, committed suicide in 2013. Her death occurred after she had been gang-raped two years earlier at a party. The images of the rape had been posted online, and for the next two years, she was subjected to bullying online, at school, and in the community. The RCMP investigated the case but there were no arrests or charges. Anonymous posted messages online threatening to release the names of the alleged offenders. Two years later, in 2015, Anonymous identified four individuals who they stated were responsible for the sexual assault on Rehteah Parsons. Two men, who were identified by Anonymous, were subsequently charged and convicted in the case. The father of Rehteah Parsons credited Anonymous for pressuring the police to reopen the investigation and to lay charges against the two men.[23]

An independent review of the case found that the Halifax police and the Crown counsel's office both mishandled the investigation, including taking too long to complete the investigation and failing to address the cyberbullying that the young woman experienced.

CREEP CATCHERS

The activities of another group called Creep Catchers (http://ttacc.ca) raise a number of issues concerning the role of the community in crime-fighting and whether such initiatives violate citizen's rights. See At Issue 6.1.

CREEP CATCHERS: PROTECTING THE COMMUNITY AND POTENTIAL VICTIMS OR PREDATORY VIOLATORS OF PRIVACY?

Members of the group, which has "chapters" across the country, pose on the Internet as underage youth. When an adult responds, a meeting is set for a public place, at which time members of Creep Catchers confront the person. The entire encounter is video-recorded as evidence to be provided to the police. Among the persons caught in a sting was an off-duty police officer.

The group has been criticized for violating the privacy rights of citizens. In 2017, for example, the BC Privacy Commissioner ordered the Surrey (British Columbia) Creep Catchers to destroy all videos and to stop the collection, use, and disclosure of information on two persons they had busted.[a] The privacy commissioner had found that Creep Catchers had violated the provincial *Privacy Act* by shaming the two individuals. A Canadian police scholar has criticized the group, arguing that the videos that are made violate due process and could interfere with police investigations that may have been underway at the time of the sting.[b]

Others have praised the group as providing a service to the community and protecting potential victims, the majority of which would be underaged girls.

Although the police have publicly discouraged the group from its activities, a number of persons have been charged after Creep Catcher stings. Among them was a 31-year-old Charlottetown, Prince Edward Island, man, charged in 2017 with making an agreement or arrangement to commit a sexual offence against a child. This after the man was lured by Creep Catchers to a public location and video-recorded by the Cape Breton Creep Catchers.[c]

Watch the video, "Predator Tries to Destroy the Evidence and Gets Arrested," from June 2017 (https://www.youtube.com/watch?v=7HjNh2aQPT0).

Creep Catchers film one of their suspects.
Courtesy of Rafal Gerszak

QUESTIONS

1. What are your views on Creep Catchers? Are they guardians of public safety or intruders on citizens' privacy?

2. What are the positive and problematic factors associated with this type of activity by a community group?

---

[a] H. Mooney. 2017, July 26. "'I Told Them to Go F--k Themselves': Surrey Creep Catchers Ordered to Destroy Videos," *Toronto Sun*. http://www.torontosun.com/2017/07/26/i-told-them-to-go-f--k-themselves-surrey-creep-catchers-ordered-to-destroy-videos.

[b] R. Laychuk. 2017, May 9. "Creep Catcher Confrontation Part of Problematic Trend, Manitoba Professor Says," *CBC News*. http://www.cbc.ca/news/canada/manitoba/manitoba-creep-catcher-confrontation-reaction-1.4105467.

[c] C. MacKay. 2017, August 15. "Charlottetown Man Charged Following 'Creep Catchers' Sting," *CBC News*. http://www.cbc.ca/news/canada/prince-edward-island/pei-charlottetown-man-charged-1.4248178.

CRIME PREVENTION

Crime prevention programs are generally aimed at reducing crime, generating community involvement in addressing general and specific crime problems, and heightening citizens' perceptions of safety. The three main approaches to crime prevention are primary, secondary, and tertiary prevention. Police departments are most extensively involved in primary crime prevention programs, although they do participate in secondary and (to a lesser extent) tertiary crime prevention as well.

The majority of crime prevention programs operated by Canadian police services have not been evaluated, and, in some cases, programs that have been determined by evaluative studies to be ineffective are still being sponsored by police. This has led a number of observers to call for the implementation of evidence-based crime prevention.[24]

PRIMARY CRIME PREVENTION PROGRAMS

Primary crime prevention programs identify opportunities for criminal offences and alter those conditions to reduce the likelihood that a crime will be committed. CCTVs

Primary crime prevention programs

Programs that identify opportunities for criminal offences and alter those conditions to reduce the likelihood that a crime will be committed.

"We're from the Neighborhood Watch committee. We've heard you're wearing a fake Rolex."

(closed-circuit television cameras) are perhaps the most controversial of the primary crime prevention programs. CCTVs have been used extensively in Britain and the United States for many years and have been installed in some Canadian municipalities. While concerns over privacy have been expressed, Canadian society is well on the way to becoming a "surveillance" society. The movements and behaviour of citizens are recorded tens or perhaps hundreds of times per day as they move around the community. There are cameras on buses, in taxis, in most private businesses, not to mention in every smartphone.

SECONDARY AND TERTIARY CRIME PREVENTION PROGRAMS

Secondary crime prevention programs

Programs that focus on areas that produce crime and disorder.

Secondary crime prevention programs focus on areas that produce crime and other types of disorder. Some initiatives focus on identifying high-risk offenders and include analyses that target high-crime areas. Others are designed to help vulnerable groups avoid becoming the victims of crime. One example is Camp Little Buffalo, sponsored by the Grande Prairie (Alberta) RCMP Detachment in collaboration with partners in the community. This five-day leadership camp is for at-risk youth between the ages of 11 and 13. The camp, which focuses on the development of communication, goal-setting, and problem-solving skills, among other skills sets, includes a variety of sports and outdoor activities. The program is also designed to foster positive interactions between the police and youth (http://www.cityofgp.com/index .aspx?page=995).

Tertiary crime prevention programs

Programs designed to prevent youth and adults from reoffending.

Tertiary crime prevention programs are designed to prevent youth and adults from reoffending. Most tertiary programs are directed towards first-time, less serious offenders, and typically have a high degree of success. Tertiary crime prevention programs are often collaborative efforts of justice and social service agencies and community groups. An example are the various diversion programs for first-time youth offenders, discussed in Chapter 13. These include intensive support programs (ISPs) that provide an alternative to custody for high-risk youth.

The effectiveness of several of the more common primary and secondary police crime prevention programs are set out in Research File 6.2.

RESEARCH FILE 6.2

THE EFFECTIVENESS OF SELECTED PRIMARY AND SECONDARY CRIME PREVENTION PROGRAMS

Primary Crime Prevention Programs

Program	Strategy	Effectiveness
Crime Prevention Through Environmental Design (CPTED)	Altering the physical environment of structures and places (e.g., improved lighting) to reduce criminal opportunities	In some jurisdictions, altering the designs of buildings and pedestrian routes have helped to reduce levels of robberies, assaults, and residential break-and-enters.
Closed circuit television (CCTV)	Placing cameras in business and/or residential areas to provide live images 24/7	Pilot projects in Calgary and Toronto and cities in the U.S. and U.K. found that CCTVs are most effective and can assist in investigations when targeted at specific locales, such as drug-dealing spots and parking garages.[a,b,c] May be most effective in reducing levels of disorder and in providing evidence to assist police in apprehending perpetrators after a crime has been committed.[d,e]

(continued)

Program	Strategy	Effectiveness
Neighbourhood Watch	Organizing residents to make them aware of strangers and criminal activities in their neighbourhood	This program is effective in reducing crime in some communities, although little is known about the factors that influence its effectiveness.[f] Implementation is most successful in low-crime, middle-class neighbourhoods.[g]

Secondary Crime Prevention Programs

Program	Strategy	Effectiveness
Drug Abuse Resistance Education (DARE) for youth	School-based program that provides information to youth about the perils of drug use	While the program generally has high levels of participation among educators, parents, and youth, the program has no impact on student attitudes and beliefs about drugs or drug use.[h] There is some evidence that the program may improve youth attitudes toward the police, particularly among youth from minority groups.[i]
Police school liaison officer programs	Police officers are assigned to schools on a residential (full-time, in school) or non-residential (periodic officer visits) basis. Officers make class presentations and participate in school activities. Objectives are primary and secondary crime prevention.	Few evaluations have been done. Programs may increase the legitimacy of the police with students and have indirect benefits (e.g., identifying at-risk youth, providing intelligence to patrol and investigative units); no demonstrated impact on school safety or crime rates.[j] Programs may result in criminalization of disciplinary situations.
Community mobilization	A strategy designed to reduce crime and victimization; strengthens at-risk communities and families and increases community wellness; involves government agencies (e.g., health, education, social services), community groups, the police, and others working collaboratively to address larger social issues and the needs of at-risk families and individuals.	The Prince Albert, Saskatchewan, program (commonly known as "The HUB"), the first of its kind in Canada, resulted in fewer calls for police service, reduced rates of violent and property crime, and a decline in emergency room visits.[k] It is being implemented in other Canadian cities.

[a] M. Barkley. 2009. *CCTV Pilot Project Evaluation Report.* Toronto: Toronto Police Service. http://geeksandglobaljustice.com/wp-content/TPS-CCTV-report.pdf.

[b] B.C. Welsh and D.P. Farrington. 2009. "Public Area CCTV and Crime Prevention: An Updated Systematic Review and Meta-Analysis," *Justice Quarterly, 26*(4), 716–745.

[c] J.H. Ratcliffe, T. Taniguchi, and R.B. Taylor. 2009. "The Crime Reduction Effects of Public CCTV Cameras: A Multi-Method Spatial Approach," *Justice Quarterly, 26*(3), 746–770.

[d] S.J. McLean, R.E. Worden, and M. Kim. 2013. "Here's Looking at You: An Evaluation of Public CCTV Cameras and Their Effects on Crime and Disorder," *Criminal Justice Review, 38*(3), 303–334.

[e] J. Ratcliffe. 2009. *Video Surveillance of Public Places.* Washington, DC: U.S. Department of Justice, Center for Problem-Oriented Policing. https://cops.usdoj.gov/pdf/pop/e02061006.pdf.

[f] C. Gill. 2016. "Community Interventions," in *What Works in Crime Prevention and Rehabilitation: Lessons from Systematic Reviews,* edited by D. Weisburd, D.P. Farrington, and C. Gill, 77–110. New York: Springer at p. 109.

[g] T. Bennett, K. Holloway, and D.P. Farrington. 2006. "Does Neighborhood Watch Reduce Crime? A Systematic Review and Meta-Analysis," *Journal of Experimental Criminology, 2*(4), 437–458.

[h] D.P. Rosenbaum. 2007. "Just Say No to D.A.R.E," *Criminology and Public Policy, 6*(4), 815–824.

[i] A.M. Schuck. 2013. "A Life-Course Perspective on Adolescents' Attitudes to Police," *Journal of Research in Crime and Delinquency, 50*(4), 579–607.

[j] C. Na and D.C. Gottfredson. 2013. "Police Officers in Schools: Effects on School Crime and the Processing of Offending Behaviors," *Justice Quarterly, 30*(4), 619–650.

[k] Public Safety Canada. 2013. "Community Mobilization Prince Albert (Synopsis)." http://www.publicsafety.ca/cnt/cntrng-crm/plcng/cnmcs-plcng/ndx/snpss-eng.aspx?n=152.

There is strong support for crime prevention among Canadians. The results of a national survey ($N = 1,863$), which included a question on spending priorities, are presented in Figure 6.1.

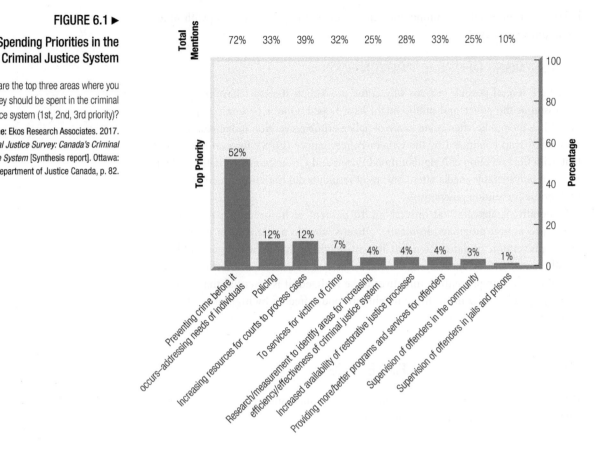

FIGURE 6.1 ▶

Spending Priorities in the Criminal Justice System

What are the top three areas where you think money should be spent in the criminal justice system (1st, 2nd, 3rd priority)?

Source: Ekos Research Associates. 2017. *National Justice Survey: Canada's Criminal Justice System* [Synthesis report]. Ottawa: Department of Justice Canada, p. 82.

CRIME PREVENTION IN INDIGENOUS COMMUNITIES

Developing and implementing effective crime prevention programs in Indigenous communities has proven to be a challenge both for police services (Indigenous and non-Indigenous) and communities themselves. The crime prevention initiatives that have been developed to date fall into one of two categories: (1) programs that are part of an overall crime prevention strategy, developed by senior police administrators, and implemented in both Indigenous and non-Indigenous communities; and (2) programs that are developed by police officers at the local level in collaboration with chiefs, band councils, and community residents. Needless to say, these latter programs have been the most effective. The effectiveness of programs is increased when community residents have a significant role in the design and delivery of the interventions.

There are a variety of programs across the country. The Six Nations Police (Ontario) operate Police Athletic League for Students (PALS) and Life Skills 101. This program is directed at high-risk youth and targets youths in the 6- to 12-year age range. One afternoon per week, youths from participating schools are with police officers in a variety of athletic activities. Life Skills 101 assists youths to gain insights into their behaviour and to avoid future conflicts and violence. It includes field trips, drug awareness programming, and assistance with school studies (http://snpolice.ca/pals).

In a national consultation, Indigenous communities highlighted the need for a policing model that emphasized an integrated, problem-oriented approach that was reflective of the needs of communities and involved the police working with other community services.[25]

CHALLENGES IN CRIME PREVENTION

There are several possible reasons why crime prevention strategies have not been as successful as the police and public might have hoped. One is community participation. First, the public often is not aware of police crime prevention initiatives. An environmental scan conducted by the Ottawa Police Service (OPS), for example, found that, with the exception of Neighbourhood Watch and Crime Stoppers (both of which received considerable media attention), most residents did not know much about the OPS crime prevention programs.[26]

Generally, it appears that only about 10 percent of households participate in crime prevention programs. Ironically, citizens who do participate in community crime prevention initiatives tend to live in neighbourhoods with few problems; in other words, they are among those *least* at risk of victimization. For the full potential of crime prevention initiatives to be realized, it is essential that there be participation by residents in those neighbourhoods affected by high rates of crime and trouble.

CRIME RESPONSE STRATEGIES

Police services use a variety of strategies to respond to crime. Among the more important strategies are presented in the following sections.

THE BROKEN WINDOWS APPROACH

The **broken windows approach** emerged in New York City in the 1980s and was a metaphor for neighbourhood deterioration. It was based on the observation of patrol officers that if a window in a building was broken and had not been replaced, in very short order all the windows would be broken. According to this approach, a broken window that remains in place is a statement that no one cares enough about the neighbourhood's quality of life to bother fixing the little things that go wrong. A broken window is a small thing, yet it may trigger further neglect and result in the progressive deterioration of the entire neighbourhood.

The central thesis of the broken windows theory, then, is that "the existence of unchecked and uncontrolled minor incivilities in a neighborhood—for example, panhandling, public drunkenness, vandalism and graffiti—produces an atmosphere conducive to more serious crime."[27]

This model of policing emphasizes rapid deployment of officers and relentless follow-up. The broken windows approach was developed in New York City and was associated with a significant reduction in crime in New York City. It has been adopted by many police services in Canada.

Considerable controversy has surrounded the broken windows theory, and questions have been raised as to the effectiveness of the various policing strategies that are based on its tenets. Among the questions that have been raised are whether policing initiatives targeting disorder are effective in reducing the levels of crime and, if so, at what cost, including the potential of over-policing and increases in public concern with safety.[28,29]

Broken windows approach

The view that if minor crimes are left unaddressed in an environment, more serious crime will emerge.

▼ A derelict, "broken windows" neighbourhood

david soulsby/Alamy Stock Photo

ZERO-TOLERANCE POLICING AND QUALITY-OF-LIFE POLICING

Zero-tolerance policing

A crime response strategy centred on the premise that a strict order-maintenance approach by the police will reduce more serious criminal activity.

A policing strategy that has gained popularity in the past decade or so is **zero-tolerance policing**, also referred to as *confident policing, proactive policing,* or *community policing with the gloves off.* The key principle is that a strict order-maintenance approach by the police in a specific area, coupled with high police visibility and presence, with a focus on disorder and minor infractions, will reduce more serious criminal activity.[30]

Increased police visibility is a core component of **quality-of-life policing**, which involves efforts to improve conditions in an area by targeting disruptive and annoying behaviour such as panhandling, loitering, and public drug and alcohol use.

Quality-of-life policing

Police efforts to improve conditions in an area by targeting disruptive and annoying behaviour.

These aggressive police strategies have often resulted in charges that the police are over-policing in certain communities and neighbourhoods and racial profiling. In New York City, the police employed "stop and frisk" in an attempt to reduce the levels of violent crime. Persons were stopped and frisked for weapons and other contraband. Police officers were required to have only "reasonable suspicion" that a crime was about to occur. Critics pointed to data indicating that a disproportionate number of African Americans and Latinos were targeted, and a report by the state attorney general found that only 3 percent of 2.4 million stops resulted in a conviction.[31] A federal court ruled in 2013 that the practice violated the constitutional rights of minorities in the city.[32]

A similar controversy has surrounded the police practice of street checks in Canada. This is discussed in Chapter 5.

PROBLEM-ORIENTED POLICING (POP)

Problem-oriented policing (POP)

A tactical strategy based on the idea that the police should address the causes of recurrent crime and disorder.

Problem-oriented policing (POP), which is based on the idea that policing should address the root causes of recurring problems of crime and disorder and then fashion solutions to those problems, often in collaboration with the community.

A central tenet of POP is the iceberg (or 80/20) rule, the view that crime (20 percent of the iceberg) is only a visible symptom of invisible, much larger problems (the 80 percent of the iceberg that lies below the water's surface).

The SARA (scanning, analysis, response, and assessment) problem-solving model helps officers identify and respond to problems, with the assistance of various agencies and organizations and community groups. It involves identifying the problem; determining the cause, scope, and effect of the problem; developing a plan to address and solve the problem; and determining whether the intervention was successful.

Problem-solving is central to the RCMP's CAPRA model. The letters stand for focusing on **C**lients, **A**cquiring and **A**nalyzing information, developing and maintaining **P**artnerships, generating an appropriate **R**esponse, and **A**ssessing the intervention.

The particular problem to be addressed may be community-wide and require a long-term plan of action, or it may involve a single individual and a situation that can be addressed in relatively short order. A good example is what is known as "problem premises," which consume considerable police resources. In Vancouver, for example, one relatively small rooming house was flagged as a problem premise: Police were called to the address a total of 259 times during an 18-month period. A total of 413 officers were on scene for more than 320 hours, and the overall cost to the taxpayers was $25,000. The Vancouver Police Department targeted specific individuals living in the rooming house, and the number of calls for service was reduced.[33]

CRIME ATTACK STRATEGIES

Crime attack strategies are proactive operations used by the police to target and apprehend criminal offenders, especially those deemed likely to reoffend, and to identify specific areas or neighbourhoods. These include increased patrol visibility, including foot patrols; proactive policing by patrol officers; and rapid patrol response.

Crime attack strategies

Proactive operations by the police to target and apprehend criminal offenders.

TACTICAL-DIRECTED PATROL

One widely used strategy is the tactical-directed patrol, which involves saturating high-crime areas (often referred to as *hot spots*) with police officers, or targeting individuals engaged in specific types of criminal activity. These may include areas that generate frequent hard crime calls (e.g., for holdup alarms, shootings, stabbings, auto thefts, thefts from autos, assaults, sexual assaults) or soft crime calls (e.g., for audible break-in alarms, disturbances, drunks, noise, unwanted individuals, vandalism, prowlers, fights). These hot spots, which are often identified through intelligence-led policing, are plotted on crime maps.

Directed forms of patrol are usually either location- or person-oriented. Tactical patrol strategies give police managers greater control over their most valuable resource—the time and activities of patrol officers. Foot and bicycle patrols may also be used in hot spot areas. The Vancouver Police Department, for example, deploys dedicated foot patrol officers in beat enforcement teams in the troubled Downtown Eastside area of the city.

TARGETING HIGH-RISK OFFENDERS

Many police services have developed initiatives designed to target high-risk offenders. Examples include the following:

- *Calgary Police Service Serious Habitual Offender Program (SHOP) and Multi-Disciplinary Resource Team (MDRT)*: SHOP is a multiagency (police, probation, Crown, social services agencies, and corrections) information and case management program for youths and adults designated as serious habitual offenders. SHOP monitors the activities of offenders both during custody and upon release in an attempt to reduce serious crime. The MDRT initiative is designed for early intervention and support for high-risk youths in the city.

- *Repeat Offender Program Enforcement Squad (ROPE)*: The ROPE squad, with officers from a number of municipal, provincial, regional, and federal police services, locates and apprehends criminal offenders who are unlawfully at large because they have violated the conditions of their release from custody, have failed to return to custody, or have escaped from correctional authorities.

- *Integrated Police-Parole Initiative (IPPI)*: This program places police officers in parole offices of Correctional Service Canada (CSC). These officers work side-by-side to monitor the activities of high-risk offenders released into the community. A preliminary evaluation of the program found that there was a reduction in technical violations of condition release by offenders in those CSC offices participating in the IPPI program, suggesting that this approach may assist with reintegration of offenders.[34] This is a good example of a tertiary crime prevention program (discussed earlier), as the efforts of the police and their partners are directed toward preventing re-offending.

These types of police strategies have not been without controversy. The Toronto Police Service Anti-Violence Intervention Strategy (TAVIS) was created to reduce the high levels of gun violence and to enhance public safety in high-crime neighbourhoods in Toronto. Its strategies included intervention, prevention, and community support and mobilization. A key strategy was building relationships with the residents in at-risk neighbourhoods.

Community meetings, high-profile police patrols, and the identification of crime hot spots and individuals involved in gun violence are all components of TAVIS.

Critics, including representatives of racialized groups, alleged that TAVIS engaged in over-policing and racial profiling. There were concerns that Black youth in particular were arbitrarily stopped and searched. These concerns led to the renaming and restructuring of the program and a shift in focus toward community policing and a focus on crime prevention.[35]

For a summary of the effectiveness of selected crime response and crime response strategies, see Research File 6.3.

RESEARCH FILE 6.3

THE EFFECTIVENESS OF SELECTED CRIME RESPONSE AND CRIME ATTACK STRATEGIES

Crime Response Strategies

Strategy	Technique	Effectiveness
Problem-oriented policing (POP)	Police attempt to address the root causes of crime and disorder and fashion solutions to those problems in collaboration with community residents. The use of SARA.[a]	Has the potential to reduce crime and disorder and to reduce the fear of crime. Can improve police–community relations and develop skills in patrol officers.[b]
Broken windows theory	The existence of unchecked and uncontrolled minor infractions/incivilities in a neighbourhood produces an environment conducive to serious crime.[c]	Studies on the impact of broken windows have produced mixed results. Some studies have found no impact on crime rates, while others have found a reduction in property crime rates.[d, e] It is likely that the broken windows approach may work in some types of neighbourhoods and that its impact may be increased if it is combined with community policing initiatives. There are concerns that in adopting the broken windows approach, the increased police activity may result in elevated levels of fear in the community. The legitimacy of the police may be compromised if certain segments of the community perceive they are being targeted.[f]
Zero-tolerance/ quality-of-life policing	Influenced by broken windows, these strict order-maintenance approaches are taken in specific areas, including high police visibility and a focus on disorder and minor infractions. Often involve police crackdowns on specific criminal activities, such as drug dealing.	Police presence may alter offenders' behaviour. Increased police visibility increases citizens' sense of security, may deter criminal behaviour, and increases police legitimacy.[g]

Crime Attack Strategies

Strategy	Technique	Effectiveness
Tactical-directed patrol	Proactive, aggressive patrol in high-crime areas. Patrol officers use unallocated time to engage in purposeful activities directed by analysis of crime data. May be location-focused or person (offender)-oriented. Often applied in conjunction with crackdowns, focusing on specific types of criminal activities, such as drug dealing.	Increasing the number of uniformed police officers in patrol cars in hot spots and during hot times (crime peaks) may significantly reduce levels of criminal activity. Proactive police arrests, including zero-tolerance arrest policies that focus on high-risk people and offences, can reduce the levels of serious violent crime. The impact of crackdowns may depend upon the community. Are resource-intensive and difficult to sustain positive results over the long term. May undermine the legitimacy of the police, particularly among young men and other groups who are more likely to be the targets of police attention.[h]

(continued)

Strategy	Technique	Effectiveness
Hot spot policing	Police focus on areas that have a high concentration of crime and/or disorder and a high risk of criminal victimization.[i]	Can reduce crime and disorder without displacing crime to surrounding areas; long-term effectiveness is enhanced by the use of POP.[j]
Foot patrols	Officers walk a "beat" in a neighbourhood or district. Some police services have dedicated foot patrols, while others encourage officers to park their patrol cars and walk when they have the opportunity.	Emerging evidence that strategically directed foot patrols can reduce the levels of crime and disorder in neighbourhoods.[k] Reduce citizens' fear of crime and calls for service. Improve officers' familiarity with neighbourhoods. To be effective, must be deployed as part of a comprehensive community policing strategy rather than as an add-on.

[a] J.E. Eck. 2004. "Why Don't Problems Get Solved?" in *Community Policing: Can It Work?* edited by W.G. Skogan, 185–206. Belmont, CA: Wadsworth/Thomson Learning.

[b] S.N. Durlauf and D.S. Nagin. 2011. "The Deterrent Effect of Imprisonment," in *Controlling Crime: Strategies and Tradeoffs,* edited by P.J. Cook, J. Ludwig, and J. McCrary, 43–94. Chicago: University of Chicago Press.

[c] R.H. Burke. 1998. "The Socio-political Context of Zero Tolerance Policing Strategies," *Policing, 21*(4), 666–682.

[d] B.E. Harcourt and J. Ludwig. 2006. "Broken Windows: New Evidence from New York City and a Five-City Social Experiment," *The University of Chicago Law Review, 73*(1), 271–320.

[e] J. Hyunseok, L.T. Hoover, and B.A. Lawton. 2008. "Effect of Broken Windows Enforcement on Crime Rates," *Journal of Criminal Justice, 36*(6), 529–538.

[f] J.C. Hinkle and D. Weisburd. 2008. "The Irony of Broken Windows: A Micro-Place Study of the Relationship Between Disorder, Focused Police Crackdowns, and Fear of Crime," *Journal of Criminal Justice, 36*(6), 503–512.

[g] M.S. Scott. 2003. *The Benefits and Consequences of Police Crackdowns.* Washington, DC: Office of Community Oriented Policing Services, U.S. Department of Justice. http://www.popcenter.org/responses/police_crackdowns.

[h] J.M. Gau and R.K. Brunson. 2010. "Procedural Justice and Order Maintenance Policing: A Study of Inner-City Young Men's Perceptions of Police Legitimacy," *Justice Quarterly, 27*(2), 255–279.

[i] J.E. Eck, S. Chainey, J.G. Cameron, M. Leitner, and R.E. Wilson. 2005. *Mapping Crime: Understanding Hot Spots.* Washington, DC: National Institute of Justice, U.S. Department of Justice. http://discovery.ucl.ac.uk/11291/1/11291.pdf.

[j] Durlauf and Nagin, "The Deterrent Effect of Imprisonment."

[k] J.H. Ratcliffe, T. Taniguchi, E.R. Goff, and J. Wood. 2011. "The Philadelphia Foot Patrol Experiment: A Randomized Controlled Trial of Police Patrol Effectiveness in Violent Crime Hotspots," *Criminology, 49*(3), 795–831.

THE POLICE AND VULNERABLE/AT-RISK GROUPS

A key theme in this text is the experience of Indigenous and racialized persons, members of visible/cultural/religious minority groups, and other at-risk and vulnerable persons with the criminal justice system. It is police officers who have the most contact with persons who are vulnerable or members of at-risk groups, and many of the controversies that surround policing in the early 21st century revolve around this issue: "To what extent do police services respond appropriately to the needs of these groups, which may include PwMI (persons with mental illness), sex trade workers, Indigenous persons, including Indigenous women, and others?"

RESPONDING TO PERSONS WITH MENTAL ILLNESS

It was noted in Chapter 5 that patrol officers are encountering more and more persons with mental illness (PwMI). A number of these encounters have ended tragically. The number of incidents involving mentally ill persons increased significantly when provincial governments failed to provide enough community-based treatment programs and facilities following the massive deinstitutionalization of the mentally ill during the 1960s and 1970s. This has resulted in massive downloading onto the police, who have become de facto community mental health workers and are the first responders to the mentally ill on the streets and in neighbourhoods. Responding to mental health costs is also resource-intensive. In 2014, mental health–related calls to the London (Ontario) police increased 40 percent and consumed 15 percent of the police budget for the year.[36]

In contrast to the portrayal of the police in the popular media, officers are as likely to be called to a mental illness crisis as to a robbery. In Vancouver, a study found that 31 percent of the calls for service received by the department had some mental health component, and there were individuals who had near daily contact with the police.[37]

The Toronto Police Service is dispatched to approximately 20,000 calls for service annually involving a person in crisis. This is between 2.0 and 2.5 percent of all occasions on which police are dispatched. Approximately 8,000 of these events involve apprehensions under the *Mental Health Act* (R.S.O. 1990, c. M.7). Some of these encounters, sadly, result in the application of lethal force by police. Between 2002 and 2012, five persons who were described as "emotionally disturbed persons" were fatally shot by police.[38]

Among the findings of a review of police encounters with PwMI in Toronto were that there had been a failure of provincial mental health system to provide adequate community-based treatment resources. In the view of this report, the police alone could not effectively address the needs of PwMI, and a robust response was required by the provincial mental health system and other agencies.[39]

Police File 6.1 profiles several cases that illustrate the types of cases of persons in crisis that come to the attention of municipal police services.

POLICE FILE 6.1

CALLS TO A MUNICIPAL POLICE SERVICE IN 2014 REGARDING CHRONIC/REPEAT PERSONS WITH MENTAL HEALTH CONCERNS: FOUR CASE STUDIES

Case 1: Suicidal Female	Case 2: Elderly Male with Dementia
A chronically suicidal female has generated over 48 police files in 2014 alone, 19 of which occurred between April 10 and May 14, 2014. Police have apprehended this female 12 times under section 28 of the *Mental Health Act*. This female suffers from full spectrum FASD (fetal alcohol spectrum disorder), addiction issues, and borderline personality disorder.	An elderly male suffering from dementia has made over 154 unfounded calls to police over the past two years. Although each call is deemed unfounded, police must attend every time a report is called in.

Case 3: Mother Concerned for Her Son	Case 4: Homeless Man with Psychotic Disorder
A mother concerned for her son called the police to help with her son who is currently living with her. The male has no previous mental health diagnosis. Upon police review, this male has generated over 233 calls for service since 2006. Police attended his home with a psychiatrist and the male was certified and taken to hospital.	A 30-year-old homeless man with a psychotic disorder has generated 2,048 calls for service between 2005 and 2014, 507 of which occurred in the city. The calls range from the male acting bizarrely, talking to himself, aggressively panhandling, sleeping in business alcoves, or being found in women's washrooms.

Source: Materials provided to author from a municipal police service.

Concerns have been raised that the police inappropriately use arrest to resolve encounters with mentally disordered people; this is most commonly referred to as the "criminalization" of the mentally ill. Research studies, however, have not supported this assertion.[40] Rather, Canadian police officers generally demonstrate high levels of benevolence and empathy toward mentally ill people, as well as a strong interest in linking them with appropriate services.[41]

Police services have been strong advocates for adequate funding for community mental health programs and services that will address the needs of this vulnerable population. Across the country, there are a variety of collaborative partnerships involving the police, mental health services, and community organizations that are designed to address the unique needs of PwMI, many of whom have extensive contact with the police.[42,43] Most major police services ensure that officers receive crisis intervention training (CIT) where they learn about mental illness and various strategies for managing encounters with PwMI.[44]

Police services have developed innovative initiatives with mental health agencies. The Durham Regional Police Service, Toronto Police Service, and Vancouver Police Department, among others, operate patrol units staffed by a police officer and a mental health worker. Watch the video, "Inside Toronto Police Service's Mobile Crisis Intervention Team" (CBC News, July 5, 2017) available at https://www.youtube.com/watch?v=osrzI06wT5E.

The Vancouver Police Department (VPD) and a number of the other larger police services participate in *assertive outreach teams*. These teams are comprised of a police officer and a psychiatrist who intervene in the 72 hours after a person is released from the hospital psych unit.[45] See the video on the Vancouver team ("Assertive Outreach Team Looks to Fill in Critical Mental Health Gap") in the Media Links section.

The VPD also participates in the *assertive community treatment* (ACT) teams. These teams include psychiatrists, social workers, nurses, and vocational counsellors, among others. The teams focus on addressing the needs of persons who have had extensive contact with the health system and the police. This includes assistance with housing and access to employment and health services (http://vancouver.ca/police/organization/investigation/investigative-support-services/youth-services/mental-health.html).

Positive outcomes have been reported by police services that have adopted the CIT model, including lower rates of arrest of PMI.[46] The Edmonton Police Service has developed a training program to improve interaction and communication between PwMI and the police. The training has resulted in less use of force with PwMI.[47] See the video link, "Edmonton Police Using Less Force with Mentally Ill after University of Alberta Course," in the Media Links section at the end of this chapter.

A study of an integrated mobile crisis service in Halifax, involving clinicians and police officers, found that there were improved response times despite an increase in the use of this service by patients, families, and service partners and an increase in the use of follow-up services by patients, as compared to a control group.[48]

THE POLICE TREATMENT OF INDIGENOUS, VULNERABLE, AND MARGINALIZED WOMEN

There are long-standing concerns with how the police treat Indigenous, vulnerable, and marginalized women. These include how police services respond to women's allegations of sexual assault and the tragedy of missing and murdered Indigenous women and girls.

"UNFOUNDED": THE POLICE INVESTIGATION OF SEXUAL ASSAULT CASES

Sexual assault is one of the most underreported crimes. In Canada, it is estimated that only 1 in 20 incidents of sexual assault are reported to the police.[49] A major reason that women do not report are not wanting to deal with the police and/or the belief that the police would not take the allegation seriously.[50]

When women do report, it is critical that the police take the allegations seriously and conduct a thorough investigation. Care must be taken to ensure that the woman is not revictimized by the investigative process. A high rate of dismissal of allegations of sexual assault as "unfounded" suggests that police officers are not conducting proper investigations. A case is generally considered by the police to be unfounded when the evidence gathered during the investigation does not meet the standard required to lay a criminal charge; the incident is reported but the victim chooses not to participate in the investigation; or the complaint is determined to be a false allegation.[51]

While women may have positive experiences with the police, others do not. The challenges faced by women who report having been sexually assaulted and the deficiencies in police investigations of the incidents were highlighted in a study that found that one in five allegations of sexual assault were determined by the police to be "unfounded."[52] The study found considerable variation among the provinces and territories in the percentage of sexual assault complaints that were cleared as unfounded during the period 2010–14, ranging from 11 percent in British Columbia to 32 percent in New Brunswick (the national rate is 19 percent).[53]

There were also differences between police services in the percentage of sexual assault allegations that were dismissed as unfounded during 2010–14—for example, Toronto at 7 percent, London at 30 percent, and Saint John, New Brunswick, at 51 percent.[54]

The investigation of sexual assault cases in the Canadian north is particularly challenging. Northern communities have among the highest rates of sexual assault cases determined by the police to be "unfounded."[55] Language and cultural barriers between community residents and the police, and the hesitancy of women to report sexual assault to the police due to distrust of the police or fear of repercussions from their family and community members, may serve as barriers to reporting. In addition, the frequent transfers of officers from the communities hinders the development of relationships of trust between women and the police.[56]

Following publication of the findings, many police services across the country conducted audits of their sexual assault case files. The London Police Service, for example, reviewed sexual assault cases recorded as unfounded between 2010 and 2016 (N = 1,030). The review resulted in the development of a victim-centred framework for classifying sexual assault allegations that is focused on belief in the victim.[57]

Several police services have created provisions for independent oversight of how cases involving allegations of sexual assault are investigated. In Calgary, for example, the external reviews will be conducted by representatives from the sex-assault centres in the city, medical personnel, and a person from the provincial Ministry of Status of Women. The oversight program is modelled on a similar program in Philadelphia, which resulted in a decrease in the number of sexual assault cases designated as "unfounded" from 18 percent to 4 percent.[58]

THE TRAGEDY OF MISSING AND MURDERED INDIGENOUS WOMEN

While the exact number of missing and murdered women and girls has not been established, it may range into the hundreds.[59] From its investigation, Human Rights Watch concluded, "The failure of law enforcement authorities to deal effectively with the problem of missing and murdered indigenous women and girls in Canada is just one element of the dysfunctional relationship between the Canadian police and indigenous people."[60] A study in British Columbia that involved interviews with 42 Indigenous women and eight Indigenous girls documented their experiences of abuse at the hands of the police and the absence of police action to investigate cases of domestic abuse and of missing and murdered women.[61]

In 2016, the federal Liberal government announced a National Inquiry into Missing and Murdered Indigenous Women and Girls (http://www.mmiwg-ffada.ca). The mission of the inquiry is to "learn the truth by honouring the lives and legacies of Indigenous women, girls and members of the LGBTQ2S community. This encompasses three goals: (1) finding the truth; (2) honouring the truth; and (3) giving life to the truth as a path to healing." As part of its mandate, the commission will examine the role of police investigations. The inquiry began hearing testimony from the families of missing and murdered women and girls in summer 2017 and, despite organizational challenges, was proceeding with its work as of late 2017.

One focus of concern is Highway 16, christened "The Highway of Tears," which runs across the northern part of British Columbia. Since 1969, 32 Indigenous and non-Indigenous women have been murdered or gone missing on this stretch of highway, most while hitchhiking. Despite the investigative efforts of an RCMP special unit, the majority of the deaths remain unsolved. See the video link for the Highway of Tears in the Media Links section at the end of this chapter.

Among the challenges of investigating these cases are a lack of investigative capacities in police service, a lack of coordination among police services, the mobility of the victims, and delays in reporting.[62]

For a case study of how police services in British Columbia failed vulnerable and marginalized Indigenous and non-Indigenous women, see Police File 6.2.

There are persistent concerns with the manner in which some police officers treat Indigenous women. A study in Saskatchewan that involved conducting interviews with Indigenous women and girls ($N = 64$) about their lived experience documented instances of mistreatment and discrimination by the police, including excessive use of force and intimidation, degrading and abusive body and strip searches by male police officers, and the failure of the police to protect women and girls against violence.[63]

The allegations against the officers, none of which has been proved in court, included instances in which officers traded drugs, alcohol, and money for oral sex; conducting "starlight tours" wherein women were driven outside of town and abandoned in isolated areas; and physical assault. The findings of this report were similar to those obtained in interviews with Indigenous women ($N = 42$) and girls ($N = 8$) in British Columbia.[64] The study documented their experiences of abuse at the hands of the police and the absence of police action to investigate cases of domestic abuse and

▼ A billboard on Highway 16 in northern British Columbia. This road has been dubbed "The Highway of Tears" because of the number of women who have gone missing or been murdered there—currently at 32 since 1969.

Steve Bosch/Vancouver Sun

WILLIE PICKTON'S FARM: MASS MURDER AND A FAILURE OF POLICE INVESTIGATION

During the mid- to late 1990s, a number of sex trade workers from Vancouver's Downtown Eastside began to go missing. These women, many of whom were addicted, disappeared and did not make contact with family or friends. One suspect who emerged was a pig farmer, Robert "Willie" Pickton, whose property was in the rapidly developing suburban municipality of Coquitlam, a few kilometres from Vancouver. Coquitlam is policed under contract by the RCMP.

The pig farm of Robert "Willie" Pickton in the Vancouver-area suburb of Coquitlam (note the adjacent subdivision of new houses)

Both the Vancouver Police Department and the Coquitlam RCMP were slow to initiate investigations, and there were ongoing issues between the two police services, including a lack of communication and information-sharing. Pickton was finally arrested in 2002, and the search for evidence on his property over the next several years became the largest and most expensive police investigation in Canadian history. Over a two-year period, 235,000 pieces of DNA evidence were gathered, and the remains of 30 women were identified. It is estimated that Pickton killed 65 women over a 15-year period on his farm. In 2007, Pickton was convicted of second-degree murder of six women and given a life sentence with no possibility of parole for 25 years.

The Vancouver Police Department conducted an extensive internal review of its handling of the Pickton investigation and identified a number of organizational factors that had hindered the investigation.[a] The provincial government subsequently appointed a retired judge to conduct an examination of the missing women's investigation.

Among the findings of the final report were that the police had failed to act to protect marginalized women and that there were systematic failures in the investigative process that delayed the apprehension of Pickton.[b] More specifically, the police were criticized for a failure of leadership, a failure to consider and pursue all investigative strategies, and inadequate staffing and resources. Compounding these were the lack of a regional police service that would have facilitated communication and the sharing of information among police investigators.

[a] D. LePard. 2010. *Missing Women Investigation Review. Summary Report.* Vancouver: Vancouver Police Department. http://vancouver.ca/police/media/2010/mw-summary-report.pdf.

[b] The Honourable W.T. Oppal (Commissioner). 2012. *FORSAKEN: The Report of the Missing Women Commissioned of Inquiry, Executive Summary.* Victoria: Minister of Justice and Attorney General of British Columbia. http://www.missingwomeninquiry.ca/wp-content/uploads/2010/10/Forsaken-ES-web-RGB.pdf.

of missing and murdered women. Watch the video, "Enquete Investigation into Val-d'Or Now Available in English," listed in the Media Links section at the end of this chapter.

In 2017, the province of Quebec announced that it was undertaking a comprehensive review of the treatment of Indigenous persons by the police, the criminal justice system, social services and health systems, and child protection agencies.[65] The announcement followed the decision of Crown prosecutors not to charge six Quebec provincial police officers in Val-d'Or for alleged abuse of Indigenous women.[66]

THE POLICE AND THE LGBTQ COMMUNITY

Historically, the relationship between the police and the LGBTQ communities and relations were characterized by conflict and mistrust. Police officers were generally drawn from the working classes and held conservative, inflexible attitudes toward non-heterosexual persons, views that were reinforced by a "macho" police culture. Recall from the discussion in Chapter 3 that the police historically have been involved in policing morality in enforcing laws that prohibited consensual homosexual conduct. This led to police raids on gay clubs, cinemas, and bath houses and the arrests of patrons in these facilities. The high-profile raids of gay bath houses by the Toronto police in the early 1980s prompted legal action and the beginning of a change in police attitudes and behaviour, as well as changes in legislation. Today, it is not uncommon for chief constables to walk in Gay Pride parades and for police services to engage with the LGBTQ communities on a variety of issues.

Officers were often unsympathetic to gay victims, and police services were slow to respond to crimes that were hate-motivated. The members of these communities were often reluctant to report victimization, and this has been compounded by the attitudes of the investigation officers. The most common experience with the police was negative, and there is often the perception that police services are not aware of the issues in the LGBTQ communities.[67]

Canadian police services have made efforts to improve the relationships with the LGBTQ communities and, at the same time, increase awareness through training programs for officers. The Windsor Police Service, in collaboration with the advocacy group Equality for Gays and Lesbians Everywhere (EGALE), implemented a mandatory training program (the first of its kind in Canada) for its officers and staff, designed to build awareness of homophobic violence and to facilitate the development of positive relationships with the LGBTQ communities. The Ottawa Police Service has a liaison committee for the lesbian, gay, bisexual, and transgender communities. The committee facilitates contact between the OPS and these communities and advocates for issues of mutual interest (https://www.ottawapolice.ca/en/news-and-community/ GLBT-Liaison-Committee.asp). See the Media Link, "Andre Goh – Building the Asian LGBT Community," at the end of this chapter.

The RCMP has produced a video featuring 20 LGBTQ officers directed toward "building a bridge of understanding for youth undergoing similar experiences" and "sharing the eventual joy of knowing that life, indeed, does get better." See the Media Link, "It Gets Better Canada," at the end of this chapter.

There has also been an increased focus by police services on hate committed against persons, which are defined as "a criminal offence committed against a person or property where the motivation is bias prejudice or hate, based on the victim's race, national or ethnic origin, language, colour, religion, sex, age, mental or physical disability, sexual orientation, or any other similar factor" (see Canadian *Criminal Code* [R.S.C. 1985, c. C-46], sections 318/319 and 718.2(a)(i)). The Toronto Police Service, for example, has a Hate Crime Unit and Hate-Crime Coordinators who are located in each police division who are responsible for investigating hate crime occurrences.

In 2017, the relations between the police and the LGBTQ communities were challenged by a controversy over whether police officers should participate, in uniform, in the annual Gay Pride parades that occur across the country. See At Issue 6.2.

SHOULD UNIFORMED POLICE OFFICERS BE ALLOWED TO PARTICIPATE IN GAY PRIDE PARADES?

As part of the improving relationships between the police and the LGBTQ communities, police officers in a number of Canadian police services for many years have participated in uniform in annual Gay Pride parades.

In 2016, the group Black Lives Matter blockaded the Toronto Gay Pride parade and refused to allow the parade to continue until the Gay Pride organizers agreed to disallow uniformed police officers from participating in future parades. This decision, and those of Gay Pride organizing committees in other communities, divided the LGBTQ communities.[a] In 2017, Calgary Pride organizers announced that uniformed police were no longer welcome to participate in the parade, stating that the policy was an acknowledgement of "[t]he historical oppression and institutionalized racism faced by queer/trans people of colour and Indigenous persons, and the potentially negative association with weapons, uniforms, and other symbols of law enforcement."[b] The decision to ban uniformed officers from Gay Pride parades divided the LGBTQ community, as reflected in the following comments of one gay activist in Vancouver:

For those of us who are older and were part of that first generation to come out, at some cost, we grew up in an era where people were barred, lost their homes, jobs, were subjected fairly regularly to beatings, and where the police were not our friends. So a lot of people worked very hard to build relationships, and to build trust with the law enforcement and the justice community.... To see that thrown away is for us who come from that generation a tragic error in strategy, and it flies in the face of the way that we gained acceptance in society.[c]

I do not see this decision as exclusion. I see this decision as accountability. I see this decision as supporting the most racialized and marginalized members of our community. ... I absolutely believe that accountability must be had, and we cannot have the same people who are beating us, who are harassing us, who're responsible for violent encounters with us, dancing with us in revelry in uniform with their guns on their side while being paid to participate.[d] (board member, Pride Toronto)

Toronto's police chief and officers participate in the 2016 Gay Pride parade.

In 2017, members of the Toronto Police Service were invited by New York's Gay Officers Action League to participate in uniform in the NYPD Gay Pride March in that city, a move that a Toronto Black Lives Matter leader described as "disgraceful."[e]

QUESTIONS

1. What is your position on whether uniformed police officers should be allowed to participate in Gay Pride parades?

2. Read the open letter sent by a gay Toronto police officer to Pride Toronto at http://www.cbc.ca/news/canada/toronto/gay-cop-black-lives-matter-letter-1.3663323. What is your response to letter?

a, b, c G. Hamilton. 2017, July 28. "Push to Bar Police from Pride Parade Divides LGBTQ," *National Post.* http://nationalpost.com/news/canada/a-tragic-error-growing-push-to-exclude-police-from-pride-parades-divides-lgbtq-community. Material republished with the express permission of Postmedia Network Inc.

d T. Simmons. 2017, January 23. "'Enough is Enough:' Pride Toronto Board Members Explains Decision to Ban Police from Parade," *CBC News.* http://www.cbc.ca/news/canada/toronto/pride-board-member-response-1.3947820.

e M. Rodriquez. 2017, May 25. "BLM Activist Calls NYPD Gay Pride March Invitation to Toronto Police 'Disgraceful,'" *mic.com.* https://mic.com/articles/178051/blm-activist-calls-gay-nypd-pride-march-invitation-to-toronto-police-disgraceful#.aTQwyXKWk.

SUMMARY

This chapter has examined the various strategies that the police use to prevent and respond to crime, with particular emphasis on the efforts of police services to build sustainable partnerships with communities and to utilize the latest technologies for detecting crimes and investigating cases. The traditional professional model of policing has evolved into community-based strategic policing, which incorporates elements of community policing with crime prevention, crime response, and crime attack strategies. This model of police work makes extensive use of data analysis, which allows police policies and operations to be intelligence-led. A number of these have been found to be effective in preventing and reducing levels of crime and social disorder, although some of the more aggressive police tactics have been criticized for being disproportionately focused on racialized groups.

There are challenges surrounding the relationship between the police and vulnerable/at-risk groups. Police services have been strong advocates for addressing the needs of PwMI with whom they have contact and participate in a variety of collaborative initiatives designed to address the unique needs of this group. The high rates of dismissal of sexual assault complaints and the issues that surround police treatment of Indigenous women illustrate the challenges that exist in the relationships between the police and the community. Significant progress has been made in improving the relationship between the police and the LGBTQ community although this has been put to the test in some cities when uniformed police were prevented from participating in Gay Pride parades.

The increasing use of high technology in policing, including the use of unmanned drones, has raised privacy issues and is another example of the tensions that exist between the need to maintain order while ensuring the rights of citizens.

KEY POINTS REVIEW

1. Most police services continue to use crime rates and clearance rates as measures of performance and developing measures of police performance that capture the variety of activities of the police has proven to be a challenge.

2. The traditional (or professional) model of police work is based on random patrol, rapid response, and reactive investigation.

3. The community policing model is premised on the three Ps: prevention, problem-solving, and partnership.

4. Community-based strategic policing is the predominant model in Canadian policing in the early 21st century.

5. Police services are increasingly adopting new technologies to improve their effectiveness.

6. Research studies have found strong community support for increased visibility and accessibility of the police, including foot patrol and that community policing has the potential to increase citizens' feelings of safety and to increase police legitimacy.

7. Police officers often participate in restorative justice programs, including circle sentencing and family group conferencing.

8. Recent years have witnessed the rise of groups such as Anonymous and Creep Catchers that use the Internet to become involved in cases that they perceive the criminal justice system has not adequately addressed.

9. There are a variety of primary and secondary crime prevention programs, some of which have proven successful.

10. Police services are involved in a wide range of programs and partnerships with the community, although there are often challenges in developing and sustaining partnerships.

11. Many of the crime response and crime attack strategies used by the police have been shown to reduce crime and citizens' fear of crime.

12. There are increasing concerns with how the police treat Indigenous women and vulnerable and marginalized women.

13. The large number of cases involving alleged sexual assault that were dismissed as "unfounded" by police services was the catalyst for revising police policy and practice.

14. The tragedy of missing and murdered Indigenous women has raised issues related to police treatment of Indigenous women.

15. In the case of the mass murderer Willie Pickton, the police were found to have failed to act to protect marginalized women, and there were systematic failures in the investigative process.

16. While the relationship between the LGBTQ community and the police historically was marked by conflict and mistrust, police services have made significant progress in improving relationships with the LGBTQ community.

KEY TERM QUESTIONS

1. What role do **clearance rates** and **crime displacement** play in discussions of measuring police performance?

2. Compare and contrast the **professional model of policing, community policing,** and **community-based strategic policing.**

3. What role do **intelligence-led policing, Compstat,** and **predictive policing** play in community-based strategic policing?

4. Define and discuss **primary** and **secondary crime prevention programs** and note the effectiveness of these initiatives.

5. What are **tertiary crime prevention programs,** and what is an example of this approach?

6. Describe the **broken windows approach, zero-tolerance policing, quality-of-life policing,** and **problem-oriented policing (POP),** and discuss their effectiveness in reducing crime and disorder.

7. Describe the **crime attack strategies** used by police and the effectiveness of these approaches.

CRITICAL THINKING EXERCISE

Critical Thinking Exercise 6.1

"To Drone or Not to Drone…"

Assume that your municipality is holding a referendum on whether or not the local police service should be allowed to use drones in police operations.

Your Thoughts?

1. Would you vote in favour of allowing the police to use drones, or against?

2. If you would vote in favour, what restrictions, if any, would you place on how drones were used?

3. What oversight structures would you put in place? If you voted against the police being able to use drones, what are the primary reasons for your position?

CLASS/GROUP DISCUSSION EXERCISE

Class/Group Exercise 6.1

The Experience of Women Who Report Being the Victim of Sexual Assault

Access the article, "What It's Like to Report Sexual Assault," by R. Doolittle, *Globe and Mail*, March 17, 2017, at https://www.theglobeandmail.com/news/investigations/what-its -like-to-report-a-sexual-assault-36-people-share-their-stories/article34338353.

Your Thoughts?

1. After reading the stories of the women, what would you identify as the common themes in their experience with the police?

2. What were the features of the cases in which women had a positive experience with the police?

MEDIA LINKS

"How Predictive Policing Software Works," *The Verge*, February 3, 2016, https://www.youtube.com/watch?v=YxvyeaL7NEM

"Amanda Todd's Story: Struggling, Bullying, Suicide, Self-Harm," October 11, 2012, https://www.youtube.com/watch?v=ej7afkypUsc

"Amanda Todd's Final Video (4 Hours Before Death) Unseen Footage," October 21, 2012, http://www.youtube.com/watch?v=wjvq23sPrHA

"#OpJustice4Rehtaeh Statement Anonymous," Anonymous Canada, April 10, 2013, https://www.youtube.com/watch?v=7_D_zvizzKA

"Assertive Outreach Team Looks to Fill in Critical Mental Health Gap," November 14, 2014, https://globalnews.ca/news/1673094/assertive-outreach-team-looks-to-fill-in-critical-mental-health-gap

"Highway of Tears," *CBS 48 Hours*, May 28, 2016, https://www.cbsnews.com/videos/highway-of-tears-3

"Enquete Investigation into Val-d'-Or Now Available in English," *CBC News*, December 12, 2015, http://www.cbc.ca/news/indigenous/investigation-into-val-d-or-now-available-in-english-1.3362534

"Who Killed Alberta Williams?" *CBC News*, October 20, 2016, http://www.cbc.ca/missingandmurdered/podcast

"Edmonton Police Using Less Force With Mentally Ill After University of Alberta Course," *Edmonton Sun*, March 18, 2013, http://edmontonsun.com/2013/03/18/edmonton-police-using-less-force-with-the-mentally-ill-after-university-of-alberta-course/wcm/0ab36288-828a-4185-b0a2-664235cd3c42

"Police Surveillance Drones Coming Soon to Local Law Enforcement," January 25, 2011, http://www.youtube.com/watch?v=NW3DLfXHCXU

"Predator Tries to Destroy the Evidence and Gets Arrested," June 22, 2017, https://www.youtube.com/watch?v=7HjNh2aQPT0

"Andre Goh—Building the Asian LGBT Community," Ontario Human Rights Commission, August 9, 2013, https://www.youtube.com/watch?v=yzF50RIGeb8

"It Gets Better Canada," November 2, 2010, https://www.youtube.com/watch?v=5p-AT18d9lU

REFERENCES

1. D. Lilley and S. Hindjua. 2006. "Officer Evaluation in the Community Policing Context," *Policing*, 29(1), 19–37.

2. N. Robertson. 2012. "Policing: Fundamental Principles in Canadian Context," *Canadian Public Administration*, 55(3), 343–363.

3. P.-P. Pare, R. Felson, and M. Ouimet. 2007. "Community Variation in Crime Clearance: A Multilevel Analysis with Comments on Assessing Police Performance," *Journal of Quantitative Criminology*, 23(3), 243–258.

4. T.I. Gabor. 2003. *Assessing the Effectiveness of Organized Crime Strategies: A Review of the Literature*. Ottawa: Department of Justice Canada, p. 6. http://www.justice.gc.ca/eng/rp-pr/csj-sjc/jsp-sjp/rr05_5/rr05_5.pdf.

5. R.T. Guerette. 2009. *Analyzing Crime Displacement and Diffusion*. Washington, DC: U.S. Department of Justice, Office of Community Oriented Policing Services. https://ric-zai-inc.com/Publications/cops-p167-pub.pdf.

6. C.T. Griffiths. 2016. *Canadian Police Work* (4th ed.). Toronto: Nelson.

7. B. Whitelaw and R.B. Parent. 2013. *Community-Based Strategic Policing in Canada* (4th ed.). Toronto: Nelson.

8. D. Osborne and S. Wernicke. 2003. *Introduction to Crime Analysis: Basic Resources for Criminal Justice Practice*. New York: Haworth Press, p. 6.

9. K. Hickey. 2015, March 17. "Report: CompStat Does Reduce Crime," *GCN*. https://gcn.com/Articles/2015/03/17/Compstat-report.aspx.

10. J.J. Willis, S.D. Mastrofski, and T. Kochel. 2010. "The Co-Implementation of Compstat and Community Policing," *Journal of Criminal Justice*, 38(5), 969–980.

11. W.L. Perry, B. McInnis, C.C. Price, S.C. Smith, and J.S. Hollywood. 2013. *Predictive Policing: The Role of Crime Forecasting in Law Enforcement Operations*. Santa Monica, CA: RAND. https://www.rand.org/content/dam/rand/pubs/research_reports/RR200/RR233/RAND_RR233.pdf.

12. L. Kretzel. 2017, July 22. "Program Helps VPD Predict Property Crimes," *NEWS 1130*. http://www.news1130.com/2017/07/22/program-helps-vpd-predict-property-crimes.

13. C. Smith. 2017, July 22. "Vancouver Police Rely on Artificial Intelligence to Combat Residential Break-Ins," *Georgia Straight*. https://www.straight.com/news/939891/vancouver-police-rely-artificial-intelligence-combat-residential-break-ins.

14. Ontario Human Rights Commission. 2017. *Under Suspicion: Research and Consultation Report on Racial Profiling in Ontario*. Toronto: Author, p. 44. http://ohrc.on.ca/sites/default/files/Under%20suspicion_research%20and%20consultation%20report%20on%20racial%20profiling%20in%20Ontario_2017.pdf.

15. R.B. Santos. 2014. "The Effectiveness of Crime Analysis for Crime Reduction: Cure or Diagnosis?" *Journal of Contemporary Criminal Justice*, 30(2), 147–168.

16. S.M. Bucerius, S.K. Thompson, and K. Hancock. 2016. *The Somali Experience in Alberta: Interviews with Members of the Edmonton Police Service on Community Outreach Strategies and Their Experiences with the Somali Diaspora in Edmonton*. Ottawa: Public Safety Canada. www.edmontonpolice.ca/~/media/8A960BDCAE274B7DA78F473A4725E576.ashx.

17. L. Cao. 2011. "Visible Minorities and Confidence in the Police," *Canadian Journal of Criminology and Criminal Justice*, 53(1), 1–26.

18. J. Sprott and A.N. Doob. 2009. "The Effect of Urban Neighborhood Disorder on Evaluations of the Police and Courts," *Crime and Delinquency*, 55(3), 339–362.

19. A. Rix, F. Joshua, M. Maguire, and S. Morton. 2009. *Improving Public Confidence in the Police: A Review of the Evidence. Research Report 28*. London, UK: Home Office. https://www.gov.uk/government/uploads/system/uploads/attachment_data/file/115846/horr28-key-implications.pdf.

20. *The Economist*. 2014, November 4. "How Guy Fawkes Became the Face of Post-Modern Protest," https://www.economist.com/blogs/economist-explains/2014/11/economist-explains-3.

21. J. Davison. 2012, October 22. "Online Vigilantes: Is 'Doxing' a Neighbourhood Watch or Dangerous Witch Hunt?" *CBC News*. http://www.cbc.ca/news/technology/story/2012/10/19/f-doxing-tracking-online-identity-anonymity.html.

22. T. Alamenciak and P. Fong. 2012, October 17. "Amanda Todd: Online Group Anonymous Now Accuses U.S. Man of Tormenting Amanda Todd," *Toronto Star*. http://www.thestar.com/news/canada/2012/10/17/amanda_todd_online_group_anonymous_now_accuses_us_man_of_tormenting_amanda_todd.html.

23. G. Ormand. 2015, August 3. "Rehteah Parsons's Father Credits Anonymous for Reopening Investigation," *Canadian Press*. http://www.cbc.ca/news/canada/nova-scotia/rehteah-parsons-s-father-credits-anonymous-for-reopening-investigation-1.3177605.

24. B.C. Welsh and D.P. Farrington. 2005. "Evidence-Based Crime Prevention: Conclusions and Directions for a Safer Society," *Canadian Journal of Criminology and Criminal Justice*, 47(2), 337–354.

25. DRPA. 2016. *A Renewed Approach to Policing in Indigenous Communities – Engagement Summary Report: What We Heard*. Ottawa: Public Safety Canada. https://www.publicsafety.gc.ca/cnt/rsrcs/pblctns/rnwd-pprch-plcng-ndgns-cmmnts/rnwd-pprch-plcng-ndgns-cmmnts-en.pdf.

26. Ottawa Police Service. 2012. *Environmental Scan: 2012*. Ottawa: Author. https://www.ottawapolice.ca/en/news-and-community/resources/enviroscan.pdf.

27. R.H. Burke. 1998. "The Socio-political Context of Zero Tolerance Policing Strategies," *Policing*, 21(4), 666–682 at p. 667.

28. B.E. Harcourt and J. Ludwig. 2006. "Broken Windows: New Evidence from New York City and a Five-City Social Experiment," *The University of Chicago Law Review*, 73(1), 271–320.

29. J.C. Hinkle and D. Weisburd. 2008. "The Irony of Broken Windows: A Micro-Place Study of the Relationship Between Disorder, Focused Police Crackdowns, and Fear of Crime," *Journal of Criminal Justice*, 36(6), 503–12.

30. T. Romeanes. 1998. "A Question of Confidence: Zero Tolerance and Problem-Oriented Policing," in *Zero Tolerance Policing*, edited by R. Hopkins Burke, 39–48. Leicester: Perpetuity Press.

31. A. Gabbat. 2013, November 14. "Stop and Frisk: Only 3% of 2.4 Million Stops Result in Conviction, Report Finds," *The Guardian*. https://www.theguardian.com/world/2013/nov/14/stop-and-frisk-new-york-conviction-rate.

32. J. Goldstein. 2013, August 12. "Judge Rejects New York's Stop and Frisk Policy," *New York Times*. http://www.nytimes.com/2013/08/13/nyregion/stop-and-frisk-practice-violated-rights-judge-rules.html.

33. J. Keating. 2010, July 20. "City Rooming House Costs a Whopping $25,000 for Police," *The Province*. https://www.pressreader.com/canada/the-province/20100720/281582351907854.

34. M. Axford and R. Ruddell. 2010. "Police-Parole Partnerships in Canada: A Review of a Promising Programme," *International Journal of Police Science and Management*, 12(2), 274–286.

35. W. Gillis. 2016, June 14. "Toronto Police Anti-Violence Unit to Be Restructured," *Toronto Star*. https://www.thestar.com/news/crime/2016/06/14/toronto-police-anti-violence-unit-to-be-restructured.html.

36. J. O'Brien. 2014, March 31. "Mental Health Calls Cost London Cops More Than $14 Million a Year – Roughly 15% of Their Budget," *London Free Press*. http://www.lfpress.com/2014/03/30/the-calls-are-costing-london-cops-about-14-million-a-year--roughly-15-of-their-budget.

37. F. Wilson-Bates. 2008. *Lost in Transition: How a Lack of Capacity in the Mental Health System Is Failing Vancouver's Mentally Ill and Draining Police Resources*. Vancouver: Vancouver Police Department. https://vancouver.ca/police/assets/pdf/reports-policies/vpd-lost-in-transition.pdf.

38. The Honourable F. Iacobucci. 2014. *Police Encounters with People in Crisis*. Toronto: Toronto Police Service, p. 6. http://www.torontopolice.on.ca/publications/files/reports/police_encounters_with_people_in_crisis_2014.pdf.

39. Ibid.

40. R.S. Engel and E. Silver. 2001. "Policing Mentally Disordered Suspects: A Reexamination of the Criminalization Hypothesis," *Criminology*, 39(2), 225–252.

41. D. Cotton. 2004. "The Attitudes of Canadian Police Officers Toward the Mentally Ill," *International Journal of Law and Psychiatry*, 27(2), 135–146.

42. D. Cotton and T.G. Coleman. 2010. "Canadian Police Agencies and Their Interactions with Persons with a Mental Illness: A Systems Approach," *Police Practice and Research*, 11(4), 301–314.

43. J.D. Livingston, C. Weaver, N. Hall, and S. Verdun-Jones. 2008. *Criminal Justice Diversion for Persons for Mental Disorders. A Review of Best Practices*. Vancouver: The Law Foundation of British Columbia, B.C. Mental Health & Addiction Services, Canadian Mental Health Association BC Division. https://cmha.bc.ca/wp-content/uploads/2016/07/DiversionBestPractices.pdf.

44. A.C. Watson and A.J. Fulambarker. 2012. "The Crisis Intervention Team Model of Police Response to Mental Health Crises: A Primer for Mental Health Practitioners," *Best Practices in Mental Health*, 8(2), 71–81.

45. P. Baker. 2014, November 14. "Assertive Outreach Teams Looks to Fill in Critical Mental Health Gap," *Global News*. https://globalnews.ca/news/1673094/assertive-outreach-team-looks-to-fill-in-critical-mental-health-gap.

46. S. Franz and R. Borum. 2010. "Crisis Intervention Teams May Prevent Arrests of People with Mental Illness," *Police Practice and Research*, 12(3), 265–272.

47. P. Roth. 2013, March 18. "Edmonton Police Using Less Force with the Mentally Ill After University of Alberta Course," *Edmonton Sun*. http://edmontonsun.com/2013/03/18/edmonton-police-using-less-force-with-the-mentally-ill-after-university-of-alberta-course/wcm/0ab36288-828a-4185-b0a2-664235cd3c42.

48. S. Kisely, L.A. Campbell, S. Peddle, S. Hare, M. Psyche, D. Spicer, and B. Moore. 2010. "A Controlled Before-and-After Evaluation of a Mobile Crisis Partnership Between Mental Health and Police Services in Nova Scotia," *Canadian Journal of Psychiatry*, 55(10), 662–668.

49. Statistics Canada. 2017, July 11. "Self-Reported Sexual Assault in Canada, 2014," *The Daily*. https://www.statcan.gc.ca/daily-quotidien/170711/dq170711a-eng.pdf.

50. Ibid.

51. London Police Service. 2017. "Review of 'Unfounded' Sexual Assault Cases." https://www.londonpolice.ca/en/about/review-of--unfounded--sexual-assault-cases.aspx.

52. R. Doolittle. 2017, February 3. "Why Police Dismiss 1 in 5 Claims of Sexual Assault as Baseless," *Globe and Mail*. https://www.theglobeandmail.com/news/investigations/unfounded-sexual-assault-canada-main/article33891309.

53. Ibid.

54. R. Doolittle, M. Pereira, L. Blenkinsop, and J. Agius. 2017, February 3. "Will the Police Believe You?" *Globe and Mail*. https://www.theglobeandmail.com/news/investigations/compare-unfounded-sex-assault-rates-across-canada/article33855643.

55. R. Doolittle. 2017, February 28. "The Challenge of Handling Sex Assault in Canada's North," *Globe and Mail.* https://www.theglobeandmail.com/news/investigations/the-challenges-of-handling-sex-assault-in-canadas-north/article34159543.

56. Ibid.

57. London Police Service, "Review of 'Unfounded' Sexual Assault Cases."

58. R. Doolittle. 2017, May 18. "Calgary Begins Canada's First External Audit of Sexual-Assault Case Files," *Globe and Mail.* https://www.theglobeandmail.com/news/national/unfounded-calgary-begins-canadas-first-external-audit-of-sexual-assault-case-files/article35055413.

59. Human Rights Watch. 2013. *Those Who Take Us Away. Abusive Policing and Failures in Protection of Indigenous Women and Girls in Northern British Columbia, Canada.* Toronto: Author, p. 7. http://www.refworld.org/docid/5209e6e94.html.

60. Ibid.

61. Ibid.

62. Vancouver Police Department. 2011. *The Tragedy of Missing and Murdered Aboriginal Women in Canada. We Can Do Better. A Position Paper by the Sisterwatch Project of the Vancouver Police Department and the Women's Memorial March Committee.* Vancouver: Author. https://vancouver.ca/police/assets/pdf/reports-policies/missing-murdered-aboriginal-women-canada-report.pdf.

63. Ontario Human Rights Commission. *Under Suspicion: Research and Consultation Report on Racial Profiling in Ontario.*

64. Human Rights Watch. *Those Who Take Us Away.*

65. B. Noel. 2017, April 3. "Anger and Hope in Val-d'Or," *Vice News Canada.* https://news.vice.com/story/anger-and-hope-in-val-dor.

66. B. Neill. 2016, November 15. "No Charges Against Quebec Provincial Police in Val-d'Or Abuse Scandal," *CBC News.* http://www.cbc.ca/news/canada/montreal/police-abuse-charges-val-d-or-1.3852390.

67. K.B. Wolff and C.L. Cokely. 2007. "'To Protect and To Serve?' An Exploration of Police Conduct in Relation to the Gay, Lesbian, Bisexual, and Transgender Community," *Sexuality and Culture, 11*(2), 1–23.

PART III
THE CRIMINAL COURTS

Chapter 7: The Structure and Operation of the Criminal Courts
Chapter 8: The Prosecution of Criminal Cases
Chapter 9: Sentencing

The criminal courts occupy a strategic position in the Canadian criminal justice system. Important decisions are made at all stages of the court process: the decision of Crown counsel to take a case forward; plea negotiations between the Crown and defence lawyers that may result in a guilty plea in exchange for certain considerations, including dropping some charges; the decisions of judges and juries; and perhaps the most important decision in the entire justice system, whether the charged person is guilty.

In this part, we'll consider the structure and operation of the criminal courts, as well as how cases are processed through the criminal courts. Chapter 7 sets out the structure of the criminal courts in Canada, including the specialized problem-solving courts that have been created in recent years. The flow of cases through the criminal courts is examined, and the issues surrounding the oversight and accountability of the judiciary are considered.

Chapter 8 examines the prosecution of criminal cases, beginning with the pre-trial process. Among the topics discussed are the role of Crown counsel, the laying of an information and laying of a charge, the ways in which an accused can be compelled to appear in court, plea negotiations, the trial, and other topics.

Chapter 9 considers sentencing in the criminal courts, including the purpose and principles of sentencing, the discretion exercised by judges, and Indigenous peoples and sentencing.

© Laurie Justus Pace, Graphics One Design, 2014

CHAPTER 7
THE STRUCTURE AND OPERATION OF THE CRIMINAL COURTS

LEARNING OBJECTIVES

After reading this chapter, you should be able to

- Discuss the structure and operation of the criminal courts.
- Describe specialized problem-solving courts and their effectiveness in addressing the needs of vulnerable accused persons.
- Discuss the operation and objectives of Indigenous courts.
- Describe the challenges that surround providing judicial services in remote areas of the country by the circuit courts.
- Identify and describe the professionals who comprise the courtroom workgroup.
- Describe the process by which judges are appointed in Canada and discuss the issues surrounding this process.
- Identify and discuss the issues surrounding judicial ethics and accountability.
- Discuss the issue of case delay and the impact of the Supreme Court of Canada decision in *R. v. Jordan*.

THE CRIMINAL COURTS IN CANADA

The criminal courts play an important, multifaceted role in Canada's criminal justice system, yet for many Canadians, the courts remain something of a mystery. This vagueness is due, in some measure, to the fact that the deliberations of judges and the activities of Crown counsel and defence lawyers are much less visible than the activities of the police.

Although the process for disposing of cases has changed little over the past two centuries, the cases coming into the courts are more complex than they once were, the legal issues are more challenging, and workloads are heavier. Many observers attribute these increased workloads and the resulting strains to the impact of the *Charter of Rights and Freedoms*.

The courts are responsible for determining the guilt or innocence of accused persons and for imposing an appropriate sentence on those who are convicted. They are also responsible for ensuring that the rights of accused persons are protected; this often involves monitoring the activities of the various agents of the criminal justice system (including the police and systems of corrections). The decisions of the courts reflect ongoing efforts to balance the rights of the accused with the need to protect society.

The principle of *judicial independence* is viewed as being essential to the proper functioning of the courts. This principle holds that citizens have the right to have their cases tried by tribunals that are fair, impartial, and immune from political interference (more on judicial independence later in the chapter).

Canada does not have a uniform court system. This often leads to considerable confusion when the various provincial/territorial and federal courts are discussed. This chapter attempts to clearly and concisely describe the system of courts; that said, students are well advised to familiarize themselves with the structure and names of the various courts in their own jurisdiction. Each province and territory maintains a website that provides detailed information on its court system.

With the exception of Nunavut, there are four levels of courts that deal with criminal cases: provincial/territorial courts, provincial/territorial superior courts, provincial appellate courts, and the Supreme Court of Canada (SCC). Nunavut has a unified, or single-level, court, the Nunavut Court of Justice, in which the powers of the lower courts have been combined into one superior court where all judges can hear all types of cases. The SCC is the highest court for all jurisdictions. Figure 7.1 provides an outline of the Canadian criminal court system.

In Figure 7.2, the court system in the province of Ontario is provided as an example of a provincial court structure. The provincial court system in Ontario has two divisions: the Superior Court of Justice and the Ontario Court of Justice. Each of these divisions has a number of other courts.

Figure 7.3 presents an overview of the cases completed in adult criminal courts in 2014–15. Note the large percentage of cases that are related to "Administration of Justice Offences." Figure 7.4 contains statistics from adult criminal courts in Canada for 2014–15. A detailed breakdown of the procedure in criminal cases is presented in Chapter 8 (Figure 8.1). The information in Figure 7.3 indicates that non-violent offences represented more than three-quarters (77 percent) of all cases completed in adult criminal court in 2014–15. Overall, approximately two-thirds (63 percent) of all cases completed in adult criminal court resulted in a finding of guilt. Of those cases that went to trial, the acquittal rate was 4 percent.[1]

Supreme Court of Canada
- established by Parliament
- became the final court of appeal for criminal cases in 1933 and for civil cases in 1949
- has judges who are federally appointed by the prime minister
- operates under the *Supreme Court* Act
- is the final court of appeal for criminal and civil law

Provincial and Territorial Courts of Appeal
- are administered by the provinces and territories
- have judges who are federally appointed
- hears appeals from decisions in superior courts and provincial and territorial courts
- some jurisdictions have a single court with a trial division and an appellate rather than a court of appeal and superior court

Provincial and Territorial Superior Courts
- administered by the provinces
- have judges who are federally appointed
- try the most serious cases
- are the court of first appeal for the provincial and territorial courts

Provincial and Territorial Courts
- are administered by the provinces and territories
- have judges who are provincially or territorially appointed
- hear cases involving federal or provincial and territorial laws (exception is Nunavut where the Court of Justice deals with both territorial and superior court cases)
- have jurisdiction over most criminal offences, traffic violations, and provincial or territorial regulatory offences (i.e., fish and wildlife)
- hear preliminary hearings in serious cases to determine whether there is sufficient evidence to proceed to trial

Federal Court of Appeal
- established by Parliament
- hears appeal from the federal courts
- has judges who are federally appointed
- has some limited criminal jurisdiction

Federal Court
- established by Parliament
- has judges who are federally appointed
- hears matters subject to federal statutes
- has some limited criminal jurisdiction

THE PROVINCIAL/TERRITORIAL COURT SYSTEM

There is some variation in the specific names given to the provincial courts across the country; even so, the system is much the same in all jurisdictions. In every province and territory, except Nunavut, as noted earlier, the court system has two levels: provincial and superior.

The provincial and territorial courts are the lowest level of courts; nearly all criminal cases begin and end in them. Their judges are appointed by the provinces and territories, which also fund these courts and have jurisdiction over them. Provincial and territorial court judges sit without juries. These courts also hear cases under the *Youth Criminal Justice Act* (S.C. 2002, c. 1), as well as cases involving alleged offences against provincial statutes. Provincial and territorial courts may also include family courts and small claims courts. Provincial/territorial court judges (along with justices of the peace)

ONTARIO COURT OF JUSTICE (OCJ)
Provincially Appointed Judges and Justices of the Peace

Criminal Law: Less serious indictable offences (s. 553 of the *Criminal Code*) and summary offences are heard by one judge.

Family Law: Custody, access and support (not during divorce), enforcement of child support, child protection, and adoption matters are heard (where there is no Unified Family Court).

Superior Court of Justice
Federally appointed judges

Drug Treatment Court: This specialist court provides court-supervised treatment for individuals addicted to drugs who have been charged with drug-related offences.

Domestic Violence Court: This court hears cases involving domestic violence.

Mental Health Court: Specialized court for persons with mental health issues who have been charged with a crime. Mental health workers, case managers, and psychiatrists are involved in determining the appropriate treatment or sentence.

Gladue Court: Throughout Canada, judges take into account the unique circumstances of Indigenous accused and Indigenous offenders (includes status and non-status Indians, Métis, and Inuit), based on the *Gladue* decision. Some areas have these specialist courts for Indigenous people facing criminal charges.

Bail Court: Determines whether a person charged with crime(s) should be held in jail until his or her trial is completed. JPs preside over bail hearings.

Youth Court: Presided over by Youth Court judges, hears cases of youths charged under the *Youth Criminal Justice Act*.

COURT OF APPEAL FOR ONTARIO
Federally appointed judges hear appeals from the Superior Court of Justice. Appeals from the Court of Appeal are heard by the Supreme Court of Canada

Family Law: Where there is no Unified Family Court, individual judges hear divorce and property issues, support, and custody and access matters.

Appeals: Appeals of summary offences and family matters from the OCJ are also heard by the Superior Court of Justice.

Unified Family Court: Hears all family matters including divorce (federal) and separation (provincial), presided over by a single judge.

Divisional Court: Hears appeals of interim and final orders and judicial reviews of administrative tribunals, government agencies and boards, and appeals of civil cases where the monetary values is less than $50,000.

Criminal Law: Major offences (s. 469, *Criminal Code*) and hybrid offences are heard by a judge and jury unless the parties consent to judge alone.

Small Claims Court: Civil claims of less than $25,000 are heard by a judge or in some cases a master.

▲ FIGURE 7.2

The Ontario Court System

Source: Ontario Justice Education Network. n.d. "Handout: The Courts of Ontario Flowchart." http://ojen.ca/wp-content/uploads/The-Courts-of -Ontario-Flowchart.pdf. Reprinted by permission of The Ontario Justice Education Network.

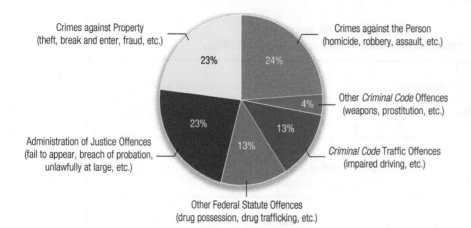

◄ FIGURE 7.3

Cases Completed in Adult Criminal Court, by Type of Offence, 2014–15

Source: A. Maxwell. 2017. "Adult Criminal Court Statistics in Canada, 2014/2015," *Juristat, 37*(1). Statistics Canada Catalogue no. 85-002-X. Ottawa: Minister of Industry, p. 18. http://www .statcan.gc.ca/ pub/85-002-x/2017001/article/ 14699-eng.pdf.

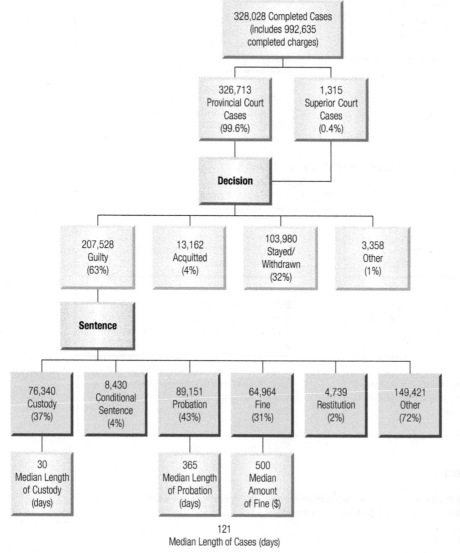

◄ FIGURE 7.4

Adult Criminal Court Statistics in Canada, 2014–15

Questions: (1) What are some of the more significant features of the data presented in Figure 7.4? (2) What do the data indicate about the flow of cases through the courts?

Source: A. Maxwell. 2017. "Adult Criminal Court Statistics in Canada, 2014/2015," *Juristat, 37*(1). Statistics Canada Catalogue no. 85-002-X. Ottawa: Minister of Industry, p. 4. http://www.statcan.gc.ca/ pub/85-002-x/2017001/article/14699-eng.pdf.

may preside over preliminary inquiries, which are held to determine whether there is sufficient evidence to warrant a trial.

Historically, the provincial and territorial courts dealt with less serious cases. This limit has changed in recent years, however; the judges in these courts now hear increasingly serious offences. As well, provincial/territorial court judges are confronted with specialized populations that may strain court resources and challenge judges to apply more appropriate sentences (see Chapter 9). Some observers now argue that the traditional distinction between the provincial/territorial courts and the higher-level superior courts has blurred somewhat in recent years. For example, research has found that although the superior courts hear proportionately more serious offences and more cases involving multiple offences, provincial and territorial courts hear more of these cases in terms of absolute numbers.[2]

PROVINCIAL AND TERRITORIAL SPECIALIZED PROBLEM-SOLVING COURTS

> The current criminal justice system is flawed and people get misguided in it, because once they're labelled an addict or a drug criminal, it's hard for them to claw their way back into society. That's why we do what we do. . . . There's no reason why someone who's been charged with a crime who suffers from a drug problem can't be offered rehabilitation in tandem with their proceedings.
>
> —addiction clinician, Drug Court[3]

Problem-solving courts

Specialized courts that are designed to divert offenders with special needs from the criminal justice system.

In recent years, a number of specialized, **problem-solving courts** have been developed that attempt to divert offenders with special needs from the criminal justice system. These specialized courts include community courts, drug courts, and mental health courts, among others. In addition, several provinces have created courts specifically for Indigenous persons. These courts operate on First Nations reserves, in the north, and in urban centres.

The three defining attributes of problem-solving courts are (1) a focus on addressing the underlying problems of offenders, victims, and communities; (2) interagency and interdisciplinary collaboration; and (3) accountability to the community.[4]

These principles are complementary to those of restorative justice. Unlike traditional courts, these community-based courts have the potential to improve the quality of life in communities, increase resident familiarity with the court process, and increase community satisfaction with the response to persons in conflict.[5]

The intent of these problem-solving courts is to shift from an adversarial or legalistic approach to one centred on treatment and rehabilitation. The focus is on addressing the underlying issues that contributed to criminal offending and developing an intervention plan to address the behaviour as well as the circumstances that contributed to it, while also holding offenders responsible for their behaviour.[6] Unlike the traditional court process, problem-solving courts involve offenders as active participants in addressing their behaviour and needs.

All of these courts are designed to address the revolving door syndrome that affects many offenders, facilitate a collaboration among justice and social service agencies, and formulate and implement problem-solving interventions. Many of the principles of restorative justice are reflected in the practice of problem-solving courts. Table 7.1 provides a comparison of traditional courts with problem-solving courts.

Specialized problem-solving courts incorporate the concept of **therapeutic justice**, which involves the use of the law and the authority of the court as change agents in promoting the health and well-being of offenders while ensuring that their legal rights are protected and that justice is done.[7]

Therapeutic justice

An approach in problem-solving courts that uses the law and the court's authority as change agents to promote the health and well-being of offenders, while ensuring that their legal rights are protected and that justice is done.

TABLE 7.1

TRADITIONAL COURTS COMPARED WITH PROBLEM-SOLVING COURTS

Traditional Court Accountability	Problem-Solving Court Accountability
Use of resources within the court system (probation officers)	Collaboration with professionals outside of the court system (e.g., drug treatment staff, victim services, employment programs)
Impersonal, procedural	Personal, individualized
Little involvement outside of the court (case handed off by judge, no further involvement)	Involvement outside of the court (monitoring, continued supervision)
Focus on processing cases through the system.	Focus on effectiveness of methods (evaluating court effectiveness and if outcomes are being reached
Focus on adjudicating	Focus on problem-solving
Communication through lawyers	Judge communicates directly with "client"

Sources: Criminal Justice. n.d. *Problem-Solving Courts.* http://criminal-justice.iresearchnet.com/system/problem-solving-courts/4; L. Eaton and L. Kaufman. 2005, April 26. "In Problem-Solving Court, Judges Turn Therapist," *New York Times.* http://www.nytimes.com/2005/04/26/nyregion/in-problemsolving-court-judges-turn-therapist.html.

Offender participation in problem-solving courts is voluntary, but there is considerable variation among the problem-solving courts in the types of cases that are handled, eligibility criteria, the sanctions that are imposed, the length and type of supervision, and the involvement of justice, social service, and community agencies.[8] Some take only offenders who have committed less serious crimes, while others accept more serious offenders. The Drug Treatment Courts (DTCs) in Canada, for example, will accept only those offenders who have committed non-violent, drug-related offences.[9] Some courts operate at the pre-plead level, while others require an admission of guilt and the acceptance of responsibility. All of the courts have established screening protocols to ensure that only those persons who meet specific criteria are selected.

To illustrate, Drug Treatment Courts (DTCs) target the needs of addicted persons in conflict with the law; mental health courts attempt to address the needs of mentally ill persons who come into conflict with the law; a Downtown Community Court in Vancouver focuses on offenders in the highly troubled Downtown Eastside area of the city; in Toronto, the Integrated Violence Court handles both criminal and family law cases; and there is an Indigenous community court in Toronto.

In these courts, offenders may avoid incarceration by agreeing to abide by specified conditions. In DTCs, for example, the offender may agree to participate in a drug-abuse treatment program and to submit to regular drug testing.[10]

In Yukon, the Community Wellness Court (CWC) focuses on persons with mental health issues, addiction issues, and other factors that may be related to their offending. Participation by offenders in the CWC is voluntary, and they must admit guilt. Persons who have committed sex offences and serious and violent offences are excluded from the court. The CWC incorporates the principles of therapeutic justice and restorative justice and offers supervision that is culturally relevant, while addressing the needs of the victim and the community. A key feature of the CWC is providing offenders with a support network during and after the program and sentencing.

The CWC has had an impact on the sentencing in Yukon. In one case, both the territorial court and the CWC agreed to let two men afflicted with fetal alcohol spectrum disorder (FASD) remain in supportive housing rather than being sent to jail for their crimes.[11] This decision was also supported by the federal prosecutor.

In 2017, the city of Buffalo, New York, opened the first court for opioid addicts. Watch the video, "Inside the First Court Designed to Keep Opioid Addicts Alive," listed in the Media Links at the end of this chapter.

THE EFFECTIVENESS OF SPECIALIZED COURTS

> She makes me feel like she really cares. I mean, she's always complementing me on doing everything that I'm supposed to be doing, and she lets me know that she's aware of what I am doing, and I feel like I'm a name, not a number.[12]

Assessing the effectiveness of various types of specialty courts is difficult because of the wide variations in admissions criteria, services provided, and how success is measured.[13]

Ongoing issues with many of the courts are high rates of non-compliance, the conditions imposed by the court, and non-completion of programs (84 percent in one study of the Toronto Drug Treatment program).[14] Many of the courts have had difficulty attracting Indigenous men and women.[15]

The use of specialized courts by visible minorities is also unknown, as are the factors that may facilitate or hinder the effectiveness of these courts in a diverse community. Canadian and U.S. research studies suggest that persons who do not have a stable residence, who have substance abuse issues, and who have a severe mental illness were less likely to complete or partially complete a program.[16] The relationship between gender and ethnicity and program completion has not been examined in Canada.

There are also the concerns that the therapeutic approach of the problem-solving courts compromises the fact-finding mandate of the court and that judges may assume the role of therapist, which is outside of their mandated judicial role.[17]

Despite these concerns, there is evidence that these courts may be an effective alternative to the traditional criminal justice system.[18] The courts appear to be most effective in reducing reoffending when the principles of risk, needs, and responsivity (discussed in Chapter 10) are followed—that is, when attention is given to selecting offenders who are most suited for the program in terms of their level of risk, their needs, and their motivation or ability to complete the requirements imposed by the courts.[19,20]

Table 7.2 provides a brief summary of the objectives, processes, and effectiveness of specialized courts. Note that much of the research has been conducted in the U.S. and that studies vary considerably in their design and in the data sets used for the analysis. So caution should be exercised in generalizing these findings.

INDIGENOUS COURTS

Section 718.2(e) of the *Criminal Code* (R.S.C. 1985, c. C-46) requires judges to consider sentencing options other than incarceration, particularly for Indigenous offenders. The principle that the judiciary should make efforts to explore alternative sentencing options—including the use of restorative justice—was affirmed by the Supreme Court of Canada in *R. v. Gladue* ([1999] 1 SCR 688). To address the needs of Indigenous offenders more effectively, several provinces have created courts specifically for Indigenous people.

First Nations communities are becoming increasingly involved in developing community-based courts that are centred on traditional Indigenous spirituality and cultural practices.[21]

The rise of Indigenous courts was also given impetus by the Calls to Action of the Truth and Reconciliation Commission to eliminate the overrepresentation of Indigenous peoples in custody using alternative justice mechanisms.[22]

TABLE 7.2

THE OBJECTIVES, PROCESS, AND EFFECTIVENESS OF SPECIALIZED COURTS

Type of Court	Objective/Process	Outcomes
Mental Health Court (MHC)	Reduce the criminalization of the mentally ill; operate at pre- and post-charge stage	Reduce reoffending by 10 to 75 percent; can reduce the amount of time offenders spend in custody, increase access to treatment services, and change life circumstances (e.g., homelessness), particularly for persons who complete the program and "graduate";[a] court personnel perceive that MHCs improve clients' lives, reduce reoffending, reduce Criminal Court workloads, and hold offenders accountable;[b] an evaluation of the Calgary Diversion Program for mentally disordered offenders found high rates of client satisfaction, and a significant reduction in charges and court appearances and in the need for acute care services;[c] potentially significant reductions in reoffending. An evaluation of the Mental Health Court in St. John's, Newfoundland, found reduced rates of recidivism for participants who completed the program.[d]
Drug Treatment Court (DTC)	Address alcohol/drug addiction of offenders and reduce reoffending; treatment-oriented approach with specified conditions (e.g., abstinence)	May significantly reduce participants' drug use and criminal offending during and following program completion;[e] helps even offenders with lengthy criminal records;[f] offenders who do not complete the program tend to lack family support, have unstable housing, and lack motivation to complete the program;[g] per-client costs are less than in traditional courts;[h] high rates of non-completion; women and Indigenous persons less likely to participate and to complete[i]
Domestic Violence Court (DV)	Stop the cycle of domestic violence; assist victims, their families, and offenders; reduce revictimization	Cases may be heard more quickly than in traditional court; potential increase in guilty pleas; may reduce Crown stay of proceedings; evaluation of Yukon Domestic Violence Treatment Option found low rates of re-assault, effectiveness in dealing with domestic violence cases, but problems connecting with victims.[j] An evaluation of the domestic violence court pilot project in Sydney, Nova Scotia, found strong support from all stakeholders, offender participation in treatment programs, but challenges in engaging victims; however, changes in offender behaviour, rates of reoffending, and rates of revictimization were not assessed[k]; an evaluation of the DV Court pilot project in Moncton, New Brunswick, found that 69 percent ($N = 478$) of offenders reoffended during the three-year pilot period but that the number of victims accessing services increased throughout the pilot period.[l]
Community Wellness Court (CWC; Yukon)	Established to address the needs of offenders with alcohol and drug problems, mental health issues, and other underlying issues that may be related to their offending. Participation is voluntary, and the offender must admit guilt. Incorporates the principles of therapeutic justice and restorative justice, and offers a multifaceted approach to reduce reoffending, while at the same time addressing the needs of victims and the community.	An evaluation found that the CWC is a valuable alternative to the traditional criminal court and was effective in meeting its objectives. Offenders who completed the program felt that it was very helpful to them and provided an opportunity for them to change life direction. A major challenge is the high rate of non-completion.[m]

[a] S. Lange, J. Rehm, and S. Popova. 2011. "The Effectiveness of Criminal Justice Diversion Initiatives in North America: A Systematic Literature Review," *International Journal of Forensic Mental Health, 10*(3), 200–214; R.D. Schneider. 2010. "Mental Health Courts and Diversion Programs: A Global Survey," *International Journal of Law and Psychiatry, 33*(4), 201–206; C.M. Sarteschi, M. G. Vaughn, and K. Kim. 2011. "Assessing the Effectiveness of Mental Health Courts: A Quantitative Review," *Journal of Criminal Justice, 39*(1), 12–20.

[b] D.E. McNiel and R.L. Binder. 2010. "Stakeholder Views of a Mental Health Court," *International Journal of Law and Psychiatry, 33*(4), 227–235.

[c] C. Mitton, L. Simpson, L. Gardner, F. Barnes, and G. McDougall. 2007. "Calgary Diversion Program: A Community-based Alternative to Incarceration for Mentally Ill Offenders," *Journal of Mental Health Policy Economic, 10*(3), 145–51. https://www.ncbi.nlm.nih.gov/pubmed/17890831.

[d] D. Orr. 2017. "A Criminal or Therapeutic Justice System? Examining Specialized Treatment Courts," *Criminal Law Quarterly, 64*(1–2), 180–199.

[e] J. Roman. 2013. "Cost-Benefit Analysis of Criminal Justice Reforms," *NIJ Journal, 272*, 31–38. https://www.ncjrs.gov/pdffiles1/nij/241929.pdf.

[f] Public Safety Canada. 2007. *Toronto Drug Treatment Court Project.* Ottawa: National Crime Prevention Centre. https://www.publicsafety.gc.ca/cnt/rsrcs/pblctns/drgtrtmnt-trnt/drgtrtmnt-trnt-eng.pdf.

(continued)

[g] B. Newton-Taylor, L. Gliksman, and J. Patra. 2009. "Toronto Drug Treatment Court: Participant Intake Characteristics as Predictors of 'Successful' Program Completion," *Journal of Drug Issues, 39*(4), 965–988.

[h] M.W. Finigan, S.M. Carey, and A. Cox. 2007. *Impact of a Mature Drug Court Over 10 Years of Operation: Recidivism and Cost.* Washington, DC: U.S. Department of Justice, National Institute of Justice. https://www.ncjrs.gov/pdffiles1/nij/grants/219225.pdf.

[i] P. Allard, P.T. Lyons, and R. Elliott. 2011. *Impaired Judgment: Assessing the Appropriateness of Drug Treatment Courts as a Response to Drug Use in Canada.* Toronto: Canadian HIV/AIDS Legal Network. http://www.aidslaw.ca/site/wp-content/uploads/2013/09/DTCs-Oct11-E.pdf; Department of Justice Canada. 2015. *Drug Treatment Court Funding Program Evaluation: Final Report.* Ottawa: Author. http://www.justice.gc.ca/eng/rp-pr/cp-pm/eval/rep-rap/2015/dtcfp-pfttt/dtcfp-pfttt.pdf.

[j] J.P. Hornick, M. Boyes, L. Tutty, and L. White. 2005. *The Domestic Violence Treatment Option (DVTO), Whitehorse, Yukon: Final Evaluation Report.* Ottawa: National Crime Prevention Centre. http://www.yukoncourts.ca/pdf/cwc_evaluation_june_2007_to_december_2013.pdf.

[k] D. Crocker, B. Crocker, and M. Dawson. 2016. *Domestic Violence Court Pilot Project, Sydney, Nova Scotia.* Halifax: Department of Justice, Nova Scotia.

[l] C.R. Dilworth and T.G. Dilworth. 2011. *The Domestic Violence Court (DV Court) Pilot Project, Moncton, New Brunswick.* Saint John, NB: New Brunswick Department of Public Safety. https://www.gnb.ca/0012/Womens-Issues/DomesticViolenceCourt/2011-01VictimsOffenders.pdf.

[m] J.P. Hornick, K. Kluz, and L.D. Bertrand. 2011. *An Evaluation of Yukon's Community Wellness Court.* Whitehorse: Yukon Justice. http://www.yukoncourts.ca/pdf/cwc_final_report_05-10-11.pdf

These courts operate in both rural and urban centres. Some are referred to as "Gladue Courts," referring to an SCC decision in *R. v. Gladue* (discussed in Chapter 9), which held that specific attention must be given by the criminal justice system to the unique circumstances of Indigenous persons whenever their liberty is at stake. These courts provide an opportunity to consider the special circumstances of Indigenous offenders and to utilize alternative sentencing options.[23]

There are a number of Indigenous courts operating across the country under the auspices of provincial courts.

GLADUE COURTS (TORONTO)

The Gladue Courts are a component of the Ontario Court of Justice. These courts deal with the cases of Indigenous people who have been charged in Toronto, and handle bail hearings, remands, trials, and sentencing. The judge, the Crown, and the defence lawyers, court clerks, and court workers are all Indigenous persons. When the cases are processed, every attempt is made to explore all possible sentencing options and alternatives to imprisonment.

TSUU T'INA NATION PEACEMAKER COURT (ALBERTA)

This provincial court, located on the Tsuu Nation near Calgary, is centred on peacemaking circles. This provincial court has an Indigenous judge, Crown prosecutor, and court clerks. Adult and youth cases (except those involving homicide and sexual assault) can be referred to peacemaking circles by the court. To be eligible for referral, the offender must admit responsibility for his or her actions, and the victim must agree to participate.

Eligible cases are assigned to a peacemaker, who facilitates a circle healing process involving Elders, the victim, the offenders, and others. In the circle, the participants discuss what happened, the impact of the offender's actions, and what should be done. Final agreements may require the offender to provide restitution, attend counselling, and/or to complete a number of community service hours. A final ceremony is held when the offender has completed the provisions in the agreement. A report is sent to the Tsuu T'ina court, where the Crown counsel reviews the case and, if satisfied, drops the charges against the offender. If the charge is not dropped, the report from the peacemaking circle will be submitted to the judge at sentencing.

INDIGENOUS PEOPLE'S COURT IN (THUNDER BAY, ONTARIO)

This court is a collaborative initiative of the Thunder Bay Indian Friendship Centre, in partnership with Nishnawbe-Aski Legal Services. It uses a restorative justice approach to sentencing and draws upon Indigenous culture and traditions to help persons who self-identify as First Nation, Indigenous, Inuit, or Métis and are in conflict with the law.

Elders play a key role in the court. To qualify to appear in the court, persons must plead guilty and accept responsibility for their offences. The initial focus of the court is on non-violent offences. At the opening of the court, the executive director of the Thunder Bay Indian Friendship Centre stated, "This court will be a powerful process to promote healing and reconciliation in our community and to use the teachings of Indigenous people to provide a holistic approach to justice."[24]

Gladue Courts continue to be established across the country, including, in 2017, a Wellness and Gladue Court in Cape Breton, Nova Scotia, based on a partnership between the Wagmatcook and Wacobah First Nations. Listen to an interview with one of the founders of the court at http://www.cbc.ca/player/play/929008707950.

In an attempt to make the justice system more relevant to Indigenous people, Saskatchewan has established a Cree Court in Prince Albert. This court travels to remote communities to hear cases. Its judges and lawyers are Cree speakers, and it is often attended by a Cree-speaking probation officer. Translators are provided when necessary. This court makes it possible for crime victims, witnesses, and defendants to speak in their own language.

The Cree Court and similar initiatives are designed to address the serious issues that surround the delivery of justice services in many rural and remote Indigenous communities.

Critics have argued that, despite the development of alternative Indigenous-centred justice forums, there is still in Canadian criminal justice the absence of an "Aboriginal voice" that would legitimize the court process and reduce what is referred to by one observer as the "illegitimate colonial control over Aboriginal Canadians."[25]

PROVINCIAL/TERRITORIAL CIRCUIT COURTS

In many northern and remote areas, judicial services are often provided via circuit courts. Circuit court parties, composed of a judge, a court clerk, a defence lawyer, a Crown counsel, and perhaps a translator, travel to communities (generally by plane) to hold court. Many communities are served every month; others are visited quarterly or even less often if there are no cases to be heard or if the weather or mechanical

▲ A circuit court party (left) arrives in the community of Qikiqtarjuaq, Nunavut (see map).

Courtesy of C. John Thompson

problems with the court plane prevent a scheduled visit. The most extensive provincial/territorial circuit court systems are in the Northwest Territories, northwestern Ontario, northern Quebec, and Nunavut.

Most of the communities are too small to have courthouses, and so the court is held in schools, community centres, or other buildings that are available. Unlike in more urban areas, the circuit court hearings are often a community event, and there are often many persons from the community, of all ages, observing the proceedings.

Concerns about the circuit court system include the lengthy court dockets resulting from the backlog of cases; time constraints on the court party, which often preclude effective Crown and defence preparation and result in marathon court sessions, frequently lasting up to 12 hours; the shortage of interpreters as the Indigenous person accused may understand little English or French and even less of the legal terminology spoken in court; and the general difficulties arising from the cultural differences between Canadian law and its practitioners and Indigenous offenders, victims, and communities.[26] The issue of case delay in these types of cases may become even more of an issue with the ruling of the SCC in the case of *R. v. Jordan* that set timelines for cases to be resolved in the criminal courts (see below).

Circuit court judges often face a difficult decision: Should they remove the convicted person from the community and place him or her in confinement hundreds or even thousands of kilometres away? To address this concern, the circuit courts are encouraging community Elders to participate in the court process and are supporting the development of community forums for dispute resolution and for alternatives to incarceration. Restorative justice strategies are often applied in this environment. However, circuit court judges must balance the need to develop culturally and community-relevant approaches to conflict resolution and case processing with the need to ensure that the rights and safety of crime victims are protected. This balance is especially important in cases involving women and young girls who have been the victims of spousal or sexual assault. For a description of a typical circuit court hearing day, see Court File 7.1.

THE PROVINCIAL/TERRITORIAL SUPERIOR COURTS

The superior courts are the highest level of courts in a province/territory and are administered by provincial and territorial governments; however, superior court judges are appointed and paid by the federal government. The name of the superior court generally identifies its location (for example, the Court of Queen's Bench of Manitoba). About 10 percent of criminal cases are heard in the superior courts.

Superior courts generally have two levels: trial and appeal. These two levels may be included in the same court, with two divisions (trial and appeal), or they may involve two separate courts. In Ontario, however, the Court of Appeal is independent and separate from the Superior Court of Justice and the Ontario Court of Justice, which are the main two trial courts in the province.

The trial-level superior court hears cases involving serious criminal offences; the appeal-level superior court hears criminal appeals (and civil appeals as well) from the superior trial court. The trial court may be known as the Supreme Court or the Court of Queen's Bench; the appeal court is usually called the Court of Appeal. These courts

CIRCUIT COURT DAY, NORTHERN SASKATCHEWAN

August 15, 2002: It's a nice day, so people amble about outside, waiting for the judge to arrive. A big fellow wears a black shirt which taunts: "I DID NOT ESCAPE. THEY GAVE ME A DAY PASS." On one side of the building is located the community hall, which serves as both bingo parlour and courtroom—when a trial runs too long, the bingo players bang on the door to be let in—and on the other side is the village office. All the windows have bars or are covered with wire mesh, which is why it seems such a dismal place. The railing on the stairs has mostly fallen away, and the floor of the entryway has a gaping hole in it. How someone hasn't broken their leg is a wonder. On the outside wall of the village office, in bright blue paint, is scribbled "F***" in huge letters; on the community-hall side, there's a smaller "F***" painted in the same painful blue. Piles of garbage and rubble are scattered around.

The interior is not much better. The walls are streaked and need a paint job, the grey-white floor has tiles missing. An old, faded red Christmas decoration hangs from the Exit sign, which has not lit up in years. The smell of cigarettes, smoked during frantic rounds of bingo, hangs in the air. A steel door right near the judge's chair opens onto the "executive washroom," a small space with toilet, sink, and one chair. This is the defence lawyer's consultation room, where he or she discusses a client's case—often for the first time. The lawyer sits on the toilet, the client on the chair, or the other way around.

The first group of accused file in. Since they are being held in custody, all are handcuffed and shackled, looking haggard from lack of sleep...The captives sit in chairs directly behind the prosecutor, which, he admits, makes him very nervous. Quietly, a toddler escapes from his stroller and runs toward his father. Despite his fetters, he lifts the child to his knee and kisses him. Another young prisoner, wearing a red Indian Posse bandana, sits and smooches with his girl, who is about seven months pregnant. She is oblivious to his chains. Another shackled captive explains that he is trying to get back into school: the judge listens as he munches on an apple. An attractive young woman is called to the witness stand, which consists of a rickety chair. She wobbles, obviously inexperienced at walking with her legs chained. The court is told that, under the influence of alcohol, she stabbed her husband twice. The wounds were not life-threatening. She has a history of depression—twice she has tried seriously to commit suicide—and no previous record. She is given a suspended sentence, and ordered to attend an alcohol treatment centre. The RCMP officer undoes her handcuffs and shackles and she joins the crowd in the back of the room.

Source: M. Siggins. 2005. *Bitter Embrace: White Society's Assault on the Woodland Cree.* Toronto: McClelland & Stewart, pp. 291–292. Copyright © 2005 by Maggie Siggins. Reprinted by permission of McClelland & Stewart, a division of Penguin Random House Canada Limited and by permission of the author.

hear cases involving the most serious offences, such as murder. Trials at this level may involve juries.

After a case has been decided at the trial level, the accused has the right to appeal the verdict or the sentence, or both, to a higher court. Appeals of provincial court decisions may have to be heard first in a superior court. Appeals from the trial divisions of the superior courts go directly to the provincial or territorial court of appeal. There is one court of appeal in each province and territory, except in Quebec and Alberta, where there are two. In all provinces, these courts are called the Court of Appeal (for example, the British Columbia Court of Appeal or the Quebec Court of Appeal).

The primary activities of appeal courts centre on reviewing decisions of the lower courts. The focus is on how the law was applied to the facts in the case.[27] While many preliminary matters are dealt with by a single judge, certain final hearings require at least three judges to hear the appeal, and the final decisions rests with the majority. Oral arguments are made to a three-judge panel by lawyers for both parties. However, it has been pointed out that appeal court judges are much more isolated than trial court judges, spending most of their time "researching and writing their opinions in their own chambers, enjoying only limited contact with others (primarily their own law clerks)."[28]

There are instances in which appeal courts have chastised lower court judges. In one case, a judge of the Ontario Court of Justice was rebuked by an Ontario Superior Court judge for contributing to the "culture of complacency" that afflicts the criminal justice system. The Superior Court judge cited noted that the lower-court judge ended court sessions when there were still witnesses waiting to testify, resulting in lengthy delays in the case.[29]

THE SUPREME COURT OF CANADA

If at least one appellate judge dissents (that is, does not agree with the majority), the unsuccessful party may pursue another appeal at the federal level. The "court of last resort"—the Supreme Court of Canada—is located in Ottawa but hears cases from all provinces and territories. The Supreme Court was established under the *Constitution Act* (1867), which authorized Parliament to establish a general court of appeal for Canada, although the bill creating the court was not passed until 1875.

The governor in council appoints the nine judges of the Supreme Court; those chosen must be superior court judges or lawyers with at least 10 years' standing at the bar in a province or territory. The appointees are selected from the major regions of the country; however, three of the judges on the court must be from Quebec (http://www .scc-csc.gc.ca). The decisions of the Supreme Court are final and cannot be appealed. However, in some instances Parliament has passed legislation in response to a decision of the Supreme Court that has effectively changed the result of the decision. This occurred in the case of *R. v. Feeney* ([1997] 3 SCR 1008).

Two other federal courts are the Federal Court and the Tax Court. The Federal Court has a Trial Court and a Court of Appeal, and hears all cases that concern matters of federal law, including copyright law, maritime law, the *Canadian Human Rights Act* (R.S.C. 1985, c. H-6), the *Immigration and Refugee Protection Act* (S.C. 2001, c. 27), and appeals from the Parole Board of Canada.

While the Supreme Court receives hundreds of applications for cases to be considered, it generally grants only about 10 percent of requests. Cases are heard by an odd number of judges—five, seven, or nine—to avoid ties. The cases that are decided by the Supreme Court of Canada often involve interpretations of the *Charter of Rights and Freedoms* or complicated issues in private and public law.

In many cases that come before the Supreme Court, either the defendant or the Crown asks for permission, or *leave*, to appeal the decision of a lower court. In some instances, the federal government asks the Supreme Court for a legal opinion on an important legal question, a process that is referred to as a *reference*. In 1998, the federal government asked

▶ The Supreme Court of Canada sitting

CP PHOTO/Jonathan Hayward

the Court to decide whether Quebec could secede unilaterally from Canada under the Constitution and whether international law gives the province of Quebec the right to secede unilaterally from Canada (*Reference re Secession of Quebec*, [1998] 2 SCR 217). In another case, the federal government asked the Supreme Court for a non-binding opinion as to whether the government could redefine marriage to allow for same-sex marriages. The court ruled (*Reference re Same-Sex Marriage*, 2004 SCC 79) that the federal government could do so; this resulted in legislation giving gays and lesbians the right to marry.

In many of the cases heard by the SCC, there is a tension between individual rights as set out in the *Charter of Rights and Freedoms* and the need to protect the general public. This tension is illustrated in *R. v. Sharpe* (2001 SCC 2). In *Sharpe*, the Supreme Court upheld the law relating to the possession of child pornography (with certain exceptions; see Court File 7.2). In other cases, laws have been struck down. In *R. v. Morgentaler* ([1988] 1 SCR 30), for example, the SCC held that the procedures for obtaining a therapeutic abortion as defined in section 287 of the *Criminal Code* infringed on the right to security of the person because of the uneven availability of services across the country. And, in *R. v. Zundel* ([1992] 2 SCR 731), the court held that the offence of spreading false news (s. 181) and even hate literature is constitutionally invalid because it infringes the fundamental freedoms of thought, belief, opinion, and expression and is not a reasonable limit in a democratic society. Although the laws referred to in these cases are still part of the *Criminal Code*, they cannot be used to prosecute anyone.

The decisions of the Supreme Court in Charter-related cases can also affect legal procedures. In *R. v. Stinchcombe* ([1991] 3 SCR 326), for example, the SCC held that the prosecution must give all relevant evidence gathered by the police to the defence to permit a defendant to make a full answer and defence to the charges.

COURT FILE 7.2

R. V. SHARPE: A CASE OF COMPETING RIGHTS

In *R. v. Sharpe* (2001 SCC 2), the accused was charged with two counts of possession of child pornography under section 163.1(4) of the *Criminal Code* and two counts of possession of child pornography for the purposes of distribution or sale under section 163.1(3). Among other materials, Sharpe had in his possession pictures of young boys engaged in sexual activities and a collection of child pornography stories (titled "Kiddie Kink Classics") that he had written.

At trial, the B.C. Supreme Court acquitted Sharpe of the charge of possession of child pornography. The acquittal was later upheld by the B.C. Court of Appeal, which stated that the *Criminal Code* section on possession of child pornography was "one step removed from criminalizing simply having objectionable thoughts."

The case was appealed to the Supreme Court of Canada by the province of British Columbia. The federal government, most provincial governments and police associations, and a variety of child advocate and child protection organizations argued that the need to protect children from sexual exploitation outweighed any protections that might be offered to Sharpe under the *Canadian Charter of Rights and Freedoms*. In a unanimous ruling, the Supreme Court upheld the law that makes it a crime to possess child pornography. Sharpe was

convicted of possessing more than 400 photographs that met the legal definition of child pornography. "Freedom of expression," the chief justice stated, "is not absolute," given the constitutional limitations provided under section 1 of the Charter, which expressly permit the court to consider "reasonable limits in a free and democratic society."

The controversial part of the Supreme Court's decision was its creation of two exceptions. The first of these asserted the right to protect private works of the imagination or photographic depictions of one's own body; the second permitted the possession of child pornography by those who create sexually explicit depictions of children for their own personal pleasure. The Supreme Court of Canada directed that Sharpe be retried on the charge of possessing child pornography and be required to prove that his case met the requirements of one of the two exceptions. Some critics asserted that the court's decision was tantamount to a legalization of child pornography. In March 2002, a B.C. Supreme Court justice ruled that Sharpe's written work, which contained descriptions of child sex and violence, had "artistic value," and Sharpe was acquitted.

Source: *R. v. Sharpe*, 2002 BCSC 423.

The SCC also hears cases that are surrounded by controversy. In 2011, the SCC ruled in favour of PHS Community Services Society, a non-profit organization that operates Insite, the supervised injection site for drug users in Vancouver. In the case of *Canada (Attorney General) v. PHS Community Services Society* (2011 SCC 44), the court held that efforts of the federal government to close the facility violated the rights of life and security of the person under section 7 of the *Charter of Rights and Freedoms*.[30]

Recall from Chapter 2 that interest groups often play a role in the formulation and application of the criminal law. The Supreme Court frequently permits intervenors (persons or parties not directly involved in the case) to file written materials and, in some instances, to make oral arguments in support of their position. The extent to which these intervenors affect the final outcome of a case is uncertain.

THE COURTROOM WORKGROUP

The professionals who populate the criminal court courtroom can be described as the **courtroom workgroup**.[31] Its permanent members have traditionally been the presiding judge, Crown counsel, and defence lawyer. Other professionals may appear on occasion (e.g., expert witnesses). The advent of problem-solving courts (discussed earlier in the chapter) has resulted in an expansion of the courtroom workgroup to include representatives from agencies and community organizations; various restorative justice approaches include members of the community as well.

Courtroom workgroup

The criminal justice professionals, including the judge, Crown counsel, and defence lawyer, who are present in the criminal court courtroom.

THE JUDGE

The presiding judge in a criminal case is a "trier of fact" and plays a variety of roles. These include interpreting the law, assessing whether evidence can be admitted, ruling on motions made by the Crown counsel and defence lawyer, and determining the truthfulness of evidence. In most cases, it also includes making a decision on the guilt or innocence of the accused and passing sentence. A key role of the judge is serving as a "gatekeeper" of evidence presented during the trial, including expert testimony, one legal scholar noting,

"As gate-keepers, judges serve to balance the utility of [expert testimony] against its possible prejudicial effects."[32]

In cases involving a jury, it is the jury that is the trier of fact, and the judge assumes the role of explaining legal procedures and specifics about the law, as well as giving the jury instructions on how the law is to be applied in reaching its decision on the guilt or innocence of the accused.[33] In all cases, it is the judge who determines the sentence. For each sentence, judges are expected to provide oral and written reasons for their decision.

▼ The Honourable Steve A. Coroza, the first Filipino-Canadian appointed to the Ontario Superior Court of Justice

Courtesy of Michael Shaw, Ashley & Crippen Photographers

JUSTICES OF THE PEACE

Justices of the peace (JPs) play a significant, but often overlooked, role in the criminal justice system. The legal authority of JPs is set out in federal and provincial/territorial statutes and regulations, including provincial/territorial justice of the peace acts and the *Criminal Code*. There are notable differences between judges and justices of the peace. Although both are appointed by their respective provincial/territorial government, judges are required to be experienced lawyers, while JPs are not lawyers. Other qualifications for JPs are set out in provincial/territorial legislation.

JPs play a variety of roles depending upon the jurisdiction. In Ontario, JPs and provincial court judges compose the Ontario Court of Justice, one of Ontario's two trial courts have primary responsibility for issuing search warrants and conducting bail hearings. In addition, JPs preside over hearings involving provincial/territory regulatory offences, including those that are liquor and traffic-related. JPs may also preside in small claims courts, work in court registries, and handle court scheduling. JPs are also involved in hearing applications for, and granting or denying applications by the police for, search warrants. One JP in Ontario referred to their role with respect to search warrants as that of a middleman "between an overactive policeman, and a member of the public."[34]

Given their role, there has in recent years been an increased focus on the qualifications and training of JPs. Critics contend that some JPs are appointed based on political patronage rather than qualifications and also that legal errors made by JPs result in accused persons being improperly detained at their bail hearing.[35]

DEFENCE LAWYERS

Defence lawyers represent persons who are charged with a criminal offence(s). The primary responsibility of the defence lawyer is to ensure that the rights of the accused person are protected throughout the criminal justice process. Defence lawyers are often actively involved in attempting to negotiate a plea for their client outside of the formal court process (see Chapter 8). At trial, the defence lawyer presents evidence and questions witnesses, experts, and others (and less often, the accused) to build a case as to the innocence of the accused. The defence lawyer is also involved in cross-examining witnesses for the prosecution and challenging the evidence that is presented by the Crown. Some accused persons are represented by legal aid lawyers (see Chapter 8).

There are concerns with the lack of diversity among defence lawyers and with the challenges faced by women lawyers in pursing the profession. A report by the Criminal Lawyers Association of Ontario[36] focusing on the retention of women in criminal law found that women lawyers who participated in focus group discussions identified a number of challenges, including the unpredictability of work hours, the unpredictability of income, and the difficulties of having and raising children while working in criminal law, as probable reasons why women may choose to leave the private practice of criminal law.

The results of a survey (N = 224) conducted as part of the study found that women were treated differently from men in the courtroom by judges, Crown counsel, and other court staff, with only 22 percent of respondents viewing women and men as treated the same. Sixty-one percent of women reported that they had considered leaving the practice of criminal law, citing low pay, long hours, and the challenges of dealing with Legal Aid as reasons that had fuelled that consideration.[37] The study also found that women were leaving the practice of criminal law at a much higher rate than their male colleagues.[38]

Listen to a panel discussion of the issue at http://www.cbc.ca/radio/thecurrent/the-current-for-march-7-2016-1.3478812/women-leaving-criminal-defence-law-due-to-discrimination-new-report-says-1.3478945.

DUTY COUNSEL

The duty counsel lawyer is first point of contact for a person who has been detained or arrested. The duty counsel's advice can be provided via telephone or in person. Duty counsel may also represent an accused in court. These services are often provided as part of a provincial or territorial legal aid plan to ensure that persons who cannot afford to hire a private lawyer have representation.

CROWN COUNSEL

Crown attorneys are lawyers who represent the Crown (or government) in court and who are responsible for prosecuting criminal cases. The responsibility for prosecuting cases is shared between the provinces and the federal government, with provincially appointed Crown attorneys prosecuting *Criminal Code* offences and federally appointed Crown attorneys prosecuting persons charged with violating other federal statutes, such as the *Controlled Drugs and Substances Act* (S.C. 1996, c. 19). In Yukon, the Northwest Territories, and Nunavut, federally appointed Crown attorneys are responsible for prosecuting all cases.

Crown counsel have been described as being a "cornerstone of the criminal justice system."[39] Crown counsel carry out their tasks on behalf of the community, rather than the victims of crime. These lawyers are responsible for laying charges against the accused in some provinces and are also involved in the prosecution of accused persons.

The role, duties, and responsibilities of provincial Crown counsel are set out in legislation. Federal prosecutors are employed by the Public Prosecutor Service of Canada and operate within the framework of the *Director of Public Prosecutions Act* (S.C. 2006, c. 9, s. 121). These Crown attorneys prosecute cases under federal statutes, including drugs, organized crime, and terrorism.[40]

Crown attorneys are involved in a range of activities. They provide advice to police officers at the pre-charge stage; they prepare for trial (for example, they collect evidence from the police and other sources, research case precedents, and interview victims, witnesses, and experts who may be called to testify); and they prepare for post-trial appeals. Crown counsel are also involved in plea bargaining (see below), developing trial strategies, managing witnesses, arguing conditions of bail, recommending sentences to the court, and appealing sentences deemed too lenient. Crown attorneys must also remain up-to-date on changes in the law and in judicial precedent, including decisions in Charter cases.

Crown prosecutors exercise a considerable amount of discretion in case processing, and this power has been reaffirmed by the Supreme Court of Canada (*R. v. Jolivet*, 2000 SCC 29).

At trial, the Crown presents the state's case in an attempt to prove beyond a reasonable doubt that the accused is guilty of the offence with which he or she has been charged. Historically, the role of Crown counsel was viewed as one of being a "representative of justice" rather than that of "partisan advocate": "Their role is not to win convictions at any cost but to put before the court all available, relevant, and admissible evidence necessary to enable the court to determine the guilt or innocence of the accused."[41]

This principle was established nearly 60 years ago by the SCC in *Boucher v. The Queen* ([1955] SCR 16): "It cannot be overemphasized that the purpose of a criminal prosecution is not to obtain a conviction. . . . The role of prosecutor excludes any notion of winning or losing; his function is a matter of public duty."[42] How this view of the Crown's role is reconciled with the demands of an adversarial system remains to be explored.

The challenge of increasing workloads in the criminal justice system is reflected in the work of Crown counsel, many of whom process up to 50 cases a day and work

90 hours a week. In the words of one Crown counsel, "You know I've winged many cases. I've seen me do trials when the first time I ever read the file was when I was calling my first witness 'cause I never had time. Just didn't have time to prepare for it. I'll call my witness, and while he's walking up to the stand I'll read his statement, and then I'll find out what he's got to say and then I'll question him. I did that many times."[43]

Increasingly, prosecutors must deal with sensitive cases involving sexual offences, family violence, and the victimization of children. New technologies, such as DNA evidence, require prosecutors to have specialized knowledge (or access to it). When prosecutors travel with circuit courts or to satellite court locations, they often have little time for case preparation. Other challenges are the cultural and language barriers that are encountered in northern and remote Indigenous communities as well as in some urban centres.

In recent years, Crown counsel have experienced increasing workloads due to the complexity of criminal cases, budget reductions, and legislation enacted by the federal government, including mandatory minimum sentences that may encourage accused persons to take their case to trial.[44] The role of Crown counsel in prosecuting cases is discussed in further detail in Chapter 8. Note that the PPSC is not an investigative agency and does not conduct investigations.[45]

OTHER COURTROOM PERSONNEL

Besides lawyers and judges, other court personnel play important roles in the processing and disposition of cases. Court administrators—also known as court registrars or court clerks—perform a variety of administrative tasks. For example, they appoint staff, manage court finances, sign orders and judgments, receive and record documents filed in the court, and certify copies of court proceedings. On request, the court reporter can make a verbatim (word for word) transcript of everything that is said during the trial. This is possible because the proceedings are tape recorded.

Sheriffs support the court by assisting in jury management, escorting accused and convicted persons, and providing security in the courtroom. In some provinces, they serve legal documents, seize goods, and collect fines.

FEATURES OF THE COURTROOM WORKGROUP

The members of the courtroom workgroup—the judge, Crown counsel, and defence lawyer—are permanent fixtures in the court, have professional and often personal relationships, and, it is argued, share a common commitment to the adversarial system of criminal justice.[46] The diversity of Canadian society is generally not reflected in the courtroom workgroup.

Significantly, and in contrast to restorative justice approaches, most accused persons play little or no role in the court process, are merely visitors (albeit for some accused, frequent visitors) to the court, and have no relationships with the others. Too often, offenders are also peripheral to the courtroom workgroup and are merely passive bystanders. As one offender with a lengthy criminal record commented, "When I go to court, my lawyer tells me to 'shut up' and not say a word. He gets me the best possible deal" (personal communication with C.T Griffiths).

This results in a situation where offenders may have numerous convictions on their record, and periods of incarceration, yet have never spoken in court or engaged in a discussion about their behaviour and what they understand about why they commit crimes and the impact of their criminality on them, their families, victims, and the community. This lessens the likelihood that significant changes will be made in their attitudes and behaviour.

The power differential between the decision makers and the persons who become involved in the criminal justice system has been extensively documented and is often cited as a reason for the failures of the criminal justice system. Nearly two-thirds of defendants plead guilty, and many of these pleas are a result of plea negotiations (see Chapter 8). Accused who appear in criminal courts are disproportionately Indigenous, Black, and disenfranchised persons from lower socio-economic levels of the community. Many are mentally ill. Two key issues for many accused persons are the access to legal representation and access to legal aid (discussed in Chapter 8).

Concerns with the vulnerabilities of accused persons and the inability of the criminal courts to address the needs of persons with special challenges have been a major catalyst for the development of several types of specialized courts, discussed above. As well, it is argued that restorative justice approaches hold considerably more promise to address the needs of the community, the victim, and the offender. A key feature of restorative justice is the involvement of the community and a reduced role for criminal justice professionals.

WHERE DO JUDGES COME FROM?

Judges at the provincial court level are appointed by provincial governments, while judges of the superior courts are appointed by the federal government. Appointments are for life so that once on the bench, judges need not consider the career implications when making controversial decisions. The appointment of judges is the historical legacy from England, "The courts were the King's courts and the judges were the King's judges."[47] A current issue is the delay associated with appointing new judges, which would assist in ensuring that cases are heard in a timely manner.

Each province/territory has in place a Judicial Advisory Committee composed of lawyers and laypersons generally appointed by the attorney general. These screening committees forward nominations to the justice minister, who makes the final appointments. At the federal level, regional committees are composed largely of members of the legal profession and community members appointed by Ottawa, who create lists of candidates who are forwarded to the Department of Justice and debated in cabinet. It is argued that this process mitigates diversity in the judiciary.

Under the Canadian Constitution, SCC judges are to be appointed by the governor general of Canada. In practice, however, it is the prime minister and cabinet who make the selections, and approval by the governor general is a formality. The prime minister is not required to seek approval of the selection via a vote in Parliament nor is required to consult with provincial or territorial leaders as to whom should be recommended for appointment. The *Supreme Court Act* (R.S.C. 1985, c. S-26) does require that the potential appointee be a judge in a provincial superior court or have at least 10 years' experience as a lawyer. As noted earlier, the Act also stipulates that at least three of the judges on the nine-judge court must be from Quebec.

Concerns about the lack of consultation led in 2004 to the creation of an ad hoc Parliamentary committee that reviews a list of seven candidates, and shortlists three from which the prime minister will select one. However, the final decision rests with the prime minister in the executive branch of government. The prime minister's selection cannot be blocked by either the committee or Parliament. This process is in contrast to the procedure in the U.S., where presidential appointments to the U.S. Supreme Court must be confirmed by the U.S. Senate, which is a part of the legislative branch.[48]

Observers have noted that judicial appointments to the SCC and to the provincial courts may be influenced by the politics of the government of the day.[49] Concerns have also been raised about the absence of transparency in who applies to become a judge, their qualifications, and the deliberations of the judicial advisory committees who make recommendations for appointments.[50,51]

DIVERSITY (OR THE LACK THEREOF) IN THE JUDICIARY

An ongoing issue is the absence of diversity in the judiciary where older, white males are most prominent. Several observers have referred to a "judiciary of whiteness," reflecting the underrepresentation of women, visible minorities, and Indigenous persons in the judiciary (lack of racial diversity among judges).[52] This underrepresentation is highlighted in the two graphs in Figure 7.5.

This underrepresentation is evident in the very small number of visible minority judges in the provinces: only three of more than 500 judges in Quebec, 24 of 334 judges in Ontario, and four visible minority judges out of 99 in Nova Scotia, including two Blacks (in a province where Blacks are overrepresented in the justice system).[53]

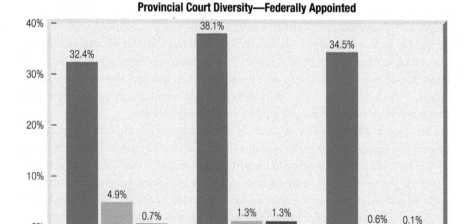

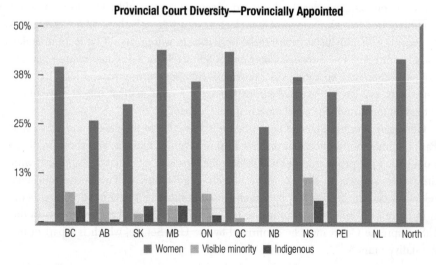

◄ **FIGURE 7.5**

The Lack of Diversity in the Canadian Judiciary

Source: A. Griffith. 2016, May 4. "Diversity among Federal and Provincial Judges," *Policy Options.* http://policyoptions.irpp.org/2016/05/04/diversity-among-federal-provincial-judges. Reprinted by permission of the Institute for Research on Public Policy.

Concerns with the selection process and the lack of diversity on the bench are reflected in the comments of an Indigenous lawyer in Halifax: "While the law is objective, a person's assessment of the facts, including another's behaviour, motives and justifications, is inevitably coloured by who we are and where we come from."[54] This is of particular concern given the overrepresentation of Indigenous persons and Blacks in the criminal justice system.[55]

A milestone for the judiciary and the criminal justice system was the appointment of the first transgender person as a judge of the Manitoba court in 2015.[56]

JUDICIAL ETHICS AND ACCOUNTABILITY

Key themes in this text are ethics and accountability in the criminal justice system. These are often-contentious issues with respect to the legal profession generally and, more specifically, the judiciary.

Provincial, territorial, and federal court judges are guided by ethical principles that are set out in various provincial and territorial documents and, for federally appointed judges, by the Canadian Judicial Council. The standards centre on integrity in personal and professional conduct and highlight impartiality and objectivity, a duty to follow the law, and the importance of appropriate personal conduct.

Judicial independence

The notion that judges are not subject to pressure and influence and are free to make impartial decisions based solely on fact and law.

Historically, the focus in Canada has been on **judicial independence** rather than on judicial accountability although the focus on accountability has increased in recent years. Provincial and territorial court judges are held accountable to various bodies. In Ontario, for example, the Ontario Judicial Council (OJC) operates under the *Courts of Justice Act* (R.S.O. 1990, c. C.43) and investigates complaints made by the general public about provincial courts judges (http://www.ontariocourts.ca/ocj/ojc). See the annual report of the OJC for case summaries of complaints (http://www.ontariocourts.ca/ocj/files/annualreport/ojc/2014-2015-EN.pdf).

The primary structure of accountability for federally appointed judges is the Canadian Judicial Council (CJC) (http://www.cjc-ccm.gc.ca), created under the *Judges Act* (R.S.C. 1985, c. J-1), which is chaired by the chief justice of Canada and is composed of judges.

Complaints about judges arise from intemperate remarks and/or inappropriate conduct either on or off the bench. Displays of gender bias, racial bias, religious bias, conflict of interest, and cultural insensitivity are grounds for complaint, as is undue delay in rendering a decision (which should usually take no more than six months). Cases investigated by the CJC have involved alleged drug use by judges, as well as other types of misconduct or illegal behaviour. In one case, a judge in Ontario faced a disciplinary hearing after wearing a Donald Trump campaign hat with the words "Make America Great Again" into the courtroom.[57]

In another case, the Quebec Court of Appeal ordered a new trial due to the sexist comments made by a male Quebec Superior Court judge toward a woman Crown counsel. In one exchange during discussions with the jury absent, the judge said to the Crown, "It would perhaps be a good thing if Ms. Pinsonnault listened to us." She replied, "I'm sorry, your honour . . . I can do two things at the same time." To which the judge responded, "That's what women are doing all the time. It does not mean that it is always done well."[58]

Sanctions range from removal from the bench (an extremely rare occurrence) to a leave of absence with pay or a letter of reprimand. Alternatives to these include counselling, educational workshops, or the requirement that the judge apologize to the complainant. In more serious cases, judges often choose to resign before the council completes its inquiry. In reality, there are only a very few instances in which judges have been removed from the bench for misconduct.

In one case, a complaint was filed against a provincial court judge who allegedly sped up a sexual assault trial at an out-of-town courthouse, saying that he would like to sleep that night in his own bed.[59]

These and other cases highlight the increasing scrutiny of judicial behaviour, particularly in cases involving sexual assault. The discussion in Chapter 6 revealed a similar focus on the police handling of sexual assault cases. It also suggests that members of the judiciary should be carefully vetted to ensure their personal attitudes and beliefs do not compromise their role as an impartial arbiter in criminal trials.

PUBLIC COMPLAINTS ABOUT JUDGES

Recall from Chapter 5 the discussion of public complaints against the police and the initiatives that have been taken in recent years to make the complaint process more transparent and to include civilian oversight of the handling of complaints. These developments stand in contrast to the complaint process for judges.

Judges who have been sanctioned by the Canadian Judicial Council can appeal to the Supreme Court of Canada. Some observers have questioned the adequacy and impartiality of the structures for judicial accountability, especially in view of the fact that judges are generally appointed for life. See At Issue 7.1.

Critics have argued that the disciplinary process for judges should be more transparent. Generally, only case summaries, without the names of the judge involved in

---

AT ISSUE 7.1

SHOULD THERE BE INDEPENDENT OVERSIGHT OF THE JUDICIARY?

Earlier in this book, it has been noted that the police are the only criminal justice agency that is subjected to outside civilian oversight. The legal profession, including the judiciary, is self-regulated; that is, the only structures of accountability exist within the legal profession. Concerns have been raised about the ability of provincial and territorial law societies to both represent and regulate the profession and the effectiveness of the Canadian Judicial Council as oversight bodies.[a] As well, it is noted that most complaints that are made to the Canadian Judicial Council are not made public but rather are kept private between the complainant, the CJC, and the judge.

A key argument that is made against outside oversight of judges is that of *judicial independence*, which means that "judges are not subject to pressure and influence, and are free to make impartial decisions based solely on fact and law."[b] Judicial independence has been cited as a primary reason why most Canadian judges do not allow cameras in their courtrooms. This issue is discussed in Chapter 8.

One question is whether the notion of judicial independence should extend to independence from oversight. Arguments in support of ensuring judicial independence distinguish between judges and the police and prosecutors, noting that the latter "are in the employ and within the authority of the executive branch of government and . . . are agents of the Crown," whereas judges "are

not subject to the direction or control of the executive branch of government."[c]

A review of the record indicates that few complaints ultimately result in the removal of a judge from the bench. As well, since the disciplinary procedure was established in 1971, there have been very few public inquiries by the council into the behaviour of a federal judge. Most complaints (which average less than 200 per year) are handled by the chairperson of the council and are not publicized but kept between the complainant, the judge, and the CJC. It might be argued that this practice limits the transparency of the council's work.

QUESTIONS

1. In your view, should judges be subject to independent oversight, similar to the police?

2. What arguments could be made in support of, and in opposition to, establishing independent oversight of the police?

---

[a] R.F. Devlin and P. Herrernan. 2008. "The End(s) of Self-Regulation?" *Alberta Law Review*, 45(5), 169–213.

[b] Chief Justices of British Columbia Courts. 2012, March 15. "Judicial Independence (And What Everyone Should Know About It)," p. 1. http://www.courts.gov.bc.ca/about_the_courts/Judicial%20Independence%20Final%20Release.pdf.

[c] Ibid., p. 4.

THE CASE OF JUSTICE ROBIN CAMP

In 2014, Alexander Wagar, a homeless youth, was on trial for sexually assaulting a 19-year-old woman. During the proceedings, Justice Robin Camp questioned the victim about the incident, on one occasion stating, "Why couldn't you just keep your knees together?" These and other comments by the judge, including several instances in which the victim was referred to as the "accused," raised concerns among legal observers and victims groups. Wagar was found not guilty by Justice Camp, who ruled that his testimony was more credible than that of the victim. The Crown appealed the case, and the Alberta Court of Appeal overturned the acquittal and ordered that Wagar be retried. At retrial, he was found not guilty.[a]

Justice Camp was subsequently appointed to the federal court. The Canadian Judicial Council launched an investigation and hearing into his alleged misconduct. In reviewing the transcripts from the trial, the committee found that the comments and questions asked by Justice Camp showed "antipathy toward laws designed to protect vulnerable witnesses, promote equality, and bring integrity to sexual assault trials."[b] The committee also found that in his reasons for judgment in the case, Justice Camp "relied on discredited myths and stereotypes about women and victim-blaming during the trial and in his reasons for judgment."[c]

In his defence, Justice Camp apologized to the complainant for this conduct and indicated that, having been educated in South Africa, he had very little knowledge of the law relating to sexual assault in Canada.

Justice Camp's questions to the alleged victim were found by the panel to be "condescending, humiliating and disrespectful."[d] The committee concluded that Justice Camp's behaviour had seriously compromised the judicial principles of impartiality, integrity, and independence. The committee's recommendation was that Justice Camp should be removed from the bench. Justice Camp subsequently resigned his position in March 2017, making his one of three cases in which judges have been removed from their position by the CJC since 1971.[e] An interview with the victim, whose identity is protected, can be viewed at https://www.youtube.com/watch?v=VPrM0xn-1EQ.

QUESTIONS

1. In your view, did the committee make the right decision in the case of Justice Robin Camp?
2. In November 2017, Camp applied to the Alberta Law Society for reinstatement as a lawyer, which would allow him to practise law. If you were on the law society's panel, would you vote to reinstate him? Camp indicated that he had grown from the experience and had been helped by counselling and, further, that he had wanted to deliver a personal apology to the woman, but had been advised not to.

---

[a] B. Graveland. 2017, January 31. "Alexander Wagar Not Guilty in Alberta 'Knees Together' Retrial," Global News. http://globalnews.ca/news/3216107/alberta-judge-to-give-verdict-in-alexander-wagar-knees-together-retrial.

[b] Canadian Judicial Council. 2016. Report to the Canadian Judicial Council of the Inquiry Committee Appointed Under Subsection 63(3) of the Judges Act to Conduct an Investigation into the Conduct of the Honourable Robin Camp, A Justice of the Federal Court. Overview. Ottawa: Author, p. 3. https://www.cjc-ccm.gc.ca/cmslib/general/Camp_Docs/2017-03-08%20Report%20to%20Minister.pdf.

[c] Ibid.

[d] Canadian Judicial Council. 2017. In the Matter of S. 63 of the Judges Act, R.S., c. J-1 Canadian Judicial Inquiry into the Conduct of the Honourable Robin Camp. Report to the Minister of Justice, p. 7. https://www.cjc-ccm.gc.ca/cmslib/general/Camp_Docs/2016-11-29%20Camp%20Inquiry%20Report%20to%20CJC%20OVERVIEW.pdf.

[e] R. Fletcher. 2016, November 30. "Federal Court Justice Robin Camp Should Be Removed from Bench, Judicial Committee Recommends," CBC News. http://www.cbc.ca/news/canada/calgary/robin-camp-federal-court-judge-inquiry-committee-report-1.3874314.

---

the case, are reported by provincial and territorial judicial councils.[60] The majority of the complaints received by the CJC are dismissed or resolved behind closed doors.[61]

A rare instance in which a public hearing was held on whether a judge should be removed from the bench was the case of Judge Robin Camp, presented in Court File 7.3.

Some instances of judicial misconduct never come to the attention of the federal and provincial or territorial councils, owing to potential complainants feeling intimidated by the judge in question, the justice system, and the complaint process. This may be felt particularly by people in vulnerable and at-risk groups and even members of visible minorities where a lack of knowledge of the complaint process, suspicion of the justice system, and language barriers may deter complaints.

It is likely that this occurred in the case of Judge David Ramsay, a provincial court judge in British Columbia, presented in Court File 7.4. This case highlights the power that judges wield in the community, as well as the vulnerability of women, especially young women—in this case, Indigenous young women.

THE CASE OF JUDGE DAVID RAMSAY

On June 1, 2004, former British Columbia Provincial Court Judge David Ramsay was sentenced to seven years in prison for sexually assaulting several teenage Indigenous girls in Prince George. He pleaded guilty to one count of sexual assault causing bodily harm, three counts of buying sex from minors, and one count of breach of trust. The sentence was two years longer than Crown counsel had asked for. During the sentencing hearing, Ramsay apologized to four of his victims, who were in court.

Evidence presented to the court indicated that Ramsay had sexually abused the young women, who were involved in the sex trade, over a 10-year period, intimidating them into remaining silent about his violent attacks on them. The girls, some as young as 12, had appeared in court before Judge Ramsay, who was aware of their life circumstances and their vulnerabilities. Ramsay was found guilty and sentenced to seven years in prison. His application for day parole was denied in 2007, and in 2008, he passed away of an illness in a New Brunswick jail.

The RCMP authorities in Prince George were criticized for their slow response to the allegations against Ramsay; reports of his abuses had been circulating in the city for several years. After Ramsay was sentenced, two RCMP officers who had at one time been stationed in Prince George were themselves investigated for misconduct amidst allegations that they had covered up Ramsay's exploits. It was alleged that one of these officers had had sex with underage prostitutes in Prince George as well; he was suspended with pay while his case was being investigated by the RCMP Major Crime section. Because of delays in the RCMP investigating the case, no further action was taken against the officer.

The Assembly of First Nations and the Native Women's Association of Canada called for an inquiry into the administration of justice in cases involving sexual assault against Indigenous women and young women. The government did not act on this suggestion.

CASE DELAY IN THE COURTS

The length of time to complete adult criminal court cases varies across the country. As would be expected, cases involving more serious criminal offences or multiple charges take longer to complete.[62] However, case delay has been endemic in the Canadian criminal justice system and, until recently, appeared to be immune from reform efforts designed to improve the case process. The staying (that is, suspension or discontinuance) of nearly 100,000 criminal cases a year in Canada is due in part to failures to get the cases to court within a reasonable period. Numerous enquiries have documented the "culture of delay" that exists in the justice system, wherein it is often years before a final decision is reached in a case.[63,64]

Periodic efforts by the provinces and territories to address the issue of case delay have been largely unsuccessful. In Ontario, for example, the Justice on Target initiative was designed to improve case flow in the criminal courts and set benchmarks for processing various types of cases that were met only approximately 60 percent of the time.[65]

THE SOURCES OF CASE DELAY

Case backlog and case delay are due to a number of factors, including a lack of judicial resources, ineffective use of resources, too few judges, the complexity of criminal cases (multi-charge cases compose a majority of the cases in criminal court), inadequate case flow management by chief judges and trial judges, and the efforts of defence counsel to lengthen the period of time that accused persons are confined prior to trial on remand. Persons on remand are given 1.5 for one day credit for jail time served prior to sentencing. Ironically, case delay has not been reduced despite the overall decline in crime rates over the past decade.

Case delay has had a significant impact on the administration of justice. In 2013, a British Columbia Supreme Court judge stayed charges against a high-ranking member of the Hell's Angels on the grounds that his Charter rights had been violated due to the two-and-a-half-year delay in the case coming to trial.[66] Also, in British Columbia, it took four years after a BC Ferries vessel sunk in 2006 with the loss of two lives for charges of criminal negligence causing death to be laid by Crown counsel, another three years for the trial to begin, and another six months before a verdict was rendered (guilty) and sentence passed.

Case delay also has an impact on crime victims and witnesses to crime, with the potential that victims are revictimized by the process and prevented from reaching closure on the incident.[67]

ADDRESSING CASE DELAY: THE SCC *R. V. JORDAN* DECISION

A watershed event in case delays in the criminal courts was the landmark ruling of the SCC in *R. v. Jordan* (2016 SCC 27). Jordan was a British Columbia man who experienced a four-year delay before being brought to trial on drug charges. Criticizing what it characterized as a "culture of complacency" in the criminal justice system, the court dismissed the charges against Jordan and set presumptive timelines for the disposition of cases in the courts from the time the person is charged to the actual or anticipated end of trial: 18 months for cases tried in provincial court and 30 months for cases in the superior court (or cases tried in the provincial court after a preliminary inquiry). Beyond these time limits, the delay will be deemed to be unreasonable, unless there are exceptional circumstances. The Jordan decision had an immediate impact on thousands of cases across the country.

The Jordan case redefined the constitutional right to a trial within a reasonable time. Prior to the Jordan decision, judges could determine that case delay violated a person's constitutionally guaranteed right "to be tried within a reasonable time" under section 11(b) of the *Canadian Charter of Rights and Freedoms* and could order a stay of proceedings or dismissal of the charges.[68]

This SCC decision has resulted in hundreds of cases being thrown out by the courts due to excessive delays. This included cases involving violence and death. The case of Lance Regan, a prisoner at the Edmonton Institution, a federal correctional facility, was one such case. Regan was charged with first-degree murder in the death of another inmate. It had been five years since Mr. Regan had been charged; the judge dismissed the case against him due to the delay. In another case, charges of first-degree murder against Adam Picard were stayed after he had been in jail for four years and the case had not been concluded.[69] In 2017, the Crown appealed the decision in the Picard case, requesting a new trial on the basis that the trial judge erred in the decision.[70]

In another case, *R. v. Williamson* (2016 SCC 28), the SCC threw out the conviction over a delay just slightly longer than 30 months. Williamson had been convicted of sexual offences involving multiple (100 times) assaults of a boy during the ages of 10 to 12.

As of the end of 2017, there were potentially thousands of cases that could be dismissed or stayed due to excessive delay.

The federal, provincial, and territorial governments pushed back against the Jordan decision. Federal prosecutors and attorneys general from several provinces argued that the timelines were too onerous and did not provide enough flexibility to deal with complex cases.[71] The Jordan ruling has also been criticized on a number of counts, including that the time guidelines were not based on any analysis, the failure of the court to distinguish between the seriousness of offences, and its impact on crime victims who may be revictimized by cases being dismissed.[72]

One question is "How did the SCC come up with the timelines in the Jordan case?" A review of the record indicates that the origins of the timelines is quite interesting. It occurred during an exchange between Supreme Cout Justice Michael Moldaver and Jordan's lawyer when the justice asked the lawyer what he would think of having time limits:

> The usually eloquent lawyer stumbled. "I don't know, it's probably better than what we have now."
>
> "What about 30 months?" Justice Moldaver replied.
>
> "I don't know—how about 24?" Mr. Gottardi said.

The court subsequently adopted the 30-month time limit for indictable offences.[73]

In spring 2017, the SCC was presented with a case that provided it with an opportunity to revisit and clarity its decision in the Jordan case.[74] James Cody was one of six persons arrested following a drug investigation; he faced numerous charges, including drug trafficking and possession of a prohibited weapon. It took five years for the case to come to trial, during which time Cody was on bail in the community. Prosecutors cited a number of reasons for the delay, including over 20,000 pages of evidence, 89 warrants that were used during the investigation, all of which took 1,700 hours of police overtime. In a 7–0 vote, the SCC unanimously dismissed drug and weapons charges against Cody.

It is uncertain how the provinces and territories are going to address this issue. Suggestions to speed up the flow of cases in the courts have included dispensing with preliminary hearings, which have been on the decline for the past decade, and having prosecutors offer early plea bargains to accused in minor criminal cases.[75] In 2017, prosecutors in Ontario were instructed to skip preliminary hearings and go straight to trial to avoid lengthy case delays.[76]

A 2017 report from the Senate of Canada recommended the expanded use of restorative justice approaches and highlighted the potential of problem-solving courts to speed the flow of cases and to address the risk and needs of offenders with specific challenges.

In 2017, Ontario announced a new initiative to speed up case flow, including hiring more judges, Crown prosecutors, duty counsel, and court staff, as well as an increased focus on the early resolution of cases. Whether this initiative will be more successful than previous efforts remains to be seen. It is likely that the Jordan decisions will have the greatest impact on the processing of cases in the criminal courts. It will be interesting to follow developments as jurisdictions attempt to meet the SCC-imposed guidelines.

The use of alternative dispute measures, specialized courts, and restorative justice approaches hold considerable promise in assisting court systems to reduce the case delays and backlogs. There has also been an increased focus on the role that judges can play in reducing case delay. A report from the Canadian Senate indicated that judges can exercise much more control over proceedings in their courtrooms in an attempt to avoid case delay.

The actions of criminal lawyers as a contributor to case delay have also come under judicial scrutiny. In a 2017 decision, the SCC (*Quebec Criminal and Penal Prosecutions v. Jodoin*, 2017 SCC 26) upheld a ruling of a Quebec judge who had awarded court costs of $3,000 against a defence lawyer who had engaged in a number of delay tactics, including attempting to have two trial judges recused for alleged bias in the case in the same day, and a number of other motions designed to delay the proceedings. The SCC ruling established the right of judges to resist

"The way I see it, justice delayed is that many more billable hours."

efforts to delay cases and that such conduct was an abuse of the criminal justice process. This ruling, in conjunction with the court's ruling in *R. v. Jordan*, is likely to reduce case delay.

One issue is whether the solution to case delay resides in pouring more resources into the criminal justice system as it is currently structured rather than making significant reforms to the system.

In response to continual requests from the judiciary for more judges, Crown counsel, and legal counsel, one media observer wondered how, if the system in Ontario was so overwhelmed, the trial of an animal rights activist for providing water to a truckload of pigs on their way to slaughter took a full seven days. The activist had been charged with mischief, and was subsequently acquitted at trail.[77]

THE CHALLENGES OF MEGA-TRIALS

The criminal courts may be overwhelmed in certain cases that result from a major tragedy or police enforcement initiative. Stronger enforcement efforts against outlaw motorcycle gangs and criminal syndicates have resulted in criminal trials involving multiple defendants, lengthy witness lists, and thousands of pages (and in many instances, thousands of pieces) of evidence.[78] Also, these types of cases are expensive.

Canada's most costly trial was the case involving Air India Flight 182, which exploded and crashed into the Atlantic Ocean off the west coast of Ireland in 1985 while on a flight from Montreal to London. All 329 passengers on board, most of whom were

Canadian citizens, were killed. The investigation into the bombings centred on certain individuals in British Columbia's Sikh community, who were involved in the struggle for an independent Khalistan in India. An Air India Task Force, led by the RCMP and working alongside police agencies in Europe, India, the United States, and Asia, spent 15 years investigating the case, at one point offering a $1 million reward for evidence that would help convict the perpetrators.

The Crown proceeded by direct indictment against the remaining two defendants. The trial began in April 2003 and went on for 19 months and 232 court days until December 2004. It was held in the B.C. Supreme Court in Courtroom 20, in Vancouver, which had been built at an estimated cost of $7.2 million, specifically for the Air India trial and for future megatrials. In March 2005, the presiding judge found the two defendants not guilty on all charges. By that time, the Air India case had cost the federal government and the Government of British Columbia a total of nearly $60 million.

SUMMARY

The discussion in this chapter has centred on the structure and operation of the Canadian criminal courts. The four levels of courts that deal with criminal cases were discussed, as well as the role and activities of judges, defence counsel, and Crown counsel. The issues surrounding the appointment of judges were examined, including the role of politics in the selection process. Problem-solving courts, centred on the notion of therapeutic justice, have emerged as an alternative to the traditional adversarial model of justice for vulnerable persons accused of criminal offences. Unique challenges surround the delivery of court services in remote and northern communities.

The cases heard by the Supreme Court of Canada often reflect the tension between balancing the rights of citizens as enshrined in the *Charter of Rights and Freedoms* with the need to protect the general public. There has been an increasing focus on the judiciary, including the lack of diversity among judges and judicial accountability. This concern has been heightened by a number of high-profile cases in which judges behaved in a disrespectful and biased manner toward accused, particularly in cases involving alleged sexual assault. The SCC decision in *R. v. Jordan* is having a significant impact on the processing of cases through the criminal justice system.

KEY POINTS REVIEW

1. The criminal courts play an important, multifaceted role in the criminal justice system.

2. There are four levels of courts that deal with criminal cases: provincial/territorial courts, provincial/territorial superior courts, provincial appellate courts, and the Supreme Court of Canada.

3. In recent years, a number of problem-solving courts have been created which attempt to divert offenders with special needs from the criminal justice system.

4. Unique challenges are confronted by provincial/territorial circuit courts that provide court services to northern and remote communities.

5. There is an inherent tension between individual rights as set out in the *Charter of Rights and Freedoms* and the needs to protect the general public, and this is often evident in the cases heard by the Supreme Court of Canada.

6. The courtroom workgroup is composed of the professionals who work in the criminal courts and include judges, defence lawyers, and Crown counsel.

7. Defendants in the criminal courts are disproportionately Indigenous, Black, and disenfranchised persons from the lower socio-economic levels of the community.

8. Judges at the provincial/territorial court level are appointed by their respective governments, while judges of the superior courts are appointed by the federal government.

9. There are concerns about the process by which judges are nominated and appointed.

10. An ongoing issue is the absence of diversity in the judiciary.

11. There are arguments in favour of, and opposed to, the election of judges.

12. Judicial ethics and the structures of judicial accountability have come under increased scrutiny in recent years.

13. In contrast to the police, there is no civilian oversight of the judiciary and the complaint process is far less transparent than in policing.

14. The longstanding issue of case delay in the courts was addressed in the SCC decision of *R. v. Jordan*.

KEY TERM QUESTIONS

1. Describe the approach of **problem-solving courts**, provide an example, and discuss the effectiveness of these courts.

2. What is **therapeutic justice** and how does it differ from the traditional approaches of the criminal court?

3. What is meant by the **courtroom workgroup** and why is this notion important in understanding the operation of the criminal courts?

4. Define **judicial independence** and discuss how it assists in understanding the role of the judiciary.

CRITICAL THINKING EXERCISE

Critical Thinking Exercise 7.1

Are Specialized Courts Just "Band-Aids?"

Despite the proliferation of specialized courts across the country, questions have been raised about their objectives and effectiveness. Access the article, "Do 'Specialized Courts' Have a Real Purpose, or Are They Just Well-Meaning Band-Aids?" at http://vancouversun .com/opinion/columnists/ian-mulgrew-do-specialized-courts-have-real-purpose-or-are-they -just-well-meaning-band-aids.

Your Thoughts?

1. What is your response to the arguments being made in this article?

2. What would you consider to be the strengths and weaknesses of the argument that is being made?

CLASS/GROUP DISCUSSION EXERCISE

Class/Group Discussion Exercise 7.1

Addressing the Lack of Diversity in the Judiciary

A key feature of the Canadian judiciary is a lack of diversity. Despite numerous reports identifying the problem, governments have not successfully addressed it. Among the options for increasing diversity in the judiciary are quotas, which would require the judiciary to reflect the diversity of Canadian society. This would include the objective of having 50 percent women judges.

Your Thoughts?

1. What is your opinion on having quotas to increase the diversity of the Canadian judiciary?
2. What other options would you suggest for addressing this issue?

MEDIA LINKS

Cameras in the Courtroom

"Cameras in the Courtroom," *The Fifth Estate*, CBC News, http://uvideoplay.com/video/Cameras-in-the-courtroom-the-fifth-estate-VideoDownload_UnVUVWZLby1QSFE.html. Note: In this video, a CBC producer speaks about the experience of cameras in the courtroom in the case presented in "A Mother's Trial."

"A Mother's Trial," *The Fifth Estate*, CBC News, http://uvideoplay.com/video/A-Mother-s-Trial-the-fifth-estate-VideoDownload_b2tyQlg2OFJuTVU.html.

Problem-Solving Courts

"Vancouver's Downtown Community Court," https://www2.gov.bc.ca/gov/content/justice/criminal-justice/vancouver-downtown-community-court/the-community-court-s-story.

"Mental Health Court," King County TV (Seattle, WA), therapeutic court for mentally ill offenders, http://www.youtube.com/watch?v=DFIDmuevXQQ

"Drug Courts: Personal Stories," https://www.courtinnovation.org/publications/drug-courts-personal-stories

"Inside the First Court Designed to Keep Opioid Addicts Alive," *Vice News*, August 7, 2017, https://www.youtube.com/watch?v=v5-yeP5_KZo

REFERENCES

1. A. Maxwell. 2017. "Adult Criminal Court Statistics in Canada, 2014/2015," *Juristat*, 37(1). Statistics Canada Catalogue no. 85-002-X. Ottawa: Minister of Industry, pp. 5–6. http://www.statcan.gc.ca/pub/85-002-x/2017001/article/14699-eng.htm.

2. C.M. Webster and A.N. Doob. 2003. "The Superior/Provincial Court Distinction: Historical Anachronism or Empirical Reality?" *Criminal Law Quarterly*, 48(1), 77–109.

3. Cited in R. Browne. 2016, December 7. "Inside the Canadian Court That Handles Drug Crime Differently," *Vice News*. https://news.vice.com/story/inside-the-canadian-court-that-handles-drug-crime-differently.

4. R. Porter, M. Rempel, and A. Mansky. 2010. *What Makes a Court Problem-Solving? Universal Performance Indicators for Problem-Solving Justice*. Washington, DC: Center for Court Innovation. http://www.courtinnovation.org/sites/default/files/What_Makes_A_Court_P_S.pdf.

5. R. Saner. 2010. *Community Perceptions of Red Hook, Brooklyn: Views of Quality of Life, Safety, and Services*. New York: Center for Court Innovation. http://www.courtinnovation.org/sites/default/files/Community_Perceptions.pdf.

6. A.J. Lurigio and J. Snowden. 2009. "Putting Therapeutic Jurisprudence into Practice: Growth, Operations, and

Effectiveness of Mental Health Court," *Justice System Journal*, 30(2), 196–218.

7. S. Goldberg. 2011. *Problem-Solving in Canada's Courtrooms: A Guide to Therapeutic Justice*. Ottawa: National Judicial Council.

8. F. Sirotich. 2009. "The Criminal Justice Outcomes of Jail Diversion Programs for Persons with Mental Illness: A Review of the Evidence," *Journal of the American Academy of Psychiatry and Law*, 37(4), 461–472.

9. E. Slinger and R. Roesch. 2010. "Problem-Solving Courts in Canada: A Review and a Call for Empirically-Based Evaluation Methods," *International Journal of Law and Psychiatry*, 33(4), 258–264.

10. J. Weekes, R. Mugford, G. Bourgon, and S. Price. 2007. *Drug Treatment Courts: FAQs*. Ottawa: Canadian Centre on Substance Abuse. http://www.ccsa.ca/2007%20CCSA%20Documents/ccsa-011348-2007.pdf.

11. P. Morin. 2016, July 11. "'Jail Is Not the Answer': Yukon Courts Keep 2 Convicts with PTSD Out of Prison," *CBC News*. http://www.cbc.ca/news/canada/north/jail-fasd-wellness-court-yukon-1.3667117.

12. MHC participant cited in K.E. Canada and A.C. Watson. 2013. "'Cause Everybody Likes to Be Treated Good': Perceptions of Procedural Justice Among Mental Health Court Participants," *American Behavioral Scientist*, 57(2), 209–230.

13. Lurigio and Snowden, "Putting Therapeutic Jurisprudence into Practice," p. 207.

14. B. Newton-Taylor, L. Gliksman, and J. Patra. 2009. "Toronto Drug Treatment Court: Participant Intake Characteristics as Predictors of 'Successful' Program Completion," *Journal of Drug Issues*, 39(4), 965–988.

15. Department of Justice Canada. 2009. *Drug Treatment Court Funding Program Summative Evaluation. Final Report*. Ottawa: Evaluation Division, Office of Strategic Planning and Performance Management. http://www.justice.gc.ca/eng/rp-pr/cp-pm/eval/rep-rap/09/dtcfp-pfttt/P2.html.

16. A. Verhaaff. 2011. "Individual Factors Predicting Mental Health Court Diversion Outcome," Unpublished MA Thesis, University of Ontario Institute of Technology. http://ir.library.dc-uoit.ca/bitstream/10155/164/1/Verehaaf_Ashley.pdf.

17. D. Orr. 2017. "A Criminal or Therapeutic Justice System? Examining Specialized Treatment Courts," *Criminal Law Quarterly*, 64(1–2), 180–199.

18. P. Bowen and S. Whitehead. 2016. *Problem-Solving Courts: An Evidence Review*, London, UK: Centre for Justice Innovation. http://justiceinnovation.org/wp-content/ uploads/2016/08/Problem-solving-courts-An-evidence-review.pdf.

19. L. Gutierrez and G. Bourgon. 2009. *Drug Treatment Courts: A Quantitative Review of Study and Treatment Quality*. Ottawa: Public Safety Canada. https://www.publicsafety.gc.ca/cnt/rsrcs/pblctns/2009-04-dtc/2009-04-dtc-eng.pdf.

20. C.T. Lowenkamp, J. Pealer, P. Smith, and E.J. Latessa. 2006. "Adhering to the Risk and Needs Principles: Does It Matter for Supervision-Based Programs?" *Federal Probation*, 70(3), 3–8.

21. S. Johnson. 2014. "Developing First Nations Courts in Canada: Elders as Foundational to Indigenous Therapeutic Jurisprudence," *Journal of Indigenous Social Development*, 3(2), 1–14.

22. Truth and Reconciliation Commission of Canada. 2012. *Truth and Reconciliation Commission of Canada: Calls to Action*. Winnipeg: http://www.trc.ca/websites/trcinstitution/File/2015/Findings/Calls_to_Action_English2.pdf.

23. P. Maurutto and K. Hannah-Moffat. 2016. "Aboriginal Knowledges in Specialized Courts: Emerging Practices in Gladue Courts," *Canadian Journal of Law & Society*, 31(3), 451–471.

24. T. Spence and H. Jones. 2017, March 12. "Thunder Bay Indigenous Peoples' Court: Where Healing Takes Place," *The Argus*. http://theargus.ca/features/2017/thunder-bay-indigenous-peoples-court.

25. D. Vermette. 2008–2009. "Colonialism and the Suppression of the Aboriginal Voice," *Ottawa Law Review*, 40(2), 225–265 at p. 228.

26. P. de Jong. 2003. *Legal Aid Provision in Northern Canada: Summary of Research in the Northwest Territories, Nunavut, and the Yukon*. Ottawa: Department of Justice Canada. http://www.justice.gc.ca/eng/rp-pr/aj-ja/rr03_la15-rr03_aj15/rr03_la15.pdf

27. L. Hausegger, M. Hennigar, and T. Riddell. 2009. *Canadian Courts: Law, Politics, and Process*. Toronto: Oxford University Press, p. 104.

28. Ibid., p. 105.

29. S. Fine. 2017, February 17. "Ontario Judge Rebuked for Ending Day Early as Delays Pile Up," *Globe and Mail*. https://www.theglobeandmail.com/news/national/ontario-judge-censured-for-short-sitting-hours-adding-to-delays/article34062449.

30. D. Small. 2012. "Canada's High Court Unchains Injection Drug Users; Implications for Harm Reduction as Standard of Health Care," *Harm Reduction Journal*, 9(1), 34.

31. J. Eisenstein and H. Jacobs. 1991. *Felony Justice*. Lanham, MD: University Press of America.

32. K.M. Campbell. 2011. "Expert Evidence from 'Social' Scientists: The Importance of Context and the Impact on Miscarriages of Justice," *Canadian Criminal Law Review*, *16*(1), 13–35 at p. 34.

33. Canadian Superior Court Judges Association. 2013. "The Role of the Judge." http://www.cscja-acjcs.ca/role_of_judge -en.asp?l=5.

34. J. Cameron. 2013. *A Context of Justice: Ontario's Justices of the Peace – From the Mewett Report to the Present.* Toronto: Osgood Hall Law School of York University, p. 27. http://digitalcommons.osgoode.yorku.ca/cgi/viewcontent .cgi?article=1286&context=clpe.

35. B. Powell. 2009, April 16. "No Legal Training, but JPs Earn $150k," *Toronto Star.* https://www.thestar.com/news/ gta/2009/04/16/no_legal_training_but_jps_earn_150k.html.

36. M.S. Madon. 2016. *The Retention of Women in the Private Practice of Criminal Law: Research Report.* Toronto: Criminal Lawyers' Association. http://www.criminallawyers.ca/wp-content/ uploads/2016/03/CLA-Womens-Study-March-2016.pdf.

37. Ibid., p. 8.

38. Ibid., p. 26.

39. Ontario Attorney General. 2005. *Role of the Crown Counsel. Preamble to the Crown Policy Manual.* Toronto: Author. http://www.attorneygeneral.jus.gov.on.ca/english/crime/ cpm/2005/CPMPreamble.pdf.

40. Public Prosecution Service of Canada. 2016. *Annual Report 2015-2016.* http://www.ppsc-sppc.gc.ca/eng/pub/ar-ra/2015 _2016/index.html#section_1_5.

41. Public Prosecution Service of Canada. 2013. *Annual Report 2012-2013.* http://www.ppsc-sppc.gc.ca/eng/pub/ar-ra/2012 _2013/03.html, 1.

42. *Boucher v. The Queen.* [1955] SCR 16, pp. 23–24. https:// scc-csc.lexum.com/scc-csc/scc-csc/en/item/2741/index.do.

43. I. Gomme and M.P. Hall. 1995. "Prosecutors at Work: Role Overload and Strain," *Journal of Criminal Justice*, 23(2), 91–200 at p. 194.

44. S. Fine. 2017, March 2. "Alberta Prosecutors at 'Breaking Point' as Abandoned Cases Pile Up," *Globe and Mail.* https://www.theglobeandmail.com/news/national/alber- ta-prosecutors-push-back-against-new-trial-length-rules/ article34181397.

45. Public Prosecution Service of Canada, *Annual Report 2015-2016.*

46. J. Eisenstein and H. Jacobs. 1991. *Felony Justice.* Lanham, MD: University Press of America.

47. L. Hausegger, M. Hennigar, and T. Riddell. 2009. *Canadian Courts: Law, Politics, and Process.* Toronto: Oxford University Press, p. 145.

48. J. Makarenko. 2007, February 1. "Supreme Court of Canada Appointment Process." *Mapleleafweb.com* [blog]. http:// www.mapleleafweb.com/features/supreme-court-canada -appointment-process.html.

49. C. Forcese and A. Freeman. 2005. *The Laws of Government: The Legal Foundations of Canadian Democracy.* Toronto: Irwin Law.

50. D. Butt. 2016, April 19. "It's Time to Judge the Judges," *Globe and Mail,* https://www.theglobeandmail.com/opinion/its -time-to-judge-the-judges/article29668267.

51. P. McCormick. 2012. "Judging Selection: Appointing Canadian Judges," *Windsor Yearbook of Access to Justice,* 30(2), 39–58. http://ojs.uwindsor.ca/ojs/leddy/index.php/ WYAJ/article/view/4368/3445.

52. M. Tutton. 2016, July 18. "Canada Must Boost Racial Diversity in 'Judiciary of Whiteness,' Advocates Urge," *Toronto Star.* https://www.thestar.com/news/queenspark/2016/07/18/ canada-must-boost-racial-diversity-in-judiciary-of-whiteness -advocates-urge.html.

53. Ibid.

54. Quoted in K. Makin. 2012, April 17. "Of 100 Federally Appointed Judges 98 Are White, Globe Finds," *Globe and Mail.* https://www.theglobeandmail.com/news/politics/of-100 -new-federally-appointed-judges-98-are-white-globe -finds/article4101504.

55. A. Griffith. 2016, May 4. "We Need a Baseline of Information About Diversity in Judicial Appointments, In Order to Evaluate the Government's Promises," *Policy Options.* http://policyoptions.irpp.org/2016/05/04/diversity -among-federal-provincial-judges.

56. C. Holmes. 2016, February 12. "'Breaking Barriers': Canada's First Transgender Judge Sworn in at Manitoba Court," *CTV News.* http://winnipeg.ctvnews.ca/breaking-barriers-canada-s -first-transgender-judge-sworn-in-at-manitoba-court -1.2775472.

57. A. Kassam. 2017, April 21. "Canada Judge Who Wore Trump Hat to Court Faces Disciplinary Hearing," *The Guardian,* https://www.theguardian.com/ world/2017/apr/21/canada-judge-bernd-zabel-trump- hat-hearing.

58. G. Hamilton. 2014, August 5. "Court Finds Quebec Judge's 'Intrinsically Sexist Attitude' toward Female Defence Lawyer Grounds for New Trial," *National Post.* http:// nationalpost.com/news/canada/court-finds-quebec-judges -intrinsically-sexist-attitude-toward-female-defence-lawyer -grounds-for-new-trial/wcm/80fddc63-269a-4522-90f2 -cef5456696d5.

59. S. Dhillon. 2017, March 23. "British Columbia Judge's Handling of Sexual-Assault Trial Sparks Complaint," *Globe*

and *Mail*. https://www.theglobeandmail.com/news/british -columbia/british-columbia-judges-handling-of-sexual -assault-trial-sparks-complaint/article34413039.

60. J. Gallant. 2017, February 11. "Reports Shed Light on Secretive Discipline Process for Ontario Judges, JPs," *Toronto Star*. https://www.thestar.com/news/gta/2017/02/11/ reports-shed-light-on-secretive-discipline-process-for-ontario -judges-jps.html.

61. S. Lambert. 2016, September 11. "Judicial Hearings Rare: Most Complaints About Judges Never Get to Public Hearing," *CBC News*. http://www.cbc.ca/news/canada/ manitoba/judicial-hearings-judge-complaints-manitoba -1.3757735.

62. Department of Justice Canada. 2017, April. "JustFacts: Jordan: Statistics Related to Delay in the Criminal Justice System." http://justice.gc.ca/eng/rp-pr/jr/jf-pf/2017/apr01.html.

63. D.G. Cowper (Chair). 2012. *A Criminal Justice System for the 21st Century. Final Report to the Minister of Justice and Attorney General Honourable Shirley Bond*. Victoria: Ministry of Justice and Attorney General. https://www2 .gov.bc.ca/assets/gov/law-crime-and-justice/about-bc-justice -system/justice-reform-initiatives/cowperfinalreport.pdf.

64. The Honourable B. Runciman (Chair) and The Honourable G. Baker (Co-Chair). 2017. *Delaying Justice Is Denying Justice. An Urgent Need to Address Lengthy Court Delays in Canada. Final Report of the Standing Committee on Legal and Constitutional Affairs*. Ottawa: Senate of Canada. https://sencanada.ca/content/sen/committee/421/LCJC/ reports/Court_Delays_Final_Report_e.pdf.

65. Ontario Ministry of the Attorney General. 2013. *Annual Report, 2012-2013*. Toronto: Author. https://www.attorneygeneral.jus .gov.on.ca/english/about/pubs/mag_annual/annual-rpt_2012 _13.php.

66. K. Bolan. 2013, June 4. "Nanaimo Hells Angel Sees Criminal Charges Stayed after Court Delays," *Vancouver Sun*. http://www.vancouversun.com/news/Nanaimo+Hells +Angel+sees+criminal+charges+stayed+after+court/ 8477653/story.html.

67. Runciman and Baker, *Delaying Justice Is Denying Justice*.

68. Ibid.

69. S. Fine. 2016, November 18. "Charges Thrown Out Due to Trial Delays a Growing Problem in Justice System," *Globe and Mail*. https://www.theglobeandmail.com/news/national/

serious-charges-thrown-out-due-to-trial-delays-a-growing -problem-in-justice-system/article32941014.

70. P. Loriggio. 2017, June 11. "Prosecutors Seek New Trial for Accused Murderer Freed Due to Court Delays," *Globe and Mail*. https://www.theglobeandmail.com/news/ national/prosecutors-seek-new-trial-for-accused-murderer -freed-due-to-court-delays/article35280219.

71. T. MacCharles. 2017, April 25. "Provinces Urge Supreme Court to Relax Tough New Deadlines for Criminal Trials," *Toronto Star*. https://www.thestar.com/news/canada/2017/04/ 25/provinces-urge-supreme-court-to-relax-tough-new -deadlines-for-criminal-trials.html.

72. B. Perrin. 2017, February 20. "Victims of Crime Pay the Real Price for Unreasonable Delays," *Globe and Mail*, https:// www.theglobeandmail.com/opinion/victims-of-crime -pay-the-real-price-of-unreasonable-delay/article34077444.

73. S. Fine. 2017, March 10. "Courts Shaken by Search for Solutions to Delays," *Globe and Mail*. https://www .theglobeandmail.com/news/national/courts-shaken -by-search-for-solutions-todelays/article34275019.

74. T. MacCharles. 2017, April 3. "Supreme Court of Canada to Revisit Trial Delays Ruling in Upcoming Session," *Toronto star*. https://www.thestar.com/news/canada/2017/ 04/03/supreme-court-of-canada-to-revisit-trial-delays-ruling -in-upcoming-session.html.

75. Department of Justice Canada. 2017, June. "JustFacts: Preliminary Inquiries." http://justice.gc.ca/eng/rp-pr/jr/jf-pf/ 2017/jun01.html.

76. S. Fine. 2017, February 22. "Ontario Prosecutors Told They Can Skip Preliminary Inquiries to Avoid Delays," *Globe and Mail*. https://www.theglobeandmail .com/news/national/ontario-crowns-told-they-can-skip -preliminary-inquiries-to-avoid-delays/article34116312.

77. C. Blatchford. 2017, May 5. "Why Did the Crown Waste Resources Prosecuting Woman Who Gave Water to Pigs?" *National Post*. http://news.nationalpost.com/full-comment/ christie-blatchford-on-anita-krajnc.

78. The Honourable P.J. LeSage and M. Code. 2008. *Report of the Review of Large and Complex Criminal Case Procedures*. Toronto: Attorney General of Ontario. http:// www.attorneygeneral.jus.gov.on.ca/english/about/pubs/ lesage_code/lesage_code_report_en.pdf.

© Laurie Justus Pace, Graphics One Design, 2014

CHAPTER 8
THE PROSECUTION
OF CRIMINAL CASES

After reading this chapter, you should be able to

- Describe the flow of cases through the criminal courts.
- Describe the pre-trial process in the criminal courts.
- Discuss judicial interim release (bail) and the issues that surround its use.
- Describe security certificates and discuss the controversy that surrounds their use.
- Discuss legal representation for defendants, the provisions for legal aid, and the issues surrounding remand.
- Describe the practices that encompass the determination of fitness to stand trial.
- Identify the issues surrounding plea bargaining.
- Discuss the role of juries in criminal trials and the research on jury decision-making.
- Identify the various defences that are used by persons charged with a crime.
- Discuss the issues that surround wrongful convictions.

The discussion in Chapter 7 revealed that not all cases in which a person is arrested end up being prosecuted in criminal court. The development of problem-solving courts and the use of restorative justice alternatives means that some accused appear in other forums.

For those whose cases are prosecuted in criminal court, there is a procedure that is followed. This is set out in Figure 8.1.

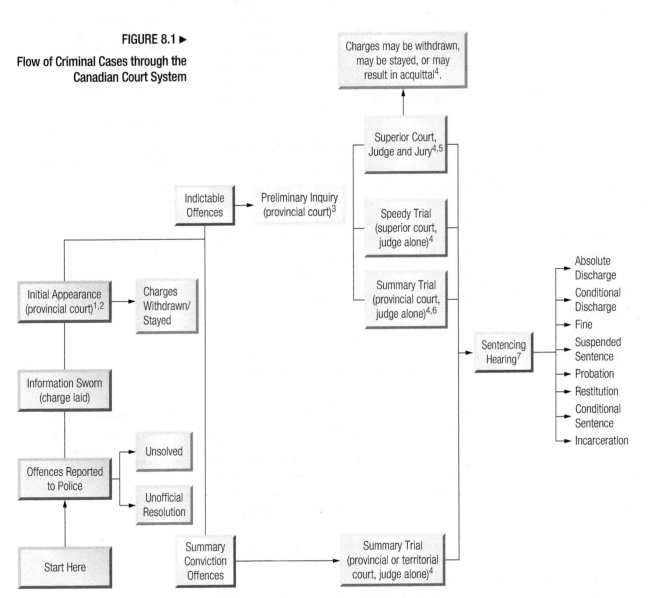

FIGURE 8.1 ▶

Flow of Criminal Cases through the Canadian Court System

[1] Appearance compelled by summons, arrest, or appearance notice.

[2] Initial sorting and judicial interim release (bail) are dealt with; election as to mode of trial may occur here or at a later hearing.

[3] Bypassed redirect indictment by the Crown, for offences within the absolute jurisdiction of the provincial or territorial court (s.483), and where accused elects a summary trial.

[4] Charges may be withdrawn, may be stayed, or may result in an acquittal in any mode of trial.

[5] This is the only mode of trial for more serious offences (s.427).

[6] This is the only mode of trial for less serious offences (s.483).

[7] Not all dispositions are available regarding all offences.

THE FLOW OF CASES THROUGH THE COURT SYSTEM

Figure 8.1 outlines the flow of cases through the criminal court system. It will be helpful to refer to this figure as you read through the materials in this chapter.

SUMMARY OFFENCES OR PROCEEDING SUMMARILY

When the case involves a **summary conviction offence**, or when the Crown proceeds summarily, it is resolved in a provincial court. Summary trials do not involve juries, and the sentences are usually less severe. When the accused is charged with an **indictable offence**, or the Crown proceeds by indictment on a **hybrid (elective) offence**, a different sequence of events unfolds. The *Criminal Code* (R.S.C. 1985, c. C-46) defines three categories of indictable offences: (1) offences under the absolute jurisdiction of provincial courts; (2) offences under the absolute jurisdiction of superior courts; and (3) electable offences. The key difference is *election*—that is, the right of the accused to choose to be tried by a judge instead of a jury.

ABSOLUTE JURISDICTION OF PROVINCIAL/TERRITORIAL COURTS

Section 553 of the *Criminal Code* lists the less serious indictable and hybrid (elective) offences wherein the accused person has no choice but to be tried in a provincial or territorial court, even if the Crown proceeds by indictment. The offences include theft (other than cattle theft), obtaining money on false pretenses, fraud, and mischief (where the subject matter of the offence is not a testamentary instrument and its value does not exceed $5,000). The list also includes keeping a gaming or betting house and driving while disqualified. There are no jury trials in provincial court.

ABSOLUTE JURISDICTION OF PROVINCIAL/TERRITORIAL SUPERIOR COURTS

Section 469 of the *Criminal Code* is a list of serious offences that are also non-electable offences. The list includes murder, treason, and piracy. These cases must be tried in a superior court before a jury unless both the accused and the provincial attorney general agree to waive this right.

The processing of non-electable offences begins with a **preliminary hearing**, sometimes called a preliminary inquiry. This (usually) short hearing is held to determine whether there is a *prima facie* case—that is, sufficient evidence to justify the time and expense of a criminal trial. A magistrate or provincial court judge listens to some (or all) of the Crown witnesses. The court may order a publication ban to protect the identity of any victim or witness and is required to order a publication ban to protect the identity of all victims of sexual offences and witnesses of sexual offenders who are less than 18 years old.[1]

The judge does not rule on the guilt of the accused at the preliminary hearing, but must decide if the Crown has evidence that could be used to prove guilt. If the judge does so decide, there is a *prima facie* case. If there is not a *prima facie* case, the judge will dismiss the case or at least dismiss the problematic charges against the accused. Usually, the matter is committed to trial, and a trial date is set. The accused person can waive the right to a preliminary hearing and go directly to trial.

In rare cases, generally involving more serious allegations, the provincial attorney general can skip the preliminary hearing and go straight to trial. This course of action is called "preferring the indictment." Recall from the discussion in Chapter 7 that dispensing with preliminary hearings has been suggested as a way to speed up the flow of cases in the courts.

Summary conviction offence

Generally, a less serious criminal offence that is triable before a magistrate or judge and, on conviction, carries a maximum penalty of a fine (not to exceed $5,000) or six months in a provincial correctional facility, or both.

Indictable offence

Generally, a more serious criminal offence that may carry maximum prison sentences of 14 years to life; examples include murder, robbery, and aggravated sexual assault.

Hybrid (or elective) offences

Offences that can be proceeded summarily or by indictment—a decision that is always made by the Crown.

Preliminary hearing

A hearing to determine if there is sufficient evidence to warrant a criminal trial.

ELECTABLE OFFENCES

Most indictable offences fall into neither of the two categories just described. These are the *electable offences*, and the accused person has three modes of trial from which to choose: (1) trial by a provincial or territorial court judge; (2) trial by a superior court judge sitting alone; or (3) trial by a superior court judge and a jury. The *Charter of Rights and Freedoms* guarantees the right to a jury trial if the alleged offence carries a maximum sentence of more than five years' imprisonment. However, not every accused person wants a jury trial.

Once an accused person has elected, he or she can re-elect another option or enter a guilty plea, in which case there will not be a trial. It is also possible (although this happens rarely) that the provincial attorney general may intervene and require a jury trial if the offence is punishable by more than five years' imprisonment and if the accused has chosen one of the first two options. Accused persons who choose option 1 do not have a preliminary hearing and waive their right to trial by jury. Accused persons who choose option 2 or 3 are entitled to a preliminary hearing unless they waive that right. Accused persons who abscond and who fail to appear for trial by jury on the appointed court date may lose their right to a jury trial.

THE PRE-TRIAL PROCESS

There are a number of steps involved in bringing a case to criminal court, and a major role is played by Crown counsel. This process must be mindful of the accused's Charter rights. Included in section 11 of the Charter, "legal rights" are the right for every citizen

(a) to be informed without unreasonable delay of the specific offence;

(b) to be tried within a reasonable time;

(c) not to be compelled to be a witness in proceedings against that person in respect of the offence;

(d) to be presumed innocent until proven guilty according to law in a fair and public hearing by an independent and impartial tribunal;

(e) not to be denied reasonable bail without just cause;

(f) except in the case of an offence under military law tried before a military tribunal, to the benefit of trial by jury where the maximum punishment for the offence is imprisonment for five years or a more severe punishment;

(g) not to be found guilty on account of any act or omission unless, at the time of the act or omission, it constituted an offence under Canadian or international law or was criminal according to the general principles of law recognized by the community of nations;

(h) if finally acquitted of the offence, not to be tried for it again and, if finally found guilty and punished for the offence, not to be tried or punished for it again; and

(i) if found guilty of the offence and if the punishment for the offence has been varied between the time of the commission and the time of sentencing, to the benefit of the lesser punishment.

Sections 12 through 14 of the Charter continue:

12. Everyone has the right not to be subjected to any cruel and unusual treatment or punishment.

13. A witness who testifies in any proceedings has the right not to have any incriminating evidence so given used to incriminate that witness in any other proceedings, except in a prosecution for perjury or for the giving of contradictory evidence.

14. A party or witness in any proceedings who does not understand or speak the language in which the proceedings are conducted or who is deaf has the right to the assistance of an interpreter.

LAYING AN INFORMATION AND LAYING A CHARGE

The police are usually responsible for laying an information, which is then ratified or rejected by the Crown. An *information* is a document that briefly outlines an allegation that a person has contravened a criminal law in a certain location during a specified period. Multiple offences are divided into separate counts.

Not all cases must be brought before a justice of the peace (JP). For certain offences, police officers are authorized to issue summons, traffic offence notices, appearance notices, and promise-to-appear notices. In such cases, accused persons are released *on their own recognizance*, which means they are responsible for ensuring that they appear in court on the designated date.

The information may be laid either after the suspect has been informed (as in the case of an arrest without a warrant or the use of an appearance notice) or before (see Figure 8.1). Remember from Chapter 5 that there are a limited number of circumstances in which the police can arrest without a warrant; there is a presumption that an appearance notice will be used for most cases. On receiving the information, the JP may not agree that the informant has made out a case; in practice, however, this rarely happens. If the JP determines there is sufficient reason to believe that a crime has been committed, the JP will issue either a warrant for the arrest of the person named in the information, or a summons that directs the named person to appear in provincial court on a specified date.

The police and the Crown exercise a considerable amount of discretion in deciding whether to lay a charge.[2] Charges are not laid in one-third of all violent crimes and property crimes that are cleared by the police, and across the country, 30 percent of all criminal cases are stayed, dismissed, or withdrawn by prosecutors and judges.[3] Reasons for not charging include the following: The victim or complainant is reluctant to cooperate; the suspect or an essential witness dies; or the suspect was committed to a psychiatric facility or was under the age of 12. The judiciary, including the Supreme Court of Canada (SCC), have been reluctant to review prosecutorial decision-making; however, the Supreme Court has held that provincial law societies are permitted to review such decisions to ensure adherence to professional standards (*Krieger v. Law Society of Alberta*, 2002 SCC 65).

Legal, administrative, and political factors may also influence the decision to lay a charge. Legal considerations include the reliability and likely admissibility of available evidence and the credibility of potential witnesses. Administrative factors include the workload and case volume of the Crown counsel's office, as well as the time and cost of prosecution relative to the seriousness of the crime. Political considerations include the need to maintain the public's confidence in the justice system.

In New Brunswick, Quebec, and British Columbia, the Crown must give approval before the police can lay a charge. Once the decision has been made to lay a charge, a police officer can initiate the process by laying an information before a JP. When doing so, the officer is called an *informant*. In practice, most informants are police officers, but any person can lay an information if they, *on reasonable grounds*, believe that a person has committed an offence.

COMPELLING THE APPEARANCE OF THE ACCUSED IN COURT

After a prosecution has been initiated, the next step is to ensure that the accused appears in court to answer the charge. This can be accomplished in a number of ways—for example, by arresting and placing the accused person in remand custody until the court appearance, or by allowing the accused person to remain at liberty in the community with a promise to appear on the court date. If the accused person does not appear, the judge can issue an arrest warrant. Figure 8.2 illustrates the various ways to compel an accused person to appear in court.

APPEARANCE NOTICE

If the alleged offence is not serious and the police have no reason to believe that the accused will fail to appear in court, an appearance notice can be issued followed by the laying of an information. The appearance notice sets out the details of the allegation against the accused person, provides the court date, and warns the accused that failure to appear in court is a criminal offence. If the charge is an indictable or elective offence, the appearance notice directs the person to appear at a specific location to be fingerprinted, pursuant to the *Identification of Criminals Act* (R.S.C. 1985, c. I-1). If the suspect is a young person, the appearance notice emphasizes the right of accused youths to legal representation.

SUMMONS

Another option is for the police to lay the information first, in which case the JP will likely issue a summons, which briefly states the allegation and directs the person to appear in court on a certain day. The fingerprint demand is also made, where applicable, as is the statement about youths' right to counsel under the *Youth Criminal Justice Act* (S.C. 2002, c. 1). The summons is then served on the accused, usually by a police officer. If the accused does not appear in court, and if there is proof that he received the summons, the judge may issue a bench warrant for his arrest; in addition, the accused may be charged criminally with failing to appear in court.

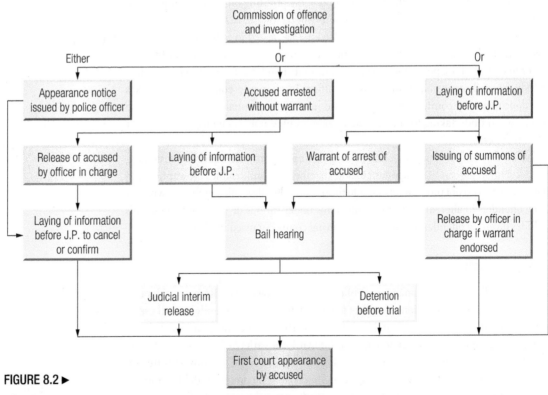

FIGURE 8.2 ▶

Compelling the Appearance of the Accused

Sources: A.W. Mewett and Mr. Justice Shaun Nakatsuru. 2001. *An Introduction to the Criminal Process in Canada* (4th ed.). Toronto: Carswell, p. 72. Reproduced by permission of Thomson Reuters Canada Limited.

ARREST

If the situation dictates, the police can arrest without a warrant (see Chapter 5) and *then* lay the information. Or, if there is time, an officer may seek an arrest warrant from a JP. Following the arrest, the next decision to be made is whether to release the accused from police custody or keep him or her in custody. Remember that the Charter protects people from arbitrary detention. The presumption is that everyone will be released from police custody after arrest.

There are only three circumstances in which immediate release might *not* occur: (1) The charge pertains to a serious indictable offence carrying a maximum sentence of more than five years in prison; (2) the police have reasonable grounds to believe the person will not appear in court; and/or (3) the police have reasonable grounds to believe it is necessary, in the public interest, to detain the accused. The public interest is defined as the need to establish the person's identity, to secure or preserve evidence, or to prevent the continuation or repetition of the offence or the commission of another offence.

A notable exception involves situations where a person is arrested pursuant to a security certificate (see below).

RELEASE BY THE POLICE

When issuing an arrest warrant, the JP usually gives the police some direction as to whether the accused person should be detained or released. When an arrest is made without a warrant, the police have the authority to release some accused persons from police custody; however, in some circumstances a bail hearing before a JP or a judge is required. When the offence is summary or elective (or one of a specified list of less serious indictable offences, including theft under $5,000), the arresting officer can simply issue an appearance notice or explain that a summons will be sought. In these circumstances, even those persons who have been arrested need not be placed in police custody.

For indictable offences carrying a maximum prison sentence of five years or less, the officer in charge of the police lockup has the authority to release the person from police custody. Several means are available to the officer in charge to compel the accused's later appearance in court. Beginning with the least consequential, they are a promise to appear, an undertaking to appear, and a recognizance not exceeding $500 (with or without deposit).

There are a number of steps involved in bringing a case to criminal court. In considering the prosecution process, it is important to note that there is considerable case attrition and that many cases do not progress very far into the system. Also, the police or the Crown send many offenders to alternative measures programs under various diversion schemes. This includes diverting offenders to the problem-solving courts discussed in Chapter 7.

THE DECISION TO LAY A CHARGE

As noted earlier in this chapter, the police and the Crown exercise a considerable amount of discretion in deciding whether to lay a charge.[4] Consequently, not all crime victims support charges being filed. Victims of domestic violence or spousal assault, for example, may refuse to cooperate with the Crown for a variety of reasons, including fear of retaliation, economic insecurity, and family pressures. Also, victims who are also involved in criminal activities (such as gang members) may be understandably reluctant to appear in court and to provide testimony against accused persons. In these circumstances, crime victims may not make use of the specialized services that are available.

JUDICIAL INTERIM RELEASE (BAIL)

[T]he bail system places heavy demands on the criminal justice system, ones that are difficult to satisfy. It is at the core of the system, not only because the outcomes of proceedings are so closely watched—although the details are protected by publication bans—but also because the system must balance the argument for detention against the presumption in favour of bail.[5]

Judicial interim release (bail) is the release of a person who has been charged with a criminal offence. It is overseen by a judicial functionary—usually a JP, but by a superior court judge if the offence is a serious one, such as murder. A person in police custody who is not released by the officer in charge must be brought to court within 24 hours or as soon as is reasonably possible. In addition, if the arrest warrant was issued by a JP, the police must bring the arrested person before a JP unless release was authorized when the warrant was issued.

Persons can be detained by the court only in situations where it is necessary to ensure attendance in court, to protect the public, and to maintain confidence in the administration of justice. The JP or judge must determine whether the accused will be released or will remain in custody until the case is disposed of. Section 11(e) of the Charter stipulates that any person charged with an offence has the right "not to be denied reasonable bail without just cause." Section 515 of the *Criminal Code*, entitled "Judicial Interim Release," requires judges to release accused persons on bail unless the Crown can show why bail should be denied.

If the Crown chooses to oppose the release of the accused, the Crown must demonstrate, at a *show cause hearing*, that detention of the accused until the trial date is necessary. In support of the recommendation that the accused be held in custody, the Crown can produce evidence of prior criminal convictions, other charges currently before the courts, or previous instances of failing to appear in court. In some cases, *reverse onus* applies; in other words, the accused must "show cause" why a release is justified. These situations include when the alleged indictable offence occurred while the person was on bail for another charge.

Detained persons seeking pre-trial release are often required to make multiple appearances in court before a ruling is made; overcrowded court dockets and a lack of personnel to participate in bail hearings are among the probable reasons for the delays.

Accused persons may also be asked to enter into a recognizance in which they agree to forfeit a set amount of money if they fail to appear in court. Generally, there is no requirement that the money be produced before the accused is released. However, a monetary deposit may be required if the accused is not normally a resident of the province or lives more than 200 kilometres away.

Another option is to release the accused on a recognizance in which a *surety* promises to forfeit a set amount of money if the accused fails to appear in court. A surety is a friend or relative who agrees to ensure the accused person's appearance for trial. In most cases involving a surety, a deposit is not required. However, if a large sum of money is involved, the existence of collateral to guarantee the payment may have to be demonstrated. If a surety withdraws support, the accused will be placed in custody unless another surety is immediately available.

Note that bail in Canada is different from the bail often seen on American television. In the United States, a deposit of money is required in order to guarantee a person's appearance in court; this practice is followed only in exceptional cases in Canada. There are in the U.S. bounty hunters who, on behalf of bail companies, track persons who have "skipped" bail. Canadian courts are generally sensitive to the possibility that

Judicial interim release (bail)

The release of a person charged with a criminal offence prior to trial.

cash bail requirements could leave accused persons of modest means to languish in custody while their more affluent counterparts remain free while awaiting trial. This principle that cash bails is not to be required in most cases was reiterated by the SCC in the case of *R. v. Kevin Antic* (2017 SCC 27). In its judgment, the court expressed concerns that persons in poverty and other marginalized persons would be unfairly penalized if cash payments were required.

THE CONDITIONS OF BAIL

If the JP or judge decides to release the accused, the conditions under which that release will take place must be determined. Again, the Crown must show cause why conditions should be attached to the release. There are "statutory" and "other" conditions of bail. Statutory conditions include reporting to a bail supervisor, while other conditions may include abstaining from alcohol or drugs, being under house arrest, and/or not having contact with certain persons. Young offenders may be required to live with a responsible person who agrees to guarantee that they will appear in court.

In some regions of the country, accused persons who are released on bail may be subject to bail supervision by probation officers and/or electronic monitoring (see Chapter 10). Accused persons who violate the conditions of release or who fail to appear in court at the designated time may have new charges filed against them for failing to comply. This offence carries a sentence of two years in jail if it is processed as an indictable offence.

There has been a trend toward increasing the number of bail conditions and the length of bail supervision due, in part, to increasing concerns with risk aversion in the criminal justice system. This has led some observers to argue that persons on bail are being "set up for failure" and are at high risk of being charged for failing to comply.[6,7] There are also concerns that low-income persons, Indigenous persons, racialized minorities, and persons with mental health and addiction issues are disproportionately impacted by the current manner in which the bail system operates.[8]

A study by the John Howard Society of Ontario found that 70 percent of the persons on bail had substance abuse issues, 40 percent had mental health issues, and 30 percent had concurrent challenges with both. The study found that "abstaining from drugs" and "abstaining from alcohol" were often imposed as conditions of bail and were closely related to failing to comply. As one lawyer commented, "The minute they don't comply, that's another offence. It's not a crime to drink alcohol but once it gets put into your bail conditions, drinking alcohol is an offence. It's an enormous pressure on people when they're on a long list of conditions."[9] In addition, considerable time and expense may be incurred by police services in rearresting offenders who have violated the conditions of their bail release. Figure 8.3 presents information on the use of bail and remand in Ontario.

ASSESSING RISK

It important that decisions to grant bail be carefully considered to ensure that the accused will abide by the conditions of the release and does not present a risk to the community. The decision of prosecutors to release an accused person on bail can have devastating consequences. In 2007, Peter Lee went on a killing spree in the community of Oak Bay, British Columbia, killing his wife, six-year-old son, his in-laws, and, finally, himself. Lee had previously attempted to kill his wife by driving his car, in which his wife was a passenger, into a pole. Over the expressed opposition of the police, Crown prosecutors allowed Lee to be released on $5,000 bail with the condition that he have no contact with his wife. Even though Lee began stalking his wife and violated other

FIGURE 8.3 ▶

The Mounting Costs of Bail and Remand in Ontario

Question: What does the information in Figure 8.3 suggest about the current use of bail and remand in Ontario, and what issues need to be addressed?

Source: Adapted from John Howard Society of Ontario. 2014. "Bail Remand Infographic." http://www.johnhoward.on.ca/wp-content/uploads/2014/10/Bail-Remand-Infographic.pdf.

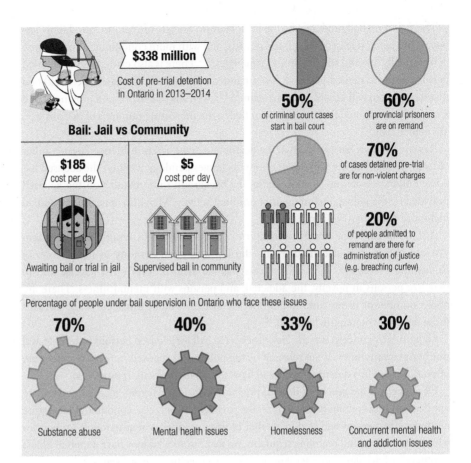

bail conditions, prosecutors did not have him arrested and he remained free, subsequently committing the murders.

In a subsequent coroner's inquiry into the incident, it was requested that the prosecutors, who did not oppose the decision to release Lee from police custody, testify before the inquest. The provincial government refused to make the prosecutors available to testify, a decision that was upheld by the B.C. Supreme Court which held that forcing the prosecutors to testify would infringe on their professional independence. Needless to say, this case generated considerable controversy. It has been suggested that risk assessments be conducted on certain accused persons, particularly in cases involving domestic violence.[10]

THE CHANGING NATURE OF JUDICIAL INTERIM RELEASE

A number of legal scholars have argued that, as currently practised, judicial interim release is not being utilized as intended under the *Bail Reform Act* (1972). More specifically, critics contend rather than being the exception as envisioned by the *Bail Reform Act*, the grounds for detention have been expanded. This has resulted in increasing numbers of accused persons being held in remand, despite falling crime rates (see Chapter 11).

A concern is that the presumption of innocence, a cornerstone of the legal system, is being undermined and that the number of "legally innocent" persons in jail has been increasing.[11] The changes in how bail is used in the criminal courts has been ascribed, in part, to a punitive penology and to an increasing aversion to risk among criminal justice decision-makers.[12]

The report on bail produced by the John Howard Society of Ontario found that "less people are being released on bail, less quickly, and with more conditions, during a time of historically low and still-declining crime rates."[13] There is also evidence that accused persons who are denied bail and are remanded into custody increases the likelihood that the accused will accept a plea bargain.[14,15] Overcrowding in certain provincial and territorial correctional facilities has been tied to the increasing numbers of persons who are denied bail.[16]

Research studies have found that the decision to grant bail is influenced by a number of factors, including the number of criminal charges pending, whether the accused has a fixed address, and any concerns raised by background information on the accused provided by the police, including prior criminal activity. Men also appear to be denied bail more often than women.

A study of eight bail courts in five provinces and territories found that the system was not operating in accordance with the law and often contrary to the *Charter of Rights and Freedoms*.[17] The bail process was found to be overly risk-adverse and to penalize persons in poverty, the addicted, and persons with mental illness. There are also a number of issues surrounding the use of bail, which, it has been argued, fails those persons who require legal aid.[18]

Of particular concern was the lack of access to bail for accused persons in remote and northern communities. If not released by the police, the accused in these regions were often flown out to a detention centre to have their bail application processed.[19]

Of concern is the revolving door of pre-trial detention, wherein accused persons are granted bail with conditions that may set the person up to fail (e.g., conditions that require abstinence by persons addicted to alcohol or drugs, residency requirements for persons who are homeless, and reporting requirements for persons who may have a mental illness or otherwise have difficulty attending an office at a specific time or location).[20]

Since the failure to comply with the conditions of bail is a criminal offence, this often creates a "revolving door" wherein accused persons are criminalized for behaviour that is otherwise not a crime.[21] These infractions are categorized as "administrative of justice" charges, and the number of these offences has also increased in recent years, due in large measure to violations of bail conditions.

A study in Vancouver found that 20 percent of the orders for persons released after being charged with a criminal offence contained a "no go" or "red zone" condition, which restricted them from certain areas of the city. These conditions disproportionately impacted poor and marginalized persons who were prevented from returning to the neighbourhoods where they could access services and shelter.[22]

PRE-TRIAL REMAND

Remand refers to accused individuals who have been charged and detained in custody and have either been denied bail, or have yet to appear before a judge, or are awaiting sentencing or the commencement of a custodial sentence. Persons are remanded into custody through the issuance of a warrant of committal by a JP or judge. Other accused are placed in custody after violating their bail conditions. All prisoners on remand are held in maximum-security facilities, regardless of the alleged offence and their criminal record, and have minimal access to programs and services.[23]

The number of persons detained on remand in provincial and territorial jails has tripled in the past three decades, and this population now represents nearly 60 percent of persons in these facilities.[24] The numbers of persons on remand outnumber sentenced offenders in confinement in most jurisdictions. There has also been an increase in the

Remand

The status of accused persons in custody awaiting trial or sentencing.

length of time spent on remand.[25] In Saskatchewan, there was a 104 percent increase in the number of persons on remand between 2006 and 2016. This was a major contributor to a 51 percent increase in provincial prison populations during this time.[26]

This means there are more persons being held on remand who have not been found guilty of any crime than there are persons who have been found guilty and sentenced. This includes an increasing number of women who are not serving sentences.[27] In Saskatchewan, for example, one-half of the persons in jail are on remand, awaiting trial.

Nearly one-quarter of those on remand are in prison for offences against the administration of justice—for example, breach of probation or bail conditions, or failure to appear in court.[28] Because offenders on remand are housed in provincial/territorial institutions, the increase in their numbers is straining resources and leading to overcrowding, an issue discussed in Chapter 11.

The costs of keeping a person awaiting trial in remand are high. In Ontario, it is $80,000 per year, compared to approximately $40,000 per year for a sentenced inmate.[29] Having persons on bail is much cheaper in Ontario as well: The per diem cost of incarcerating an adult on remand is about $183 per day, as opposed to about $5 per day if the person is on bail and under supervision in the community.[30] This is significant, given the small number of offenders on remand who are ultimately sentenced to custody (see Figure 8.3).

Remand populations include persons charged with violent offences but also persons with mental health and addiction problems. This presents challenges to correctional staff, whose role is generally limited to custody-type activities. It has been argued that the conditions faced by persons in remand violate international human rights standards, which require that those on remand who have not been convicted of a crime be held in conditions better than those for sentenced offenders.[31]

Research has found that pre-trial detention can exert pressure on accused persons to plead guilty.[32] As one accused person in remand stated:

> She [his lawyer] said, "If you're willing to pay a fine, the charges of armed assault, attempted murder, and robbery will be dropped. And if you plead guilty to dangerous driving and you pay a fine, they are willing to release you in two weeks from now. Otherwise, if you persist in pleading not guilty, you'll go back in custody waiting for a trial date and you face four years in prison." So, what do you think I said?[33]

Innovative approaches are required to reduce the larger numbers of persons on remand. In Manitoba, the John Howard Society (JHS) operates a residential facility that houses medium- to high-risk males who are on remand. This diversion program provides an opportunity for the men to take programming that would be unavailable had they been held in a provincial facility. The JHS also supervises a number of persons in the community who would otherwise be incarcerated while awaiting trial (http://www.johnhoward.mb.ca/wp/).

The persons participating in this program are more likely to observe the conditions of their bail and have a lower conviction rate than persons who are kept in remand who are subsequently released, evidence that there are lower-cost and effective remedies to the current remand situation.[34]

SECURITY CERTIFICATES

Security certificates

A process whereby non-Canadian citizens who are deemed to be a threat to the security of the country can be held without charge for an indefinite period of time.

Under the *Immigration and Refugee Protection Act* (S.C. 2001, c. 27), **security certificates** can be issued against non-citizens (visitors, refugees, or permanent residents) in Canada who are deemed to pose a threat to national security. These persons can then be held in detention, without charge, for an indefinite period of time. The certificates must be

THE CASE OF MOHAMED HARKAT

Mohamed Harkat entered Canada in 1995 from Algeria using a fake Saudi Arabian passport. In 1997, he was granted refugee status and in 2001 married a Canadian citizen. In 2002, Harkat was detained under a national security certificate, which declared him to be an agent of the terrorist organization al Qaeda and a threat to Canada. In 2006, Harkat was released on strict bail conditions. In 2013, his lawyers appeared before the SCC to argue that the process violates the Charter because it requires very little evidence about the allegations that a person poses a security threat to Canada. The SCC heard the case behind closed doors and, in its ruling in 2014, upheld the constitutionality of the security certificate. As of late 2017, the federal government was attempting to deport Harkat to Algeria.

Sources: J. Bronskill. 2016, March 17. "Facing Deportation, Mohamed Harkat Plans to Ask Government to Let Him Stay in Canada," *CTV News*. https://www.ctvnews.ca/politics/facing-deportation-mohamed-harkat-plans-to-ask-government-to-let-him-stay-in-canada-1.2820814; L. MacKinnon. 2014, May 14. "Mohamed Harkat Security Certificate Upheld by Top Court," *CBC News*. http://www.cbc.ca/news/politics/mohamed-harkat-security-certificate-upheld-by-top-court-1.2642459; *Canada (Citizenship and Immigration) v. Harkat*, 2014 SCC 37.

signed by both the Minister of Citizenship and Immigration and the Minister of Public Safety and emergency preparedness. Note that security certificates are not a criminal proceeding, but a process within the *Immigration and Refugee Protection Act*.

Foreign nationals who have a security certificate issued against them are automatically detained; permanent residents may be also detained if it is determined that they are a danger to society or are likely not to appear for court proceedings. Otherwise, permanent residents can be released under strict bail conditions.

A security certificate allows indefinite detention without charge or trial. The government is required only to provide a summary of the case against the person who is subjected to a security certificate. Case proceedings are usually conducted in secret. The reasonableness of the security certificate is reviewed by a judge of the Federal Court. If the court upholds the security certificate, it becomes a removal order from Canada and the person is deported to his or her home country. The Federal Court's decision in cases involving security certificates is final and cannot be reviewed. The case of Mohamed Harkat, who is the subject of a security certificate, is presented in Court File 8.1.

Amnesty International and other human rights groups have argued that the security certificate process violates fundamental human rights, including the right to a fair trial and the right to protection against arbitrary detention. Of concern is that much of the evidence in security certificate cases is heard *in camera* (behind closed doors), with only the Federal Court judge and government lawyers and witnesses present. Although persons who have been detained receive a summary of a portion of the evidence, the specific allegations against them and the sources of the allegations are not disclosed to the detainee. As well, evidence against the detainee may be presented in court without the detainee and his or her lawyer being present; this precludes a cross-examination of witnesses.

The ongoing controversy surrounding security certificates highlights the ongoing challenge of balancing individual rights with those of society. The debate is likely to continue.

DEFENDANTS' ACCESS TO LEGAL REPRESENTATION

All adults accused of crimes have the right to retain legal counsel. The *Charter of Rights and Freedoms* stipulates that persons who are arrested and detained must be informed of this fact, and they must be permitted to contact a lawyer before giving a statement, if they so choose. The right to retain legal counsel levels the playing field, so to speak, between the accused and the police and Crown attorney. Most Canadians are unaware of their rights or the intricacies of this country's complex legal system. In our adversarial system, the police and prosecution enjoy the home field advantage, and the lawyer is on the defendant's team.

Most accused persons require legal representation, yet not all of them can afford a lawyer. There is no blanket right to state-paid legal representation. At arrest, the police officer recites this Charter warning: "It is my duty to inform you that you have the right to retain and instruct counsel without delay" (see Police File 5.4). The right to *retain* counsel, however, does not impose an absolute duty on provincial governments to provide all accused persons with *free* counsel (see the discussion of legal aid below). However, all persons who are arrested or detained must have the opportunity to access preliminary advice from duty counsel through a toll-free telephone line, where such services exist.

In the case of *R. v. Prosper* ([1994] 3 SCR 236), the SCC ruled that detainees must be told they may qualify for free counsel if they meet the financial criteria of the local legal aid plan. However, the Supreme Court has also ruled that impoverished persons do not have a blanket right to legal counsel and that it was within the authority of the provincial/territorial governments to determine guidelines and criteria.

A major challenge in the territories is ensuring that accused persons have representation prior to their first appearance. Representation is often done over the telephone and is often of poor quality.[35]

LEGAL AID FOR THE ACCUSED

Clearly, it would be unacceptable for wealthy criminal defendants to have lawyers while poor defendants go unrepresented. At the same time, the universal provision of free legal representation would be expensive. There are also concerns about whether free representation can be as good as representation paid for by the accused.

Although every province/territory has a legal aid plan, Canada's jurisdictions vary greatly with respect to which types of cases qualify for assistance and which income levels are sufficiently low that an applicant is entitled to full or partial coverage. In recent years, several provinces have lowered the qualifying income levels as one means of stemming the dramatic rise in legal aid costs. Also, some types of cases no longer qualify for legal aid. It is not uncommon, for example, for applicants to be required to demonstrate that they face the very real prospect of being incarcerated for the offence. The stringent requirements to qualify for legal aid have been identified as a major impediment to access to justice.[36]

Across the country, legal aid services are delivered by lawyers in private practice, who are paid by a legal aid plan, by legal aid staff lawyers, and by lawyers working in legal aid clinics.[37]

There is an extensively documented crisis in legal aid in Canada, including underfunding, disparities in coverage, fragmentation wherein a client may qualify for legal aid only for a portion of their legal problem, and a lack of access to legal aid services among marginalized groups including Indigenous persons, newcomers, the poor, and others.[38]

This is a major issue in the larger debate over access to justice and the concern over the increasing numbers of persons in criminal courts who are self-represented. Judges are sensitive to the rights of persons who do not have legal counsel. In one case, the Ontario Court of Appeal ordered a new trial for a person convicted of possession and trafficking of drugs on the grounds that the trial judge failed to inform the accused, who was self-represented, about potential violations of his Charter rights by the police.[39]

FITNESS TO STAND TRIAL

A fundamental principle of the common law is that the accused person must be fit to stand trial. During the early stages of the court process, a lawyer may suspect that his or her client is suffering from some degree of mental illness. The existence of a mental disorder at the time of the offence may be integral to the defence strategy. However, mental disorder is a concern for another reason. Accused persons who cannot understand the object and consequences of the proceedings because of mental disorder are unfit to stand trial. In other words, they are unable to instruct their counsel or even fully appreciate that they are on trial.

At the request of the defence counsel or on its own initiative, the court may order that the accused person be assessed to determine fitness. That order is normally in force for no more than five working days, but a longer period can be ordered in "compelling circumstances." Section 2 of the *Criminal Code* states that an offender is unfit to stand trial when it is determined by the court that they are

> ...unable on account of mental disorder to conduct a defence at any stage of proceedings before a verdict is rendered or to instruct counsel to do so, and, in particular, unable on account of mental disorder to
>
> (a) understand the nature or object of the proceedings,
> (b) understand the possible consequences of the proceedings, or
> (c) communicate with counsel.

Almost always, the fitness of an accused person to stand trial is assessed by a psychiatrist while the accused is either remanded in custody or at a hospital or psychiatric facility. Those found unfit to stand trial may be detained in a mental health facility until deemed fit to stand trial by a body such as the Ontario Review Board. Once the accused is found fit, the trial can resume. If a person never achieves a state of fitness, the Crown may conclude that it is no longer prudent to continue the criminal prosecution. In cases where the alleged offence is not serious, an accused who is found to be unfit to stand trial may simply be diverted into the provincial/territorial mental health system. The person may subsequently become fit to stand trial at a later date.

Persons who are found fit to stand trial may still use the defence of not criminally responsible on account of mental disorder (NCRMD; discussed below), although it has been noted that the fact that an accused person is found to be mentally disordered at the time the offence was committed does not necessarily absolve him or her from being criminally responsible for the crime.[40]

ASSIGNMENT AND PLEA

The arraignment of the accused takes place early in the process, if not at first appearance. The charges are read in open court, and the accused can enter a plea. The two most common pleas are "guilty" and "not guilty." If a plea of guilty is entered, the case goes directly to sentencing (see Chapter 9); a plea of not guilty results in the case being bound over for trial. Technically, every accused person—even those who are "guilty as sin"—can plead not guilty. Remember that in our adversarial system of justice, all accused persons are presumed innocent, and the onus is on the Crown to prove guilt. Pleading not guilty, therefore, is not the same as claiming innocence.

Accused persons may plead not guilty because they are, in fact, innocent; because they have a plausible defence and want to exercise their right to a trial; and/or because their lawyer has advised them to do so. Although most cases end with a guilty plea, they do not always begin that way. Accused persons often plead not guilty at the outset of the process, in part to strengthen their position in any plea bargaining that may take place. Accused who plead not guilty can change their plea to guilty at any point before the verdict.

PLEA BARGAINING

The majority of cases that come to the criminal court are resolved not in a trial in a courtroom. In Ontario in 2014–15, for example, only 5.1 percent of all adult cases were resolved with a trial. Jury trials are even more rare.[41] Rather, cases are resolved behind-the-scenes via **plea bargaining** (also referred to as *plea negotiation*), which involves discussions between the Crown prosecutor and the defence surrounding the charge(s) facing the accused, discussions of procedure, discussions of the sentence, and discussions of the facts of the alleged offence, all of which are designed to expedite the trial of the accused.[42]

Plea bargaining is a fixture, and some would say indispensable component of the criminal justice system, despite the fact that there is no mention of plea bargaining in the *Criminal Code* and no federal, provincial, or territorial legislation or guidelines exist to regulate this practice. As one lawyer has noted, "In our Canadian justice system guilty pleas are the rule and trials the exception."[43]

These discussions may result in a plea agreement, whereby the accused gives up the right to make the Crown prove the case at trial in exchange for the promise of a benefit.

For example, the Crown can promise the possibility of a lower sentence by withdrawing some charges; by reducing a charge to a *lesser but included offence* (that is, an offence that is similar but not as serious); by proceeding summarily rather than with an indictment; by asking the judge that multiple prison sentences run concurrently rather than consecutively; or by agreeing to a joint submission to the judge about sentencing. Note that once a plea agreement has been agreed to by the Crown and defence, it can only be repudiated in exceptional circumstances.

Historically, plea bargaining was felt not to have a role in the criminal justice process, the Law Reform Commission stating in 1975 that it was "something for which a decent criminal justice system has not place."[44] However, by 2016, the court's sentiment had changed. In the case of *R. v. Anthony-Cook* (2016 SCC 43), the SCC described plea agreements as "vitally important to the well-being of our criminal justice system" and noted that without plea negotiations, the justice system would "eventually collapse under its own weight." The reasons why plea bargaining changed from pariah to accepted practice remain to be explored by Canadian scholars.

Victims' rights legislation requires that crime victims be kept informed of the status of their cases during the criminal justice process. However, only in the provinces of Ontario (S.O. 1995, c. 6) and Manitoba (2015; C.C.S.M. c. V55) do victims have the right to receive information about plea negotiations. Only in these jurisdictions is the Crown required to consult with victims during the plea bargaining process.[45]

Plea bargaining

An agreement whereby an accused pleads guilty in exchange for the promise of a benefit.

Section 606 of the *Criminal Code* requires that presiding judges determine that a guilty plea entered by an accused as a result of a plea agreement has been entered into voluntarily and that the accused understands the nature and consequences of the plea. The SCC has ruled (*R. v. Nixon*, 2011 SCC 34) that plea agreements between Crown and defence are not binding. Once the Crown and the defence have agreed upon a sentence, a joint submission is made to the presiding judge.

While judges are not legally bound to accept the recommendation contained in a joint submission, the general principle is that judges will depart from the recommendation only in instances where it is contrary to the public interest to do so.[46] This has led some observers to argue that it is the Crown prosecutors, rather than judges, who play a primary role in determining sentences.[47]

There are also concerns that plea bargaining can lead to wrongful convictions, particularly in cases where the accused is promised that the charges will be reduced and the severity of the sentence will be lessened.[48] The issue of plea bargaining continues to be a source of controversy in the criminal justice system. See At Issue 8.1.

ACCESS TO THE COURTROOM

A key concept in Canadian criminal justice is the **open court principle**, which holds that, except in special circumstances, every stage of the court process must be open and accessible to the public.

This principle has been established in various decisions of the SCC (e.g. A.G. *(Nova Scotia) v. MacIntyre*, [1982] 1 SCR 175). This principle has been described

Open court principle

The principle that, with certain exceptions, every stage of the court process must be open and accessible to the public.

by Canadian courts as "one of the hallmarks of a democratic society" (*CBC v. New Brunswick*, [1996] 3 SCR 480). Public access to court proceedings is viewed as essential to ensure the accountability of the judicial system (*A.G. (Nova Scotia) v. MacIntyre*).

This means that, with certain exceptions, court proceedings, including the testimony of witnesses, occur in courtrooms that are accessible to the general public. The decision to close a courtroom to the public is taken only when it is determined by the judge to be in the interest of public morals, the maintenance of order, or the proper administration of justice. The applicant for a closed courtroom—usually the prosecutor—must prove that public exclusion is necessary. Judges may also issue publication bans. In trials involving certain offences, including sexual offences involving children, the judge can order that the identity of the complainant or of a witness and any information that could disclose their identity not be published or broadcast.

In contrast to the U.S., however, the open court principle has not extended to cameras being allowed in the courtroom to record the proceedings. Efforts by the media to record and broadcast court proceedings have generally been met with opposition from all parties in the courtroom workgroup.[49]

There have been exceptions to the general prohibition of cameras in the courtroom. The SCC has allowed cameras to broadcast most of its proceedings since 1995, and several provinces have, on occasion, allowed cameras to record proceedings in specific cases. In 2016, an Alberta judge allowed cameras in the court for the verdict in the case of Travis Vader. Vader had pled not guilty to two counts of first-degree murder in the deaths of an elderly couple whose bodies were never found.[50] (Watch the verdict at https://www.youtube.com/watch?v=FcokRPEjOuc.)

Ironically, the presiding judge erred in finding Vader guilty of second-degree murder, using a section of the *Criminal Code* that had been found by the SCC in 1990 to be unconstitutional. The judge's verdict was subsequently changed to manslaughter, and Vader was sentenced to life in prison with no possibility of parole for seven years.

MODE OF TRIAL: TRIAL BY JUDGE ALONE OR BY JUDGE AND JURY

The key roles in criminal courts are played by the judge, the prosecutor or Crown counsel, the defence counsel, the witnesses, and the jury. The "trier of fact" in a criminal case—usually a judge—decides whether the guilt of the accused person has been proved beyond a reasonable doubt. In a small number of cases, a jury of citizens makes this decision.

The right for an accused to have a trial by jury is set out in section 11(f) of the *Charter of Rights and Freedoms*, which states that any person charged with an offence has the right "except in the case of an offence under military law tried before a military tribunal, to the benefit of trial by jury where the maximum punishment for the offence is imprisonment for five years or a more severe punishment."

Jury trials are virtually mandatory in some types of cases, an available option in many, and prohibited in others. Jury trials are not available for summary conviction offences; nor, with a handful of exceptions, are they available in youth court. In fact, there are key differences in the prosecution of summary conviction offences and indictable offences. See Figure 8.1.

Until the re-emergence of restorative justice approaches to criminal justice two decades ago (see Chapter 13), the criminal jury was the last vestige of significant community involvement in the administration of justice. Juries are involved in determining the guilt or innocence of accused persons, deciding parole eligibility for convicted offenders, and determining whether the eligibility for parole is reduced. Jury trials are actually quite rare in the justice system, and most criminal matters are tried by judge alone.

The responsibility for setting the qualifications for jurors falls under provincial jurisdiction. With the exception of Yukon, Northwest Territories, and Nunavut, where juries are composed of six persons, all juries in criminal cases have 12 jurors.

There are three important differences between trial by jury and trial by judge alone. First, in jury trials, the jury decides on the true facts and determines the person's guilt; in trials with a judge alone, the judge determines the law and the facts. Second, in a jury trial, the judge makes a "charge to the jury," during which the judge instructs the jurors about the law that applies to the case. And, third, judges give reasons for their decisions. Lawyers use these reasons to help predict outcomes in future cases with similar facts. Jurors don't give reasons with their verdict.

In cases involving trial by jury, the presiding judge must order a pre-hearing conference, which is attended by the Crown, the defence counsel, and the judge. They can discuss any "matters to promote a fair and expeditious trial." In non-jury cases, pre-trial conferences are optional. Informal "pre-trials" are becoming increasingly routine. They take place in a judge's chambers and involve an off-the-record discussion of issues surrounding the case. These discussions provide an opportunity for plea bargaining, since the presence of a judge can promote a fair resolution between the two parties (which is preferable to eleventh-hour bargaining on the courthouse steps).

The stages in a criminal trial by jury are set out in Figure 8.4.

▼ FIGURE 8.4

Stages in a Criminal Trial by Jury

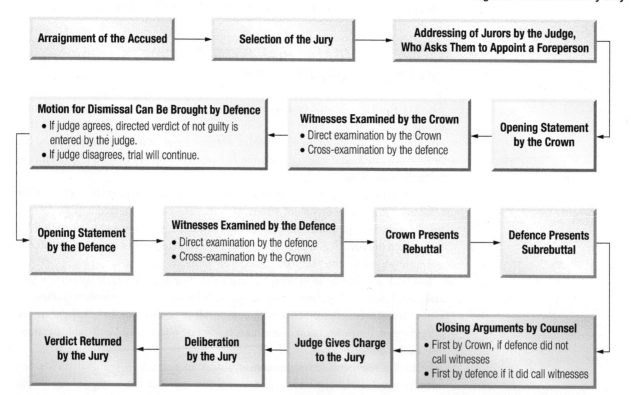

DISCLOSURE OF EVIDENCE

A key component of the prosecution of criminal cases is the disclosure of evidence. There are several SCC decisions that affect the disclosure of evidence in criminal trials. The court's ruling in *R. v. Stinchcombe* ([1991] 3 SCR 326) requires that the Crown give the defence lawyer access to all evidence that might be presented by the prosecution in a trial, especially any potentially *exculpatory evidence* (evidence that might indicate the accused did not commit the crime). As noted in Chapter 6, this requirement has placed significant resource demands on the police and has been a contributor to the delays encountered in preparing cases for trial.

The decision in *R. v. McNeil* (2009 SCC 3) places a duty on the Crown to disclosure any records of misconduct by the investigating police officers in the case. In *R. v. O'Connor* (1995 4 SCR 411), the SCC held that a defendant who had been charged with sexual assault did not have an automatic right to the medical and therapy records of his accusers. The ruling in this case prompted the federal government to enact legislation that sets out a procedure for disclosure of personal records, including medical records, in all sexual offence cases. This includes the requirement that the court take into account the privacy and equality rights of women.

This process is called *disclosure of evidence* or *discovery* and includes, among other materials, the names and addresses of persons the Crown intends to call as witnesses, the results of any examinations or tests on the accused, materials from wiretaps and surveillance, and the names of expert witnesses that the Crown intends to call.

The failure to disclose evidence can trigger a Charter remedy because it impairs an accused person's right to make full answer and defence to the charges. However, the disclosure requirement does not work in reverse: the defence is not obliged to disclose material to the prosecution. Recall from the discussion in Chapter 4 that the requirements of disclosure have placed an added resource burden on police services who may spend as much time preparing documents related to the investigation as in the investigation itself.

THE TRIAL

Stay of proceedings

An act by the Crown to terminate or suspend court proceedings after they have commenced.

A trial takes place if the accused person who pleads not guilty does not change that plea and the Crown does not withdraw the charges or terminate the matter with a **stay of proceedings**. Especially in provinces or territories where the police have sole responsibility for laying charges, a Crown attorney may review cases early in the process and screen out those that might not succeed, as well as those for which there is insufficient evidence to secure a conviction. Because of this practice of case screening, and guilty pleas on the part of accused persons, most cases do not go to trial. Trials are actually quite rare, occurring in only about 10 percent of criminal cases.[51] The majority of cases are resolved via plea bargaining or by the Crown counsel staying the proceedings or withdrawing the charges.

The accused person is generally present throughout the proceedings, and may testify but is not required to do so. To avoid media scrutiny, a "famous person" being charged may be represented by counsel, negotiate a guilty plea through a plea bargain, and/or not appear at all.

Figure 8.5 illustrates the traditional common law court setting, in this instance the Ontario Court of Justice. There are slight variations in the layout of different courts. To take a virtual tour of several provincial courts in Alberta, visit http://www.albertacourts.ab.ca.

"Your Honor, the relevance of this line of questioning will become apparent in a moment."

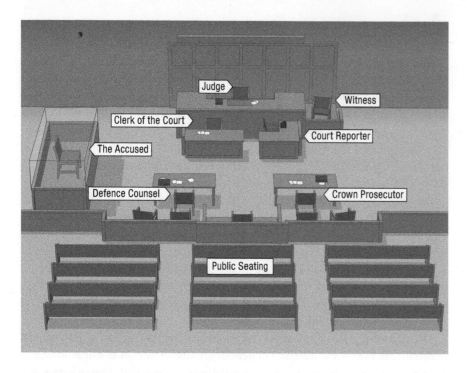

Judge

Witness

Clerk of the Court

Court Reporter

The Accused

Defence Counsel

Crown Prosecutor

Public Seating

THE CASE FOR THE CROWN

It is the task of the Crown to prove the guilt of an accused person beyond a reasonable doubt; if the Crown fails to do this, there can be no conviction. The trial begins with the prosecution calling witnesses and presenting evidence in support of the position that the accused is guilty. For interpersonal offences, the testimony of the complainant may well be the Crown's key evidence. At the very least, the Crown attorney must produce evidence covering all the major elements of the offence.

For example, in a murder case, the Crown must show that someone died and that the death was culpable homicide (that is, not an accident or death by natural causes). There should be evidence linking the accused to that death (e.g., eyewitnesses, fingerprints,

THE CANADIAN PRESS/Paul Chiasson

◄ Crown prosecutors arrive at court.

DNA evidence, or circumstantial evidence, such as a strong motive on the part of the accused). Expert witnesses may be called to interpret evidence or to present findings from the police investigation.

At trial, there is *direct evidence* and *circumstantial evidence*, best distinguished by the following analogy:

> Imagine we wake up in the morning and when we peek out of the window to look at the weather for the day (this example is obviously pre-smartphones) we notice the road, the sidewalk, and the ground is wet and rain is falling from the sky. We accept, therefore, that it is raining, and if we have been in Calgary all summer, we might even say "it is raining again."
>
> Returning to our example, if we look out of our window and we see the road is wet but the sky is clear, we cannot directly aver to what the weather was like before we woke. We can, however, draw a "rational" or "reasonable" inference from the state of wetness and say, "it was raining sometime before" but we did not observe that happen. We are not "direct" witnesses to this assumed event. In fact, we could be very wrong about our inference. For instance, if the road is wet but the sidewalk and ground is not, then we cannot safely assume it rained. A more "rational" or "reasonable" explanation may be that the City of Calgary street cleaners came by and washed the road.[52]

The first scenario is an example of direct evidence, as it is based on direct observation. The second is an example of circumstantial evidence in that it is not directly observed, but requires inferences to be drawn from the facts.

In the past, for circumstantial evidence to be admitted in court, judges required the prosecution to disprove all of the other possibilities. That changed in the SCC decision in *R. v. Villaroman* (2016 SCC 33). Images of child pornography had been found on the defendant's computer by a shop repairperson. The accused was convicted at trial based on the circumstantial evidence that he owned the computer and his was the only user name. The Alberta Court of Appeal overturned the conviction, ruling that the trial judge erred in not considering other ways that the images could have found their way onto the computer. However, the SCC reinstated the conviction, ruling that Crown does not have to disprove other possible explanations.

There is also *hearsay evidence*, which is, "Evidence that is offered by a witness of which they do not have direct knowledge but, rather, their testimony is based on what others have said to them" (http://www.duhaime.org/LegalDictionary/H/Hearsay.aspx). Hearsay evidence, also commonly referred to as "second-hand evidence," "rumour," or "gossip," is rarely admissible in court. The SCC has noted that a major problem with hearsay evidence is that "it has not been subjected to the trial by fire of cross-examination" (*R. v. Abbey*, [1982] 2 SCR 24). In a more recent case, the SCC reaffirmed the "high bar" for admitting hearsay evidence (*R. v. Bradshaw*, 2017 SCC 35).

There is no guarantee that evidence presented to the court will be admitted. The authority for courts to exclude evidence is contained in section 24(2) of the *Charter of Rights and Freedoms*. Evidence can be excluded if the accused's Charter rights were violated, including an illegal search by the police, or if admitting the evidence would bring the administration of justice into disrepute. In the case of *R. v. Neyazi* (2014 ONSC 6838), an Ontario Superior Court Justice excluded drugs that were found during an illegal search after determining the search was based on racial profiling by the police.

THE CASE FOR THE DEFENCE

At the close of the Crown's case, the defence may enter either an insufficient-evidence motion or a no-evidence motion, suggesting to the judge that the state has not made its case and that there is no point to continuing the trial. If the judge agrees, the case

◄ A defence lawyer enters the courtroom.

is dismissed. If not, the defence presents its case. The defence attorney can cross-examine Crown witnesses and challenge the admissibility of Crown evidence.

Generally, the sexual history of the victim is inadmissible as evidence in court when defendants want to show that the complainant was "more likely to have consented" to the alleged offence or "is less worthy of belief." The restriction is not absolute, and defendants can argue that the information is necessary for their defence.

As part of the case for the defence, the accused person may testify (give evidence) on his or her own behalf, but is not obliged to do so. For accused persons who testify in court, there are advantages and disadvantages. On the one hand, testifying gives defendants an opportunity to present their side of the story and establish credibility.

On the other hand, a defendant who testifies opens the door to cross-examination by the Crown prosecutor, who will attempt to point out weaknesses and inconsistencies in the testimony. In addition, if the defendant presents good character or reputation as a reason why he or she could not have committed the offence, the prosecution is free to enter into evidence any previous convictions. Otherwise, the jury or judge cannot learn if the accused has a prior criminal record (at least until the sentencing phase, if the defendant is found guilty).

An accused acting as his or her own counsel is not usually permitted to cross-examine a witness under the age of 14 in cases involving sexual offences or violent crimes. The court will appoint a lawyer to undertake that task. The judge has discretion and can permit an unrepresented defendant to conduct the cross-examination if the proper administration of justice requires it.

The more common defences that are used in the criminal court process can be generally grouped into (1) "You've got the wrong person"; (2) the mental state of the accused at the time the alleged offence occurred; (3) justifications (or excuses) for having committed a criminal act; and (4) procedural defences.

THE "YOU'VE GOT THE WRONG PERSON" DEFENCE

This defence strategy centres on one of two possibilities: that the police arrested the wrong person, or that the complainant fabricated the allegation, thus no crime was committed. To support a claim of false accusation, the defence may present evidence verifying the defendant's alibi. One example of a verified alibi is establishing that the defendant was in jail when the offence was committed.

THE MENTAL STATE OF THE ACCUSED AT THE TIME OF THE ALLEGED OFFENCE

The three most common defences that are centred on the mental state of the accused at the time of the alleged offence are (1) mental disorder (not criminally responsible on account of mental disorder, or NCRMD); (2) intoxication; and (3) automatism.

NOT CRIMINALLY RESPONSIBLE ON ACCOUNT OF MENTAL DISORDER (NCRMD)

Not criminally responsible on account of mental disorder

A defence that relieves the accused person of criminal responsibility due to a mental disorder.

Accused persons who are found fit to stand trial may use the defence of **not criminally responsible on account of mental disorder (NCRMD)**. This is contained in section 16 of the *Criminal Code* which states, "No person is criminally responsible for an act committed, or an omission made while suffering from a mental disorder that rendered the person incapable of appreciating the nature and quality of the act or omission or of knowing that it was wrong."

An assessment ordered by the court is used to determine this verdict, which is not a finding of guilt or a conviction for the offence. The accused person is determined not to have been responsible for his or her behaviour at the time the offence was committed. This may include cases in which the accused is suffering from fetal alcohol spectrum disorder (FASD), a condition of brain damage caused by a person's birth-mother drinking during pregnancy. In approximately 1 percent of the cases heard in adult criminal courts, the accused is found NCRMD.[53]

The court has a number of options for persons determined to be NCRMD: detention in a hospital, a conditional discharge, or an absolute discharge.[54] Legal observers have cautioned that NCRMD is not a true defence, as a verdict of NCRMD is not that the accused didn't commit the offence, but that the defendant is not criminally responsible for the act due to their mental state at the time.[55]

Persons who are found NCRMD are subjected to annual reviews by provincial review boards and may qualify for escorted and unescorted passes into the community. Historically, the victim's families were not notified of decisions made by the review boards. Research has found that there is considerable variability between the provinces in the number of accused persons found NCRMD, which suggests that there may be significant differences between jurisdictions in how the law is being applied.[56] The data reveal variations over time within provinces as well. In Quebec, for example, the number of NCRMD findings has increased over the years from 1992 ($N = 177$) to 2005 ($N = 407$) to 2011–12 ($N = 540$).[57]

As part of its "get tough on crime" approach, the federal Conservative government (2006–15) enacted the *Not Criminally Responsible Reform Act* (S.C. 2014, c. 6). The intent of the legislation was to place public safety as the primary consideration in managing persons found NCRMD. Those offenders determined to be at risk of committing violent offences in the future would be required to have this status revoked by a court, prior to being released by a review board. Persons designed as "high risk" are not allowed to have unescorted visits out into the community, and victims are provided with information on when the offender is being discharged and where the offender lives.[58] This legislation was designed to address what was perceived to be a review process that was too lenient on offenders who had been found NCRMD.

Critics argue that the legislation is an illustration of the politicization of the criminal justice process and runs counter to the research on persons who are designated NCRMD.[59] There is no evidence that this approach will increase public safety. Rather, it is argued, the legislation further stigmatizes mentally ill offenders, particularly those who are designated as "high risk."[60]

Research on persons found NCRMD in British Columbia, Ontario, and Quebec (N = 1,800) found that this is a heterogenous group with respect to their mental health issues and involvement in crime and that only a small percentage of this group had committed serious violent offences.[61] The overall recidivism rates of this group after three years was 17 percent, which is lower than other groups of offenders (see Chapter 12), and those persons who had committed severe violent crimes were less likely to recidivate.[62]

Cases in which an accused was found NCRMD are often high profile and surrounded by controversy. The case of Vincent Li, who was referred in some quarters as the "poster boy" for the reform of NCRMD is one example.[63] See Court File 8.2.

COURT FILE 8.2

A DEATH ON THE GREYHOUND: A CASE OF NOT CRIMINALLY RESPONSIBLE DUE TO MENTAL DEFICIENCY

On July 30, 2008, Vincent Li, a passenger on a Greyhound bus travelling through Manitoba, attacked a fellow passenger, Tim McLean, stabbing him to death, decapitating him, and cannibalizing part of the victim's body.

Li was arrested at the scene and charged with second-degree murder. He pled not guilty. Defence counsel argued that Li was not criminally responsible for his actions due to mental illness. At trial, evidence was presented by a forensic psychiatrist that Li was schizophrenic and suffered a major psychotic episode that led to the killing. Li had told the psychiatrist that God had told him that the victim was a "force of evil" who was about to stab Li unless he took action to protect himself. Testimony from the psychiatrist was that Li was not capable of understanding that his actions were wrong.

Both Crown and defence argued that Li was not criminally responsible due to his mental illness and the presiding judge agreed. In 2009, Li was sent to a provincial psychiatric facility and placed under the authority of the Manitoba Criminal Code Review Board, which has the authority to determine how long he would remain in the facility.

The case stirred considerable controversy when, in 2013, the review board accepted the recommendation from Li's mental health treatment team that he be allowed to have supervised excursions into Winnipeg and surrounding areas.[a] In 2016, Li began living on his own in an apartment in Winnipeg, while being supervised to ensure he took his medication and attended counselling.

In 2017, the review board gave Li (who had changed his name to Will Lee Baker) an absolute discharge, stating that he did not pose a threat to community safety. The board's decision was based on testimony from mental health professionals that he had been a model patient

The Greyhound bus on which Vincent Li attacked Tim McLean

THE CANADIAN PRESS/Winnipeg Free Press—Ken Gigliotti

and that the "weight of evidence" indicated that he was not a risk.[b] The board also cited a 1999 SCC ruling that required it to grant an absolute discharge if the person did not pose a risk to community safety.[c]

The decision was heavily criticized by the victim's family, politicians, and a forensic psychologist who stated that Baker's absolute discharge was not in the public interest.[d]

---

[a] J. Turner. 2013, May 17. "Greyhound Bus Killer Vince Li Gets Freedom to Travel to Winnipeg, Beaches," *Winnipeg Sun*. http://www.winnipegsun.com/2013/05/17/greyhound-bus-killer-vince-li-gets-freedom-to-travel-to-winnipeg-beaches.

[b] *CBC News*. 2017, February 10. "Vince Li, Who Beheaded Passenger on Greyhound Bus, Given Absolute Discharge." http://www.cbc.ca/news/canada/manitoba/vince-li-discharge-1.3977278.

[c] *Winko v. British Columbia (Forensic Psychiatric Institute)*, [1999] 2 SCR 625.

[d] *CBC News*, "Vince Li, Who Beheaded Passenger on Greyhound Bus, Given Absolute Discharge."

INTOXICATION

Some of the most controversial defences centre on the argument that accused persons are not criminally liable because they could not have formed *mens rea*. This mental state could have been temporary and situational or the result of a long-term mental disorder. In order to convict in most cases, the judge or jury must believe that the action under scrutiny—the *actus reus*—was a voluntary exercise of the person's will. In a 1994 decision, the Supreme Court of Canada found a man not guilty of raping a woman because he had been so intoxicated that his actions were not voluntary (*R. v. Daviault*, [1994] 3 SCR 63).

This decision triggered a public outcry, and the federal government responded by amending the *Criminal Code* to specify that self-induced intoxication cannot be used to excuse certain types of interpersonal offences, including assault and sexual assault, even if *mens rea* is absent. This was reaffirmed in the SCC ruling in *R. v. Tatton* (2015 SCC 33), wherein the court ruled that intoxication cannot be used as a defence unless the accused was drunk to the point of automatism.

AUTOMATISM

In what is considered the landmark ruling on the defence of automatism in *R. v. Stone* ([1999] 2 SCR 290), a justice of the SCC defined automatism as "a state of impaired consciousness ... in which an individual, though capable of action, has no voluntary control over that action." In one case, a Toronto-area man drove across town, fatally stabbed his mother-in-law, and promptly turned himself in to the police, confessing repeatedly to the crime. Despite overwhelming evidence that he had killed the woman, he was acquitted at trial. The jury accepted the defence evidence that the man had been sleepwalking and therefore could not have formed the requisite *mens rea*. The defence of automatism does not always result in an outright acquittal.

JUSTIFICATIONS: EXCUSE-BASED DEFENCES

The second set of defence strategies can be categorized as excuse-based defences. These are set out in Figure 8.6.

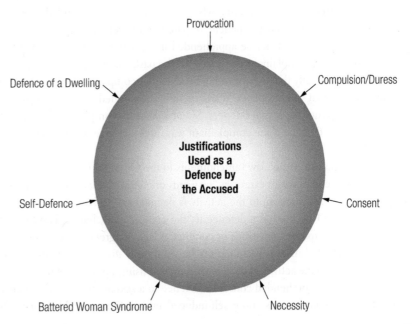

FIGURE 8.6 ▶

Justifications Used as a Defence by the Accused

A full discussion of each of these defences could consume an entire text,[64] so here only a limited comment is made. For a SCC case involving excuse-based defences, see *R. v. Ryan* (2013 SCC 3).

PROVOCATION

The defence of provocation is often associated with claims of self-defence. Persons charged with murder can claim provocation to justify a reduction to the charge of manslaughter (here, provocation is a partial defence). In recent years, the courts have heard a number of these cases and the decisions seem to turn on the specific events. Critics claim that the SCC has placed restrictions on the right of accused to use provocation as a defence.

In *R. v. Cairney* (2013 SCC 55), the SCC rejected Mr. Cairney's defence that he was provoked into killing Stephen Ferguson who was extremely abusive towards Mr. Cairney's cousin over a long period of time. On one occasion, Mr. Cairney had witnessed Mr. Ferguson kneel on his cousin's throat and threaten to kill her. Mr. Cairney argued at trial that knowing and witnessing the abuse for over a decade had caused him to lose control and shoot Mr. Ferguson.

CONSENT

The issue of consent is a contentious issue in the criminal justice system and has been at the centre of a number of high-profile cases. The defence of consent is based on the argument that the complainant voluntarily agreed to engage in the activity in question. A common example: Two individuals can consent to a fistfight if both parties appreciate the risks and neither is seriously injured. However, if one of the individuals escalates the altercation into an assault and the other party is seriously injured or killed, then consent is not generally available as a defence.

Similarly, a hockey player has consented to some level of violence and perhaps physical injury upon stepping on the ice. However, this consent does not extend to intentional acts of violence, such as being chopped across the face with the blade of a hockey stick.

However, lack of resistance to an assault or sexual assault does not constitute consent if the submission of the complainant was achieved by force, threats, fraud, or the exercise of authority. An example of this last is where there is a clear power imbalance, as in the case of teacher–student, doctor–patient, or parent–child relationships.

Consent can be real, or it can be apprehended if the accused mistakenly believed that a non-consenting complainant consented. In the past, some accused persons were able to argue successfully that they honestly believed the complainant was consenting to sexual activity—that "no meant yes." Parliament has responded by restricting the use of consent as a defence for sexual offences. Since 1988, for example, consent has not been available as a defence if the complainant was under the age of 14 at the time of the offence.

In 1992, the "no means no" law (amendments to the *Criminal Code*) was enacted. If a sexual assault complainant expresses "by words or conduct, a lack of agreement to engage in the activity," consent to the activity is deemed not to have been obtained. Neither can consent be used as a defence if "the complainant, having consented to the sexual activity, expresses, by words or conduct, a lack of agreement to continue to engage in the activity." Also, consent cannot be voluntarily given by someone who is induced to engage in the activity with a person who is abusing a position of trust, power, or authority. Nor is apprehended consent a defence to a sexual assault if the accused person's belief in consent arose from self-induced intoxication or reckless or willful disregard, or if the accused did not take "reasonable steps" to ascertain whether the complainant was in fact consenting.

The challenges surrounding the issue of consent are often most prominent in cases of alleged sexual assault. Observers have noted that there is often a disconnect between the law on sexual consent and "accepted behaviour" social norms surrounding consent in sexual relations.[65] In the case of *R. v. Ewanchuk* ([1999] 1 SCR 330), the SCC held that there was no defence of "implied consent" to sexual assault.

There have been a number of high-profile cases involving allegations of sexual assault that have sent protestors to the streets. These cases are surrounded by controversy. They illustrate the issues and controversy that often surround consent in sexual assault cases.

In one case in 2017, a judge in Nova Scotia found a taxicab driver not guilty of sexual assault. The driver had been arrested and charged after a woman was found by a police officer in the backseat of his taxi, naked from the chest down, severely intoxicated, and unconscious. The driver was found with his pants down, holding her underwear. In stating the reasons for the judgment, the judge stated that the woman may have consented to a sexual encounter prior to passing out, noting, "Clearly, a drunk can consent."[66]

The Crown appealed the decision, and the Nova Scotia Court of Appeal was scheduled to hear the case in November 2017. Criminal law experts disagreed on the ruling. Speaking in support of the finding, one criminal lawyer stated, "The principles the judge relies on are legally correct; they're just not popular." Others disagreed, with a law professor arguing that the judge himself had indicated, "there was significant circumstantial evidence of the complainant's lack of capacity."[67]

Another case that generated considerable controversy was the 2016 sexual assault trial of Jian Ghomeshi, a high-profile Canadian radio host. This case is the subject of a Class/Group Discussion Exercise at the end of this chapter.

The uncertainty and controversy surrounding the issue of consent prompted the federal government in 2017 to pass Bill C-51, which, among other provisions, amends the *Criminal Code* to state that an unconscious person is incapable of giving consent and expands the "rape shield" provisions of the *Criminal Code* to include communications of a sexual nature or for a sexual purpose.

▶ Participants in a protest against the decision of Judge Gregory Lenehan's decision in the sexual assault case involving a Halifax taxicab driver, March 2017.

THE CANADIAN PRESS/Darren Calabrese

BATTERED WOMAN SYNDROME

Experienced by women who have suffered chronic and severe abuse, battered woman syndrome (BWS) is a condition characterized by feelings of social isolation, worthlessness, anxiety, depression, and low self-esteem. In the landmark case *R. v. Lavallee* ([1990] 1 SCR 852), the Supreme Court of Canada accepted BWS as a defence, and it has since been used successfully in subsequent cases.[68,69]

In *R. v. Malott* ([1998] 1 SCR 123), the Supreme Court of Canada stated, "'Battered woman syndrome' is not a legal defence in itself, but rather is a psychiatric explanation of the mental state of an abused woman which can be relevant to understanding a battered woman's state of mind." In *R. v. Ryan* (2013 SCC 3), however, the SCC placed limits on the extent to which a woman who was in an abusive relationship could use the defence of duress. The woman had attempted to hire a hit man (who was, in fact, an RCMP undercover officer) to kill her abusive husband.[70,71]

PROCEDURAL DEFENCES

This category of defence strategies focuses not on the guilt or innocence of the accused, but rather on the conduct of the police or prosecution, or perhaps the validity of the law itself. In common parlance, this is known as "getting off on a technicality." The judge can rule on most of these issues before the trial even starts, but Charter arguments can sidetrack a trial until the issue is resolved.

Procedural defences fall roughly into four categories:

- *Challenging the validity of the applicable law.* Some successful procedural defences have attacked the constitutionality of the law used to charge the accused.

- *Challenging the validity of the prosecution.* Another strategy is to claim that the police or prosecutors acted unfairly in the investigation or charging of the accused. Entrapment and abuse of process (discussed in Chapter 3) are two examples of unfair conduct.

- *Contesting the admissibility of evidence gathered by the police.* If key evidence is excluded, not enough evidence may remain to prove guilt beyond a reasonable doubt. As noted in Chapter 5, a confession gained after an unlawful arrest may be ruled inadmissible if its use would bring the system of justice into disrepute.

- *Seeking a remedy for violation of a Charter right.* In extreme circumstances, the violation of an accused person's Charter rights can be remedied by the termination of the prosecution. There have been cases in which the Charter right to trial within a reasonable time was violated and a stay of proceedings was ordered by the presiding judge.

THE JURY

Juries are finders of fact while the role of the judge is to interpret the law, determine the admissibility of evidence, and instruct the jurors. It is the jury that will determine the guilt or innocence of the accused person. Jury decisions must be unanimous. If the jury returns a verdict of guilty, then it is the responsibility of the judge to impose the sentence.

Unlike their American counterparts, Canadian jurors are prohibited from discussing their deliberations with the media. Each province/territory has legislation that sets out the qualifications for jurors and that provides other directives for selecting juries and guiding their activities. Jury duty is still regarded as a civic duty; with a few exceptions, a person called for jury duty will be required to serve.

Courtesy of Felicity Don

The three essential attributes of a criminal jury are (1) impartiality, (2) competence, and (3) representativeness (*R. v. Bain*, [1992] 1 SCR 91). The SCC has assigned to Crown counsel the role of ensuring that the jury meets these requirements and stated that "the Crown Attorney should use the means at his or her disposal to exclude prospective jurors that could be biased in favour of the prosecution, even if the defence is not aware of this fact" (*R. v. Bain*, [1992] 1 SCR 91).

There have been concerns that juries do not reflect the diversity of the community, in particular, the lack of Indigenous representation on juries hearing cases involving Indigenous accused. In 2011, a judge in Thunder Bay, Ontario, postponed a murder trial because the jury pool did not include Indigenous persons.[72]

A subsequent inquiry, conducted for the province by a retired SCC judge, found that the criminal justice system as applied to Indigenous persons in the province, and particularly in the northern regions of the province, was in crisis and that the status quo was not sustainable.[73] The lack of representation of Indigenous persons on jury rolls was symptomatic of a larger problem of Indigenous distrust of and lack of knowledge about the criminal justice system and, more specifically, juries.

In 2013, Clifford Kokopenace's manslaughter conviction was overturned by the Ontario Court of Appeal on the basis that his rights were violated by the provincial government, which failed to ensure there was proper representation of Indigenous persons on jury rolls, even though the problem had been widely documented.[74] The appeal court upheld Kokopenace's conviction for the stabbing death of his friend on the Grassy Narrows reserve as "reasonable," but sent the case back for a new trial. The conviction was subsequently re-instated by the SCC in a 5–2 decision (*R. v. Kokopenace*, 2015 SCC 28). The court held that "reasonable efforts" had been made by the community to ensure that the jury had adequate Indigenous representation.[75]

Since jury deliberations are "secret," research on jury deliberations and decision-making is based on "mock" (pretend) juries, as no recording devices or observers are allowed into jury rooms. In contrast to the U.S., it is not permissible to interview jurors about the deliberations when the case is concluded.

It does not appear that personal characteristics of jurors play a significant role in decision-making, and non-evidentiary factors tend to play a role when the evidence presented to the jury is not clearly in favour of the prosecution or defence.[76] Individual jurors do participate differentially in deliberations, and jurors also appear to experience considerable pressure to reach a unanimous verdict and there is an effort to avoid a "hung jury," a situation in which consensus cannot be reached on the guilt or innocence of an accused.

Among the concerns that surround the use of juries is that jurors may not understand evidence that is presented at trial due to its complexity or the manner in which it is presented by the defence and prosecutor.[77] It has also been suggested that there may be a "CSI effect" (from the popular television show, *Crime Scene Investigation*), wherein jurors expect that there will be clear and unequivocal scientific evidence presented by the prosecutor that can support a conviction. Research, however, has failed to support the CSI effect, although jurors appear to have high expectations that prosecutors will present scientific evidence in support of an argument that the accused person is guilty.[78]

One area that is of concern is the instructions that are given to jurors following the trial and prior to deliberations. These instructions generally relate to the charges facing the defendant and the standard of proof that the jurors must use in weighing the evidence that has been presented at trial. From 30 to 50 percent of jury instructions that are reviewed on appeal result in orders for new trials due to errors made by the judge in giving instructions to the jury. Jury instructions are not mentioned in the *Criminal Code*, and this has resulted in considerable disparity in how this most-important component of the judicial process is managed by judges.

In rare cases, juries have engaged in nullification, failing to convict an obviously guilty accused because the laws do not represent the will of the community. This has occurred in marijuana cases and in a series of jury decisions relating to abortion (*R. v. Krieger*, 2006 SCC 47; *R. v. Morgentaler*, [1988] 1 SCR 30).

Another concern that has only recently emerged is the presence of post-traumatic stress disorder (PTSD) among persons who have served on juries.[79] It often occurs as a result of jurors being exposed to graphic crime scene photos, evidence, and testimony. Provincial and territorial governments are beginning to address the issue and, in some jurisdictions, have made assistance available for former jurors who request it.

APPEALS

There is the possibility of appeal once a case has been concluded in court. Not every case can be appealed; in fact, in the majority of cases an appeal is *not* filed. The right to appeal exists only in certain situations; in others, the Court of Appeal can grant leave (permission) to appeal. Unlike in the U.S. where only the defence can appeal, in Canada either the Crown prosecutor or the defence lawyer can file an appeal. A distinction is made between grounds for appeal which involve questions of law, and those which involve questions of fact, and those which involve both. Note also that there are different appeal procedures for summary conviction and indictable offences.

Once an appeal has been launched, the incarcerated appellant may be released on bail until the appeal is heard. The judge who hears this request considers, among other things, the *prima facie* merits of the appeal itself; this is to ensure that frivolous appeals cannot routinely be used to defer the serving of a prison sentence.

An appeal may be directed at the verdict, or the sentence, or both. However, most appeals are directed at the sentence: The incarcerated appellant thinks it is too severe, or the prosecutor thinks it is too lenient. The appellate court assesses the sentence against the prevailing norms found in reported case law. In deciding the case, the court may raise the sentence, or lower it, or refuse to interfere with what the trial judge ordered.

An appeal of the verdict usually requires some demonstration that a legal error was made at the trial or that new, exculpatory evidence has been discovered. In contrast, defendants can appeal any facet of the case that renders the verdict unreasonable.

There are five possible outcomes of verdict appeals. The appeal court can (1) decide not to hear the appeal; (2) hear the appeal and dismiss it; (3) substitute a conviction on a lesser but included offence (and probably reduce the sentence); (4) direct that the offender be acquitted; *or* (5) order a new trial. Most appeals originate from the defence side. However, in Canada it is also possible for a Crown attorney to appeal the acquittal of an accused.

CRIME VICTIMS AND THE COURT PROCESS

Criminal courts have often not adequately considered the needs of crime victims during the court process. It generally falls to the police to protect victims and ensure their appearance in court to provide testimony. The *Canadian Victims Bill of Rights* (S.C. 2015, c. 13, s. 2) entrenched a role for crime victims in the court process.

At trial, victims may be called upon to testify. They are summoned to court (by subpoena) and are paid a small fee just like any other witness. Testifying in a public courtroom, in the presence of the alleged perpetrator, is an emotionally arduous task for victims. The *Criminal Code* contains concessions to crime victims who testify in court; most of these, however, are offered at the discretion of the trial judge. These provisions (see below) were developed in response to concerns that the victims of sexual offences were often victimized a second time by the experience of testimony and cross-examination. A concern is that the victim may be re-victimized by the criminal court proceedings.

Women victims often feel that it is they who are on trial, rather than the accused, one survivor of sexual violence stating, "…the woman is guilty, she's just got to prove that she's innocent—she didn't commit the crime. So, it's reversed. It's backwards, this so-called justice system."[80]

Commenting on the sentence that her perpetrator received, one woman survivor of sexual violence stated,

> Like for me, I have a lifetime sentence. Like this will never leave me, it will always be there. We can only manage to, hope to get through our lives and have a happy and fulfilling life. But I'm forty and I'm still not there yet. So why do these people get no time, or just a little bit of time, when they could steal some money and it's considered more of a crime. Like what makes us so invaluable that we don't deserve justice…[81]

The need for training for criminal justice system personnel, including the police and judges, was also identified as being required to ensure that the needs of the victims are addressed. One survivor of sexual violence stated, "… I think they really, truly need to understand there needs to be better education on the side of law enforcement, or on the judicial side, as to why it is so under-reported; why people feel such a sense of shame; why victims will blame themselves or feel responsible […] why people tend to get away with this and why people are reluctant to come forward…"[82]

COMPENSATION FOR CRIME VICTIMS

There are a number of ways in which crime victims can seek financial redress for the harm caused by the victimization, including compensation for property offences by **restitution** paid by the offender upon an order by the court and through private insurance. Victims of personal injury offences can apply for financial compensation from the provincial government to cover expenses and damages directly related to the crime.

Criminal injury compensation programs operate in all provinces except Newfoundland and Labrador but not in the territories. Given the high rates of crime and victimization in these jurisdictions, this is of concern. Victims may be compensated for out-of-pocket expenses such as lost wages and, in some jurisdictions, for "pain and suffering" caused by the offence. This compensation is available even in cases where the charges against the alleged offender have been stayed or withdrawn. In contrast to criminal courts where guilt must be proved beyond a reasonable doubt, the standard used by compensation boards is "balance of probabilities," a far lower threshold.

One woman, a survivor of a sexual assault, reflected on her experience of taking her claim to the Ontario Criminal Injuries Compensation Board:

> Was it worth it? No, and yes. On one hand, the emotional torture of having to testify was not worth the small sum of money I got, and could never undo what had been already been done to me. On the other, hearing the "alleged offender" blatantly commit a lie to public record, and have him hear from a legal authority that yes, he indeed victimized me were two of my favourite moments of 2016. For someone who had just been denied justice through criminal court, it was satisfying to have a legal body rule in my favour.[83]

Restitution

A court-ordered payment that the offender makes to the victim to compensate for loss of or damage to property.

Criminal injury compensation

Financial remuneration paid to crime victims.

ACCOMMODATING DIVERSITY IN THE COURTROOM

Canadian courts have often struggled to accommodate accused persons who do not speak either French or English. In 2015, a Vancouver Island man accused of drug trafficking was set free by a provincial court judge because the province had failed, over two years of proceedings, to provide a Cambodian interpreter.

An issue that illustrates the challenges that the criminal justice system faces in accommodating diversity is whether a victim who is a Muslim and wears the niqab (a full face veil revealing only the eyes) should be permitted to testify against the person who allegedly committed an offence against her. See At Issue 8.2.

WRONGFUL CONVICTIONS

The criminal justice system operates within a legal and procedural framework that is designed to ensure that the rights of those accused of criminal offences are protected and that their guilt must be proved "beyond a reasonable doubt." In several cases, the SCC has reiterated that one of the primary goals of the criminal justice system is to ensure that innocent persons are not wrongfully convicted (e.g., *R. v. Trochym*, 2007 SCC 6).

Despite this, innocent persons are found guilty and, in some instances, are sent to prison for crimes they did not commit. Or, a person pled guilty when legitimate defences were available. Indigenous women who are charged with murder, for example, frequently plead guilty although they may have been able to use self-defence as a justification for the act.[84] As with plea bargaining and bail, persons who are marginal and of

SHOULD A MUSLIM WOMAN WHO WEARS A NIQAB BE ALLOWED TO TESTIFY IN COURT AGAINST HER ALLEGED PERPETRATOR?

In 2008, a preliminary hearing was held in an Ontario provincial court involving a case in which the cousin and uncle of a woman known as N.S., the alleged victim, were charged with sexual assault. When called by the prosecution as a witness, N.S., a Muslim, indicated that she wished to testify wearing her niqab. She stated that her religious belief required her to wear a niqab in public where men and other close family members might see her. N.S. indicated that she had removed her niqab for her driver's licence photo (taken by a woman) and would remove it if required to clear customs. The presiding judge held that N.S.'s religious beliefs were not that strong and ordered her to remove her niqab. N.S. objected and applied to the Superior Court of Justice to quash the provincial court order and to permit her to testify wearing the niqab.

The case moved on to Superior Court of Justice and then to the Ontario Court of Appeal, and ultimately to the SCC. In 2012, in *R. v. N.S.* (2012 SCC 72), the SCC ruled that a Muslim witness may be required to remove her niqab to testify in court, depending upon the seriousness of the case and the sincerity of her religious beliefs. Included in its ruling was the following statement:

> Always permitting a witness to wear the niqab would offer no protection for the accused's fair trial interest and the state's interest in maintaining public confidence in the administration of justice. However, never permitting a witness to testify wearing a niqab would not comport with the fundamental premise under the Charter that rights should be limited only to the extent that the limits are shown to be justifiable. The need to accommodate and balance sincerely held religious beliefs against other interests is deeply entrenched in Canadian law.

If wearing the niqab did not pose a risk to a fair trial, then it would be permitted. The case was returned to the provincial judge to make the final determination, which was to require N.S. to remove her

Women wearing niqabs

THE CANADIAN PRESS/Chris Young

niqab in order to testify.[a,b] Among the views expressed about the SCC was that it further marginalized Muslim women and ensured continued discrimination against them.[c]

QUESTIONS

1. What is your perspective on this issue?
2. Do you think that the SCC struck the right balance between the need to accommodate an individual's religious practice and the rights of the accused?

[a] M.H. Ogivlie. 2013. "Naqabs in Canadian Courts: R. v. N.S." *Ecclesiastical Law Journal*, 15(3), 334–343;

[b] S. Mulrain. 2013, May 18. "R. v. N.S. – Redux [on wearing the niqab in Court]." http://www.mondaq.com/canada/x/239016/trials+appeals+compensation/R+v +NS+Redux.

[c] L. Chambers and J. Roth. 2014. "Prejudice Unveiled: The Niqab in Court," *Canadian Journal of Law & Society*, 29(3), 381–395; *R. v. N.S.*, 2012 SCC 72.

---

lower socio-economic levels are most at risk of being wrongfully convicted. Indigenous persons are overrepresented in the group of wrongfully convicted persons.[85]

One wrongfully convicted Indigenous man stated his lawyer had urged him to plead guilty because he would have had to take the stand in the court and "my credibility would be a big problem because of my criminal record. In the end, it came down to a contest between me with my criminal record, and Dr. Smith [the Crown's expert witness] with his credentials."[86]

In another case, Anthony Hanemaayer, who was charged with assault based on an attack of a 15-year-old girl at knifepoint, pled guilty and was sentenced to two years less a day in a provincial jail. In 2006, another offender admitted to committing the crime. Hanemaayer said that he

© Frank Cotham/The New Yorker/The Cartoon Bank

"He'll do."

followed the advice of his lawyer to accept a plea bargain after his lawyer's warning that he faced a long prison sentence if convicted at trial.[87]

Wrongful convictions rarely occur as the result of a single mistake or event; they are almost always a consequence of a series of events. These include "tunnel vision" on the part of police and the Crown (that is, the focus of the investigation was too narrow); mistaken eyewitness identification and testimony; false confessions; the testimony of in-custody informers; and defective, unreliable, and unsubstantiated expert testimony.[88,89] Research studies, for example, have consistently found that eyewitness testimony is notoriously unreliable, and caution should be exercised by justice system personnel in using eyewitness testimony to establish the facts in a criminal case.[90] In other cases, accused persons have been wrongfully convicted on the basis of testimony from experts and suspect scientific evidence.

Sections 696.1 to 696.6 of the *Criminal Code*—"Applications for Ministerial Review—Miscarriages of Justice"—give the federal minister of justice the power to review criminal cases to determine whether there has been a miscarriage of justice. These regulations set out the requirements for an application for a criminal conviction review. Completed applications are forwarded to the Criminal Conviction Review Group (CCRG); lawyers on that body review and investigate the applications and make recommendations to the minister (see http://canada.justice.gc.ca/eng/cj-jp/ccr-rc/index.html).

Innocence Canada (formerly the Association in Defence of the Wrongfully Convicted; http://innocencecanada.com) has been instrumental in having the convictions of a number of persons overturned. Two of the earliest high-profile cases of wrongful conviction were those of David Milgaard and Donald Marshall. David Milgaard was convicted and given a life sentence in 1970 for the murder of a Saskatoon nursing aide. He spent 23 years in prison before the Supreme Court of Canada set aside his conviction in 1992. Five years later, he was exonerated by DNA evidence. In 1999, Larry Fisher was found guilty of the murder. Milgaard received a $10 million settlement for his wrongful imprisonment.

Donald Marshall, a Mi'kmaq, was sentenced to life imprisonment for murder in 1971 and spent 11 years in prison before being acquitted by the Nova Scotia Court of Appeal in 1983. A Royal Commission of Inquiry concluded that incompetence on the part of the police and the judiciary contributed to his wrongful conviction, as did the fact that he was an Indigenous person.[91]

THE ROLE OF THE POLICE

It was noted in Chapter 6 that police role in wrongful convictions is often associated with the interrogation of a suspect and a confession (later found to be false) to having committed the crime.

THE ROLE OF CROWN COUNSEL

Crown counsel exercise considerable control over how cases are processed in the justice system, from participating in plea bargaining with defence lawyers, to the selection of jurors, to how evidence against the accused is presented. In extreme cases, Crown counsel do not abide by the law or professional ethics, and this can lead to wrongful convictions. It has also been argued that there is a "culture of infallibility" among Crown attorneys that may hinder admission that mistakes have been made.[92]

In Manitoba, Crown prosecutor George Dangerfield presided over at least four cases in which accused persons were subsequently found to have been wrongfully convicted. Subsequent investigations discovered that Dangerfield failed to disclose exculpatory evidence, that is "evidence that may justify or excuse an accused defendant's actions, and which will tend to show the defendant is not guilty or has no criminal intent" (http://www.legaldictionary.thefreedictionary.com/Exculpatory+evidence). In addition to the shattered lives of the persons prosecuted by Dangerfield, the province of Manitoba has paid out millions of dollars to the wrongfully convicted. See the video, "The Wrong Man," in the Media Links section at the end of this chapter.

A number of accused persons were wrongfully convicted in cases prosecuted by George Dangerfield. One was Frank Ostrowski, Sr. who spent 23 years in prison before a federal investigation determined that a likely miscarriage of justice occurred. Among the findings of the investigation were that the police and Crown counsel Dangerfield had concealed the fact that a key prosecution witness had perjured himself and given a deal for testifying against Ostrowski.[93]

In a landmark decision (*Henry v. British Columbia (Attorney General)*, 2015 SCC 24), the SCC ruled that Ivan Henry, who spent 27 years in prison after being wrongfully convicted, could sue the prosecutors involved in his wrongful conviction case for non-disclosure of evidence at trial. Prior to this, Crown prosecutors had been generally immune from lawsuits.

THE ROLE OF EXPERT WITNESSES

Expert witnesses can have a significant impact on the criminal court process. Conflicting testimony may be given by experts on behalf of the Crown and the defence. Scholars have noted that historically there has been a reluctance on the part of the judiciary to examine the independence and the validity and reliability of the views of expert witnesses.[94] Traditionally, experts testifying in court were generally from the "hard sciences," including forensics. In recent years, experts from the "soft sciences," including criminology, psychology, and anthropology, are involved as expert witnesses, and this has raised concerns of the reliability and validity of the testimony.[95]

A recent high-profile case in Ontario, however, involved Dr. Charles Smith, a forensic pathologist whose expert testimony in several cases of child death contributed to the wrongful conviction of several persons. An inquiry conducted by Mr. Justice Stephen Goudge found that Smith made false and misleading statements to the court in his testimony and that Smith was an unqualified pathologist who did not acknowledge the limits of his professional expertise.[96]

▼ Frank Ostrowski, Sr. was wrongfully convicted in a case prosecuted by George Dangerfield.

THE CANADIAN PRESS/Steve Lambert

A report of the Ontario coroner concluded that there were significant problems with 20 of 44 autopsies carried out by Smith on deceased children. His testimony in court may have resulted in the wrongful conviction of 13 persons and an additional number of persons who were initially wrongfully charged with killing children.[97]

Smith had presented evidence on causes of death even though his formal training was in pediatric pathology, which is the study of disease in children and youth. Smith was subsequently stripped of his medical licence by the Ontario College of Physicians and Surgeons, which made a finding of professional misconduct and incompetence. For an excellent account of the impact of Charles Smith on the accused and their families, see *Death in the Family*.[98] One of the cases involving Dr. Smith is presented in Court File 8.3.

THE WRONGFUL CONVICTION OF TAMMY MARQUARDT

Tammy Marquardt was born in Toronto of Anishinaabe heritage. She left home at age 17 after being sexually abused by her mother's boyfriend. She gave birth two years later to a son, Kenneth, who had a number of health issues, including epilepsy. In October 1993, while living in poverty in an abusive relationship, Tammy found Kenneth, now two-and-a-half years old, gasping for air; she called emergency services. Kenneth died three days later from brain damage.

The autopsy was performed by Dr. Charles Smith who concluded that Kenneth's death was not accidental. In 1995, despite a plea of not guilty, Marquardt was convicted of second-degree murder and was sentenced to life in prison with no possibility of parole for 10 years. Her other two children were taken from her and put up for adoption.

Tammy Marquardt holding a photo of her son, Kenneth

Ten years later, Tammy's case was reviewed along with all of the other cases in which Dr. Smith had performed autopsies. Along with others, the findings in her case were found to incorrect and, in 2012, a new trial was ordered. The Crown subsequently decided not to retry her, and she was exonerated in the death of her son. She had served 14 years in prison.[a] For the story of Tammy Marquardt, see the book *Real Justice: Branded a Baby Killer: The Story of Tammy Marquardt* by J. D'Costa, 2015. Toronto: Lorimer.

[a] G. Malone. 2016, February 2. "Why Indigenous Women Are Canada's Fastest Growing Prison Population," *Vice News*. https://www.vice.com/en_ca/article/5gj8vb/why-indigenous-women-are-canadas-fastest-growing-prison-population.

Settlements in cases of wrongful conviction can amount to millions of dollars, although, it could be argued, no amount of money can compensate for the lost years. Ivan Henry of British Columbia received $8 million after spending more than 27 years in prison after being wrongfully convicted of a series of violent sexual assaults. In a ruling in 2016, a judge stated that the Crown in the case had shown a "shocking disregard" for Henry's rights by withholding evidence in the case.[99]

Cases of wrongfully convicted persons continue to emerge. In 2014, Leighton Hay was freed after serving 14 years in prison for a murder he always denied having committed. The Ontario Superior Court of Justice issued a rare apology for taking so long "to get things right."[100] Wrongful conviction cases highlight the flaws that continue to exist in the criminal justice system, often with significant consequences for the accused. It is estimated that at least one in 25 convicted persons on death row in the U.S. are innocent.[101] Another case involving a potentially innocent Indigenous man who, as of 2017, had served 34 years in prison was being heard in late 2017.

A major concern is that the criminal justice system and the SCC have not proven to be effective in preventing persons from being wrongfully convicted. Many persons who were wrongfully convicted, including David Milgaard, had their cases heard before the SCC.[102]

RESTORATIVE JUSTICE APPROACHES

There are a variety of restorative justice–centred programs that operate across the country and which can be accessed prior to the imposition of a sentence.

THE OTTAWA RESTORATIVE JUSTICE PROGRAM

The Collaborative Justice Program is a post-plea, pre-sentence restorative justice program premised on restorative justice principles. It operates in the Ottawa-Carleton judicial district and is designed to provide an alternative to the traditional criminal justice process. The program is unique in that it takes cases involving serious criminal offences. The objective is to facilitate a dialogue between the victim and the offender that can be presented to the court at sentencing.

The program considers cases of serious offending, including robbery, break and enter, assault causing bodily harm, weapons offences, and driving offences that involve death or bodily harm and in which a conviction would normally result in a period of incarceration. Cases are referred to the program by a variety of sources, including the judiciary, the Crown or defence counsel, police, probation, and victim services.

Three criteria must be met before a case is accepted by the program: (1) The crime is serious and the Crown is seeking a period of custody; (2) the accused person displays remorse and is willing to take responsibility for and work to repair the harm done; and (3) there is an identifiable victim who is interested in participating. The experience of one offender with the Collaborative Justice Program is presented in Court File 8.4.

COURT FILE 8.4

ASSAULT WITH A WEAPON: AN OFFENDER SPEAKS ABOUT THEIR EXPERIENCE WITH THE COLLABORATIVE JUSTICE PROGRAM

I was involved in an unfortunate incident months ago which resulted in criminal charges brought against me. I'm a middle-aged professional, hard-working, responsible, family-oriented, and engaged in the community who has never been involved in disputes like that, let alone with the police.

Out of frustration of experiencing the same noise situation for the last seven years, I made a mistake when I let my anger control my actions. After this happened, a new chapter started in my life. First came the extreme worry for the well-being of two individuals that suffered because of what I did, and then, the feeling that "everything was over for me," a mix of shame, regret, and lack of hope.

Soon after the incident I contacted a lawyer to represent me. I was in good hands but felt that only the "legal" side of things was being taken care of, not the "human" side of the situation: the side that included all affected by the incident.

Fortunately, eventually I got involved with the Collaborative Justice Program. Actually, I think the word "fortunately" cannot really express I mean ... getting involved with the Program has really made a big difference in my life and I believe in the lives of the other people involved. The restorative approach was really effective; in my case it provided me the opportunity to apologize to victims (in writing) and ask them what I could do to help them. It led me to seek assistance in addressing and learning techniques to manage anger. And it helped me to be a more compassionate person overall.

Source: Collaborative Justice Program: Restorative Justice Ottawa. http://www.collaborativejustice.ca/EN/testimonials/ testimonial.php?i=19. Reprinted with permission from the Collaborative Justice Program.

SUMMARY

The discussion in this chapter has focused on the prosecution of criminal cases. There are a number of events that occur prior to trial that affect the outcome of cases. Judicial interim release (bail) is available for many offenders and often has conditions attached that, in the view of some observers, set the accused person up to fail. While all accused persons have the right to legal representation, there is no obligation on the provinces/territories to pay for it and many people without means do not quality. Plea bargaining is a controversial practice in the criminal courts as it is not subject to legislative provisions or guidelines. Defence lawyers can employ a number of defences at trial, including not criminally responsible on account of mental disorder (NCRMD), which has stirred controversy. Although jury trials are rare in the criminal justice system, little is known about the challenges that juries face in understanding testimony and reaching a verdict. Cases of wrongful conviction continue to occur and are often the result of decisions made by the police, Crown prosecutors, and eyewitnesses. There are restorative justice programs that operate at the pre-sentencing phase of the criminal justice process.

KEY POINTS REVIEW

1. There are a number of steps involved in bringing a case to criminal court and a key role is played by Crown counsel.

2. The police and Crown exercise considerable discretion in deciding whether to lay a charge, and many factors may influence their decision.

3. There are a number of ways in which accused persons can be compelled to appear in court to answer the charge against them, including issuing an appearance notice, issuing a summons, and remanding the accused into custody.

4. The bail system places heavy demands on the criminal justice system, and in recent years, it has become more restrictive and has included more conditions on the person who is released on bail.

5. There are more persons in custody on remand awaiting trial than there are sentenced offenders in custody.

6. Security certificates are processes whereby non-residents of Canada who are deemed a threat to the country can be held, without charge, for an indefinite period of time with the objective of deportation.

7. There is no blanket right to state-paid legal representation, and funding cuts in legal aid have made it difficult for many accused to access legal assistance.

8. A fundamental principle of the common law is that the accused person must be fit to stand trial.

9. The most common defences for accused can be generally grouped into (1) "you've got the wrong person"; (2) the mental state of the accused at the time the alleged offence occurred; (3) justifications (or excuses) for having committed a criminal act; and (4) procedural defences.

10. Plea bargaining is a widely used, yet controversial, practice in the criminal justice process.

11. With a few notable exceptions (e.g. the SCC), cameras are not allowed in Canadian courtrooms.

12. There has been a growing emphasis on the rights of crime victims in the court process, although victims continue to experience difficulties.

13. Challenges have been experienced in accommodating diversity in the courtroom, as exemplified by the controversy over whether a victim can wear a niqab while giving testimony.

14. Increasing attention is being given to the wrongfully convicted and to the activities and decisions of the police, prosecutors, and judges that contribute to miscarriages of justice.

15. There are restorative justice programs that operate at the post-conviction, pre-sentencing phase of the criminal court process.

KEY TERM QUESTIONS

1. What is the difference between **summary conviction offences** and **indictable offences**? What is a **hybrid (elective) offence**?

2. What role does the **preliminary hearing** play in the prosecution of criminal cases?

3. What is **judicial interim release (bail)** and what are the issues that surround its use?

4. Describe **remand** and its significance for the study of the criminal court process.

5. Why are **security certificates** the focus of controversy?

6. What are the issues that surround **plea bargaining**?

7. What is the **open court principle** and why is it an important concept in the study of criminal justice?

8. In what situations would a Crown counsel enter a **stay of proceedings**?

9. Describe the defence of **not criminally responsible on account of mental disorder** and note why is it controversial.

10. What is the difference between **restitution** and **criminal injury compensation**?

CRITICAL THINKING EXERCISE

Critical Thinking Exercise 8.1

Cases of the Wrongfully Convicted: Lessons Learned?

Wrongful convictions are a problem that continues to plague the criminal justice system. Although each case is different, identifying the commonalties among the cases is important for preventing future cases. Access the list of some of the persons (as of late 2017) who have been found to have been wrongfully convicted at http://www.cbc.ca/news/canada/canada-s-wrongful-convictions-1.783998. Select two cases from the list of the wrongfully convicted persons. Read them, noting the key elements of each case.

Your Thoughts?

1. Which cases did you review?

2. Among the cases, what were the similarities and differences in the dynamics that led to the wrongful conviction?

3. Identify three recommendations that could be made from the case studies that might reduce the likelihood of wrongful convictions in the future.

CLASS/GROUP DISCUSSION EXERCISE

Class/Group Discussion Exercise 8.1

The Trial of Jian Ghomeshi: Consent and Sexual Assault

Jian Ghomeshi was a high-profile radio host at CBC. In 2014, he was arrested and charged with four counts of sexual assault and one count of overcoming resistance by choking involving three separate women.[a] In 2015, he was charged with three additional counts of sexual assault involving three additional women. Ghomeshi pled not guilty to all of the charges.

The trial proceedings were highly contentious, with the defence arguing that one of the complainant's statements to the police was different from her testimony in court, that there were lengthy delays in the complainants' reporting the alleged assaults to the police, that two of the complainants colluded about the testimony they would present in court, and other inconsistencies in their evidence about whether they had contact and sexual encounters with Mr. Ghomeshi after the alleged assaults.[b] In 2016, Ghomeshi was acquitted on all of the charges, the presiding judge noting that the inconsistency of the complainants' testimony and "outright deception" had undermined the prosecution's case. Crown counsel subsequently withdrew a charge of sexual assault on a separate incident.

The ruling in the case generated considerable debate. The judge was accused of blaming the victims and contributing to the silencing of women who have been victims of sexual assault and to the perception that the women complainants were the ones who were on trial.[c] Concerns were expressed that the intense scrutiny of the three complainants at trial by Ghomeshi's defence lawyer will dissuade women from coming forward with complaints of being sexually assaulted.[d] Watch the *Fifth Estate* documentary, "The Trial of Jian Ghomeshi," at http://www.cbc.ca/fifth/episodes/2015-2016/the-trial-of-jian-ghomeshi.

Your Thoughts?

1. What does the trial of Jian Ghomeshi reveal about the challenges surrounding consent, sexual assault, and the law?

[a] R. Doolittle, J. Mahoney, and J. Bradshaw. 2014, November 26. "Ghomeshi Faces Five Charges in Sexual Assault Case, Is Granted Bail," *Globe and Mail*. https://www.theglobeandmail.com/news/national/jian-ghomeshi-charged-with-sexual-assault/article21788631.

[b] M. Gollom. 2016, February 8. "Jian Ghomeshi Trial: Complainant Agreed to Date and Sexual Encounter after Alleged Assault," *CBC News*. http://www.cbc.ca/news/canada/toronto/jian-ghomeshi-sexual-assault-trial-1.3436593.

[c] *CBC News*. 2016, March 24. "Jian Ghomeshi Trial's Not Guilty Decision Triggers Outrage, March to Police Headquarters." http://www.cbc.ca/news/canada/toronto/jian-ghomeshi-judge-ruling-1.3504250.

[d] R. Charles. 2016, February 10. "Jian Ghomeshi Trial Could Deter Women from Reporting Sexual Assault," *CBC News*. http://www.cbc.ca/news/canada/toronto/ghomeshi-trial-sexual-assault-chill-1.3441059.

MEDIA LINKS

"A Question of Innocence," *The Fifth Estate*, CBC News, April 1, 2011, http://www.cbc.ca/player/play/1866006030

"Bus 1170: Vince Li and the Greyhound Bus Murder," *The Fifth Estate*, CBC News, January 6, 2017, https://www.youtube.com/watch?v=3gAeVysCIl8

"The Wrongful Conviction of Ivan Henry," November 25, 2014, https://www.youtube.com/watch?v=PJS-qSH46kc

"NCR: Not Criminally Responsible," *CBC Doc Zone*, October 18, 2014, http://www.cbc
.ca/doczone/episodes/not-criminally-responsible

"Diagnosis Murder: Exploring the Suspect Science behind Shaken Baby Accusations,"
The Fifth Estate, CBC News, January 13, 2012, https://www.youtube.com/
watch?v=6yuxEvN8gp0

"The Disgrace of Charles Smith," *The Agenda with Steve Palkin*, TVO, February 9, 2017,
http://tvo.org/article/current-affairs/shared-values/death-in-the-family-the-story-of
-disgraced-doctor-charles-smith-and-the-families-he-destroyed

"Charles Smith Scandal: How A Mother Wrongly Accused of Killing Her Son Fought
Back," *The Current*, CBC Radio, January 12, 2017, http://www.cbc.ca/listen/shows/
the-current/segment/11338523

"The Wrong Man," *The Fifth Estate*, CBC News, March 5, 2010, http://www.cbc.ca/fifth/
episodes/2009-2010/the-wrong-man

"Steven Truscott—His Word Against History," *The Fifth Estate*, CBC News, http://www
.cbc.ca/fifth/episodes/40-years-of-the-fifth-estate/steven-truscott-his-word-against
-history

REFERENCES

1. *Criminal Code*. R.S.C. 1985, c. C-46, s. 486(1).

2. D. Layton. 2002. "The Prosecutorial Charging Decision," *Criminal Law Quarterly*, 46(1–2), 447–482.

3. Y. Dandurand. 2009. *Addressing Inefficiencies in the Criminal Justice Process. Vancouver: International Centre for Criminal Law Reform and Criminal Justice Policy. A Preliminary Review*. http://icclr.law.ubc.ca/sites/icclr.law.ubc.ca/files/publications/pdfs/Inefficiencies PreliminaryReport.pdf.

4. Layton, "The Prosecutorial Charging Decision."

5. J. Cameron. 2013. *A Context of Justice: Ontario's Justices of the Peace – From the Mewett Report to the Present*. Toronto: Osgood Hall Law School of York University, p. 23. http://digitalcommons.osgoode.yorku.ca/cgi/viewcontent.cgi?article=1286&context=clpe.

6. John Howard Society of Ontario. 2013. *Reasonable Bail?* Toronto: Author. http://www.johnhoward.on.ca/wp-content/uploads/2014/07/JHSO-Reasonable-Bail-report-final.pdf.

7. J.B. Sprott and N.M. Myers. 2011. "Set Up to Fail: The Unintended Consequences of Multiple Bail Conditions," *Canadian Journal of Criminology and Criminal Justice*, 53(4), 404–423.

8. Legal Aid Ontario. 2016. *A Legal Aid Strategy for Bail*. http://www.legalaid.on.ca/en/publications/paper-legal-aid-strategy-for-bail-2016-11.asp

9. Quoted in G. Zochodne. 2013, August 27. "Free, But for How Long? The City That Never Fails to 'Fail to Comply,'" *Oshawa Express*.

10. M. Enright. 2013, January 27. "Bail and Violence Against Women," *The Sunday Edition*, CBC Radio. http://www.cbc.ca/radio/thesundayedition/bail-and-violence-against-women-1.2904430.

11. M.F. McLellan. 2010. "Bail and the Diminishing Presumption of Innocence," *Canadian Criminal Law Review*, 15(1), 57–74.

12. N.M. Myers. 2009. "Shifting Risk: Bail and the Use of Sureties," *Current Issues in Criminal Justice*, 21(1), 127–47.

13. John Howard Society of Ontario, *Reasonable Bail?*, p. 3.

14. L. Hausegger, M. Hennigar, and T. Riddell. 2009. *Canadian Courts: Law, Politics, and Process*. Toronto: Oxford University Press, p. 290.

15. G. Kellough and S. Wortley. 2002. "Remand for Plea: Bail Decisions and Plea Bargaining as Commensurate Decisions," *British Journal of Criminology*, 42(1), 186–210.

16. J. Gilbert. 2016, January 14. "Blame Our Bail System for Overcrowded Ottawa Jail," *Ottawa Sun*. http://www.ottawasun.com/2016/01/14/blame-our-bail-system-for-overcrowded-ottawa-jail

17. A. Deshman and N. Myers. 2014. *Set Up to Fail: Bail and the Revolving Door of Pre-Trial Detention*. Ottawa: Canadian Civil Liberties Association. https://ccla.org/dev/v5/_doc/CCLA_set_up_to_fail.pdf.

18. Legal Aid Ontario, *A Legal Aid Strategy for Bail*.

19. Deshman and Myers, *Set Up to Fail: Bail and the Revolving Door of Pre-Trial Detention*.

20. Ibid.

21. Ibid.

22. S. Seccia. 2017, March 1. "'Red Zones' Set the Marginalized Up for More Trouble, Study Finds," *The Tyee*. https://thetyee.ca/News/2017/03/01/DTES-Red-Zones.

23. P. George, T.N. Gopal, and S. Woods. 2013/2014. "Look at My Life: Access to Education for the Remand Population of Ontario," *Canadian Review of Social Policy*, 70, 34–47.

24. Correctional Services Program. 2017. "Trends in the Use of Remand in Canada, 2004/2005 to 2014/2015," *Juristat*, 37(1). Statistics Canada Catalogue no. 85-002-X. Ottawa: Minister of Industry. http://www.statcan.gc.ca/pub/85-002-x/2017001/article/14691-eng.pdf.

25. J. Reitano. 2016. "Adult Correctional Statistics in Canada, 2015/2016," *Juristat*, 37(1). Statistics Canada Catalogue no. 85-002-X. Ottawa: Minister of Industry. http://www.statcan.gc.ca/pub/85-002-x/2017001/article/14700-eng.pdf.

26. J. Ferguson. 2016. "Justice – Planning for Inmate Capacity of Adult Correctional Facilities," in *2016 Report – Volume 2: Report of the Provincial Auditor of Saskatchewan to the Legislative Assembly of Saskatchewan*. Regina: Author, 169–187. https://auditor.sk.ca/pub/publications/public_reports/2016/Volume_2/28_Justice_Inmate%20Capacity.pdf.

27. R. Gartner, C.M. Webster, and A.N. Doob. 2009. "Trends in the Imprisonment of Women in Canada," *Canadian Journal of Criminology and Criminal Justice*, 51(2), 169–198.

28. L. Porter and D. Calverley. 2011. "Trends in the Use of Remand in Canada, 2011," *Juristat*, 31(1). Statistics Canada Catalogue no. 85-002-X. Ottawa: Minister of Industry. http://www.statcan.gc.ca/pub/85-002-x/2011001/article/11440-eng.pdf.

29. K. Latimer. 2017, March 25. "'We Need to Be Better: Half of the People in Sask. Jails Are on Remand," *CBC News*. http://www.cbc.ca/news/canada/saskatchewan/remand-intake-continues-to-overcrowd-sask-jails-1.4032993.

30. D. Drummond. 2012. *Commission on the Reform of Ontario's Public Services*. Toronto: Queen's Printer for Ontario, p. 353. https://www.fin.gov.on.ca/en/reform commission/chapters/report.pdf.

31. John Howard Society of Ontario. 2007. *Standing Committee on Prison Conditions in Ontario: Second Report to the Board: Remand in Ontario*. Toronto: Author.

32. E. Euvrard and C. Leclerc. 2016. "Pre-Trial Detention and Guilty Pleas: Inducement or Coercion?" *Punishment & Society*, 19(5), 1–18.

33. Ibid., pp. 8–9.

34. *CBC News*. 2017, January 24. "Innovative Man. Remand Program Could Decrease Overcrowding in Sask. Jails." http://www.cbc.ca/news/canada/saskatoon/remand-program-overcrowding-saskatchewan-jails-manitoba-1.3949943.

35. P. de Jong. 2003. *Legal Service Provision in Northern Canada: Summary of Research in the Northwest Territories, Nunavut, and the Yukon*. Ottawa: Department of Justice. http://www.justice.gc.ca/eng/rp-pr/aj-ja/rr03_la15-rr03_aj15/rr03_la15.pdf.

36. S. Friedman. 2013, April 20. "Right to Know: Legal Aid Off Limits to All but the Poorest," *Ottawa Citizen*. http://firearmslaw.ca/2013/04/20/right-to-know-legal-aid-off-limits-to-all-but-the-poorest.

37. Attorney General of Ontario. 2015. "The Choice of Delivery Models for Legal Aid." https://www.attorneygeneral.jus.gov.on.ca/english/about/pubs/olar/ch7.php.

38. Canadian Bar Association. 2015. "Legal Aid in Canada." https://www.cba.org/Sections/Legal-Aid-Liaison/Resources/Resources/Legal-Aid-in-Canada.

39. T. Venetis. 2017, May 30. "Retrial Ordered After Judge Fails to Provide Guidance to Self-Represented Litigant," *Lawyer's Daily*. https://www.thelawyersdaily.ca/articles/3849/retrial-ordered-after-judge-fails-to-provide-guidance-to-self-represented-litigant.

40. S.N. Verdun-Jones. 2014. *Criminal Law in Canada. Cases, Questions & the Code* (6th ed.). Toronto: Nelson.

41. A.N. Doob and C.M. Webster. 2016. "Weathering the Storm? Testing Long-Standing Canadian Sentencing Policy in the Twenty-First Century," *Crime and Justice*, 45(1), 359–418.

42. M.P. Piccinato. 2004. *Plea Bargaining*. Ottawa: Department of Justice Canada. http://www.justice.gc.ca/eng/rp-pr/csj-sjc/ilp-pji/pb-rpc/pb-rpc.pdf.

43. J. Kennedy. 2016. "Plea Bargains and Wrongful Convictions," *Criminal Law Quarterly*, 63(4), 556–566.

44. Law Reform Commission of Canada. 1975. *Criminal Procedure: Control of the Process* [Working paper no. 15]. Ottawa: Information Canada, p. 14. http://www.lareau-law.ca/LRCWP15.pdf.

45. M. Manikis. 2012. "Recognizing Victims' Role and Rights During Plea Bargaining: A Fair Deal for Victims of Crime," *Criminal Law Quarterly*, 58(3–4), 411.

46. Kennedy, "Plea Bargains and Wrongful Convictions."

47. Doob and Webster, "Weathering the Storm?," p. 364.

48. Kennedy, "Plea Bargains and Wrongful Convictions."

49. I. Hanomansing. 2016, September 18. "Legal Profession 'Willing to Set Logic Aside' to Bar Cameras from Courtrooms," *CBC News*. http://www.cbc.ca/news/canada/camera-court-room-benefit-harm-travis-vader-trial-1.3767349.

50. Canadian Press. 2016, September 15. "A Look at Rare Times the Canadian Justice System Has Allowed Cameras in Court." *CTV News*. http://www.ctvnews.ca/canada/a-look-at-rare-times-the-canadian-justice-system-has-allowed-cameras-in-court-1.3070757.

51. Hausegger, Hennigar, and Riddell, *Canadian Courts: Law, Politics, and Process*, p. 293.

52. L. Silver. 2016, August 11. "Modernizing Circumstances: Revisiting Circumstantial Evidence in *R. v. Villaroman*," *ABlawg.ca*. http://ablawg.ca/2016/08/11/modernizing-circumstantial-evidence. Reprinted by permission of Lisa Silver.

53. A. Maxwell. 2017. "Adult Criminal Court Statistics in Canada, 2014/2015," *Juristat*, 37(1). Statistics Canada Catalogue no. 85-002-X. Ottawa: Minister of Industry. http://www.statcan.gc.ca/pub/85-002-x/2017001/article/14699-eng.pdf.

54. M. Sinha. 2009. *An Investigation into the Feasibility of Collecting Data on the Involvement of Adults and Youth with Mental Health Issues in the Criminal Justice System*. Ottawa: Minister of Industry. https://www.publicsafety.gc.ca/lbrr/archives/cnmcs-plcng/statcan-cjrps-no16-eng.pdf.

55. Verdun-Jones, *Criminal Law in Canada*, p. 185.

56. A.G. Crocker, T.L. Nicholls, M.C. Seto, Y. Charette, G. Cote, and M. Caulet. 2015. "The National Trajectory Project of Individuals Found Not Criminally Responsible on Account of Mental Disorder in Canada. Part 2: The People behind the Label," *Canadian Journal of Psychiatry*, 60(3), 106–116.

57. A.G. Crocker, T.L. Nicholls, M.C. Seto, G. Cote, Y. Charette, and M. Caulet. 2015. "The National Trajectory Project of Individuals Found Not Criminally Responsible on Account of Mental Disorder in Canada. Part 1: Context and Methods," *Canadian Journal of Psychiatry*, 60(3), 98–105 at p. 98.

58. Department of Justice Canada. 2014, July 11. "Coming into Force of the Not Criminally Responsible Reform Act" [News release]. http://news.gc.ca/web/article-en.do?nid=867529.

59. A.G. Crocker, T.L. Nicholls, M.C. Seto, and G. Cote. 2015. "The National Trajectory Project of Individuals Found Not Criminally Responsible on Account of Mental Disorder in Canada," *Canadian Journal of Psychiatry*, 60(3), 96–97.

60. S. Mach and K. Daniels. 2015, March 2. "The Not Criminally Responsible Reform Act: A Recap of the MLJH Annual Colloquium," *McGill Journal of Law & Health*. Online. https://mljh.mcgill.ca/2015/03/02/the-not-criminally-responsible-reform-act-a-recap-of-the-mljh-annual-colloquium/.

61. Crocker, Nicholls, Seto, and Cote, "The National Trajectory Project of Individuals Found Not Criminally Responsible on Account of Mental Disorder in Canada."

62. Y. Charette, A.G. Crocker, M.C. Seto, L. Salem, T.L. Nicholls, and M. Caulet. 2015. "The National Trajectory Project of Individuals Found Not Criminally Responsible on Account of Mental Disorder in Canada. Part 4: Criminal Recidivism," *Canadian Journal of Psychiatry*, 60(3), 127–134.

63. Mach and Daniels, "The Not Criminally Responsible Reform Act: A Recap of the MLJH Annual Colloquium."

64. S.N. Verdun-Jones. 2011. *Criminal Law in Canada: Cases, Questions and the Code*. Toronto: Nelson.

65. S. Boesveld. 2014, November 26. "Canadian Law Decisive on What Constitutes Sexual Consent: There's Nothing 'Implied' or 'Implicit' About It," *National Post*. http://nationalpost.com/news/canada/canadian-law-decisive-on-what-constitutes-sexual-consent-theres-nothing-implied-or-implicit-about-it.

66. A. Csanady. 2017, March 3. "Nova Scotia Judge Facing Formal Complaints, Petitions, for Finding Cabbie Not Guilty of Sexual Assault," *National Post*. http://news.nationalpost.com/news/canada/nova-scotia-judge-facing-formal-complaints-petitions-for-finding-cabbie-not-guilty-of-sex-assault.

67. Ibid.

68. K.-L. Tang. 2003. "Battered Women Syndrome Testimony in Canada: Its Development and Lingering Issues," *International Journal of Offender Therapy and Comparative Criminology*, 4(6), 618–629.

69. E. Sheehy, J. Stubbs, and J. Tolmie. 2012. "Battered Women Charged with Homicide in Australia, Canada and New Zealand: How Do They Fare?" *Australian & New Zealand Journal of Criminology*, 45(3), 383–399.

70. S. Neil. 2013, January 22. "Supreme Court Clarifies the Law of Duress, Ends Nicole Ryan's Tragic Ordeal," *TheCourt.ca*. http://www.thecourt.ca/supreme-court-clarifies-the-law-of-duress-ends-nicole-ryans-tragic-ordeal.

71. E. Ono. 2017. "Reformulating the Use of Battered Woman Syndrome: Testimonies in Canadian Law: Implications for Social Work," *Journal of Women and Social Work*, 32(1), 24–36.

72. CBC News. 2011, March 16. "Ont. Murder Trial Halted for Lack of Aboriginal Jurors." http://www.cbc.ca/news/canada/ont-murder-trial-halted-for-lack-of-aboriginal-jurors-1.1053442.

73. The Honourable F. Iacobucci. 2013. *First Nations Representation on Ontario Juries. Report of the Independent Review Conducted by The Honourable Frank Iacobucci*. Toronto: Government of Ontario. https://www.attorneygeneral.jus.gov.on.ca/english/about/pubs/iacobucci/First_Nations_Representation_Ontario_Juries.html.

74. C. Perkel. 2013, June 13. "Manslaughter Conviction Tossed Over Lack of Aboriginals on Ontario Juries," *National Post*. http://www.cbc.ca/news/canada/thunder-bay/manslaughter-conviction-tossed-over-lack-of-aboriginals-on-jury-1.1385058.

75. M. Blanchfield. 2015. "Supreme Court Upholds Aboriginal Man's Manslaughter Conviction," *Globe and Mail*, May 21, https://www.theglobeandmail.com/news/national/supreme-court-rules-in-ontario-case-on-lack-of-aboriginals-on-juries/article24541580.

76. D.J. Devine, L.D. Clayton, B.B. Dunford, R. Seying, and J. Pryce. 2000. "Jury Decision Making: 45 Years of Empirical Research on Deliberating Groups," *Psychology, Public Policy, and Law*, 7(3), 622–727.

77. B.P. Hrycan. 2006. "The Myth of Trial by Jury," *Criminal Law Quarterly*, 51(2), 157–168.

78. D.E. Shelton, Y.S. Kim, and G. Barak. 2006. "A Study of Juror Expectations and Demands Concerning Scientific Evidence: Does the 'CSI Effect' Exist?" *Vanderbilt Journal of Entertainment & Technology Law*, 9(2), 331–368.

79. I. Roumeliotis. 2017, January 15. "'It's Still a Nightmare': The Case of Jurors Released with PTSD and Little or No Help after Verdict," *CBC News*. http://www.cbc.ca/news/health/jury-duty-ptsd-help-1.3931643.

80. M. Lindsay. 2014. *A Survey of Survivors of Sexual Violence in Three Canadian Cities*. Ottawa: Department of Justice Canada, p. 24. http://www.justice.gc.ca/eng/rp-pr/cj-jp/victim/rr13_19/rr13_19.pdf.

81. Ibid., p. 27.

82. Ibid., p. 25.

83. From R. Talusan. 2017, May 3. "When Criminal Court Failed My Rape Case, I Tried Criminal Compensation," *Vice News*. https://www.vice.com/en_ca/article/when-criminal-court-failed-my-rape-case-i-tried-criminal-compensation. Reprinted by permission of VICE.

84. K. Roach. 2015. "The Wrongful Conviction of Indigenous People in Australia and Canada," *Flinders Law Journal*, 17(2), 203–262. https://papers.ssrn.com/sol3/papers.cfm?abstract_id=2739386.

85. Ibid.

86. Cited in Roach, "The Wrongful Conviction of Indigenous People in Australia and Canada," p. 212.

87. *CBC News*. 2009, August 8. "Canada's Wrongful Convictions." http://www.cbc.ca/news/canada/canada-s-wrongful-convictions-1.783998.

88. Federal/Provincial/Territorial Heads of Prosecutions. 2011. *The Path to Justice: Preventing Wrongful Convictions. Report of the Federal/Provincial/Territorial Heads of Prosecutions Subcommittee on the Prevention of Wrongful Convictions*. Ottawa. Public Prosecution Service of Canada. https://www.cacp.ca/law-amendments-committee-activities.html?asst_id=468.

89. R. Bajer, M. Trepanier, E. Campbell, D. LePard, N. Mahaffy, J. Robinson, and D. Stewart. 2007. *Wrongful Convictions in Canada*. Vancouver: International Society for Reform of the Criminal Law. http://www.millerthomson.com/assets/file/article_attachments/Wrongful_Convictions_in_Canada.pdf.

90. G.L. Wells, A. Memmon, and S.D. Penrod. 2006. "Eyewitness Evidence. Improving Its Probative Value," *Psychological Science in the Public Interest*, 7(2), 45–75.

91. The Honourable T.A. Hickman. 1989. *Royal Commission on the Donald Marshall, Jr. Inquiry*. Halifax: Government of Nova Scotia. https://www.novascotia.ca/just/marshall_inquiry/_docs/Royal%20Commission%20on%20the%20Donald%20Marshall%20Jr%20Prosecution_findings.pdf.

92. J. Kennedy. 2016. "Crown Culture and Wrongful Convictions," *Criminal Law Quarterly*, 63(4), 414–438.

93. N. Macdonald. 2009, October 22. "Wrong Man, Yet Again?" *Maclean's*. http://www.macleans.ca/news/canada/wrong-man-yet-again.

94. E. Cunliffe. 2013. "Independence, Reliability, and Expert Testimony in Criminal Trials," *Australian Journal of Forensic Sciences*, 45(3), 284–295.

95. K.M. Campbell. 2011. "Expert Evidence from 'Social' Scientists: The Importance of Context and the Impact on Miscarriages of Justice," *Canadian Criminal Law Review*, 16(11), 13–35.

96. The Honourable S.T. Goudge. 2008. *Inquiry into Pediatric Forensic Pathology in Ontario. Report*. Toronto: Attorney General of Ontario. https://www.attorneygeneral.jus.gov.on.ca/inquiries/goudge/report/index.html.

97. Ontario Office of the Chief Coroner. 2007. *Public Announcement of Review of Criminally Suspicious and Homicide Cases Where Dr. Charles Smith Conducted Autopsies or Provided Opinions*. Toronto: Author. http://govdocs.ourontario.ca/node/27525.

98. J. Chipman. 2017. *Death in the Family*. Toronto: Doubleday Canada.

99. A. Woo. 2016, June 8. "Ivan Henry Awarded $8-Million for 27 Years of Wrongful Imprisonment," *Globe and Mail*. https://www.theglobeandmail.com/news/british-columbia/bc-judge-awards-ivan-henry-8-million-for-wrongful-imprisonment/article30350882.

100. A. Maki. 2014, November 28. "Wrongfully Convicted of Murder, Leighton Hay Free After 12 Years," *Globe and Mail*.

https://www.theglobeandmail.com/news/national/wrongly-convicted-of-murder-leighton-hay-free-after-12-years/article21825039.

101. S.R. Gross, B. O'Brien, C. Hu, and E.H. Kennedy. 2014. "Rate of False Conviction of Criminal Defendants Who Are Sentenced to Death," *Proceedings of the National Academy of Sciences, 111*(20), 7230–7235.

102. Kennedy, "Crown Culture and Wrongful Convictions."

© Laurie Justus Pace |Graphics One Design, 2014

CHAPTER 9
SENTENCING

After reading this chapter, you should be able to
- Identify the purpose and principles of sentencing.
- Identify and discuss the goals of sentencing.
- Discuss the sentencing options available to judges.
- Discuss the judicial options of judicial determination, judicial restraint order, dangerous offender, and long-term offender designation.
- Identify and describe the considerations of judges in sentencing.
- Discuss the issues surrounding the sentencing of Indigenous offenders.
- Discuss the issues surrounding sentencing and crime victims.
- Discuss the effectiveness of various sentencing options.

THE PURPOSE AND PRINCIPLES OF SENTENCING

Section 718 of the *Criminal Code* (R.S.C. 1985, c. C-46) sets out the purpose and principles of sentencing:

> The fundamental purpose of sentencing is to protect society and to contribute, along with crime prevention initiatives, to respect for the law and the maintenance of a just, peaceful and safe society by imposing just sanctions that have one or more of the following objectives:
>
> **(a)** to denounce unlawful conduct and the harm done to victims or to the community that is caused by unlawful conduct;
>
> **(b)** to deter the offender and other persons from committing offences;
>
> **(c)** to separate offenders from society, where necessary;
>
> **(d)** to assist in rehabilitating offenders;
>
> **(e)** to provide reparations for harm done to victims or to the community; and
>
> **(f)** to promote a sense of responsibility in offenders, and acknowledgement of the harm done to victims or to the community.

An important principle in sentencing is **proportionality**: the sentence must be proportionate to the gravity of the offence and to the degree of responsibility of the offender (s. 718.1). As well, the **principle of restraint** is designed to ensure that the sentence that is imposed is "a just and appropriate punishment, and nothing more" (*R. v. M. (C.A.)*, [1996] S.C.J. no. 28, para. 80).

THE GOALS OF SENTENCING: THE CASES OF MR. SMITH AND MR. JONES

There are three primary groups of sentencing goals in the criminal courts: utilitarian, retributive, and restorative. The semi-fictitious cases of "Mr. Smith" and "Mr. Jones" (not their real names) will be used to illustrate how these sentencing goals are applied.

Mr. Smith was a Quebec police chief and swimming coach who was convicted of four counts of sexual assault for fondling two girls aged 12 and 13. Mr. Jones, a computer engineer in British Columbia, was convicted of sexual assault for fondling his young stepdaughter over a two-year period. The cases of Mr. Smith and Mr. Jones—neither of whom had a prior criminal record—were widely publicized in their respective communities, and both men eventually lost their jobs.

UTILITARIAN GOALS

Utilitarian sentencing goals focus on the future conduct of Mr. Smith, Mr. Jones, and others who might commit similar offences. These goals focus on protecting the public from future crimes in the following ways:

- by discouraging potential Mr. Smiths and Mr. Joneses from crime (*general deterrence*);
- by discouraging Mr. Smith and Mr. Jones from doing it again (*specific deterrence*);
- by addressing the reasons why Mr. Smith and Mr. Jones did it (*rehabilitation*); and
- by keeping Mr. Smith and Mr. Jones in jail to protect society (*incapacitation*).

Proportionality (in sentencing)

The sentence must be proportionate to the gravity of the offence and to the degree of responsibility of the offender.

Principle of restraint (in sentencing)

Ensures that the sentence that is imposed is a just and appropriate punishment, and nothing more.

RETRIBUTIVE GOALS

The past, rather than the future, is the focus of retributive sentencing goals, which include the following:

- to express society's disapproval of Mr. Smith's and Mr. Jones's behaviour and to validate existing laws (*denunciation*); and

- to make Mr. Smith and Mr. Jones "pay" for their offences, based on the philosophy "an eye for an eye" (*retribution*).

Central to the retributive goals of sentencing is the notion of proportionality; that is, the sentences received by Mr. Smith and Mr. Jones should be proportionate to the gravity of their offences as well as to their degree of responsibility.

RESTORATIVE GOALS

These goals are premised on the principles of restorative justice, introduced in Chapter 2. As noted, restorative justice is based on the principle that criminal behaviour injures not only victims but also communities and offenders. Any attempt to resolve the problems that the criminal behaviour has created should, therefore, involve all three parties. Restorative justice approaches also have a utilitarian function in that they are designed to protect the public from future criminal behaviour.

Since the victims in both these cases were children, they would be excluded from any restorative justice forum. However, the victims' families would have the opportunity to discuss the impact of the crimes, and Mr. Smith and Mr. Jones would be held accountable for their criminal behaviour.

WHAT SENTENCES DID MR. SMITH AND MR. JONES RECEIVE?

Under the *Criminal Code* (s. 271)

Everyone who commits a sexual assault is guilty of

(a) an indictable offence and is liable to imprisonment for a term of not more than 10 years or, if the complainant is under the age of 16 years, to imprisonment for a term of not more than 14 years and to a minimum punishment of imprisonment for a term of one year; or,

(b) an offence punishable on summary conviction and is liable to imprisonment for a term of not more than 18 months or, if the complainant is under the age of 16 years, to imprisonment for a term of not more than two years less a day and to a minimum punishment of imprisonment for a term of six months.

Although neither Mr. Smith nor Mr. Jones had a prior criminal record and both had a good job history, the offences they committed were serious and had a significant impact on the victims. One of Mr. Smith's victims suffered long-term emotional and academic problems, while Mr. Jones's former spouse and children experienced considerable emotional difficulties. The child victims in both cases had been young and vulnerable. Mr. Smith had been an authority figure in the community, and parents trusted him to supervise their children, a trust he violated. Similarly, Mr. Jones violated the trust of his stepdaughter and most likely would have continued sexually abusing her had she not informed her mother of his improper behaviour.

Mr. Smith was sentenced to two years less a day in a provincial correctional facility. The Crown appealed the sentence on the grounds that it was too lenient. But the Appeal Court upheld the sentence, in part because Mr. Smith had been fired from his job as police chief and so had already experienced a severe sanction. The Appeal Court acknowledged that child abuse typically demands a denunciatory sentence for the protection of society, but noted that each case must be judged on its merits.

Mr. Jones was not so fortunate. He was sentenced to 18 months' confinement in a provincial correctional facility and three years' probation (the maximum). In explaining the sentence, the presiding judge cited the objectives of denunciation and general and specific deterrence.

These two cases highlight the vast discretion that Canadian judges have in sentencing.

SENTENCING OPTIONS

The sentencing options from which Canadian judges may select, and a case example of each, are set out in Table 9.1. Note that offenders who receive an absolute discharge or a conditional discharge do not need to apply for a records suspension (formerly referred to as a "pardon") to have the charges removed from their records. These are the only sentences to which this proviso applies.

TABLE 9.1

SENTENCING OPTIONS AND CASE EXAMPLES

Absolute discharge	The offender is found guilty but technically not convicted. The offence will appear on the offender's criminal record for one year and then be removed.
Case example:	A young mother in Fort McMurray was given an absolute discharge after pleading guilty to stealing $638 worth of items from Wal-Mart. The items included candy and baby sleepers. The presiding judge expressed concern as to how the woman ended up in the situation and suggested that she seek professional help.[a]
Conditional discharge	The offender is found guilty and released upon the condition that he or she comply with the conditions of a probation order that may range from one to three years. If the offender fails to meet the conditions, he or she may be returned to court to be sentenced on the original charge. A conditional discharge remains on the offender's criminal record for three years after the completion of the probation order. A key requirement is that the imposition of this sentence not be contrary to the public interest.
Case example:	A student suspended from the medical school at Dalhousie University in Halifax pled guilty to a charge of possessing a high-capacity ammunition magazine for a gun. His psychiatrist had notified police after becoming concerned that persons at the university were at risk of being killed. He had also been charged with uttering threats and engaging in threatening conduct. While out on bail, he began going to counselling. A one-year period of probation was attached to the conditional discharge, including that he not possess weapons or consume drugs without a prescription and that he take counselling for mental health and anger management issues. Upon successful completion of the term of probation, he will not have a criminal record. The presiding judge stated that a conditional discharge would not be contrary to the public interest.[b]
Suspended sentence	The offender is convicted of the offence, but the imposition of the sentence is suspended pending successful completion of a period of probation that may range from one to three years. A **suspended sentence** results in a criminal record.
Case example:	A 69-year-old man from El Salvador received a three-year suspended sentence in Regina Provincial Court for incidents relating to the inappropriate touching of two women passengers on city buses. The judge held that the two incidents were "at the lower end of the sexual assault spectrum" and noted that the man was elderly, had no prior record, and was remorseful for his actions. The suspended sentence involved a three-year period of probation, including the condition that he provide a DNA sample to police. The decision means that he will have a criminal record.[c]
Fine	The offender must pay a specific amount of money within a specified time or face the prospect of imprisonment for fine default.
Case example:	A Calgary couple was fined $12,000 after being found guilty of a single charge of neglect under the provincial *Animal Protection Act*. A total of 91 pets who had been neglected were seized from their home and included 69 rabbits, 20 hamsters, a dog, and a cat. Most of the animals had to be euthanized. In the house, there were piles of rabbit feces up to 45 centimetres deep.[d]
Forfeiture	Convicted offenders may be required to forfeit goods to the Crown. For example, those found in possession of counterfeit money, narcotics, illegal pornography, hate propaganda, or some types of weapons or explosives may be required to hand over these seized goods. The items are either destroyed or sold, with the proceeds going to the government. A "proceeds of crime" provision in the *Criminal Code* also allows the government to seize money, property, vehicles, and other goods acquired as a result of crimes.

(continued)

TABLE 9.1

SENTENCING OPTIONS AND CASE EXAMPLES *(Continued)*

Case example:	Two gang members in British Columbia received lengthy prison terms for drug trafficking. The judge also ordered the forfeiture of $100,040 police received from the gang members during a 2009 undercover sting by the police.[e]
Prohibitions	These may be attached to a sentence and can include prohibition from driving, prohibition from attending places frequented by children, and prohibition from possessing firearms.
Case example:	An Ontario man was sentenced to 50 months in prison and banned from driving for seven years after being convicted of impaired driving causing death. The offender had struck a man who was standing on his parents' front lawn.[f]
Intermittent sentence	A custodial sentence served on a "part-time" basis (generally weekends, from Friday evening until Monday morning) and generally no more than 90 days in length.
Case example:	A North Vancouver, British Columbia, man received a 90-day **intermittent sentence** after pleading guilty to accessing child pornography. The man was apprehended as part of an FBI undercover operation in which an undercover officer posed as a person wanting to access child pornography. The police investigation revealed that the man had downloaded child pornography images from a file sharing network.[g]
Probation	The offender is placed under supervision in the community for a specified period of time (maximum three years), must fulfill general conditions, and may be required to adhere to or complete specific conditions (e.g., attend alcohol or drug counselling).
Case example:	A South Porcupine Ontario Provincial Police officer was sentenced to 18 months' probation for defrauding the local chapter of the Ontario Provincial Police Association of approximately $7,000. The officer had served as the treasurer for the association for a number of years. An investigation found the officer had made 65 questionable transactions from the account for personal items. The officer apologized to her family, friends, and colleagues in court. The court also required that the officer repay the remaining portion of the money that was still outstanding.[h]
Conditional sentence	The offender receives a term of confinement (less than two years) and is allowed to serve it in the community under the supervision of a probation officer, provided he or she meets certain specified conditions (although the offender is *not* on probation and may be imprisoned for violation of conditions).
Case example:	A Peterborough, Ontario, man who defrauded the Quaker Oats Company of nearly $2 million was ordered to pay restitution and given a conditional sentence of two years, less a day, to be followed by three years' probation. The former employee of the company had set up fake corporations that billed the company for work that was never completed.[i]
Imprisonment	The offender is sentenced to a period of confinement—to a provincial institution if the sentence or sentences total two years less a day, and to a federal correctional institution if the sentence or sentences total two years or more.
Case example:	A Montreal man was sentenced to five years in prison for his role in the theft of $18.7 million of maple syrup. The syrup had been stored in a warehouse that was partially owned by his wife and had been rented by the Federation of Quebec Maple Syrup Producers. The man pleaded guilty to theft and trafficking after being apprehended selling the syrup on the black market.[j]

[a] *Western Star* (Corner Brook, NL). 2016, November 23. "Fort McMurray Woman Given Absolute Discharge." http://www.thewesternstar.com/news/local/2016/11/23/fort-mcmurray-woman-given-absolute-disch-4691752.html.

[b] S. Bruce. 2016, October 26. "Suspended Med Student Gets Conditional discharge on Weapons Offence," *Local Xpress* (Halifax).

[c] B. Fitzpatrick. 2016, December 1. "Man Receives Suspended Sentence after Groping Bus Passengers," *Regina Leader-Post*. http://leaderpost.com/news/crime/man-receives-suspended-sentence-after-groping-bus-passengers.

[d] K. Martin. 2016, November 3. "Couple Fined $12,000 for Failure to Care for 91 Pets in Filthy Home," *Calgary Herald*. http://calgaryherald.com/news/local-news/couple-fined-12000-for-failure-to-care-for-91-pets-in-filthy-home.

[e] K. Bolan. 2012, December 12. "UN Gang Members Get 8 and 10 Years in Cocaine Case, Minus Pre-Trial Credit," *Vancouver Sun*. http://vancouversun.com/news/staff-blogs/un-gang-members-get-8-and-10-years-in-cocaine-case-minus-pre-trial-credit.

[f] J. Sims. 2017, January 9. "'They Lost Their Son': Ontario Drunk Driver Gets Four-Years for Running Over Man Standing on His Parents' Lawn," *National Post*. http://news.nationalpost.com/news/canada/ontario-drunk-driver-gets-four-years-for-running-over-man-standing-on-parents-lawn.

[g] J. Seyd. 2016, June 3. "Child Porn Viewer Gets 90 Days in Jail," *North Shore News*.

[h] R. Grech. 2016, November 9. "Cops Gets 18 Months' Probation for $7,000 Fraud," *Daily Press* (Timmins, ON). http://www.timminspress.com/2016/11/09/cop-gets-18-months-probation-for-7000-fraud.

[i] J. Bain. 2016, January 5. "House Arrest for Man Who Defrauded Quaker," *Peterborough Examiner*. http://www.thepeterboroughexaminer.com/2016/01/05/house-arrest-for-man-who-defrauded-quaker.

[j] G. Hamilton. 2017, April 24. "Sweet Revenge for Quebec Maple Syrup Producers: Thief Gets Five Years for Role in $18.7 Million Heist," *National Post*. http://nationalpost.com/news/canada/sweet-revenge-for-quebec-maple-syrup-producers-thief-gets-five-years-for-role-in-18-7-million-heist.

Suspended sentence

A sentencing option whereby the judge convicts the accused but technically gives no sentence and instead places the offender on probation, which, if successfully completed, results in no sentence being given.

Intermittent sentence

A sentence that is served on a part-time basis, generally on weekends.

Probation

A sentence imposed on an offender by a criminal court judge that provides for the supervision of the offender in the community by a probation officer, either as an alternative to custody or in conjunction with a period of incarceration in a provincial or territorial correctional institution.

Concurrent sentences

Sentences that are amalgamated and served simultaneously.

Consecutive sentences

Sentences that run separately and are completed one after the other.

Most of the sentencing options set out in Table 9.1 provide alternatives to confinement. Some of these options may be combined; for example, the judge may impose a period of **probation** of up to three years in conjunction with a sentence of two years less a day for offenders in provincial/territorial systems, or they may impose fines along with probation or a period of confinement. Alternatives to confinement are discussed in Chapter 10.

The large majority of people convicted of criminal offences are not sent to prison but rather are placed under some form of supervision in the community, most frequently probation (discussed in Chapter 10). This includes requiring the offender to participate in some type of restorative justice program, including victim–offender mediation (discussed in Chapter 10).

For offenders convicted of multiple offences, the judge may order that the sentences be served either concurrently or consecutively. **Concurrent sentences** received by the offender are merged into one sentence and served simultaneously. Thus, an offender sentenced to two prison sentences of nine months each will serve a nine-month sentence (not an 18-month sentence). **Consecutive sentences** are served separately: one begins after the other has expired. That is, an offender sentenced to two terms of nine months each will serve 18 months. When deciding whether a sentence should be consecutive or concurrent, the court should consider (1) the timeframe of the offences, (2) the similarity of the offences, (3) whether a new intent broached each offence, and (4) whether the total sentence is fit and proper. Whether a sentence is concurrent or consecutive will affect the offender's parole eligibility, as it will determine how long he or she must serve before being able to apply for release.[1]

Provisions in the *Criminal Code* state that all sentences are to be concurrent unless the trial judge specifies that they are to be consecutive. By contrast, sentences under the *Provincial Offences Act* (R.S.O. 1990, c. P.33) are to be consecutive unless the sentencing judge specifies that they are to run concurrently. There are exceptions to this. The *Protecting Canadians by Ending Sentence Discounts for Multiple Murders Act* (S.C. 2011, c. 5), passed in 2011, allows judges to impose consecutive sentences to offenders convicted of multiple murders. Previously, these sentences were served concurrently.

This occurred in the case of Travis Baumgartner, who in 2013 received a 40-year sentence after pleading guilty to killing three fellow security officers and critically wounding another.[2] And in 2014, Justin Bourque received five life sentences with no chance for parole for 75 years for killing three RCMP officers and wounding two other officers in a shooting spree in Moncton, New Brunswick.[3]

VICTIM FINE SURCHARGE (VFS)

The VFS was introduced in 1989 as a way to provide funding for victim services. Initially, judges were able to waive the surcharge if its imposition would impose undue hardship on an offender. In 2013, as part of the "get tough" approach to crime, the then federal Conservative government made the penalty mandatory with the enactment of the *Increasing Offenders' Accountability for Victims Act* (S.C. 2013, c. 11). This required judges to order the offender to pay a victim fine surcharge (VFS) equal to 15 percent of any fine. If there is no fine, an amount of up to $10,000 is set by the judge.

Many judges attempted to bypass the legislation by sentencing offenders to one day in jail and then counting attendance at court as "time served." In 2015, the BC Provincial Court ruled in *R. v. Barinecutt* (2015 BCPC 189) that the imposition of a victim fine surcharge on a homeless man violated his Charter rights, as it criminalized the man in perpetuity, which would violate his rights to security and liberty under the *Charter of Rights and Freedoms*.[4]

There are two common misunderstandings about the VFS. First, the surcharge is *not* a sentence in its own right and is always ordered in addition to another disposition. Second, the money is *not* paid to the victim. It goes into a provincial fund to pay for victim services. Some provinces also collect the VFS for *provincial offences*. The rate of non-payment of VFSs is unknown, although it can be anticipated that for many offenders, even a small amount may be beyond their means. It is possible for judges to incarcerate offenders who are unable to pay the victim fine surcharge, a provision which may significantly impact offenders in poverty.

ADDITIONAL SENTENCING OPTIONS

JUDICIAL DETERMINATION

Section 743.6 of the *Criminal Code* gives sentencing judges the authority to impose, on some offenders receiving a sentence of imprisonment of two years or more, the requirement that an offender receiving a sentence of two or more years, serve one-half of the sentence prior to being eligible for parole, instead of the typical one-third. The primary objectives of this provision are protection of the public and specific and general deterrence.

Indigenous offenders are overrepresented in the group of offenders receiving **judicial determination**. Offenders receiving judicial determination are more likely than other offenders to serve their entire sentence in confinement.

Judicial determination

An order by the sentencing judge that the offender serve one-half of their sentence before being eligible to apply for parole.

JUDICIAL RESTRAINT ORDER

Under Section 810 of the *Criminal Code*, you may lay an information before a justice of the peace (JP) if you have reasonable grounds to believe that another person will injure you, your spouse, your children, or your property. The person need not have a criminal history at the time of the application. Other sections—810.01(1), fear of a criminal organization offence; 810.1(1), fear of a sexual offence; and 810.2, fear of serious personal injury—require an information to be laid before a provincial court judge. Section 810 has withstood Charter challenges.

If the JP or the judge is satisfied that there are reasonable grounds for the threat, the defendant is required to enter into a recognizance to keep the peace and be of good behaviour for a period not to exceed 12 months. This is frequently referred to as a *peace bond*.[5]

The court may also impose conditions on the defendant—for example, to abstain from possessing a firearm, to avoid contact with persons under 14, or to stay away from places frequented by children (such as school or daycare grounds). Violation of the conditions of an 810 order is an offence and can result in imprisonment. A defendant can also be imprisoned for refusing to agree to an 810 order. Critics of section 810 argue that the conditions are too broad in their application in that no crime need have been committed in order for them to be imposed.

Section 810 orders can also be imposed by judges when an offender is released from custody following the completion of his or her sentence (see Chapter 12).

LIFE IMPRISONMENT

Under the *Criminal Code*, persons convicted of murder are subject to life imprisonment. This means that the offender is under sentence for life, although he or she may serve this sentence both in prison and upon release on parole in the community. The *Criminal Code* sets out the minimum number of years that an offender must serve in prison before being eligible to apply for release on parole. The key word is *apply*—there is no guarantee that the parole board will grant a release.

As part of its crime policy legislative agenda, the federal government in 2011 passed the *Protecting Canadians by Ending Sentence Discounts for Multiple Murders Act*, which permits a judge, in cases involving more than one murder, to add up parole eligibility periods within a life sentence consecutively, rather than concurrently, as had been past practice. In 2013, Travis Baumgartner, an armoured car guard who killed four of his colleagues in an on-the-job robbery, made a plea deal that would give him a life sentence with no chance of parole for 40 years. Prior to the legislation, Baumgartner would have had to serve a maximum of 25 years prior to being eligible for parole.[6]

The death penalty was abolished by Parliament in 1976 and replaced with a mandatory life sentence without possibility of parole for 25 years in cases of first-degree murder (although it was retained for a number of military offences, including treason and mutiny). Until 1976, more than 700 persons had been put to death.

SENTENCING CONSIDERATIONS

Criminal court judges consider a wide range of factors in determining the sentence to be imposed on a convicted offender. Several of the more common factors are set out in Table 9.2.

"As a mitigating circumstance, may I say that my client's getaway car was a hybrid."

© Leo Cullum/The New Yorker Collection/The Cartoon Bank

Gender may also be a consideration in sentencing. Research studies have considered the influence of the "chivalry factor" and the "evil woman" factor on the sentences received by women offenders. The chivalry theory holds that women offenders receive more lenient sentences than men offenders due to the perception that women are less threatening and dangerous, while the evil woman theory holds that women offenders are likely to be more severely punished due to their violation of gender norms and values.[7] Canadian research on sentencing women is sparse; U.S. research has found that, historically, women tended to receive more lenient sentences than men, but that in recent times it appears to be similar to men.[8] The increasing numbers of women, particularly Indigenous women, in prison populations suggests that this trend is evident in Canada as well.

TABLE 9.2
SENTENCING CONSIDERATIONS

Factor	Description
Aggravating factors	These are facts about an offender and the offence that are considered negative and tend to increase the severity of a sentence (e.g., violence, violation of a position of authority).
Mitigating factors	These are facts about the offender and the offence that may decrease the severity of a sentence (e.g., being Indigenous, being addicted).
Case law precedent	Judges will consider sentencing decisions in previous, similar cases. A general principle is that there should be similar sentences in similar cases.
Pre-sentence reports (PSRs)	The PSR, prepared by probation officers, presents information on the offender's background, present situation, and risk/needs. It also sets out options for sentencing that the judge will consider.
Victim impact statements	These contain information on the harm done to the victim (psychological and physical) as well as the consequences of the victimization.
Psychological assessments	These are completed on offenders and address the mental state and treatment needs of the offender.
Indigenous offenders	Section 718.2(e) requires judges to consider alternatives to incarceration for Indigenous offenders.
Black offenders	Defence lawyers are increasingly asking for cultural assessments to be prepared on black offenders prior to sentencing.

To reduce the numbers of women sentenced to confinement, it has been suggested that sentencing guidelines could be developed for judges to ensure that judges exercise their discretion in gender-sensitive ways. This would include considering the disproportionate impact of incarceration on women, who are most often the primary caregiver for their children, and are often confined in institutions a considerable distance from their families and friends, due to their small numbers.[9] These issues are discussed further in Chapter 11.

Given the broad discussion of judges in most cases, the extent to which any one of these sources of information impact the judge's sentence will vary on a case-by-case basis. Research indicates that judges do pay close attention to the materials contained in the pre-sentence report. These reports are prepared by probation officers on adult offenders who have been convicted. PSRs are prepared on the request of a sentencing judge; they are not mandatory. The PSR contains a wealth of information on the offender's background and offence history, as well as victim impact information and assessments completed by treatment professionals.

For Indigenous offenders, there are special considerations that the PSR must address. For example, it must include information on the offender's background and community, as well as on available community-based programs and services, including restorative justice programs such as sentencing circles and Elder-assisted interventions.

EXTRAORDINARY MEASURES: DANGEROUS AND LONG-TERM OFFENDERS

There are two dispositions that are quite different from the sentences discussed so far in that they are not time limited and are used only in the most serious and unusual cases. These dispositions involve declaring offenders either dangerous offenders or long-term offenders.

DANGEROUS OFFENDER (DO) DESIGNATION

Section 752 of the *Criminal Code* contains procedures and criteria for declaring someone a "dangerous offender." That section defines a **dangerous offender** (DO) as a person who may be given an indeterminate sentence upon conviction for a particularly violent crime and/or who has demonstrated a pattern of committing serious violent offences. In the judgment of the court, the offender's behaviour is unlikely to be controlled or prevented by normal approaches to behavioural restraint. The purpose of the section is to identify those persons with unacceptable propensities for violence and to incapacitate them in order to protect the public interest.

A person can be declared a DO by a sentencing judge only if the Crown makes a formal application after conviction but before sentencing. The provincial attorney general must approve such an application beforehand. If the Crown proves the case, the judge *may* order detention for an indeterminate period. If this happens, the offender is detained in a federal prison, but there is no set length on the sentence. The offender can be released by the Parole Board of Canada the following year, the following decade, or never (see Chapter 12). These applications are rare, and there is a high burden of proof on the Crown. Two elements are considered in making this determination: *past* offence history, and the likelihood of serious offences in the *future*.

The first threshold is that the current offences of conviction must involve at least one "serious personal injury offence"—that is, an indictable offence for which the possible sentence is at least 10 years and which involved the use or attempted use of violence against another person, *or* conduct endangering or likely to endanger the life or safety

> **Dangerous offender**
>
> A designation made by the judge after conviction that results in an indeterminate term of imprisonment in a federal correctional institution.

of another person, *or* conduct inflicting or likely to inflict severe psychological damage on another person.

The second threshold involves past behaviour of the offender, which reflects a pattern of persistent, aggressive behaviour; a failure to control sexual impulses; and other behaviour which indicates that the offenders have difficulty controlling their behaviour.

This indeterminate sentencing option is unique in that judges are explicitly called upon to predict, based on patterns of past behaviour, the likelihood of serious offences in the future. Specifically, the Crown must prove (beyond a reasonable doubt) that the offender "constitutes a threat to the life, safety or physical or mental well-being of other persons …" (*Criminal Code*, s. 753(1)(a)).

Expert witnesses are often called to help the court make these determinations. At least two psychiatrists—one nominated by the defence, the other by the prosecution—must testify. Other experts may be called, and the offender can call witnesses to testify to his or her character and reputation.

There has been a steady increase in the number of offenders designated as dangerous.[10] Of concern is the increase in the number of Indigenous offenders designated as dangerous offenders, comprising 29 percent of this group of offenders in 2016.[11]

Dangerous offenders present challenges to the criminal justice system due to the myriad factors that are associated with their offending, including low levels of education, disturbed childhoods, psychopathy, and substance abuse problems.[12] A profile of a dangerous offender is presented in Court File 9.1.

(continued)

July 2003: Miller's wife, Lesley, speaks out about her struggle to pay for her husband's care. One year later, the Alberta government decides it will cover the cost of his long-term care for the duration of his life, and the woman vows to continue fighting for further compensation for victims of crime and a change in laws around repeat offenders.

Feb. 28, 2005: Provincial court Judge Brad Kerby declares Teskey a dangerous offender. With the designation, Teskey is locked up indefinitely until the National Parole Board sees fit to let him rejoin society. During the hearing, several psychiatrists label Teskey as a psychopath who is likely to reoffend.

April 7, 2005: Demolition begins on the apartment building where Teskey attacked Miller. Years earlier, Lesley Miller sold it to pay for her husband's therapy and other costs. The property deteriorated and became a hub for criminal activity before the decision was made to tear it down.

November 2005: Lesley Miller is awarded the Alberta Centennial Medal by then Lieutenant-Governor Norman Kwong for her advocacy work.

June 2006: The Alberta Court of Appeal upholds Teskey's conviction in a 2–1 decision. The appeal, based on the lengthy delay in the judge handing down his reasons for the verdict, is sent up to the Supreme Court of Canada.

June 7, 2007: After hearing the application in February, Canada's highest court grants Teskey a new trial, which begins in Edmonton court Dec. 7, 2007.

Feb. 8, 2008: Teskey is found guilty of the assault on Miller for the second time.

May 16, 2008: Lesley Miller meets with then Alberta Premier Ed Stelmach as part of her continued petitioning of the government to improve access to funds for victims of crime.

Feb. 4, 2009: Teskey's third dangerous offender hearing gets underway. He is designated as a dangerous offender in June 2010 and Teskey is once again imprisoned indefinitely.

August 2010: Guards find cocaine and crack in Kinder-egg containers in his cell in the Edmonton Remand Centre. He is convicted in March 2012 and has five years added to his indefinite sentence.

Sept. 10, 2014: Teskey's appeal of his dangerous offender designation is dismissed in a unanimous decision by the Alberta Court of Appeal.

April 2016: Teskey's applications for day parole and full parole are both denied by the Parole Board of Canada. He is eligible to apply again in five years.

Sept. 24, 2016: Miller dies, nearly 16 years after the attack. Teskey is not charged for the death.

May 2017: Teskey is 46 and, while he is eligible to apply for release in 2021, will remain in custody in a federal correctional institution unless he can convince the Parole Board of Canada that he is no longer a danger to society.

All of the psychological assessments conducted on Teskey identified him as a highly intelligent psychopath. There have been extensive online comments on Teskey's case, and while the majority of the comments are critical of the justice system, others raise issues related to his childhood. These two views are reflected in the following comments:

> This man's file is yet another piece of evidence that our system is far too lenient on criminal filth. We must prioritize public safety over rehabilitation and reintegration.

> He should have had counselling and rehabilitation services at a young age. This was a person who was at first and victim himself. Not everyone is able to move past such horrible atrocities committed on them as children. Very sad.

> I'm not sure why being a victim of sexual, or other abuse, is a mitigating factor in adult behaviour. Indeed it is not fair, it is terrible... but it is not an excuse to abuse others.

Source: P. Parsons. 2016, October 1. "Leo Teskey's Path to Dangerous Offender Status," *Edmonton Journal*, http://edmontonjournal.com/news/crime/leo-teskeys-path-to-dangerous-offender-status-after-beating-landlord-into-coma. Material republished with the express permission of Postmedia Network Inc.

LONG-TERM OFFENDER (LTO) DESIGNATION

Section 753 of the *Criminal Code* contains provisions for declaring someone a **long-term offender** (LTO). Crown counsel may use this option when the case falls short of the stringent criteria for filing a DO application. As with dangerous offenders, evidence must be presented to indicate that there is substantial risk that the offender will commit a serious personal offence after release from prison.

The designation is available only for those offenders who have received a sentence of more than two years. At sentencing, the judge sets the length of the long-term supervision order. This means that after the sentence ends (which includes confinement and post-release supervision), the long-term supervision order comes into effect. This order requires that the offender be supervised by a parole officer for the remaining period of the order, which may be up to 10 years. The Parole Board of Canada sets the

Long-term offender

A designation under section 752 or 753 of the *Criminal Code* that requires the offender to spend up to 10 years under supervision following the expiry of his or her sentence.

PROFILE OF A LONG-TERM OFFENDER

On September 16, 2009, Ross Garland kidnapped a woman at the Halifax airport, jumping into her car after she had dropped off a friend. Garland made the victim stop and withdraw money from ATMs. The victim escaped while he was attempting to force her into the trunk. He was later apprehended. Garland had a lengthy criminal record dating back 30 years, including robbery with a weapon and assault causing bodily harm. Associated with his criminality was a long history of substance abuse. During the long-term offender hearing, the presiding judge noted that Garland's substance abuse issue were "very serious and very unrelenting."[a] The judge also noted that he had been unresponsive to treatment in previous prison terms. The judge sentenced Garland to eight years in prison, followed by eight years of supervision, noting that it would be "disastrous for both Mr. Garland and the community if he were to be released into the community without supervision."[b] At the hearing, the kidnapping victim told Mr. Garland that she forgave him and Garland apologized to her.

[a,b] D. Jeffrey. 2013, April 15. "Kidnapper Declared a Long-Term Offender," *Halifax Chronicle Herald*. http://thechronicleherald.ca/metro/1123521-kidnapper-declared-long-term-offender.

conditions under which the offender will be supervised following the expiration of his or her sentence.

The long-term offender designation, designed to deal with specific sexual offences, is another option for Crown counsel, particularly in cases in which the Crown falls short of the rigid requirements or level of evidence to file a dangerous offender application. As with dangerous offenders, there must be evidence that the offender presents a substantial risk of reoffending by committing a serious personal offence. However, there must also be risk assessment evidence demonstrating that the offender may be effectively managed in the community with appropriate supervision and treatment.[13] A profile of a long-term offender is presented in Court File 9.2.

There are differences between the designation of long-term offender (LTO) and long-term supervision orders (LTSO). The LTO designation is imposed by the sentencing judge and is the actual sentence of the court under section 753.1 of the *Criminal Code*. An LTSO refers to the administration of the sentence and is the responsibility of the Parole Board of Canada under the *Corrections and Conditional Release Act* (S.C. 1992, c. 20).

SENTENCING IN A DIVERSE SOCIETY

In Chapter 1, it was noted that the application of the criminal law is challenging in a diverse society where visible and cultural minority groups are a growing portion of the population. If found guilty, judges are confronted with how to determine the most appropriate sentence for the offender.

A key issue related to diversity is whether the cultural practices of a person's country of origin should be considered a mitigating factor in determining the sentence for an offender whose crime was committed in Canada. There may be practices and behaviour that are permitted, or at least not sanctioned, in other countries that are a violation of the *Criminal Code* in Canada. This issue arose in the case presented in Legal File 9.1.

R. V. H.E.: SENTENCING AND CULTURAL PRACTICES

An Iranian man had been convicted of repeated sexual and physical assaults of his wife and of their children during a three-year period after the family had arrived from Iran. The trial judge sentenced the man to 18 months in a provincial correctional institution, citing a number of mitigating circumstances, including difference in culture between Iran and Canada with respect to sexual and physical assaults in the family.

On appeal, the appellant court judge found the sentence of 18 months to be "manifestly unfit" and increased the sentence to four years in prison. In imposing the increased sentence, the appeals court judge stated, "Cultural norms that condone or tolerate conduct contrary to Canadian law must not be considered a mitigating factor on sentencing. A cultural practice that is criminal in Canada does not mitigate the perpetrator's conduct for sentencing purposes. Cultural differences do not excuse or mitigate criminal conduct" (*R. v. H.E.*, 2015 ONCA 531).

SENTENCING INDIGENOUS OFFENDERS

In 1996, section 718.2(e) was added to the *Criminal Code*. It states, "[A]ll available sanctions, other than imprisonment, that are reasonable in the circumstances and consistent with the harm done to victims or to the community should be considered for all offenders, with particular attention to the circumstances of Aboriginal offenders." The intent of this amendment was to have judges consider alternative sentencing options for Indigenous offenders who would otherwise be sent to prison and thereby reduce the overrepresentation of Indigenous peoples in prison.

In a decision in 1999, the SCC affirmed this principle in *R. v. Gladue* ([1999] 1 SCR 688). Jannie Tanis Gladue had pled guilty to stabbing her partner to death, but the SCC held that Indigenous persons may have "unique systemic or background factors" that must be considered in determining the sentence whenever the person's freedom is in question, such as cases in which a term of incarceration would normally be imposed by the court. In particular, courts are required to give special consideration to the background and life circumstances of Indigenous offenders and to consider a range of sentencing options. Judges must be mindful of imposing "culturally inappropriate" sentences.

These concerns are also to be considered at other stages of the criminal justice process where the offender's liberty is at stake, including parole board hearings. The Gladue principle applies at bail hearings, sentencing, parole eligibility, dangerous offender application hearings, and other decision-making points where the liberty of an Indigenous offender is at stake.[14]

A **Gladue report** may be requested by the defence counsel, Crown prosecutor, or the presiding judge at the pre-sentencing or bail hearing stage of the criminal court process. The report is prepared by specially trained persons who gather information on the accused's personal history, including residential school experience, contact with child welfare authorities, physical or sexual abuse, health issues, and other personal and traumatic events in the Indigenous person's life that may be associated with his or her conflict with the law.[15]

In the words of a Gladue report writer, "The Gladue report is not meant to secure a reduced sentence. The purpose is to provide the court with a real understanding of what the individual has been through in their lives."[16]

To illustrate, the following is an excerpt from a Gladue report, which associates an offender's charge of assault with a weapon while intoxicated with the loss of his cultural heritage:

Gladue report

A report prepared prior to sentencing of Indigenous offenders which sets out historical events and that may be related to the offender's conflict with the law and criminal behaviour.

Mr. M. lived a fairly traditional and semi-nomadic lifestyle for about the first six years of his life. After the age of six, living on the land became problematic because of the intrusion of Canadian law into the lives of the Inuit…

…. [A] kaleidoscope of debilitating social and mental health problems result[ed] from a traumatic change in a way of life….

Alcoholism is often cited as a response to, and an escape from, the physical and psychological stresses of relocation and the depressing sense of loss and powerlessness among relocates. At Easterville, for example, alcoholism became a major problem after relocation.[17]

Specifically, section 718.2(e) requires judges to consider (1) the unique systemic or background factors that may have contributed to the criminal behaviour of the Indigenous person before the court, and (2) specific sentencing procedures and sanctions (including restorative justice and traditional healing practices) that may be more appropriate for the individual Indigenous offender. This includes taking into consideration colonialism, residential schools, and the marginality of Indigenous persons in Canadian society.

The *Gladue* decision was confirmed by the Supreme Court of Canada in *R. v. Ipeelee* (2012 SCC 13). See Critical Thinking Exercise 9.3 at the end of this chapter. In 2012, the Ontario Appeal Court ruled that two Indigenous men arrested for drug smuggling at the U.S. border should not be extradited to the U.S. where their Indigenous heritage would not be considered at sentencing, as required in Canada.[18]

An example of how the criminal history of an Indigenous person found guilty in a Gladue court is reframed at the sentencing stage is illustrated in the following exchange:

> [Duty counsel]: She is 29 years old. She is First Nations. She is the first born of an alcohol and crack addicted mother. She suffered a litany of abuse–physical, sexual and then was placed into foster care where again she was physically and sexually abused. […] She has a long criminal record but she has also been victimized and re-victimized throughout her life. Her problems are so deep and longstanding.
>
> [Judge]: The Crown is seeking a substantial sentence based on a very long record. I've considered your plea, what you have had to deal with in your life… I think time serviced is appropriate. I will suspend the sentence and place you on probation for 6 months.[19]

A case involving a Gladue report is presented in Legal File 9.2.

Gladue decision

A decision by the SCC which held that in cases where a term of incarceration would normally be imposed, judges must consider the unique circumstances of Indigenous people.

LEGAL FILE 9.2

R. V. KREKO

On May 5, 2012, Andrew Kreko robbed Jason Gomes at gunpoint of his necklace and cellphone. Kreko fled on foot, but was pursued by Gomes in his vehicle. Kreko was hit by the car and then fired four shots, one of which grazed Gomme's head, causing a minor injury, and another which entered Kreko's own leg, resulting in a serious injury.

Kreko pleaded guilty to possession without lawful excuse of a loaded prohibited firearm, robbery with a handgun, and intentional discharge of a firearm while being reckless as to the life or safety of another person. The trial judge sentenced him to 13 years in prison in 2014. Although a Gladue report had been prepared and submitted to the judge to consider prior to sentencing, the judge concluded, as he would later state, that "It appeared to me that his Aboriginal connection had been irrelevant to his offences, or how he got there."[a]

The Ontario Court of Appeal (*R. v. Kreko*, 2016 ONCA 367) subsequently reduced Kreko's sentence to nine years in prison. In its

decision, the trial court judge erred in concluding that there was no link between Kreko's Indigenous background and the offences that he committed. The appeal court noted that Kreko's mother had come from a family where there had been alcohol abuse and had given birth to Andrew when she was 15 years old and in the care of the province. He was subsequently placed in foster care and adopted at age two by a non-Indigenous family. His adoptive mother left the family soon after. Andrew's adoptive father told him about his Indigenous heritage and that he was adopted when he was in his late teens, which, the appeal court noted, "came as a shock to him, and the realization of the loss of both his adoptive mother and his birth mother led to feelings of abandonment, resentment and a sense that he was unwanted."

[a] J. Gallant. 2016, May 24. "Court Erred in Sentencing Aboriginal Man, Court of Appeal Rules," *Toronto Star*. https://www.thestar.com/news/gta/2016/05/24/court-erred-in -sentencing-aboriginal-man-court-of-appeal-rules.html.

A number of issues surround the Gladue principles. There are, however, limits in the extent to which sentencing provisions such as *Gladue* can address the social, political, and economic factors that contribute to the marginalization of Indigenous and ethno-cultural groups and their disproportionate contact with the criminal justice system.[20]

Indigenous women's groups have expressed concerns about alternative models of justice, particularly in cases of violence against women.[21] Among the arguments are that culture-based community justice models do not address the multifaceted issue of violence against women, nor the over-incarceration of Indigenous offenders.[22] There are concerns that the voices of Indigenous women are not being heard in discussions surrounding the use of sentencing circles in communities.

Questions have been raised as to the extent to which the courts are following the requirements of section 718.2(e) and its effectiveness in addressing Indigenous overrepresentation in prisons. Since the creation of section 718.2(e), the number of Indigenous persons in prison has more doubled, increasing from 11 percent to nearly 25 percent.[23] In addition, there is some concern as to the availability and quality of training for justice officials, including judges, across the country.[24] See At Issue 9.1.

Judges are not obligated to follow the recommendations set forth in Gladue reports. In one case, the court rejected the argument made by the defence that their client should receive a lenient sentence after being convicted of sexual assault since he was a residential school survivor. The crimes involved several girls who were under the age of 14. The defence had asked for a sentence of less than two years in confinement,

---

AT ISSUE 9.1

IS SECTION 718.2(E) AN EFFECTIVE STRATEGY TO REDUCE THE OVERREPRESENTATION OF INDIGENOUS PERSONS IN PRISON POPULATIONS?

Supporters argue that section 718.2(e) represents enlightened sentencing policy and is only one component of a wider effort to address the overrepresentation of Indigenous people in the criminal justice system and in correctional institutions. Supporters also argue that the section requires only that judges *consider* sanctions other than confinement when sentencing Indigenous offenders. Critics counter that special sentencing provisions for Indigenous people discriminate against non-Indigenous offenders and are based on the faulty assumption that it is sentencing practices, rather than complex historical and contemporary factors, that are the primary reason for the high rates of Indigenous incarceration. To these observers, it is disconcerting that, despite initiatives and legislation, such as the *Gladue* decision, Indigenous persons continue to be overrepresented in the justice system and in corrections, proportionate to their numbers in the general Canadian population. And this representation has steadily increased over the past decade. In support of this view, research is cited which has found that various sentencing reforms in Australia and New Zealand have also not reduced the overrepresentation of Indigenous people in prison.[a]

Research studies have found that section 718.2(e) is applied inconsistently by judges across the country and that, for a variety of reasons, judges' discretion may be limited in cases where Indigenous men and women have been convicted of violent offences.[b] There have been several court decisions where judges have ruled that the

circumstances of the offences (primarily involving violence) and the accused's prior record and other background factors required that the principles of deterrence and denunciation take precedence over rehabilitation (*R. v. L.D.W.*, [2005] 215 BCAC 64; *R. v. Kakekagamick*, [2006] 211 CCC 289).[c] As well, Indigenous women's organizations have expressed concern that the legislation has negative implications for women who are sexually assaulted in their communities, with men receiving non-carceral sentences.[d]

QUESTION

1. What other arguments might be made in support of, or in opposition to, section 718.2(e)? Which of these do you find most persuasive?

---

[a] S. Jeffries and P. Stenning. 2014. "Sentencing Aboriginal Offenders: Law, Policy, and Practice in Three Countries," *Canadian Journal of Crime and Criminal Justice, 56*(4), 447–494.

[b] G. Balfour. 2013. "Do Law Reforms Matter? Exploring the Victimization—Criminalization Continuum in the Sentencing of Aboriginal Women in Canada." *International Review of Victimology, 19*(1), 85–102.

[c] B.R. Pfefferle. 2008. "*Gladue* Sentencing: Uneasy Answers to the Hard Problem of Aboriginal Over-Incarceration," *Manitoba Law Journal, 32*, 113–143.

[d] Balfour, "Do Law Reforms Matter?"

Additional source: P. Stenning, C. LaPrairie, and J.V. Roberts. 2001. "Empty Promises: Parliament, the Supreme Court, and the Sentencing of Aboriginal Offenders," *Saskatchewan Law Review, 64*(1), 137–168.

followed by community service, while the Crown had recommended a seven-year prison term. In sentencing the defendant to six years in prison, the judge acknowledged that he had been the victim of sexual abuse while in a residential school, but noted that the seriousness of the crime required a lengthy prison sentence. The judge also stated that the victims as well had suffered due to their Indigenous status.[25]

These types of cases place judges in a difficult position: on the one hand weighing the issues of systemic racism and the experience of Indigenous persons, while at the same time ensuring that a sentence is proportional and addresses the needs of victims and the community.

INDIGENOUS TRADITIONAL PUNISHMENTS

A key theme in this text is the increasing role of First Nations communities in the criminal justice process. This includes the use of traditional punishments in addition to those imposed by the criminal justice system or even in cases where the accused was not prosecuted. The Blood Tribe Indian reserve in Alberta, for example, has banished community members involved in committing sex crimes against children and gang members who had been imprisoned for a killing. The band also banished a member who was allegedly robbing gravesites of weapons and beads. Although this person was never charged by the police, the community decided that he should not remain in the community.[26] Non-Indigenous offenders have also been banished by the courts, which has generated considerable controversy. See At Issue 9.2.

Persons who are banished from a First Nations reserve may be required to complete a number of conditions, including attending treatment, doing community service, being mentored by an Elder, and remaining crime-free. There may also be a requirement that the offender appear before the community and apologize. The view is that these traditional sanctions are more effective than the "western" justice system.[27]

In other cases, the court may postpone sentencing while the offender participates in a traditional Indigenous healing program. This occurred in 2017 in the case of a couple from the Blood Tribe in Alberta who had pled guilty to the crime of failing to provide the necessities of life to their nine-year-old daughter who nearly died from neglect. The court postponed sentencing while the couple participated in the Kainai Peacemaking Centre. The program focuses on restoring personal, family, and

---

AT ISSUE 9.2

SHOULD BANISHMENT BE USED AS A SENTENCING OPTION?

In July 2017, Gordie Bishop was sentenced to time served (825 days in jail) and banished from the province of Newfoundland and Labrador as part of a probation order. Bishop, who had a 27-page criminal record, had been convicted of aggravated assault of a peace officer, assaulting a police officer with a weapon, break and enter, and other charges relating to an incident. This was in addition to a conviction for six other offences related to the same incident in which a police officer was dragged by a getaway car that Bishop was driving. Bishop must remain out of the province during the time he is on probation.

QUESTIONS

1. What is your view of the use of banishment as a component of a sentence?
2. Should banishment be used for both Indigenous and non-Indigenous offenders?
3. What issues might arise with the use of banishment?

Source: *CBC News*. 2017, July 11. "Gordie Bishop Exiled from the Province for Dragging Cop with Getaway Car." http://www.cbc.ca/news/canada/newfoundland-labrador/gordie-bishop-banishment-order-rnc-peter-eastons-1.4199640.

community relationships. The Kainai Peacemakers are Elders from the tribe who offer guidance to program participants.[28] A Gladue pre-sentencing report stated, "These people are good people and they care about their children."[29]

SENTENCING AND RACE

The race of the accused person and its role in sentencing is becoming increasingly important. In 2003, the Ontario Court of Appeal ruled in the case of *R. v. Borde* (63 OR (3d) 417) that trial judges can, in appropriate cases, take into account systemic racism as a mitigating factor in sentencing young black offenders who have been convicted of less serious crimes.

In 2016, in the case of *R. v. Reid* (2016 ONSC 954), an Ontario judge spared a young Black man jail time and imposed a **conditional sentence**, requiring the man to serve two years under house arrest and attend counselling. The man had been arrested by police for running a dial-a-dope operation and subsequently pled guilty to three counts of trafficking crack cocaine and one count of possession of the proceeds of crime. In sparing the man jail time (the Crown prosecutor had asked for a sentence of one year in jail), the judge cited the case of *R. v. Nur* (2011 ONSC 4874) which held that anti-Black discrimination played a role in the disproportionate number of Blacks in prison, and also noted that, while Blacks comprised 2.9 percent of the Canadian population, they accounted for 9.8 percent of the total prison population. The judge also cited a number of traumatic experiences in the man's background and the pre-sentence report, which indicated that Mr. Reid had taken a number of positive steps to turn his life around.

The issue of the extent to which cultural assessments should be considered in sentencing was a key element in the case of Kale Leonard Gabriel, presented in Legal File 9.3.

> **Conditional sentence (of imprisonment)**
>
> A sentence for offenders who receive a sentence or sentences totalling less than two years whereby the offender serves his or her time in the community under the supervision of a probation officer.

LEGAL FILE 9.3

R. V. GABRIEL: THE ROLE OF CULTURAL ASSESSMENTS IN SENTENCING

In 2016, a jury in Nova Scotia found Kale Leonard Gabriel guilty of second-degree murder in the shooting death of Ryan White in Mulgrave Park in north-end Halifax. Gabriel, who is part Black, had killed White in a dispute over drug turf. The conviction carried an automatic penalty of life in prison, although the judge has discretion in determining when Gabriel would be eligible to apply for parole.

The range for parole eligibility is from 10 to 25 years. Crown counsel requested that the eligibility for parole be set at 15 years, while defence argued that Gabriel should be eligible for parole after serving 10 years. A key issue was whether the history of discrimination against Blacks in Nova Scotia should be a mitigating circumstance in determining the length of time Gabriel should serve before being eligible for parole.

The judge reserved the decision for several months, indicating that a cultural assessment was required as well as an assessment of other factors in Gabriel's background that might be related to his offending. The final decision was that Gabriel would serve 13 years before being eligible for parole, the judge stating, "A period of parole eligibility for 10 years would not be enough to denounce this crime, punish the offender and deter those who see disadvantaged communities like Mulgrave Park as their turf."[a] In his reasons for the decision, the judge did acknowledge that the cultural assessment revealed that Gabriel's

background and environment as a Black man did influence his choices, although he noted that Gabriel's mother had played an active and positive role in his upbringing. In this case, the judge concluded that the seriousness of the crime was not mitigated by Gabriel's experience as an African-Nova Scotian (*R. v. Gabriel*, 2017 NSSC 90).

Although the history of discrimination against Blacks in Nova Scotia and Gabriel's background were determined by the judge in this case not to be mitigating circumstances, the use of cultural assessments for visible minorities may become more common in the criminal courts. Victims' families, on the other hand, have expressed concerns that cultural assessments diminish the responsibility of the offender.[b]

For a discussion of the case, listen to, from CBC's *The Current*, "Black Canadians Need Pre-Sentencing Cultural Assessments, Says Lawyer," http://www.cbc.ca/radio/popup/audio/listen.html?autoPlay =true&medialds=2689837423.

---

[a] B. Rhodes. 2017, March 29. "Kale Gabriel Gets Life Sentence for Murder of Ryan White," *CBC News*. http://www.cbc.ca/news/canada/nova-scotia/kale-gabriel-ryan -white-murder-sentence-halifax-1.4046493.

[b] D. Quan. 2017, April 25. "Consider Impact of Systemic Racism before Sentencing Black Offenders, Canadian Judges Urged," *National Post*. http://news.nationalpost .com/news/canada/consider-impact-of-systemic-racism-before-sentencing-black -offenders-canadian-judges-urged.

Despite the overrepresentation of African-Canadians in prison populations, the courts generally have been reluctant to extend the Gladue principles to other racialized groups. In *R. v. Hamilton* ([2004] OJ No. 3252), the presiding judge reduced the sentences of two women who had pled guilty to trafficking cocaine into Canada from Jamaica. The judge's reasoning was that Black Canadians had been the victims of historic racism not dissimilar to that experienced by Indigenous peoples, and therefore, the sentencing principles of section 718.2(e) should apply. More specifically in this case, the presiding judge found that the respondents should receive conditional sentences rather than incarceration due to their being subjected to systemic racism and gender bias. As well, their poverty made them vulnerable to becoming involved as cocaine couriers.

The Ontario Court of Appeal, however, criticized the judge's ruling, noting that sentencing in the criminal courts is not the place "to right perceived societal wrongs" or "make up for perceived social injustices by the imposition of sentences that do not reflect the seriousness of the crime." While finding the conditional sentences inadequate, the appeals court concluded that little would be accomplished by sending the women to prison, given they had already spent over a year under house arrest due the conditional sentences.

HOW DO JUDGES DECIDE?

> Sentencing is a very human process. Most attempts to describe the proper judicial approach to sentencing are as close to the actual process as a paint-by-numbers landscape is to the real thing—Ontario Court of Appeal Judge David Doherty in *R. v. Hamilton* (2004 ONCA 5549 at para. 87)

Sentencing is among the most difficult tasks that judges have to perform, and probably the most controversial. It has been described as a "delicate art which attempts to balance carefully the societal goals of sentencing against the moral blameworthiness of the offender and the circumstances of the offence, while at all times taking into account the needs and current conditions of and in the community" (*R. v. M. (C.A.)*, [1996] 1 SCR 500, at 566).

Controversy often surrounds sentencing because Canada is a diverse and open society that encompasses a broad range of religious, social, cultural, and moral values and views; thus, Canadians have widely disparate opinions on what constitutes a fit penalty for a particular offence.

There are three important steps in the decision-making of trial judges: (1) identifying the relevant factors in the case; (2) identifying the relevant law; and (3) combining the relevant facts and the law to produce the correct outcome.[30] Judges may experience difficulties in carrying out these activities: Expert witnesses may provide conflicting testimony; defence lawyers may attempt to obscure the facts in an attempt to gain advantage for their clients; and key witnesses may be unable to recollect the events that occurred, particularly if the incident occurred years previous. As noted, court decisions have also held that judges must consider the unique circumstances of Indigenous offenders, and there is an increasing awareness that cultural assessments may be required for Blacks at the sentencing stage.

JUDICIAL DISCRETION

Canadian judges have considerable discretion in selecting a sentence. Section 718.3(1) of the *Criminal Code* states: "Where an enactment prescribes different degrees or kinds of punishment in respect of an offence, the punishment to be imposed is, subject to the limitations prescribed in the enactment, in the discretion of the court that convicts a person who commits the offence."

In making a sentencing decision, a judge may sometimes seek to impose a sentence that not only fits the crime and reflects the "going rate" for similar offences, but also takes into account the offender's particular circumstances. In other cases, the sentence may reflect only the severity of the crime, with no consideration to the situation of the offender. In still other cases, judges are confronted with difficult issues that generate considerable media attention and public and political debate. Recall from Chapter 2 that there are high levels of public dissatisfaction with the criminal courts, centring primarily on what Canadians perceive as overly lenient sentences imposed on the convicted.

Judges exercise considerable discretion in making sentencing decisions, and this may result in non-legal factors playing a role in their decision-making and contributing to sentencing disparity. **Sentencing disparity** involves "different sentences being meted out for similar offences committed by similar offenders in similar circumstances."[31]

For most offences, judges have wide latitude in deciding on a sentence, and this results in variability in sentencing decisions across the country. There is, for example, considerable variation across the country with respect to the use of imprisonment. In 2011–12, for example, nearly 70 percent of convictions in Prince Edward Island resulted in a sentence of imprisonment (the majority for impaired driving), compared to 30 percent in Saskatchewan and just under 40 percent in British Columbia.[32] While a number of factors contribute to this variability (e.g., the specific mix of offences that are presented to judges), there does appear to be different approaches to the use of imprisonment across the country.

What is generally not considered by Crown, defence lawyers, and judges are the **collateral consequences of sentencing**. These are the sanctions and prohibitions that are placed on persons who have been convicted of a criminal offence and their families, in offenders who have been incarcerated).[33]

In many U.S. states, convicted felons are prohibited from accessing student loan programs, cannot be employed in certain types of businesses, may have their criminal record uploaded to the Internet, and may not be eligible to apply for government contracts. Collateral consequences also include the impact of a conviction and/or a particular sentence on the offender's family (see Chapters 11 and 12). All of these may hinder the offender's efforts at rehabilitation and, for those offenders in confinement, re-entry into the community.

The failure of the criminal justice system to consider collateral consequences may undermine its effectiveness. Many restorative justice approaches, on the other hand, consider these types of consequences and may be more effective in fashioning sanctions that produce positive outcomes (see Chapter 13).

There is evidence that the personal attributes of judges may influence their decision-making. The political party that appointed the judge, the region of the country in which the judge practises, and the gender of the judge have all been found to influence decisions. Judges in Ontario and in the western regions of the country tend to be more liberal in their decision-making.[34] Similarly, female judges have been found to vote differently than male judges in some regions, with one study of the Alberta Court of Appeal finding that female judges tended to more often support the complainant in cases involving sexual and domestic violence.[35] A Canadian study found that men who murder their wives, girlfriends, or other women family members are more likely to be convicted of the crime than men who kill strangers. However, these men also tended to receive shorter prison sentences than men who killed strangers.[36]

Sentencing disparity

Different sentences being meted out for similar offences committed by similar offenders in similar circumstances.

Collateral consequences (of sentencing)

The sanctions and prohibitions that are placed on persons convicted of criminal offences (and their families), particularly those offenders who have been incarcerated.

In contrast to other Commonwealth jurisdictions such as England and Wales that have developed more structured sentencing guidelines, Canada's judges have considerable discretion in sentencing.[37] That said, judges must be careful to balance their personal views with their mandated role.

Judges may experience challenges in balancing their personal conscience—that is, their own sense of justice, with judicial conscience, which is their duty as a judge.[38] There are cases in which a judge's personal conscience has resulted in the sentencing decision being overturned and a new trial ordered.

In one Ontario case, the Ontario Court of Appeal determined that the trial judge used insulting language toward a man accused of sexual assault, including accusing the defendant of staging a "dramatic and insincere" crying outburst in the witness box, and "let his personal feelings" about the man "overtake his objectivity."[39] The trial judge had also described the victim's mother as "utterly despicable in my view and a totally unbelievable witness." The Court of Appeal held that the presiding judge allowed his personal feelings about the defendant and his mother to compromise his objectivity.[40]

In another instance, concerns have been raised about a particular judge in the Ontario Court of Appeal, whose written decisions read like a crime novel. In one case involving murder, the judge wrote, "Handguns and drug deals are frequent companions, but not good friends. Rip-offs happen. Shootings do too. *Caveat emptor. Caveat venditor* (let the buyer beware; let the seller beware). People get hurt. People get killed. Sometimes the buyer. Other times, the seller. That happened here."[41] In the view of the judge's critics, judicial rulings should be more solemn.

STATUTORY GUIDANCE

Increasingly in recent years, judges looking for guidance in sentencing can find direction from Parliament in some statutes. However, section 718 of the *Criminal Code*, reproduced earlier in the chapter, is merely a list of the sentencing rationales typically presented in textbooks such as this one. The fundamental principle of sentencing, as stated in section 718.1 of the *Criminal Code*, is that of proportionality: A sentence must be proportionate to the gravity of the offence and to the degree of responsibility of the offender.

In what may well be the beginning of a trend, Parliament has specified factors that judges should consider when sentencing drug cases under the *Controlled Drugs and Substances Act* (S.C. 1996, c. 19). According to section 10(2) of that Act, an offender may deserve a harsher sentence when he or she carried, used, or threatened to use a weapon; used or threatened to use violence; trafficked in one of the specified substances, or possessed such a substance for the purposes of trafficking, in or near a school, on or near school grounds, or in or near any other public place usually frequented by people under 18; or trafficked one of the specified substances, or possessed such a substance for the purpose of trafficking, to a person under 18. These provisions join the principles and purposes of sentencing set out in section 718 of the *Criminal Code* and indicate that Parliament is willing to give sentencing judges some guidance by designating certain types of crime as deserving of greater punishment.

MAXIMUM SENTENCES

Every offence has a maximum sentence that a judge cannot exceed. However, these maximums are so high as to provide little practical guidance. For example, life imprisonment is the maximum sentence for manslaughter. Life imprisonment is also a possible (but not probable) sentence for offences such as piracy (s. 74), breaking and entering a dwelling house (s. 306), and stopping a mail truck to rob or search it (s. 345). If no maximum sentence is specified for an indictable offence, the maximum allowable is five years. A maximum sentence is rarely applied for an indictable offence.

For summary conviction offences, the maximum sentence is six months in prison and/or a $5,000 fine (except for sexual assault, where the maximum sentence is 18 months). The same maximum sentence applies when the Crown prosecutor elects to proceed summarily on a hybrid offence. However, these limits do not apply when the defendant elects trial in a provincial court on an indictable offence (this is a common misunderstanding). Judges cannot exceed the statutory maximum sentence, even when they disagree with the decision to proceed summarily. Prosecutorial election for summary proceedings is one way that Crown counsel can limit the severity of the sentence. Election can, therefore, be used as a bargaining chip in sentencing negotiations (plea bargaining).

LIMITS ON JUDICIAL DISCRETION

CASE LAW PRECEDENT

There are some limits to judges' discretion. A key principle of sentencing—set out in section 718.2(b) of the *Criminal Code*—is that two similar crimes committed by two similar offenders in similar circumstances should draw similar sentences. This is the notion of **case law precedent**. In their deliberations, judges consider the sentences handed down by other judges, and as just noted, the *Criminal Code* gives some guidance by setting maximum sentence limits and, for certain crimes, mandatory minimum sentences.

> **Case law precedent**
>
> Law that is established by previous court decisions and based on the rule of precedent.

The appellate courts defer to the sentencing decisions of lower court judges and are reluctant to overturn these unless the sentence is found to be "demonstrably unfit [due to] an error of principle, failure to consider a relevant factor, or overemphasis of the appropriate factors" (*R. v. McDonnell*, [1997] 1 SCR 948).

That said, the *Criminal Code* does not direct judges as to what sentences should be imposed in any one case. Judges must attempt to individualize the sentence to meet the objectives of sentencing, but have considerable discretion in fashioning the punishment to be imposed.

A consideration is how offenders view the sanctions that are imposed on them and how effective they perceive the punishments to be. A U.K. study that involved interviewing male and women prisoners ($N = 30$) and men and women on probation ($N = 9$) found that the offenders held a wide range of views about punishment and what it should be (van Ginneken and Hayes, 2017).[42] Punishment meant different things to the offenders in the sample. This led the authors to conclude, "We cannot assume that punishment holds the same meaning to every person," and that it is important to consider each offender's specific circumstances (van Ginneken and Hayes, 2017:74).[43]

MANDATORY MINIMUM SENTENCES (MMSs)

Mandatory minimum sentences are also a constraint of judicial discretion. Several offences, on conviction, carry mandatory minimum sentences. For example, use of a firearm during the commission of an offence carries a minimum sentence of one year in prison for the first conviction and three years for subsequent offences (both to be consecutive to any term of imprisonment imposed for the offence itself). Other offences with mandatory minimum sentences are a second conviction for impaired driving, and first- and second-degree murder.

MANDATORY MINIMUM SENTENCES: EFFECTIVE CRIME RESPONSE STRATEGY OR POLITICALLY MOTIVATED CRIME POLICY?

Supporters of MMSs contend that these sentences serve as a general and specific deterrent, prevent crime by removing offenders from the community, serve as a symbolic denunciation for certain behaviours, and reduce sentencing disparity.[a]

In contrast, opponents of MMSs have raised concerns that MMSs have little or no deterrent value, serve to limit judicial discretion with a resulting impact on individual cases, have significant cost implications, and may lead to unfair sentencing practices. There are a number of potentially adverse effects of mandatory minimum sentences, including increased costs due to an increase in "not guilty" pleas and an increase in prison populations[b,c] Opponents argue that MMSs are an example of a politically driven crime policy, citing research studies that have found that MMSs have only a modest effect on crime prevention, no effect on drug consumption or drug-related crime, and no effect in reducing sentencing disparity, due primarily to the increased role of prosecutorial discretion in MMS situations. Further, there is no evidence that increasing the number of offences eligible for mandatory minimums results in increased public confidence in the justice system.[d]

QUESTIONS

1. Which arguments regarding MMSs do you find most persuasive?
2. Would you support (1) having no MMSs, or (2) having MMSs for certain offences?

---

[a] L. Caylor and G.G. Beaulne. 2014. *A Defence of Mandatory Minimum Sentences.* Ottawa: MacDonald-Laurier Institute. http://www.macdonaldlaurier.ca/files/pdf/MLIMandatoryMinimumSentences-final.pdf.

[b] T. Gabor and N. Crutcher. 2002. *Mandatory Minimum Penalties: Their Effects on Crime, Sentencing Disparities, and Justice System Expenditures.* Ottawa: Research and Statistics Division, Department of Justice Canada. http://www.justice.gc.ca/eng/rp-pr/csj-sjc/ccs-ajc/rr02_1/rr02_1.pdf.

[c] A.K. Malik. 2007. "Mandatory Minimum Sentences: Shackling Judicial Discretion for Justice or Political Expediency?" *Criminal Law Quarterly, 53*(2), 236–259.

[d] K.N. Varma and V. Marinos. 2013. "Three Decades of Public Attitudes Research on Crime and Punishment in Canada," *Canadian Journal of Criminology and Criminal Justice, 55*(4), 555–556.

As part of its "get tough" approach to crime, the federal Conservative government (2006–15) expanded the number of offences that, on conviction, require a mandatory minimum sentence. However, in recent years the judiciary has pushed back against this, with judges in a number of cases finding that mandatory minimum penalties violated the *Charter of Rights and Freedoms*. In *R. v. Smickle* (2013 ONCA 678), for example, the Ontario Court of Appeal ruled that a three-year mandatory minimum sentence for gun possession was "cruel and unusual punishment." In the view of the court, there was a "cavernous disconnect" between the severity of such an offence and the severity of the sentence.[44] Considerable controversy has surrounded mandatory minimum sentences. See At Issue 9.3.

SENTENCING AND CRIME VICTIMS

It was noted in Chapter 3 that there have been increased efforts to involve victims in the criminal justice process and to ensure that the interests of crime victims are addressed. These efforts have included allowing victim impact statements, collecting "fine surcharges" from offenders for use in supporting victim services programs, and establishing mediation programs as forums for victim–offender reconciliation (see Chapter 13). Crime victims are often not happy with the sentencing decisions of judges. This is reflected in the comments of the father following the decision of a judge to sentence a man who had killed his son in an unprovoked attack to two years less a day in a provincial jail, "Two f—ing years—that's f—ing ridiculous."[45] While there are concerns that victims may have unrealistic expectations as to the impact of their statement on the sentence that is imposed, it is generally accepted that the benefits of having victim input at the sentencing stage outweigh any potential drawbacks.[46]

While the adversarial system of criminal justice may result in victims feeling re-victimized or dissatisfied with the process and the sentence, restorative justice often results in different outcomes. Victims are part of, rather than ancillary to, the process, and this is discussed later in the chapter.

VICTIM IMPACT STATEMENTS

Section 722.1 of the *Criminal Code* provides that, at the sentencing stage, a crime victim can submit to the court a **victim impact statement (VIS)** explaining his or her personal/emotional reaction to being victimized, any physical injuries caused by the victimization, and the financial impact of the victimization. There are no limitations on the kinds of offences for which a VIS can be submitted. However, it is most commonly used for crimes against the person.

A VIS can take the form of a letter to the judge. Many provinces distribute standard forms, which typically ask the victim to itemize physical injuries and any permanent disability, as well as the dollar value of financial losses, such as property loss or damage, lost wages, or medical expenses not covered by insurance. There is also space to express personal reactions to the crime, including any need for counselling. At the discretion of the judge, victims may read their VIS aloud in court or testify about the impact of the crime; they are not allowed to request specific penalties or directly address the issue of sentencing. Despite this, Canadian research has shown that a significant portion of VISs include a sentencing recommendation.

The VIS presented to the court by a woman whose father and three children were killed by a drunk driver is reproduced in Court File 9.3. It speaks of the silence that now envelops her home.

Although VISs are enshrined in the *Criminal Code*, no guidance is provided as to how the courts should utilize the information they contain and what role VISs should play in sentencing.[47]

It is estimated that VISs are presented to the court is as few as 10 percent of cases.[48] A study (N = 96) of the use of VISs by judges in British Columbia, Alberta, and Manitoba found that two-thirds of the judges felt that the VISs contained information that was useful in sentencing. There was, however, considerable variability in the percentage of

Victim impact statement (VIS)

Submission to a sentencing court explaining the emotional, physical, and financial impact of the crime.

COURT FILE 9.3

A MOTHER'S VICTIM IMPACT STATEMENT

I am listening in vain for my kids to call out my name and I don't hear them. I don't have anyone left to call me mom. Not one left.... Where there was once joy in waking up and greeting the day there is only despair and heartache. The soothing night time sounds of my children's gentle breathing, of their little footsteps coming into my room are all gone.... When you killed my children you took away my identity as a mother and without my kids, I'm nothing anymore.... When I begin to cry over one of my dead, I feel so guilty because I am crying for one and not the other. I don't know how to even begin to sort out the grief for my dad, my rock, my protector.... [E]very waking moment is haunted by what was and what can never be again.

Source: *R. v. Muzzo*, 2016 ONSC 2068.

SHOULD VICTIM IMPACT STATEMENTS BE CONSIDERED IN SENTENCING CONVICTED OFFENDERS?

Advocates of the introduction of victim impact statements (VISs) at sentencing contend that they ensure that victims are involved in the justice process, make the justice system more accountable, help the victim recover from the victimization, and educate both offenders and judges about the real-life consequences of crime. Opponents of VISs argue that they are emotionally charged and thus undermine the objectivity of the justice process. Research studies indicate that VISs have little influence on the sentence a convicted offender receives.

In reality, victim impact statements are submitted in only a small percentage of cases, and there are even fewer cases where crime victims present an impact statement in court. As well, judges appear to value the information contained in victim impact statements, although it is uncertain as to the impact of this information on the sentence that is imposed.[a] A number of provincial court decisions have held that crime victims should have no role in determining the type of sentence imposed although appeal courts have set aside sentences in a number of cases where it was determined that important information from the victim impact statement had not been considered.[b]

QUESTION

1. In your view, what are the strongest arguments for and against the use of victim impact statements in sentencing?

---

[a] J.V. Roberts and A. Edgar. 2007. "Victim Impact Statements at Sentencing: Judicial Experiences and Perceptions—A Survey of Three Jurisdictions," *JustResearch, 14,* 14–17. http://www.justice.gc.ca/eng/rp-pr/jr/jr14/jr14.pdf.

[b] S.N. Verdun-Jones and A.A. Tijerino. 2002. "The Influence of Victim Impact Statements on the Sentencing Process: The Emerging Canadian Jurisprudence," in *Victim Participation in the Plea Negotiation Process in Canada: A Review of the Literature and Four Models for Law Reform.* Ottawa: Policy Centre for Victim Issues. http://canada.justice.gc.ca/eng/rp-pr/cj-jp/victim/rr02_5/rr02_5.pdf.

Additional source: B. Anderson and D. Coletto. 2016, July 9. "Canadians' Moral Compass Set Differently from That of Our Neighbours to the South" [news release]. *Abacus Data.* http://abacusdata.ca/canadians-moral-compass-set-differently-from-that-of-our-neighbours-to-the-south.

---

judges who held this view, with Manitoba at 47 percent, British Columbia at 36 percent, and Alberta at 12 percent.[49] This suggests that there is uncertainty surrounding the role of VISs in the sentencing process. See At Issue 9.4.

Rather, how the information is used is left to the discretion of individual judges, with some judges considering the VIS in formulating the sentence, and others viewing the VIS as an opportunity to express the emotional impact that the crime has on the victim and their family, which can assist the judge in understanding the consequences of the offence but which is not meant to influence the sentence.[50] In the latter case, this may result in disillusionment among crime victims due to unmet expectations.

COMMUNITY IMPACT STATEMENTS (CISs)

Section 722.2 of the *Criminal Code* provides that communities can also present impact statements in court. A community impact statement describes to the court how the crime committed by the offender impacted the community.[51]

Providing for community impact statements is a recognition that the effects of crime can be far-reaching. Sometimes the victim of an offence is more than one person—it is a community. The purpose of community impact statements is to allow the community to explain to the court and the offender how the crime has affected the community. For example, in the case of *R. v Muzzo* (2016 ONSC 2068), which involved the death of three children in an accident caused by a drunk driver, community impact statements were provided by the town mayor, the president and CEO of the mother's place of employment, a school board trustee from the area in which the family lived, and a representative from the scouting group in which the children participated.

PUBLIC PERCEPTIONS OF SENTENCING

Recall from the discussion in Chapter 2 that the Canadian public is often misinformed about the criminal justice system and is subject to being influenced by the media and high-profile crimes. The sentencing decisions of judges, particularly in high-profile cases, are often highly publicized in the media.

A survey of Canadians (N = 4,200) found concerns about sentencing practices, focused on violent offenders who were perceived not to receive severe enough penalties, and punishments that were too harsh for offenders convicted of non-violent offences, including selling drugs.[52] The survey also found that, for the respondents, two of the most important considerations in sentencing were the harm done to the victim and the offender's criminal history.[53] These findings suggest that the Canadian public may not be as punitive as is often assumed, particularly with respect to persons who have committed less serious offences.

RESTORATIVE APPROACHES AND SENTENCING

Questions surrounding the effectiveness of sentencing have provided an opportunity for restorative justice approaches to be used. One of the most important provisions of Section 718 was the introduction of restorative justice principles in the context of sentencing.[54] In particular, subsection (e) states, "to provide reparations for harm done to victims or to the community," and subsection (f) states, "to promote a sense of responsibility in offenders, and acknowledgement of the harm done to victims or to the community."

Section 718 provides the opportunity to apply the principles of restorative justice in determining the sentence for a convicted offender. One of the more well-known approaches is circle sentencing, which draws from traditional Indigenous practices.

CIRCLE SENTENCING

Circle sentencing is a restorative justice strategy that involves collaboration and consensual decision-making by community residents, the victim, the offender, and justice system personnel to resolve conflicts and sanction offenders. The process for circle sentencing was established in two court cases, *R. v. Gingell* (1996 50 CR (4th) 326 (QL) (Y Terr Ct) and *R. v. Moses* (71 CCC (3rd) 347, [1992] 3 CNLR 116 (QL)(Y Terr Ct).

Circle sentencing originally developed in several Yukon communities as a collaboration between community residents and territorial justice personnel, primarily RCMP officers and judges from the Territorial Court of Yukon. Circle sentencing is premised on traditional Indigenous healing practices and has multifaceted objectives, including addressing the needs of communities, victims, the families of victims, and offenders through a process of reconciliation, restitution, and reparation. A fundamental principle of circle sentencing is that the sentence is less important than the process used to select it.

In circle sentencing, all of the participants, including defence lawyer, prosecutor, police officer, victim and family, offender and family, and community residents, sit facing one another in a circle. The presiding judge may or may not be present. Through discussions, those in the circle reach a consensus about the best way to dispose of the

Circle sentencing

A restorative justice strategy that involves collaboration and consensual decision-making by community residents, the victim, the offender, and justice system personnel to resolve conflicts and sanction offenders.

TABLE 9.3

DIFFERENCES BETWEEN CRIMINAL COURT AND CIRCLE SENTENCING PRINCIPLES

Criminal Court	Circle Sentencing
The crime.	Crime is a small part of a larger conflict.
The sentence resolves the conflict.	The sentence is a small part of the solution.
The focus is on past conduct.	The focus is on present and future conduct.
Takes a narrow view of behaviour.	Takes a larger, holistic view of behaviour.
Not concerned with social conflict.	Focuses on social conflict.
The sentence is the most important part of the process.	The sentence is the least important part of the process; most important is the process itself, which shapes the relationship among all parties.

Source: Reprinted by permission of Justice Barry D. Stuart.

case, taking into account both the need to protect the community and the rehabilitation and punishment of the offender. Note that judges are not bound by the recommendations of a sentencing circle and maintain control over sentencing at all times. Circle sentencing has spawned a number of variations, including community sentence advisory committees, healing circles sentencing panels, and community mediation panels. There are significant differences between the principles of sentencing in the criminal courts and those of circle sentencing. These are highlighted in Table 9.3.

In contrast with the adversarial approach to justice, circle sentencing has the potential to reacquaint individuals, families, and communities with problem-solving skills; rebuild relationships within communities; and focus on the causes, not just the symptoms of problems.

Circle sentencing is generally available only to offenders who plead guilty. The operation of the circle sentencing process is specific to communities, meaning that it may (and should) vary between communities, and the circle-sentencing process relies heavily upon community volunteers for its success. Both Indigenous and non-Indigenous victims, offenders, and community residents participate in sentencing circles. An example of a circle sentencing hearing is presented in Court File 9.4.

It should be pointed out that circle sentencing is not appropriate for all offenders or for all crimes. Moreover, the success of a given circle will depend on the extent to which all of its participants are committed to the principles of restorative justice.[55] There are general concerns about the use of restorative justice approaches in First Nations communities in cases involving intimate partner violence.[56] Specific concerns have been raised, for example, as to whether crime victims—especially Indigenous women who have been the victims of sexual assault and domestic abuse—may be pressured into participating in circle sentencing.[57] Also, sentencing circles are not part of Inuit tradition, so there may be limits in the extent to which this approach can be used in these communities. Note also that presiding judges are not obligated to follow the recommendations of sentencing circles.

THE POLITICS OF SENTENCING

Commenting on the absence of research-informed sentencing policy in Canada, the criminologist Julian Roberts stated, "Politics is stronger than evidence."[58]

A CIRCLE SENTENCING IN SHESHATSHIU, NEWFOUNDLAND AND LABRADOR

NEWFOUNDLAND
AND LABRADOR

Natuashish

Sheshatshiu

St John's

Sheshatshiu, Newfoundland and Labrador

In June 2015, a man in the Innu community of Sheshatshiu, charged with two counts of assault, opted to have circle sentencing as part of the court proceedings. Both the victim and the accused agreed to the process and the accused admitted his guilt. The circle sentencing hearing was attended by the judge, the Crown, the defence, the accused, the victim, persons affected by the crime, and other community members. Everyone was called upon to speak, including community members who shared their stories and, for some, their struggles

with substance abuse and their efforts to address it. The value of this approach was noted by the Sheshatshiu Innu First Nation justice coordinator, who stated, "I think there is a situation where the accused is asking the court to hear the history, and also echo some of the challenges in terms of what he has gone through and set a picture. He's not making excuses in terms of more leniency. But more of a process where we can have a dialogue between the court system and the Innu and have that discussion. It's much more inclusive."[a]

Contrast the dynamic of a circle sentencing with the advice given to accused persons as to how to behave at sentencing in the criminal court by Student Legal Services of Edmonton. Under the section "Speak to Sentence," it states:

> As a general rule, you should say nothing about the offence unless there are mitigating circumstances that should be brought to the attention of the Judge. If you had a really good reason to commit the offence (i.e. shoplifting to feed your hungry children) or if it was completely out of character for you to commit such an offence, then you should explain your circumstances to the Judge to give him/her an understanding of why you committed the offence. If there is no acceptable reason for why you committed the offence, then you are better off saying nothing.[b]

[a] J. Barker. 2016, June 11. "Sheshatshiu Man Opts for Rare Innu Sentencing Circle," *CBC News*. http://www.cbc.ca/news/canada/newfoundland-labrador/sheshatshiu-man-opts-for-rare-innu-sentencing-circle-1.3630921.

[b] Student Legal Services of Edmonton. 2015. "Guilty Pleas and Sentencing." http://www.slsedmonton.com/criminal/how-to-plead-guilty/#SPEAK_TO_SENTENCE.

Recall the discussion in Chapter 2 that the criminal justice system is often affected by politics. In that chapter, the "get tough," American-style approach of the federal Conservative government (2006–15) resulted in a number of significant changes to sentencing in Canada. One of the overall objectives of the legislation that was passed by the government was to limit the discretion of judges. This included an expansion in the number of offences subject to mandatory minimum sentences. As one judge stated, the legislation marked "a move away from individualized discretion in sentencing."[59]

This included legislation that included the following provisions:

- restrictions on judges as to what types of offences can be considered for a conditional sentence, which is generally served at home

- elimination of "two-for-one" (two days credit for one day served) for time served by offenders in pretrial custody (Bill C-25: *The Truth in Sentencing Act*, 2009)

- the introduction of mandatory minimum sentences for 60 criminal offences, including crimes involving guns and drugs (Bill C-10: *The Safe Streets and Communities Act*, 2012)

- provisions that encouraged Crown counsel to consider adult sentences for young offenders who have committed certain offences, and changes in the rules of pretrial detention for this offender population (Bill C-10: *The Safe Streets and Communities Act*, 2012)

The extent to which this approach to responding to offenders will remain intact is questionable. In decisions made in 2014 through 2016, the SCC

- held that a provision of the *Truth in Sentencing Act* (2009) that prohibited judges from giving more than one-for-one pretrial credit was deemed to be unreasonable and unconstitutional (*R. v. Summer*, 2014 SCC 26);

- struck down a provision in the *Criminal Code* that prevented sentencing judges from crediting more than the time the offender actually served in pre-trial detention against the sentence imposed when the offender had been denied bail because of a past criminal record. (*R. v. Safarzadeh-Markhali*, 2016 SCC 14); and

- struck down the three-year minimum sentence for illegal gun possession, calling the law "cruel and unusual punishment" (*R. v. Nur*, 2015 SCC 15), and the one-year minimum term for drug traffickers with a previous conviction for trafficking (*R. v. Lloyd*, 2016 SCC 13).

THE EFFECTIVENESS OF SENTENCING

Despite the critical role of sentencing in the criminal justice system, there are questions about its effectiveness in addressing the needs of victims, offenders, and the community. Some of the research on the effectiveness of sentencing is summarized in Research File 9.1.

RESEARCH FILE 9.1

THE EFFECTIVENESS OF SENTENCING

Does increasing the severity of punishment have a deterrent effect on offenders? Generally, no. It is the certainty of punishment, rather than the severity of punishment, that has the most significant deterrent effect on offenders and others. While persons with a stake in conformity may fear lost opportunities if they are criminally sanctioned, marginal persons who perceive that they have few legitimate opportunities (and who in fact do not have many) may not engage in this calculus.[a]

Persons with strong family and community ties are much more likely to be deterred by the fear of being caught than persons without those ties.[b]

Is there consistency in sentencing? Not always. With a few exceptions involving mandatory minimum sentences, most offences have only a maximum penalty, and this provides judges with considerable discretion in deciding both the objective of the sentence and the specific penalty. This makes it difficult to predict with any accuracy what type of sentence will be imposed for offences, even though judges are guided by case precedents.

Does the threat of longer prison terms reduce crime? Not likely. Mandatory minimum sentences do not appear to have a deterrent impact on criminal offending.[c]

Are sentences matched effectively to individual offenders? Often, no. Matching specific sentencing options with the needs and risks of offenders is, at best, an inexact science. Few research studies have examined which types of sentences are most effective—that is, which ones serve as a deterrent and address risk and needs—with specific types of offenders.

Is there continuity from criminal courts to corrections? Not always. Once the offender leaves the courtroom, he or she becomes the responsibility of corrections. Judicial recommendations for placement and treatment programming are not binding on correctional decision-makers. However, this continuity is increased in specialized courts.

Do problem-solving courts work? Potentially. They can be effective at reducing rates of reoffending. See Table 7.1.

Are circle sentencing and peacemaking effective? Potentially. There have been few controlled evaluations of these programs. Most of the literature on circle sentencing is anecdotal, which makes it difficult to develop evidence-based practices and to determine the factors that may facilitate (or hinder) the effective use of this restorative justice strategy. This includes whether the community itself has the capacity to support circle sentencing and whether the rights of the victim will be protected.[d] Concerns have surrounded the use of circle sentencing in cases involving domestic violence, with critics arguing that the power imbalances between the accused and the accuser may result in the revictimization of women.[e]

---

[a] National Institute of Justice. 2014. *Five Things About Deterrence*. Washington, DC: U.S. Department of Justice. https://www.ncjrs.gov/pdffiles1/nij/247350.pdf; S.N. Durlauf and D.S. Nagin. 2011. "The Deterrent Effect of Punishment," in *Controlling Crime: Strategies and Tradeoffs*, edited by P.J. Cook, J. Ludwig, and J. McCrary, 43–94. Chicago: University of Chicago Press.

[b] A.E. Perry. 2016. "Sentencing and Deterrence," in *What Works in Crime Prevention and Rehabilitation: Lessons from Systematic Reviews*, edited by D. Weisburd, D.P.F. Arrington, and C. Gill, 169–191. New York: Springer.

[c] P. Menedez and D.J. Weatherburn. 2015. "Does the Threat of Longer Prison Terms Reduce the Incidence of Assaul," *Australian & New Zealand Journal of Criminology, 49*(3), 389–404.

[d] C.T. Griffiths and R. Hamilton. 1996. "Sanctioning and Healing: Restorative Justice in Canadian Aboriginal Communities," in *Restorative Justice: Theory, Practice, and Research*, edited by J. Hudson and B. Galaway, 175–191. Monsey, NY: Criminal Justice Press.

[e] A. Cameron. 2006. "Sentencing Circles and Intimate Violence: A Canadian Feminist Perspective," *Canadian Journal of Women and the Law, 18*(2), 479–512; A. Shagufta. 2010. "Should Restorative Justice Be Used for Cases of Domestic Violence?" *International Journal of Restorative Justice, 6*(1), 1–48.

YOU BE THE JUDGE

Even with a number of offences that, upon conviction, carry a mandatory minimum sentence, Canadian judges exercise considerable discretion in sentencing. To gain an appreciation of the challenges judges face in making sentencing decisions, review the summaries of actual cases presented in Court File 9.5. Place yourself in the position of the sentencing judge.

COURT FILE 9.5

YOU BE THE JUDGE

Read each of the following case summaries. Then decide on a sentence and note the purpose of your sentence. Record your sentencing decisions and the reasons why you selected each particular sentence. Once you have completed all five cases, check at the end of the chapter in Class/Group Discussion Exercise 9.1 and see the actual sentences imposed by the judges for these cases.

Case 1 Appearing before you is the former mayor of a large Canadian city. He has been found guilty of eight criminal charges related to pocketing nearly $37,000 in kickbacks from property developers and engineering firms in the city through his former aide. The former aide testified at trial that he led developers and business persons to believe that their projects would be delayed or not approved unless they made cash contributions. The cash "donations" were then split between the aide and the mayor. The prosecution is asking for a sentence of two years in prison, followed by two years on probation. Defence counsel has proposed that either a suspended sentence be imposed, or a mixed sentence that would include probation, community service work, and non-consecutive jail time. The maximum sentence that can be imposed for this offence is five years in prison.

Case 2 Appearing before you is a 38-year-old man who has been convicted of assault causing bodily harm. The conviction is the result of an incident that occurred during a 3-on-3 non-contact Ice Hockey Challenge tournament in Fort Erie, Ontario. The goalie had left the crease and, using two hands, used his goalie stick to smash the face of an onrushing player who was on a breakaway. The hit resulted in severe damage to the victim's face, which required numerous surgeries and reconstructions. Evidence showed that the goalie had been celebrating his birthday and had been binge-drinking prior to the game. The accused has no prior record and a stable employment record, although he came from a troubled background. His father had spent 20 of his 44 years in prison and was beaten to death by members of a biker gang when the accused was 12 years old. The accused has written a letter of apology to the victim and has started counselling for his alcohol problems. The Crown prosecutor has asked for a sentence from between 30 days and nine months, while the defence lawyer has asked the judge to place the accused on probation, or to give him a conditional discharge.

Case 3 In court for sentencing is a 38-year-old man who has pled guilty to two counts of aggravated assault, dangerous driving

causing bodily harm, mischief over $5,000, and assault with a weapon. The man had gotten into an argument with employees at a gas station about how to pre-pay for gas. He left the gas station, but then returned and, several minutes later, drove his truck through the front entrance of the store at a high rate of speed, hitting four people. All of the victims suffered significant injuries. Crown counsel is requesting that you impose a sentence of five to seven years and a ten-year driving ban. The defence lawyer is seeking a jail term of two years less a day and a five-year driving ban. In the *Criminal Code*, aggravated assault is an indictable offence punishable by period of imprisonment not to exceed 14 years; dangerous driving causing bodily harm is punishable by a period of imprisonment not to exceed 10 years; mischief over $5,000 is punishable by a period of imprisonment up to 10 years; and assault with a weapon has a maximum sentence of 18 months in jail if a summary conviction, and 10 years in prison if an indictable conviction. Evidence presented in court revealed that it was the man's first criminal offence and that he had a "chaotic upbringing."

Case 4 Before you is an Indigenous man who is a resident of the Yellow Quill First Nation in Saskatchewan. While severely intoxicated, the man led his two daughters—aged three and one—into a blizzard and then blacked out. The two girls perished in the −30°C weather. The man has pled guilty to criminal negligence causing death. For this offence, the penalty is life imprisonment. The man has a criminal record involving 52 convictions, primarily related to not following court orders. Crown counsel has suggested that an appropriate sentence would be two-and-a-half to five years in prison, while the defence has asked for a conditional sentence to be served at home in the community. (Note: This case was heard prior to the change in the law that prohibited the use of conditional sentences in cases involving violence.) In considering an appropriate sentence, you have directed that a sentencing circle be formed, composed of police, Crown counsel, defence lawyers, Elders, and others from the community, including family members. Following lengthy deliberations, which included conversations with the man, the sentencing circle has recommended to you that he not be sent to prison but rather he should remain in the community to heal under the guidance of Elders and participate in alcohol and drug treatment. The record also indicates that the man violated his bail conditions while awaiting sentencing by drinking and also has been charged with assaulting his common-law wife.

The purposes of sentencing and the various sentencing options available to judges were presented earlier in this chapter. Recall from the discussion of sentencing options that you can combine some options; that is, you can sentence the offender to a period of custody in a provincial correctional facility and, as well, add on a period of probation of up to three years. Probation cannot be used in conjunction with a sentence of more than two years, which places the offender under the jurisdiction of federal corrections. As well, the various objectives of sentencing were discussed earlier.[60]

A JUDGE DELIBERATES ON A SENTENCE: THE CASE OF *R. V. BURGESS*

Selected materials from the case of *R. v. Burgess* (2016 NSPC 1) are presented below to illustrate how judges consider the various types of information in determining a sentence. The case involved a 34-year-old woman who had been found guilty of manslaughter in 2016 for pushing her elderly father down a flight of stairs during a domestic argument. The judge imposed a sentence of four years.

The materials include the presiding judge's comments on the victim impact statement submitted to the court, the findings of the pre-sentence report, and what the judge identified as the aggravating and mitigating factors in the case.

VICTIM IMPACT STATEMENTS

Mr. Burgess's death and the circumstances under which it occurred have had a devastating effect on the individual members of his family and their relationships. Six family members provided victim impact statements in which they movingly expressed their profound grief and heartache. Mr. Burgess's wife, Lynda, referring to him as her "soulmate," spoke of how much she misses him. His three sisters described their brother as loving and caring. They grieve their loss and the broken family relationships. Mr. Burgess's youngest sister, Christine, has experienced a deterioration in her health since he died. She characterized the description of her brother as "a good guy," offered by many people who have spoken to her since her brother's death, as a perfect description. In her words, "not perfect, but a good guy." Mr. Burgess's sister-in-law, the sister of Lynda Burgess, mourns someone she loved and, as with everyone else who provided statements, laments the deeply painful divisions that now exist in the family.

VANESSA BURGESS'S BACKGROUND AND CIRCUMSTANCES

Interviewed for her pre-sentence report, Ms. Burgess described an unhappy and stressful childhood and adolescence. She was bullied at school and verbally abused at home. She felt emotionally deprived by her parents, saying they were not affectionate with her or with each other. Ms. Burgess had a better relationship with her father than with her mother.

She left home at 15 and developed a substance abuse problem. She used illegal drugs and became an alcoholic. Around the age of 20, she overcame her substance abuse dependency and has been sober for over eight years. The evidence at trial indicated Ms. Burgess's belief that her father was resentful of her successful recovery. Although he had been sober for many years while Ms. Burgess was growing up, about 11 years before his death he began drinking again, which led to a pronounced deterioration in their relationship.

Ms. Burgess moved back to live with her parents about 15 to 16 months prior to July 2011 so that she could focus on obtaining her high school diploma. She told police that the atmosphere at home prior to July 20 had been "very, very toxic." In her police interrogation and her testimony at trial, Ms. Burgess said her father had subjected her to name-calling and disparaging comments. Ms. Burgess is now 32. She is involved in a dating relationship with a 39-year-old man who is very supportive of her. He is aware that Ms. Burgess has been convicted of manslaughter. He provided a letter of support for her sentencing.

Ms. Burgess told the author of the pre-sentence report that her boyfriend is "a strong person with strong family values which is good for her...." She believes the relationship will continue. Ms. Burgess advised the author of the pre-sentence report that she obtained her Grade 12 with very good marks and attended Maritime Business College in 2013 for a business development certification. She has worked in various jobs, including most recently as a house painter, but is currently unemployed.

The foreman with the painting company where Ms. Burgess had been employed told the author of the pre-sentence report that Ms. Burgess was a reliable and responsible worker who got along well with the other employees and established positive relationships with clients. Ms. Burgess has been an active and enthusiastic volunteer with Search and Rescue and her church. She was an energetic contributor to the activities of the Student Association at the Nova Scotia Community College where she took her Grade 12.

As I will mention shortly, Ms. Burgess is highly valued by her friends, a number of whom have submitted supportive letters on her behalf. Ms. Burgess has accessed various counselling programs and services in the past, including substance abuse counselling and anger management. She has been attending sessions with an Elizabeth Fry Society support worker since 2013, and her family doctor has prescribed medication to help with sleep disturbance issues and mild depressive symptoms. Ms. Burgess also reports significant grief over her father's death, telling the author of the pre-sentence report, "I miss him so much. I have had no closure...."

Ms. Burgess's Elizabeth Fry Society support worker described her as a "very spiritual person" whose spirituality has been helping her cope with the stress of the court proceedings. The pre-sentence report concludes by stating that Ms. Burgess's "level of commitment to maintaining abstinence from drugs and alcohol is commendable; however, that level of commitment to addressing her grief and mental health would benefit [her] as well."

AGGRAVATING FACTORS

My trial findings identify a number of aggravating factors:

- Ms. Burgess used considerable force against her father in objectively dangerous circumstances at the top of a steep set of stairs.
- Ms. Burgess was larger, stronger, and sober. Her father was of slight stature and intoxicated.
- Ms. Burgess did not do anything to have Mr. Burgess assessed for injuries he might have sustained in such a serious fall, a fall from the top to the bottom of the stairs. She did not tell her mother the truth about how Mr. Burgess had fallen until the next morning after they had both left the house and Mr. Burgess was still at the bottom of the stairs.

MITIGATING FACTORS

Ms. Burgess's previous good character and lack of a prior record are mitigating factors. She has endeavoured to be a contributing member of the community through her Search and Rescue volunteer work and has been supportive and helpful to her friends. She has shown herself to be a good, reliable employee. She is to be credited for attending counselling sessions through the Elizabeth Fry Society and for maintaining sobriety after a struggle with substance abuse issues.

Ms. Burgess's remorse is also a mitigating factor entitled to some, albeit limited, weight. Ms. Burgess is described as remorseful in the pre-sentence report, which indicates that she accepts responsibility for her actions and does not rationalize or deny her behaviour. However, Ms. Burgess qualified her role by stating, "Apparently, my push pushed him down the stairs but there was no intent to hurt him. I would never hurt my father. This hurts me a great deal...." As I mentioned earlier in these reasons, she also told the author of the pre-sentence report, "...I am a good person. Something bad happened to me and I am willing to take responsibility for it." It seems obvious that Ms. Burgess has not fully recognized the extent of her responsibility for her father's death (*R. v. Burgess*, 2016 NSPC 1).

SUMMARY

The discussion in this chapter has focused on sentencing in the criminal courts. The purposes and principles of sentencing were set out along with the various judicial sentencing options. Canadian judges also have additional authority to use judicial determination, issue judicial restraint orders, and designate offenders as dangerous offenders or long-term offenders.

The factors that judges taken into account in making decisions were discussed, and it was noted that extra-legal variables may come into play as well. The challenges of sentencing in a diverse society were discussed, including the issue surrounding the sentencing of Indigenous offenders within the framework of section 718.2(e) of the *Criminal Code* and the *Gladue* decision. These require judges to consider alternatives to incarceration for Indigenous offenders; it is applied unevenly across the country and may not be a consideration in cases involving violent offending. The discussion also considered the increasing role of cultural assessments in sentencing. Judges have considerable discretion in imposing sentences, and their decision-making may be influenced by case law precedent, by statutory guidance, and by their own biases.

Victim impact statements and federal legislation are designed to increase victim involvement in the sentencing process, although restorative justice approaches may hold more potential for ensuring that the needs of crime victims are met.

Excerpts from the case of *R. v. Burgess* were used to illustrate the role of victim impact statements, the pre-sentence report, and the judge's determination of aggravating and mitigating factors in the case on the sentence imposed on a convicted person.

KEY POINTS REVIEW

1. Among the statutory objectives of sentencing are denunciation, deterrence, the separation of offenders from society, rehabilitation, and reparation for harm done.

2. The sentencing goals in the criminal courts fall into three main groups: utilitarian, retributive, and restorative.

3. Judges can select among a number of sentencing options.

4. Judges can impose a number of additional conditions on offenders, including judicial determination, judicial restraint orders, and dangerous offender and long-term offender designations.

5. Criminal court judges consider a wide range of factors in determining the sentence to be imposed on an offender.

6. There are several offences that, upon conviction, carry mandatory minimum sentences.

7. Efforts have been made to reduce the overrepresentation of Indigenous peoples in correctional institutions by considering alternatives to confinement in sentencing, although the impact of section 718.2(e) of the *Criminal Code* and the *Gladue* decision is questionable.

8. Sentencing is among the most difficult tasks that judges have to perform and probably the most controversial.

9. Mandatory minimum sentences may not serve as a deterrent or make communities safer and can best be viewed as a politically driven crime policy.

10. There is evidence that the personal attributes of judges may influence their decision-making.

11. Judges in the criminal courts can select from a range of sentencing options, which include various alternatives to confinement and varying terms of imprisonment in correctional institutions.

12. There have been increasing efforts to involve victims in the sentencing process.

13. Circle sentencing is an example of a restorative justice approach that can be an alternative to traditional sentencing.

14. Politics can have a significant impact on the legislative framework of sentencing.

15. Excerpts from the case of R. v. Burgess illustrate how judges weigh information in a case in reaching a decision.

16. Research evidence is for the most part inconclusive as to the effectiveness of the various sentencing options, although it appears that incarceration is not an effective general or specific deterrent.

KEY TERM QUESTIONS

1. What is meant by **proportionality** in sentencing, and what is the **principle of restraint**?

2. What is a **suspended sentence**, a **conditional sentence**, and an **intermittent sentence**?

3. Define **probation**.

4. What is the difference between a **concurrent** and a **consecutive** sentence?

5. What is **judicial determination** and what role does it play in sentencing?

6. How do the designations of **dangerous offender** and **long-term offender** impact convicted persons?

7. What was the *Gladue* **decision** and what is a **Gladue report** role do they play in the sentencing of Indigenous offenders?

8. Describe what is meant by **sentencing disparity** and provide examples.

9. What are the **collateral consequences of sentencing**?

10. What role does **case law precedent** play in sentencing?

11. What is a **victim impact statement (VIS)**, and what role does it play in the criminal justice process?

12. Describe **circle sentencing** and then contrast its principles with those of the traditional criminal court.

CRITICAL THINKING EXERCISES

Critical Thinking Exercise 9.1

Sentencing Options

With the exception of those offences that, upon conviction, require the judge to impose a mandatory minimum sentence, Canadian judges exercise consideration discretion in sentencing. Review the case examples for each of the sentencing options that are set out in Table 9.1. Consider the sentencing option that was selected in the case by the presiding judge.

Your Thoughts?

1. Considering the brief information presented for each of the case examples, in your view, was the appropriate sentencing option selected?

2. Provide the basis for your opinion of each case.

Critical Thinking Exercise 9.2

Predictability in Sentencing versus Individualized Discretion in Sentencing

Bill C-10, the *Safe Communities and Streets Act* (2012), was designed, in part, to reduce the discretion of judges in sentencing. In expressing concerns about this legislation, one judge stated that it undermined a longstanding principle of sentencing that had been established by the SCC, most notably that:

> There is no such thing as a uniform sentence for a particular crime.... Sentences for a particular offence should be expected to vary to some degree across various communities and regions in this country, as the "just and appropriate" mix of accepted sentencing goals will depend on the needs and current conditions of and in the particular community where the crime occurred.[a]

Your Thoughts?

1. What is your response to this judge's comments?

2. What arguments could be offered in support of, and in opposition to, the notion of individualized decision-making?

3. A critic of individualized decision-making might raise the issue as to whether the notion of variability in sentencing, considering "the needs and current conditions of and in a particular community," might lead to decisions that are discriminatory against certain groups or persons. How would you respond to this criticism?

[a] R.M. Pomerance (Justice). 2013. "The New Approach to Sentencing in Canada: Reflections of a Trial Judge," *Canadian Criminal Law Review, 17*(3), 305–326 at p. 307.

Critical Thinking Exercise 9.3

A Critique of *Gladue*

Following are excerpts from an editorial about the *Gladue* principle that appeared in the *Toronto Sun* newspaper:

> The courts must consider as mitigating factors the effects of colonialism, residential schools, displacement and other historical wrongdoings, including what impact those may have had on aboriginal offenders.
>
> There are no similar provisions for non-aboriginal offenders, including those who may have come from war-torn countries or suffered directly or indirectly from human atrocities such as the Holocaust or Cambodia's Khmer Rouge mass-killings of the 1970s.
>
> No, the sentencing provisions are based on the race of the offender only. Which is racism. And in a free, just and democratic country like Canada, it's appalling we have these kinds of laws on the books.
>
> Instead of creating racist laws, Parliament should address some of the root causes of why so many aboriginals are in jail—like the effects of another racist law, the

Indian Act, and the continued segregation of aboriginal people. How about the squalid and inhumane conditions of many reserves in Canada?[a]

Your Thoughts?

1. How would you respond to this editorial?

[a] T. Brodbeck. 2012, December 16. "Federal Justice Minister Rob Nicholson Backs Gladue Racist Sentencing Laws," *Winnipeg Sun.* http://www.winnipegsun.com/2012/12/15/federal-justice-minister-rob-nicholson-backs-gladue-racist-sentencing-laws. Material republished with the express permission of Postmedia Network Inc.

CLASS/GROUP DISCUSSION EXERCISE

Class/Group Discussion Exercise 9.1

You Be the Judge Results from the Cases in Court File 9.5

Case 1 Decision On March 30, 2017, Judge Louise Provost of the Quebec Court sentenced the former mayor of Montreal, Michel Applebaum to one year in prison, followed by two years on probation. The judge rejected the submission of the defence, noting that defendant did not express remorse for the offences and had not accepted responsibility for his actions. In passing sentence, the judge stated, "The court considers that the accused will probably not be able to hold an elected position in the future, thereby reducing the risk of recidivism. But the crime is serious because it has an element of corruption. This reprehensible behaviour violates the fundamental values of our society."

Applebaum was granted parole in March 2017 after serving one-sixth of his one-year sentence. Among the conditions of his release were that he seek employment, perform at least 20 hours of community service per week, and report twice a week to the police for two months. He will then be subject to a two-year period of probation.

Source: S. Banerjee. 2017, March 30. "Ex-Montreal Mayor Applebaum Sentenced to One Year in Prison for Corruption," *Globe and Mail.* http://www.theglobeandmail.com/news/national/ex-montreal-mayor-applebaum-sentenced-to-one-year-in-prison-for-corruption/article34501569; S. Banerjee. 2017, June 6. "Ex-Montreal Mayor Michael Applebaum Granted Parole," *Toronto Sun.* http://www.torontosun.com/2017/06/06/ex-montreal-mayor-michael-applebaum-granted-parole.

Case 2 Decision On March 30, 2017, Judge Tory Calvin sentenced Todd Ball to serve an intermittent sentence of 30 days on weekends and one year of probation for assault causing bodily harm. The probation order included a requirement of alcohol counselling. The judge noted that Ball had written a letter of apology and was in counselling. The judge also noted that on-ice assaults within a hockey game present challenges for the justice system, as there may be some level of violence associated with the game and by stepping onto the ice, and players accept that they may be subject to injury. The judge stated, "In my mind, the significant fact is that this was a non-contract, fun tournament. It makes it very different from cases involving competitive play, for instance in the NHL or the AHL." Following the sentencing, the victim stated, "I feel they should have made an example out of him. He only got 30 days for breaking someone's face. My life has never been the same."

Source: B. Sawchuk. 2017, March 30. "Ontario Goalie Who Destroyed Hockey Player's Face to Serve 30-Day Jail Sentence on Weekends," *National Post.* http://news.nationalpost.com/sports/ontario-goalie-who-destroyed-hockey-players-face-to-serve-30-day-jail-sentence-on-weekends.

Case 3 Decision On January 16, 2017, Alberta provincial court judge Mike Allen sentenced Steven Cloutier to six years in prison and also imposed a ten-year driving ban. The judge described the event as "a bomb hitting the station" and added, "It became a terrifying, life-altering day." In determining the sentence, the judge indicated that he had taken into account that it was Cloutier's first offence and also the findings of a psychological report indicating neglect during childhood.

Source: M. Dhariwal. 2017, January 16. "Six-Year Sentence for May Who Drove Truck into Edmonton Gas Station," *CBC News.* http://www.cbc.ca/news/canada/edmonton/six-year-sentence-for-man-who-drove-truck-into-edmonton-gas-station-1.3937908.

Case 4 Decision On March 6, 2009, Christopher Pauchay was sentenced to three years in prison. The judge's rationale for not following the recommendations of the sentencing

circle was that Pauchay lacked insight into his behaviour and didn't accept responsibility for the deaths. Pauchay subsequently served two-thirds of his sentence in confinement and was released on statutory release in 2011. His sentence expired in January 2012.

Source: *CBC News*. 2009, March 6. "Father of Girls Who Froze to Death Gets 3 Years in Prison." http://www.cbc.ca/news/canada/saskatchewan/father-of-girls-who-froze-to-death-gets-3-years-in-prison-1.840881.

Your Thoughts?

For each of the four cases, ask yourself these questions:

1. Did my sentence match the sentence of the judge?

2. Was it more lenient or harsher?

3. Did the judge in the actual case make a good decision?

4. With respect to the Pauchay case:

    a. In your view, was the judge correct in directing that a circle sentencing process be conducted in this case?

    b. Do you agree with the final sentencing decision of the judge in this case?

    c. Critics of the judge's decision might argue that the court's decision undermines the efforts of communities to be involved in the justice process. In your view, is this a valid concern?

MEDIA LINK

"Crime and Punishment—The Story of Capital Punishment," https://www.youtube.com/watch?v=0hWcX9vZiKc

REFERENCES

1. *The Canadian Criminal Law Notebook*. 2017. http://criminalnotebook.ca/index.php/Concurrent_and_Consecutive_Sentences.

2. *CBC News*. 2013, September 11. "Travis Baumgartner Gets 40 Years without Parole for Killing Co-Workers." http://www.cbc.ca/news/canada/edmonton/travis-baumgartner-gets-40-years-without-parole-for-killing-co-workers-1.1706464.

3. *CBC News*. 2014, October 31. "Justin Bourque Gets 5 Life Sentences, No Chance for Parole for 75 Years." http://www.cbc.ca/news/canada/new-brunswick/justin-bourque-gets-5-life-sentences-no-chance-of-parole-for-75-years-1.2818516.

4. D. Dias. 2015, July 2. "Mandatory Victim Surcharges Unconstitutional: B.C. Court," *Canadian Lawyer*. http://www.canadianlawyermag.com/legalfeeds/2773/mandatory-victim-surcharges-unconstitutional-b-c-court-main.html.

5. Department of Justice. 2017. "Peace Bonds Fact Sheet." http://www.justice.gc.ca/eng/cj-jp/victims-victimes/factsheets-fiches/peace-paix.html.

6. C. Purdy. 2013, September 11. "Armoured Car Shooter Won't Get Out of Prison for at Least 40 Years," *Globe and Mail*. http://www.theglobeandmail.com/news/national/armoured-car-shooter-wont-get-out-of-prison-for-at-least-40-years/article14255049.

7. S. Bontrager, K. Barrick, and E. Stupi. 2013. "Gender and Sentencing: A Meta-Analysis of Contemporary Research," *Journal of Gender, Race, & Justice*, 16(2), 349–372.

8. Ibid.

9. J.V. Roberts and G. Watson. 2017. "Reducing Female Admissions to Custody: Exploring the Options at Sentencing," *Criminology and Criminal Justice*, 17(5), 546–567.

10. Public Safety Canada Portfolio Corrections Statistics Committee. 2016. *Corrections and Conditional Release Statistical Overview: 2015 Annual Report*. Ottawa: Public Safety Canada. https://www.publicsafety.gc.ca/cnt/rsrcs/pblctns/ccrso-2015/ccrso-2015-en.pdf.

11. N. Macdonald. 2016, February 18. "Canada's Prisons Are the 'New Residential Schools,'" *Macleans*. http://www.macleans.ca/news/canada/canadas-prisons-are-the-new-residential-schools.

12. R. Langevin and S. Curnoe. 2014. "Are Dangerous Offenders Different from Other Offenders? A Clinical Profile,"

International Journal of Offender Therapy and Comparative Criminology, 58(7), 780–801.

13. Public Safety Canada. 2008. *Corrections and Conditional Release Statistical Overview: Annual Report 2008*. Ottawa: Public Works and Government Services Canada, p. 109. https://www.publicsafety.gc.ca/cnt/rsrcs/pblctns/ccrso -2008/2008-ccrs-eng.pdf.

14. C. Murdocca. 2013. *To Right Historical Wrongs: Race, Gender, and Sentencing in Canada*. Vancouver: UBC Press, p. 8.

15. Legal Services Society of B.C. 2011. *Gladue Primer*. Vancouver: Author. http://www.legalaid.bc.ca/resources/ pdfs/pubs/Gladue-Primer-eng.pdf.

16. M. Erskine. 2015, April 15. "Gladue Report Writer Opens a Window on the Process," *Manitoulin Expositor*. http://www.manitoulin.ca/2015/04/15/gladue-report -writer-opens-a-window-on-the-process.

17. P. Maurutto and K. Hannah-Moffat. 2016. "Aboriginal Knowledges in Specialized Courts: Emerging Practices in Gladue Courts," *Canadian Journal of Law & Society*, 31(3), 451–471 at p. 464.

18. Canadian Press. 2012, September 21. "Court Quashes Extradition Order of Two Aboriginal Men," *CTV News*. http://toronto.ctvnews.ca/court-quashes-extradition -orders-of-two-aboriginal-men-1.966997.

19. Maurutto and Hannah-Moffat, "Aboriginal Knowledges in Specialized Courts," p. 466.

20. Murdocca, *To Right Historical Wrongs*.

21. Ibid., p. 64.

22. Ibid., p. 65.

23. F.T. Green. 2017, April 5. "Native Injustice Comes Full Circle," *Now Toronto*. https://nowtoronto.com/news/native -injustice-comes-full-circle/.

24. S. April and M.M. Orsi. 2013. *Gladue Practices in the Provinces and Territories*. Ottawa: Department of Justice Canada. http://www.justice.gc.ca/eng/rp-pr/csj-sjc/ccs-ajc/ rr12_11/rr12_11.pdf.

25. G. Hamilton. 2016, October 12. "Former First Nations Police Chief's Request for Lenient Sentence Over 'Abhorrent' Rapes Rejected," *National Post*. http://news.nationalpost .com/news/canada/former-first-nations-police-chiefs-request -for-lenient-sentence-over-abhorrent-rapes-rejected.

26. C. Graef. 2015, April 21. "Indigenous Tribes Are Abandoning American Style 'Justice' in Favor of Traditional Punishments," *Mint Press News*. http://www.mintpressnews .com/indigenous-tribes-are-abandoning-american-style -justice-in-favor-of-traditional-punishments/204612.

27. Ibid.

28. K. Marvin Tail Feathers. "The Development of the Kainai Peacemaking Centre." Unpublished MA Thesis. Athabasca University. Athabasca, Alberta, p. 30. http://dtpr .lib.athabascau.ca/action/download.php?filename=mais/ Kelly+Tail+Feathers+Final+Project.pdf.

29. S. Lawrynuik. 2017, March 14. "Sentencing Delayed for Blood Tribe Parents Charged with Failing to Provide Necessaries of Life," *CBC News*. http://www.cbc.ca/news/ canada/calgary/blood-tribe-necessaries-of-life-1.4024607.

30. L. Hausegger, M. Hennigar, and T. Riddell. 2009. *Canadian Courts: Law, Politics, and Process*. Toronto: Oxford University Press, p. 104.

31. Ibid., p. 300.

32. J. Boyce. 2013. "Adult Criminal Court Statistics in Canada, 2011/2012," *Juristat*, 33(1). Statistics Canada Catalogue no. 85-002-X. Ottawa: Minister of Industry, p. 13. http://www.statcan.gc.ca/pub/85-002-x/2013001/article/ 11804-eng.pdf.

33. S.B. Berson. 2013, September. "Beyond the Sentence– Understanding Collateral Consequences," *NIJ Journal*, 272, 26–28. https://ncjrs.gov/pdffiles1/nij/241927.pdf.

34. D.R. Songer and S.W. Johnson. 2007. "Judicial Decision Making in the Supreme Court of Canada: Updating the Personal Attribute Model," *Canadian Journal of Political Science*, 49(4), 911–934 at p. 927.

35. J. Stribopoulos and M.A. Yahya. 2007. "Does a Judge's Party of Appointment or Gender Matter to Case Outcomes? An Empirical Study of the Court of Appeal for Ontario," *Osgoode Hall Law Journal*, 45(2), 315–363.

36. M. Dawson. 2016. "Punishing Femicide: Criminal Justice Responses to the Killing of Women over Four Decades," *Current Sociology*, 64(7), 996–1016.

37. J.V. Roberts. 2012. "Structuring Sentencing in Canada, England and Wales: A Tale of Two Jurisdictions," *Criminal Law Forum*, 23(4), 319–345 at p. 330.

38. R.M. Pomerance (Justice). 2013. "The New Approach to Sentencing in Canada: Reflections of a Trial Judge," *Canadian Criminal Law Review*, 17(3), 305–326 at p. 320.

39. C. Blatchford. 2017, May 3. "Sexual Assault Verdict Overturned from Judge Who Calls Accused 'Dramatic and Insincere.'" *National Post*. http://news.nationalpost.com/news/ canada/christie-blatchford-sexual-assault-verdict-overturned -from-judge-who-called-accused-dramatic-and-insincere.

40. Ibid.

41. K. Makin. 2011, March 10. "The Judge Who Writes Like a Paperback Novelist," *Globe and Mail*. http://www.theglobeandmail.com/news/national/ the-judge-who-writes-like-a-paperback-novelist/article570811.

42. E.F.J.C. van Ginneken and D. Haynes. 2017. "'Just' Punishment? Offenders' Views on the Meaning and Severity of Punishment," *Criminology & Criminal Justice, 17*(1), 62–78.

43. Ibid., p. 74.

44. Canadian Press. 2013, November 12. "Mandatory Minimum Sentences for Gun Crimes Ruled Unconstitutional," *Globe and Mail.* http://www.theglobeandmail.com/news/national/mimimun-sentencing-law-for-gun-crimes-ruled-unconstitutional/article15387142/#dashboard/follows.

45. L. Hendry. 2009, September 9. "Sentence Outrages Victim's Father (Comment)," *The Intelligencer* (Belleville, ON). September 9. http://www.intelligencer.ca/2009/09/09/sentence-outrages-victims-father-comment

46. J.V. Roberts. 2008. "Victim Impact Statements: Lessons Learned and Future Priorities," *Victims of Crime Research Digest, 1,* 3–16. http://www.justice.gc.ca/eng/rp-pr/cj-jp/victim/rr07_vic4/rr07_vic4.pdf.

47. T. Markin. 2017. "Victim Rights in Sentencing: An Examination of Victim Impact Statements," *Canadian Criminal Law Review, 22*(1), 95–119.

48. K. Egan. 2012, October 9. "Just How Much Impact Does the Impact Statement Make?" *Ottawa Citizen.* http://www.ottawacitizen.com/Just+much+impact+does+impact+statement+make/7215570/story.html.

49. J.V. Roberts and A. Edgar. 2007. "Victim Impact Statements at Sentencing: Judicial Experiences and Perceptions—A Survey of Three Jurisdictions," *JustResearch, 14,* 14–17. http://www.justice.gc.ca/eng/rp-pr/jr/jr14/jr14.pdf.

50. M. Manikis. 2015. "Victim Impact Statements at Sentencing: Toward a Clearer Understanding of their Aims," *University of Toronto Law Journal, 65*(2), 85–123.

51. Department of Justice. 2015. "Victims' Rights in Canada: Community Impact Statements" [Fact sheet]. http://www.justice.gc.ca/eng/cj-jp/victims-victimes/factsheets-fiches/pdf/community-collectivite.pdf.

52. Ekos Research Associates. 2017. *National Justice Survey: Canada's Criminal Justice System.* Ottawa: Department of Justice Canada, p. 27. http://epe.lac-bac.gc.ca/100/200/301/pwgsc-tpsgc/por-ef/justice_canada/2017/015-16-e/report.pdf.

53. Ibid., p. 37.

54. Murdocca, *To Right Historical Wrongs,* p. 59.

55. J. Dickston-Gilmore and C. LaPrairie. 2005. *Will the Circle Be Unbroken? Aboriginal Communities, Restorative Justice and the Challenges of Conflict and Change.* Toronto: University of Toronto Press.

56. J. Dickson-Gilmore. 2014. "Whither Restorativeness? Restorative Justice and the Challenge of Intimate Violence in Aboriginal Communities," *Canadian Journal of Criminology and Criminal Justice, 56*(4), 417–46.

57. A. Acorn. 2004. *Compulsory Compassion: A Critique of Restorative Justice.* Vancouver: UBC Press.

58. Roberts, "Structuring Sentencing in Canada, England and Wales," p. 332.

59. Pomerance, "The New Approach to Sentencing in Canada," p. 307.

60. Author's note: While these case summaries do not provide all of the materials that a sentencing judge would have access to (e.g., the pre-sentence report), the exercise does provide you with a sense of the challenges faced by sentencing judges.

PART IV
CORRECTIONS

Chapter 10: Corrections in the Community: Alternatives to Confinement
Chapter 11: Correctional Institutions
Chapter 12: Release, Re-entry, and Reintegration

Corrections

Structures, policies, and programs to sanction, punish, treat, and supervise in the community and in correctional institutions, persons convicted of criminal offences.

Non-carceral corrections

That portion of systems of correction relating to offenders in non-institutional settings (e.g., parole officers, halfway houses, etc.).

Carceral (institutional) corrections

That portion of systems of correction relating to correctional institutions (e.g., inmates, correctional officers, etc.).

This part examines the corrections component of the criminal justice system. **Corrections** can be defined as the structure, policies, and programs delivered by governments, not-for-profit organizations, and members of the general public to sanction, punish, treat, and supervise in the community and in correctional institutions, persons convicted of criminal offences.

Correctional systems and the other components of the criminal justice system have as their primary mandate the protection of society. However, there is often disagreement over how this goal can best be accomplished. Historically, the corrections "pendulum" has swung back and forth between more punitive policies and those that are more focused on rehabilitation. In the early 21st century, a more punitive penology emerged under the federal Conservative government (2006–15), although court decisions and legislative and policy changes by the federal Liberal government (2015–present) have mitigated this to some degree.

All correctional systems have both **non-carceral** (non-institutional) and **carceral** (institutional) components. Non-carceral corrections, often referred to as *community corrections*, includes both alternatives to confinement and programs for offenders released from correctional institutions. Carceral corrections includes jails and correctional institutions operated by the provinces and territories and the federal government.

Chapter 10 explores strategies that provide alternatives to confinement and provide for the supervision and control of offenders in the community, including sentencing options such as conditional discharge, suspended sentences, diversion programs, conditional sentences, and probation.

Chapter 11 examines the attributes of correctional institutions that pose challenges for inmates, correctional officers, management, and treatment staff.

Chapter 12 examines the release of offenders from confinement and their re-entry and reintegration back into the community.

An excellent resource for non-carceral and carceral corrections is the Criminalization and Punishment Education Project run by the University of Ottawa and Carleton University (http://tpcp-canada.blogspot.ca).

© Laurie Justus Pace, Graphics One Design, 2014

CHAPTER 10
CORRECTIONS IN THE COMMUNITY:
ALTERNATIVES TO CONFINEMENT

LEARNING OBJECTIVES

After reading this chapter, you should be able to

- Describe the sentencing options that provide an alternative to incarceration.
- Discuss the issues that surround the use of diversion.
- Describe conditional sentences and their use as an alternative to confinement.
- Identify the ways in which an offender can be on probation and compare and contrast probation with parole and with conditional sentences.
- Discuss the recruitment, training, role, and responsibilities of probation officers.
- Describe how the principles of risk, need, and responsivity are used in probation practice.
- Discuss the experience of persons on probation.
- Identify and discuss the challenges of probation practice.
- Describe the use of electronic monitoring and GPS with probationers and discuss the issues surrounding the use of high technology for supervision.

Many challenges may be encountered by persons who are in conflict with the law and are placed on probation. Probation officers may also have difficulties providing effective supervision and intervention.

Recall from the discussion at the beginning of Part IV that *community corrections* includes both alternatives to confinement (e.g., diversion, probation) and programs for offenders released from correctional institutions (e.g., parole), as well as a variety of intermediate sanctions and restorative justice initiatives.

The large majority of offenders who are found guilty are not sent to correctional institutions but rather are given a non-custodial sanction to be completed in the community. The then federal Conservative government (2006–15) enacted legislation that restricted the use of several alternative measures, although subsequent court decisions have found some of these to be a violation of the *Charter of Rights and Freedoms*. A quick review of the sentencing options set out in Table 9.1 reveals a variety of sanctions that do not involve incarceration. These include absolute discharges, conditional discharges, suspended sentences, conditional sentences, and probation.

A quick summary of "who's who" in non-carceral and carceral corrections in Canada can be seen in Table 10.1.

Figure 10.1 presents a breakdown of the admissions to adult correctional services by type of supervision and by jurisdiction (federal and provincial/territorial). Note that approximately 23 percent of all offenders are in some type of custody, while 77 percent are under some form of community supervision.

Figure 10.2 presents a breakdown of offenders under the jurisdiction of Correctional Service Canada (CSC). Note that a majority of federal offenders are in custody (61.9 percent), while just over 30 percent are under active supervision in the community.

The following sections discuss the variety of sentencing options that result in convicted persons not being sent to a correctional institution.

TABLE 10.1

THE "WHO" OF NON-CARCERAL AND CARCERAL CORRECTIONS

Non-carceral	Carceral
Judges	Judges
Probationers	Inmates
NGOs (e.g., John Howard Society, Elizabeth Fry Society)	Superintendents and wardens
Community counsellors/treatment professionals	Correctional officers; institutional parole officers
Indigenous friendship centres	Spiritual advisers (e.g., chaplains, Indigenous Elders)
Community volunteers	Native prison liaison workers
Offender's family	Citizen Advisory Committees
Parole board members	Treatment professionals
Parolees	Community volunteers
Federal offenders on statutory release	Offender's family
Parole officers	
Halfway house staff	

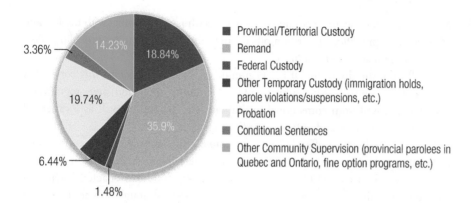

◄ FIGURE 10.1

Admissions to Adult Correctional Services, by Type of Supervision and Jurisdiction, 2015–16

Source: J. Reitano. 2017. "Adult Correctional Statistics in Canada, 2015/2016," *Juristat, 37*(1). Statistics Canada Catalogue no. 85-002-X. Ottawa: Minister of Industry, p. 15. http://www.statcan.gc.ca/pub/85-002-x/2017001/article/14700-eng.pdf.

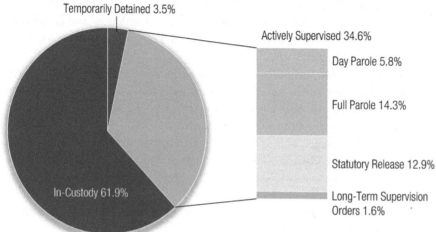

◄ FIGURE 10.2

Offenders under the Responsibility of the CSC, 2015

Source: Public Safety Canada Portfolio Corrections Statistics Committee. 2016. *Corrections and Conditional Release Statistical Overview: 2015 Annual Report.* Ottawa: Public Works and Government Services Canada, p. 33. https://www.publicsafety.gc.ca/cnt/rsrcs/pblctns/ccrso-2015/ccrso-2015-en.pdf. This information was reproduced with the permission of the Minister of. Public Safety and Emergency Preparedness Canada, 2017.

ABSOLUTE AND CONDITIONAL DISCHARGES

Section 730(1) of the *Criminal Code* (R.S.C. 1985, c. C-46) states that the presiding judge may discharge an offender in cases where an accused person either pleads guilty or is found guilty for an offence other than one for which there is a mandatory minimum penalty or the offence is punishable by a term of imprisonment for a period of 14 years to life. Note that although the person is found guilty, he or she is not "convicted," meaning that the offence will not be permanently on the person's record.

In *R. v. MacFarlane* (1976 ALTASCAD 6), the court stated that discharges should only be used in exceptional circumstances. The standard that is used in determining the appropriateness of a discharge is that it would be "in the best interests of the accused and not contrary to the public interest." The "best interests of the accused" was defined by the court in *Regina v. Sanchez-Pino* (1973 11 CCC (2d) 53 (ONCA) at p. 59) as being "a good person of good character, or at least of such character that the entry of a conviction against him may have significant repercussions." And if allowing the conviction to remain on the offender's record would "have a prejudicial impact on the accused disproportionate to the offence committed."[1] The "public interest" has been defined by the courts as whether any benefit would accrue if the community would benefit by knowing of the person's criminal activity.[2]

Absolute discharges are discharges without conditions, while conditional discharges have conditions attached to them, including to keep the peace and be of good behaviour, to appear before the court when requested, to report to a probation officer, to seek and maintain employment, and others. If the offender fails to comply with these and any other specific conditions, which may include abstaining from the use of drugs or alcohol, the offender can be returned to court and the conditional discharge may be cancelled. In such cases, a more severe sentence may be imposed. The courts have established that conditional discharges can even be used where a violent offence has been committed (*R. v. Knowlton*, 2005 ABPC 29).

SUSPENDED SENTENCE

Convicted offenders who receive a suspended sentence are provided with the opportunity to avoid incarceration by abiding by conditions of a probation order for a period from one to three years. Upon completion of the period of supervision, the offender will have a criminal record (which distinguishes suspended sentences from a conditional discharge).

FINES

Fine option programs provide an opportunity for offenders to pay off their fines by working on various community service projects. Fines can be levied alone or in conjunction with another sanction such as probation or even incarceration (in which case it doesn't serve as an alternative to confinement).

The Supreme Court of Canada (SCC) has ruled (*R. v. Wu*, 2003 SCC 73) that an offender is not to be imprisoned for the non-payment of a fine where there is a genuine inability to pay. The court held that poverty is a reasonable excuse for non-payment of a fine. The court further held that imprisonment is only appropriate where the offender has demonstrated a refusal to pay without reasonable excuse and that persons should be given a reasonable time to pay and to do so by participating in a fine options program.

All provinces and territories except Ontario, Newfoundland and Labrador, and British Columbia have fine option programs. These programs provide an opportunity for offenders to work off their fines by earning credits for working, unpaid, for various community groups and organizations. Offenders in some jurisdictions can also pay off the victim fine surcharge by participating in a fine options program.[3]

Due to fiscal restraints, the government of Saskatchewan announced in 2017 that, with exceptions for those offenders who were truly destitute, offenders would not be allowed to work off their fines but must pay in cash. The government noted that only 44 percent of offenders worked the agreed-upon hours to pay off their fines.[4]

DIVERSION PROGRAMS

Diversion

Programs that are designed to keep offenders from being processed further into the formal criminal justice system.

Diversion programs have been a feature of Canadian criminal justice for decades. Offenders can be diverted from the formal criminal justice process at several points — there are diversion programs at the pre-charge, post-charge, and post-sentencing. The problem-solving courts discussed in Chapter 7 are designed to divert offenders with special needs from the traditional court system. There are also many diversion programs for youth offenders, and these are discussed in Chapter 13.

Generally speaking, the objective of all diversion programs is to keep offenders from being processed further into the formal criminal justice system and, in so doing, to reduce costs, minimize social stigmatization, and assist offenders in addressing the specific factors related to their offending. Most diversion programs require that offenders acknowledge responsibility for their behaviour and agree to fulfill certain conditions within a specified time. This may include attending an alcohol or drug treatment program, completing a number of community service hours, or other requirements. If these conditions are successfully met, the charges are withdrawn and the person does not have a criminal record.

Traditional diversion programs are focused on low-risk, first-time offenders, although cases involving more serious offences have been referred to diversion programs.

A major concern with diversion programs is **net-widening**—a situation wherein persons who would otherwise have been released outright by the police or not charged by Crown counsel are involved in the justice system.

There are also concerns that diversion programs can be coercive and punitive. Also, there is some ambiguity surrounding the notion of "choice" in the operations of diversion programs and whether diversion programs may infringe on the rights of accused persons.

Although there are no recent Canadian studies, research in the U.S. suggests that diversion programs can reduce the seriousness and frequency of reoffending.[5,6] The factors associated with successful outcomes for offenders involved in diversion programs include stable employment and a supportive environment.[7]

VICTIM–OFFENDER MEDIATION

Many diversion programs are centred on the principles of restorative justice. Victim–offender mediation (VOM) programs (often referred to as victim–offender reconciliation [VOR] programs) take a restorative approach in which the victim and the offender are provided with the opportunity to express their feelings and concerns. With the help of a neutral mediator, the offender and the victim resolve the conflict, address the consequences of the offence, and, ultimately, come to understand each other. In recent years, VOM and VOR programs have been extended to cases involving crimes of violence and have included incarcerated offenders.

Restorative justice approaches that provide an opportunity for the victim to meet face-to-face with the offender receive high marks from crime victims and have a positive impact on the psychological and physical health of crime victims. A study ($N = 34$) of victims of violent crime in Canada and Belgium who participated in victim–offender mediation, family group conferencing, or victim–offender encounters found high levels of victim satisfaction.[8] These were ascribed to the perception that the process was procedurally just, was flexible, provided care, and was empowering. These views existed regardless of the outcome of the intervention.

A number of these types of programs operate in First Nations communities. One is profiled in Corrections File 10.1.

CONDITIONAL SENTENCES

Section 742 of the *Criminal Code* states that a convicted person who would otherwise be incarcerated for less than two years can be sentenced to a conditional term of imprisonment, to be served in the community rather than in custody. The offender is required to fulfill certain conditions, although the offender is not on probation. Failure to comply with the conditions of a conditional sentence order (CSO) results in the offender being returned to court, where the sentencing judge has a variety of options, including sending the offender to prison. Offenders on CSOs are supervised in the community by probation officers, even though they are not on probation. See Table 10.3 for a comparison of CSOs and probation.

Net-widening

A potential, unanticipated consequence of diversion programs in which persons who would otherwise have been released outright by the police or not charged by Crown counsel are involved in the justice system.

THE MIIKANAAKE COMMUNITY (ONTARIO) JUSTICE PROGRAM

The Miikanaake Commuity Justice Program is a pre- and post-charge diversion program for youth and adult Indigenous offenders who reside in Simcoe County in southern Ontario. Referrals may come from the police at the pre-charge stage, or from Crown counsel after the person has been charged. Offenders are diverted from the criminal justice system and referred to a community council, which is composed of members of the community. The council works with the offender to address the underlying causes of the offender's behaviour in order to facilitate reintegration back into the community. Among the options available to the council are counselling, requiring the offender to pay restitution, and recommending treatment or community service. Upon successful completion of an agreed-upon plan, persons who have been referred to the program at the pre-charge phase will not be charged by the police; for those persons referred to the program at the post-charge phase, the Crown may stay or withdraw the charges upon successful completion of the agreed-upon plan.

Miikanaake Community Justice program

Source: Breaking Trail: Miikanaake Community Justice Program. http://enaahtig.ca/Program%20Brochures/Miikanaake%20Community%20Justice%20Program.pdf.

In its ruling in *R. v. Proulx* (2000 SCC 5), the SCC directed that two factors be taken into account in determining whether a conditional sentence is appropriate: (1) the risk that the offender will reoffend, and (2) the amount of harm the offender would cause in the event of offending again.

All CSOs contain standard, compulsory conditions that are similar to those contained in probation orders. Optional conditions may also be set down and may be added to or reduced by the court over time. These may include abstaining from alcohol or drugs, providing for the support or care of dependents, performing community service work, and/or attending a treatment program.

Non-compliance with the conditions of a CSO can result in the offender being incarcerated. If an allegation is made that a condition has been breached, the offender may have to appear in court to prove that the allegation is false. This is a reverse onus situation; in other words, it is up to the offender to prove that the breach did *not* occur.

The *Safe Streets and Communities Act* (S.C. 2012, c. 1) prevents judges from imposing a conditional sentence in cases where the offender has been convicted of an offence involving bodily harm, drug trafficking, or the use of a weapon (along with a variety of other offences in which the Crown had proceeded by indictment). As of late 2017, it remains to be seen whether these restrictions on the use of conditional sentences will be overturned by the courts.

Offenders who are given a CSO and placed under house arrest are often viewed by the media and the general public as having received a "slap on the wrist" and as having escaped the negative experiences of incarceration. Yet adhering to a CSO's requirements, which may include 24-hour house arrest, presents challenges for offenders that may be no less intense than those of incarceration. In interviews, offenders on CSOs mention the negative impact on their working lives and on those who are close to them, including their children.[9]

CSOs have been surrounded by controversy since their inception in 1996. While popular with judges, concerns have been raised about high violation rates and, initially, the use of CSOs by judges for offenders who had committed crimes of violence. These concerns prompted the then federal Conservative government to restrict the use of CSOs for certain offences. This may have resulted in a decrease in the use of CSOs; in British Columbia, the number of persons supervised on CSOs declined by nearly one-half between 2011 and 2015.[10]

Although the use of CSOs has been credited with contributing to the reduction of prison populations, there is variability among the provinces and territories in their use. However, although CSOs could serve to reduce the high numbers of Indigenous offenders in prison, research has found that only in the provinces of Quebec and Ontario has there been an elevated use of this sentencing option. In the remaining jurisdictions, non-Indigenous offenders are most likely to be the beneficiaries of this alternative to incarceration.[11]

PROBATION

Section 731 of the *Criminal Code* provides that in cases in which no minimum penalty is prescribed, the sentencing judge may place the offender on probation for a period of up to three years. Probation is the most frequently used strategy for supervising offenders in the community as an alternative to incarceration, although it is used in conjunction with other sanctions as well. See Table 10.2.

The proportion of offenders who receive a sentence of probation has remained in the 43 to 45 percent range in recent years.[12] Probation is popular largely because it is so versatile. The specific conditions of a probation order can be tailored to the risk and needs of the offender and may include the requirement that the probationer attend specialized programs.

A probation order will contain compulsory conditions as set out in section 732.1(2) of the *Criminal Code*. These include the requirement that the probationer "keep the peace and be of good behaviour," to "appear before the court when required to do so," and to notify the court or supervising probation officer of any change in employment status, residence, and so on.

In addition, the probation order may contain **optional conditions** that are tailored to the offender's specific circumstances and, under section 732.1(3) of the *Criminal*

Optional conditions

Conditions attached to offenders who are supervised in the community that are tailored to their specific risk and needs.

TABLE 10.2

THE USES OF PROBATION

Adult offenders can be on probation under the following scenarios:

- as part of a conditional discharge (mandatory)
- as a condition of a suspended sentence (mandatory)
- as part of an intermittent sentence (mandatory)
- as a sentence on its own (the most common)
- following a prison term of two years or less
- in conjunction with a conditional sentence
- as a federal offender who received a sentence of *exactly* two years (little known)

Code, include not possessing, owning, or carrying a firearm; performing up to 240 hours of community service over a period not exceeding 18 months; remaining within the jurisdiction of the court unless written permission is received from the court or supervising probation officer; and, with the agreement of the probationer, participating in an approved treatment program.

Additional conditions can include the requirement that the probationer provide restitution to the victim; restrictions on whom the probationer can contact; travel restrictions, including "red-zone, no-go areas"; and the requirement that the offender attend alcohol and/or drug counselling.

Offenders who fail to comply with the conditions of their probation order can be found guilty of an indictable offence and imprisoned for not more than four years, or found guilty of a summary conviction offence, subject to incarceration for not more than 18 months, and a fine, or both. In reality, few offenders who violate the conditions of their probation suffer these consequences.

PROBATION AND CONDITIONAL SENTENCES: WHAT'S THE DIFFERENCE?

Although conditional sentences and probation might appear to be indistinguishable, there are significant differences between the two. These are set out in Table 10.3.

PROBATION VERSUS PAROLE: WHAT'S THE DIFFERENCE?

Probation and parole both involve an offender being supervised in the community. However, there are considerable differences between them. These are set out in Table 10.4.

TABLE 10.3

PROBATION VERSUS CONDITIONAL SENTENCES

Probation	Conditional Sentence
Imposed by a criminal court judge	Imposed by a criminal court judge
Designed as an alternative to custody, although may be used in conjunction with a period of incarceration in a provincial or territorial jail	Designed for offenders who would be custody-bound but allows offenders to serve period of custody in the community, generally under house arrest
Can be imposed for any type of offence	Cannot be used when the offender has been convicted of a crime that carries a mandatory minimum penalty and for certain offences, including drug trafficking, offences causing body harm, and use of a weapon
Used for offenders receiving a sentence of less than two years	Used for offenders receiving a sentence of less than two years
Maximum length is three years	Maximum length must be less than two years
Objective is rehabilitation	Objective is rehabilitation and punishment (*R. v. Wu*, 2003 SCC 73).
Supervision by probation officers	Supervision by probation officers, although the offender is *not* on probation
Offender must abide by certain conditions	Offender must abide by certain conditions
Breach of conditions may result in offender being returned to court where additional conditions may be imposed	Breach of conditions may result in offender being sent to jail
The offender on probation must consent to treatment (*R. v. Rogers* (1991), 2 CR (4th) 192 (BCCA))	The offender must attend any treatment program ordered by the court

TABLE 10.4

PROBATION VERSUS PAROLE: WHAT'S THE DIFFERENCE?

Probation	Parole
Imposed by a criminal court judge	Granted by an administrative tribunal (a parole board)
Available only for provincial/territorial offenders (except federal offenders who received a sentence or sentences totalling exactly two years)	Available to federal and provincial/territorial offenders
Maximum length is three years	Continues until warrant expiry date (end of sentence)
May be used in conjunction with a period of confinement in a provincial/territorial institution (and following a sentence of exactly two years in a federal correctional facility)	A form of conditional release from confinement in a provincial/territorial/federal correctional facility
Requires offender to abide by general conditions (e.g., obey the law and keep the peace) and perhaps specific conditions tailored to the offender's individual risk factors (e.g., abstain from alcohol)	Requires offender to abide by general and perhaps also specific conditions that are designed to reduce risk factors (e.g., no-contact provisions)
Breach of condition can be a charge under the *Criminal Code* that requires evidence for conviction of breach of probation; additional conditions may be imposed and the terms of probation extended; offenders found in breach of conditions rarely incarcerated	Breach of condition may result in suspension or revocation, resulting in a return to custody; the offender may be re-released with additional conditions. (Note: Suspension of parole occurs when there has been a breach of conditions, to prevent a breach of conditions, or to protect society; a parole revocation occurs when the Parole Board of Canada terminates an offender's release either due to violation of a condition or the commission of a new offence. See Chapter 12.)

RECRUITMENT AND TRAINING OF PROBATION OFFICERS

Since probation falls under the authority of the provinces and territories, each jurisdiction has developed its own procedures and standards for recruiting and training probation officers. Applicants for probation officer positions are often required to hold a university degree and have strong verbal and written communication skills, among others. In the province of Alberta, applicants must demonstrate a number of core competencies, including managing information and people, organizational skills, and problem-solving skills, among others.[13]

In Ontario, to apply for the position of probation officer, an applicant must

- hold a degree, from an institution authorized by the province to grant degrees, in one of the following disciplines: social work, psychology, sociology, and criminology; or a degree from an institution authorized by the province to grant degrees; and experience, greater than five years in total, in a social services or correctional organization, in a role(s) that involves the formal assessment of human behaviour and the application of structured interventions aimed at supporting the changing of human behaviour;

- possess strong verbal and written communication skills, as well as counselling and assessment skills; and,

- be able to establish and maintain client and stakeholder relationships.[14]

There are similar qualifications to become a probation officer in other jurisdictions.

Most often there is pre-employment training, during which potential applicants must complete a number of courses (many of which are offered online), often at their own expense, before being eligible to apply for a position as a probation officer.

There are also ongoing in-service training courses for probation officers. These focus on the supervision of special populations (such as sex offenders and the mentally disordered) and the use of assessment instruments.

Probation officer salaries vary between the provinces/territories. In Ontario in 2016, the median salary was $37.98 per hour, while in Saskatchewan, the hourly wage ranges from $27.219 to $34.110 an hour. In Manitoba, probation officer salaries range between $45,335 and $71,775 per year.

ROLE AND RESPONSIBILITIES OF PROBATION OFFICERS

The activities of probation officers largely involve assessing clients with respect to their needs and the risks they pose, providing individualized case management with the objective of reducing criminal behaviour, and supervising offenders on probation as well as persons who have been released on bail while awaiting trial. In Quebec and Ontario, probation officers supervise offenders who have been released on provincial parole; in the other provinces and territories, these offenders are supervised by federal parole officers. Some probation officers supervise offenders involved in diversion programs (i.e., who have been diverted from the criminal justice system).

A typical workday for a probation officer involves writing reports, meeting with offenders, and reporting their findings to judges or other criminal justice personnel. The majority of the "supervision" of probationers is done in the office. Home visits may be rare, due to a variety of factors, including security concerns, high caseloads, and a lack of resources.

A core component of the probation officer's role is completing assessments, which are designed to identify the offender's needs, evaluate risk, and assist in formulating a plan of supervision. These assessments are used not only in the case management process but also by provincial parole boards in determining whether to grant conditional release to offenders in custody. There are various assessment instruments that measure risk factors for adult and youth offenders as well as specialized measures for specific groups of offenders, including sex offenders.

Probation officers prepare pre-sentence reports (PSRs) on adult offenders who have been convicted and are submitted to the presiding judge at sentencing. The PSR contains a wealth of information on the offender's background and offence history, as well as victim impact information and assessments completed by treatment professionals. For Indigenous offenders, there are special considerations that the PSR must address per the requirements of the *Gladue* decision, discussed in Chapter 9. For example, it must include information on the offender's background and community, as well as on available community-based programs and services, including restorative justice programs such as sentencing circles and Elder-assisted interventions.

It has been noted that there has been a shift in emphasis in PSRs from a focus on rehabilitation and individualized treatment to a focus on risk.[15] There are concerns

---

PERSPECTIVE

Probation Officer

I think it is our responsibility to try to help individuals and to identify the issues that they have so they can begin working on themselves. For the offenders on my caseload, I try to help them with basic needs, such as food, shelter, employment training, and core programming that will help them develop their self-confidence and address their issues. It is important to have empathy and to understand the client's needs while also having realistic expectations of them. I try to see that the conditions of the probation order are followed while at the same time respecting the person.

Source: Personal communication with C.T. Griffiths

◄ Probation officer facilitating a session with a probationer

that PSRs lead to "statistical justice"—that is, with the information provided to judges focusing on risk assessments to the exclusion of other types of information.[16]

CASE MANAGEMENT AND SUPERVISION

The probation officer–client relationship has been found to be critical to the success of this correctional strategy. Key elements of successful probation supervision include establishing and maintaining rapport, considering the risk and needs of the offender, and adjusting the balance between control and assistance as required. Research has found that firm, fair, and caring relationships between probation officers and offenders reduce the risk of re-arrest, even after accounting for the offender's level of risk and pre-existing personality attributes.[17]

A study of probationer's perspectives on probation found that relationships built on trust, mutual respect, and the pursuit of mutually agreed upon goals were directly related to the offender's perceptions of the helpfulness of probation.[18] When the probation officer can focus on addressing the problems the probationer is experiencing, there is often a reduction in reoffending.[19]

Many probation offices now have specialized supervision units composed of specially trained officers for offenders convicted of spousal assault, sex offences, and other specific types of crime. Studies suggest that specially trained probation officers are less likely to be punitive in responding to violations of a probation order, perhaps due to their more in-depth understanding of the cognitive thinking patterns and behaviours of specific groups of offenders.[20]

PROGRAMS AND SERVICES FOR PROBATIONERS

Provincial/territorial systems of corrections and not-for-profit organizations offer probationers a variety of programs and services. Probation officers in many jurisdictions are also involved in facilitating programs for offenders. In British Columbia, for example, these include programs on violence prevention, substance abuse management, respectful relationships, living skills, cognitive skills, and educational upgrading, as well as a program for sex offenders.

THE WARRIORS AGAINST VIOLENCE PROGRAM, VANCOUVER

The Warriors Against Violence program in Vancouver is a prevention program designed to end family violence in Indigenous communities by assisting men to heal. The men who participate in the program may attend voluntarily, or be referred by lawyers, social workers, probation officers, or the Court.

In discussing the objectives of the program, the co-founder of the program stated, "We help the men learn how to respect all women. To help them look at themselves—about why we are so pissed off at the world and angry." The men meet in a healing circle and discuss their involvement in violence as well as the trauma they experienced growing up. As one participant stated, "I grew up almost like every other child on a reserve—severe poverty, severe abuse, severe alcoholism. I thought it was a regular way to live."

Listen to the interview with staff from the Warriors Against Violence program at http://wav-bc.com and watch the video at http://www.cbc.ca/news/indigenous/warriors-against-violence-tries-to-heal -aboriginal-men-1.3136168.

Source: D. McCue. 2015, July 6. "'Warriors Against Violence' Tries to Heal Aboriginal Men," *CBC News.* http://www.cbc .ca/news/indigenous/warriors-against-violence-tries-to-heal-aboriginal-men-1.3136168.

There is an increasing recognition that many offenders are suffering from trauma and that efforts must be made to facilitate their healing. One program for Indigenous men, operated by a non-governmental organization, is profiled in Corrections File 10.2.

THE DUAL ROLE OF PROBATION OFFICERS

Probation officers play a dual role: They provide assistance and support for offenders, and at the same time they enforce the conditions of the probation order. In carrying out the assistance and support role, the probation officer may help the offender address issues that have contributed to the offence and identify resources in the community such as alcohol and drug treatment programs, education upgrading courses, and mental health services.

However, the probation officer must at the same time ensure compliance with the general and specific conditions of the probation order. For offenders who are less cooperative, an approach based on control may be effective; whereas for offenders who are motivated to change, the probation officer can provide encouragement, support, and assistance. Probation officers have the discretion to tailor their style of supervision to the needs and risks of the individual probationer. To be effective, probation officers must, to the greatest extent possible, balance enforcement with treatment and balance a client-centred approach with meeting organizational requirements, such as completing assessments and other paperwork.[21]

It is often difficult for probation officers to focus equally on both roles, and this may be a barrier to effective case management. For example, a probationer with a history of drug addiction who has relapsed and started "using" again (or who never ceased using drugs) may want to ask his or her probation officer for help finding a treatment program. However, that person could trigger a charge of breach of probation by disclosing the illegal drug use to the probation officer. On the other hand, failing to disclose the drug relapse could result in the commission of further criminal acts to support the addiction.

Over the past decade there has been a shift in the role and orientation of probation officers toward control and surveillance in probation supervision.[22] This shift has been due in large measure to increasing caseloads, the focus on risk assessment in order to ensure accountability and reduce liability, and the increasing number of special higher risk categories of offenders—such as sex offenders and assaultive male offenders—who are receiving sentences of probation.

COLLABORATION WITH OTHER AGENCIES

A notable trend in probation is collaboration with other agencies. In Alberta, for example, probation officers work with the police and the courts in the Alberta Priority Prolific Offender Program (P-POP), which focuses on prosecuting and rehabilitating repeat offenders.[23]

Increasingly, probation officers are working with others in an interdisciplinary context. Most community police stations in Alberta, for example, have probation and parole officers working out of them. The personnel collaborate to prosecute and rehabilitate repeat offenders.[24] The role of probation officers includes ensuring that prolific offenders have access to appropriate treatment resources and working with offenders to implement a plan for successful re-entry into the community and a change in life direction.

For two participants in the P-POP, one with 135 convictions and 34 periods of custody and the other with 100 convictions for property-related offences and 27 stints in jail, the P-POP provided an opportunity for them to change. One stated, "I wanna deal with everything because in a year I want to be working, renting a place, owning my own car, being accepted back into the community ... and that's what my goal is."[25]

Probation officers in Alberta also participate in the Integrated Justice Services Project (IJSP) wherein probation officers are paired with Alberta Health and Alberta Human Services professionals, police, and other municipal professionals in a single office.[26]

These partnerships assist in breaking down the silos that have traditionally existed between criminal justice and social service and health agencies and can be a more effective and efficient approach to addressing the needs of probation clients as well as facilitating information sharing on materials related to serious and prolific offenders.

THE RISK, NEED, AND RESPONSIVITY MODEL IN PROBATION

A key set of concepts that have gained prominence in non-carceral and carceral corrections are the principles of risk, need, and responsivity (RNR).

The **risk principle** states that correctional interventions have a greater chance of success when they are matched with the offender's level of risk, because higher-risk offenders benefit more than medium- and low-risk offenders.

The **need principle** says that correctional interventions should target the criminogenic needs (dynamic risk factors) of offenders, including substance abuse, peer relations, and pro-criminal attitudes.

The **responsivity principle** states that correctional interventions should be matched to the learning styles and abilities of individual offenders, with particular emphasis on cognitive-behavioural interventions.

Although RNR has most frequently been associated with institutional treatment programs, it is now recognized that this model may have validity in community corrections, as well as in providing supervision and programs for offenders who have avoided

Risk principle

Correctional interventions are most effective when matched with the offender's level of risk, and higher-risk offenders benefit from interventions more than medium- and low-risk offenders.

Need principle

To be effective, correctional interventions must address the criminogenic needs of offenders.

Responsivity principle

Correctional interventions should be matched to the learning styles of individual offenders, with particular emphasis on cognitive-behavioural interventions.

a custodial sentence and those released into the community following a period of confinement.[27] Programs and interventions that utilize RNR have been proven to be more successful than those based on traditional practice.[28]

Application of the responsivity principles may be problematic, as many offenders have disabilities that may present obstacles to learning. Unfortunately, for a variety of reasons, including mental deficiency or learning disability, a deeply rooted attitudinal and behavioural pattern centred on a criminal lifestyle, an extensive history of confinement in institutions, and/or a general lack of interest in making the effort to change, not all inmates are receptive to treatment.

Despite research studies that have validated this approach to reducing reoffending, RNR has not been without its critics. There are specific concerns with the responsivity principle, given that many offenders have mental disabilities that may present obstacles to successful participation in programs. As well, the receptivity of offenders to treatment who are deeply entrenched in a criminal lifestyle may undermine the responsivity principle. There is also the concern that, too often, the RNR model has been used as a "one-size-fits-all" approach that fails to take individual factors such as an offender's level of motivation to change.[29,30]

THE APPLICATION OF RNR TO PROBATION PRACTICE: THE STRATEGIC TRAINING INITIATIVE IN COMMUNITY SUPERVISION (STICS)

A core component of probation practice in several jurisdictions is the Strategic Training Initiative in Community Supervision (STICS) program. The STICS program focuses on the principles of RNR and teaches probation officers ways to utilize those principles when supervising probationers, with particular attention to criminogenic factors such as relationships with peers and criminal thinking patterns. The STICS approach is centred on relationship building and establishing trust between the probation officer and client. The probation officer assumes the role of a change agent, as opposed to merely "managing" the offender and ensuring compliance with conditions.[31]

The STICS initiative is a good example of applying evidence-based correctional strategies—in this case the principle of RNR—to correctional practice— in this instance, probation. As one observer has noted, "The STICS directive allows probation officers to 'think outside the box' and as a consequence, allows them the ability to exercise creativity with policy in regard to the responsivity needs of offenders and subsequent service delivery."[32] This is particularly important when the probation officer is supervising persons with impairments, including FASD. For these individuals, the cognitive-behavioural approach that is widely used in correctional interventions, may not be effective, requiring the probation officer to adapt to the needs of the probationer.

In the words of one probation officer:

> My STICS program tells me that I am going to try something else. I am going to go out of the box a little bit. I'm going to say "listen, I do have to breach you on this, but I am going to recommend that no action be taken." Or I might not breach at all and I am going to tell him "you know what? I want you to go to AA for maybe about 2 months and then I will re-refer you and we will see how that works". . . and I am willing to go out of the box like that.[33]

Research studies have found that probation officers who utilize STICS have better outcomes with their probationers and that there are lower levels of re-offending.[34]

INTENSIVE SUPERVISION PROBATION

Intensive supervision probation (ISP) entails increased surveillance of probationers, various treatment interventions, efforts to ensure that offenders are employed, and reduced caseloads for probation officers. In Canada, ISP is used primarily with youth offenders. In ISP programs, offenders are monitored closely, and rigorous conditions are imposed on them, such as multiple weekly reporting requirements, strict enforcement of the mandatory and optional conditions on the probation order, and the requirement that offenders secure and maintain employment. ISP is more suited for offenders who are classified as posing a greater risk to reoffend in the community. An underlying premise of these programs is that they can help reduce the number of prison admissions, cut operational costs, and protect the public, while providing increased supervision of more serious offenders.

An example of an ISP is the Criminal Organization and High Risk Offender Unit (COHROU) program in Manitoba. The COHROU targets high-risk offenders and involves intensive supervision and programming for serious, high-risk offenders, most of whom have committed violent offences and are assessed as being high risk. An evaluation of the COHROU found relatively high rates of reoffending among a sample ($N = 409$) of probationers in the program; including breaches of probation conditions, 27.4 percent of the offenders did not commit an offence during the program or during the two-year follow-up. On the other hand, if violation of probation conditions are not included, 57.5 percent of the offenders successfully complete the COHROU without committing a new offence, while 46.2 percent did not commit a new offence during their entire period of supervision.[35]

THE EXPERIENCE OF PROBATIONERS

Few studies have examined the experience of persons on probation. There is some evidence to suggest that many probationers believe that their sentence served as a deterrent and that being on probation was beneficial.[36] A survey of offenders on probation in British Columbia ($N = 1,121$) found that probationers had a positive overall experience on probation (81 percent), a majority (90.5 percent) felt that their probation officer treated them fairly, and they did not have difficulty accessing programs (91.3 percent). Similarly, a majority of the probationers surveyed (63.5 percent) indicated that they were involved in their supervision plan. Overall client satisfaction did not vary by the gender or Indigenous status of the probationer, nor the region of the province in which they resided.[37]

On the other hand, there is evidence that some offenders may experience **pains of probation**. Depending upon the specific conditions attached to the probation order, these may include restrictions on where they can travel, having to change their daily life routine, the stigma associated with being on probation, and possible difficulties with employment.

In contrast to inmates in correctional institutions, who may experience physical pains, those associated with probation tend to be more economic and emotional.[38] Intensive supervision programs in particular may place restrictions on the probationer, who may then view probation negatively.

Research in the U.S. has found that some offenders rate being on probation as more punitive than short-term prison sentences.[39,40] Offender perceptions of probation may be due, in part, to their previous experience in prison and on probation: Offenders who have been previously incarcerated may not find confinement as punitive as close supervision in the community.

THE CHALLENGE OF PROBATION PRACTICE

Historically, little attention has been given to the challenges faced by probation officers in carrying out their duties. Research has identified a number of areas of concern, including those discussed in the following sections.

OCCUPATIONAL STRESS

Studies have found that probation officers have higher stress levels than in the general population. Studies indicate that the most satisfying aspect of a probation officer's job is working with offenders, and the least satisfying are the ever-increasing administrative duties, including paperwork and dealing with agency management.[41,42]

Women probation officers may have higher levels of stress than their male counterparts, related in part to safety concerns when supervising male probationers.[43,44] There is evidence that incidents involving probation officer safety are vastly underreported. A major reason why probation officers do not conduct home visits is safety concerns.

One probation officer's reflection on the impact of occupational stress on his life is presented in Corrections File 10.3.

SUPERVISING HIGH-RISK AND HIGH-NEED PROBATIONERS

There has been an increase in the needs and risk levels of offenders placed on probation and in the numbers of offenders who are mentally disordered or who have been convicted of sex-related crimes and crimes of violence. Today, more probationers have been convicted of a violent crime and many probationers have been assessed as being high risk.[45]

This may make it difficult for probation officers to access programs and services for their clients. One probation officer noted:

> I have a client on my caseload who called 9-1-1 hundreds of times one weekend. He is mentally disabled, but forensic services will not do an assessment on him until his alcohol addiction problems have first been addressed. (probation officer, personal communication with C.T. Griffiths, 2012)

CORRECTIONS FILE 10.3

A PROBATION OFFICER'S ACCOUNT OF THE IMPACT OF OCCUPATIONAL STRESS

As a probation officer, part of my job is to write presentencing reports. To do so I [pored] over documents related to crimes committed. I've always thought of myself as a tough guy. Lately though, when I deal with cases where the victim was a child, I can't shake the anger I feel. I find myself wanting to punch something. Sometimes I've even felt like crying, but I just won't allow myself to do that, because I'm not weak. Instead I end up hating the world. More than once I've caught myself putting off looking through files. Frequently on my way home I buy a six-pack. I then go to take care of my horses, drinking while I do that. I stay away from my family's happy chatter as much as I can. They are so naïve and ignorant! I don't want to burst their bubble, so I don't talk to them about my work. But I worry constantly about my children's safety. I am very strict with them, especially about where they go and who they hang out with. I get into arguments with my wife who objects to my repetitive coaching of my kids to not trust anyone outside immediate family. I often fantasize about what I would do to an offender if he hurt one of my kids.

Source: From C. Spinaris. 2013, January 7. "Occupational Exposure to Primary and Secondary Trauma in Corrections," *Corrections.com*. http://www.corrections.com/news/article/31682-occupational-exposure-to-primary-and-secondary -trauma-in-corrections. Reprinted by permission of the author.

HEAVY WORKLOADS AND HIGH CASELOADS

The duties of probation officers have continued to expand and now include providing bail supervision for adult criminal courts, preparing PSRs for sentencing courts, supervising offenders on conditional release orders, and liaising with social services, the police, and the courts.

Probation officers in many jurisdictions have experienced increases in their caseloads, some of which are in the 100+ range per officer. The average caseload is often in the 60 to 70 probationers per officer range.[46,47] High caseloads have been cited as a major factor in why probation officers generally do not do home visits.[48]

A LACK OF PROBATION OFFICER–OFFENDER CONTACT AND INTERVENTION

Probation officers may have only limited in-person contact with the individual offenders on their caseloads. Contact may be by telephone, and when the officer does meet with the offender, the session may be short. Close supervision is particularly important for offenders on probation who are designated as high risk. Several U.S. and Canadian jurisdictions have attempted to address this issue by setting up "probationer kiosks." See At Issue 10.1.

AT ISSUE 10.1

PROBATIONER KIOSKS: AN IDEA FOR CANADA?

The majority of offenders in Canada and the U.S. are on probation, and systems of corrections are exploring ways to provide cost-effective services to probationers. This has led to the creation of "reporting kiosks" in a number of U.S. states and Canadian jurisdictions.[a] These kiosks are either ATM-like machines or stand-alone computers, placed in convenient locations, such as probation offices or police departments. Biometric identification, such as fingerprints, are used to verify the probationer, who logs in and is prompted to answer a number of questions related to his or her employment, as well as any contact with the criminal justice system. After answering the questions, the probationer is provided with a receipt indicating that he or she had "reported in." Lower-risk probationers, as determined by the RNR model, are most often designated to use the kiosks. An evaluation of the program in New York state found that lower-risk probationers who use the kiosks have lower re-arrest rates than higher-risk probationers who meet face-to-face with a probation officer.[b] A study of reporting kiosks in Maryland involving 103 low-risk offenders, including sex offenders, found that 2 percent reoffended within 90 days of being on probation, compared to the typical rare of 10 percent.[c] Another U.S. study found widespread support for the kiosks among probation officers.[d] This suggests that reporting kiosks may be a viable alternative for lower-risk probationers.

As of 2017, self-reporting kiosks for probationers were being piloted in several sites in British Columbia. Probationers log on via a biometric scan of their fingers. Here are the instructions that are provided to probationers in order to "report in":

Welcome to eServices

Step 1—Enter your CS # on the touch screen and press
Step 2—Put your finger on the reader
Step 3—You now have access to your information and services:

QUESTIONS

1. In view of the challenges that surround providing supervision for probationers in Canada, would you support a pilot project using reporting kiosks?

2. What are the potential strengths and limitations of the use of this technology in probation?

3. What are the potential issues that might surround the increasing use of technology in corrections, in this case, for the "supervision" of probationers?

---

[a] J. Jannetta and R. Halberstadt. 2011. *Kiosk Supervision for the District of Columbia*, Washington, DC: Urban Institute. https://justnet.org/pdf/Kiosk%20Supervision%20 for%20the%20District%20of%20Columbia%20-%202011.pdf.

[b] J.A. Wilson, W. Naro, and J.F. Austin. 2007. *Innovations in Probation: Assessing New York City's Automated Reporting System*. Washington, DC: The JFA Institute. http://www.pbpp.pa.gov/Information/Documents/Research/OSR3.pdf.

[c] Maryland Department of Public Safety and Correctional Services. 2002. *Kiosk Reporting System: A Report to the Budget Committees of the Maryland General Assembly*. Annapolis, MD: Author.

[d] E.M. Ahlin, C.A. Hagen, M.A. Harmon, and S. Crosse. 2016. "Kiosk Reporting among Probationers in the United States," *The Prison Journal, 96*(5), 688–708.

PROBATION SERVICES IN REMOTE AND NORTHERN REGIONS

Unique challenges are involved in providing effective probation services in northern and remote communities where community services and support may be limited or non-existent. This, and the isolation, may make it difficult to recruit and retain probation officers. At one point, for example, only one-half of the 25 communities in Nunavut had full-time probation officers.[49] These difficulties are particularly acute given the high rates of crime and violence that afflict many northern and remote communities. Concerns about the effectiveness of probation in these regions were reflected in the comments of an Inuit woman who had been the victim of violence in one of the communities:

> He was charged with assault. Then, a few weeks later, he was in JP court and he got six months probation. I thought it was going to be ok because after the JP court he said he would quit beating me up. But after one month he started again. That was against his probation. He'd go see his probation officer every month and when he still had six or eight months to go, he quit going. Nobody said anything and nothing happened. He was still drinking when he was on probation. It's just a lot of words, no action.[50]

As noted in Chapter 7, circuit court judges sentencing offenders in northern and remote communities may be reluctant to sentence offenders to custody in correctional institutions that may be hundreds of kilometres from the offender's home community.

SUPERVISING A DIVERSE CLIENTELE

An unstudied dimension of probation practice in Canada is the challenge presented by factors such as language, culture, religion, and ethnicity. Most probation officers in Canada are Caucasian, yet their probation caseloads may reflect the diversity of Canadian society. English- or French-speaking probation officers can expect to encounter difficulties when supervising newly arrived Canadians, who may have limited language skills; similarly, cultural differences may impede the development of therapeutic relationships with probationers as well as with community partners. Research in the United States found that probationers who were supervised by an officer of their own race had more positive perceptions of that officer.[51] This question has not yet been explored in Canada.

THE NEED FOR REFORM: FINDINGS FROM ONTARIO AND BRITISH COLUMBIA

Enquiries into probation practice in Ontario and British Columbia illustrate the challenges facing this correctional strategy. In 2017 in Ontario, approximately 45,000 offenders were serving sentences in the community on probation or parole, supervised by 865 probation and parole officers. In its 2014 report, the Office of the Auditor General of Ontario identified a number of issues surrounding probation and provincial parole, including risk assessments not being completed on offenders within the specified time limits, the lack of information on offenders who breached the conditions of their probation, lower-risk offenders being over-supervised while high-risk probationers were under-supervised, and a failure to track offender participation in, and the effectiveness of various treatment programs.[52] A follow-up study by the Office of the Auditor General found that many of these issues had not been addressed.[53]

The challenges facing the probation system in Ontario were subsequently highlighted by a media investigation. It found that offenders, including those who had been convicted of violent crimes, were not being properly supervised in the community.[54] One probation officer stated, "In some cases we are talking about violent, serious offenders that aren't properly being monitored in the community." An offender who had been placed on probation following conviction for sexual assault noted, "Nobody, nobody has ever come [to his home]. No police, no probation officer. . . . You don't know what is happening, what I am doing. You don't know because you never come to my house. . . . They [offenders] think it's a joke."[55] A Crown attorney in Ontario noted that probation officials often did not charge offenders for breaches of conditions, stating, "They'd prefer they [charges] weren't laid. They want them to disappear."[56]

Similar findings have been reported from audits of community corrections in other jurisdictions. The Office of the Auditor General of British Columbia, for example, found that there were shortcomings in training for probation officers, and that there was no consistency in the identification of the risk and needs of probationers and access to interventions.[57] In addition, the study found that only 35 percent of offenders with a condition on their probation order to complete a treatment program did so.[58] In a follow-up investigation, the Office of the Auditor General found that many of the problems persisted and that many of the previous recommendations that the Community Corrections Division indicated had been "fully or substantially implemented" had only been "partially implemented."[59]

The findings in Ontario and British Columbia raise significant concerns as to whether systems of corrections are able to engage in the reforms required to be more effective in achieving their objectives. The discussion in Chapters 11 and 12 will reveal that this same question can be asked of institutional corrections and of community corrections for offenders released from confinement.

SURVEILLANCE IN THE COMMUNITY: THE USE OF ELECTRONIC MONITORING (EM) AND GPS TRACKING

> Ultimately, Maurice started to reflect on the quality of life under EM: "I'm free but actually am I free?" He concluded that the monitor was "like holding something over a dog's nose, teasing him with food . . . like hitting the lottery and losing the ticket. You are still incarcerated, no matter how you look at it." (offender on GPS-enabled ankle bracelet)[60]

A key trend in corrections is the increasing surveillance of offenders under supervision in the community. This has been made possible by technology that allows authorities to track offenders via various forms of electronic monitoring and Global Positioning Systems (GPS). While the use of these technologies may provide alternatives to confinement and allow the offender to remain in the community, there are serious issues surrounding privacy and human rights.

Electronic monitoring (EM) is used by provincial and territorial systems of corrections and Correctional Service Canada to monitor offenders who are under supervision in the community. This has resulted in an increasing number of persons who are under this type of surveillance.

Electronic monitoring

A correctional strategy that involves placing an offender under house arrest and then using electronic equipment to ensure that the conditions of supervision are fulfilled.

▲ Electronic monitoring anklet with GPS

In some provinces, EM is imposed by the sentencing judge, while in others, EM is used as a condition of early release from incarceration. Where EM is used in support of an alternative to confinement, its primary objective is to ensure public safety while at the same time allowing the offender to remain in the community. Generally, only offenders who have been convicted of less serious, non-violent offences and who have a stable residence and a telephone are eligible to participate in EM programs.

There is an increased focus on the use of EM to monitor persons on bail who, due to their risk factors, would have otherwise been kept in remand. In Ontario, this is done via compliance monitoring provided by a private company (Recovery Science Corporation; www.recoveryscience.ca). The expanded use of EM for bail could potentially reduce the numbers of persons on remand, which currently exceed those in sentenced custody.

Increasingly, GPS tracking systems are being used to monitor the location and movements of high-risk offenders, including sex offenders. GPS technology has the capacity to track an offender's movements on a continuous basis and makes it possible to determine where an offender is at any given moment. In addition, it is possible to "customize" tracking and to specify the boundaries of an offender's movements and to set out locations where the offender is not permitted (e.g., a sex offender may be prohibited from going near schools or playgrounds). A monitoring program can be designed that will alert both the offender and the agency if the offender violates certain area restrictions.

Electronic monitoring has not been without its critics. In particular, there are concerns with the expansion of surveillance and the impact of EM on offenders, with one observer calling it a "flawed alternative."[61] Critics contend that EM must be used as a true alternative to incarceration—that is, instead of confinement, rather than an additional condition to release into the community—and that it should facilitate, rather than hinder, a person's integration into the community.[62]

A concern is that advances in technology will allow the enhancement of surveillance to include the capacity to monitor a person's physiological and brain activity, to remotely administer drugs, and to provide a video record of a person's movements. It is likely that the surveillance of offenders will remain a highly controversial issue. See Critical Thinking Exercise 10.1.

There are also concerns that the expansion of EM will come at the expense of probation and parole officers developing relationships with offenders that will facilitate change.[63] It was previously noted that, in many jurisdictions, probation supervision is often limited to office visits. The expansion of the use of surveillance technology may further reduce face-to-face contact.

THE EFFECTIVENESS OF ALTERNATIVES TO CONFINEMENT

Research File 10.1 sets out what is known about the effectiveness of alternatives to confinement. Note that community corrections agencies often do not gather the information required to determine the effectiveness of probation practice.[64] And few of the more common programs for probationers, including those operated by private contractors, have been evaluated.

THE EFFECTIVENESS OF ALTERNATIVES TO CONFINEMENT

Does Traditional Diversion Work? Hard to tell. There are few formal evaluations. There is some evidence from U.S. studies that diversion can reduce the seriousness and frequency of reoffending. It may "widen the net" by focusing on low-risk, first-time offenders. There is no evidence that diversion has any impact on correctional populations. It may increase the justice system's workload and costs.[a,b] Problem-solving courts as an alternative to the justice system have shown promise. See Chapter 7.

Do Electronic Supervision and GPS Work? Uncertain. Research, conducted primarily in the U.S., has produced mixed results. Some studies have found that EM can play a significant role in reducing rates of recidivism, even among more serious offenders, including sex offenders.[c,d] A California study ($N = 516$) found that sex offenders on parole monitored by GPS had their parole revoked less often and committed fewer crimes than a matched set of sex offenders who were not monitored by GPS.[e] However, other studies have concluded that it is uncertain whether the use of GPS tracking prevents sex offending and that GPS tracking may be most useful in investigating offences.[f]

In many jurisdictions, EM is not being used as a true alternative to confinement.[g] There is no evidence that EM programs reduce prison admissions, but they are less costly than incarceration. The perception among probation officers and offenders in a U.S. study was that EM had a negative impact on personal and family relationships and hindered efforts to secure housing and employment.[h]

Are Conditional Sentences Effective? Potentially. There is research evidence to suggest that conditional sentences may be more effective than imprisonment in reducing recidivism.[i] Concerns with CSOs centre on the high of violations of conditions (up to 40 percent of cases)[j] and the inappropriate use of CSO as a sentencing option by judges.

Is Probation Effective? There is no evidence that traditional probation practice reduces reoffending.[k] This is due to a variety of factors, including the lack of training of probation officers in strategies that may improve probation outcomes, in particular the absence of the principles of RNR in probation practice. While many probationers who have committed less serious crimes successfully complete, less positive results are reported for offenders with lengthy criminal records and who have additional issues, such as addiction and mental illness.[l]

Research studies suggest that probation is most effective with those offenders who are in a stable personal relationship, are employed, have higher levels of education, and do not have an extensive criminal record. Specialized supervision units can be effective in increasing offender accountability and reducing rates of reoffending, and have a positive impact on victim satisfaction.[m] There is growing evidence that incorporating the principles of RNR into probation practice improves the quality of supervision and case outcomes.[n]

Potential obstacles to effective probation practice are a lack of training for probation officers, the failure to identify the risk and needs of offenders and to design appropriate interventions, and low program completion rates by offenders.

Does Intensive Supervision Probation Work? Yes. These programs can manage risk while providing probationers with access to treatment. ISP may be more cost-effective than incarceration and produce better outcomes.[o]

------

[a] J. Bonta. 1998. "Adult Offender Diversion Programs: Research Summary." *Corrections Research and Development, 3*(1). http://www.publicsafety.gc.ca/cnt/rsrcs/pblctns/ffndr-dvrsn/ffndr-dvrsn-eng.pdf.

[b] J. Nuffield. 1997. *Diversion Programs for Adults.* Ottawa: Solicitor General Canada.

[c] W. Bales, K. Mann, T. Blomberg, G. Gaes, K. Barrick, K. Dhungana, and B. McManus. 2010. *A Quantitative and Qualitative Assessment of Electronic Monitoring.* Washington, DC: National Institute of Justice, U.S. Department of Justice. http://www.criminologycenter.fsu.edu/p/pdf/EM%20Evaluation%20Final%20Report%20for%20NIJ.pdf.

[d] S. Bottos. 2007. *An Overview of Electronic Monitoring in Corrections: Issues and Implications.* Ottawa: Correctional Service of Canada. http://www.csc-scc.gc.ca/research/r182-eng.shtml.

[e] P. Bulman. 2013, February. "Sex Offenders Monitored by GPS Found to Commit Fewer Crimes," *NIJ Journal, 271,* 22–25. https://www.nij.gov/journals/271/pages/gps-monitoring.aspx.

[f] M. Meloy. 2009. "You Can Run But You Cannot Hide: GPS and Electronic Surveillance of Offenders," in *Sex Offender Laws: Failed Policies, New Directions,* edited by R. Wright, 165–179. New York: Spring Publishing Company.

[g] J. Bonta, S. Wallace-Capretta, and J. Rooney. 2000. "Can Electronic Monitoring Make a Difference? An Evaluation of Three Canadian Programs," *Crime and Delinquency, 46*(1), 61–75.

[h] Bales et al., *A Quantitative and Qualitative Assessment of Electronic Monitoring.*

[i] J. Cid. 2009. "Is Imprisonment Criminogenic? A Comparative Study of Recidivism Rates Between Prison and Suspended Prison Sanctions," *European Journal of Criminology, 6*(6), 459–480.

[j] D. North. 2001. "The Catch-22 of Conditional Sentencing," *Criminal Law Quarterly, 44*(3), 342–374.

[k] J. Bonta, G. Bourgon, T. Rugge, T-L. Scott, A.K. Yessine, L. Gutierrez, and J. Li. 2011. "An Experimental Demonstration of Training Probation Officers in Evidence-Based Community Supervision," *Criminal Justice and Behavior, 38*(11), 1129.

[l] M. DeLisi and P.J. Conis. 2013. *American Corrections: Theory, Research, Policy, and Practice* (2nd ed.). Burlington, MA: Jones & Bartlett Learning, p. 248.

[m] A.R. Klein, D. Wilson, A.H. Crowe, and M. DeMichele. 2008. *Evaluation of the Rhode Island Probation Specialized Domestic Violence Supervision Unit,* Washington, DC: U.S. Department of Justice. http://www.ncjrs.gov/pdffiles1/nij/grants/222912.pdf.

[n] Bonta et al., "An Experimental Demonstration of Training Probation Officers in Evidence-Based Community Supervision."

[o] DeLisi and Conis, *American Corrections,* p. 251.

SUMMARY

This chapter has provided an overview of the sentencing options that provide an alternative to incarceration and the strategies that are used by systems of corrections to manage this population of offenders. These include diversion, conditional sentences, and probation, which is the most frequently used alternative to custody. The recruitment and training of probation officers and the role and responsibilities of probation officers were examined. It was noted that probation officers play a dual role of providing support for probationers while at the same time enforcing the conditions of probation orders. A number of challenges in probation practice were identified and discussed, and the need for reform was highlighted by enquiries into probation practice in Ontario and British Columbia. The increasing use of technology for monitoring offenders in the community was noted and questions were posed as to whether there should be limits on the surveillance of offenders in the community. The chapter concluded with a review of research on the effectiveness of various alternatives to confinement.

KEY POINTS REVIEW

1. Corrections includes both non-carceral (non-institutional) and carceral (institutional) programs and services.

2. There are a variety of sentencing options that keep persons out of confinement.

3. Conditional sentences are a widely used and often controversial alternative to incarceration.

4. Probation is the most frequently used alternative to incarceration and is different from conditional sentences and from parole.

5. Probation falls under the jurisdiction of the provincial and territorial governments and each has developed their own standards for recruitment and training.

6. Probation officers have a wide range of responsibilities, including preparing pre-sentence reports (PSRs), conducting risk and needs assessments and supervising offenders. Probation officers confront a number of challenges in carrying out their mandate.

7. Probation officers play a dual role in providing assistance and support for offenders and enforcing the conditions of the probation order, although in recent years there has been an increasing emphasis on control and surveillance.

8. The principles of RNR are widely used in probation practice, including in the STICS initiative.

9. Probationers may experience emotional and economic challenges due to the conditions imposed on them while under supervision in the community.

10. Probation offices experience a number of challenges in carrying out their responsibilities, including stress associated with their jobs, heavy workloads and high caseloads, the challenges of supervising high-risk and high-needs offenders, and maintaining in-person contact with their clients.

11. Inquiries into probation in Ontario and British Columbia found significant issues, including shortcomings in probation officer training, a failure to complete risk assessments on offenders, and the failure of probation to track offender participation in treatment programs and to assess the effectiveness of the interventions.

12. The increasing use of technology to monitor offenders in the community, electronic monitoring and GPS, has raised a number of issues.

13. Research on the effectiveness of alternatives to confinement has produced mixed results.

14. Probation appears to be most effective with offenders who are employed, have stable family relationships, and who do not have an extensive criminal record.

KEY TERM QUESTIONS

1. How is **corrections** best defined?

2. Describe **non-carceral** and **carceral corrections** and provide examples of each type.

3. Identify and discuss the objectives of **diversion** programs.

4. What is **net-widening** and why is it a concern associated with diversion programs?

5. What are **optional conditions**, why are they important for offenders being supervised in the community, and what are some examples of these types of conditions?

6. Describe the **risk**, **need**, and **responsivity** (RNR) model and its use in probation practice.

7. Describe **intensive probation supervision (ISP)** and provide a program example.

8. What are the **pains of probation** and how do they manifest themselves among probationers?

9. Describe the use of **electronic monitoring**, including the potential role of GPS technology, as a corrections strategy.

CRITICAL THINKING EXERCISE

Critical Thinking Exercise 10.1

Should There Be Limits on the Surveillance of Offenders under Community Supervision?

It is likely that, in the coming years, advances in technology will allow authorities to not only track offenders but also control their behaviour. Sophisticated tracking devices and chip implants in offenders, for example, would allow authorities to determine not only the location of an offender who is under supervision, but also whether the offender is impaired by alcohol or drugs and, potentially, the offender's thought patterns. The use of this type of technology could result in significant reductions in the number of offenders confined in correctional institutions and even allow offenders who have been convicted of serious crimes to remain in the community under supervision. However, the use of technology in this manner would also raise ethical and privacy issues as well as questions about the limits of government control over persons under supervision.

Your Thoughts?

1. What would be your position on the potential use of technology that would track offenders as well as monitor their physiology and thoughts?

2. Indonesia is considering implanting tracking "chips" into offenders, which would allow them to be "followed" at all times. Should this be considered in Canada for certain high-risk offenders who are released into the community?

3. Should the Canadian federal government pass legislation placing limits on the use of technology for monitoring offenders under supervision in the community?

CLASS/GROUP DISCUSSION EXERCISE

Class/Group Discussion 10.1

Should All Sex Offenders in Canada Who Are under Supervision in the Community Be Required to Wear an Electronic Monitoring and GPS Tracking Device?

Watch the following videos:

> "Keeping Tabs on Sex Offenders with GPS Monitoring," December 18, 2010, https://www.youtube.com/watch?v=_k6dR2jmMhA

> "All Sex Offenders on GPS under California Parole Division Supervision," December 18, 2010, https://www.youtube.com/watch?v=Cc74MVlBwzM (note that probation officers in California are armed)

Your Thoughts?

1. What are the arguments for and against legislation requiring all sex offenders in Canada to wear electronic monitoring and GPS tracking devices?

2. What is your view on this issue?

MEDIA LINKS

"Warriors Against Violence," *CBC News*, July 6, 2015, http://www.cbc.ca/news/indigenous/warriors-against-violence-tries-to-heal-aboriginal-men-1.3136168

"Who's Watching? 4,500 Outstanding Warrants for Alleged Probation and Conditional Sentence Violations in Ontario," *Global News*, May 10, 2017. Follow the links in this article for a several part media series on probation in Ontario, http://globalnews.ca/news/3430313/4500-outstanding-warrants-for-alleged-probation-and-conditional-sentence-violations-in-ontario.

"Who's Watching? Ontario's Probation System 'a Joke,' Say Offenders" (Part 1), *Global News*, May 9, 2017, http://globalnews.ca/news/3429225/ontarios-probation-system-a-joke-say-offenders

REFERENCES

1. P. Bowal, S. Callbeck, and B. Lines. 2014, September 5. "Absolute and Conditional Discharges in Canadian Criminal Law," *LawNow*. http://www.lawnow.org/absolute-conditional-discharges-canadian-criminal-law.

2. Ibid.

3. M. Spratt. 2013, November 4. "Canadian Debtors' Prison, Victim Fine Surcharges, and Half Truths" [blog post]. http://www.michaelspratt.com/law-blog/2013/11/4/zv95us1eopwzwbsray6o2ubzau2ind.

4. C. Hamilton. 2017, May 4. "No Longer Allowing Community Service in Lieu of Paying Traffic Tickets Could Hurt Sask. Non-Profits," *CBC News*. http://www.cbc.ca/news/canada/saskatoon/fine-option-rules-could-hurt-non-profits-1.4098904.

5. L. Butler, J. Goodman-Delahunty, and R. Lulham. 2012. "Effectiveness of Pre-Trial Community-Based Diversion in Reducing Reoffending by Adult Intrafamilial Child Sex Offenders," *Criminal Justice and Behavior*, 39(4), 493–513.

6. D.E. Roe-Sepowitz, K.E. Hickle, M.P. Loubert, and T. Egan. 2011. "Adult Prostitution Recidivism: Risk Factors and Impact of a Diversion Program," *Journal of Offender Rehabilitation*, 50(5), 272–285.

7. A. Verhaff and H. Scott. 2015. "Individual Factors Predicting Mental Health Court Diversion Outcome," *Research on Social Work Practice*, 25(2), 213–228.

8. T. Van Camp and J.-A. Wemmers. 2013. "Victim Satisfaction with Restorative Justice: More Than Simply Procedural Justice," *International Review of Victimology*, 19(2), 117–143.

9. J.V. Roberts. 2012. "Serving Time at Home: The Conditional Sentence of Imprisonment," in *Criminal Justice in Canada: A Reader* (4th ed.), edited by J.V. Roberts and M.G. Grossman, 178–186. Toronto: Nelson.

10. Office of the Auditor General of British Columbia. 2016. *Progress Audit Report. The Effectiveness of B.C. Community Corrections*. Victoria: Author. http://www.bcauditor.com/sites/default/files/publications/reports/OAGBC_Progress_Community_Corrections_FINAL.pdf.

11. A.A. Reid. 2017. "The (Differential) Utilization of Conditional Sentences among Aboriginal Offenders in Canada," *Canadian Criminal Law Review*, 22(2), 133–258.

12. Department of Justice Canada. 2017, January. "JustFacts: Sentencing in Canada." http://justice.gc.ca/eng/rp-pr/jr/jf-pf/2017/jan01.html.

13. Alberta Justice and Solicitor General. 2017. "Probation Officer." https://www.solgps.alberta.ca/careers/probation_officer/Pages/default.aspx.

14. Ontario Ministry of Public Safety and Correctional Services. 2016. "Careers in Corrections: Becoming a Probation and Parole Officer." https://www.mcscs.jus.gov.on.ca/english/corr_serv/careers_in_corr/careers_pp_officer/careers_pp_officer.html.

15. K. Hannah-Moffat and P. Maurutto. 2010. "Re-Contextualizing Pre-Sentence Reports: Risk and Race," *Punishment & Society*, 12(3), 262–286 at p. 272.

16. Ibid., p. 279.

17. P.J. Kennealy, K.L. Skeam, S.M. Manchuk and J.E. Louden. 2012. "Firm, Fair, and Caring Officer-Offender Relationships Protect against Supervision Failure," *Law and Human Behavior*, 36(6), 496–505.

18. B. DeLude, D. Mitchell, and C. Barber. 2012. "The Probationer's Perspective on the Probation Officer-Probationer Relationship and Satisfaction with Probation," *Federal Probation*, 67(1), 35–39.

19. J. Bonta, T. Rugge, T.-L. Scott, G. Bourgon, and A.K. Yessine. 2008. "Exploring the Black Box of Community Supervision," *Journal of Offender Rehabilitation*, 47(3), 248–270.

20. J. Louden, J.L. Skeem, J. Camp, and E. Christensen. 2008. "Supervising Probationers with Mental Disorder: How Do Agencies Respond to Violations?" *Criminal Justice and Behavior*, 35(7), 832–847.

21. J. Matthews. 2009. "'People First: Probation Officer Perspectives on Probation Work'–A Practitioner's Response," *Probation Journal*, 56(1), 61–67.

22. R. Burnett and F. McNeill. 2005. "The Place of the Officer-Offender Relationship in Assisting Offenders to Desist from Crime," *Probation Journal*, 52(3), 221–242.

23. Alberta Justice and Solicitor General. 2017. "Priority Prolific Offender Program (P-POP)." https://justice.alberta.ca/programs_services/safe/Pages/p-pop.aspx.

24. Ibid.

25. N. Hixt. 2013, May 27. "Breaking the Cycle: Repeat Offenders Who Are Changing Their Ways," *Global News*. http://globalnews.ca/news/593752/breaking-the-cycle-a-repeat-offender-who-is-changing-his-ways.

26. P. Thompson and J. Schutte. 2010. *Integrated Justice Services Project: Implementing Problem-Solving Justice*. Edmonton: Government of Alberta. http://www.courtinnovation.org/sites/default/files/documents/Integrated%20Justice%20Service%20Project.pdf.

27. J. Bonta, G. Bourgon, T. Rugge, T-L. Scott, A.K. Yessine, L. Gutierrez, and J. Li. 2011. "An Experimental Demonstration of Training Probation Officers in Evidence-Based Community Supervision," *Criminal Justice and Behavior*, 38(11), 1127–1148.

28. D.A. Andrews and J. Bonta. 2010. *The Psychology of Criminal Conduct* (5th ed.). New Providence, NJ: LexisNexis Matthew Bender.

29. J.L. Skeem, H.J. Steadman, and S.M. Manchak. 2015. "Applicability of the Risk-Need-Responsivity Model to Persons with Mental Illness Involved in the Criminal Justice System," *Psychiatric Services*, 66(9), 916–922.

30. T. Ward, J. Mesler, and P.M. Yates. 2007. "Reconstructing the Risk-Need-Responsivity Model: A Theoretical Elaboration and Evaluation," *Aggression and Violent Behavior*, 12(2), 208–228.

31. J. Bonta, C. Gress, and L. Gutierrez. 2013. "Taking the Leap: From Pilot Project to Wide-Scale Implementation of the Strategic Training Initiative in Community Supervision (STICS)," *Justice Research and Policy*, 15(1), 17–35.

32. B.L. Gerger. 2011. "'Now You See Me, Now You Don't'–Service Delivery of Fetal Alcohol Spectrum Disorder (FASD) Offenders: A Study of Policy and Practice in Saskatchewan Community Corrections." Unpublished MA Thesis. Regina: Justice Studies, University of Regina, p. 102. http://ourspace.uregina.ca/bitstream/handle/10294/3540/Gerger_Bonny_Lynn_192303351_MA_JUST_Spring2012.pdf?sequence=1.

33. Ibid.

34. G. Bourgon, L. Gutierrez, and J. Ashton. 2012. *From Case Management to Change Agent: The Evolution of 'What Works' in Community Supervision*. Ottawa: Public Safety Canada. https://www.publicsafety.gc.ca/cnt/rsrcs/pblctns/2012-01-cmc/2012-01-cmc-eng.pdf.

35. M. Weinrath, M. Doerksen, and J. Watts. 2015. "The Impact of an Intensive Supervision Program on High-Risk Offenders:

Manitoba's COHROU Program," *Canadian Journal of Criminology and Criminal Justice*, 57(2), 253–288.

36. B.K. Applegate, H.P. Smith, A.H. Sitren, and N.F. Springer. 2009. "From the Inside: The Meaning of Probation to Probationers," *Criminal Justice Review*, 34(1), 80–95.

37. R.A. Malatest & Associates Ltd. 2008. *BC Community Corrections Client Survey Research. Client Satisfaction– Community Corrections Services*. Victoria, BC: Ministry of Public Safety and Solicitor General.

38. I. Durnescu. 2011. "Pains of Probation: Effective Practice and Human Rights," *International Journal of Offender Therapy and Comparative Criminology*, 55(4), 530–545.

39. B.M. Crouch. 1993. "Is Incarceration Really Worse? Analysis of Offender's Preferences for Prison over Probation," *Justice Quarterly*, 10(1), 67–88.

40. J. Petersilia and S. Turner. 1993. "Intensive Probation and Parole," in *Crime and Justice: A Review of the Research*, edited by M. Tonry, 281–335. Chicago: University of Chicago Press.

41. J. Annison, T. Eadie, and C. Knight. 2008. "People First: Probation Officer Perspectives on Probation Work," *Probation Journal*, 55(3), 259–271.

42. Matthews, "'People First: Probation Officer Perspectives on Probation Work.'"

43. C. Simmons, J.K. Cochran, and W.R. Blount. 2007. "The Effects of Job-Related Stress and Job Satisfaction on Probation Officers' Inclination to Quit," *American Journal of Criminal Justice*, 21(2), 213–229.

44. R.N. Slate, T.L. Wells, and W.W. Johnson. 2003. "State Probation Officer Stress and Perceptions of Participation in Workplace Decision Making," *Crime and Delinquency*, 49(4), 519–541.

45. L. Landry and M. Sinha. 2008. "Adult Correctional Services in Canada, 2005/2006," *Juristat*, 28(6). Statistics Canada Catalogue no. 85-002-X. Ottawa: Minister of Industry. http://www.statcan.gc.ca/pub/85-002-x/2008006/article/ 10593-eng.htm.

46. Office of the Auditor General of British Columbia. 2011. *Effectiveness of BC Community Corrections*. Victoria: Author. http://www.bcauditor.com/sites/default/files/publications/ 2011/report_10/report/OAGBC-BC-Community -Corrections%20for%20print.pdf.

47. J. Hamilton-McCharles. 2015, January 5. "Insight into Probation and Parole," *The Nugget* (North Bay, ON). http://www.nugget.ca/2015/01/05/insight-into-probation -and-parole.

48. *CBC News*. 2015, September 26. "Ontario Probation Officers Say Workload Too Great to Do Home Visits." http://www.cbc.ca/news/canada/ottawa/ontario-probation -officers-understaffed-1.3245289.

49. *CBC News*. 2009, June 16. "More Than Half of Nunavut's Communities Lack Probation Officers." http://www.cbc.ca/ news/canada/north/more-than-half-of-nunavut-s-communities -lack-probation-officers-1.778474.

50. C.T. Griffiths, E. Zellerer, D.S. Wood, and G. Saville. 1995. *Crime, Law, and Justice Among Inuit in the Baffin Region, N.W.T., Canada*. Burnaby, BC: Criminology Research Centre, Simon Fraser University.

51. N.F. Springer, B.K. Applegate, H.P. Smith, and A.H. Sitren. 2009. "Exploring the Determinants of Probationers' Perceptions of Their Supervising Officers," *Journal of Offender Rehabilitation*, 48(3), 210–227.

52. Office of the Auditor General of Ontario. 2014. *Annual Report 2014*. Chapter 3. "Adult Community Corrections and Ontario Parole Board." Toronto: Author. http://www.auditor .on.ca/en/content/annualreports/arreports/en14/301en14 .pdf.

53. Office of the Auditor General of Ontario. 2016. *Annual Report 2016*. Chapter 1. "Adult Community Corrections and the Ontario Parole Board." Toronto: Author. http:// www.auditor.on.ca/en/content/annualreports/arreports/ en16/v2_101en16.pdf.

54. C. Jarvis and L. Young. 2017, May 9. "Who's Watching? Ontario's Probation System 'a Joke,' Say Offenders," *Global News*. http://globalnews.ca/news/3429225/ontarios -probation-system-a-joke-say-offenders.

55. Ibid.

56. Ibid.

57. Office of the Auditor General of British Columbia, *Effectiveness of BC Community Corrections*.

58. Ibid.

59. Ibid.

60. J. Kilgore. 2016, October 20. "E-Carceration: The Problematic World of Being on an Electronic Monitor," *AlterNet*. http://www.alternet.org/human-rights/electronic -monitoring-restrictive-and-wrong.

61. J. Kilgore. 2015. *Electronic Monitoring Is Not the Answer: Critical Reflections on a Flawed Alternative*. Urbana, IL: Urbana-Champaign Independent Media Center. http:// centerformediajustice.org/wp-content/uploads/2015/10/ EM-Report-Kilgore-final-draft-10-4-15.pdf.

62. Ibid.

63. M. Nellis. 2014. "Upgrading Electronic Monitoring, Downgrading Probation: Reconfiguring 'Offender Management' in England and Wales," *European Journal of Probation*, 6(2), 169–191.

64. Office of the Auditor General of British Columbia, *Effectiveness of BC Community Corrections*.

© Laurie Justus Pace, Graphics One Design, 2014

CHAPTER 11
CORRECTIONAL INSTITUTIONS

After reading this chapter, you should be able to

- Describe the circumstances surrounding the creation of the first penitentiary in Canada.
- Describe the federal and provincial/territorial systems of corrections.
- Discuss how prison architecture reflects philosophies of punishment and correction.
- Describe the types of correctional institutions and how security is maintained.
- Identify and discuss the challenges in managing correctional institutions.
- Provide a profile of the Canadian inmate population, including women inmates and Indigenous inmates.
- Identify several special inmate populations and the challenges they present.
- Discuss overcrowding in correctional institutions and its implications for staff, inmates, and treatment programs.
- Describe the use of segregation, the issues that surround this correctional management strategy, and three cases that changed the use of solitary confinement.
- Describe the recruitment and training of correctional officers, their role and relationships, activities in the prison, and sources of occupational stress.
- Describe the dynamics of life inside prisons, including the inmate code, violence and victimization, and the experience of prison inmates.
- Discuss the classification of offenders, the role of risk/needs profiles, and case management.
- Discuss the effectiveness of correctional treatment programs.

For 150 years in Canada, correctional institutions (as they are now called) have been a core component of the response to criminal offenders and their use shows no sign of decline. These facilities have endured despite ongoing challenges, many of which emerged within the walls of Canada's first penitentiary in the early 1830s—overcrowding, the lack of classification of offenders, limited programming, and inadequate provisions for inmate safety, among others.

Although the architecture of correctional institutions has changed over the centuries, and living conditions are greatly improved, many inmates still live in fear and have difficulty avoiding the more negative features of life inside. And, similar to their earlier counterparts, Canadian institutions in the 21st century continue to hold a disproportionate number of persons who are marginalized in society: the poor, Indigenous persons, and the mentally ill. The dynamics of life inside correctional institutions pose challenges to efforts to address the needs of inmates and to prepare them for release back into the community.

While space considerations prevent an in-depth examination of the history and evolution of Canada corrections, it is possible to present some of the more significant events that contributed to the current state of corrections. (For a more detailed discussion, see Griffiths and Murdoch, *Canadian Corrections*, 5th ed., published by Nelson.)

One way to track the changes in corrections philosophies is to study prison architecture. As an example, see the images in Corrections File 11.1 of Kingston Penitentiary, which was the first prison constructed in Canada in 1835 and which closed in 2013; Pê Sâkâstêw Aboriginal Healing Centre, a federal correctional institution located in Hobbema, Alberta; and Central East Correctional Centre, a 1,184-bed provincial correctional facility located in Lindsay, Ontario.

THE KINGSTON PENITENTIARY, ONTARIO; PÊ SÂKÂSTÊW HEALING LODGE, ALBERTA; CENTRAL EAST CORRECTIONAL CENTRE, ONTARIO

An aerial view of the federal Kingston Penitentiary, constructed in 1835 and closed in 2013

© iStockphoto.com/SkyF

The Pê Sâkâstêw federal minimum security correctional facility for Indigenous offenders is located in Hobbema, Alberta, and based on a healing lodge design.

Courtesy of Correctional Service Canada

Elgin Middlesex Detention Centre

Graig Glover/London Free Press. Material republished with the express permission of Postmedia Network Inc.

QUESTION

1. Compare and contrast the images of the three facilities. What does the architecture of each convey about correctional philosophy?

THE CREATION OF THE CANADIAN PENITENTIARY

The events surrounding the building of the first penitentiary in Kingston, Ontario, in the early 1800s illustrate how changes in the response to crime and criminal offenders can be influenced by social, economic, and political forces. There were influences from the U.S., where between 1790 and 1830, crime came to be viewed as a consequence of community disorder and family instability rather than as a manifestation of individual afflictions. The Americans built penitentiaries in an attempt to create settings in which the criminals could be transformed into useful citizens through religious contemplation and hard work. Some of these institutions operated on a "separate and silent" system, in which prisoners were completely isolated in their cells from one another. This came to be known as the **Pennsylvania model**.

Pennsylvania model (for prisons)

A separate and silent system in which prisoners were completely isolated from one another, eating, working, and sleeping in separate cells.

**Auburn model
(for prisons)**

A system that allowed prisoners to work and eat together during the day and housed in individual cells at night.

In other penitentiaries, in what became known as the **Auburn model** (originating in New York state), prisoners worked and ate together during the day and slept in individual cells at night. A system of strict silence, which forbade prisoners from communicating or even gesturing to one another, was enforced at all times. The Auburn model was the system on which most prisons in the United States and Canada were patterned.

In Canada, the building of the first penitentiary in Kingston, Ontario, was the result of a number of influences, including developments in the U.S., overcrowding in the local jails where there was a lack of classification of inmates, and the view that corporal punishment was improper and degrading.[1] When completed in 1835, the Kingston Penitentiary was the largest public building in Upper Canada. It symbolized a **moral architecture**, one that reflected the themes of order and morality.

Moral architecture

The term used to describe the design of the first penitentiary in Canada, the intent of which was to reflect themes of order and morality.

It was to be a model for those confined in it, as well as for society, and among its goals were the eradication of the underlying causes of crime: intemperance, laziness, and a lack of moral values. Hard labour and a strong emphasis on religion were the focal points of the reformation process within the penitentiary. A strict silent system was enforced. Breaches of prison regulations brought swift and harsh punishment, including flogging, leg irons, solitary confinement, and rations of bread and water.

The conditions in Kingston led to the creation of a Royal Commission in 1848, 13 years after it opened. The **Brown Commission** investigated, and substantiated, charges of mismanagement, theft, and mistreatment of the inmates, including flogging of men, women, and children, some as young as 11.

Brown commission

An investigation into the operation of the Kingston Penitentiary that condemned the use of corporal punishment against inmates and emphasized the need for rehabilitation.

Despite efforts to reform Kingston, corporal punishment, the silent system, and hard labour remained prominent features of prison life. In retrospect, the Brown Commission can perhaps best be viewed as a missed opportunity for Canadians to reconsider the use of imprisonment and to explore potentially more effective ways to prevent crime and reform offenders. For several documentary films on the Kingston Penitentiary, see the Media Links section at the end of this chapter.

LOCAL JAILS AND PROVINCIAL PRISONS

Conditions in the local jails and provincial institutions at this time were generally deplorable. Prisoners were required to pay for their meals, liquor, and rent—and, upon release, for the jailer's fee for his services. Those inmates unable to pay the fee were often confined for additional periods of time or allowed to panhandle on the streets to raise the necessary funds.[2]

Efforts were made to improve the operation of prisons in the 1880s. Federal legislation provided for the appointment of federal prison inspectors and outlined their powers and duties; addressed the need for the separate confinement of women offenders, mentally disordered inmates, and young offenders; and provided for the use of solitary confinement in federal penitentiaries. However, inmates continued to be subjected to a variety of physical disciplinary sanctions, many of which continued in use until the 1930s.[3]

Following World War II, there was a shift toward the treatment model of corrections. The federal prison system introduced vocational training, education, and therapeutic intervention techniques. These included group counselling and individual therapy. The decade of the 1960s was the height of the treatment model and Canadian corrections. However, by the late 20th and early 21st century, there was a shift towards a more conservative model of correctional practice, driven in part by the political agenda of the then federal Conservative government (2006–15). This was noted as a major trend in Canadian criminal justice in Chapter 2. Since 2015, there appears to be a swing back toward a less punitive corrections regimen, aided by the decisions of the courts that have found many of the "get tough on crime" initiatives unconstitutional, including a number of mandatory minimum sentences.

FEDERAL CORRECTIONS

The federal system of corrections is operated by Correctional Service Canada (CSC), an agency of Public Safety Canada. It is responsible for offenders who receive a sentence of two or more years. The CSC, headquartered in Ottawa, has five regions: Atlantic, Quebec, Ontario, Prairie, and Pacific. It operates a variety of facilities, including federal penitentiaries, halfway houses, healing lodges and treatment centres for Indigenous offenders, community parole offices, psychiatric hospitals, reception and assessment centres, health care centres, palliative care units, and an addiction research centre. Also, CSC has partnered with not-for-profit organizations such as the John Howard Society, St. Leonard's Society, and the Elizabeth Fry Society to operate its halfway houses across the country.

PROVINCIAL AND TERRITORIAL CORRECTIONS

The large majority (96 percent) of convicted offenders receive sentences that place them under the jurisdiction of provincial/territorial correctional authorities. Just more than half the custodial sentences imposed by the courts are for less than one year.[4] As a result, the larger percentage of offenders in Canada are confined in provincial and territorial facilities.

The provincial/territorial governments operate correctional facilities and remand centres. The provinces also operate specialized institutions for offenders with severe mental health issues. For an inside look at a specialized institution for offenders with severe mental health issues in Ontario, view the documentary film, "Out of Mind, Out of Sight: Inside the Brockville Psych," listed in the Media Links section at the end of this chapter.

FACILITIES OPERATED BY NON-PROFIT ORGANIZATIONS

There are a variety of correctional facilities and programs operated by non-profit organizations across the country, the most well-known being the Elizabeth Fry Society, the John Howard Society, and St. Leonard's Society. The Native Counselling Service of Alberta focuses its efforts on Indigenous offenders. As examples, the St. Leonard's Society operates the eight-bed, multi-level Madame Justice Louise Arbour House (named after the former chief justice of the Supreme Court of Canada), which provides a residence for women who are challenged by mental health, substance abuse, and other issues.

In Edmonton, the Native Counselling Services of Alberta operates the Stan Daniels Healing Centre, a 72-bed facility for male offenders, and the Buffalo Sage Wellness

House for women offenders. These offenders are on conditional release (day parole, full parole, or statutory release) or have inmate status.

THE USE OF INCARCERATION

The materials presented in Chapter 2 revealed that only a very small percentage of offenders who are found guilty are sentenced to a period of confinement in a correctional institution. The majority of adult offenders (80 percent) are on probation or serving conditional sentences.[5] The federal incarceration rate has declined somewhat in recent years, although there have been increases in the number of offenders being sent to provincial and territorial institutions. Northwest Territories, Yukon, and Nunavut have the highest incarceration rates in Canada, and comparatively speaking, Nunavut and Northwest Territories have higher rates of incarceration than many countries, including Russia and South Africa.[6]

Although more offenders are held in provincial and territorial institutions, the time spent in confinement is short: Thirty percent of sentenced offenders spent less than one week in confinement, while nearly 60 percent were incarcerated for one month or less.[7] The majority of custodial sentences (81 percent) are for less than six months.[8]

TYPES OF CORRECTIONAL INSTITUTIONS

Federal correctional facilities are categorized in terms of these security levels: **minimum-security institutions**, which generally have no perimeter fencing and allow unrestricted inmate movement, except during the night; **medium-security institutions**, which are surrounded by high-security perimeter fencing with some restrictions on inmate movement; and **maximum-security institutions**, which have highly controlled environments, high-security perimeter fencing, and an environment in which inmates' movements are strictly controlled and constantly monitored by video surveillance cameras.

There is also one Special Handling Unit (SHU) in Canada. This is a high-security institution for inmates who present such a high level of risk to staff and other inmates that they cannot be housed in maximum-security facilities. CSC also operates a number of regional health centres. These facilities house violent offenders and offer treatment programs that focus on violence and anger management.

For an inside look at the New Toronto South Detention Centre, see the Media Link, "Inside Toronto's New Maximum Security Detention Centre," at the end of this chapter.

All correctional facilities have two types of security: (1) **static security**, which includes perimeter fencing, video surveillance, and alarms, as well as fixed security posts, such as control rooms and position posts, where officers remain in a defined area; and (2) **dynamic security**, which includes ongoing interaction, beyond observation, between correctional officers and inmates. It includes working with and speaking with inmates, making suggestions, providing information, and—in general—being proactive.

The personnel in correctional institutions include the warden, who has overall responsibility for the operation of the institution; other senior managers, including the deputy warden, who are responsible for overseeing various areas of the prison; and program managers, correctional officers, treatment staff, and intelligence officers, among others.

Minimum-security institutions

Federal correctional facilities that generally have no perimeter fencing and allow unrestricted inmate movement except at night.

Medium-security institutions

Federal correctional facilities that have a less highly controlled institutional environment than maximum-security institutions and in which the inmates have more freedom of movement.

Maximum-security institutions

Federal correctional institutions with a highly controlled institutional environment.

Static security

Fixed security apparatus in correctional institutions, including fixed security posts wherein correctional officers are assigned to and remain in specific areas, such as a control room or perimeter patrol.

Dynamic security

A variety of ongoing, meaningful interactions between staff and inmates.

▼ Ferndale Institution is a federal minimum-security correctional facility located east of Vancouver.

Jeff Vinnick/Vancouver Sun. Material republished with the express permission of Postmedia Network Inc.

THE CHALLENGES OF MANAGING CORRECTIONAL INSTITUTIONS

MEETING THE REQUIREMENTS OF LAW, POLICY, AND LEGISLATION

The senior management, correctional officers, treatment staff, and others must meet the requirements of legislation and policy, including ensuring that the rights of inmates under the *Charter of Rights and Freedoms* are protected. Corrections authorities are accountable to ensuring that inmates are treated fairly and that the rule of law prevails in correctional institutions.

Wardens in charge of correctional institutions must address a number of challenges. These include meeting the requirements of legislation and policy, being accountable for their decisions, and being aware of the requirements of the **rule of law**. This means they are accountable for treating inmates in a way that protects their fundamental rights, including those under the *Charter of Rights and Freedoms*. Corrections officials also have a **duty to act fairly** when managing offenders. This means that decisions must be fair and equitable and that offenders must have the opportunity to respond to any assessments made by correctional personnel about their conduct and performance.

Provincial and territorial ombudspersons, auditor generals, and the federal Office of the Correctional Investigator provide a degree of oversight of institutional corrections, although the findings from their investigations are not binding. However, the rulings of the courts are, and there is an increasing number of cases initiated by inmates and by inmate families coming before the courts.

THE PRISON AS A TOTAL INSTITUTION

Prisons are what the sociologist Erving Goffman referred to as **total institutions**. All aspects of life are conducted in the same place, and the activities of a group of persons with similar status (inmates, in the case of prisons) are tightly scheduled and controlled by an administrative hierarchy.[9] This regimen may prevent inmates from developing the skills to function independently once released into the community.

While all correctional institutions share a common identify as total institutions, some are more "total" than others. Correctional facilities vary in terms of their affiliation (federal/provincial/territorial), security classification, size, management style, inmate characteristics and other key factors that affect the dynamics of institutional life. This can be described as a **continuum of correctional institutions**. At one end of such as continuum would be minimum-security and community corrections facilities; at the other end would be maximum-security institutions. As one might expect, the dynamics of life inside institutions at either end of the continuum would be considerably different. Even institutions at the same security level have their own "personalities"—a function of history, the attitudes and behaviour of administrators and staff, the specific attributes of the inmate population, and other less tangible factors.

THE "SPLIT PERSONALITY" OF CORRECTIONS

Prisons are asked to pursue conflicting goals, which include protecting society while at the same time preparing offenders for release. This is often referred to as the "split personality" of corrections. The features of correctional institutions, centred on controlling every facet of the inmate's life, may make it difficult to prepare them for life on the outside.

Rule of law

The requirement that governments, as well as individuals, be subjected to and abide by the law.

Duty to act fairly

The obligation of correctional authorities to ensure that offenders are treated fairly by corrections personnel.

Total institutions

Correctional institutions, psychiatric hospitals, and other facilities characterized by a highly structured environment in which all movements of the inmates or patients are controlled 24 hours a day by staff.

Continuum of correctional institutions

The differences in institutional environments among correctional institutions located at either end of the security spectrum—maximum to minimum.

THE IMPACT OF LEGISLATION AND POLITICAL AGENDA

Politicians, provincial legislatures, and the federal government exercise considerable control over how correctional institutions are operated, the goals they are asked to pursue, and the resources that are made available to corrections personnel. This is illustrated by the legislation that was passed by the federal Conservative government (2006–15), including the introduction of more mandatory minimum sentences (many of which have since been ruled unconstitutional by the courts).

CONDITIONS IN CORRECTIONAL INSTITUTIONS

> The first was the deplorable physical condition of the Penitentiary. The cleanliness or lack of it is horrendous. There is a buildup of dirt and grime throughout the Penitentiary.... Washrooms were filthy and staff often had to resort to cleaning them on their own. While some cells had been renovated, others had been plastered at some point and had gaping holes in the walls.[10]

A description of a Canadian prison in the 1800s? No. The 2008 findings of a committee that visited Her Majesty's Penitentiary in St. John's, Newfoundland, opened in 1859 and added on to over the decades. The institution has been described as a "tinderbox," with overcrowding, a lack of programs, and understaffed conditions.[11] Critics have called the institution, "A Victorian-era throwback that should be bulldozed."[12] The conditions in the Baffin Correctional Centre were found to be so deplorable that the decision was made in 2016 to build a new facility.[13] View the video, "'Welcome to Hell': Inside Canada's Most Decrepit Prison, Baffin Correctional Centre," in the Media Links section at the end of this chapter.

The physical condition of a correctional facility can have a significant impact on the dynamics that develop among inmates and between inmates and staff, and can cause higher rates of serious violence.[14,15] Assaults in the previously described correctional institution doubled between 2014 (20) to 2016.

In a potentially precedent-setting case, a Quebec judge in 2012 reduced an offender's sentence from 53 months to 44 months after calling a provincial correctional facility "unhygienic" and commenting, "There are rats and vermin (in the jail)." The judge also cited gang activity and the high rate of drug use in the prison as imposing unnecessarily severe punishment on offenders in the facility.[16]

For additional materials on issues surrounding incarceration, visit the Criminalization and Punishment Education Project (http://cp-ep.org).

THE CHANGING OFFENDER PROFILE

Offenders confined in correctional institutions tend to be male, young, single, poorly educated, and marginally skilled. They are disproportionately Indigenous and Black, they are likely to have a history of unstable lives, and many have grown up in dysfunctional families. Their problem-solving skills are minimal.

Most are serving time in provincial/territorial institutions, and more than half of the sentences are for less than one month. Although many of these attributes have long been a feature of inmates in correctional institutions, there are disturbing trends. The federal offender population, for example, is becoming more diverse, with decreases in the number of Caucasian offenders and increases in other groups. See Figure 11.1.

There has been a significant increase in the number of federal offenders who are classified as maximum security at admission, as well as an increase in the proportion of offenders serving a sentence for a violent offence. Although the majority of offenders

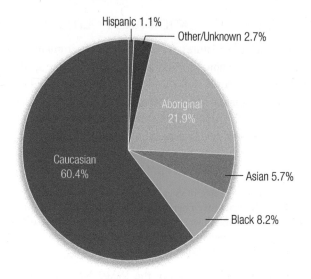

Hispanic 1.1%

Other/Unknown 2.7%

Aboriginal 21.9%

Caucasian 60.4%

Asian 5.7%

Black 8.2%

◄ FIGURE 11.1

Percentage of the Total Offender Population

Source: Public Safety Canada Portfolio Corrections Statistics Committee. 2016. *Corrections and Conditional Release Statistical Overview: 2015 Annual Report.* Ottawa: Public Works and Government Services Canada, p. 49. https://www .publicsafety.gc.ca/cnt/rsrcs/pblctns/ccrso-2015/ ccrso-2015-en.pdf. This information was reproduced with the permission of the Minister of Public Safety and Emergency Preparedness Canada, 2017.

committed to provincial and territorial institutions have been convicted of non-violent offences, these populations pose challenges as well.

There are high rates of alcohol and drug problems, unstable work histories, and inmates who have been convicted of violent offences. There are also high rates of communicable diseases, including HIV/AIDS, tuberculosis, and hepatitis B and C, in institutional populations.[17] In addition, these offenders have a variety of treatment needs. Over 90 percent are assessed as requiring substance abuse treatment, and nearly 90 percent in federal custody have treatment needs in the personal/emotional domain.[18]

The increasing diversity is reflected in the overall federal inmate population, which increased by just under 14 percent during the decade from 2005 to 2015. Other notable trends during this time included

- a significant increase (+77.4 percent) in the number of women incarcerated as compared to males (+11.6 percent);
- a significant increase in the incarcerated Indigenous population (+52.4 percent) compared to non-Indigenous persons (+4.9 percent); and,
- a significant increase in the Black population (+77.5 percent) as compared to the Caucasian population (+6.8 percent).[19]

The number of Black inmates is growing, and this group now represents nearly 10 percent of the total federal prison population, while comprising only 3 percent of the Canadian population.[20] The significant increases in the number of women, Indigenous persons, and Blacks suggest the need for understanding why these groups are more prone to becoming involved in the criminal justice system and to being incarcerated.

WOMEN INMATES

Women offenders present unique challenges for systems of corrections. There is the recognition that the pathways to crime for women offenders are in many ways distinct from that of male offenders, which requires the development of gender-specific programs and interventions. Some of the general attributes of women offenders are set out in Corrections File 11.2.

Generally speaking, women offenders share with their male counterparts a marginalized background of poverty, alcohol and/or drug dependency, limited

CORRECTIONS FILE 11.2

A PROFILE OF WOMEN OFFENDERS IN CORRECTIONS

- Women offenders represent about one in ten offenders admitted to custody and, in many respects, present a different profile than male offenders.

- The number of women admitted to federal custody increased 40 percent in the past decade, and the number of Indigenous women admitted to federal correctional facilities increased 90 percent during that time.

- An increasing number of women are admitted to custody for violent crimes.

- One in ten women are gang-affiliated, compared to one in six for male offenders.

- One in four federal women inmates have been incarcerated on drug-related charges, and HIV and HCV infection is generally higher among women inmates.

- In contrast to male offenders, a high percentage of women offenders have been the victims of physical and sexual abuse and exhibit high rates of eating disorders, depression, and sleep disorders.

- Federal women offenders are twice as likely as male offenders to have been previously hospitalized for psychiatric reasons and to have a mental-health challenge.

- Women offenders generally have greater health and mental-health needs than male inmates and are more likely to have experienced sexual or physical victimization prior to incarceration.

- The number of federal women offenders over the age of 50 has increased over the past decade. Compared to younger women, these offenders had lower overall risk/needs, were less likely to have substance abuse issues, but have more personal/emotional issues.

- Indigenous women continue to be overrepresented in correctional institutions, and their numbers have been steadily increasing. While less than 5 percent of the total Canadian population, they represent 39 percent of women admitted to federal custody and 38 percent of admissions to provincial and territorial custody.

- The physical and mental health of Indigenous women offenders is particularly precarious, with histories of victimization and substance abuse.

Sources: Canadian HIV/AIDS Legal Network. 2012. *Women in Prison, HIV and Hepatitis C, Toronto* [Info sheet]. http://sagecollection.ca/en/system/files/women _in_prison_hiv_and_hepatitis_c.pdf; D. Calverley. 2010. "Adult Correctional Services in Canada, 2008/2009," *Juristat, 30*(3). Statistics Canada Catalogue no. 85-002-X. Ottawa: Minister of Industry. http://www.statcan.gc.ca/pub/85-002-x/2010003/ article/11353-eng.htm; D.D. DeHart. 2008. "Pathways to Prison: Impact of Victimization in the Lives of Incarcerated Women," *Violence Against Women, 14*(12), 1362–1381; Department of Justice. 2017, January. "JustFacts: Indigenous Overrepresentation in the Criminal Justice System." http://justice.gc.ca/eng/rp-pr/ jr/jf-pf/2017/jan02.html; L. Greiner and K. Allenby. 2010, November. "A Descriptive Profile of Older Women Offenders [Research report R-229]." http://www.csc-scc .gc.ca/research/005008-0229-01-eng.shtml; T.H. Mahony, J. Jacob, and H. Hobson. 2017. "Women and the Criminal Justice System" in *Women in Canada: A Gender-Based Statistical Report* (7th ed.). Statistics Canada Catalogue no. 89-503-X. Ottawa: Minister of Industry, p. 7. http://www.statcan.gc.ca/pub/89-503-x/2015001/ article/14785-eng.pdf; C. Plourde, A. Gendron, and N. Brunelle. 2012. "Profile of Substance Use and Perspective on Substance Use Pathways Among Incarcerated Aboriginal Women," *Pimatisiwin: A Journal of Aboriginal and Indigenous Community Health, 10*(1), 83–95; L. Stone. 2012, May 25. "Gangs Starting to 'Infect' Women's Prisons," *Calgary Herald.* http://www.calgaryherald.com/news/ Gangs+starting+infect+women+prisons/5553864/story.html.

education, and minimal employment skills. Women offenders may have suffered sexual and physical abuse and may be responsible for children or stepchildren. There are numerous documented instances in which the human rights of women have been violated, including violations of Canada's obligations under international law.[21]

The pains of imprisonment may be much more severe for women offenders than for their male counterparts. This is for a number of reasons. Many federally sentence women (FSW) are housed in facilities that are far from their home communities. Three in four of the incarcerated women are mothers to children under the age of 18, and at the time of arrest almost all of them were the single caregivers. Being confined can also have a strong impact on women who have experienced physical and emotional abuse as children and/or adults.[22,23] As one woman inmate in a provincial correctional institution stated:

> Women don't get visits. And it's really hard not to get visits. They put us so far away that there's no way our families can afford to come. Women have children and yet we're the farthest they place. What are our families supposed to do?[24]

Women offenders adapt to life inside correctional institutions differently than their male counterparts. Generally speaking, women inmates are far less likely than male inmates to verbally and/or physically assault correctional staff, regardless of their criminal history, mental health, and addiction issues.[25] This may change with the influx of increasing numbers of women offenders convicted of violent crimes and women who are gang-affiliated.

INDIGENOUS INMATES

Managing Indigenous inmates presents unique challenges because of the challenges they themselves have had to face. The challenges faced by these offenders are highlighted in the profile of Indigenous offenders ($N = 316$) enrolled in the Aboriginal Offender Substance Abuse Program in a federal correctional institution:

- Half of the sample indicated that they had been in the care of the child welfare system—71 percent had spent time in foster care and 39 percent in a group home.
- 61 percent had family members who had spent time in prison.
- 73 percent reported a familial history of involvement with the residential school system; 18 percent said they themselves were residential school survivors.
- Almost all (96 percent) indicated that substance use was related to their current offence; 85 percent reported they were under the influence at the time of their offence.
- 88 percent reported they had a family member struggling with alcohol or drug addiction issues.
- Significantly, nearly one-third of the sample indicated they were first introduced to Indigenous cultural teachings in prison.[26]

Indigenous inmates now comprise 25 percent of the inmates in federal institutions while only comprising 4.3 percent of the Canadian population. Indigenous women now represent approximately 36 percent of all federal women in custody.[27] See Figure 11.2.

SPECIAL INMATE POPULATIONS

In addition to women offenders, Indigenous persons, and Blacks and other racialized groups, there are groups of inmates who require special attention. See Table 11.1.

Many inmates are homeless or under-housed prior to their incarceration.[28] A large number of them have lengthy criminal histories. The treatment needs of persons incarcerated in correctional institutions are high: Many suffer from alcohol and/or drug addiction; many have a mental impairment or other affliction such as FASD. The Baffin Regional Correctional Centre has been referred to as a "homeless shelter," holding inmates who did not have access to alternative services when they were in the community.[29]

These offenders often have few connections to "mainstream" Canadian society, and in this manner, they are very similar to the predecessors in previous centuries.

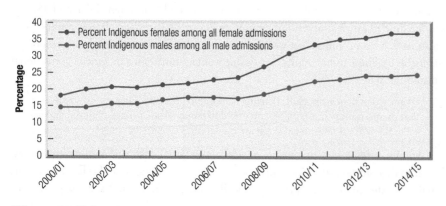

◄ FIGURE 11.2

Adult Admissions to Sentenced Custody, by Gender and Indigenous Status, 2000/2001 to 2014/2015

Source: T.H. Mahony, J. Jacob, and H. Hobson. 2017. "Women and the Criminal Justice System" in *Women in Canada: A Gender-Based Statistical Report* (7th ed.). Statistics Canada Catalogue no. 89-503-X. Ottawa: Minister of Industry, p. 40. http://www.statcan.gc.ca/pub/89-503-x/2015001/article/14785-eng.pdf.

TABLE 11.1

THE CHALLENGES OF SPECIAL INMATE POPULATIONS

Elderly inmates	The number of federal offenders over the age of 50 has doubled in the past decade (25 percent of federal inmates and 30 percent of offenders under supervision in the community). They are more likely to be convicted of violent offences and sex offences (many of which are historical); more likely to be afflicted with chronic diseases and disabilities that require special attention and resources; and are vulnerable to psychological and physical victimization by younger inmates.[a] Some observers have called for the creation of senior-only units in correctional institutions.[b]
Mentally ill	The number of offenders entering correctional institutions with mental health issues is growing. It is estimated that 40 percent of inmates in Ontario provincial institutions have at least one severe mental health symptom. Women and Indigenous inmates in the province are more likely than other inmates to have two or more severe mental health symptoms.[c] It is estimated that 35 percent of federal inmates have a mental impairment that requires treatment.[d] Correctional institutions have been called the "asylums of the 21st century." The death of Ashley Smith in a federal women's correctional centre spotlighted deficiencies in the response to persons with mental illness who become involved in the justice and corrections systems.
Offenders with fetal alcohol spectrum disorder (FASD)	FASD is a condition of brain damage caused by alcohol consumption by the birth mother during pregnancy; the symptoms include impulsive violence, aggression, and learning disabilities. It is estimated that between 10 and 23 percent of federal inmates are afflicted with FASD.[e] A study of federal inmates in Stony Mountain Institution (Manitoba) found the incidence of FASD was ten times greater than found in the general population.[f]

[a] Office of the Correctional Investigator. 2011. *38th Annual Report to Parliament. Summary of Issues and Challenges Facing Older and Aging Offenders in Federal Custody*. Ottawa: Author. http://www.oci-bec.gc.ca/cnt/comm/presentations/presentationsAR-RA0911Info-eng.aspx.

[b] A. Iftene. 2017. "The Pains of Incarceration: Aging, Rights, and Policy in Federal Penitentiaries," *Canadian Journal of Criminology and Criminal Justice, 59*(1), 63–93.

[c] G.P. Brown, J.P. Hirdes, and B.E. Fries. 2015. "Measuring the Prevalence of Current, Severe Symptoms of Mental Health Problems in a Canadian Correctional Population: Implications for Delivery of Mental Health Services for Inmates," *International Journal of Offender Therapy and Comparative Criminology, 59*(1), 27–50.

[d] K. Makin. 2011, January 21. "Why Canada's Prisons Can't Cope with Flood of Mentally Ill Inmates," *Globe and Mail*. https://www.theglobeandmail.com/news/national/why-canadas-prisons-cant-cope-with-flood-of-mentally-ill-inmates/article563604.

[e] Office of the Correctional Investigator. 2016. *Annual Report, 2015-2016*. Ottawa: Author, p. 4. http://www.oci-bec.gc.ca/cnt/rpt/pdf/annrpt/annrpt20152016-eng.pdf.

[f] P. MacPherson and A.E. Chudley. 2007. *FASD in a Correctional Population: Preliminary Results from an Incidence Study*. Montague, PEI: Addictions Research Centre. http://download.docslide.net/download/link/fasd-in-a-correctional-population-preliminary-results-from-an-incidence-study.

Additional sources: Office of the Correctional Investigator. 2011. *Annual Report, 2010-2011*. Ottawa: Author. http://www.oci-bec.gc.ca/cnt/comm/presentations/presentationsAR-RA0911-eng.aspx; Mental Health Commission of Canada. 2012. *Changing Directions, Changing Lives: The Mental Health Strategy for Canada*. Calgary: Author, p. 60. http://strategy.mentalhealthcommission.ca/pdf/strategy-images-en.pdf; K. Makin. 2010, November 19. "Senator Fights for Mentally Ill in Prison," *Globe and Mail*, p. A9.

They have needs and present risks that place significant demands on systems of corrections, in particular provincial/territorial institutions that tend to have fewer resources than their federal counterparts and must attempt to respond in a highly compressed timeframe.

Although some of the specific attributes of prison populations have changed (e.g., an increase in the number of inmates with HIV/AIDS), the general profile of inmates has not changed over the centuries: Prisons are still populated by the poor, disabled, and disenfranchised persons who reside at the margins of mainstream society.

OVERCROWDING IN CORRECTIONAL INSTITUTIONS

Overcrowding has plagued correctional institutions since the Kingston Penitentiary was constructed in 1835. Today, many Canadian prisons are beyond 100 percent capacity; for example, Saskatchewan facilities are operating at twice their capacity.[30] And in 2016, it was reported that the Ottawa-Carleton Detention Centre was so overcrowded that some inmates were forced to sleep in the showers.[31]

In the federal system, where over one-half of federal prisons operate at, or over, their rated capacity of inmates, an increase in the number of long-term prisoners, including lifers (who represent 20 percent of the inmate population), also contributed to overcrowding.[32] The Baffin Correctional Centre in Iqaluit, Nunavut, was originally built for 68 minimum-security inmates, but has held as many as 115 inmates at all security levels.[33]

There are many factors that cause overcrowding in correctional institutions, including changes in legislation, mandatory minimum sentences, inmates remaining in custody longer due to parole board decisions, the decision of offenders not to apply for release at their eligibility date, the absence of new facilities, and poor strategic planning.[34]

Overcrowding in provincial and territorial institutions is also caused by the increasing numbers of offenders in remand, which, in turn, is due, in part, to delays in the criminal court process. A former inmate in the Prince Albert Provincial Correctional Centre recalled:

> Towards the end of my stay, more inmates started coming in on remand, and they started taking the school classroom, and the church, and they started just putting beds in there, and TVs, just to house inmates while they were waiting on remand. So they were taking our [rehabilitative] programs away just to make room for sleep.[35]

Overcrowding results in the warehousing of offenders to the extent that the focus is on managing the prison populations rather than on rehabilitation.[36] It may be difficult to keep separate persons on remand with the convicted inmate population.[37] Overcrowding often limits inmate access to programs, and many offenders leave the institution without completing a full course of treatment.[38] This is particularly problematic for sex offenders, who may not be confined long enough to complete a treatment program. Inmates may spend longer periods of time in their cells.[39] And it can lead to double-bunking—two offenders being confined to a cell designed for one. Double-bunking is now considered standard practice in federal institutions and in most provincial/territorial institutions.[40] Double-bunking violates the United Nations Minimal Standards for Prisoners.

Overcrowding can affect daily prison life by heightening tensions among inmates and between inmates and correctional officers (COs).[41] The impact of overcrowding is reflected in the incidence of inmate-on-inmate assault, which in federal prisons increased 93 percent from 2006–07 to 2014–15.[42] In many provinces, there have been double-digit increases in inmate-on-inmate violence.[43] In Manitoba, for example, where provincial institutions are as much as 145 percent over capacity, there was a 43 percent increase in "serious incidence" security events between 2009 and 2012.[44] In Ontario, overcrowding in provincial institutions has resulted in a significant increase in lockdowns, wherein inmates are confined in their cells for lengthy periods of time.[45]

PREVENTING DISORDER AND DISTURBANCES

A primary responsibility of senior management and the COs is to maintain "good order" in the institution, ensuring that the staff and inmates move through the daily routine or schedule with no or minimal conflict.[46]

A number of factors may influence the level of order or disorder in an institution, including overcrowding, the composition of the inmate population, the behaviour of COs, the prison's physical design, and the management style of prison administrators.[47]

The presence of inmates from rival gangs and tensions between ethnic groups can spark inmate-on-inmate attacks. A study of misconduct (N = 18,085) among Indigenous and non-Indigenous federal inmates found that inmates who were younger, male, higher risk, and Indigenous were more extensively involved in misconduct.[48] Conflict between inmate gang members may also spark violence. It is estimated that one in six federal inmates is affiliated with a known gang or with organized crime.[49]

In some instances, disturbances, which are generally limited in scope, escalate into riots, during which inmates, correctional officers, and correctional staff may be at risk of serious injury or death. Riots continue to be a feature of Canadian federal and provincial correctional facilities, including a six-hour riot in the maximum-security Central North Correctional Centre in Ontario in June 2015, and a riot at the federal Saskatchewan Penitentiary in December 2016, during which one inmate was killed and several were injured.[50,51]

ENSURING INMATE SAFETY

The accountability of corrections officials extends to ensuring the safety of inmates in their charge—an onerous task, particularly in federal maximum-security institutions. Although wardens have little say in how many inmates are sent to their facility, the types of inmates they receive, and when inmates will leave their institution via transfer, conditional release, or statutory release, they are responsible for the safety and security of the inmates once they have arrived.

Recent years have seen a number of high-profile incidents within prisons, some of them involving inmates murdered by fellow inmates. This has increased the pressure on CSC to ensure that its policies and procedures provide protection for inmates. Inmates may be placed in administrative segregation (see below) for their protection. This may include inmates who have "snitched out" or testified against other inmates, inmates who have drug debts or other outstanding obligations, and inmates convicted of sexual offences.[52]

Canadian courts have become more active in addressing inmates' rights, which include the right to serve time in a safe and secure environment. The federal government is being sued more and more frequently by inmates who have been victimized while serving their time. In 2013, inmates in a detention centre in London, Ontario, launched a $300 million suit against the Ontario government claiming that overcrowded conditions and violence violated their rights and freedoms under the Charter. The courts have also intervened in cases where inmates have been victimized while in custody.

The challenges of keeping inmates safe were highlighted by the murder of Denise Fayant. Thirty hours after arriving at the Edmonton Institution for Women, 21-year-old Denise Fayant was strangled by her former lover with a bathrobe sash. She died two days later in hospital. An investigation into the death, which was originally ruled a suicide, found that she had been slain by two inmates, one of whom had been her former lover and against whom she was scheduled to testify. A subsequent inquiry conducted by an Alberta provincial court judge found that Fayant had repeatedly told corrections officials that she would fear for her safety if they transferred her to the newly opened institution. Prison officials insisted that they had been assured by inmates in the prison that no harm would come to Fayant.

Two inmates were later convicted and sentenced to additional federal time for the death. The investigating judge concluded that Fayant's death was avoidable and was a result of "callous and cavalier" actions on the part of Corrections Canada.[53] For additional materials on this case, see Critical Thinking Exercise 11.1 at the end of this chapter.

Protective custody (PC) involves the use of a section of the prison that may hold inmates who are at risk in the general population. It may include inmates who have snitched out or testified against other inmates, inmates who have drug debts or other outstanding obligations, and inmates convicted of sexual crimes such as rape and child molestation. It is also possible for an inmate who is feeling at risk to "check themselves in" to PC to protect themselves.

Correctional authorities must also ensure that inmates do not do self-harm. Self-injurious behavior (SIB) includes head-banging and skin-cutting. Women offenders are at high risk of SIB, and Indigenous offenders account for 45 percent of all self-harm incidents in federal prisons, while comprising 39 percent of the prison population.[54] The suicide rate among inmates incarcerated in federal (70 per 100,000) and provincial (43 per 100,000) institutions is much higher than for the Canadian general population (10.2 per 100,000).[55] The number of federal inmates who engage in SIB more than tripled from 2006 to 2016.[56]

INMATE HEALTH AND INFECTIOUS DISEASES

Correctional systems face challenges providing short- and long-term health care, dispensing medication, and developing policies to combat high-risk behaviours.[57]

Perhaps the most critical challenge facing correctional authorities is the spread of communicable diseases, including HIV/AIDS, tuberculosis, and hepatitis B and C.[58,59] There are alarmingly high rates of infection among Canadian inmates. Estimates are that the rate of HIV/AIDS infection in federal prisons is 15 times higher than in the general population. As many as 75 percent of the women in the federal Edmonton Prison for Women are known to be HIV-positive, compared to less than 1 percent of the Canadian population. For Indigenous offenders in federal, provincial, and territorial institutions, the rates are even higher.[60,61]

Systems of corrections have developed a number of prevention strategies in their efforts to prevent and reduce high-risk behaviours among inmates and to reduce levels of infection. For example, CSC provides inmates with condoms, lubricants, dental dams, and bleach kits for needles (though not needles). In several federal institutions, inmates have been trained as peer health counsellors to educate others on how to reduce the risk of infection. The federal government has also expanded its methadone maintenance program for heroin-addicted offenders. Provincial/territorial systems of correction have undertaken similar efforts, though there is considerable variation in the harm reduction resources provided to inmates. The challenges are considerable, given the higher turnover of inmates in the latter system and the short periods of confinement.

The non-profit Prisoner's HIV/AIDS Support Action Network (PASAN) (www.pasan.org) has been instrumental in advocating for changes in correctional policy and for inmate rights in this area. This includes providing support services for prisoners and their families, conducting HIV prevention programs in correctional institutions in Ontario, and advocating to change correctional policies with respect to HIV/AIDS issues. Another organization that is active in this area is the Canadian AIDS Treatment Information Exchange (CATIE) (www.catie.ca).

To reduce the risk, correctional authorities employ a number of interdiction strategies, including frequent searches, a urinalysis program, drug dogs, video surveillance, and ion scanners that can detect drug residue on clothing and other objects on visitors as well as on inmates returning from absences in the community. The effectiveness of interdiction strategies in reducing the availability of drugs and the rates of infectious diseases is uncertain.[62] See At Issue 11.1.

THE USE OF SEGREGATION

One strategy that is used by correctional managers to maintain security in the institution or to discipline an inmate for misconduct is **segregation** (also often referred to as *solitary confinement*, although solitary confinement is a place and segregation is a status). Inmates placed in segregation may be locked in a cell for 23 hours a day and generally do not have access to programming or to normal inmate privileges.

The *Corrections and Conditional Release Act* (CCRA; S.C. 1992, c. 20) includes provisions for two types of segregation: disciplinary and administrative. *Disciplinary segregation* is imposed in cases where an inmate has been found in violation of an institutional rule, whereas *administrative segregation* is imposed when an inmate has attempted or intends to act in a way that is deemed to threaten the prison population.

While there are strict guidelines for the use of disciplinary segregation, including time limits and mandatory independent oversight, these safeguards do not apply

Segregation

A correctional management strategy that is used for disciplinary or administrative reasons and often involves an inmate being locked in a cell for 23 hours a day; also referred to as *solitary confinement*.

to inmates who are in administrative segregation. Many inmates who have been held in solitary confinement for lengthy periods of time, and some who have died while in solitary (including Ashley Smith, whose case is discussed below), were classified as being in administrative segregation. In early 2018, the Court of Appeal in Ontario set at 15 days the maximum amount of time that a federal inmate could be kept in administrative segregation and it is anticipated that this guideline will be implemented.

There have been increases in the number of Indigenous and Black admissions to segregation, while the number of Caucasian inmates confined in segregation has declined. Indigenous inmates are represented in segregation in federal institutions at a rate that is approximately seven times that of their proportion of the Canadian population (30 percent in segregation; 4.3 percent of the Canadian population). Indigenous women are much more likely to be labelled as high risk and to be placed in segregation. Among federal offenders, the large majority (95 percent) of admissions to administrative segregation are men.[63]

▲ For those in solitary confinement, human contact can be limited to a slot in the door and disjointed voices of inmates nearby.

Inmates with a history of self-injury and who have been identified as having mental health, behavioural, and cognitive issues are more likely to have a history of being in segregation. These offenders are also more likely to be rated as high needs/high risk and to be assessed as having low motivation and low reintegration potential.[64] There are concerns that segregation is increasingly being used to manage overcrowding in provincial institutions and as a management strategy to deal with inmates with physical and mental issues.[65]

THE CONTROVERSY OVER AND REFORM OF SOLITARY CONFINEMENT

The use of solitary confinement in federal and provincial and territorial correctional institutions has been at the centre of controversy for many years.[66] There is considerable evidence that solitary confinement causes "psychotic disturbances," the symptoms of which include "anxiety, depression, anger, cognitive disturbances, perceptual distortions, paranoia and psychosis and self-harm."[67] Given these adverse effects, the use of solitary confinement can constitute a violation of the UN Convention against Torture and Other Cruel, Inhuman or Degrading Treatment or Punishment.[68] The Canadian Medical Association labelled the placement of inmates in solitary confinement as "cruel and usual punishment" and recommended that the practice be severely restricted.[69] Others have called for an outright abolition of solitary confinement.[70]

The effects of solitary confinement are reflected in the recollection of BobbyLee Worm, an Indigenous federally sentenced woman incarcerated for robbery, who spent 3½ years in segregation for fighting with other inmates and prison staff. She recalled that, during her time in solitary, the only human contact she'd had was when a small slot in the door opened and a guard passed her a tray of food. Reflecting on the experience, she stated:

> You feel like you're losing your mind. Days turn into nights and into days and you don't know if you'll ever get out. The more time I spent in solitary confinement, the more trouble I had in prison. They told me solitary confinement would help me but it made me even worse.[71]

Several high-profile cases involving the lengthy periods of time in solitary confinement and, in some cases, death prompted the federal government to pass legislation in 2017 that restricted the use of solitary confinement. See Corrections File 11.3.

THREE CASES THAT CHANGED THE USE OF SOLITARY CONFINEMENT

Ashley Smith

On October 19, 2007, 19-year-old Ashley Smith was found unconscious in her segregation cell at the Grand Valley Institution for Women. She died later that day. She had more than 800 incident reports, more than 500 institutional charges, and 168 self-harm incidents. Ms. Smith was transferred to the penitentiary at age 19 and was subsequently moved 17 times between 9 different federal correctional facilities. She had spent 1,047 days in solitary confinement.

An investigation by Office of the Correctional Investigator found that the actions of CSC violated the law and CSC policy. More specifically, it found that Ms. Smith's mental health issues had not been addressed either in the youth facility or in the federal institutions in which she was confined. The report concluded that Ms. Smith's death might have been prevented had she been provided with proper care. For a timeline of Ashley Smith's involvement in the corrections system, related documents, and interviews, see the web page of *The Fifth Estate*, regarding the episodes "Out of Control" and "Behind the Wall: The Ashley Smith Story," at http://www.cbc.ca/fifth. See Class/ Group Discussion Exercise 11.1 for more materials on the death of Ashley Smith.

Eddie Snowshoe

A note written by Eddie Snowshoe prior to his taking his own life says, "I want all my personal property to be trashed. Tell my mom that I have no blame at all towards her and that I know she will be strong for the boys."

On August 30, 2010, Eddie Snowshoe, an Indigenous man from the Northwest Territories, hung himself after 162 days in solitary confinement at the Edmonton federal maximum-security prison. He had attempted to commit suicide on a number of previous occasions and had slowly deteriorated during his three years in prison. It was noted that, "Mr. Snowshoe had morphed from a shy but hale young man into a chronically suicidal inmate suffering from a dangerous brew of mental-health issues." A Board of Investigation found that there had been little interaction between Mr. Snowshoe and correctional staff during his time in solitary. His mental health issues were not addressed and there was no plan developed to reintegrate him back into the general inmate population. Further, the investigation found that his continued placement in segregation was not justified. See Class/ Group Discussion Exercise 11.1 for further materials on the death of Eddie Snowshoe.

Jessica Doria-Brown / CBC. Reprinted by permission of CBC.

Ashley Smith's grave

Adam Capay

Adam Capay, a 24-year-old member of the Lac Seul First Nations in Northwestern Ontario, spent 4½ years in solitary confinement in a provincial jail in Thunder Bay, Ontario, while awaiting trial. His trial had been delayed three times. During this time:

> Capay said he spent much of his time in a kind of half sleep, drifting in and out of consciousness. The lights were on 24 hours a day. Reality was difficult to discern. He was constantly hungry. He went into the yard once or twice a month. A psychiatrist talked to him for a couple of minutes every few months, mostly to approve his continued segregation. He'd engaged in self-harm, and had lacerations on his wrists and puncture wounds on his scalp. He'd recently been restrained after bashing his head against the wall.

Adam Capay's detention was in violation of provincial regulations and United Nations standards. View the film "Inside Canada's Corrections System. Prisons: The Case of Adam Capay" at http://tvo.org/ video/programs/the-agenda-with-steve-paikin/inside-canadas -corrections-system.

Sources: Office of the Correctional Investigator. 2008. *A Preventable Death.* Ottawa: Author. http://www.oci-bec.gc.ca/cnt/rpt/pdf/oth-aut/oth-aut20080620-eng.pdf; P. White. 2014, December 5. "Confined: The Death of Eddie Snowshoe," *Globe and Mail.* https://www.theglobeandmail.com/news/national/confined-the-death-of-eddie -snowshoe/article21815548; M. Patriquin. 2016, November 2. "Why Adam Capay Has Spent 1,560 Days in Solitary," *Maclean's.* http://www.macleans.ca/news/why-adam -capay-has-spent-1560-days-in-solitary.

These cases and the increasing chorus of criticism of the practice prompted legal action that resulted in the prohibition against keeping inmates in administrative segregation longer than 15 days. The CSC has also introduced new regulations prohibiting the use of segregation cells for vulnerable inmates. This includes inmates who are at a high risk of suicide or self-harming behaviour and those with serious mental illness and those who are physically disabled, terminally ill, or pregnant.[72] It is anticipated that these policies will contribute to a significant drop in the number of inmates held in solitary confinement in the coming years.

THE INCIDENT AT THE KINGSTON PRISON FOR WOMEN (P4W): A WATERSHED EVENT IN WOMEN'S CORRECTIONS

On April 22, 1994, a brief but violent physical confrontation took place between six inmates and several correctional officers at the Kingston Prison for Women (which has since been closed). A lack of leadership from the prison's warden contributed to the events that unfolded over the next several days. This included sending an all-male Institutional Emergency Response Team (IERT) to extract eight inmates in the segregation unit from their cells and strip-search them, stripping the women in the presence of male members of the IERT, body cavity searches, and the use of leg irons. Several of the women were subsequently placed in solitary confinement for many months.

An independent judicial inquiry was subsequently conducted, headed by the Honourable Louise Arbour, then a highly respected member of the Quebec judiciary. The inquiry's final report was extremely critical of the actions taken by correctional staff, the IERT personnel, and the warden.[73] The same report sharply criticized the response of senior CSC officials. In the end, the commissioner of corrections resigned.

The inquiry's report documented numerous violations of policy, the rule of law, and institutional regulations. The **Arbour Report** made 14 key recommendations relating to the following: cross-gender staffing in correctional institutions for women; the use of force and of IERTs; the operations of segregation units; the needs of Indigenous women in correctional institutions; ways of ensuring accountability and adherence to the rule of law by correctional personnel; and procedures for handling inmate complaints and grievances.

The Arbour Report had a significant impact on CSC's operations and on the development of women's corrections.[74] A deputy commissioner for women was appointed, a use-of-force policy was developed that stipulates that all-male institutional emergency response teams are never to be used as a first response in women's correctional institutions, and it is now forbidden for male staff to be present when women inmates are being strip-searched. The report also accelerated the closing of the Prison for Women in the year 2000 and the opening of smaller, regional facilities for federal women offenders.[75] Despite these reforms, a number of scholars have argued that CSC has failed to develop a correctional practice for women that is empowering and rehabilitative.[76] It has been argued that the experience of women offenders in institutions has remained largely unchanged, and the focus of the system is on punishment and control.[77] Particular criticism has been directed toward the treatment of women offenders with mental illness.

Arbour Report

The report of an inquiry into events at the Kingston Prison for Women in April 1994 which documented violations of policy, the rule of law, and institutional regulations, and had a significant impact on the development of women's corrections.

WORKING INSIDE: THE EXPERIENCE OF CORRECTIONAL OFFICERS

Correctional officers play a pivotal role in correctional institutions, and their responsibilities have grown more complex in recent years. On a daily basis, it is COs who have the most contact with inmates. Though systems of corrections make extensive use of high technology, such as video surveillance and various warning devices (static security), COs are the primary mechanism by which institutional policies and regulations are implemented and by which the inmates are controlled (dynamic security). COs are also a key part of efforts to rehabilitate offenders. There are concerns that the advent of the high-tech prison with increased surveillance and restricted inmate movement will reduce the levels of dynamic security, wherein COs have frequent contact with inmates, and increase static security.

RECRUITMENT AND TRAINING

Ensuring that suitable candidates are recruited for the position of CO and providing training that prepares the recruits for work inside correctional institutions are key to COs successfully meeting the challenges of working inside. A feature of Canadian corrections is the variability between the training for federal correctional officers and their provincial and territorial counterparts. Another is the lack of diversity among COs, despite the fact that Indigenous persons and Blacks are overrepresented in prison populations.

At the federal level, each of CSC's five regions (Atlantic, Quebec, Ontario, Prairie, Pacific) is responsible for recruiting, selecting, assessing, and hiring correctional officers using national standards. Persons who are seeking an entry-level CO position must apply to the region where they want to work (www.jobs.gc.ca). Potential applicants are encouraged by the CSC to complete the self-assessment questionnaire for the position of CX-01, which is the entry-level correctional officer position. The questionnaire can be found at http://www.csc-scc.gc.ca/careers/092/003001-3021-eng.pdf.

Successful applicants are required to complete the Correctional Training Program, composed of a combination of online and classroom training. CSC has developed a special process for selecting and training staff to work in institutions for federally sentenced women. Specific criteria are used to identify personnel who are sensitive to women's issues, their life histories, and their unique needs. In addition to the training provided to all new COs, staff selected to work in women's facilities must complete a "women-centred training" course. This course consists of a number of modules covering areas such as women's criminality and its links to personal history, self-injury, and suicide; same-sex relationships; cultural sensitivity; and dealing effectively with lifers.[78]

In contrast to federal corrections, there are no national standards for recruiting and training COs for provincial/territorial systems of corrections. Each province and territory has its own procedures, standards, and training courses, some of which are more thorough than others.

THE AUTHORITY OF CORRECTIONAL OFFICERS

The authority of COs in prisons is both legal and moral. With respect to legal authority, though COs do not have the power to discipline inmates, in enforcing the policies and regulations of the institution, officers are able to initiate the punishment process. Equally important is their moral authority, which is based on establishing functional relationships with the inmates.

COs have considerable discretion in carrying out their daily activities and in determining when and how they will enforce the rules and regulations of the institution. Officers are well aware that full enforcement of all institutional regulations at all times would make life unbearable for both themselves and the inmates. Studies have revealed that COs can have one of two agendas: custodial or correctional. The custodial agenda of COs centres on control and the enforcement of regulations, while the correctional agenda involves COs functioning as change agents by assisting inmates in their efforts to access programs and services and to deal with personal issues.[79]

Research studies suggest that, similar to inmates, there is a correctional officer subculture that includes a code of behaviour designed to maintain occupational solidarity and, in some instances, shield inappropriate and sometimes criminal behaviour.[80] There are attributes of the CO subculture that may contribute to officers abusing their authority and mistreating inmates. The solidarity of officers may make it difficult to detect, investigate, and prosecute officers who are involved in activities that violate professional standards, institutional regulations, or the law.

In an investigation of 55 use-of-force complaints filed by inmates in Ontario provincial institutions during the time period 2010–12, the Ontario ombudsman found that the allegations were substantiated in 26 cases. From the investigations, the ombudsman concluded that there were acts of violence against inmates, a code of silence among correctional officers to lie and falsify records, and harassment and threats directed toward COs who did not abide by the code of silence.[81]

RELATIONSHIPS WITH INMATES

> When I first went to work as a correctional officer, everything inside seemed to be in chaos. You wonder what the heck is going on. It takes a few months to get in tune with the place. After you've been there awhile you get to know who the major players are, how different correctional officers approach situations. You develop a rapport with the inmates and begin developing relationships with them. I've always said that being a correctional officer is an art…to know how to balance the authority you have with the realities of life inside. (former CO, now deputy warden of a federal correctional institution, personal communication with C.T. Griffiths)

COs must learn the subtle non-verbal cues that will help them "read" individual inmates. They must also become familiar with the various intricacies of the inmate social system, the methods used to distribute and use contraband goods and drugs, and other activities such as gambling, strong-arming, and debt collection. Early on, the inmates will "test" new COs to determine how they will exercise their discretion and authority. These processes of adaptation and learning and of developing strategies to cope with the pressures and demands of everyday life in the prison are similar to those undergone by new inmates.[82]

Even though a core principle of correctional officers is "never trust an inmate," the unique features of daily life inside institutions create pressures for COs and inmates to develop accommodative relationships, which, for inmates, help reduce the pains of imprisonment, and, for COs, ensure daily stability and order. A key requirement is that COs treat inmates fairly and with respect. An inmate on remand commented, "A good correctional officer shows you respect, not somebody who talks down to you like you're a piece of garbage."[83] A CO in a federal institution agreed that respect was important, stating, "If you treat people with respect, they'll do the same."[84]

The specific patterns of interaction that develop between COs and inmates depend on a variety of factors, including the individual CO, the size of the inmate population, the security level of the facility, and the policies and management style of the senior administration. Research suggests that there is variation among COs in their attitude toward and performance on the job.[85]

This diversity among officers is reflected in the comments of a former inmate who served time in Central East Correctional Centre in Ontario:

> I must say that the guards in Lindsay are one extreme to the next, you got goldie locks over on 2 pod who will shove his hand down the toilet to try to get your package and he loves the bend over and cough shit. then you got the older laid back guys that leave you alone if you are just doing your own thing that dont disrespect you like your some dog in a cage (easter bunny).[86]

CORRECTIONS OFFICER ABUSE OF AUTHORITY

The interactions between COs and inmates may also be affected by the inmate's offence and criminal history. A study of Canadian male and women COs in several provinces ($N = 100$) found that sex offenders were viewed negatively by COs and as objects of fear and distrust.[87]

The low visibility of daily life inside correctional institutions, combined with the broad discretion exercised by COs, may lead to situations where COs abuse their authority and sometimes even violate the law. Visible minority inmates, in particular, may perceive that COs are abusing their discretionary powers. Interviews ($N = 73$; 30 women, 43 men) with Black inmates in Canadian federal institutions found that nearly all had experienced discrimination by corrections officials, the report finding, "Their needs did not appear to be a priority; their concerns were often ignored and many felt as though there were a 'different set of rules' for Black inmates."[88]

The Black inmates also reported feeling targeted for infractions of institutional regulations more frequently than other inmates, and institutional records revealed that these inmates were overrepresented in categories of infractions where COs had discretion, such as "being disrespectful to staff" and "jeopardizing the safety/security of the institution or another person."[89]

An Indigenous inmate recalled an instance of overt racism on the part of one CO at Prince Albert Provincial Correctional Centre:

> I remember one guard came out to give a job to somebody. The guy had only been there two weeks and another guy had been there three months on the range and he comes out and he says, "Yeah—new guy gets the job." And buddy who's been there for three months says, "Why didn't I get the job?" And the guard plainly says, "cause you're Indian." And he says, "Are you serious?" He says, "Yeah"—and walks away."[90]

Not all COs think and act the same way. Individual COs can be placed on a continuum based on how they exercise their discretionary authority and their relationships with inmates. There are officers who are more compassionate and others who are more punitive in their approach.[91]

Research studies have found that the design of a prison can have a significant impact on inmate–staff and inmate–inmate relationships. Newer institutions and those in which there were few inmates who were double-bunked evidenced more positive relationships and interactions.[92]

RELATIONSHIPS WITH THE ADMINISTRATION AND TREATMENT STAFF

Administrators may be viewed with a mixture of distrust and cynicism, as distant from the everyday realities of the prison, and being more concerned with fiscal and administrative issues that have little relevance to line-level officers. COs may also be concerned that, in applying policies set out by the administration, they might be held responsible. As one provincial CO stated, "I'm scared to do a mistake and to get the finger."[93] This occurred in the case of the death of Ashley Smith, discussed in elsewhere in this chapter.

Many COs hold a rather dim view of treatment programs, with many officers feeling that rehabilitation programs are a waste of time and money. The COs' view that few inmates have the ability, resources, and motivation to make significant changes in their attitudes and behaviour may limit the potential of COs to be effective change agents in the institution. There may also be a perception that many inmates become involved in treatment programs primarily to improve their chances of release on parole, rather than for self-improvement.

STRESSORS FOR CORRECTIONAL OFFICERS

During the course of their careers, COs may be exposed to a wide variety of critical incidents, including disturbances and riots, hostage takings, inmate murder, inmate self-mutilation and suicide, threats to the officer's safety, and injury to the officer. COs' concerns with security extended to their personal lives, including the threat of victimization of themselves and their family.[94] This included the fear of being followed and being watched by ex-inmates.

These factors, along with conditions in the prison and shiftwork, contribute to the high levels of stress and burnout experienced by COs.[95,96] This may have a significant impact on the COs' level of support for treatment programs, with officers who are burned out expressing less support; the amount of sick leave and absenteeism; how the COs interaction with the inmates; and the levels of support for management.[97,98]

These incidents may also result in symptoms associated with post-traumatic stress disorder (PTSD), an extreme form of critical incident stress, the symptoms of which include nightmares, hypervigilance, intrusive thoughts, and other forms of psychological distress.[99] Research has found that 36 percent of male federal COs are suffering from PTSD.[100] This is compared to between 1.1 and 3.5 percent of the Canadian general population.

Women correctional officers may experience additional stressors from working in a largely male-dominated environment that has traditionally valued toughness and physicality over communication skills and tact. There are cases in which woman COs have been subjected to sexual harassment, discrimination, and abuse of authority in many federal institutions.[101] A former woman federal CO referred to a "hush-or-hurt culture," where women victims of harassment often did not report it due to fear of reprisal.[102] The discriminatory treatment may extend to COs who are LGBT: In 2013, the Grievance Settlement Board in Quebec awarded $100,000 to a gay correctional officer who had been subjected to taunts and homophobic slurs by his colleagues in a provincial correctional facility.[103]

DOING TIME: THE WORLD OF THE INMATE

ENTERING THE PRISON

> I remember the day that I came in; the first time I went to the cafeteria and I could feel a hundred sets of eyes on me. I could see everybody wondering who you are, what you're in for, how long you're doing. (lifer)[104]

The specific impact that entry into the prison has on the individual offender will vary, depending on a variety of factors, including his/her personality, offence history, and previous incarcerations. First-time offenders may experience severe cultural shock, whereas offenders with extensive criminal histories and previous confinements are likely to be relatively unaffected. For these inmates, the processes and procedures related to entry into the institution and confinement are well-known, as are many of the correctional officers (COs) and inmates in the facility. Indeed, returning to the prison may be more of a homecoming than a banishment. For the uninitiated inmate, however, adjusting to the regimen of prison life can be stressful and frightening.

Regardless of background, there is a psychological and material stripping of the individual, which involves a series of **status degradation ceremonies**. This includes the issuing of prison clothing, the assignment of an identification number, the loss of most personal possessions, and the end of unhindered communication with the outside community.[105] These procedures are the mechanism by which the offender is moved from

Status degradation ceremonies

The processing of offenders into correctional institutions whereby the offender is psychologically and materially stripped of possessions that identify him or her as a member of the "free society."

residency in the community, with its attendant freedoms, to the world of the prison, with its rules, regulations, informal economy, and social system.

It can be argued that many of the persons entering correctional institutions have already had their "status" degraded, through a life of poverty, addiction, mental health issues, and growing up in dysfunctional environments. Degradation is associated with marginalization, and the above-noted profile of offenders suggests that it is persons from vulnerable groups who are most likely to end up incarcerated.

Though all incoming inmates are provided with copies of the institutional regulations and an orientation, each inmate is left to his or her own devices (and wits) to adjust to life inside and to develop strategies and techniques of coping and survival.

Following is a portion of the advice given by one inmate to a second inmate who had just arrived at Millhaven, a federal correctional facility in Ontario:

> Drugs and alcohol are everywhere and I urge you to avoid that trip. Ninety percent of all killings revolve around the dope scene.... Don't accept anything from anyone, because you don't want to put yourself in a position where you'll have to repay the favour. Nothing is free. It's in your best interest to avoid cliques. You'll be spending a lot of time on your own—it's much safer that way.... Don't encourage conversation with anyone. Be brief and polite.... Don't promise anyone anything.... Stay quiet and mind your own business.[106]

Unfortunately, though systems of corrections have perfected the mechanisms for transforming citizens into inmates, there are no *status restoration ceremonies* at the end of the inmate's confinement that would function to convert the inmate back into a citizen. The consequences of this for the re-entry and reintegration of offenders released from correctional institutions will be explored in Chapter 12.

LIVING INSIDE

A key concept in understanding the carceral experience is the **pains of imprisonment**. In his classic study of a maximum-security prison, presented in the book *Society of Captives*, Gresham Sykes identified a number of deprivations experienced by inmates.[107] These include the loss of liberty, loss of access to goods and services, and loss of access to heterosexual relationships, as well as the loss of personal autonomy

▶ A maximum-security cell in Collins Bay Institution, a federal institution in Ontario

THE CANADIAN PRESS/Lars Hagberg

and personal security. There are also the collateral effects of confinement, which include the loss of personal relationships and social networks in the outside community, the acquisition of self-defeating habits and attitudes, and the loss of personal belongings.

Inmates also attempt to cope with the deprivation of heterosexual relationships and to secure sexual gratification. Masturbation and consensual sexual relations with another inmate are the two most common types of sexual activity in correctional institutions. Consensual sex, while technically homosexual, is an adaptation to a unique circumstance; inmates revert to heterosexual sexual activity when they return to the community.

The pains of imprisonment are particularly acute for inmates serving life sentences. Realistically, it is highly unlikely that most long-term offenders will be able to sustain their pre-prison relationships, especially if relations with a spouse and/or children were unstable. The pains of imprisonment, combined with the challenges faced by individual inmates, may lead to **self-injurious behaviour (SIB)**, including cutting and slashing, and, in some cases, to suicide.[108] Women offenders are at higher risk of SIB as a way to cope with emotional pain, distress, and isolation.[109] And Indigenous offenders account for 45 percent of all self-harm incidents in federal prisons.[110]

THE INMATE SOCIAL SYSTEM

A universal attribute of correctional institutions is the existence of an inmate social system, often referred to as the **inmate subculture**. For decades, criminologists have attempted to determine the origins, components, and functions of the inmate social system. Explanations generally centre on the role that the subculture plays in providing inmates with illicit goods and services and the impact of the pre-prison experiences and attitudes that offenders may bring into the institution.

There are a number of other key concepts that assist in understanding the inmate social system. One is **prisonization**, which is the process by which inmates become socialized into the norms, values, and culture of the prison.[111]

Offenders are said to be **institutionalized** when they have become prisonized to such a degree that they are unable to function in the outside, free community. There are offenders who have spent most of their youth and adult lives confined in correctional institutions. These **state-raised offenders** have experienced only limited periods of freedom in the community and may have neither the social skills nor the ability to function outside the total institutional world of the prison. For these offenders, the prison provides security, friends, room and board, and a predictable routine, none of which is guaranteed in the outside community. The prison, not the community, is their home.

A key component of the inmate social system is the **inmate code**, a set of behavioural rules that govern interactions among the inmates and with institutional staff.[112] The rule sets include "do your own time" (i.e., mind your own business), "don't exploit other inmates," and "don't weaken."[113] A former federal inmate described the inmate code as follows:

> Keep your mouth shut, keep your nose out of other people's business and, you know, don't talk to the guards or nothing because then people are figuring you're going to be a rat. Not to be a rat or an informant, that's a big one. To hold your own if somebody tries to get at you. You gotta defend yourself, or you're a punk.... If you can't stand up for yourself then you're not a man in there.... Just honour your word, that's the big thing, and pay your debts when you owe, and mind your own business.[114]

Self-injurious behaviour (SIB)

Deliberate self-inflicted bodily harm or disfigurement.

Inmate subculture

The patterns of interaction and the relationships that exist among inmates confined in correctional institutions.

Prisonization

The process by which inmates become socialized into the norms, values, and culture of the prison.

Institutionalized

Inmates who have become prisonized to such a degree that they are unable to function in the outside, free community.

State-raised offenders

Inmates who have spent the majority of their adult (and perhaps young adult) lives confined in correctional institutions and, as a consequence, may have neither the skills nor ability to function in the outside, free community.

Inmate code

A set of behavioural rules that govern interactions among inmates and with institutional staff.

There is considerable evidence that the inmate code is no longer adhered to by all of the inmates, particularly among younger offenders. This is reflected in the comments of two inmates and one staff member in provincial institutions:

> You know, it used to be how nobody stole from each other in the old days. Now, it's like holy f*! You know what I mean?... Yeah, there is so little of the code in here right now. (remand inmate, Fort Saskatchewan Correctional Centre, Alberta)

> The unwritten rules of jail are basically gone. There's so much rattin' and shit on these ranges. It's f*-in' sickening. (sentenced inmate, Headlingley Correctional Centre, Manitoba)

> I think it's there, but definitely not as big as before. Years back, there used to be an inmate code of conduct, and they respected each other's privacy. Now, there is a very limited code because they are pretty much stealing from each other—unheard of back in, say, the early eighties. (staff member, Headlingly Correctional Centre, Manitoba)[115]

The breakdown of the inmate code has been attributed to a variety of factors, including the increasing number of state-raised inmates with lengthy histories of involvement in foster homes and social services and increasing communication between inmates and staff.[116]

While most inmates pay at least "lip service" to the code, an inmate's greatest source of danger is other inmates. Prison assaults are disproportionately committed by younger inmates and in institutions that are overcrowded.[117] Inmates convicted of sex offences are at a high risk of being verbally and/or physically abused and victimized.[118]

A number of **social (or argot) roles** are associated with the inmate social system. These roles are based on the inmate's friendship networks, sentence length, current and previous offences, degree of at least verbal support for the inmate code, and participation in illegal activities such as gambling and drug distribution.

For example, "square johns" exhibit prosocial attitudes and behaviour and are positive toward staff and administration. "Right guys," on the other hand, are antisocial and have negative attitudes toward authority. "Snitches" ("rats" or "squealers") play a risky game of providing information on inmates and their activities to correctional staff.[119] A related feature of inmate society is a specialized vocabulary: A "bit" is the inmate's sentence (e.g., a five-year "bit"); "beef" is the type of crime; a "fish" is a new inmate; while a "goof" is an inmate who behaves inappropriately in the institution (e.g., whistles; for some unknown reason, whistling is not permitted among inmates).

Contributing to the lack of loyalty and solidarity among inmates is the rat (or snitch) system, by which inmates may improve their own position and prospects with COs and the administration, often at the expense of fellow inmates.

A defining feature of life in contemporary correctional institutions is that inmates tend to group themselves into niches, or friendship networks. These networks may be based on associations formed during previous incarcerations or in the outside

Social (or argot) roles

Roles that inmates assume based on their friendship networks, sentence length, and other factors related to their criminal history and activities in the institution.

PERSPECTIVE

Deputy Warden, federal correctional institution

The long-term inmates are more manageable than short-term inmates. They understand they are going to have to get along with other inmates and the staff. The long-term guys are the ones that end up being on the inmate committees and taking a more balanced view of things. It's the short-term guys that are the most difficult to manage. It's this group that causes all of the problems.

Source: Personal communication with C.T. Griffiths, 2007.

community; on shared ethnicity or culture; or on length of sentence (e.g., lifers may group together). It is this friendship group, rather than the inmate population as a whole, that provides the individual inmate with security and support and that is the recipient of the inmate's loyalty. Inmates and correctional staff distinguish between "convicts" and "inmates" (or "new school kids"), and perceive the latter as not respecting the traditional inmate social system.

The longer an inmate is confined, the more difficult it may be to retain prosocial attitudes and behaviours, especially when the inmate is confined with offenders with more criminal orientations. A major challenge confronting systems of correction is preventing offenders from becoming so immersed in the culture of the prison that the efforts of the individual inmate and the correctional staff to promote change are impeded.

Ironically, it could be argued that those inmates who adjust well in the highly structured environment of correctional institutions may encounter the most difficulties upon release. And there is the larger issue as to whether lengthy sentences serve as a general and specific deterrent to further criminality.

THE EXPERIENCE OF LGTBQ AND TRANSGENDER INMATES

Historically, inmates were sent to correctional institutions based on their identified gender at birth. The numbers of LGBTQ and transgender inmates in Canadian correctional institutions is unknown. What is known is that these inmates may experience hardships in correctional institutions due to correctional policies and mistreatment by staff and other inmates. In the U.S., it is estimated that one-third of transgender inmates have been the victims of sexual assault.[120]

In 2017, CSC announced that transgender inmates would be considered for placement based on their gender identity rather than their genitalia and that inmates would be allowed to wear clothing appropriate to their gender identity.[121] A number of provinces have adopted a similar policy, and other provincial and territorial corrections systems are likely to follow.[122]

INMATE FAMILIES

Family members may feel isolated and neglected by correctional authorities.[123] The families of inmates may also be stigmatized and marginalized in the community.[124] Other concerns relate to finances, housing, isolation from the community, and fears related to the offender's return to the community.[125] The partners of offenders may experience trauma, shame, isolation, and depression.[126,127] Children whose parents are incarcerated can suffer from emotional, behavioural, and academic problems, the type and severity of which vary with the child's age, gender, and length of separation from parents.[128,129]

For the inmate, the loss of regular family contact is one of the pains of imprisonment. Research suggests that inmate participation in family visitation programs has a positive impact on the inmate's family life, reduces institutional misconduct, and lowers the rates of reoffending.[130]

INMATE GRIEVANCES AND COMPLAINTS

Thousands of complaints and grievances are filed every year by inmates in federal and provincial correctional facilities. A very small number (as little as 5 percent) of the inmate population is responsible for nearly 70 percent of the complaints and grievances that are filed. The most frequent complaints received by the federal correctional investigator relate to health care, the conditions of confinement, and institutional transfers.[131]

DOES INCARCERATION WORK?

Very little is known about whether incarceration reduces recidivism.[132] The research evidence suggests that prisons should not be used with the expectation of reducing reoffending and that the excessive use of incarceration as a sanction can have substantial cost implications as well as increase criminal behaviour among some offenders.[133] Individuals sent to prison may be further marginalized and socially and economically stigmatized.[134] The threat of custody is unlikely to deter state-raised offenders.

There is some research to suggest that incarceration can be effective in interrupting the crime trajectory of individual offenders and result in reduced offending upon release. This seems to depend on the criminal history and age of the offender: Offenders with lengthy criminal records may continue offending upon release; older inmates with a criminal history are less likely to reoffend.[135]

Of concern is that sentencing to custody persons with little or no prior involvement in crime and the justice system may result in increased criminality when they return to the community, particularly if they are confined in higher security institutions.[136] There is some evidence that, all things being equal, inmates housed in higher levels of security and in harsh conditions are more likely to reoffend upon release.[137]

There is evidence that offenders who spend their time under supervision in the community have lower rates of reoffending than offenders released from correctional institutions, even considering the types of offences committed.[138] And incarceration is much more expensive than community supervision and may not make the community safer or increase the potential of offenders to return to the community as law-abiding citizens.

These findings suggest that incarceration should be used very selectively and that there may be alternatives to confinement that not only are more cost-effective but also can address the risk and needs of offenders while at the same time ensuring community safety.

CLASSIFICATION AND TREATMENT

There are three major trends in offender classification and treatment: (1) the increasing use of sophisticated risk/needs assessment instruments; (2) the increasing domination of treatment research, policy, and programs from a psychological perspective—in particular, a cognitive-behavioural approach; and (3) a differentiated treatment approach for women, Indigenous persons, and specific categories of offenders such as sex offenders.

Classification is the process by which inmates are subdivided into groups based on a variety of factors such as risk and needs, and it is used to determine institutional placement and programming. It is a core component of correctional treatment. While the classification process in federal corrections is well-established, there are major challenges in provincial/territorial facilities.[139]

The assessment process continues throughout the offender's sentence, from intake to incarceration to release from custody and up to sentence expiry. Offenders have a variety of criminogenic needs that must be addressed both within the institution and later in the community. These include education, mental health, social networks, employment, accommodation, drugs and alcohol, attitudes, and cognitive skills. All of these criminogenic needs are *dynamic* risk factors; that is, they are amenable to change and have been found to be important factors to address in order to reduce the likelihood of reoffending.[140]

As an example, Figure 11.3 presents data on the type of rehabilitative need of offenders admitted to correctional facilities in Saskatchewan in 2010–11. The majority of offenders had four of the six rehabilitative needs. Note the high percentage of

Classification

The process by which inmates are categorized through the use of various assessment instruments to determine the appropriate security level of the inmate and program placement.

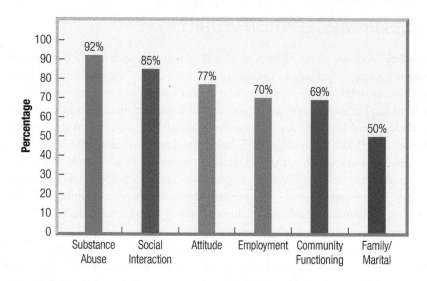

◄ FIGURE 11.3

Adults in Sentenced Custody, by Type of Rehabilitative Need, Saskatchewan, 2010–11

Source: M. Dauvergne. 2012. "Adult Correctional Statistics in Canada, 2010/2011," *Juristat, 32*(1). Statistics Canada Catalogue no. 85-002-X. Ottawa: Minister of Industry, p. 13. http://www.statcan.gc.ca/pub/85-002-x/2012001/article/11715-eng.pdf.

offenders with substance issues and social interaction (criminal peers and companions) among this population.[141]

The classification systems used by federal and provincial/territorial corrections generally include psychological, personality, and behavioural inventories that attempt to categorize offenders.

Risk assessment and risk management are the mantras of contemporary corrections, and the assessment of risk is a key component of classification and case management. Risk assessments are designed to identify those offenders who are most likely to reoffend upon release from the institution if no treatment intervention occurs.[142] In assessing the degree of risk posed by an offender, corrections personnel generally consider **static risk factors** and **dynamic risk factors**.

Static risk factors include the offender's criminal history, including prior convictions, seriousness of prior offences, and whether the offender successfully completed previous periods of supervision in the community. Dynamic risk factors are those attributes of the offender that can be altered through intervention, and include vocational training and education, addiction issues, attitude and motivation, and cognitive thinking abilities among others.

Research studies have identified eight factors that reliably predict involvement in criminality: (1) lack of attachment to family/marital supports; (2) school/employment problems; (3) lack of prosocial leisure or recreational activities; (4) antisocial peers; (5) antisocial attitudes; (6) antisocial personality; (7) substance abuse; and (8) history of antisocial behaviour.[143]

CASE MANAGEMENT

Correctional **case management** is the process by which the needs and abilities of offenders are matched with correctional programs and services.

At the core of the case management process is the **correctional plan,** which is developed for most inmates, the exception being those serving short sentences. This plan determines the offender's initial institution placement, specific training or work opportunities, and release plan. The *Canadian Victims Bill of Rights* (S.C. 2015, c. 13, s. 2) provides that crime victims can receive information about an offender's progress in fulfilling the objectives of their correctional plan.

A major challenge for treatment staff is that most adult custodial sentences ordered by the court are short—nearly 60 percent are one month or less.[144]

Static risk factors

Attributes of the offender that predict the likelihood of recidivism but are not amenable to change, including criminal history, prior convictions, seriousness of prior offences, and performance on previous conditional releases.

◄ **Dynamic risk factors**

Attributes of the offender that can be altered through intervention, including level of education, employment skills, addiction issues, and cognitive thinking abilities, among others.

Case management

The process by which the needs and abilities of offenders are matched with correctional programs and services.

Correctional plan

A key component of the case management process that determines the offender's initial institution placement, specific training or work opportunities, and preparation for release.

INSTITUTIONAL TREATMENT PROGRAMS

The programs most frequently offered in correctional institutions include substance abuse management, family violence, sex offender programming, violence prevention, anger management, GED (high school equivalency) courses, and various vocational programs. There may also be programs that target specific groups of offenders, such as sex offenders. In addition, there are programs facilitated by outside groups, including Alcoholics Anonymous (AA) and Narcotics Anonymous (NA). There are also specific programs for women offenders and Indigenous offenders. Sex offenders in particular present challenges for treatment staff, especially those classified as high risk. Their patterns of deviance are often deeply entrenched.[145]

There are also a variety of other innovative programs that bring community members together with incarcerated offenders. These include book clubs, writing programs for offenders, and mother–child programs. Several universities participate in the "Inside-Out" program, in which students from the outside take courses with inmates inside institutions.[146] The inmates enroll in the course and receive credit upon completion.

A Toronto organization, Book Clubs for Inmates, runs 17 book clubs in 17 federal institutions that involve volunteers leading monthly discussions with inmates.[147] Another program, Walls to Bridges (W2B), is highlighted in Corrections File 11.4.

The short time that most offenders spend in provincial and territorial institutions makes it difficult to address alcohol, drug, and mental health issues, as well as to develop specialized programs (e.g., for offenders with FASD). As a former inmate in

---

CORRECTIONS FILE 11.4

THE WALLS TO BRIDGES PROGRAM: CREATING COLLABORATIVE AND INNOVATIVE LEARNING COMMUNITIES IN CORRECTIONAL INSTITUTIONS

The Walls to Bridges (W2B) program is a collaborative partnership between the Grand Valley Institution for Women (GVI), a federal correctional facility in Kitchener, Ontario, and the Faculty of Social Work at Wilfrid Laurier University. The program is centred on college and university courses that are taught in jails, prisons, and community corrections facilities. The courses are attended by offenders who are incarcerated or under supervision in the community, along with college and university students. All of the participants earn college or university credit for completing the courses. W2B program materials highlight, "All participants in the class are peers, learning the class content together through innovative, experiential and dialogical processes" (http://wallstobridges.ca/what-we-do/). Courses recently offered in GVI include Sociology of Race and Ethnicity, Public Policy and Native Peoples in Canada, and Walls to Bridges: Prisons and Punishment.

PERSPECTIVE

Sex Offender Treatment Therapist

Sex offenders are the ones who have the greatest difficulty taking responsibility for what they have done. Groups are a good way to get to them. When you facilitate a group of sex offenders, there is a certain dynamic that goes on. Sex offenders in the group have an understanding of behaviour that I will never have. With sex offenders, the biggest strength of the group was their being able to help each other accept responsibility for their behaviour.

Source: Personal communication with C.T. Griffiths

a provincial institution in Saskatchewan stated, "Usually you're not in an institution long enough to get into their program, and they design it like that for a reason. You get on a waiting list for a program. It's not designed to get you the program, it's designed to get you back."[148]

There is a question as to whether treatment is a priority for correctional authorities. CSC, for example, spends less on correctional programming than on staff overtime—about 2 percent of its multibillion-dollar budget. Programs for inmates in provincial/territorial facilities are often limited and the first to be reduced in times of fiscal restraint.[149] This despite the fact that offenders in custody are generally higher risk and have more needs than those under supervision in the community.

There is also increasing evidence that a large number of offenders in correctional institutions are suffering from some type of trauma. This may be related to critical physical and psychological abuse as a child, exposure to traumatic events, and physical injuries, including traumatic brain injury as a result of head injuries.[150] This disability may have a significant effect upon the ability of the inmate to adjust to life in the institution and to participate in, and benefit from, correctional programs and services.

WOMEN OFFENDERS AND TREATMENT

A number of task forces have identified the need for a gender-specific approach to treatment, one that centres on empowerment and that recognizes the broader, systemic barriers facing women in general: poverty, unemployment, lack of education, and sexism.[151,152]

The use of the risk, need, and responsivity principles (RNR) have been found to be equally important for the treatment of male and female offenders.[153] Studies have found that women offenders who are exposed to intensive treatment interventions have lower rates of reoffending than women who are not.[154] Several evaluations of gender-specific interventions targeting high-risk/needs women offenders in Canada have found that RNR programs can reduce reoffending.[155,156]

At the federal level, gender-responsive substance abuse programs have produced lower rates of reoffending among women. The Women Offender Substance Abuse Program (WOSAP) is a gender-specific program designed to empower women to make healthy lifestyle choices in order to reduce reoffending upon release.

THE PRINCIPLES OF EFFECTIVE CORRECTIONAL TREATMENT

To be effective, correctional treatment programs must (1) be based on empirically supported models of correctional change; (2) incorporate the principles of risk, need, and responsivity (RNR); (3) be focused on the dynamic risk factors associated with the offender's criminal behaviour; (4) be monitored, evaluated, and accredited; and (5) be implemented by well-trained, dedicated program staff.[157,158,159] Following the risk principle, treatment interventions are focused primarily on higher-risk inmates.[160]

For any program to have a significant impact, the offender must be amenable to treatment. Not all inmates are receptive to treatment. This can be for a variety of reasons, including mental deficiency or learning disability, a deeply rooted attitudinal and behavioural pattern centred on a criminal lifestyle, an extensive history of confinement in institutions, and/or a general lack of interest in making the effort to change.[161] Conversely, the benefits of treatment programs can be enhanced if the background culture of the inmates is considered. Programs for Indigenous inmates that consider the cultural attributes and are delivered by knowledgeable staff have produced more positive outcomes than generic programs.[162]

It is also important that inmates have timely access to treatment programs so as to be able to complete the programs prior to release. This is particularly problematic for inmates in provincial and territorial institutions. Nearly 60 percent of adult offenders served a term of one month or less.[163] In Ontario, 76 percent of persons sentenced to provincial correctional facilities in 2015 received a sentence of three months or less.[164] This makes it extremely difficult for inmates to participate in, or to complete, treatment programs.

A long-standing challenge for correctional systems has been to ensure continuity between treatment interventions in institutional settings and those in the community following release. This is the concept of **throughcare**. Studies have found that the effectiveness of institution-based treatment programs is enhanced when there is a "seamless" transition to community-based treatment when the offender is released from confinement.[165]

Throughcare

The notion that there should be continuity between institutional treatment and programs and community-based services for offenders.

RESTORATIVE JUSTICE IN CORRECTIONAL INSTITUTIONS

Restorative justice approaches can also be used after offenders have been incarcerated for an offence. This may involve the victim and/or the victim's family meeting with the offender. There is an opportunity for the victim or the victim's family to reach closure on the incident and assist the victim and/or the victim's families to continue the healing. Given the intensity of emotions that surround these meetings, it is important that the mediator meet with both parties separately prior to the meeting to assess their motivations and to ensure that the victims are not re-victimized by the experience. See Corrections File 11.5.

INDIGENOUS HEALING CENTRES AND LODGES

Corrections systems have made some efforts to address the specific treatment needs of Indigenous offenders. Among the more common Indigenous-specific programs found in correctional institutions across the country are sweat lodges, healing circles, and modules that focus on cultural awareness, substance abuse, and family violence.

Under section 81 of the CCRA, the federal government has entered into agreements with First Nations groups across the country to develop and operate healing lodges. These include Pê Sâkâstêw (Cree for "new beginnings" and pronounced "Bay Sah-ga-stay-o"); a minimum-security facility for male offenders near Hobbema, Alberta, on the Samson Cree Nation; the Prince Albert (Saskatchewan) Grand Council Spiritual Healing Lodge for male Indigenous offenders on the Wahpeton Dakota First Nation;

A VICTIM'S FAMILY MEETS THE MAN WHO KILLED THEIR SISTER/MOTHER

On February 20, 2010, Coral Forslund's sister, Martha, and her boyfriend were riding on a motorcycle when they were hit and killed by a driver who made an illegal turn on the highway. The car, stolen earlier that day, was driven by a 25-year-old man who had a lengthy history of substance abuse and of offending, including weapons offences, assault, and failure to provide a breath sample. In July 2011, the man was found guilty of seven counts, including two counts of criminal negligence causing death. He was sentenced to seven years in prison and given credit for 3½ years for time he had already served.

Coral recalled that when the offender was sent to prison, she had considerable hatred for him. However, she always wondered whether he was remorseful. With assistance from a federal program called Restorative Opportunities (http://www.csc-scc.gc.ca/restorative-justice/003005 -1000-eng.shtml), she and several members of her extended family met with the offender in a session with a mediator. During the five-hour session, they asked the offender a range of questions, at times cutting him off when they felt he was being less-than-honest with them. When she pointed to her nephew and said, "This guy doesn't have a mother," the offender broke down and sobbed. He spoke directly to them, stating, "I killed your mother. I killed your sister." The offender was released in March 2014 and, on release, was attending counselling and school. The session brought the families of the victims a newfound peace, Coral's sister stating, "He did accept responsibility. He did apologize and it seemed sincere."

Source: D. Quan. 2015, February 8. "How Restorative Justice Changed a Grieving Family's Opinion of a Hit-and-Run Driver," *Canada.com.* http://o.canada.com/news/national/how-restorative-justice-changed-a-grieving-familys-opinion -of-a-hit-and-run-driver.

the Okimaw Ohci Healing Lodge (Saskatchewan) for federal Indigenous women offenders, which incorporates Indigenous culture and spirituality; and the Waseskun Healing Centre, near Montreal, which offers residential therapy for men and women referred from First Nations and from provincial and federal correctional institutions. Healing lodges operate under CSC but are also accountable to a governing council composed of Elders and other First Nations representatives.[166]

At healing lodges, the needs of Indigenous offenders are addressed in a holistic manner. They receive individualized programming, engage with the community, partake in Indigenous teachings and ceremonies, and engage with Elders.[167]

TREATMENT PROGRAMS FOR INDIGENOUS INMATES

Indigenous offenders generally have greater criminogenic needs than non-Indigenous offenders. The risk factors for chronic Indigenous offenders—whose deviant behaviour typically begins in childhood, escalates in the adolescent years, and continues throughout adulthood—include substance abuse, a dysfunctional family environment, and negative peer group associations.

Indigenous offenders have access to the same treatment programs as other inmates, including interventions focusing on substance abuse, domestic violence, sexual offending, violence prevention, emotions management, and cognitive skills training. There are also specific interventions directed toward Indigenous inmates.

The Ma Mawi Wi Chi Itata Family Violence Program at Stony Mountain Prison in Manitoba, for example, is a program for Indigenous inmates designed to address issues related to violent behaviour toward spouses, partners, and

▼ Kwìkwèxwelhp Healing Lodge in Harrison Mills, British Columbia

Courtesy of the Correctional Service Canada

family members. Similarly, the Pathways Units program, which operates in a number of federal correctional institutions across the country, are living units led by small teams composed of Indigenous Elders and correctional staff. The approach is grounded in Indigenous culture and spirituality.

Provincial and territorial systems of corrections have far fewer programs and services for Indigenous inmates, even though these offenders may account for as much as 90 percent of the inmate population.

MEASURING THE EFFECTIVENESS OF CORRECTIONAL TREATMENT

Recidivism rates

The number of offenders released from confinement who, once released from prison, are returned to prison.

The traditional method used to determine success is **recidivism rates**—that is, the number of offenders who, once released from confinement, are returned to prison either for a technical violation of their parole or statutory release or for the commission of a new offence. There is, however, no Canada-wide guideline for measuring the rate of reoffending of offenders who are under supervision. Some jurisdictions do not track offenders, and, among others, there are differences in the period of time that offenders are monitored for new offences and whether offences committed after the end of community supervision ends are counted.

Using recidivism rates as a measure of success is problematic for a number of reasons. For one, it prevents an assessment of the "relative" improvement of the offender; for example, an offender who previously committed serious crimes and is subsequently returned to confinement for a relatively minor offence might be viewed as a "relative success" rather than as a failure. Or an offender's return to the community may have been successful due to factors unrelated to the treatment intervention. On the other hand, the offender may have returned to criminal activity and not have been detected.

One issue that surrounds the effectiveness of correctional treatment is whether offenders should be required to participate in treatment programs while they are confined in correctional institutions. See At Issue 11.2.

AT ISSUE 11.2

THE ETHICS OF CORRECTIONAL TREATMENT: SHOULD PRISON INMATES HAVE THE RIGHT TO REFUSE TREATMENT?

It was previously noted that offenders on probation must consent prior to participating in treatment programs while under supervision in the community. The same issue exists for incarcerated offenders.

Consider the following scenario: An inmate convicted of a sex offence is sentenced to 15 years in prison. During confinement, he refuses to participate in treatment programs. As a consequence, he does not receive any form of conditional release, is denied statutory release after having served two-thirds of the sentence, and serves his entire sentence in prison. On his warrant expiry date, he is released, untreated, from the correctional institution, at high risk of reoffending.

The Canadian *Charter of Rights and Freedoms* guarantees that all persons have the right to life, liberty, and security of the person, rights that would most likely be violated by any provision of mandatory treatment.[a] A provision in the CCRA states that inmates must provide informed consent, both at the outset and during treatment, and that

the inmate has the right to refuse treatment or to withdraw from a treatment program at any time. Research suggests that mandated (coerced) participation in treatment programs is ineffective in reducing reoffending as compared to voluntary participation in treatment.[b]

QUESTIONS

1. What is your position on the right of inmates to refuse treatment?

2. Would you support an attempt to impose mandatory treatment on certain categories of offenders, such as sex offenders and violent offenders?

---

[a] C. McKinnon. 1995. "The Legal Right of Offenders to Refuse Treatment," *Forum on Corrections Research, 7*(3), 43–47. http://www.csc-scc.gc.ca/research/forum/e073/e073n-eng.shtml.

[b] K.K. Parhar, J.S. Wormith, D.M. Derkzen, and A.M. Beauregard. 2008. "Offender Coercion in Treatment: A Meta-Analysis of Effectiveness," *Criminal Justice and Behavior, 35*(9), 1109–1135.

DOES CORRECTIONAL TREATMENT WORK?

Since the introduction of treatment programs into correctional institutions in the 1950s, there has been an ongoing debate over their effectiveness. The debate has involved politicians, community interest groups, correctional scholars, and senior and line-level corrections personnel. The debate was originally sparked by the pronouncement of the scholar Robert Martinson nearly 40 years ago that "nothing works"—that treatment programs did not reduce reoffending.[168] No mind that upon re-analysis of the data, Martinson recanted his original conclusion.[169] The "nothing works" mantra has long been used as a political tool to justify cutting treatment programs and services for inmates and other offenders.

Despite the challenges of doing time, inmates are able in some instances to take advantage of programs to improve their education and skill sets. As former inmate in Collins Bay Penitentiary, a federal correctional institution in Ontario, recalled:

> When I came into the system, I couldn't read or write hardly. I had no trades, and I took advantage when I was in and went back to school and I went and got my grade 6, grades 7, 8, 9, 10, 11, 12 at Collins Bay. I ended up getting my welding licence and my apprenticeship in Collins Bay, and I ended up walking out of there with 89 credits [toward a welding certificate].[170]

With the usual caveats that studies vary widely in their design and analytics and that there are relatively few Canadian studies, some of what we know about the effectiveness of correctional treatment interventions are set out in Research File 11.1.

RESEARCH FILE 11.1

THE EFFECTIVENESS OF CORRECTIONAL TREATMENT INTERVENTIONS

Do correctional treatment programs work? The general consensus among researchers is that *some programs work to reduce reoffending of some offenders*; treatment programs that adhere to the RNR principles can reduce rates of reoffending from 10 percent to 40 percent.[a,b,c]

Do correctional programs successfully address the risk and needs of offenders? Perhaps not. A large study of federal offenders ($N = 24,315$) released on conditional release between 2005 and 2010 found no change in the offender's risk level (93.5 percent), nor in needs (88.2 percent). This suggests that whatever programming these offenders received while incarcerated did not alter their risk or needs ratings between their entry into a correctional institution and their release.[d]

Do adult basic education and vocational/work programs reduce reoffending? They can. Participation in prison education programs can reduce the levels of misconduct in institutions and reduce rates of reoffending.[e,f] A key requirement is throughcare—continuity between the institutional program and programs and services in the community.

Do programs for offenders with mental health issues work? Potentially. An evaluation of the CSC Mental Health Strategy, designed to provide a continuum of care from the institution to the community, found that offenders who had access to mental health specialists were less likely to have their conditional release revoked or suspended.[g]

Do drug treatment programs for federal offenders work? Some appear to. There is evidence that the programs for violent offenders, sex offenders, and inmates with substance abuse issues can be successful in reducing reoffending.[h] Federal inmates who reside in "drug-free" intensive supervision unit (ISU) programs are less likely to be returned to custody than other offenders and less likely to be returned to custody for a new offence.[i] The CSC ISUs have strong support from inmates and correctional staff but their long-term impact on drug use and recidivism is uncertain.[j] Multistage residential programs that provide a bridge between the prison and the community can also reduce reoffending.[k]

Do treatment programs in provincial and territorial institutions work? Unknown. Despite the fact that most offenders in confinement are in these facilities, program evaluations are virtually non-existent.

Do sex offender treatment programs work? Difficult to determine, due in part to the wide variety of offenders that are classified as "sex offenders." Some interventions appear to work to reduce reoffending among certain groups of sex offenders. Sex offenders who participate in treatment programs generally have lower rates of reoffending than comparison groups that received no intervention.[l] Programs for sex offenders based on the principles of RNR are the most effective in reducing reoffending, as are cognitive-behavioural interventions that focus on dysfunctional thoughts and feelings.[m,n]

(continued)

Does effective correctional treatment save money? Yes. An evaluation of programs in federal institutions found that for every $1 invested in correctional programming, there was a return of $1 to $8; for every $1 of sex offender programming, a return of $6.59; and for every $1 of substance abuse programming, a return of $2,69. "Return" was measured by the cost savings associated with achieved correctional outcomes; that is, offenders are supervised in the community and do not reoffend.

In addition, the cost of participating in institutional employment programs equals $779 in terms of good correctional outcomes, versus offenders not participating in institutional employment programs in terms of poor correctional outcomes, which is $15,662.[o]

[a] J. Bonta. 1997. *Offender Rehabilitation: From Research to Practice.* Ottawa: Department of the Solicitor General of Canada. https://www.publicsafety.gc.ca/cnt/rsrcs/pblctns/ffndr-rhblttn-rsrch/ffndr-rhblttn-rsrch-eng.pdf.

[b] L.W. Sherman, D. Gottfredson, D. MacKenzie, J. Eck, P. Reuter, and S. Bushway. 1997. *Preventing Crime: What Works, What Doesn't, What's Promising.* Washington, DC: Office of Justice Programs, U.S. Department of Justice. https://www.ncjrs.gov/pdffiles/171676.pdf.

[c] P. Smith, P. Gendreau, and K. Swartz. 2009. "Validating the Principles of Effective Intervention: A Systematic Review of the Contributions of Meta-Analysis in the Field of Corrections," *Victims and Offenders, 4*(2), 148–169.

[d] M. Olotu, D. Luong, C. MacDonald, M. McKay, S. Heath, N. Allegri, and E. Loree. 2011. *Report of the Evaluation of CSC's Community Corrections.* Chapter 1, "Correctional Interventions." Ottawa: Correctional Service Canada, p. 48. http://www.csc-scc.gc.ca/publications/092/005007-2008-eng.pdf.

[e] J.H. Esperian. 2010. "The Effect of Prison Education on Recidivism," *Journal of Correctional Education, 61*(4), 316–334.

[f] John Howard Society of Alberta. 2002. *Inmate Education.* Edmonton: Author. http://www.johnhoward.ab.ca/pub/old/respaper/educa02.pdf.

[g] N. Allergi, K. Deleveus, D. Loung, H. Li, T. Jensen, D. Batten, . . . M. Henighan. 2008. *Evaluation Report: Community Mental Health Initiative.* Ottawa: Correctional Service of Canada. http://publications.gc.ca/collections/collection_2013/scc-csc/PS84-33-2008-eng.pdf.

[h] S. Belenko, C. Foltz, M.A. Lang, and H-E. Sung. 2004. "Recidivism among High-Risk Drug Felons: A Longitudinal Analysis Following Residential Treatment," *Journal of Rehabilitation, 40*(1), 105–132.

[i] D.D. Varis, D. Lefebvre, and B.A. Grant. 2006. "Intensive Support Units for Federal Offenders with Substance Abuse Problems: An Impact Analysis," *Forum on Corrections Research, 18*(1). http://www.csc-scc.gc.ca/research/r151-eng.shtml.

[j] D.D. Varis. 2001. "Intensive Support Units for Federal Inmates: A Descriptive Review," *Forum on Corrections Research, 13*(3). http://www.csc-scc.gc.ca/research/forum/e133/133m_e.pdf.

[k] J.A. Inciardi, S.S. Martin, and C.A. Butzin. 2004. "Five-Year Outcomes of Therapeutic Community Treatment of Drug-Involved Offenders after Release from Prison," *Crime and Delinquency, 50*(1), 88–108.

[l] F. Losel and M. Schmucker. 2005. "The Effectiveness of Treatment for Sex Offenders: A Comprehensive Meta-Analysis," *Journal of Experimental Criminology, 1*(1), 117–146.

[m] F. Cortoni and K.L. Nunes. 2007. *Assessing the Effectiveness of the National Sexual Offender Program.* Ottawa: Correctional Service of Canada. http://publications.gc.ca/collections/collection_2010/scc-csc/PS83-3-183-eng.pdf.

[n] R. Hanson and K.E. Morton-Bourgon. 2009. "The Accuracy of Recidivism Risk Assessments for Sexual Offenders: A Meta-Analysis of 188 Prediction Studies," *Psychological Assessment, 21*(1), 1–21.

[o] Olotu et al., "Correctional Interventions," p. 106.

SUMMARY

The discussion in this chapter has focused on correctional institutions. The origin, evolution, and management of correctional institutions were discussed. It was noted that there are a number of challenges that are encountered in operating correctional institutions. These include the profile of inmates, who tend to be poorly educated and marginally skilled, disproportionately Indigenous and Black, and increasingly, designated as having special needs. Overcrowding and the use of segregation were identified as two major issues.

The role of COs was examined, and their relationships with one another, with inmates, and with the administration and treatment staff were discussed. There are instances in which COs may abuse their considerable powers and authority. The experiences of inmates were examined, focusing on entering and living in the prison. The classification and treatment of offenders with a particular focus on the principles of effective correctional treatment and the effectiveness of correctional programs in reducing reoffending were considered.

KEY POINTS REVIEW

1. The events surrounding the building of the first Canadian penitentiary in the early 1800s illustrate how changes in the response to crime and criminal offenders can be influenced by social, economic, and political forces.

2. One way to trace the changing philosophy of corrections and punishment is by examining the architecture of correctional institutions over the past 200 years.

3. Among the challenges of managing correctional institutions are that of being a total institution, having a split personality of punishment and treatment, and being a public and political institution.

4. Offenders in correctional institutions tend to be male, young, single, poorly educated, and marginally skilled.

5. Indigenous persons and Blacks are overrepresented in institutional populations.

6. The profile of offenders has changed, including an increase in special needs populations.

7. Overcrowding contributes to unsafe environments for correctional staff and inmates and hinders correctional treatment programs.

8. The use of segregation is highly controversial and has resulted in a number of deaths in custody.

9. A pivotal role in correctional institutions is played by correctional officers who have both legal and moral authority.

10. Correctional officers must develop accommodative relationships with inmates to ensure daily stability and order.

11. Correctional officer relationships with treatment staff and the administration may be characterized by distrust and cynicism.

12. Persons confined in correctional institutions tend to have low levels of education, limited employment skills, and addiction issues, and are disproportionately Indigenous and Black.

13. Inmates experience many challenges, including adjusting to life inside, coping with the pains of imprisonment, navigating the inmate social system, staying safe, and maintaining personal relationships.

14. Classification is a core component of correctional treatment, and risk assessments are used to identify the degree of risk posed by the offender upon release from the institution.

15. The core principles of effective correctional treatment centre on risk, need, and responsivity (RNR).

16. The use of recidivism rates to measure the success of correctional treatment programs is problematic.

17. Research studies indicate that correctional treatment programs can be effective in reducing reoffending.

KEY TERM QUESTIONS

1. Compare and contrast the **Pennsylvania model** and the **Auburn model** of prisons.

2. What is **moral architecture**, and how does it help us understand the goals of the first penitentiaries that were built in Canada and how architecture can reflect correctional philosophies?

3. What was the **Brown Commission**, and why is it important in the study of Canadian corrections?

4. Describe the attributes of the **minimum-**, **medium-**, and **maximum-security** facilities and the multilevel institutions and the Special Handling Unit, operated by the federal Correctional Service Canada.

5. Compare and contrast **static security** and **dynamic security**.

6. What is meant by the **rule of law** and the **duty to act fairly**, and how do these concepts apply to corrections?

7. Why are prisons viewed as **total institutions**, and why is this an important concept in the study of corrections?

8. What is the **continuum of correctional institutions**, and how does this concept assist our understanding of life inside prisons?

9. Discuss the use of **segregation** and the controversy that has surrounded its use.

10. What was the **Arbour report**, and what is its significance in Canadian corrections and, more specifically, correctional policy and practice for women inmates?

11. Define and discuss the importance of the following concepts for the study of corrections and life inside correctional institutions: (1) **status degradation ceremonies**; (2) **pains of imprisonment**; (3) **inmate subculture**; (4) **prisonization**; (5) **state-raised offenders**; (6) **inmate code**.

12. Discuss **self-injurious behavior (SIB)** among inmates and the factors that place inmates at risk of this behaviour.

13. How does the concept of **social (or argot) roles** assist in understanding the dynamics among inmates in correctional institutions?

14. Define **classification** and its role in corrections.

15. Compare and contrast **static risk factors** and **dynamic risk factors**, and note the role of each type of factor in the classification process.

16. Discuss the role of **case management** and the **correctional plan** in correctional treatment.

17. Describe **throughcare** and its importance in correctional treatment.

18. What are the issues that surround the use of **recidivism rates** as a measure of the success of correctional treatment programs?

CRITICAL THINKING EXERCISE

Critical Thinking Exercise 11.1

The Death of Denise Fayant: A Closer Look

The death of Denise Fayant in a federal correctional institution was discussed earlier in the chapter. Read the public inquiry that was held on the death, available at https://open.alberta.ca/dataset/f60a2dfe-5dd8-49d3-b430-77b22db88ed8/resource/bf3c045a-cba7-42bf-b33b-778857b9126a/download/01000-Report-into-death-of-Denise-Leanne-Fayant.pdf.

Your Thoughts?

1. What were the key events that led to the death of Denise Fayant?

2. What role did corrections personnel play in this incident?

3. What are the "lessons learned" from this tragedy?

Source: Province of Alberta. 1998. *Report to the Attorney General. Public Inquiry. The Fatalities Inquiry Act.* Edmonton: Author. https://open.alberta.ca/dataset/f60a2dfe-5dd8-49d3-b430-77b22db88ed8/resource/bf3c045a-cba7-42bf-b33b-778857b9126a/download/01000-Report-into-death-of-Denise-Leanne-Fayant.pdf.

CLASS/GROUP DISCUSSION EXERCISE

Class/Group Discussion Exercise 11.1

The Deaths of Ashley Smith and Eddie Snowshoe: A Systemic Failure of Corrections?

The in-custody death of Ashley Smith was discussed in this chapter. Another inmate, Eddie Snowshoe, also died in federal custody. The cases are similar in many respects. Access materials that compare the circumstances of the two deaths in *The Globe and Mail* article "Confined: The Death of Eddie Snowshoe," written by Patrick White (http://www.theglobeandmail.com/news/national/confined-the-death-of-eddie-snowshoe/article21815548/). In Part 5 of the article, titled "The Gorilla House at the Zoo," under the title "Where did the system fail?" review the comparison between the two cases.

Your Thoughts?

Consider the similarities between the two cases.

1. How could the issues that are identified have been addressed so that the likelihood of the deaths of Ashley Smith and Eddie Snowshoe could have been reduced?
2. Now, read the report of the federal correctional investigator on the death of Matthew Ryan Hines (*Fatal Response: An Investigation into the Preventable Death of Matthew Ryan Hines. Final Report,* available at http://www.oci-bec.gc.ca/cnt/rpt/pdf/oth-aut/oth-aut20170215-eng.pdf). What are the similarities between the Hines case and the cases of Ashley Smith and Eddie Snowshoe?

MEDIA LINKS

History

"Corrections in Canada: A Historical Timeline," http://www.csc-scc.gc.ca/about-us/006-2000-eng.shtml

The Kingston Penitentiary

"Kingston Penitentiary Tour," November 26, 2013, https://www.youtube.com/watch?v=cjUTEE-TVx4

"Tales from Kingston Pen," CBC, April 6, 2013, https://www.youtube.com/watch?v=3YbFOOD5Nlk

"Kingston Pen: Secrets and Lies," *The Fifth Estate,* CBC, May 4, 2014, https://www.youtube.com/watch?v=f5oEe8r2fYs

Correctional Institutions

"Behind Bars: Overcrowded Prisons in Canada," *16x9 on Global,* Global News, April 13, 2012, www.youtube.com/watch?v=2mDOof6H6cc

"Beyond the Fence: A Virtual Tour of a Canadian Penitentiary," http://www.csc-scc.gc.ca/csc-virtual-tour/index-eng.shtml

"Inside Toronto's New Maximum Security Detention Centre," *Globe and Mail,* October 4, 2013, http://www.theglobeandmail.com/views/news/videos/video-inside-torontos-new-maximum-security-detention-centre/article14698079

"'Welcome to Hell': Inside Canada's Most Decrepit Prison, Baffin Correctional Centre," *National Post,* May 19, 2015, http://news.nationalpost.com/news/canada/welcome-to-hell-inside-canadas-most-decrepit-prison-baffin-correctional-centre

Perspectives on the Ottawa-Carleton Detention Centre

"A Look Inside the Ottawa-Carleton Detention Centre," *CBC News*, October 28, 2016, http://www.cbc.ca/news/canada/ottawa/look-inside-ottawa-carleton-detention-centre-1.3824336

"Life at Ottawa's Jail: Perspectives from Prisoners' Loved Ones," Criminalization and Punishment Education Project (CPEP), April 26, 2016, https://www.youtube.com/watch?v=QwG8m7l3_gU

"Life Inside Ottawa's Jail: A Woman's Perspective," Criminalization and Punishment Education Project (CPEP), April 14, 2016, https://www.youtube.com/watch?v=gDyfxQQd8xw

"Life at Ottawa's Jail: A Recent Prisoner's Perspective," Criminalization and Punishment Education Project (CPEP), April 2, 2016, https://www.youtube.com/watch?v=uZsAJVO9_8w

"Life Inside Ottawa's Jail: An Aboriginal Perspective," Criminalization and Punishment Education Project (CPEP), May 13, 2016, https://www.youtube.com/watch?v=xvNDzcllcrI

"Unprecedented Footage from Inside an Ontario Penitentiary," *CTV News*, May 16, 2016, https://www.youtube.com/watch?v=76Y45-7jcfE

"A Tour of the New Toronto South Detention Centre," *Torontoist*, October 3, 2013, http://torontoist.com/2013/10/a-tour-of-the-new-toronto-south-detention-centre

"Revealed in Photos: Take a Tour Inside Ottawa's Notorious Jail," *Ottawa Citizen*, October 27, 2016, http://ottawacitizen.com/news/local-news/inside-the-ottawa-jail-tour-of-the-ocdc

Mentally Ill Offenders

"'It's Not Always Easy': A Rare Look at Life Inside the Shepody Healing Centre," *CTV News*, June 20, 2017, http://atlantic.ctvnews.ca/it-s-not-always-easy-a-rare-look-at-life-inside-the-shepody-healing-centre-1.3467844

"Institutionalized: Mental Health Behind Bars," *Vice News*, April 7, 2015, https://www.youtube.com/watch?v=-fQ50a-m92Y

"Out of Mind, Out of Sight: Inside the Brockville Psych," TVO, November 26, 2017, http://tvo.org/video/documentaries/out-of-mind-out-of-sight-inside-the-brockville-psych

"Death Behind Bars," *Global News*, May 1, 2014, http://globalnews.ca/news/1301910/investigation-canadas-psychiatric-prisons-have-highest-death-assault-rates

Doing Time

"What Is Prison Like? Prisoner's HIV/AIDS Support Action Network," GoodEvidenceChannel, January 30, 2012, https://www.youtube.com/watch?v=9R7B1nGKICE

"A Canadian Prisoner's Perspective," *Toronto Star*, July 2008, https://www.youtube.com/watch?v=y-daYflbwc8

"End Solitary Confinement, Says Former Female Inmate," *CBC News*, May 23, 2013, http://www.cbc.ca/news/canada/british-columbia/end-solitary-confinement-says-former-female-inmate-1.1337374

"Shocking Video Released of Canadian Prison Riot," March 13, 2012, http://www.youtube.com/watch?v=YLLdJJA6QwY

"The Devil You Know," *The Fifth Estate*, CBC, February 18, 2011, http://www.cbc.ca/fifth/episodes/2010-2011/the-devil-you-know

"Family Visits Important for Inmate Rehabilitation, Reintegration: Warden," *Toronto Star*, February 1, 2017, https://www.thestar.com/news/canada/2017/02/01/family-visits-important-for-inmate-rehabilitation-reintegration-warden.html

Indigenous Offenders

"House to Home—The Buffalo Sage Wellness House," Native Counselling Services of Alberta, August 31, 2016, https://www.youtube.com/watch?v=hqaGX-8TEuk

REFERENCES

1. R. Baehre. 1977. "Origins of the Penitentiary System in Upper Canada," *Ontario History*, 69(3), 185–207.

2. D. Coles. 1979. *Nova Scotia Corrections: An Historical Perspective*. Halifax: Corrections Services Division, Province of Nova Scotia, p. 8.

3. M. MacGuigan. 1977. *Report to Parliament by the Sub-Committee on the Penitentiary System in Canada*. Ottawa: Supply and Services Canada, p. 12.

4. Public Safety Canada Portfolio Corrections Statistics Committee. 2016. *Corrections and Conditional Release Statistical Overview: 2015 Annual Report*. Ottawa: Public Works and Government Services Canada. https://www.publicsafety.gc.ca/cnt/rsrcs/pblctns/ccrso-2015/ccrso-2015-en.pdf.

5. J. Reitano. 2017. "Adult Correctional Statistics in Canada, 2015/2016," *Juristat*, 37(1). Statistics Canada Catalogue no. 85-002-X. Ottawa: Minister of Industry, p. 3. http://www.statcan.gc.ca/pub/85-002-x/2017001/article/14700-eng.pdf.

6. A. Brockman. 2017, March 6. "Incarceration Rates in Canada's North among Highest in G20," *CBC News*. http://www.cbc.ca/news/canada/north/incarceration-rates-canada-s-north-1.4010379.

7. Reitano, "Adult Correctional Statistics in Canada, 2015/2016," p. 5.

8. Department of Justice. 2017, January. "JustFacts: Indigenous Overrepresentation in the Criminal Justice System." http://justice.gc.ca/eng/rp-pr/jr/jf-pf/2017/jan02.html.

9. E. Goffman. 1961. *Asylums: Essays on the Social Situation of Mental Patients and Other Inmates*. Garden City, NJ: Doubleday, p. 6.

10. S. Poirier (Chairperson). 2008. *Decades of Darkness: Moving Towards the Light. A Review of the Prison System in Newfoundland and Labrador*. St. John's: Ministry of Justice, p. 17. http://www.justice.gov.nl.ca/just/publications/ac_report.pdf.

11. Canadian Press. 2017, January 15. "'It's a Tinderbox': Assaults Soar in 158-Year Old Prison," *Edmonton Sun*. http://www.edmontonsun.com/2017/01/15/its-a-tinderbox-assaults-soar-in-158-year-old-prison.

12. Ibid.

13. Office of the Correctional Investigator. 2013. *Report of the Office of the Correctional Investigator (Canada) on the Baffin Correctional Centre and the Legal and Policy Framework of Nunavut Corrections*. Iqaluit: Nunavut Corrections. http://assembly.nu.ca/library/GNedocs/2013/001193-e.pdf.

14. D.M. Bierie. 2012. "Is Tougher Better? The Impact of Physical Prison Conditions on Inmate Violence," *International Journal of Offender Therapy and Comparative Criminology*, 56(3), 338–355.

15. W.W. Franklin, C.A. Franklin, and T.C. Pratt. 2006. "Examining the Empirical Relationship Between Prison Crowding and Inmate Misconduct: A Meta-Analysis of Conflicting Research Results," *Journal of Criminal Justice*, 34(4), 401–412.

16. QMI Agency. 2012, October 12. "'Unhygienic' Prison Conditions Leads to Less Time for Prisoner," *Toronto Sun*. http://www.torontosun.com/2012/10/13/unhygienic-prison-conditions-leads-to-less-time-for-prisoner.

17. M. Dauvergne. 2012. "Adult Correctional Statistics in Canada, 2010/2011," *Juristat*, 32(1). Statistics Canada Catalogue no. 85-002-X. Ottawa: Minister of Industry, p. 12. http://www.statcan.gc.ca/pub/85-002-x/2012001/article/11715-eng.pdf.

18. D. Calverley. 2010. "Adult Correctional Services in Canada, 2008/2009," *Juristat*, 30(3). Statistics Canada Catalogue no. 85-002-X. Ottawa: Minister of Industry. http://www.statcan.gc.ca/pub/85-002-x/2010003/article/11353-eng.htm.

19. Office of the Correctional Investigator. 2016. *Annual Report, 2015-2016*. Ottawa: Author. http://www.oci-bec.gc.ca/cnt/rpt/pdf/annrpt/annrpt20152016-eng.pdf.

20. Office of the Correctional Investigator. 2013. *Annual Report, 2012-2013*. Ottawa: Author. http://www.oci-bec.gc.ca/cnt/rpt/annrpt20122013-eng.aspx.

21. E. Bingham and R. Sutton. 2012. *Cruel, Inhuman, and Degrading? Canada's Treatment of Federally Sentenced Women with Mental Health Issues*. Toronto: International Human Rights Program, University of Toronto. http://www.dawncanada.net/main/wp-content/uploads/2013/12/Cruel-and-Inhuman_FINAL_Print.pdf.

22. W. Lamb. 2004. *Couldn't Keep It to Myself: Wally Lamb and the Women of York Correctional Institution*. New York: HarperCollins.

23. W. Lamb. 2007. *I'll Fly Away: Further Testimonies from the Women of York Prison*. New York: HarperCollins.

24. J. Demers. 2014. *Warehousing Prisoners in Saskatchewan: A Public Health Approach*. Regina: Canadian Centre for Policy Alternatives, p. 26. https://www.policyalternatives.ca/sites/default/files/uploads/publications/Saskatchewan%20Office/2014/10/warehousing_prisoners_in_saskatchewan.pdf.

25. M. Solinas-Saunders and M.J. Stacer. 2012. "Prison Resources and Physical/Verbal Assault in Prison: A Comparison of Male and Female Inmates," *Victims and Offenders*, 7(3), 279–311 at p. 302.

26. Office of the Correctional Investigator. 2014. *Annual Report, 2013-2014*. Ottawa: Author, p. 43. http://www.oci-bec.gc.ca/cnt/rpt/pdf/annrpt/annrpt20132014-eng.pdf. Reprinted by permission of the Office of the Correctional Investigator.

27. Ibid., p. 53.

28. John Howard Society of Toronto. 2010. *Homeless and Jailed: Jailed and Homeless*. Toronto: Author. http://johnhoward.ca/wp-content/uploads/2016/12/Amber-Kellen-Homeless-and-Jailed-Jailed-and-Homeless.pdf.

29. B. Brown. 2017, May 24. "Senator Says Nunavut Jail System Acts as Homeless Shelter," *Nunatsiaq Online*. http://www.nunatsiaqonline.ca/stories/article/65674senator_says_nunavut_jail_system_acts_as_homeless_shelter/.

30. Office of the Auditor General Manitoba. 2014. *Managing the Province's Adult Offenders*. Winnipeg: Author, p. 237. http://www.oag.mb.ca/wp-content/uploads/2014/03/Chapter-6-Managing-the-Provinces-Adult-Offenders-Web.pdf.

31. T. Khandaker. 2016, March 30. "A Canadian Jail Is So Overcrowded That Inmates Have Been Sleeping in Showers," *Vice News*. https://news.vice.com/article/a-canadian-jail-is-so-overcrowded-that-inmates-have-been-sleeping-in-showers.

32. Office of the Correctional Investigator, *Annual Report, 2015–2016*.

33. B. Weber. 2015, May 19. "'Welcome to Hell': Inside Canada's Most Decrepit Prison, Baffin Correctional Centre," *National Post*. http://news.nationalpost.com/news/canada/welcome-to-hell-inside-canadas-most-decrepit-prison-baffin-correctional-centre.

34. Office of the Auditor General of British Columbia. 2015. *An Audit of the Adult Custody Division's Correctional Facilities and Programs*. Victoria: Author. http://www.bcauditor.com/pubs/2015/special/audit-adult-custody-divisions-correctional-facilities-and

35. Demers, *Warehousing Prisoners in Saskatchewan: A Public Health Approach*, p. 12.

36. Ibid.

37. Office of the Auditor General Manitoba, *Managing the Province's Adult Offenders*, p. 248.

38. C.T. Lowenkamp, E.J. Latessa, and P. Smith. 2006. "Does Correctional Program Quality Really Matter? The Impact of Adhering to the Principles of Effective Intervention," *Criminology & Public Policy*, 5(3), 575–594.

39. Office of the Correctional Investigator. 2010. *Annual Report, 2009–2010*. Ottawa: Author. http://www.oci-bec.gc.ca/cnt/rpt/annrpt/annrpt20092010-eng.aspx.

40. Demers, *Warehousing Prisoners in Saskatchewan: A Public Health Approach*, p. 11.

41. Office of the Correctional Investigator, *Annual Report, 2009–2010*.

42. M. Tutton. 2016, December 12. "Inmate Violence Steadily Increasing throughout Canadian Prison System," *Globe and Mail*. http://www.theglobeandmail.com/news/national/inmate-violence-steadily-increasing-throughout-canadian-prison-system/article33295905.

43. Ibid.

44. Office of the Auditor General Manitoba, *Managing the Province's Adult Offenders*, p. 248.

45. A.M. Paperny. 2015, July 9. "Rough Justice: Lockdowns Skyrocket at Short-Staffed Ontario Jails," *Global News*. http://globalnews.ca/news/2091102/rough-justice-lockdowns-skyrocket-at-short-staffed-ontario-jails.

46. B. Steiner. 2008, July. *Maintaining Prison Order: Understanding Causes of Inmate Misconduct within and Across Ohio Correctional Institutions*. Unpublished doctoral dissertation. University of Cincinnati, p. 10.

47. R. Ricciardelli and V. Sit. 2016. "Producing Social (Dis)Order in Prison: The Effects of Administrative Control on Prisoner-on-Prisoner Violence," *The Prison Journal*, 96(2), 210–231.

48. R. Ruddell and S. Gottschall. 2014. "The Prison Adjustment of Aboriginal Offenders," *Australian & New Zealand Journal of Criminology*, 47(3), 336–354.

49. R. Sampson (Chair). 2007. *Report of the Correctional Service of Canada Review Panel: A Roadmap to Strengthening Public Safety*. Ottawa: Minister of Public Works and Government Services Canada. https://www.publicsafety.gc.ca/cnt/cntrng-crm/csc-scc-rvw-pnl/report-rapport/cscrprprt-eng.pdf.

50. H. Alam. 2016, December 15. "Inmate Dead, Others Injured after Riot in Saskatchewan Prison," *Toronto Star*. https://www.thestar.com/news/canada/2016/12/15/inmate-dead-others-injured-after-riot-in-saskatchewan-federal-prison.html.

51. V. Ferreira. 2015, June 21. "Six-Hour Inmate Riot at Penetanguishene Superjail under Investigation," *Barrie Examiner*. http://www.thebarrieexaminer.com/2015/06/19/six-hour-inmate-riot-at-penetanguishene-superjail—under-investigation.

52. R. Ricciardelli and M. Moir. 2013. "Stigmatized among the Stigmatized: Sex Offenders in Canadian Penitentiaries," *Canadian Journal of Criminology and Criminal Justice*, 5(53), 353–386.

53. P. Cowan and D. Sheremata. 2000, February 9. "Death in Experimental Prison Unit—'She Was Helpless,'" *Edmonton Sun*.

54. Office of the Correctional Investigator. 2012. *Annual Report, 2011-2012*. Ottawa: Author, p. 36. http://www.oci-bec.gc.ca/cnt/rpt/pdf/annrpt/annrpt20112012-eng.pdf.

55. Public Safety Canada Portfolio Corrections Statistics Committee. 2012. *Corrections and Conditional Release Statistical Overview: 2012 Annual Report*. Ottawa: Public Works and Government Services Canada, p. 67. http://www.publicsafety.gc.ca/cnt/rsrcs/pblctns/2012-ccrs/2012-ccrs-eng.pdf.

56. M. Devlin. 2017, May 22. "Number of Federal Inmates Who Self-Harm Tripled in the Last Decade," *Globe and Mail*. https://www.theglobeandmail.com/news/national/number-of-federal-inmates-who-self-harm-tripled-in-last-decade/article35079038.

57. Le Protecteur du Citoyen. 2016. *2015–2016 Annual Report*. Quebec: Author, p. 82. https://protecteurducitoyen.qc.ca/sites/default/files/pdf/rapports_annuels/2015-2016-annual-report-ombudsman.pdf.

58. R. Jurgens, M. Novak, and M. Day. 2011. "HIV and Incarceration: Prisons and Detention," *Journal of the International AIDS Society*, 14(1), 26–42.

59. A.M. Nolan and L.A. Stewart. 2017. "Chronic Health Conditions among Incoming Canadian Federally Sentence Women," *Journal of Correctional Health Care*, 23(1), 93–103.

60. T. Campbell. 2011. *Pros and Cons: A Guide to Creating Successful Community-Based HIV and HCV Programs for Prisoners* (2nd ed.). Ottawa: Prisoners with HIV/AIDS Support Action Network (PASAN), p. 22. http://www.pasan.org/resources.html.

61. D. McLay and A. Silversides. 2011. "Behind the Walls: Living with HIV in Prison Comes with Its Own Set of Challenges, and Some Aren't the Ones You'd Expect," *The Positive Side*, Canadian AIDS Treatment Information Exchange. http://www.catie.ca/en/printpdf/positiveside/winter-2011/behind-walls.

62. S.K.H. Chu and R. Elliott. 2009. *Clean Switch: The Case for Prison Needle and Syringe Programs in Canada*. Toronto: Canadian HIV/AIDS Legal Network. http://www.aidslaw.ca/site/wp-content/uploads/2013/09/PNSPs-ENG.pdf

63. Public Safety Canada Portfolio Corrections Statistics Committee, *Corrections and Conditional Release Statistical Overview, 2015 Annual Report*, p. 65.

64. Office of the Correctional Investigator, *Annual Report, 2015–2016*.

65. John Howard Society of Ontario. 2015. *Unlocking Change. Decriminalizing Mental Health Issues in Ontario*. Toronto: Author. http://www.johnhoward.on.ca/wp-content/uploads/2015/07/Unlocking-Change-Final-August-2015.pdf.

66. M. Warzecha. 2016, April 13. "'Solitary Horrors': The Grim History of Solitary Confinement and Its Modern-Day Comeback," *National Post*. http://nationalpost.com/g00/news/world/solitary-horrors-the-grim-history-of-solitary-confinement-and-its-modern-day-comeback.

67. United Nations General Assembly. 2011. "Interim Report of the Special Rapporteur of the Human Rights Council on Torture and Other Cruel, Inhuman or Degrading Treatment or Punishment," 66th Session, Resolution 65/205, p. 18. http://solitaryconfinement.org/uploads/SpecRapTortureAug2011.pdf.

68. Ibid. pp. 19–20.

69. D. Kelsall. 2014. "Cruel and Usual Punishment: Solitary Confinement in Canadian Prisons," *Canadian Medical Association Journal*, 186(18), 1345.

70. West Coast Prison Justice Society. 2016. *Solitary: A Case For Abolition*. Vancouver: Author. https://prisonjusticedotorg.files.wordpress.com/2016/11/solitary-confinement-report.pdf.

71. CBC News. 2013, May 22. "End Solitary Confinement, Says Former Female Inmate." http://www.cbc.ca/news/canada/british-columbia/end-solitary-confinement-says-former-female-inmate-1.1337374.

72. P. White. 2017, August 7. "Prisons See Drop in Solitary Confinement Use as Vulnerable Groups Granted Immunity," *Globe and Mail*. https://www.theglobeandmail.com/news/national/prisons-see-drop-in-solitary-confinement-use-as-vulnerable-groups-granted-immunity/article35897637.

73. L. Arbour (Honourable). 1996. *Report of the Commission of Inquiry into Certain Events at the Prison for Women in Kingston*. Ottawa: Public Works and Government Services Canada. http://www.justicebehindthewalls.net/resources/arbour_report/arbour_rpt.htm.

74. C. Glube (Chair). 2006. *Moving Forward with Women's Corrections*. Ottawa: Correctional Service Canada. http://www.csc-scc.gc.ca/text/prgrm/fsw/wos29/wos29-eng.shtml.

75. S. Hayman. 2006. *Imprisoning Our Sisters: The New Federal Women's Prisons in Canada*. Kingston, ON: McGill-Queen's University Press.

76. J. Ferrari. 2011. *Federal Female Incarceration in Canada: What Happened to Empowerment?* Unpublished master's thesis. Kingston, ON: Queen's University. https://qspace.library.queensu.ca/bitstream/1974/6352/3/Ferrari_Jacqueline_201104_MA.pdf.

77. Ibid., p. 115.

78. T. Lajeunesse, C. Jefferson, J. Nuffield, and D. Majury. 2000. *The Cross Gender Monitoring Project: Third and Final Report*. Ottawa: Correctional Service Canada. http://www.csc-scc.gc.ca/publications/fsw/gender3/toc-eng.shtml.

79. K. Kauffman. 1988. *Prison Officers and Their World*. Cambridge, MA: Harvard University Press.

80. J.M. Pollock. 2014. *Ethical Dilemmas in Criminal Justice* (8th ed.). Belmont, CA.: Wadsworth, pp. 342–343.

81. A. Marin. 2013. *The CODE: Investigation into the Ministry of Community Safety and Correctional Services Response to Allegations of Excessive Use of Force Against Inmates*. Toronto: Ombudsman Ontario, p. 9. https://www.ombudsman.on.ca/Files/sitemedia/Documents/Investigations/SORT%20Investigations/The-Code-EN.pdf.

82. M. Welch. 2011. *Corrections: A Critical Approach* (3rd ed.). New York: Routledge.

83. M. Weinwrath. 2016. *Behind the Walls. Inmates and Correctional Officers on the State of Canadian Prisons*. Vancouver: UBC Press, p. 144.

84. Ibid., p. 155.

85. M.A. Farkas. 2000. "A Typology of Correctional Officers," *International Journal of Offender Therapy and Comparative Criminology*, 44(4), 431–449.

86. Anonymous online comment (username easter bunny). n.d. InsidePrison.com. www.insideprison.com/prison_stories.asp?story_id=1130&pNum=2.

87. D. Spencer and R. Ricciardelli. 2016. "'They're a Very Sick Group of Individuals': Correctional Officers, Emotions, and Sex Offenders," *Theoretical Criminology*, 21(3), 380–394.

88. Office of the Correctional Investigator, *Annual Report, 2012–2013*.

89. Ibid.

90. Demers, *Warehousing Prisoners in Saskatchewan: A Public Health Approach*, p. 19.

91. R. Ricciardelli. 2014. "Canadian Prisoners' Perceptions of Correctional Officer Orientations to their Occupational Responsibilities," *Journal of Crime and Justice*, 39(2), 324–343.

92. K.A. Beijersbergen, A.J.E. Dirkzwager, P.H. van der Laan, and P. Nieuwbeerta. 2016. "A Social Building? Prison Architecture and Staff–Prisoner Relationships," *Crime & Delinquency*, 62(7), 843–874.

93. H. Crichton and R. Ricciardelli. 2016. "Shifting Grounds: Experiences of Canadian Provincial Correctional Officers," *Criminal Justice Review*, 41(4), 427–445 at p. 436.

94. R. Ricciardelli and A. Gazso. 2013. "Investigating Threat Perception Among Correctional Officers in the Canadian Provincial Correctional System," *Qualitative Sociology Review*, IX(3), 96–119 at p. 111.

95. G. Keinan and A. Malach-Pines. 2007. "Stress and Burnout Among Prison Personnel: Sources, Outcomes, and Intervention Strategies," *Criminal Justice and Behavior*, 34(3), 380–398.

96. W. Millson. 2002. "Predictors of Work Stress Among Correctional Officers," *Forum on Corrections Research*, 14(1), 45–47. http://www.csc-scc.gc.ca/research/forum/e141/141l_e.pdf.

97. E.G. Lambert, N. L. Hogan, I. Altheimer, S. Jiang, and M.T. Stevenson. 2010. "The Relationship between Burnout and Support for Punishment and Treatment: A Preliminary Examination," *International Journal of Offender Therapy and Comparative Criminology*, 54(6), 1004–1022.

98. E.G. Lambert, S.M. Barton-Bellessa, and N.L. Hogan. 2015. "The Consequences of Emotional Burnout among Correctional Staff," *Sage Open*, 15(2), 1–15.

99. L. Rosine. 1995. "Critical Incident Stress and Its Management in Corrections," in *Forensic Psychology—Policy and Practice in Corrections*, edited by T.A. Leis, L.L. Motiuk, and J.R.P. Ogloff, 213–226. Ottawa: Correctional Service Canada, 1995.

100. G. Galloway. 2016, July 27. "PTSD Affects 36 Percent of Male Prison Officers, Federal Data Reveal," *Globe and Mail*, https://www.theglobeandmail.com/news/politics/ptsd-prevalent-among-male-prison-officers-federal-data-reveal/article31145169.

101. M. Warnica. 2016, November 24. "Edmonton Prison Guards' Taped Sexual Phone Chats Highlight 'Culture of Fear,'" *CBC News*. http://www.cbc.ca/news/canada/edmonton/edmonton-prison-guards-taped-sexual-phone-chats-highlight-culture-of-fear-1.3865242.

102. Ibid.

103. J. Rankin and S. Contenta. 2013, November 18. "Gay Ontario Jail Guard Bob Ranger Suffered Poisoned Workplace," *Toronto Star*. https://www.thestar.com/business/2013/11/18/gay_ontario_jail_guard_bob_ranger_suffered_poisoned_workplace.html.

104. P.J. Murphy and L. Johnsen. 1997. *Life 25: Interviews with Prisoners Serving Life Sentences*. Vancouver: New Star, p. 41.

105. R.A. Cloward. 1969. "Social Control in the Prison," in *Prison within Society: A Reader in Penology*, edited by L. Hazelrigg, 78–112. Garden City: Doubleday.

106. R. Dube. 2002. *The Haven: A True Story of Life in the Hole*. Toronto: HarperCollins, pp. 238–239.

107. G.M. Sykes. 1958. *Society of Captives—A Study of a Maximum Security Institution*. Princeton: Princeton University Press.

108. J. Power and S.L. Brown. 2010. *Self-Injurious Behaviour: A Review of the Literature and Implications for Corrections*. Ottawa: Correctional Service Canada, p. 1. http://www.csc-scc.gc.ca/005/008/092/005008-0216-01-eng.pdf.

109. C.A. Dell and T. Beauchamp. 2006. "Self-Harm among Criminalized Women" [Fact sheet]. Canadian Centre on Substance Abuse. http://www.ccsa.ca/Resource%20Library/ccsa-011338-2006-e.pdf.

110. Office of the Correctional Investigator, *Annual Report, 2011–2012*, p. 36.

111. D. Clemmer. 1940. *The Prison Community*. Boston: Christopher.

112. G.M. Sykes and S.L. Messinger. 1960. "The Inmate Social System," in *Theoretical Studies in the Social Organization of the Prison*, edited by R.A. Cloward, D.R. Cressey, G.H. Grosser, R. McCleery, L.E. Ohlin, G.M. Sykes, and S.L. Messinger, 5–19. New York: Social Science Research Council.

113. Welch, *Corrections: A Critical Approach*, p. 137.

114. R. Ricciardelli. 2014. *Surviving Incarceration. Inside Canadian Prisons*. Waterloo, ON: Wilfred Laurier Press, pp. 115–116.

115. Weinwrath, *Behind the Walls*, pp. 103–104.

116. Ibid.

117. K.F. Lahm. 2008. "Inmate-On-Inmate Assault: A Multi-level Examination of Prison Violence," *Criminal Justice and Behavior*, 35(1), 120–137.

118. Ricciardelli and Moir, "Stigmatized Among the Stigmatized: Sex Offenders in Canadian Penitentiaries."

119. Welch, *Corrections: A Critical Approach*, pp. 137–138.

120. A. Stahl. 2017, June 12. "Transgender Prisoners Suffer Abuse at Record Numbers," *Vice News*. https://www.vice.com/en_us/article/43g5jd/why-is-ice-closing-its-only-detention-center-for-transgender-detainees-v24n5.

121. K. Harris. 2017, January 13. "Correctional Service Flip-Flops on Transgender Placement Policy," *CBC News*. http://www.cbc.ca/news/politics/transgender-inmates-placement-policy-1.3934796.

122. T. Lupick. 2015, December 13. "Living Nightmare for Transgender Inmate at All-Male Prison," *Toronto Star*. https://www.thestar.com/news/canada/2015/12/13/living-nightmare-for-transgender-inmate-at-all-male-prison.html.

123. R. Light and B. Campbell. 2006. "Prisoners' Families: Still Forgotten Victims?" *Journal of Social Welfare & Family Law*, 28(3–4), 297–308.

124. S. Hannem. 2011. "Stigma and Marginality: Gendered Experiences of Families of Male Prisons in Canada," in *Critical Criminology in Canada: New Voices, New Directions*, edited by A. Doyle and D. Moore, 183–217. Vancouver: UBC Press.

125. D. Braman. 2007. *Doing Time on the Outside: Incarceration and Family Life in Urban America*. Ann Arbour: University of Michigan Press.

126. Light and Campbell, "Prisoners' Families: Still Forgotten Victims?"

127. S. Moroney. 2011. *Through the Glass*. Toronto: Doubleday Canada.

128. R.C. Johnson. 2009. "Ever-Increasing Levels of Parental Incarceration and the Consequences for Children," in *Do Prisons Make Us Safer? The Benefits and Costs of the Prison Boom*, edited by S. Raphael and M.A. Stoll, 177–206. New York: The Russell Sage Foundation.

129. J. Murray. 2010. "The Cycle of Punishment: Social Exclusion of Prisoners and Their Children," *Criminology and Criminal Justice*, 7(1), 55–81.

130. D. Derkzen, R. Gobeil, and J. Gileno. 2009. *Visitation and Post-Release Outcome Among Federally-Sentenced Offenders*. Ottawa: Correctional Service Canada. http://publications.gc.ca/collections/collection_2010/scc-csc/PS83-3-205-eng.pdf.

131. Public Safety Canada Portfolio Corrections Statistics Committee, *Corrections and Conditional Release Statistical Overview, 2015 Annual Report*, p. 31.

132. D.P. Mears, J.C. Cochran, and F.T. Cullen. 2015, October 15. "We Are Still Largely in the Dark as to Whether Incarceration Reduces Recidivism" [Blog post], *American Politics and Policy*. http://eprints.lse.ac.uk/64303/1/blogs.lse.ac.uk-We%20are%20still%20largely%20in%20the%20dark%20as%20to%20whether%20incarceration%20reduces%20recidivism.pdf.

133. F.T. Cullen, C.L. Jonson, and D.S. Nagin. 2011. "Prisons Do Not Reduce Recidivism: The High Cost of Ignoring Science," *Prison Journal*, 91(3), 48–65.

134. S.N. Durlauf and D.S. Nagin. 2011. "The Deterrent Effect of Punishment," in *Controlling Crime: Strategies and Tradeoffs*, edited by P.J. Cook, J. Ludwig, and J. McCrary, 43–94. Chicago: University of Chicago Press.

135. A.S. Bhati and A.R. Piquero. 2008. "Estimating the Impact of Incarceration on Subsequent Offending Trajectories: Deterrent, Criminogenic, or Null Effect?" *Journal of Criminal Law and Criminology*, 98(1), 207–254.

136. S.D. Bushway and R. Paternoster. 2009. "The Impact of Prison on Crime," in *Do Prisons Make Us Safer? The Benefits and Costs of the Prison Boom*, edited by S. Raphael and M.A. Stoll, 119–150. New York: Sage.

137. M.K. Chen and J.M. Shapiro. 2007. "Do Harsher Prison Conditions Reduce Recidivism? A Discontinuity-Based Approach," *American Law and Economics Review*, 9(1), 1–29.

138. J. Cid. 2009. "Is Imprisonment Criminogenic? A Comparative Study of Recidivism Rates Between Prison and Suspended Sentence Sanctions," *European Journal of Criminology*, 6(6), 459–480.

139. Poirier, *Decades of Darkness: Moving Towards the Light*, p. 17.

140. G. Harper and C. Chitty. 2005. *The Impact of Corrections on Re-Offending: A Review of "What Works."* Home Office Research Study 291. London: Development and Statistics Directorate, Home Office. http://webarchive.nationalarchives.gov.uk/20110218135832/rds.homeoffice.gov.uk/rds/pdfs04/hors291.pdf.

141. Dauvergne, *Adult Correctional Statistics in Canada, 2010/2011*, p. 12.

142. G. Taylor. 1997. "Implementing Risk and Needs Classification in the Correctional Service of Canada," *Forum on Corrections Research*, 9(1), 32–35.

143. D.A. Andrews and J. Bonta. 2010. *The Psychology of Criminal Conduct* (5th ed.). New Providence, NJ: Matthew Benders & Company.

144. Public Safety Canada Portfolio Corrections Statistics Committee, *Corrections and Conditional Release Statistical Overview: 2012 Annual Report*, p. 11.

145. J. Lee. 2017, June 17. "Can a Child Sexual Offender Be Cured?" *The Age*. http://www.theage.com.au/victoria/can-a-child-sexual-offender-be-cured-20170608-gwnmux.html.

146. Kwantlen Polytechnic University. 2017, July 5. "KPU Breaks Down Barriers with Prison Exchange Program" [News release]. http://www.kpu.ca/news/2017/07/05/kpu-breaks-down-barriers-prison-exchange-program.

147. K. Taylor. 2014, November 21. "The Book Club at the Big House: How Reading Makes a Difference in Prison," *Globe and Mail*. https://www.theglobeandmail.com/arts/books-and-media/the-book-club-at-the-big-house-how-reading-makes-a-difference-in-prison/article21691700.

148. Demers, *Warehousing Prisoners in Saskatchewan: A Public Health Approach*, p. 14.

149. Office of the Correctional Investigator. 2011. *Annual Report, 2010-2011*. Ottawa: Author, p. 32. http://www.oci-bec.gc.ca/cnt/comm/presentations/presentationsAR-RA0911-eng.aspx.

150. Centers for Disease Control. n.d. "Traumatic Brain Injury in Prisons and Jails: An Unrecognized Problem." https://www.cdc.gov/traumaticbraininjury/pdf/prisoner_tbi_prof-a.pdf.

151. Glube, *Moving Forward with Women's Corrections*.

152. Task Force on Federally Sentenced Women. 1990. *Creating Choices: The Report of the Task Force on Federally Sentenced Women*. Ottawa: Correctional Service Canada. http://www.csc-scc.gc.ca/text/prgrm/fsw/choices/toce-eng.shtml.

153. K. Heilbrun, D. DeMatteo, R. Fretz, J. Erickson, K. Yasuhara, and N. Anumba. 2008. "How 'Specific' Are Gender-Specific Rehabilitation Needs? An Empirical Analysis," *Criminal Justice and Behavior*, 35(11), 1382–1397.

154. L.B. Lovins, C.T. Lowenkamp, E.J. Latessa, and P. Smith. 2007. "Application of the Risk Principle to Female Offenders," *Journal of Contemporary Criminal Justice*, 23(4), 383–398.

155. N. Messina, C.E. Grella, J. Cartier, and S. Torres. 2010. "A Randomized Experimental Study of Gender-Responsive

Substance Abuse Treatment for Women in Prison," *Journal of Substance Abuse Treatment*, 38(2), 97–107.

156. S.J. Tripodi, S.E. Bledsoe, J.S. Kim, and K. Bender. 2011. "Effects of Correctional-Based Programs for Female Inmates: A Systematic Review," *Research on Social Work Practice*, 21(1), 15–31.

157. Andrews and Bonta, *The Psychology of Criminal Conduct*.

158. J. Bonta and D.A. Andrews. 2010. "Viewing Offender Assessment and Treatment Through the Lens of the Risk-Need-Responsivity Model," in *Offender Supervision: New Directions in Theory, Research and Practice*, edited by F. McNeil, P. Raynor and C. Trotter, 19–40. New York: Willan Publishing.

159. Office of the Correctional Investigator, *Annual Report, 2010–2011*, p. 44.

160. P. Smith and P. Gendreau. 2007. "The Relationship Between Program Participation, Institutional Misconduct, and Recidivism among Federally Sentenced Adult Male Offenders," *Forum on Corrections Research*, 19(1). http://www.csc-scc.gc.ca/research/forum/Vol19No1/v19n1-chap2-eng.pdf.

161. C.T. Griffiths and D. Murdoch. 2018. *Canadian Corrections* (5th ed.). Toronto: Nelson.

162. G. Luther, M. Mela, and V.J. Bae. 2013. *Literature Review on Therapeutic Justice and Problem Solving Courts*. Saskatoon: University of Saskatchewan. https://www.usask.ca/cfbsjs/documents/Lit%20Review%20MHC%20Saskatoon%20Academic%20Dec%202013.pdf.

163. Reitano, *Adult Correctional Statistics in Canada, 2015/2016*, p. 5.

164. John Howard Society of Ontario. 2016. *Fractured Care: Public Health Opportunities in Ontario's Correctional Institutions*. Toronto: Author, p. 14. http://johnhoward.on.ca/wp-content/uploads/2016/04/Fractured-Care-Final.pdf.

165. A.L. Solomon, K.D. Johnson, J. Travis, and E.C. McBride. 2004. *From Prison to Work: The Employment Dimensions of Prisoner Reentry*. Washington, DC: Justice Policy Center, Urban Institute. http://www.urban.org/sites/default/files/publication/58126/411097-From-Prison-to-Work.PDF.

166. Correctional Service Canada. 2016. *Correctional Service Canada Healing Lodges*. Ottawa: Author. http://www.csc-scc.gc.ca/aboriginal/002003-2000-eng.shtml.

167. M.M. Mann. 2009. *Good Intentions, Disappointing Results: A Progress Report on Federal Aboriginal Corrections*. Ottawa: Office of the Correctional Investigator. http://www.oci-bec.gc.ca/cnt/rpt/pdf/oth-aut/oth-aut20091113-eng.pdf.

168. R.M. Martinson. 1974. "What Works? Questions and Answers About Prison Reform," *Public Interest*, 35, 22–54.

169. R.M. Martinson. 1979. "New Findings, New Views: A Note of Caution Regarding Sentencing Reform," *Hofstra Law Review*, 7, 243–258.

170. M. Munn and C. Bruckert. 2013. *On the Outside: From Lengthy Imprisonment to Lasting Freedom*. Vancouver: UBC Press, p. 49.

© Laurie Justus Pace. Graphics One Design, 2014

CHAPTER 12
RELEASE, RE-ENTRY, AND REINTEGRATION

LEARNING OBJECTIVES

After reading this chapter, you should be able to

- Discuss the purpose and principles of conditional release.
- Discuss the release options for provincial/territorial and federal inmates.
- Describe the issues surrounding crime victims and conditional release.
- Describe the dynamics of parole board decision-making and the issues that surround this process.
- Discuss the effectiveness of conditional release options.
- Discuss the challenges that offenders, including high-risk and special-needs offenders, have re-entering and reintegrating into the community.
- Discuss the role of parole officers.
- Describe the challenges of special offender populations on parole.
- Discuss the factors influencing success and failure of offenders on conditional release.
- Discuss the effectiveness of community supervision and control strategies.

PERSPECTIVE

An Inmate Reflects on Leaving Collins Bay Penitentiary

As I travelled down the highway in a Greyhound bus to London, Ontario, I started to feel uneasy. I wondered if anybody on this bus could tell if I had been in prison. Everybody here had tablets and smartphones in front of their faces except me. Would they think that was weird?

On layover in Toronto, I left the bus station to buy a pack of cigarettes and I felt like a fugitive. I remembered how uncomfortable I felt my first week at the last prison I was in and how I felt nervous in the open exercise yard there. Except now I was afraid to cross the street in a pleasant Canadian city. I felt I'd really gotten out just in time—I was only slightly institutionalized.

. . .

And now I was about to do the rest of my time as a federal inmate on conditional release, commonly known as parole. I knew that if people found out they may look at me differently. I knew some people would think I wasn't punished enough, they may even believe I don't deserve a second chance. I knew some would even be so ignorant as to judge my children for the sins of their father. But I didn't care what they thought, because I knew I deserved my sentence, and now it was time to prepare for when it ended.

Source: K. Martin. 2016, June 7. "What I Learned from My Time in Canadian Prison," *Vice News*. https://www.vice.com/en_ca/article/what-i-learned-from-my-time-in-canadian-prison. Reprinted by permission of VICE.

The vast majority of offenders confined in correctional institutions are ultimately released back into the community. Federal offenders are more likely to apply for a **conditional release** since their sentences are longer.

Provincial/territorial inmates, on the other hand, are often serving such short sentences that they do not qualify for conditional release; many of those who do waive their right to a hearing are released outright without any supervision until their **warrant expiry date**. For many of these offenders, conditional release is viewed by many offenders as being "set up to fail" and a form of "custody without walls."[1]

The underlying premise of conditional release programs is that the likelihood of recidivism is reduced as the offender is reintegrated back into the community under supervision. Release on parole is not a statutory right—it is a privilege. Though inmates have the right to apply for parole when eligible, there are no guarantees of a positive outcome.

Recall from Chapter 2 that the public has little confidence and trust in the criminal justice system, due in part to media reports. Canadians often hear about parole in the media and sensational headlines, particularly in cases where a violent crime has been committed by an offender on conditional release.

Common:

"Parolee Sought on Canada-Wide Warrant," *Sudbury Star*, May 2017

"Parolee Arrested on Drug Charges," *Niagara This Week–St. Catharines*, March 20, 2017

Not So Common:

"20 Parolees Successfully Completed Parole This Week!" *The Daily Planet*

THE PURPOSE AND PRINCIPLES OF CONDITIONAL RELEASE

Section 100 of the *Corrections and Conditional Release Act* (CCRA; S.C. 1992, c. 20) states:

> The purpose of conditional release is to contribute to the maintenance of a just, peaceful and safe society by means of decisions on the timing and conditions of

Conditional release

A generic term for the various means of leaving a correctional institution before warrant expiry whereby an offender is subject to conditions that, if breached, could trigger revocation of the release and return to prison; parole is one type of conditional release.

Warrant expiry date

The end of an offender's sentence.

release that will best facilitate the rehabilitation of offenders and their reintegration into the community as law-abiding citizens.

The process of determining which inmates qualify for conditional release is forward-looking and predictive, asking two basic questions that are set out in section 102 of the *Corrections and Conditional Release Act*, which states that the Parole Board of Canada or a provincial parole board may grant parole to an offender if, in the board's opinion, (1) the offender will not, by reoffending, present an undue risk to society before the expiration, according to law, of the sentence the offender is serving; and (2) the release of the offender will contribute to the protection of society by facilitating the reintegration of the offender into society as a law-abiding citizen.

The Parole Board of Canada (PBC) makes conditional release decisions for federal offenders and for provincial/territorial offenders in all provinces except Quebec and Ontario, which have their own provincial parole boards.

THE RELEASE OPTIONS FOR FEDERAL AND PROVINCIAL/TERRITORIAL INMATES

The release of an offender from custody can occur at one of three points in the sentence: (1) the parole eligibility date, for either **day parole** or **full parole**; (2) the **statutory release** date, which generally occurs at the two-thirds point in a sentence; or (3) the warrant expiry date, which marks the end of the sentence imposed by the court. The specific conditional release options available to inmates depend on the length of the sentence and on whether offenders are under the supervision and control of the provincial/territorial or federal systems of corrections. The release options for federal and provincial or territorial inmates are set out in Corrections File 12.1.

Day parole

The authority granted by a parole board that provides an opportunity for inmates to be at large in order to prepare for full release (e.g., for job search) while returning at night to an institution or, more typically, to a community residential facility.

Full parole

The authority granted by a parole board for an inmate to be at large under supervision in the community for the remainder of his or her sentence.

Statutory release

A type of conditional release (made by the CSC and not the PBC) that allows incarcerated federal offenders to be released at the two-thirds point in their sentence and to serve the remaining one-third of their sentence under supervision in the community.

CORRECTIONS FILE 12.1

RELEASE OPTIONS FOR FEDERAL AND PROVINCIAL/TERRITORIAL INMATES

Type of Release	Federal	Provincial or Territorial
Temporary absences	Usually the first type of release granted; escorted (ETA) or unescorted (UTA); for medical, family, employment, education purposes.	Most common type of release.
Eligibility	ETA anytime; UTA varies with length and type of sentence; maximum-security inmates not eligible for UTAs; sentences of three years or more: may apply for UTA after serving one-sixth of sentence; sentences of two to three years: may apply for UTA six months into sentence; life sentences: may apply for UTA three years before full parole eligibility date.	Varies; in some jurisdictions, inmate can apply immediately; others require waiting period; may require electronic monitoring (EM).
Day parole	Prepares offender for release on full parole by allowing participation in community-based activities; offender must return nightly to an institution or halfway house unless otherwise authorized by the PBC or a provincial parole board.	
Eligibility	Sentences of two years or more; inmate can apply six months prior to full parole eligibility date or six months, whichever is greater; inmates serving life sentences eligible to apply three years before parole eligibility date.	Day parole not an option for provincial inmates in Ontario and Quebec. Provincial/territorial inmates serving sentences of six months or more in remaining jurisdictions are eligible for day parole after serving one-half of the portion of the sentence that must be served before full parole eligibility.

(continued)

Type of Release	Federal	Provincial or Territorial
Full parole	Provides an opportunity for offenders to serve remainder of the sentence under supervision in the community; usually follows successful completion of day parole, where available; parolee must report to a parole supervisor on a regular basis and abide by conditions.	
Eligibility	After serving one-third of sentence (except for offenders serving life sentences for murder); after 25 years if serving a life sentence for first-degree murder; between 10 and 25 years (set by judge at sentencing) for offenders serving life sentences for second-degree murder.	In Ontario, inmates sentenced to less than six months may apply for full parole at any time; those receiving sentences of longer than six months must serve one-third of their sentence before being eligible; in other jurisdictions, inmates are eligible after serving one-third of their sentence.
Statutory release	Mandatory conditional release of federal offenders by law; not a decision of the PBC. For offenders who have not applied for, or not been granted, parole. Offenders serve the remainder of their sentence under the supervision of parole officers and must abide by conditions.	Not available for provincial/territorial inmates who may serve their entire sentence in custody, minus **remission** that is earned at a rate of one day for every two days served and allows for **discharge** from the institution.
Eligibility	By law, for most federal offenders after serving two-thirds of their sentence (if not released on parole); offenders serving life or indeterminate sentences not eligible; Correctional Service Canada (CSC) may recommend that an offender be denied statutory release if it believes the offender is likely to (a) commit an offence causing death or serious harm to another person, (b) commit a sexual offence against a child, or (c) commit a serious drug offence before the end of the sentence.*	Not applicable to provincial/territorial inmates.

* PBC may detain the offender, which is called **detention during the period of statutory release**; inmates detained in this manner will have their case reviewed on an annual basis.

Source: National Parole Board. 2010. *Fact Sheet: Types of Release.* http://pbc-clcc.gc.ca/infocntr/factsh/rls-eng.shtml. Reprinted by permission of the Parole Board of Canada.

Federal offenders may also be released under **one-chance statutory release**. In this case, if the conditions of the release are violated, the offender is returned to custody to service the remainder of his or her sentence. Offenders on this type of release are generally higher risk. Figure 12.1 illustrates the sentencing milestones for federal offenders.

THE PAROLE PROCESS

The different stages of the parole process are depicted in Figure 12.2.

The staff in correctional institutions participate in the parole process by helping inmates to develop a **release plan**. In provincial/territorial institutions, this function is performed by staff variously called inmate liaison officers, parole coordinators, or conditional release coordinators. In federal institutions, case management officers and

Remission/discharge

Available to provincial inmates who have served two-thirds of their sentence.

Detention during the period of statutory release

A decision by the Parole Board of Canada (after an application by CSC) that a federal inmate be denied statutory release and be detained in the institution until warrant expiry date.

◄ **FIGURE 12.1**

Sentencing Milestones for Federal Offenders with Fixed Sentences

Source: Public Safety Canada. 2007. *Sentencing Milestones (A Roadmap to Strengthening Public Safety).* Ottawa: Minister of Public Works and Government Services Canada, p. 108. http://www.publicsafety.gc.ca/cnt/cntrng-crm/csc-scc-rvw-pnl/report-rapport/trnstn-comm-eng.aspx. This information was reproduced with the permission of the Minister of Public Safety and Emergency Preparedness Canada, 2017.

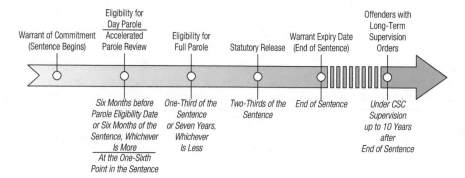

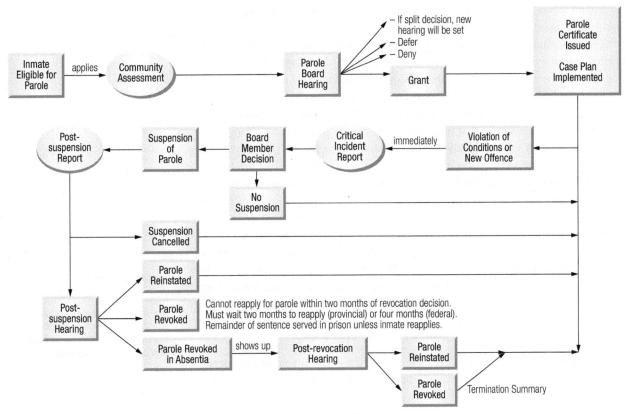

▲ FIGURE 12.2

Parole Flow Chart

Source: Justice Institute of BC, Corrections and Community Justice Division. 1998. Reprinted with permission.

One-chance statutory release

A release option whereby offenders who violate the conditions of a statutory release are required to serve the remainder of their sentence in confinement.

Release plan

A plan setting out the residential, educational, and treatment arrangements made for an inmate who is applying for conditional release.

Community assessment

An evaluation of the feasibility of the release plan, the level of supervision required, and the availability of community resources.

institutional parole officers prepare release plans and other materials that will be used by parole boards in their deliberations. The release plan contains information about where the prospective parolee will live, employment prospects, and any arrangements for community-based support (such as residence in a halfway house or residential drug treatment facility). Release plans must be vetted by probation or parole officers in the community into which the offender will be released.

A key component of the release plan is the **community assessment**. Prepared by the probation or parole officer, this report evaluates the feasibility of the offender's proposed community plan in terms of the level of supervision required and the availability of community resources. Among the areas examined in the assessment are the proposed residence; education, employment, and/or treatment plans; family and other support networks in the community; the extent to which the offender accepts responsibility for and understands the offending behaviour; information supplied by the victims; and any recommended special conditions the parole board may attach to the parole.

Parole board members use the information contained both in the release plan and the community assessment to determine whether an inmate should be granted a conditional release and, if so, the special conditions that should be attached to it.

An offender who presents little risk of reoffending would typically have a favourable background and no previous criminal convictions. Offenders who present a high risk must demonstrate that they have taken steps to address those aspects of their lives that would increase the likelihood of reoffending. However, as discussed later in the chapter, the general nature of the conditional release provisions gives parole board members a considerable amount of discretion in deciding whether to grant or deny parole.

Pre-release planning is an important part of the inmate's correctional plan and is directed toward managing the risk posed by offenders and, ideally, providing access to programs and services in the community. Despite its importance in the correctional process, pre-release planning is often minimal in provincial/territorial institutions. A small sample (N = 12) of provincial inmates in Nova Scotia, some of whom had also served federal time, indicated that there was no pre-release planning, no information provided on support services in the community, and they were not generally aware of the assistance that was available to them.[2] There may also be a lack of pre-release planning for inmates with particular challenges, such as mental illness. This hinders successful reintegration into the community upon release.[3]

Federal inmates, who are incarcerated for longer periods compared to their provincial or territorial counterparts, have greater access to pre-released assistance. These inmates tend to be released in gradual stages, beginning with escorted or unescorted **temporary absences**. Long-term studies have shown that offenders who are gradually released from prison on conditional release are more likely to become law-abiding citizens than those offenders who stay in prison until the end of their sentence.

THE CHANGING FACE OF CONDITIONAL RELEASE

Statistics indicate that after several years of decline, the percentage of provincial/territorial and federal offenders released on day and full parole increased beginning in 2013 to 2014.[4]

Figure 12.3 illustrates the trend lines for the number of offenders in federal correctional institutions and on some type of conditional release.

PAROLE BOARD GRANT RATES

The parole board grant rates for federal and provincial day parole and full parole are presented in Figures 12.4 and 12.5.

The data in Figure 12.4 and Figure 12.5 indicate that the day parole grant rate is 71 percent for federal and 57 percent for provincial offenders, while the full parole grant rate is 30 percent for federal inmate-applicants and 32 percent for provincial applicants.

Within these overall grant rates, however, there is disparity in the grant rates for women and male applicants as well as for Indigenous and Black inmate-applicants:

- Compared to other offenders, Black federal inmates are less successful in their application for day parole and have a much lower grant rate for provincial full parole.

Temporary absence

A type of conditional release that allows an inmate to participate in community activities, including employment and education, while residing in a minimum-security facility or halfway house.

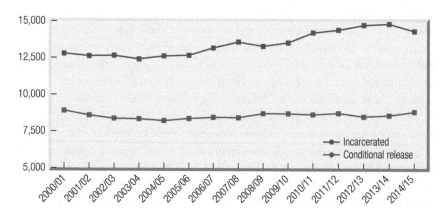

◀ FIGURE 12.3

The Federal Offender Population

Source: Parole Board of Canada. 2016. *Performance Monitoring Report 2014/2015.* Ottawa: Author, p. 7. https://www.canada.ca/content/dam/canada/parole-board/migration/005/009/093/005009-3000-2015-en.pdf. Reprinted by permission of the Parole Board of Canada.

FIGURE 12.4 ▶

Grant Rates for Federal and Provincial Day Parole, 2010–11 to 2014–15

Note: Accelerated parole review (APR) was abolished in 2011 although persons eligible for APR prior to 2011 continued to have their cases heard under that provision.

Source: Parole Board of Canada. 2016. Performance Monitoring Report 2014/2015. Ottawa: Author, p. 27. https://www.canada.ca/content/dam/canada/parole-board/migration/005/009/093/005009-3000-2015-en.pdf. Reprinted by permission of the Parole Board of Canada.

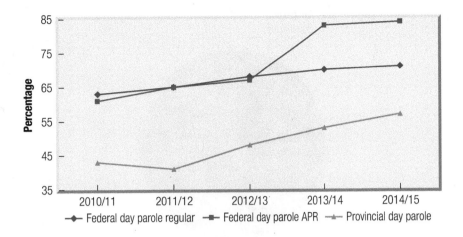

FIGURE 12.5 ▶

Grant Rates for Federal and Provincial Full Parole, 2010–11 to 2014–15

Source: Parole Board of Canada. 2016. *Performance Monitoring Report 2014/2015.* Ottawa: Author, p. 30. https://www.canada.ca/content/dam/canada/parole-board/migration/005/009/093/005009-3000-2015-en.pdf. Reprinted by permission of the Parole Board of Canada.

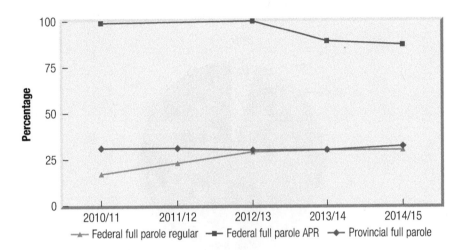

Indigenous offenders serve a higher proportion of their sentences prior to day or full parole release than their non-Indigenous counterparts, including Blacks, and have the lowest federal and provincial full parole grant rates.

- Asian offenders have the highest federal and provincial full parole grant rates.
- Indigenous offenders are more likely to be released on statutory release than other types of release, and are more likely than non-Indigenous offenders to be released on statutory release.
- Women offenders have higher federal and provincial parole grant rates than male offenders.[5]

The reasons for these disparities in grant rates has yet to be explored.

The majority of inmates in provincial/territorial institutions do not apply for parole; instead, they serve out their sentences in custody. With earned remission, these inmates are eligible to be released after serving two-thirds of their time in custody. In contrast to federal offenders, provincial/territorial inmates who are released on earned remission are not supervised by parole officers. For these inmates, the parole board must often decide whether to release an offender on parole who may present a risk, and with a plan that is not optimal, or to have the inmate serve until the statutory date and then leave custody with no supervision or plan.

Figure 12.6 provides a breakdown of the federal conditional release population in 2014 to 2015. Note that there are nearly as many offenders on statutory release as are on

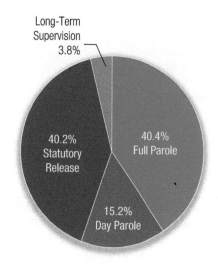

◄ **FIGURE 12.6**

Federal Conditional Release Population, 2014

Source: Adapted from Parole Board of Canada. 2016. *Performance Monitoring Report 2014/2015.* Ottawa: Author, p. 67. https://www.canada.ca/content/dam/canada/parole-board/migration/005/009/093/005009-3000-2015-en.pdf. Reprinted by permission of the Parole Board of Canada.

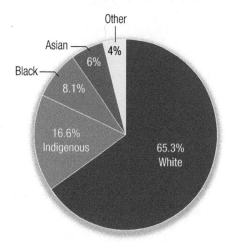

◄ **FIGURE 12.7**

Federal Conditional Release Population by Group, 2014–15

Note: All of the groups, except Caucasians, have recorded increases in recent years.

Source: Adapted from Parole Board of Canada. 2016. *Performance Monitoring Report 2014/2015.* Ottawa: Author, p. 68. https://www.canada.ca/content/dam/canada/parole-board/migration/005/009/093/005009-3000-2015-en.pdf. Reprinted by permission of the Parole Board of Canada.

full parole. This reflects both the decline in the full parole grant rate (discussed below) and the increasing levels of risk posed by federal offenders who are incarcerated and who may be less likely to receive parole. The diversity of offenders on federal conditional release is illustrated in Figure 12.7, which depicts the federal correctional release populations by Indigenous groups and race in 2012.

VICTIMS AND CONDITIONAL RELEASE

For crime victims and their families, the parole hearing is the first public forum since the court where they have an opportunity to speak to the impact of the crime and to confront the offender. There is legislation that gives victims rights with respect to conditional release. Under section 142 of the CCRA, victims can request a variety of types of information, including the offender's eligibility dates for conditional release, including temporary absences; hearing dates for conditional release; the offender's destination upon release; and, if the offender is transferred from a federal institution to a provincial or territorial institution, the name and location of that facility.

The *Canadian Victims Bill of Rights* (S.C. 2015, c. 13, s. 2) also contains provisions that require authorities to inform crime victims of any hearings related to the conditional release of an offender and any conditions that are attached to a conditional release. Victims also have the right to attend parole hearings, with the exception of the provincial parole board in Quebec, and to submit a victim impact statement, either in person at the hearing, or via audio or video, or a written statement.

Despite these rights, the participation of crime victims in the conditional release process is sporadic. It is rare for a victim impact statement to be submitted to the board and even less common for victims to appear at parole board hearings. There are a variety of possible reasons for this.

The institution where the parole hearing is held may be a considerable distance from the victim's home, or the victim may not have access to a victim support person. In addition, despite the efforts of the provincial/territorial and federal governments, most victims have little knowledge of the parole process and how hearings are conducted. And that the decision of the board is forward-looking and predictive; and that the focus is on whether the offender, if released, will reoffend prior to his or her warrant expiry date (end of sentence). And that the parole hearing is not a retrial of the case.

It can also be very intimidating for the victim to sit in a parole hearing room with the offender present and to speak candidly about the offender's potential release. The victim may fear reprisals when the offender is released. For these and a variety of other reasons, some victims choose to make a written submission to the parole board to be considered during the hearing, while a smaller number submit videotaped statements for parole board members to view. There are no guidelines as to how much "weight" victim submissions or presentations in parole hearings should be given in making the conditional release decision.

An excerpt from a victim's written submission to a parole board is presented in Corrections File 12.2.

Most crime victims are not harassed or threatened by offenders on conditional release; however, some victims are at great risk. It is in these cases that victim notification is most crucial, for both officially sanctioned releases and unauthorized absences from community supervision.

To facilitate the sharing of information with crime victims on the movement and release of their perpetrator, CSC operates a National Victim Services Program. This

---

CORRECTIONS FILE 12.2

A VICTIM'S WRITTEN SUBMISSION TO A PAROLE BOARD

I have just received notification that [name removed], if granted parole, will be released as soon as [date removed]. I am writing this letter to express my strong opposition to his release on parole. I am one of victims of the crimes for which [name removed] was most recently convicted. I was in a relationship with [name removed] for a number of months. During this relationship, [name removed] was emotionally and physically abusive toward me. This ultimately resulted in him physically assaulting me, resulting in a serious concussion, multiple bruises and lacerations. For my safety, I had to leave the province. I am still suffering the physical and psychological impact of [name removed] abuse.

[Name removed] is a very manipulative person. He may tell the parole board that he needs to be released on parole so that he can get treatment for his issues. He is not sincere in this. I am certain that if he is released, he will re-offend. It is my belief that [name removed] should serve his entire sentence in custody. The more time he is kept from society, then the safer it will be. If the parole board releases [name removed] then this will send him the wrong message that he can be abusive without any fear of punishment.

Source: Anonymous. Provided to the author.

program provides registered crime victims with updated information on the offender's status, notifications of parole board hearings, and release dates and conditions. An evaluation of the program found that it was successfully achieving these objectives.[6] Similar programs are operated by provincial/territorial systems of corrections, although the effectiveness of these initiatives is unknown. As well, in certain high-profile cases, the board may be presented with petitions signed by community residents opposing the release of the offender. See At Issue 12.1.

PAROLE BOARD DECISION-MAKING

Parole hearings are usually presided over by two board members and are generally held in the institution where the inmate is being held. In federal parole hearings, the inmate-applicant is accompanied by his or her case manager, who serves as an assistant. Lawyers also may attend, although the parole board is an administrative tribunal and not a court of law. Different rules apply. Federal Indigenous offenders may have an Elder or cultural advisor present at the hearing. The number of these hearings has declined over the years to just over one-third of hearings, with a slight increase seen in 2016.[7] This fact has stirred some controversy, critics arguing that this practice undermines the integrity of Indigenous-centred corrections.

In its deliberations, the parole board considers a number of documents contained in the inmate-applicant's parole file. These generally include, but are not limited to, police reports, an official record of convictions, classification reports, reports from institutional staff on the inmate's behaviour and performance, correctional plan progress report, victim impact statements, pre-sentence reports, letters of support, and the community assessment prepared by a probation or parole officer.

For a description of a day in the life of a Parole Board of Canada parole board member, see https://www.canada.ca/en/parole-board/services/board-members/ a-day-in-the-life-of-a-board-member.html.

During the hearing, the board members ask the inmate about the release plan and other questions to ascertain suitability of release. Board members are

▼ A parole board hearing

AP Photo/Jessica Hill, Pool

interested in the insights the offender has gained about the offence, the decisions that led to the criminal behaviour, and the steps the offender has taken to address the issues that were associated with the criminal activity. This includes the programs that the inmate has completed and the extent to which the inmate has addressed issues related to alcohol or drug abuse, anger management, or life skills. Indications of remorse and of empathy for the victim are considered important by board members. The file review and the interview are meant to determine whether the offender can be managed at an acceptable level of risk in the community.

The *Gladue* decision, discussed in Chapter 9, has also impacted the decision-making of parole boards. Boards are required to consider the unique circumstances of Indigenous applicants and the effects of the residential school system, as well as the inmate-applicant's family history, experience with social services and child welfare, and other factors related to the loss of culture.[8]

If the parole board determines that the level of risk the inmate-applicant presents is not manageable in the community, the application for release on day parole or full parole will be denied. If parole is denied, the board will set out for the inmate the steps that can be taken to improve chances of release in the future. This is particularly important for inmates in federal institutions, as these offenders are serving longer sentences. Inmates in provincial/territorial institutions who are denied parole will most likely be released at their two-thirds date and so will not re-apply for parole.

If parole is granted, a certificate of parole is prepared. The parole certificate contains both mandatory conditions, such as obeying the law and keeping the peace, and additional conditions such as abstaining from intoxicants. Regardless of the board's decision, it is required to write a report stating the reasons for the denial or granting of conditional release. For inmates whose application for release has been denied, the CCRA (s. 147) sets out grounds for appeal. As parole boards are tribunals rather than courts of law, appeals are generally made on the grounds that proper procedures were not followed by the board.

The decision of a parole board to release an inmate back into the community is, along with the verdict of the criminal court, perhaps the most important decision that is made in the correctional process. Despite this, little attention has been given to the composition of parole boards, the relationship between member characteristics and conditional release decisions, how board members use the information contained in offender case files, and the consequences of decisions for the offender, the victims, and the community.

INMATE APPLICANTS AND THE PAROLE HEARING

For inmates applying for conditional release, the appearance before the parole board can be stressful, intimidating, and anxiety-provoking. Inmates have little or no understanding of the role of the parole board and may be intimidated by the more sophisticated language skills of board members. Other inmate-applicants may be veterans of parole hearings. A lifer on parole who had appeared before the parole board on numerous occasions offered the following observation on parole hearings:

> Parole hearings for me now are old hat. I know how to present myself, what to do, what they want to hear, why they want to hear it. I have a good understanding of what their role is, and what they think their role is and how to approach that . . .[9]

Parole board members, for their part, may not realize that the inmate-applicant is mentally disordered or, in the case of a post-suspension hearing, the offender is still in withdrawal following a relapse into drug use while on conditional release. Board members can ask the inmate-applicant literally anything. For most inmates who plead guilty in criminal court, this is the first time they have been asked detailed questions about their crimes, their personal history, and their future intentions. The severe time constraints under which many parole boards operate place an added burden on both board members and the inmate-applicant, and that may lead to superficial coverage of some topics.

In jurisdictions where the PBC is responsible for provincial/territorial parole hearings (all except Ontario and Quebec, which operate their own provincial parole boards), *paper decisions* are common, and no hearing is held. This method denies inmate-applicants the opportunity to meet face to face with the board and discuss their application. It also denies the victims of crime the chance to appear before the parole board and discuss the impact of the crime, and to offer their opinion on the inmate's application for release.

Under the best of circumstances, parole board members face the daunting task of determining whether the release of the inmate-applicant will be manageable in the community and will facilitate their reintegration into the community. This must be accomplished within a hearing that may last no longer than one hour. As one observer has noted, "As the last 'stop' in an offender's carceral journey, there may be little that the parole process can do to respond to or to address the factors contributing to her or his incarceration in the first place."[10]

THE DYNAMICS OF PAROLE BOARD DECISION-MAKING

Despite the important role that parole boards play in the correctional process, little is known about the interactions that occur between the inmate-applicants and parole board members. A journalist's account of the hearings of the PBC in the Ontario region, presented in Corrections File 12.3, provides some insights.

CORRECTIONS FILE 12.3

A JOURNALIST'S OBSERVATIONS OF THE PAROLE BOARD OF CANADA, ONTARIO REGION

Like Santa, a parole board is supposed to know who's been good or bad, and so by the time the hearing arrives, parole panellists (called directors) already know more about the prisoner than they perhaps care to—and a lot of it is not very nice.

On this particular day, three board directors—former prison warden Kenneth Payne, career correctional-service employee Sheila Henriksen, and social worker John Brothers—have the final say.

Armed with documents describing the parole-seeker's criminal history, psychological assessments, education, family situation, other relationships, behaviour while in prison, and the recommendation from Correctional Service Canada, the members try to evaluate what risk these individuals pose to society and determine if that risk is manageable in the community.

The first up to bat on this day is a 36-year-old Kingston man who was sentenced to life on a charge of second-degree murder for killing a friend in a dispute over a woman.

At 8:30 a.m., the slight, frail-looking man is waiting outside the hearing with his case management officer and a university law student

as the morning announcements play over the intercom. The atmosphere is weirdly like high school.

When the door to the hearing room opens, the brief window of opportunity has arrived that the convict has been waiting for—make-or-break time. The parole panel will soon begin its gruelling interview. No holds are barred, and no part of a convict's life is off limits.

Sitting a couple of metres from the convicts, looking them in the face, panel members have to sift through what they're hearing and judge what is sincere and what is contrived, remembering that people seldom get to this point in their lives by being totally honest.

The members take in the convict's appearance and mannerisms, dissect his answers, ask questions in different ways to get a better read, and compare the answers to facts provided by the professions.

They often caution the convicts against lying, because their replies must be consistent with what's in their files.

This morning, the murderer from Kingston slouches, his hair slicked back tightly like people wore in the 1950s. He is wearing dark clothes, a tweed sports jacket, and unmatching, light-coloured socks.

(continued)

The case management officer sits at a table to his left. Right as the hearing starts, the convict withdraws his application for full parole. He says day parole will suffice.

The man has spent time in a number of jails and prisons since the murder. He stares straight ahead as the case management officer outlines his criminal record, all of it minor and non-violent up to the killing. He also relates how the convict was granted full parole twice, in 1992 and again in 1995, and violated it both times.

A doctor's report rates the probability he will reoffend within a year of release at 40 percent, saying he suffers from an antisocial personality disorder.

A panel member asks why he withdrew his application for full parole. In a low, frail voice, the convict states the obvious: "In a realistic view, I don't think you guys would send me to full parole."

A member jokes, "You have already done some of our work for us." Mr. Payne asks the convict about the bad choices he has made through his life, and there are many. The convict says his worst was getting involved in a relationship with the woman he killed for and, as he puts it, his "negative thinking."

The focus shifts to what he might have learned from his failures. "I needed to change the way I view things," the convict says. "I used to go through distorted thinking patterns. I have a problem over-complicating things. I used to take on other people's problems and make them my own."

In discussing an anger-management course he has just repeated, he is asked: "When was the last time you felt really angry?" "When I got the letter from the parole board that media would be at my hearing," he answers. He adds, "Nothing personal," as he turns toward the observers behind him.

Asked about the killing, the convict says he doesn't recognize the man who did it, that there are "some pretty blank spots surrounding that time."

Ms. Henriksen questions his integrity. "I have got a sense you have an ability to fool people," she says. He replies: "Sitting in the position I am in, it doesn't seem right for me to say, 'Trust me.'"

But the board chooses to trust him anyway. Following brief deliberations, it grants the man once-a-month [unescorted temporary absences]. If he does well on those, the next step will be day parole and then full parole without any further hearing.

"The board is satisfied you have benefited from our programs," says Mr. Payne.

The convict thanks the directors and, as he leaves, passes the bank robber waiting outside. And the process repeats itself.

The day ends with the case of the Stratford father, a 29-year-old first-time offender who smashed up his truck after a night of partying and nearly killed his passenger. His sentence was two years for criminal negligence causing bodily harm. He has served about a year.

If there is a common thread among these convicts it is the way they handle stress: Drugs and alcohol are their mainstays.

Oddly enough, the convict doesn't do a very good job of selling his case. Lucky for him it sells itself.

The case management officer gives an exemplary report on his prison behaviour, noting he attends night school and wants to pursue a trade in college.

The convict shakes as he appears before the panel members, who at times try to relax him.

One thing that works against him is a compelling victim impact statement. The victim is suing the convict. "I know he's mad but I have gone and tried to talk with him and all he does is yell at me or make rude gestures when he drives by," the convict explains. "I just wish it was me who got injured that night."

"All I know is I have two young kids I haven't seen in a month and I want to get back to them," says the man. "I can't wait."

Another quick verdict: immediate full parole. The directors deliver their judgment. And then they just hope.

Source: D. Campbell. 1997, November 3. "A Journalist Goes to Prison to See for Himself How Parole Boards Decide Which Convicts Are Good Risks and Which Ones Are Not," *Ottawa Citizen*, p. A3. Material republished with the express permission of Postmedia Network Inc.

ISSUES IN PAROLE BOARD DECISION-MAKING

There are a number of issues that surround parole boards and their decision-making. These include issues discussed in the following sections.

THE LACK OF DIVERSITY AMONG PAROLE BOARD MEMBERS

A major criticism of the PBC has been the lack of diversity among its members. One observer noted, "Unless you understand what you're dealing with, you don't make an informed decision. . . . Board members need an awareness of the offender's community, what's unique to the community, what may be the impediments to communications, what may be the cultural impediments to change."[11] Of concern is that board members may not be knowledgeable about gender issues and women offenders and the dynamics that are associated with women in conflict with the law.[12]

Diversity is also important in assessing risk. A major challenge is that the composition of parole boards does not reflect the majority of inmate-applicants who are from vulnerable, marginalized, and racialized groups. This raises the issue as to how board members can understand and make decisions that consider the life history and circumstances of the persons who appear before it.

The PBC has made efforts to increase sensitivity to diversity issues, although an investigation of these efforts found that "diversity issues were not effectively integrated into the existing organizational structures of the PBC but, rather, were constituted as peripheral to the organization's 'real' work."[13]

Some efforts have been made to address the challenges faced by Indigenous inmates applying for conditional release. Members of the PBC must undergo cultural sensitivity and awareness training, learn about the traditions and cultures of the Inuit, Métis, and First Nations populations, and complete training with Elders. How this training is applied in parole hearings and the impact it has had on parole board decisions has not been examined.

Federal Indigenous offenders have the opportunity to participate in parole hearings with an Indigenous cultural advisor, and there are also Elder-assisted parole hearings. The Elder may say a prayer or perform a ritual (such as smudging) to open and/or close the parole hearing. Experience has been that Elder-assisted parole board hearings have resulted in hearings being more fair, culturally sensitive, and respectful.[14]

There is also provision for parole hearings to be held in the community rather than the penitentiary, as a means to restore the relationship between the offender and the community.

CONSIDERING THE CIRCUMSTANCES OF OFFENDERS FROM MARGINALIZED AND RACIALIZED GROUPS

The inmate-applicants who appear before parole boards present a broad spectrum of risk and needs. Most, however, are from marginalized and racialized groups or are Indigenous.[15] The Gladue decision requires that parole boards consider the unique circumstances of Indigenous inmate-applicants who apply for conditional release.

An important question is whether the parole board, at such a late stage in the criminal justice system, can address the historical and contemporary factors that contribute to the conflict with the law and that may mitigate successful reintegration back into the community.[16] For many inmate-applicants, the parole hearing is the first instance in which they will have spoken about their crime and the circumstances surrounding it.

PUBLIC AND POLITICAL INFLUENCE ON THE BOARD

Parole board members are appointed by governments and, traditionally, positions on parole boards have been patronage appointments—that is, rewards for supporters of the government. Members are not required by legislation to have any special training or expertise in law, criminology, psychology, or corrections. As concerns with risk management and negative publicity surrounding high-visibility crimes committed by offenders on conditional release increase, this is likely to affect the decision-making of the PBC.[17] There is a concern that too much discretion has been vested in non-judicial personnel whose decisions are subjected to very little oversight.

It has been argued that there is a need to staff parole boards with persons with specialized professional competence.[18] See Critical Thinking Exercise 12.1 at the end of this chapter.

THE ABSENCE OF CASE INFORMATION FEEDBACK TO PAROLE BOARD MEMBERS

Few if any mechanisms are in place for parole board members to receive feedback on the outcomes of their decisions—that is, what happens to offenders while they are under supervision in the community and after warrant expiry and the end of supervision. Generally, parole board members learn of an inmate's behaviour on conditional release only when that person commits a high-profile crime or, by happenstance, reappears during a parole suspension hearing before one of the board members involved in the original decision.

THE ABSENCE OF CLEARLY DEFINED RELEASE CRITERIA

One criticism often levelled against parole boards is that too much discretion has been vested in non-judicial decision-makers whose decisions are not subject to judicial appeal. The two general criteria that are to guide release decisions, as outlined in the *Corrections and Conditional Release Act* (see above), have long been a source of difficulty for correctional staff, for inmates, and for parole board members themselves. Board members have access to a great deal of information on each inmate-applicant—including police reports, pre-sentence reports, the presiding judge's reasons for the sentence, materials produced by case managers (including risk/needs assessments), and parole officers' community assessments—yet it is often difficult for them to prioritize this information and make a predictive decision.

This lack of guidance, combined with the discretion exercised by board members, can result in individual styles of decision-making, which may, in turn, lead to disparity in decisions on applications for conditional release between boards as well as among board members, even within the same jurisdiction. Whether a particular inmate-applicant is successful may depend upon which board members happen to sit the hearing.

IS PAROLE BOARD DECISION-MAKING EFFECTIVE?

The effectiveness of parole boards should be measured by more than rates of success/reoffending of offenders. The lack of standardized criteria for board membership, the potential impact of public and political influences, the absence of feedback, and broad decision-making guidelines all potentially undermine the effectiveness of parole boards. As well, offenders with FASD, with a mental illness, who are a visible minority, or who are Indigenous may be at a disadvantage in parole hearings. Many offenders, particularly in provincial/territorial institutions, do not apply for parole but rather serve their time to their discharge date (two-thirds of their sentence) and leave the institution with no supervision or access to community-based programs and services for the balance of their sentence.

THE REINTEGRATION PROCESS

Reintegration

The process whereby an inmate is prepared for and released into the community after serving time in prison.

Reintegration is a process, not an event. It has been defined as "all activity and programming conducted to prepare an offender to return safely to the community as a law-abiding citizen."[19]

The term should not be used too literally, as it suggests that before their incarceration, offenders had been successfully integrated into the community. Many inmates come from marginalized backgrounds and have not acquired the resources or skill sets to participate in mainstream society.[20] While offenders sent to custody experience a variety of status degradation ceremonies as they move from citizen in the community to inmate, there are no status restoration ceremonies and "rituals of reintegration" that would build on the offender's accomplishments rather than being focused solely on risk.[21] As a consequence, many newly released offenders are left to their own devices to adapt and survive.

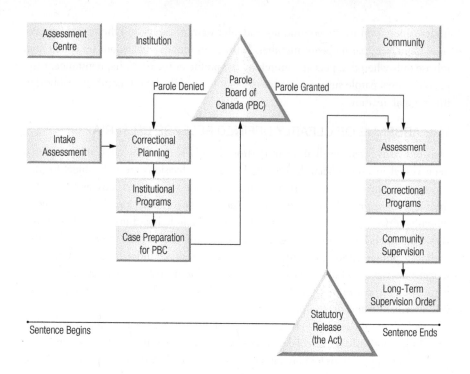

◄ FIGURE 12.8

The Reintegration Process for Federal Offenders

Source: Adapted from Office of the Auditor General of the Canada. 1996. *Report of the Auditor General of Canada – November 1996.* Ottawa: Author, pp. 30–31. Reproduced with the permission of Her Majesty the Queen in Right of Canada, as represented by the Auditor General of Canada, 2017.

The reintegration process for federal offenders is illustrated in Figure 12.8.

The flow diagram in Figure 12.8 indicates that reintegration begins when the offender is first assessed and continues with institutional programming and preparation for applying for conditional release. The goal of reintegration is to avoid recidivism in the short term (i.e., until the warrant expiry date) as well as afterwards. When required, yet another goal is to address the interests of crime victims. There are a variety of community correctional centres operated by CSC and provincial/territorial governments directly, or via contract, across the country. There are also residential treatment centres and recovery houses that specialize in alcohol and substance abuse intervention.

Most inmates who reoffend do so within the first two years following release from a correctional institution, and this highlights the importance of providing support in the community.

For integration to succeed, continuity is required between the programs and services in the institution and those in the community.[22,23] This is the notion of throughcare. A seamless transition in treatment from the institution to the community is particularly important for offenders with special needs, such as substance abuse issues.[24]

In Chapter 11, *throughcare* was identified as an important strategy in assisting inmates to make the transition from custody to the community. In British Columbia, the Integrated Offender Management (IOM) program is designed to facilitate collaborative case planning and management between adult custodial and community corrections to achieve the successful reintegration of offenders back into the community.[25] This is an example of throughcare.

An exit survey of offenders ($N = 466$) who participated in the IOM program found that 96 percent found the program was helpful to them, while 79 percent felt that the program would assist them in avoiding reoffending. However, there was no attempt to track these offenders to determine the actual rate of reoffending.

COMING BACK: THE CHALLENGES OF RE-ENTRY AND REINTEGRATION

> Going to jail had such an impact on me 'cause I lost everything. I lost my identity. I lost my family. I lost my place in my community. I lost everything. (an inmate)[26]

> Reintegrating individuals are expected to turn their lives around, but are consistently denied access to opportunities that would allow them to do so. This results in diminished self-worth, disillusionment and a sense of hopelessness and futility.[27]

In Chapter 11, the various pains of imprisonment experienced by offenders who are confined in correctional institutions were discussed. Upon their release from confinement, some offenders may also experience **pains of re-entry**.[28] Correctional institutions, particularly those at the maximum-security level, are closed, highly structured, and artificial environments where an antisocial value system predominates and where inmates have few responsibilities. Upon release, these same individuals are expected to resume life in a community that values independence of thought and an ability to cope with the complexities of daily existence. Life on the outside is everything prison is not: unpredictable, fast-paced, and filled with choices. The challenges are captured in the following observation:

> I can go where I want to go and do what I want to do, but I was kind of nervous. . . . You know, if I was going to walk down the road, get run over by a car, or . . . I think I was really nervous to . . . how I would react to people. . . . I grew up in jail . . . so that's the only life I knew. . . . You do this, you do that, you do this, and you hope you don't get killed. . . . It's how you live in there. And then when I got out . . . it was different.[29]

Re-entry is made even more difficult for long-term offenders, who have had little opportunity to become familiar with changes that have occurred in the community since they were confined. This includes how to navigate technology. As a former federal inmate recalled:

> The first time that I had a paycheque and I had to put it in 'cause the bank was closed. And I'm standing there with the cheque in my hand. I didn't sign it. No signature, nothing on it—and I still don't know how to use this machine [ATM] so I'm trying to figure this out and I hit a button—and I guess—I was just holding my cheque, I guess it was close enough and whoosh all of a sudden, it's gone. I went into a panic.[30]

Offenders who have served lengthy periods of time in confinement may experience symptoms of PTSD, which may include flashbacks, suicidal thoughts, and depression. With respect to reintegration, there are challenges with finding housing and employment due to their criminal record and the stigma associated with having been in prison. Increasingly, employers are requiring background record checks that may present barriers to ex-offenders seeking employment. Although ex-offenders can apply for a record suspension (formerly known as a pardon), this requires a wait time of five years for summary offences and 10 years for indictable offences.

Imagine the difficulty you would have adjusting to a law-abiding lifestyle in the community if you were a parolee with a grade 9 education, a poor record of employment, tenuous or non-existent family support, a substance abuse problem, and/or few or no non-criminal friends (not to mention a criminal record). Unfortunately, earning a record of positive conduct inside the correctional institution (including completion of various treatment programs) may not adequately prepare you for the challenges of adapting to life in the community. Planning a day without the rigid timetable of prison routine can be a daunting task.

Pains of re-entry

The difficulties that inmates released from prison encounter as they try to adjust to life in the community.

© Leo Cullum/The New Yorker Collection/The Cartoon Bank

"Actually, there were a number of messages while you were in prison."

A newly released offender can feel like a stranger—inadequate, acutely self-conscious, and convinced that every person on the street can tell from appearance alone that he or she has been in prison. As one woman ex-offender recounted:

> It's like you're on the bus and you think it's written on your forehead that you just came out of prison. It's terrible, it is. You got no one around. It's much easier in prison because all of the guards were around. They cared about you somewhat. Out here it just seems like you are by yourself. Just thrown out. And you are always being judged.[31]

For a released inmate who has no friends on the outside who can be relied on for assistance, protection, and security, the institution may exert a stronger pull than freedom itself. As one ex-offender who had served over 20 years in prison stated to your author: "I have never had the intensity of friendships, the trust, the companionship, in the outside community that I had when I was incarcerated" (personal communication).

A transition this dramatic would challenge even the most gifted individual, and it is especially difficult for marginalized and socially isolated offenders who have been incarcerated for long periods. One long-term offender commented to C.T. Griffiths: "The values, attitudes, and behaviours that I learned inside were just the opposite of what I needed to make it in the free world." Complicating this is that many offenders have few, if any, non-criminal friends or access to legitimate opportunities.

The pressures on released offenders may place them at risk of suicide. In a study ($N = 1,025$) of inmates during the time period 1995 to 2006, there were a total of 47 deaths from all causes among the sample: 26 (2.54 percent) died by suicide and of these 77 percent occurred outside the prison. This suggests that offenders are more at risk of suicide in the community than in correctional institutions, a finding that highlights the need for programs and services for offenders released into the community.[32]

THE CHALLENGES OF NEWLY RELEASED OFFENDERS

A sentence of imprisonment triggers a process whereby individuals are extracted from society and forced to adjust to a closed, structured, and artificial environment, one in which an antisocial value system predominates and inmates have little responsibility. Then, upon release, these same inmates are expected to resume/assume a law-abiding life in the community and to hold prosocial values, exercise independence of thought and decision-making, and display life skills that enable them to cope with the complexities of daily life in a fast-paced society.

All the plans to "go straight" can crumble like a New Year's resolution in February. The newly released offender may face social, economic, and personal challenges that make it difficult to avoid returning to criminal activity. A significant minority of parolees commit a criminal offence within three years of their release.

The majority of federal offenders released on conditional release have difficulties associated with the seven dynamic need domains: attitudes, community functioning, employment, marital/family, personal and emotional, associates, and substance abuse.[33]

The most frequently mentioned problems facing offenders upon re-entry are a lack of education and job skills, finding suitable housing, the absence of family support, poverty, drug and alcohol problems, and low self-esteem.[34] Criminal records preclude entry into some professions, including those requiring the employee to be bonded (insured). Some employers may have less stringent requirements but still be reluctant to hire someone with a criminal record. The job-seeking parolee may not have suitable clothes for interviews or may not possess job-specific gear such as steel-toed boots and special tools. Family reunification can be another source of stress. The longer the term of confinement, the less prepared the parolee is to resume family relations.

There is an emerging awareness of homelessness and the challenges that this poses to offenders released from institutions. There is evidence that homelessness is related to reoffending, with four out of ten admissions of homeless persons to one Toronto-area jail during one year being returnees.[35] It is estimated that 30 percent of released offenders are homeless and have no stable residence to go to when they are released.[36] Compounding the problem are provincial laws that allow landlords to deny accommodation to persons with a criminal record.[37]

Offenders often find themselves in Catch-22 situations, illustrated by one released offender: "You need to meet with a worker first to get money, you need to get out of jail to meet with a worker ... you need an address to get a cheque, and a cheque to get an address."[38] There is often a lack of continuity between programs in the institution and in the community. Offenders who were in a methadone maintenance program in the institution, for example, may not have access to this program in the community, particularly those offenders from rural and remote communities.[39] Additional challenges may exist owing to mental illness, the presence of FASD, and substance abuse issues.[40]

Interviews with offenders and service providers ($N = 35$) involved in community corrections in Hamilton, Ontario, identified housing, employment opportunities, mental health counselling, and addiction services as major challenges for offenders on conditional release. Speaking to the difficulties experienced upon release, one client stated, "I didn't overcome these challenges. I went back to sex trade work. Most girls, that's what they do."[41] Another commented on what happens when the ex-offender's needs are not met: "They wander the streets. They don't know how to address their needs."[42]

Particular challenges were faced in staying away from old friendship networks, as were the consequences of not having timely access to treatment programs. Comments on this from the clients included the following:

- "People have big plans coming out of jail but they don't happen because of the time lag between being released from jail and arriving at the first service provider."
- "A girl gets out of jail, she wants to get into rehab right away. She can't go so she gets frustrated and decides, 'Well, if I can't get clean now I might as well still do drugs.'"[43]

In an attempt to cope with the pains of re-entry, a parolee may revert to such high-risk behaviour as heavy drinking, drug use, fighting, and spending time with old friends from prison. Watch the video, "A Homecomer's Confession – Eddie B. Ellis Jr.," listed in the Media Links section at the end of this chapter.

STRANGERS IN A STRANGE LAND: THE ISOLATION OF OFFENDERS RETURNING TO THE COMMUNITY

> I guess my biggest problem coming back into the community was a misunderstanding in that I thought people in the community wanted me to come back. . . . I paid my penalty but I was not welcomed back into the community with open arms. I had to fight for and establish my place. (ex-offender)[44]

Newly released offenders can feel like the proverbial "stranger in a strange land"—embarrassed and inadequate, and convinced that every person on the street can tell at a mere glance that they have been in prison. In the words of a woman parolee with a life sentence: "I didn't feel like I was back. I didn't feel like I belonged. . . . I didn't feel part of this world anymore, I was still inside. In some respects, part of me will always be inside."[45] Ironically, offenders may experience feelings of paranoia and fear for their safety upon re-entering the community. Another offender commented, "I was always more nervous getting out than going in."[46]

Securing employment, stable housing, and education have been found to be critical for the successful reintegration of offenders.[47] In addition, offenders with special needs require access to programs and services, including mental health services, addition programs and counselling, and in some instances, family counselling.[48]

Ex-offenders may face discrimination from employers, one recalling:

> And then the boss that I worked for found out about my background. . . . He found out and this guy made my life miserable. Every dirty job there was after that, he gave me. And I told him, right to his face, I said, "You don't have the balls to break me," I said. "CSC tried for ten years. You don't have the balls and neither did they."[49]

Ex-offenders, particularly those who have been incarcerated for a lengthy periods of time, may struggle in social interactions and in personal relationships. As one ex-offender recalled:

> I think that it [prison] skewed my development and my ability to have open and honest relationships with women because of the prison mentality and the objectifying of women in that environment . . . because all interactions with women were forced, strained, over-supervised. There was no natural ability to learn how to talk to women.[50]

In addition, there is concern that offenders who are released from incarceration may suffer from **post-incarceration syndrome (PICS)**.[51] This syndrome is a consequence of offenders having lived in the total institution world of the prison amidst all of the dynamics that were discussed in Chapter 11. It can include PTSD, including depression or anxiety, and antisocial personality traits, including defiance of authority and the victimization of others. It may be particularly severe for offenders who have served lengthy prison terms and presents challenges to successfully reintegrating back into the community. The ex-offender may have difficulty establishing or re-establishing personal and family relationships, including contact with their children. Problems may be compounded if the released offender has mental health and/or addiction issues.

These difficulties are reflected in the account of a family member whose uncle came to live with their family after serving 21 years in prison for murder. See Corrections File 12.4.

Post-incarceration syndrome (PICS)

A condition of offenders in custody and in the community that is caused by prolonged exposure to the dynamics of life inside correctional institutions.

CORRECTIONS FILE 12.4

LIVING WITH MY UNCLE'S POST-INCARCERATION SYNDROME

Ever since he got here he has been impossible to live with. He is rude, dismissive, abrasive, disrespectful, inconsiderate, and tactless. He does not seem to care about the effect he is having on other people. He has severe entitlement issues that cause him to place unreasonable demands on others' time and patience.

Sometimes, I feel as though I have to walk on eggshells in my own house because I am afraid that if I really let him know how I feel, it will result in a confrontation that will escalate and cause him to have to leave our home. I have been trying to understand his situation and what it must have been like for him in prison and what it must be like for him now trying to cope with residual feelings of injustice, trauma, and bitterness, but it is becoming emotionally taxing to the point where I dread coming home at night. This is no way to live for both him and I.

I took it upon myself to Google all the things I have been noticing with him. The irritability, short fuse, outbursts of anger, hypersensitivity to sounds, increased appetite, disagreeableness, combativeness, history of substance abuse, arrested development, and child-like expectancies and behaviours, and it all began to formulate a psychological profile that was consistent with post-incarceration syndrome (PICS).

Given what I understand about my uncle's condition, I would not go so far as to say that I don't like him. I will say that I don't like what the world has turned him into. I don't like the fact that he has become another man that I cannot genuinely get close to and cultivate a loving relationship with due to his trauma-ridden past. I also don't like the fact that I don't know how to help him.

Source: L. Pabon. 2013, November 22. "Living With My Uncles Post Incarceration Syndrome," *Luis Speaks*. https://luisspeaks.wordpress.com/2013/11/22/living-with-my-uncles-post-incarceration-syndrome. Reprinted with permission from Luis Pabón.

WOMEN OFFENDERS AND REINTEGRATION

> The system doesn't support reintegration.... You see them being released into the community with nothing. And how surprised should we be that they reoffend?
>
> —executive director, Elizabeth Fry Society, Ottawa[52]

Women offenders re-entering the community face many of the same challenges as their male counterparts, including issues related to employment, housing, and access to programs and services. However, women offenders may be more likely to experience gender discrimination and more stigma as ex-offenders than their male counterparts, in part because of societal attitudes toward "misbehaving women."[53]

Similar to their male counterparts, women offenders re-entering the community must attempt to establish stability in their lives. This requires supportive family and friendship networks as well as access to programs and services. Finding employment may be even more challenging for women than it is for men, because women are less likely to have completed their education, often have little job experience, and may have to find and pay for daycare.[54,55]

Women released from confinement may also have to address difficult issues with respect to their partners/spouses who may also have been involved in criminal activity. This may place additional strains on women and increase the "pains of re-entry."

Among the factors that appear to be associated with reoffending among women offenders are a high-risk rating, unemployment, substance abuse, and failure to complete community-based programs.[56] Successful reintegration is facilitated by a conscious decision on the part of the woman offender to live a crime-free/drug-free life; support from families, partners/spouses, and children; and a positive relationship with her parole officer.[57]

For inmate-mothers, the challenges may include re-establishing contact with their children, finding suitable accommodation with sufficient space, and attempting to regain custody if the children have been placed in care during the mother's confinement. Especially when the inmate-mother is the sole caregiver, child protection authorities may require that the mother obtain stable employment and suitable accommodation before being allowed to reapply for custody.

The frustrations that mothers may encounter upon release are reflected in the following comments of an ex-offender on parole in Ontario:

> I took parole to get my kids back. Parole agreed to my present location, but now the Children's Aid Society is saying it's not suitable for the kids. I can't rent before I know whether I am going to get my kids, and I can't get them back until I rent. I can't get mother's allowance until I have my kids, and without it I can't rent. I never know what I have to do for who. There are just so many hoops to jump through.[58]

It can be assumed that the challenges are even greater for women released from provincial/territorial institutions since these women will have only served a short time in confinement and may not have access to programs and services upon release. Recall that provincial/territorial offenders who serve two-thirds of their sentence are released without any form of supervision in the community. This may be particularly problematic for women who have extensive histories of abuse, addiction, and mental illness.

INDIGENOUS OFFENDERS AND REINTEGRATION

Indigenous offenders serve a higher proportion of their sentence before being released on parole, partly because of the seriousness of the crimes they have committed but also because of the lack of community supports available to them, especially in rural and remote communities.

Many parole-eligible Indigenous inmates do not apply for conditional release. This may be for a number of reasons, including not understanding the parole process, a lack of support in the outside community, and/or a lack of confidence in their ability to successfully complete conditional release. There may also be limited access to Indigenous-specific treatment programs, particularly in provincial/territorial institutions and in rural and northern communities upon release. A report of the Auditor General of Canada found that only 20 percent of Indigenous offenders were able to complete treatment programs prior to their eligibility date for conditional release.[59] These factors contribute to the situation where Indigenous inmates are more likely than non-Indigenous inmates to be on statutory release or to be held into custody until their warrant expiry date.

Provincial/territorial and federal day parole and full parole completion rates are high, generally in the 70 percent to 95 percent range. There are differences, however, in the rates of completion between various groups of inmates:

- Compared to non-Indigenous offenders, Indigenous offenders have a lower successful completion rate for both federal day and full parole.
- Federal women offenders have higher successful completion rates than male offenders.
- Asian offenders have the highest rates of completion of both day and full parole.
- For offenders serving determinate sentences, the successful completion rate on federal full parole is in the 85 percent range.[60]

The reasons for the disparities in parole completion outcomes between women, male, Asian, and Indigenous offenders have not been explored.

STRATEGIES TO INVOLVE FIRST NATIONS IN THE RELEASE AND REINTEGRATION OF INDIGENOUS OFFENDERS

Several provisions in the CCRA are designed to increase the involvement of First Nations communities in the release and reintegration of federal Indigenous offenders. Section 81 authorizes the federal government to enter into agreements with First Nations communities whereby the community will take over the "care and custody" of some Indigenous inmates. Section 84 provides an opportunity for First Nations to participate in a community-assisted hearing in front of the PBC, to propose a plan for the conditional release and reintegration of the Indigenous offender into their community. This provision also allows for offenders under a long-term supervision order to be supervised in an Indigenous community. There is also a policy providing for the involvement of Elders in parole hearings.

In practice, there is variable use of Elder-assisted parole hearing across the country. There is disagreement as to how best to integrate Indigenous status into the policies and practices of the Parole Board of Canada.[61]

Community-assisted parole hearings are rare as well. There is often resistance in the community to becoming involved, and there may not be the capacity in the community to take responsibility for assisting in the reintegration of the offender.

HIGH-RISK AND SPECIAL-NEEDS OFFENDERS ON CONDITIONAL RELEASE

Although it is likely that all offenders re-entering the community from correctional institutions encounter challenges in reintegrating back into the community, certain groups of offenders may encounter particular difficulties.

HIGH-RISK OFFENDERS

A key concern for corrections is managing the risk that offenders may pose to the safety and security of the community. To manage the risk posed by high-risk offenders, CSC collaborates with several police departments across the country (including the Regina Police Service and the Hamilton Police Service). It involves police officers being hired to work as community corrections liaison officers (CCLOs). These officers monitor the activities of high-risk/high-needs offenders in the community and liaise between police officers and parole officers.[62] Larger police services across the country also have specialized teams that focus on chronic and high-risk offenders.

PERSONS WITH MENTAL ILLNESS

Federal and provincial/territorial systems of corrections have been slow to address the challenges faced by persons with mental health issues upon re-entry into the community. This often leads to a cycle of release/reoffending/reincarceration.[63] Offenders with mental health issues may be more likely to commit technical violations of their parole.[64]

Offenders with mental illness present special challenges upon returning to the community, including social isolation, co-occurring substance abuse disorder, and finding suitable employment and housing. A study of offenders with mental illness in detention in Quebec, for example, found that these individuals were poorly prepared to re-enter the community, they had difficulty accessing services, and there was little continuity between programs in the institution and in the community.[65] Programs and services for special-needs populations are less developed by provincial/territorial corrections systems, and offenders with specific needs who reside in northern and remote areas of the country have limited access to assistance.

SEX OFFENDERS

Sex offenders on conditional release are often high profile in the media and present governments and corrections with unique challenges. Their release from prison is often front-page news in the local press or even announced over the Internet. Correctional systems use a variety of techniques to manage the risks of this offender group. Treatment interventions include the use of drugs such as antiandrogens to reduce sex drive and a CSC-operated high-risk offender program, which includes a maintenance program for managing sex offenders who are on conditional release. This program is cognitive behaviour–oriented and includes individual and group counselling. It is designed to provide continuity to programs for sex offenders in correctional institutions.

Governments and systems of corrections also employ a variety of strategies to monitor and control high-risk sex offenders (and other high-risk offenders on parole) in the community. This includes the use of electronic monitoring (EM) and GPS tracking (discussed in Chapter 10).

Several provinces, including British Columbia and Ontario, have established sex offender registries that require these offenders to register 15 days prior to release into the community (or upon conviction if they receive a non-custodial sentence), and they must then re-register annually as well as 15 days prior to any change of address. The centralized register database includes information on the offender, such as their name, date of birth, current address, and identifying marks, as well as photographs. Offenders remain on the registry indefinitely unless they are acquitted on appeal or receive a pardon.

Community notification (CN) is a widely used, yet controversial, strategy designed to manage risk and protect the community from high-risk sex offenders. The practice

Community notification

The practice, usually carried out by police agencies, of making a public announcement that a high-risk offender has taken up residence in an area.

of CN generally involves the police making a public announcement that a high-risk sex offender has taken up residence in an area. The premise of CN policies is that by warning potential victims and the community at large, the ability of the community to protect itself is strengthened and offenders who know they are being watched will be deterred from reoffending.[66] On the other hand, CN can enflame community residents who may take a "not in my backyard" (NIMBY) view of offenders returning to the community. See Class/Group Discussion 12.1.

CN can involve proactive measures, such as distributing leaflets door to door and placing signage on the sex offender's property, or it can be passive, involving the posting of the information on the Internet to be accessed by interested parties, including persons in the market to purchase real estate. Several American states post the names and home address of all sex offenders on the Web. Information can be accessed to determine if, and how many, sex offenders live in proximity to a specific piece of property. In Canada, police departments periodically place public warnings on their websites.

This strategy may also be viewed as a hardening of attitudes against certain categories of offenders and reflective of a punitive penology. The negative aspects of CN are that it may prevent the offender from re-establishing a stable residence and relationships in the community, thereby increasing the possibility of reoffending.

These challenges were highlighted in a case in British Columbia. A sex offender with 42 prior offences, including sexual and violent attacks against victims as young as nine, was forced out of a community after being released from custody. He had refused to participate in treatment programs during his time in prison. The RCMP had issued a CN, releasing his photo and warning that he was a high risk to reoffend. In the words of the town's mayor: "Basically, our community did what the judicial system wouldn't. . . . We said, 'You have no rights. Get out of town.'" As the threats against him mounted, the offender decided to move to another community 70 kilometres away. "I'm in a small town right now," he commented, "and I've had the support of [the town] for long time here and I'm going to lose it over the media [coverage]. . . . Then what do I do from here, go to someone else's community?"[67]

The use of CN raises the issue of how to balance the rights of the community with the privacy rights of the offender, as well as ethical questions as to how intrusive the State can be in a person's private life. See Class/Group Discussion 12.1.

THE STATE-RAISED OFFENDER AND RE-ENTRY

The stress of re-entry may be especially acute for the state-raised offender (see Chapter 11). These individuals have very little experience living in the outside community, have few or no family ties, and—a key point—have no "stake" in the community. Their friends, identity, status, and power are all inside the correctional institution. Outside in the free community, there are no guarantees of status, of security, or of a routine that provides for one's basic needs. In such cases, the pull of the institution may be greater than that of freedom on the streets.

Close friendships are in danger of being lost, and inmates may feel that they are abandoning close friends, confidants, and/or lovers inside. These feelings may be especially acute when soon-to-be-released inmates realize that they have no network of support on the outside who can be relied on for assistance, protection, and security and who are not involved in criminal behaviour.

▼ Community residents in British Columbia protest the return of a sex offender to the community.

Arlen Redekop/Vancouver Sun. Material republished with the express permission of Postmedia Network Inc.

Even offenders who, prior to confinement, had relatively conventional lifestyles (with the exception of their law-breaking) can find it hard to unlearn the automatic responses acquired in an environment where physical aggression is a survival skill.

In an attempt to cope with the pains of re-entry, the parolee may revert to high-risk behaviour, including heavy drinking, drug use, resuming friendships with former criminal associates, or spending time with old friends from prison. Though most will complete their period of conditional release without committing a new offence, many will be reconvicted of a criminal offence within three years of release.

PAROLE OFFICERS AND THE SUPERVISION OF OFFENDERS

Offenders on parole are generally required to report regularly to a correctional agent such as a parole officer. Parole officers are also involved in supervising offenders who are placed on long-term supervision orders by the court. Not all offenders who are released into the community require the same level of supervision. Assessments are made to determine the need and risk level of the offender—low, medium, or high—and these are used to determine the level and intensity of supervision. Supervision by parole officers may range from periodic telephone calls to the offender's residence to the requirement that the parolee reside in a community-based residential facility with 24-hour monitoring and attend frequent face-to-face meetings with a parole officer.[68] Electronic monitoring and GPS tracking, discussed in Chapter 10, are also used as a supervision tool.

The activities and responsibilities of parole officers include conducting assessments of offenders to determine their risk and needs; preparation of materials for the parole board, including the community assessment; monitoring the offender's behaviour and enforcing the conditions of the parole certificate; counselling; and serving as an officer of the court, which includes giving testimony in court in cases where the parolee has been charged with a new offence.

THE DUAL FUNCTION OF PAROLE SUPERVISION

Like probation officers, parole officers have a dual role in their relations with clients. The first involves being a resource person and confidant to counter the pains of re-entry. In this regard, the supportive activities of parole officers can include offering job search advice, referring clients for counselling, and advocating with welfare authorities on their behalf. The second role involves monitoring and enforcing parole conditions. To be effective, parole officers must have the capacity to understand their clients.

Each parole officer has his or her own style of supervision. Some are more lenient and give the parolees assigned to them a longer "leash"; others are much stricter. To be effective, parole officers must adapt their supervision style to the risk/needs of the offender.

There are concerns that the increasing emphasis on risk management in corrections and the rise of a punitive penology may transform the role of parole officers into one of monitoring and enforcing compliance with release conditions and periodically reassessing changes in risk and need.[69]

ADDITIONAL PROVISIONS FOR SUPERVISION

The *Criminal Code* (R.S.C. 1985, c. C-46) contains a number of provisions that can be used to impose conditions and supervision on offenders once they have completed their custodial sentence and/or parole. One is the long-term offender designation (section 753 of the *Criminal Code*; see also Chapter 9). If certain criteria are met indicating that the offender will present a substantial risk of committing a serious personal offence following release from custody, the sentencing judge can impose the designation of long-term offender and require the offender to be under the supervision of a parole officer for up to 10 years.

The other provision is found in section 810 of the *Criminal Code*, which can be used for offenders who have not been granted parole and who have served their entire sentence in custody. Section 810.1 may be used in situations where there is fear that the offender poses a risk to persons under 14. Under section 810.2, prosecutors may ask the court to impose restrictions on persons who are considered a high risk to commit a violent offence in the community.

FACILITIES AND PROGRAMS FOR OFFENDERS ON CONDITIONAL RELEASE

The conditional release may include a requirement that the parolee reside in a community-based residential facility with 24-hour monitoring and frequent face-to-face meetings with a parole officer. Correctional Service Canada (CSC) operates a number of community correctional centres (CCCs) across the country. These facilities house offenders on various types of conditional release, including day and full parole, statutory release, and offenders who are on long-term supervision orders.

The CCCs serve as a transition between the institution and the community and offer a variety of programs and also provide offenders with access to programs and services in the community. These and other facilities (often referred to as *halfway houses*), many of which are operated by non-profit organizations such as the John Howard Society, Elizabeth Fry Society, St. Leonard's Society, and the Salvation Army, provide an opportunity for offenders on conditional release to have stable accommodation and to slowly adjust to being back in the community. The facility provides a safe space and the experience may be viewed positively, as being "halfway out of prison" rather than halfway in.[70]

An investigation of the CCCs by the Office of the Correctional Investigator identified several factors that hindered their effectiveness in assisting offenders to successfully reintegrate back into the community.[71] These included an increase in the number of high-risk offenders, many of whom were on statutory release, having been denied parole due to risk factors; the majority of offenders were sent to a CCC directly from maximum- or medium-security facilities; three-fourths of the residents at the CCCs were deemed at a high risk to reoffend; half of the residents were identified as having low reintegration potential; and 70 percent were deemed to have high needs in areas such as employment and education. CCC staff also indicated there were an increasing number of offenders being sent to CCCs who had mental health and addiction issues.[72] Among the conclusions of the study were that the needs of the most vulnerable offenders, including the elderly and those with mental health issues, were not being adequately met.

NON-PROFIT ORGANIZATIONS AND OFFENDER REINTEGRATION

A significant role in the reintegration of offenders into the community is played by not-for-profit organizations, including the Elizabeth Fry Society, the John Howard Society, St. Leonard's Society, the Mennonite Central Committee, various faith-based programs, and a variety of other organizations across the country.

The John Howard Society of Ontario (JHSO), for example, operates the South Etobicoke Reintegration Centre, a "one-stop shop" providing assistance to men released from the Toronto Intermittent Centre and the Toronto South Detention Centre which, combined, comprise the largest jail in Canada. Services provided by the JHSO include housing, employment, mental health, and legal services. The JHSO also operates a peer support program staffed by persons who have themselves been involved in the correctional system and who have substance abuse issues.[73]

In Manitoba, the Elizabeth Fry Society provides a variety of program and services for women and transgender offenders, including a Provincial Reintegration Worker program that assists women in preparing for release and transition back to the community (http://www.efsmanitoba.org/Prisons.page). Across the country, the St. Leonard's Society operates community residential facilities as well as a variety of reintegration programs (http://www.slcs.ca).

Despite the positive feedback from both offenders and staff, programs operated by non-profit organizations are vulnerable to funding cuts. Lifeline, a high-profile program for persons serving a life sentence released into the community (and who will be on parole for the remainder of their life), was terminated in 2012 when the then federal Conservative government ended its funding.[74] This despite positive reports on the program from CSC. View the documentary film, "A Life After Life," listed in the Media Links section at the end of this chapter.

CSC also contracts private operators (including not-for-profit organizations such as the 7th Step Society) to provide beds in community residential facilities (CRFs). In each province/territory, there are parallel systems of residences that the government operates either directly or under contract with private operators. These CRFs are often called halfway houses. Most released offenders do not reside in halfway houses, but rather live on their own or with their families.

CSC also operates an intensive supervision program for offenders on conditional release who have a history of violence and confinement in correctional institutions, who exhibit little motivation to change, who may have psychological disorders, and who present a high risk of reoffending. Many of these offenders were denied parole and subsequently granted statutory release. The objectives of the program are to ensure the safety of the community through a regimen of intensive supervision, to help offenders access resources and services in the community, and to manage the risk presented by the offender.

There are also peer mentoring programs, wherein ex-offenders assist offenders re-entering the community, including the Gates Peer Health Mentoring Program for women offenders released from provincial institutions in British Columbia.[75]

To assist offenders in transitioning from the correctional institution to the community, a number of U.S. states have developed re-entry courts. These specialized courts operate much the same as the problem-solving courts discussed in Chapter 7. At present, there are no re-entry courts in Canada.[76]

MAKING IT OR GOING BACK: FACTORS IN THE SUCCESS OR FAILURE OF OFFENDERS ON RELEASE

It took me 34 years to get lucky, a lot of people don't get that opportunity, and they get really frustrated and they get really angry and down on themselves. They resort to alcohol and drugs, and that is sometimes why they are there in the first place, and then they just get out of control, they don't care about their life. They don't care if they get into trouble. When I look back in my life, going out on those mandatory supervision releases, I would be doing things like getting really drugged and getting high, and then hurting somebody. I think people, a lot of people, are doing that just because they don't have any positive things happening in their life, and they can't see a positive future. (ex-offender, personal communication with C.T. Griffiths)

Even the most institutionalized state-raised inmate does not leave a correctional institution with the intent of returning. And correctional systems have as a primary objective the reduction of recidivism among offenders released into the community. Statistics indicate that most federal offenders successfully complete conditional release and do not reoffend prior to warrant expiry.

Among the factors that increase the likelihood of success on parole are a supportive network of family and friends, stable housing and employment, participation in education and treatment programs, and a conscious decision to move out of a criminal lifestyle.[77,78,79,80,81] There is some evidence that the ethnicity, age, and gender of the parolee may influence the decisions of supervising parole officers.[82]

Research studies have also found that inmates who have a sustained pattern of visitation while incarcerated are less likely to recidivate.[83] This highlights the importance of offenders maintaining social networks with persons outside the institution. Unfortunately, many male and women offenders have no visitors during their period of incarceration.

Over the past decade, the rate of conviction for violent offences for offenders under supervision in the community has declined. This includes offenders on day parole, full parole, and statutory release.[84] Unfortunately, it is the handful of offenders who commit heinous crimes again who receive the attention of the media. It is they who often have a significant impact not only on victims but also on corrections policies and practices—who encourage tougher sentencing laws and tighten the decision-making of parole boards. The "silent majority" of offenders who successfully complete conditional release is invisible to the community. Contrary to the images portrayed in the media, the majority of sex offenders are not rearrested for new sex crimes.

When asked about the connotations attached to the word "parolee," community residents tend to respond in one of two ways: "got out too soon" or "dangerous to the public." These responses reflect the fact that most citizens get their information on crime, criminal justice, and corrections from the media.

SUSPENSION AND REVOCATION OF CONDITIONAL RELEASE

Failing to abide by any of the set conditions, including committing a new criminal offence or failing to adhere to the conditions of the parole certificate, may result in a **suspension of conditional release**.

When a parolee is suspended, two outcomes are possible: (1) the parole supervisor cancels the suspension and releases the person from custody, or (2) the case is referred back to the provincial parole board or the PBC for a hearing to determine whether there should be a **revocation of conditional release** (which usually means a transfer back to a correctional facility).

Parole officers have considerable discretion in the use of suspensions. The law states that officers *may* suspend a parolee for violating a parole condition or when new offences are alleged. The number of cases in which technical violations occur or new offences are alleged but a suspension is not imposed is unknown.

Suspension of conditional release

A process initiated by the supervising parole officer (or in some instances by the parole board) in cases whether the parolee has allegedly failed to abide by the conditions of release.

Revocation of conditional release

A decision by a releasing authority, such as a parole board, made in connection with an offender whose release has been suspended.

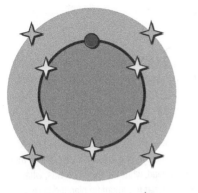

● Core Member ✦ Volunteers ✦ Professionals

▲ **FIGURE 12.9**

Circles of Support and Accountability

Source: *Circles of Support & Accountability: An Evaluation of the Pilot Project in South-Central Ontario.* Reproduced with the permission of Correctional Service Canada.

Circles of Support and Accountability (COSAs)

Community-based committees composed of criminal justice personnel and community members that provide mentoring for high-risk sex offenders whose sentences have expired.

▼ A Circle of Support and Accountability

Radius Images/Alamy Stock Photo

Offenders who have had their conditional release suspended are returned to the correctional facility to await a post-suspension hearing before the parole board. The board will review the report on the incident that triggered the suspension and the post-suspension report prepared by the supervising parole officer. The parole board has a number of options, including cancelling the suspension and reinstating the parole (with additional conditions if required), or end the parole which means that the offender remains in confinement.

Most offenders whose releases are revoked have committed *technical* violations; that is, they have violated the general and/or specific conditions attached to their conditional release. These include having a positive urinalysis test, being in an unauthorized area, or making contact with prohibited persons. About 10 percent of cases involve a revocation for a new offence. This does not mean that only 10 percent of offenders on conditional release commit new offences. It is not known how many offences are committed but not discovered by the police or corrections authorities, how many offences are discovered but classified as technical violations because such charges are more easily proved, or how many suspensions are cancelled for other reasons when in fact an offence has been committed. It would be useful as well to develop recidivism profiles and to identify the factors that are associated with the length of time the offender was on conditional release and the commission of a technical violation or a new offence (e.g., "low-risk or slow recidivists," "high-risk or rapid recidivists").[85]

CIRCLES OF SUPPORT AND ACCOUNTABILITY (COSAS): A RESTORATIVE, REINTEGRATIVE PROGRAM FOR HIGH-RISK SEX OFFENDERS

Circles of Support and Accountability (COSAs) were first developed by the Canadian Mennonite Community in the early 1990s and were based on the traditional Indigenous practice of healing circles. They provide support for sex offenders who are released from federal institutions at warrant expiry or whose period of supervision on conditional release has ended through warrant expiry. See Figure 12.9.

These offenders are the most likely targets of judicial recognizances and community notification (CN). Any offender who participates in the program does so on a voluntary basis; no legal mechanism can compel an offender to be subject to monitoring.

COSAs are centred on the principles of restorative justice, including the importance of positive relationships that can facilitate positive change in the offender while at the same time addressing the injury caused to the victim and the community.[86] The efforts of COSAs are designed to extend contact with the offender beyond the warrant expiry date (end of sentence and parole supervision) and to engage the community in efforts to reintegrate high-risk offenders.[87]

A circle of support is a team of five or six volunteers assigned to an offender to assist him or her as the offender takes up residence in their community. Volunteers can include teachers, social workers, police officers, businesspeople, and other community residents. They help with all facets of reintegration, including housing, employment, budgeting and financial management, spiritual development, and moral support. The offender may call only in times of stress or may have daily contact with the circle members. Circle members can also mediate between the offender and the community. Mediation took place in the case of Joe, whose arrival in the community was the subject of a community notification. See Corrections File 12.5.

JOE AND HIS CIRCLE OF SUPPORT

It began with a telephone call. "Can you help me?" the caller asked. "I'm just out of prison, and the police have already been warning everyone that I am in town. Where am I going to find a quiet place to live?" Joe, 54, had been released at warrant expiry from prison after serving a six-year sentence for sexual assault against a child. It was his eighth conviction.

Joe wanted to come to our city for several reasons. He knew us, he had met public resistance in another town when he attempted to settle there before his parole was [revoked], and he suspected that he could get help in relapse prevention. We agreed to help him find accommodation, help him find a job, and try to build a Circle of friendship and support in his new city. We thought of people that we knew who could help him in each of these areas and who would be willing to work with us. We also agreed to make contact with the police.

The detectives, when we met with them, candidly said, "We don't want him here." Based on institutional reports, the police felt that Joe was likely to reoffend. There had been a lot of negative publicity recently about released prisoners reoffending, and they didn't want any of that kind of publicity for their department.

When Joe came to stay with us for the weekend while beginning the apartment search, the police quickly made his picture available to the media and warned the community of his presence among us.

The media descended upon us because we had been identified as providing support for Joe. Pickets of irate and concerned parents arrived in front of our home. After a number of angry and threatening phone calls, we finally bought a telephone answering machine.

The police mounted a plan of surveillance. They felt sure he would reoffend within a short period. They were concerned about the safety of the children in the neighbourhood, but they also wanted to ensure Joe's safety.

One of the neighbours had called the police and had a lengthy discussion with the detective. She later called to talk with me. Ann had small children and was very concerned for their safety and that of the many other children living in the area. After a discussion with her, and later with Joe, we agreed that he would meet with her to discuss her concerns. Lengthy negotiations ensued, finally resulting in a meeting proposed in a neutral site, and several other neighbours were invited to participate. The police detectives would also be present. They would be there not only as a resource, but also as people who could add to the participants' feelings of security.

Joe, accompanied by two of his friends, was the first to arrive at the meeting and take a seat on the far side of the room. Soon the neighbours began to arrive. Then the detectives entered. The ground rules of the meeting were outlined. We would go around the circle to allow everyone an opportunity to share their first name and a particular concern they brought with them. We would have a statement from the neighbourhood group, followed by an opportunity for Joe to share, and from there we would move to addressing the issues presented. Only one person at a time would speak, and they would follow our direction and instructions for the orderly addressing of the issues.

Before the end of the meeting, we would decide together what of this meeting would be appropriate to share with other people, outside of this meeting.

As we began to go around the circle, the first person began by saying how much she appreciated the willingness of Joe and his friends to attend such a meeting. Ann outlined the questions she had heard the others discussing with her. There was a long list of questions: they wanted to know what had happened, what the sentence was, what treatment he had obtained, and what treatment he planned to receive now that he was released. "From your experience, what is the best way to avoid the behaviour you were charged with?" "How do you plan to deal with the negative reactions and anger of some individuals in the community?"

Joe responded, outlining in general terms his offences. Appreciation was expressed for the constructive method the residents had chosen to address their concerns, which he acknowledged were understandable. He indicated that he had received some treatment while in the institution and was planning to arrange suitable community-based therapy and had indeed made arrangements for that already. He had also set up an accountability system through his Circle of Support, by which he had daily contact with us, and we were able to make inquiry as to his faithfulness to his commitments in specific relevant areas.

We talked, and the earlier tension in the room eased as we got on with the task of problem-solving around the various issues at hand. Though all the questions were not answered, by the end of the 2½-hour meeting, there was a feeling of accomplishment and a readiness to move on.

Out of that meeting and others we had, some bridges were built. Neighbourhood residents, some of whom were vocally angry, began to see Joe as a person and recognized the difficulties with which he coped.

Throughout this time, Joe's Circle of Support met regularly with him. At least one of the Circle Members contacted him every day. After a year, we still talk to him daily. We took him to do his laundry, to shop for groceries and furnishings for his apartment.

The police have been partners with us in Joe's Circle of Support. Without the patient, humorous, understanding commitment of the detectives with whom we dealt most frequently, our efforts might not have reached this point. They came to our Circle meetings. They checked in with us frequently and we trusted their openness with us. Similarly, the police served as a buffer with the community, correcting rumours and diffusing problems.

Joe's life has settled into a comfortable pattern. He maintains a clean, comfortable apartment and has developed some close relationships. He is finding ways to spend his time and is slowly developing a small network of friends, although trust takes a long time.

QUESTION

1. If you had been asked to become a member of Joe's CoSA, would you have agreed? Why or why not?

Source: Courtesy of the Mennonite Central Committee of Ontario.

In Ontario, the Mennonite Central Committee operates the Community Reintegration Project (CRP), which provides the COSA program offering support for sex offenders who are released from federal institutions at warrant expiry.

THE EFFECTIVENESS OF COMMUNITY SUPERVISION STRATEGIES

The importance of conditional release for the community and the offender requires effective supervision and control strategies. It was previously noted that recidivism rates are the primary measure of effectiveness in corrections and this is no less true for assessing conditional release strategies.

Research File 12.1 sets out what is known about the effectiveness of selected community supervision strategies. The file indicates that there are successful strategies and also that some of the more highly publicized strategies, such as community notification, are generally not effective in reducing reoffending.

RESEARCH FILE 12.1

THE EFFECTIVENESS OF SELECTED SUPERVISION/CONTROL/REINTEGRATION STRATEGIES

Do Temporary Absences (TAs) Work? Yes. For provincial/territorial offenders, the rates of successful completion of escorted and unescorted TAs have consistently been in the 95 percent+ range, while 99 percent of federal offences successfully completed their TA.[a] A study ($N = 27,098$) of federal offenders found that TAs were an effective strategy for reducing reoffending and for gradually reintegrating offenders back into the community. TAs were particularly beneficial for higher-risk offenders who had served longer sentences.[b]

Is Day Parole an Effective Conditional Release Option? Yes. Day parole is an important part of the graduated release of offenders from confinement. It provides inmates with access to community services, employment, and educational opportunities. The overall successful completion rates for federal day parole are around 90 percent, although there are differences between groups of offenders.[c]

Is Parole an Effective Conditional Release Option? In the short term, yes. Long term, unknown. Although most parolees successfully complete their sentence, it is unknown whether the needs of offenders have been addressed and whether their quality of life (e.g. addiction issues, housing, family stability, employment) have been addressed. Recall that one of the two criteria for granting release is that the offender will not constitute an undue risk to the community prior to the expiration of their sentence. This means the parole board is not responsible for what happens beyond that point in time. (Parole boards are not required to weigh the short- and long-term impact of their decisions.)[d] Success rates are generally higher for low-risk offenders without lengthy criminal histories and those who have not committed a sexual offence or another crime of violence.[e] Ex-offenders may remain marginal and vulnerable.

Little is known about the challenges faced by Indigenous and Black offenders, offenders from other racialized groups, and LGBTQ offenders on parole and their efforts to reintegrate back into the community. The level of assistance provided by parole officers may be hindered by high caseloads and an emphasis on control and surveillance.

Is Statutory Release (SR) a Useful Strategy? Yes. Although the PBC is generally not involved in this decision, SR does provide for supervision of the highest-risk offenders. Without SR, these offenders would serve their entire sentence in custody and be released without any supervision (except if they are subject to a long-term supervision order). The successful completion rates of offenders on SR is around 60 percent.[f]

Do EM and GPS tracking reduce reoffending? There is no conclusive evidence that the use of EM reduces reoffending, and the adoption of GPS tracking for parolees in Canada is too recent to have produced any conclusive findings. Evidence of the effectiveness of GPS in reducing reoffending in the U.S. is mixed: While some studies have found no impact on reoffending, a California study ($N = 516$) found that sex offenders on parole monitored by GPS had their parole revoked less often and committed fewer crimes than a matched group of offenders who were not monitored by GPS.[g,h,i]

The use of these technologies may increase the workload and be very time-consuming for parole officers. There are also concerns that the use of this technology may create a false sense of security among the public.[j]

Do Community-Based Programs for Offenders Work? Yes, in certain conditions. Research studies indicate that community-based programs for parolees are most effective when premised on the principles of risk, need, and responsivity (RNR).[k] A study of high-risk, high-needs federal

(continued)

offenders with psychiatric conditions in CCCs found that treatment interventions including counselling had a significant impact on reducing the rates of reoffending.[l]

A challenge is access to programs and services, particularly for provincial/territorial offenders. Audits of community corrections in Ontario, for example, found that many offices did not offer core programs and only a relatively small percentage of designated offenders attended rehabilitation programs.[m,n] Problems were particularly acute in northern regions of the provide.

Does Community Notification (CN) Work? Although CN appears to have strong support from the public, there have been few studies (none of them Canadian) about the impact of CN on reoffending among high-risk offenders. Nor have there been any about whether CN improved feelings of personal safety in the community. Studies in the U.S. have found no differences in the recidivism rates (commission of new offences and/or violations of release conditions) of male sex offenders.[o] Community notification can lead to vigilantism and hinder offenders' efforts to reintegrate.[p]

Do Sex Offender Registries Work? Not likely. There are no Canadian studies; however, research in other jurisdictions has not demonstrated that sex offender registries reduce reoffending.[q,r]

Do COSAs Work? Yes. Canadian studies have found that offenders who participated in COSAs had significantly lower rates of sexual recidivism, recidivism for violent crimes, and general reoffending.[s,t] Offenders and community members who participated in COSAs had a positive view of the program and COSAs provided a network of support for high-risk offenders in the community. Similar outcomes have been reported from studies of COSAs in the U.S.[u]

[a] Public Safety Canada Portfolio Corrections Statistics Committee. 2017. *Corrections and Conditional Release Statistical Overview: 2016 Annual Report.* Ottawa: Public Works and Government Services Canada, p. 101. https://www.publicsafety.gc.ca/cnt/rsrcs/pblctns/ccrso-2016/ccrso-2016-en.pdf.

[b] L.M. Helmus and M. Ternes. 2016. "Temporary Absences from Prison in Canada Reduce Unemployment and Reoffending: Evidence of Dosage Effects from An Exploratory Study," *Psychology, Public Policy, and Law, 23*(1), 23–38.

[c] Public Safety Canada Portfolio Corrections Statistics Committee, *Corrections and Conditional Release Statistical Overview: 2016 Annual Report*, p. 93.

[d] A.N. Doob, C.M. Webster, and A. Manson. 2014. "Zombie Parole: The Withering of Conditional Release in Canada," *Criminal Law Quarterly, 61*(3), 301–328.

[e] B.M. Huebner and M.T. Berg. 2011. "Examining the Sources of Variation in Risks for Recidivism," *Justice Quarterly, 28*(1), 146–173.

[f] Public Safety Canada Portfolio Corrections Statistics Committee, *Corrections and Conditional Release Statistical Overview: 2016 Annual Report*, p. 97.

[g] P. Bulman. 2013, February. "Sex Offenders Monitored by GPS Found to Commit Fewer Crimes," *NIJ Journal, 271.* 22–25. http://www.nij.gov/journals/271/gps-monitoring.htm.

[h] California Sex Offender Management Board. 2010. *Recommendations Report.* Sacramento: Author, p. 48. http://www.casomb.org/docs/CASOMB%20Report%20Jan%202010_Final%20Report.pdf.

[i] M.L. Meloy. 2009. "You Can Run but You Cannot Hide: GPS and Electronic Surveillance of Offenders," in *Sex Offender Laws: Failed Policies, New Directions*, edited by R. Wright,
165–179. New York: Spring Publishing Company.

[j] K.M. Budd and C. Mancini. 2015. "Public Perceptions of GPS Monitoring for Convicted Sexual Offenders: Opinions on Effectiveness of Electronic Monitoring to Reduce Sexual Recidivism," *International Journal of Offender Therapy and Comparative Criminology, 61*(12), 1335–1353.

[k] C.T. Lowenkamp, J. Pealer, P. Smith, and E.J. Latessa. 2006. "Adhering to the Risk and Need Principles: Does It Matter for Supervision-Based Programs?" *Federal Probation 70*(3), 3–8.

[l] J. Abracen, A. Gallo, J. Looman, and A. Goodwill. 2016. "Individual Community-Based Treatment of Offenders with Mental Illness: Relationship to Recidivism," *Journal of Interpersonal Violence, 31*(10), 1842–1858.

[m] Office of the Auditor General of Ontario. 2014. *Annual Report, 2014.* Chapter 3. Adult Community Corrections and Parole Board. Toronto: Author. http://www.auditor.on.ca/en/content/annualreports/arreports/en14/301en14.pdf.

[n] Office of the Auditor General of Ontario. 2016. *Annual Report, 2016.* "Ontario Community Corrections and Parole Board. Follow-Up of VFM Section 3.01, 2014 Annual Report." Toronto: Author. http://www.auditor.on.ca/en/content/annualreports/arreports/en16/v2_101en16.pdf.

[o] R.G. Zevitz. 2006. "Sex Offender Community Notification: Its Role in Recidivism and Offender Reintegration," *Criminal Justice Studies, 19*(2), 193–208.

[p] Y.N. Brannon, J.S. Levenson, T. Fortney, and J.N. Baker. 2007. "Attitudes about Community Notification: A Comparison of Sexual Offenders and the Non-Offending Public," *Sexual Abuse: A Journal of Research and Treatment, 19*(4), 369–379.

[q] J. Vess, A. Day, M. Powell, and J. Graffam. 2014. "International Sex Offender Registration Laws: Research and Evaluation Issues Based on a Review of Current Scientific Literature," *Police Practice and Research, 15*(4), 322–335.

[r] J. Vess, A. Day, M. Powell, and J. Graffam. 2013. "International Sex Offender Registration Laws: Research and Evaluation Issues Based on a Review of Current Scientific Literature," *Police Practice & Research, 14*(3), 205–18.

[s] J.A. Chouinard and C. Riddick. 2014. *An Evaluation of the Circles of Support and Accountability Demonstration Project: Final Report.* Regina: Collaborative Centre for Justice and Safety, University of Regina. http://www.justiceandsafety.ca/rsu_docs/cosa-final-report-with-cover.pdf.

[t] R.J. Wilson, F. Cortoni, and A.J. McWhinnie. 2009. "Circles of Support and Accountability: A Canadian National Replication of Outcome Findings," *Sex Abuse, 21*(4), 412–430.

[u] G. Duwe. 2012. "Can Circles of Support and Accountability (COSA) Work in the United States? Preliminary Results from a Randomized Experiment in Minnesota," *Sexual Abuse: A Journal of Research and Treatment, 25*(2), 143–165.

DECISIONS AND OUTCOMES: ONE MAN'S JOURNEY THROUGH THE CRIMINAL JUSTICE SYSTEM

A synopsis of one offender's journey through the criminal justice system illustrates the issues that surround the decision-making of criminal justice professionals and accountability for these decisions in corrections. See Corrections File 12.6.

THE CLINTON SUZACK CASE

The Offender

In September 1992, 27-year-old Clinton Suzack pleaded guilty to 17 charges in Sault Ste. Marie, Ontario. His record to that point dated back to 1981 and included robbery with violence, unlawful confinement, and assault. There was an Alberta-wide arrest warrant (not valid outside of Alberta) on charges of breach of probation and assault. He had a serious, long-standing alcohol problem and an explosive temper, but was bright and articulate.

The 17 charges stemmed from 5 incidents, involving 9 victims, that had been committed between 1987 and 1992. In December 1987, Suzack assaulted a bar employee who refused to serve him. He failed to attend court and did not comply with the conditions of his bail. In June 1991, he punched a man three times in the face at a house party and viciously assaulted another partygoer with a broken bottle. The injuries to the second man's neck required surgery and a stay in the hospital's intensive care unit. Later in the evening, after the ambulance left, Suzack attacked a woman in the bathroom, punched her several times, and broke her nose. Two men who intervened were also assaulted, but they managed to subdue Suzack, who was subsequently arrested.

Another assault occurred in October 1991. Then in January 1992, Suzack assaulted and threatened a cocktail waitress and a women bar patron. In April, he assaulted a woman acquaintance following an argument.

The Crown Attorney

In September 1992, Suzack's lawyer negotiated an arrangement whereby the Crown would recommend a prison sentence of two years less a day in exchange for a guilty plea.

The Judge

The plea bargain was not binding on the sentencing judge. The judge said he was inclined to hand down a sentence of four-and-a-half years, but conceded to the joint submission of the Crown and the defence attorney. He called Suzack a "vicious, violent person" but saw the guilty plea as a mitigating factor and handed down a 729-day sentence. He also ordered three years' probation—the maximum available—to follow the prison term. In addition, the judge recommended that Suzack attend the Northern Treatment Centre in Sault Ste. Marie, although with the acknowledgment that the recommendation was not binding on the provincial correctional system.

The Correctional System

Suzack began his sentence in September 1992. He was classified as a high-risk inmate and sent to Millbrook, the most secure provincial institution. He repeatedly requested a transfer to a lower security facility, but none were willing to take him. His institutional misconduct record was one obstacle. He played tackle football when only touch football was permitted, refused an assigned job as a cleaner, was rude to a guard, and was found in his cell with two other inmates after being warned this was against the rules. For these infractions,

he lost seven days of recreational privileges and three days of earned remission and was reprimanded twice.

While at Millbrook, Suzack took computer and woodworking courses. He attended Alcoholics Anonymous (AA) meetings, participated in an anger management group, and engaged in educational upgrading. A report from the institution's psychologist noted the pattern of alcohol-related violence, but concluded that Suzack was "a bright, articulate individual with considerable potential [who] has demonstrated to staff that he has insights into many of his problem areas and motivation to make some changes." The release plan Suzack devised for presentation to the parole board included an intention to live with three friends in Sudbury, one of whom would employ him in his computer equipment company.

The Probation/Parole System

A Sudbury probation/parole officer, in a pre-parole investigation, confirmed the release plan by contacting the people with whom Suzack intended to live. The opposition of one of his crime victims to the release was noted in the report, as was the alcohol problem and outstanding warrant. As is typically the case, the officer had never met Suzack. He recommended that parole be denied.

The Parole Board

With a 729-day sentence, Suzack would be eligible for parole on June 2, 1993, having served one-third of the sentence (or eight months). If denied parole, he would be automatically released at the two-thirds point in his sentence (February 1994). Three members of the Ontario Board of Parole interviewed him on May 5, 1993. Before the hearing, they reviewed the pre-parole report, his prior record, and the institution's file, including the psychiatrist's report, training reports, and the reports on institutional misconducts. The Sault Ste. Marie police sent descriptions of most but not all of the offences for which Suzack had been convicted. The police "strongly opposed" parole, calling Suzack a "menace to society and a threat to the safety of the public."

The board denied Suzack parole, primarily because the proposed living arrangement would not meet his needs for community-based treatment for anger management and alcohol abuse. Also weighing against Suzack were his prior record, the severity of the current offences, his minimization of the role of alcohol in his offences, and his previous failures under community supervision (for example, his failure to comply with conditions of bail).

The Correctional System

One month later, Suzack lost 14 days' recreational privileges for fighting. He then reapplied for a transfer to the Sudbury jail, which offered a temporary absence program.

The psychiatrist updated the first report by noting that since being denied parole, Suzack had completed an alcohol awareness program, a woodworking course, and an anger management program (re-enrolling in the latter). Moreover, he was chairman of both the

(continued)

Native Sons Program and the institutional AA group, was doing schoolwork, and had volunteered in the prison chapel. While noting the seriousness of Suzack's offences, the report concluded: "He will gain little else by remaining at this facility.... He has exhausted the relevant treatment services here and the positive structured plan he currently has in place may not be there on discharge [in February]." Despite the positive report, Suzack was denied admittance on the grounds of institutional misconduct.

Salvation Army Rehabilitation Centre

To have any chance of parole, Suzack had to devise a better release plan. He applied to the Salvation Army program in nearby Hamilton. When interviewed by a staff member at the centre, Suzack indicated that all his offences stemmed from the one house party. The centre agreed to admit him into a 90-day program once he was released on parole.

The Probation/Parole System

Suzack's new release plan had to be confirmed. The Sudbury probation/parole officer conducted another investigation and again recommended that parole be denied. A Hamilton probation/parole officer confirmed the availability of the Salvation Army program. He had never met Suzack and had little information about him (because of a computer error), and therefore he was not able to offer an opinion on the suitability of parole.

The Parole Board

Suzack got a second hearing, at the discretion of the board, because of his new release plan and recent program participation. All the above-mentioned documents were available to the board, along with a social work report and a letter from a Hamilton-based Indigenous centre that offered Suzack the opportunity to explore Native culture. At the August 17 hearing, he was seen by three other board members (one of whom was Indigenous). He described the programs he had taken, expressed a willingness to learn about Native culture, and articulated some insights into his past behaviour.

Board members asked Suzack about his alcohol problem, past treatment, misconducts, and outstanding charges, but little about the offences. Again, he implied that all the charges stemmed from one incident. The board granted him parole, citing his participation in all available institutional programs and the offer of admittance into the 90-day treatment program operated by the Salvation Army in Hamilton, far away from his victims.

Probation/Parole System

On August 26, Suzack was released from Millbrook and took up residence at the Salvation Army Rehabilitation Centre in Hamilton. He was on the caseload of the Hamilton probation/parole officer who had written the pre-parole report. This officer met Suzack for the first time five days after his release on parole. By then, the officer had gathered background information about Suzack and had begun to question whether the Salvation Army program was an appropriate placement for him. It was not a secure facility and was designed for motivated parolees who did not require close supervision.

Salvation Army Rehabilitation Centre

The Salvation Army Rehabilitation Centre in Hamilton is one of many centres contracted by the Ontario government to provide services to released offenders. Upon Suzack's admission, the director assumed case management responsibility, instead of delegating the case to a staff member. The following day, the director and the parole officer discussed their mutual concerns. A program involving AA and attendance at the Indigenous centre was established.

On September 9, Suzack asked to be excused from an AA meeting. The request was denied. Suzack left the Salvation Army centre later that day. The director learned of, and reported, the parole violation on the following day. An arrest warrant was issued, and his previous victims were notified.

The Offender

Suzack eluded arrest until October 7, 1993, when he and an accomplice, Peter Pennett, fatally shot a Sudbury Regional Police Constable Joe MacDonald in the back of the head after an altercation during a routine traffic stop. Convicted of first-degree murder, Suzack was sentenced to life with no eligibility for parole for 25 years. At sentencing, the judge indicated that Suzack should serve his entire sentence in maximum security. Suzack was initially housed in a maximum-security facility in Ontario and was later moved to Joyceville, a medium-security correctional facility. He was transferred back to maximum security after being suspected in an escape plot. He was then moved back to Joyceville.

In the fall of 2001, after serving six years of his life sentence, Suzack was moved to William Head Institution, a medium-security correctional facility at the southern tip of Vancouver Island. This transfer was criticized by several police groups in Ontario, including the Ontario Association of Police Chiefs, as well as by municipal councils throughout the province. All called on the federal solicitor general to return Suzack to maximum security to serve his life sentence. As of late 2017, Suzack was still incarcerated.

The Victim

The estate of the police constable filed a civil suit against the various justice agencies that had been involved in making decisions about Suzack, including the provincial parole board and probation/parole service. The case was settled out of court for an undisclosed sum.

QUESTIONS

1. Identify the key decisions that were made in this case? Are there decisions that could have been made that would have prevented what happened?
2. If you were a member of a panel reviewing this case, would you recommend that any of the justice personnel and agencies involved in making decisions about Suzack be held civilly liable for their decisions? Explain.
3. If you believe that the decision-making process in the Suzack case was flawed, which decision-makers were most responsible?

SUMMARY

The discussion in this chapter has focused on the release of offenders from confinement and their re-entry into the community. The purpose and principles of conditional release are set out in the *Corrections and Conditional Release Act* but provide only a broad framework within which release decisions are made. There are a variety of types of release that are designed to reintegrate offenders back into the community. This presumes that offenders were integrated into the community prior to their incarceration, a questionable assumption for many offenders who are sent to correctional institutions. For inmate-applicants, the parole hearing process can be intimidating, and there are often socio-economic and cultural disparities between board members and inmate-applicants. There are a number of issues that surround parole board decision-making, which makes it, at best, an inexact science.

The reintegration process for offenders was explored, and it was noted that offenders often experience pains of re-entry that are associated with the challenges of adjusting to community life. The dual role of parole officers was noted, and the strategies used to control and manage high-risk offenders were examined. The effectiveness of selected supervision and control strategies was discussed. A case study was presented to illustrate the journey of one offender through the justice and corrections system, highlighting the decisions that were made and the consequences of these decisions.

KEY POINTS REVIEW

1. The purpose and principles of conditional release are set out in the *Corrections and Conditional Release Act*.

2. The specific conditional release options that are available to inmates depends on the length of the offender's sentence and whether they are under the supervision and control of provincial/territorial or federal systems of corrections.

3. There is often little pre-release planning for provincial/territorial offenders.

4. Statistics indicate that conditional release is being used less often than in previous years.

5. The role of crime victims in the conditional release is sporadic and is most often limited to providing written impact statements to the board.

6. In making release decisions, the parole board is interested in whether the offender can be managed at an acceptable level of risk in the community.

7. For inmate-applicants, appearing before a parole board can be stressful.

8. Issues surrounding parole board decision-making include these: Boards may be subject to public and political influence; there is an absence of clearly defined release criteria; and feedback on case decisions to parole board members is lacking.

9. Research suggests that some conditional release options are more successful than others in reducing the likelihood of reoffending.

10. Reintegration is best understood as a process rather than as an event.

11. Many inmates experience challenges in re-entering the community.

12. Women offenders experience unique challenges upon re-entry, including, for many women, attempting to re-establish contact and relationships with their children.

13. Parole officers play a dual role in providing assistance and monitoring offenders, although there is an increasing focus on control.

14. Mentally ill offenders and sex offenders on conditional release present unique challenges for parole supervisors and community-based service providers.

15. There are a number of factors that are related to the success of offenders on conditional release.

16. There is some question as to the effectiveness of supervision/control strategies used for offenders on conditional release.

KEY TERM QUESTIONS

1. Define the following types of **conditional release**: **temporary absence, day parole, full parole, remission/discharge**, and **statutory release**.

2. Describe the procedures and objectives of **detention during the period of statutory release** and then define **one-chance statutory release**.

3. What is the **warrant expiry date**?

4. Discuss the role of the **release plan** and the **community assessment** in conditional release.

5. Define **reintegration** and its objectives.

6. How do the **pains of re-entry** and **post-incarceration syndrome (PICS)** affect offenders returning to the community?

7. Describe **community notification** and discuss the issues surrounding its use.

8. Define **suspension of conditional release** and **revocation of conditional release** and explain how these affect the status of an offender on conditional release.

9. What are **Circles of Support and Accountability** and how do they work?

CRITICAL THINKING EXERCISE

Critical Thinking Exercise 12.1

"Justice Shouldn't Be Political"

The following editorial was published in the *Ottawa Citizen* on February 23, 2011, following the then federal Conservative government's announcement that new members had been appointed to the Parole Board of Canada:

> The recent appointment of eight new members to the National Parole Board of Canada by the Minister of Public Safety, Vic Toews, raises important questions about the appointment process to administrative boards and tribunals in Canada. Of the eight new appointees, five are former police officers.
>
> There is no reason to believe that all the appointees are not "highly qualified and committed people" as claimed by the minister. There is also no reason why former police officers are not deserving candidates to serve on this important federal board.
>
> What is troubling about the appointments is the apparent attempt to create a perception that the current federal government is going to be tough on prospective parolees by putting their fate in the hands of enforcement-minded individuals. . . . The role of appointed members of the tribunal is not to be tough or lenient but to be fair and objective.
>
> Federal and provincial boards and tribunals have long been a repository for politicized appointments. . . . These quasi-judicial tribunals play an extremely important role in deciding critical issues of life, liberty and public safety. Any perception by the public that the impartiality or competence of these rights-oriented boards and tribunals has been compromised by partisan political appointments will necessarily bring the administration of justice into disrepute.

Your Thoughts?

1. What is your response to this editorial?

2. What reforms could be undertaken to address the issues that are raised in the editorial?

Source: Excerpt from J. Morton and M.M. Persaud. 2011, February 23. "Justice Shouldn't Be Political," *Ottawa Citizen*, p. A13. http://jmortonmusings.blogspot.ca/2011/02/justice-shouldnt-be-political.html. Reprinted by permission of James C. Morton.

CLASS/GROUP DISCUSSION EXERCISE

Class/Group Discussion 12.1

Should the Practice of Community Notification Be Discontinued?

Proponents of community notification (CN) contend that the practice alerts the neighbourhood to a potential risk, thereby reducing the likelihood of another offence; that public safety overrides any expectation the offender has for privacy; and that it serves to protect victims. Opponents of CN counter that CN is not an innovative correctional practice, but rather reflective of penal populism; that there is no evidence that it is effective in reducing reoffending; that it increases public fear and paranoia; and that it makes it difficult for offenders to reintegrate into the community and, in so doing, raises the risk of reoffending.

▲ A lawn sign at a sex offender's residence in the U.S.

Your Thoughts?

1. Which arguments do you find most persuasive?

2. Would you want to be notified of the presence of a sex offender in your neighbourhood? Explain. If so, what would the knowledge cause you to do differently?

3. Does your province/territory have a community notification law? Check the statute books, because several do and more are planned. Check out the website of your local police. Many now have community notification pages.

4. In many states in the U.S., the law requires that signage be placed at the residence of convicted sex offenders. What arguments could be made in support of, and in opposition to, this practice? What is your view on this practice? Would you support this approach in Canada?

Sources: A. Bain. 2011. "Please Recycle: Continuities in Punishment," *International Journal of Law, Crime, and Justice, 39*(2), 121–35; Y.N. Brannon, J.S. Levenson, T. Fortney, and J.N. Baker. 2007. "Attitudes about Community Notification: A Comparison of Sexual Offenders and the Non-Offending Public," *Sexual Abuse: A Journal of Research and Treatment, 19*(4), 369–379; G. Duwe and W. Donnay. 2008. "Impact of Megan's Law on Sex Offender Recidivism: The Minnesota Experience," *Criminology, 46*(2), 411–446.

MEDIA LINKS

Parole Board of Canada

"Virtual Tour of a [Parole Board of Canada] Hearing Room," https://www.canada.ca/en/parole-board/services/parole/virtual-tour-of-a-hearing-room.html

"Elder-Assisted Hearings," https://www.canada.ca/en/parole-board/corporate/publications-and-forms/videos/elder-assisted-hearings.html

John Howard Society

"Luke on How JHS Helped Him to Get a Second Chance to Succeed," October 28, 2013, https://www.youtube.com/watch?v=-iW7SKCg8Qg

"John Howard Societies of Ontario—What You Need to Know," April 4, 2012, https://www.youtube.com/watch?v=xUt-4j5Z45Y

"John Howard Society of Ontario—Ottawa's ACElinks Program & Jeannie," December 17, 2014, https://www.youtube.com/watch?v=hqgaIFy4__M

"Sue, Former JHS Client, Speaks to the Importance of Public Education," October 29, 2013, https://www.youtube.com/watch?v=Ww9WQQWDofc

"A Man Changed: Tom's Home with Calgary John Howard Society," August 10, 2015, https://www.youtube.com/watch?v=KoEhCDbHtdc

Elizabeth Fry Society

"Hearts for Homes: Stories from the Elizabeth Fry Society," Shaw TV, November 14, 2016, https://www.youtube.com/watch?v=Qt4HwbNkzzk

"Elizabeth Fry Society—Client Stories," Elizabeth Fry Society of Ottawa, January 24, 2014, https://www.youtube.com/watch?v=QehalpHHF1M

"Elizabeth Fry Society Calgary," August 30, 2016, https://www.youtube.com/watch?v=-6HQmGHl_lQ

Native Counselling Services of Alberta

"Journey of a Warrior—The Stan Daniels Healing Centre," July 18, 2016, https://www.youtube.com/watch?v=xsqoIrKdnRk

"Journey of a Warrior (Ep. 2)—Readiness," July 8, 2015, https://www.youtube.com/watch?v=H7DoxxlkCnY

"Journey of a Warrior (Ep. 3)—In Search of Your Warrior," August 10, 2015, https://www.youtube.com/watch?v=jl6ieEJ2lpg

"Stan Daniels—Journey of a Warrior (Ep. 4)—Reintegration," December 4, 2015, https://www.youtube.com/watch?v=YfQ-k1rjClE

Salvation Army

"The Salvation Army Toronto," http://www.salvationarmyjustice.ca/about-us.html

Indigenous Women, Re-entry and Reintegration

"The BANG You Feel," Native Counselling Services of Alberta, April 8, 2015, https://www.youtube.com/watch?v=xRoc4AvWpL0

Offenders on Parole

"'A Homecomer's Confession—Eddie B. Ellis Jr.," February 18, 2011, https://www.youtube.com/watch?v=EmrQcMzwz6E

"The Released," *Frontline*, PBS, April 28, 2009, www.pbs.org/wgbh/pages/frontline/released

"A Life After Life," *The National*, CBC, August 30, 2012, https://www.youtube.com/watch?v=Br_rkmWdZz0

"Tracked: A Week Under GPS Supervision," News21, August 10, 2010, http://www.youtube.com/watch?v=QBAT07UEWug

REFERENCES

1. M. Halsey. 2007. "Assembling Recidivism: The Promise and Contingencies of Post-Release Life," *Journal of Criminal Law and Criminology*, 97(4), 1209–1260 at p. 1256. http://scholarlycommons.law.northwestern.edu/cgi/viewcontent.cgi?article=7276&context=jclc.

2. C. Marshall. 2008. *HIV/AIDS and Hepatitis in Correctional Facilities: Reducing the Risks*. Halifax: The Nova Scotia Advisory Commission on AIDS, p. 26. http://www.gov.ns.ca/AIDS/documents/HIV-AIDS-Hepatitis-C-Correctional%20Facilities.pdf.

3. Schizophrenic Society of Ontario. 2012. *Provincial Correctional Response to Individuals with Mental Illness in Ontario: A Review of the Literature*. Toronto: Author, p. 4. http://www.schizophrenia.on.ca/getmedia/c2af5aea-1bf8-40fd-86ad-1fd9b928f40a/Provincial_.

4. Public Safety Canada Portfolio Corrections Statistics Committee. 2016. *Corrections and Conditional Release Statistical Overview: 2015 Annual Report*. Ottawa: Public Works and Government Services Canada, pp. 77, 81. https://www.publicsafety.gc.ca/cnt/rsrcs/pblctns/ccrso-2015/ccrso-2015-en.pdf.

5. Parole Board of Canada. 2016. *Performance Monitoring Report 2014-2015*. Ottawa: Author. https://www.canada.ca/content/dam/canada/parole-board/migration/005/009/093/005009-3000-2015-en.pdf

6. M.K. Olotu and M.G. Beaupre. 2010. *Evaluation Report. National Victim Services Program*. Ottawa: Correctional Service of Canada. http://csc-scc.gc.ca/text/pa/nvsp/index-eng.shtml.

7. Public Safety Canada Portfolio Corrections Statistics Committee. 2017. *Corrections and Conditional Release Statistical Overview: 2016 Annual Report*. Ottawa: Public Works and Government Services Canada, p. 87. https://www.publicsafety.gc.ca/cnt/rsrcs/pblctns/ccrso-2016/ccrso-2016-en.pdf

8. S. Turnbull. 2016. *Parole in Canada: Gender and Diversity in the Federal System*. Vancouver: UBC Press, pp. 98–99.

9. P.J. Murphy, L. Johnsen, and J. Murphy. 2002. *Paroled for Life: Interviews with Parolees Serving Life Sentences*. Vancouver: New Star, p. 93.

10. Turnbull, *Parole in Canada: Gender and Diversity in the Federal System*, p. 200.

11. Ibid., p. 73.

12. Ibid., pp. 182–183.

13. Ibid., p. 54.

14. Ibid., p. 126.

15. Ibid., p. 185.

16. Ibid., p. 200.

17. I. Zinger. 2012. "Conditional Release and Human Rights in Canada: A Commentary," *Canadian Journal of Criminology and Criminal Justice*, 54(1), 117–135 at p. 121.

18. M.A. Paparozzi and R. Guy. 2009. "The Giant That Never Woke: Parole Authorities as the Lynchpin to Evidence-Based Practices and Prisoner Reentry," *Journal of Contemporary Justice*, 25(4), 397–411.

19. A. Thurber. 1998. "Understanding Offender Reintegration," *Forum on Corrections Research*, 10(1), 14–18 at p. 14.

20. C.T. Griffiths, Y. Dandurand, and D. Murdoch. 2007. *The Social Reintegration of Offenders and Crime Prevention*. Ottawa: National Crime Prevention Centre, Public Safety Canada. http://publications.gc.ca/site/eng/318886/publication.html.

21. S. Maruna. 2011. "Reentry as a Rite of Passage," *Punishment & Society*, 13(1), 3–28.

22. K. Bumby, M. Carter, S. Gibel, L. Gilligan, and R. Stroker. 2007. *Increasing Public Safety Through Successful Offender Reentry: Evidence-Based and Emerging Practices in Corrections*. Washington, DC: Center for Effective Public Policy and Bureau of Justice Assistance. http://www.ct.gov/opm/lib/opm/cjppd/cjresearch/forecastresearchworkgroup/resources/svori_cepp.pdf.

23. P.B. Burke. 2008. *TPC Reentry Handbook: Implementing the NIC Transition for Prison to the Community Model*. Washington, DC: National Institute of Corrections, U.S. Department of Justice. https://s3.amazonaws.com/static.nicic.gov/Library/022669.pdf.

24. L. Gideon. 2009. "What Shall I Do Now? Released Offenders' Expectations for Supervision Upon Release," *International Journal of Offender Therapy and Comparative Criminology*, 53(1), 43–56.

25. British Columbia Ministry of Justice. 2014. *Integrated Offender Management Participant Exit Survey Report. Survey Results*. Victoria: Author. http://www2.gov.bc.ca/assets/gov/law-crime-and-justice/criminal-justice/corrections/research-evaluation/iom-client-exit-survey-report.pdf.

26. Excerpted from M. Munn and C. Bruckett. 2013. *On the Outside: From Lengthy Imprisonment to Lasting Freedom*. Vancouver: UBC Press, p. 89. Reprinted by permission.

27. John Howard Society of Ontario, W. O'Grady, and R. Lafleur. 2016. *Reintegration in Ontario: Practices, Priorities, and Effective Models*. Toronto: Author, p. 38. http://johnhoward.on.ca/wp-content/uploads/2016/11/Reintegration-in-Ontario-Final.pdf.

28. C.T. Griffiths and D. Murdoch. 2018. *Canadian Corrections* (5th ed.). Toronto: Nelson.

29. Excerpted from M. Munn and C. Bruckett. 2013. *On the Outside: From Lengthy Imprisonment to Lasting Freedom*. Vancouver: UBC Press, p. 70. Reprinted by permission.

30. Excerpted from M. Munn and C. Bruckett. 2013. *On the Outside: From Lengthy Imprisonment to Lasting Freedom*. Vancouver: UBC Press, p. 72. Reprinted by permission.

31. M.R. Maidment. 2006. *Doing Time on the Outside: Deconstructing the Benevolent Community*. Toronto: University of Toronto Press, p. 103.

32. M.S. Daigle and H. Naud. 2012. "Risk of Dying by Suicide Inside or Outside Prison: The Shortened Lives of Male Offenders," *Canadian Journal of Criminology and Criminal Justice*, 54(4), 511–528.

33. M. Olotu, D. Luong, C. MacDonald, M. McKay, S. Heath, N. Allegri, and E. Loree. 2011. *Report of the Evaluation of CSC's Community Corrections*. Chapter 1: Correctional Interventions. Ottawa: Correctional Service Canada, p. 47. http://www.csc-scc.gc.ca/publications/092/005007-2008-eng.pdf.

34. J.B. Helfgott and E. Gunnison. 2008. "The Influence of Social Distance on Community Corrections Officer Perceptions of Offender Reentry Needs," *Federal Probation*, 72(1), 2–12.

35. S. Novac, J. Herner, E. Paradis, and A. Kellen. 2006. *Justice and Injustice: Homelessness, Crime, Victimization, and the Criminal Justice System* [Research paper #207]. Toronto: Centre for Urban and Community Studies, University of Toronto. http://www.urbancentre.utoronto.ca/pdfs/researchprojects/Novacet-al-207-JusticeHomeless2006.pdf.

36. R. Zorzi, S. Scott, D. Doherty, A. Engman, C. Lauzon, M. McGuire, and J. Ward. 2006. *Housing Options Upon Discharge from Correctional Facilities*. Ottawa: Canada Mortgage and Housing Corporation. http://www.cmhc-schl.gc.ca/odpub/pdf/65340.pdf?fr=1343101698796.

37. H. Echenberg and J. Jensen. 2009. *Risk Factors for Homelessness*. Ottawa: Social Affairs Division, Parliamentary Information and Research Service, p. 2. http://www.parl.gc.ca/Content/LOP/ResearchPublications/prb0851-e.pdf.

38. Marshall, *HIV/AIDS and Hepatitis in Correctional Facilities*, p. 27.

39. Ibid., p. 30.

40. Griffiths, Dandurand, and Murdoch, *The Social Reintegration of Offenders and Crime Prevention*.

41. Social Planning & Research Council of Hamilton. 2010. *Hamilton Community Correctional Services Needs Assessment*. Hamilton: Author, p. 15. http://www.sprc.hamilton.on.ca/wp-content/uploads/2010/02/Hamilton-Community-Correctional-Services-Needs-Assessment-February-2010.pdf.

42. Ibid., p. 16.

43. Ibid.

44. Excerpted from M. Munn and C. Bruckett. 2013. *On the Outside: From Lengthy Imprisonment to Lasting Freedom*. Vancouver: UBC Press, p. 73. Reprinted by permission.

45. Murphy, Johnsen, and Murphy, *Paroled for Life: Interviews with Parolees Serving Life Sentences*, pp. 166–167.

46. Marshall, *HIV/AIDS and Hepatitis in Correctional Facilities*, p. 26

47. John Howard Society of Ontario, O'Grady, and Lafleur, *Reintegration in Ontario: Practices, Priorities, and Effective Models*.

48. Ibid.

49. Excerpted from M. Munn and C. Bruckett. 2013. *On the Outside: From Lengthy Imprisonment to Lasting Freedom*. Vancouver: UBC Press, p. 110. Reprinted by permission.

50. Excerpted from M. Munn and C. Bruckett. 2013. *On the Outside: From Lengthy Imprisonment to Lasting Freedom*. Vancouver: UBC Press, p. 158. Reprinted by permission.

51. T.T. Gorski. n.d. "Post Incarceration Syndrome and Relapse." http://www.tgorski.com/criminal_justice/cjs_pics_&_relapse.htm.

52. L. Stone. 2012, May 25. "After an Inmate's Release, the Struggle Begins," *Calgary Herald*.

53. T.P. LeBel. 2011. "'If One Doesn't Get You Another One Will': Formerly Incarcerated Persons' Perceptions of Discrimination," *The Prison Journal*, 92(1), 63–87.

54. C. Glube (Chair). 2006. *Moving Forward with Women's Corrections*. Ottawa: Correctional Service of Canada. http://www.csc-scc.gc.ca/text/prgrm/fsw/wos29/wos29-eng.shtml.

55. R. Sampson (Chair). 2007. *Report of the Correctional Service of Canada Review Panel*. Ottawa: Minister of Public Works and Government Services Canada. http://www.publicsafety.gc.ca/csc-scc/cscrprprt-eng.pdf.

56. F.I. Matheson, S. Doherty, and B. A. Grant. 2009. *Women Offender Substance Abuse Programming and Community Reintegration*. Ottawa: Correctional Service of Canada. http://www.csc-scc.gc.ca/text/rsrch/reports/r202/r202-eng.shtml.

57. R. Gobiel. 2008. *Staying Out: Women's Perceptions of Challenges and Protective Factors in Community Reintegration*. Ottawa: Correctional Service of Canada. http://www.csc-scc.gc.ca/text/rsrch/reports/r201/r201-eng.shtml.

58. S. Wine. 1992. *A Motherhood Issue: The Impact of Criminal Justice System Involvement on Women and Their Children*. Ottawa: Solicitor General, p. 111.

59. Auditor General of Canada. 2016. *Fall Reports of the Auditor General of Canada. Report 3 – Preparing Indigenous Offenders for Release – Correctional Service Canada.* Ottawa: Author. http://www.oag-bvg.gc.ca/internet/English/parl_oag_201611_03_e_41832.html#.

60. Parole Board of Canada, *Performance Monitoring Report 2014-2015*, p. 48.

61. Turnbull, *Parole in Canada: Gender and Diversity in the Federal System*, p. 114.

62. M. Axford and R. Ruddell. 2010. "Police–Parole Partnerships in Canada: A Review of a Promising Programme," *International Journal of Police Science and Management*, 12(2), 274–286.

63. Griffiths, Dandurand, and Murdoch, *The Social Reintegration of Offenders and Crime Prevention.*

64. S. Steen, T. Opsal, P. Lovegrove, and S. McKinzey. 2012. "Putting Parolees Back in Prison: Discretion in the Parole Revocation Process," *Criminal Justice Review*, 38(1), 70–93.

65. Le Protecteur du Citoyen. 2011. *Report by the Québec Ombudsman: Toward Services That Are Better Adjusted to Detainees with Mental Disorders.* Québec City: Author, p. 6. https://protecteurducitoyen.qc.ca/sites/default/files/pdf/rapports_speciaux/10-05-11_Rapport_sante_mentale_FINAL_EN.pdf.

66. R.G. Zevitz. 2006. "Sex Offender Community Notification: Its Role in Recidivism and Offender Reintegration," *Criminal Justice Studies*, 19(2), 193–208.

67. CBC News. 2005, October 19. "'You Have No Rights. Get Out' B.C. Town Tells Sex Offender." http://www.cbc.ca/news/canada/you-have-no-rights-get-out-b-c-town-tells-sex-offender-1.522283.

68. Correctional Service Canada. 2013. "Commissioner's Directive: Community Supervision." Ottawa: Government of Canada. http://www.csc-scc.gc.ca/policy-and-legislation/715-1-cd-eng.shtml.

69. M. Lynch. 1998. "Waste Managers? The New Penology, Crime Fighting, and Parole Agent Identity," *Law and Society Review*, 32(4), 839–870.

70. Munn and Bruckett, *On the Outside: From Lengthy Imprisonment to Lasting Freedom*, p. 81.

71. Office of the Correctional Investigator. 2014. *Overcoming Barriers to Reintegration: An Investigation of Federal Community Correctional Centres.* Ottawa: Author. http://www.oci-bec.gc.ca/cnt/rpt/oth-aut/oth-aut20141008-eng.aspx.

72. Ibid.

73. John Howard Society of Ontario, O'Grady, and LeFluer, *Reintegration in Ontario: Practices, Priorities, and Effective Models*, p. 9.

74. CBC News. 2012, April 16. "Prison Rehab Program Axed Due to Budget Cuts." http://www.cbc.ca/news/canada/prison-rehab-program-axed-due-to-budget-cuts-1.1179484.

75. V. Hrvatin. 2017, March 13. "For B.C.'s Female Prisoners, This Peer Mentor Program is a Leg Up on the Outside," *Globe and Mail.* https://www.theglobeandmail.com/news/british-columbia/for-bcs-female-prisoners-this-peer-mentor-program-is-a-leg-up-on-the-outside/article34294343.

76. E. McGrath, E. 2012. "Reentry Courts: Providing a Second Chance for Incarcerated Mothers and Their Children," *Family Court Review*, 50(1), 113–127.

77. S.J. Bahr, L. Harris, J.K. Fisher, and A.H. Armstrong. 2010. "Successful Reentry: What Differentiates Successful and Unsuccessful Parolees?" *International Journal of Offender Therapy and Comparative Criminology*, 54(5), 667–692.

78. LeBel, "'If One Doesn't Get You Another One Will': Formerly Incarcerated Persons' Perceptions of Discrimination."

79. John Howard Society of Ontario, O'Grady, and Lafleur, *Reintegration in Ontario: Practices, Priorities, and Effective Models.*

80. M. Makarios, B. Steiner, and L.T. Travis. 2010. "Examining the Predictors of Recidivism Among Men and Women Released from Prison in Ohio," *Criminal Justice and Behavior*, 37(12), 1377–1391.

81. C.A. Visher, S.A. Debus-Sherrill, and J. Yahner. 2011. "Employment After Prison: A Longitudinal Study of Former Prisoners," *Justice Quarterly*, 28(5), 698–718.

82. S. Steen, T. Opsal, P. Lovegrove, and S. McKinzey. 2012. "Putting Parolees Back in Prison: Discretion in the Parole Revocation Process," *Criminal Justice Review*, 38(1), 70–93.

83. J.C. Cochran. 2014. "Breaches in the Wall: Imprisonment, Social Support, and Recidivism," *Journal of Research in Crime and Delinquency*, 51(2), 220–229.

84. Public Safety Canada Portfolio Corrections Statistics Committee, *Corrections and Conditional Release Statistical Overview: 2016 Annual Report*, p. 99.

85. R. Fitzgerald, A. Cherney, and L. Heybroek. 2016. "Recidivism among Prisoners: Who Comes Back?" *Trends & Issues in Crime and Criminal Justice*, 530. Canberra: Australian Institute of Criminology. http://www.aic.gov.au/media_library/publications/tandi_pdf/tandi530.pdf.

86. C. Wilson. 2011. "The Realities of Practice," in *A Community-Based Approach to the Reduction of Sexual Reoffending*, edited by S. Hanvey, T. Philpot, and C. Wilson, 58–71. London: Jessica Kingsley.

87. S. Hanvey, T. Philpot, and C. Wilson. 2011. *A Community-Based Approach to the Reduction of Sexual Reoffending.* London: Jessica Kingsley.

© Laurie Justus Pace, Graphics One Design, 2014

YOUTH JUSTICE

Chapter 13: The Youth Justice System

There is one chapter in this part and it focuses on the youth justice system. There are a number of reasons for including these materials in a criminal justice text. Among these are the fact that some youth who become involved in the youth justice system continue into the adult criminal justice system. This requires a consideration of the response to youth in conflict through legislation, policies, and programs. The discussion will reveal that, as with adult offenders, there has historically been different philosophies as to how best to respond to youth who come into conflict with the law. It will also reveal that, similar to the adult system, Indigenous youth and youth from racialized groups are overrepresented in the youth justice system. There are a variety of programs for youth in custody and under supervision in the community. A notable feature of the current *Youth Criminal Justice Act* is the emphasis on seeking alternatives to custody whenever possible and the involvement of community members in responding to youth in crisis. The effectiveness of these programs will often determine the life journey of youth, many of whom are vulnerable and at risk.

© Laurie Justus Pace, Graphics One Design, 2014

CHAPTER 13
THE YOUTH JUSTICE SYSTEM

LEARNING OBJECTIVES

After reading this chapter, you should be able to

- Describe and compare the legislation that has provided the framework for the response to young offenders from 1908 to the present.
- Discuss the types of programs that have been developed for at-risk youth and justice-system-involved youth.
- Describe the differences between the adult and youth criminal justice systems.
- Identify and discuss the four levels of the youth justice system.
- Describe and provide an example of a specialized problem-solving youth court.
- Discuss the role of the community in the youth justice system.
- Describe the non-custodial and custodial sentencing options for young offenders.
- Discuss the experience of young men and women in custody and following release.
- Describe the various types of restorative justice programs for young offenders.

Shane's Story

Shane, 16, is an Indigenous young man who lives with his mother in social housing. The family is on social assistance. When Shane was eight years old and his sister was two years old, his family moved from their First Nations community to a nearby city in southwestern Ontario. His father left the family when he was 10 and his mother has suffered from depression since then. His younger sister was taken into care at the age of four under a voluntary agreement with Child Welfare Services. Unfortunately, his sister died in care six months later due to an unfortunate car accident.

Shane has had a history of self-harming behaviour since his father left the family and the loss of his sister. He was struggling in school and claimed to be affiliated with an Indigenous urban gang as a fringe member. One day Shane was hanging out with a friend who was his "big brother" in the gang. The two of them went into a large electronic retail store. A staff of the store witnessed Shane's friend have a conversation with him in front of the cellphone accessories aisle. The friend then left the store by himself. Shortly after Shane's friend left shortly, Shane started putting some cellphone accessories in his backpack and headed out of the store. Shane was stopped at the exit by a security guard who searched Shane's backpack and found unpaid cellphone accessories in the amount of $500.

Both Shane's mother and the police were called. Shane was taken to the police station where he had a meeting with his mother and an Indigenous police officer. During the intake interview, Shane shared that he still struggles with issues of loss over his younger sibling, the absence of his father, and displacement from this home community and culture.

After talking to Shane and his mother and understanding more about his family background and situation, the police officer decided to not press charges. Instead, the officer offered Shane an opportunity to participate in an extrajudicial measures (EJM) diversion program that is designed for Indigenous youth.

The program Shane was referred to has been running for 15 years and has supported hundreds of youth to regain community and cultural connections. Youth involved in the program build relationships with Elders and peer mentors. It offers healing supports through a sweat lodge and counselling to work through unprocessed grief and loss. The program offers referral services for Shane's mother to support her on her healing journey. The program takes a restorative approach to youth justice and hosts healing and sharing circles that can include family and community members. Shane will have support to finish school as well as opportunities to learn skills and enroll in a program that provides on-the-job training. Shane agreed to voluntarily participate in the EJM program and contacted the community agency that runs the program to get started.

Source: S.M. Kwok, R. Houwer, H. HeavyShield, R. Weatherstone, and D. Tam. 2017. *Supporting Positive Outcomes for Youth Involved with the Law*. Toronto: Youth Research and Evaluation eXchange (YouthREX). http://exchange.youthrex.com/report/supporting -positive-outcomes-youth-involved-law. Reprinted by permission of S.M. Kwok.

In Chapter 3, it was noted that the study of Indigenous persons, Blacks, and other racialized groups in the criminal justice system must consider their historical and contemporary experience. This applies to youth involved with the justice system as well.

Three legislative acts have provided the framework for the response to youth in conflict with the law: the *Juvenile Delinquents Act* (1908), the *Young Offenders Act* (1984), and the *Youth Criminal Justice Act* (2003–present; S.C. 2002, c. 1). The legislation reflects changing philosophies about youth misbehaviour, its causes, and how best to respond to young persons who are at risk or in conflict with the law. The philosophy and approach of each of these acts is set out in Table 13.1.

The philosophy and approach of the province of Quebec has historically been somewhat different from the rest of the country.[1] The provincial *Youth Protection Act* (1984, c. 4, s. 1) was passed in 1977 and set youth justice within a child welfare/social development framework. Rehabilitation and reintegration are the primary goals of the youth justice system.[2] *Centres jeunesse* (youth centres), which are located across the province, have responsibility for both youth who are in need of protection and those who are in conflict with the law.[3]

This approach does not distinguish between youth in need of protection and youth offenders. Both groups of youths are viewed as requiring special assistance given their level of maturity and early stage of development.[4] Quebec's approach to youth and risk and young offenders has been credited with contributing to a low police-reported crime rate, a high rate of diversion under the YCJA, and a low number of cases in youth court.[5]

"It seems like only yesterday you were a juvenile offender."

TABLE 13.1

YOUTH OFFENDER LEGISLATION, 1908–PRESENT

Legislation	Philosophy/Approach
Juvenile Delinquents Act (JDA) (1908)	Reflected a social welfare approach to youth offenders who were viewed as suffering from a lack of parental and social guidance and as requiring assistance and intervention to address the personal, social, and familial factors that had contributed to their offending behaviour. The underlying philosophy of the JDA was *parens patriae*, Latin for "parent of the country." Youth courts had broad discretion in dealing with youth who were deemed to be at risk, including those who had not committed any crime. Under the JDA, youth could be sent to court and sentenced, even to custody, for "status offences"—behaviour that was not illegal for an adult, such as truancy from school.[a] Youth could remain under supervision until they were deemed to have been rehabilitated.[b]
Young Offenders Act (1984)	This legislation attempted to balance the protection of young offenders' special needs and legal rights and freedoms with the protection of the public, while ensuring young offenders were held accountable for their behaviour. Criticized for too great a focus on rights and rehabilitation of the youth and less on accountability, thereby placing the community at risk.[c]
Youth Criminal Justice Act (YCJA) (2003–present)	Objectives of the legislation include crime prevention, rehabilitation and reintegration, and "meaningful consequences." Affirmed the rights of youth under the *Charter of Rights and Freedoms* and directed the youth justice system to, whenever possible, use alternatives to incarceration via extrajudicial measures so that youth could avoid going through the formal youth justice system.[d] The legislation reflected the belief that "youth may be more deserving of leniency due to their psychological and moral immaturity."[e]

[a] M. Alain and J. Desrosiers. 2016. "A Fairly Short History of Youth Criminal Justice in Canada," in *Implementing and Working with the Youth Criminal Justice Act across Canada*, edited by M. Alain, R. R. Corrado, and S. Reid, 23–40. Toronto: University of Toronto Press.

[b] L. Casavant, R. MacKay, and D. Valiquet. 2008. *Youth Justice Legislation in Canada*. Ottawa: Library of Parliament. https://lop.parl.ca/Content/LOP/ResearchPublications/2008-23-e.pdf.

[c] S.J. Bell. 2012. *Young Offenders and Youth Justice: A Century After the Fact* (4th ed.). Toronto: Nelson.

[d] John Howard Society of Alberta. 2007. *Youth Criminal Justice Act Handbook*. Edmonton: Author. http://www.johnhoward.ab.ca/pub/old/youthcrim/youth.pdf.

[e] J. Umamaheswar. 2012. "Bringing Hope and Change: A Study of Youth Probation Officers in Toronto," *International Journal of Offender Therapy and Comparative Criminology*, *57*(9), 1158–1182 at pp. 1163–1164.

In addition to federal legislation, the UN Convention on the Rights of the Child applies to all children under the age of 18. It sets out the rights of children, including children with disabilities.[6] Two articles in the convention are particularly applicable to youth and the justice system:

Article 2.1. Parties shall respect and ensure the rights set forth in the present Convention to each child within their jurisdiction without discrimination of any kind, irrespective of the child's or his or her parent's or legal guardian's race, colour, sex, language, religion, political or other opinion, national, ethnic or social origin, property, disability, birth or other status.[7]

Article 3.1. In all actions concerning children, whether undertaken by public or private social welfare institutions, courts of law, administrative authorities or legislative bodies, the best interests of the child shall be a primary consideration.[8]

THE RISK AND NEEDS OF YOUTH

A high percentage of the youth who come into contact with the police and the youth justice system grew up in, and live in, high-risk environments. This includes communities that may be afflicted by substance abuse and violence, and families that are fractured

Juvenile Delinquents Act (JDA; 1908)

Legislation centred on a social welfare approach to youth crime that gave judges considerable discretion to intervene in the lives of young offenders.

Young Offenders Act (YOA; 1984)

Youth legislation that attempted to balance the protection of young offenders' special needs and legal rights and freedoms with the protection of the public, while ensuring young offenders would be held accountable.

and do not provide a supportive and nurturing environment for youth. Youth with disabilities are also overrepresented in the youth justice system. This includes youths with learning disabilities, fetal alcohol spectrum disorder (FASD), and mental health issues, among others.[9] Being homeless may also increase the risk of youth of self-harm and of having mental health.[10] These factors, may, in turn, increase the likelihood that these youth come into conflict with the law.

Mental health symptoms are typically more prevalent amongst the young women offender population.[11] Further, young women offenders typically have experienced higher rates of sexual, emotional, and physical abuse than their young male counterparts.[12]

Many of the youth who come into contact with the youth justice system have experienced various forms of trauma in the form of physical and sexual abuse and other critical incidents. Others have disabilities—intellectual, physical, sensory, and psychological—that must be addressed.[13]

PROGRAMS FOR AT-RISK YOUTH

I would say the most challenging part is when you're not able to steer a young person away from whatever the situation is because of the environment that they're in. We've been to funerals where you sometimes feel like, is there something more that could have been done, but we try and use those opportunities where we haven't succeeded to challenge ourselves to do better with the next group of young people that are coming along because we know that they really need that positive adult ally, that role model, in their life, and so we need to be that person at times. It just makes us work harder. (youth outreach worker, East Metro Youth Services, Toronto)[14]

Across the country, there are myriad programs and services operated by provincial and territorial governments and non-profit organizations, often with support from the federal government. These are designed to prevent at-risk youth from becoming involved in the youth justice system, or to assist those who are involved in the system in changing directions in their lives. Some programs focus on youths 11 years and under who are not yet subject to the youth justice system, but who are at risk of becoming involved once they reach the age of 12. Outreach teams and youth street workers work to establish contact and relationships with at-risk youth and serve as a resource, identifying programs and services that the youth may access.

Many of the initiatives involve multi-agency collaboration, often involving child welfare, health services, police, and others. To illustrate the range of programs, several are highlighted in Table 13.2.

There are also concerns with the group of youth who are at risk of becoming chronic or persistent offenders. The individual youth, and their family, peer group, school, and community have all been found to be important factors in the development of this behaviour pattern.[15] Effective intervention strategies address all of these factors, and this is often best done through multi-agency collaboration.

A concern is that, in some jurisdictions, there are not adequate programs and services for youth, particularly those in need of special assistance. A review of the provincial response to youth with disabilities found a "large disconnect" between the approach set out in the YCJA and the experience of children and their parents and service providers.[16]

TABLE 13.2

SELECTED PROGRAMS FOR AT-RISK AND JUSTICE-SYSTEM-INVOLVED YOUTH

Program	Philosophy/Approach
The "SNAP" (Stop Now and Plan) program	A mental health program designed for youth six to ten years of age.[a] It is a cognitive-behavioural strategy designed to teach children and parents how to control their feelings of anger and to pause and consider alternatives before they react to a situation or event. The SNAP program has been shown to reduce impulsive and aggressive behaviour in children under the age of 12.[b]
The "YIP" (Youth Inclusion Program)	Neighbourhood-based program for ages 11 to 14 that is designed to prevent youth from entering the justice system and to assist those youth who are already involved in the youth justice system. The program offers a variety of activities led by mentors and role models, including arts, culture, drug education, and sports, among others.[c]
The MST (multisystemic therapy) intervention model	Designed for youths 15 to 17 years of age to address issues related to antisocial behaviour and eliminate the risk factors that contribute to this behaviour. These include ineffective discipline, poor relationship skills, and lack of education, among others. The parents and family of the youth may be included in certain interventions.[d]
Community Empowering Enterprises (CEE) (Toronto)	A United Way–supported program that offers a seven-month intensive entrepreneurship program focusing on career development for Black youth in the city.[e]
Multi-agency Preventative Program (MAPP) (Brandon, Manitoba, and other municipalities in the province)	A non-profit organization involving a network of agencies, including the schools; Addictions Foundation Manitoba; provincial child and family services; Métis Child, Family and Community Services; Dakota-Ojibway Child and Family Services; and others. Provides a framework for information-sharing on youth at risk that is used to support agency interventions.[f]
Ooskahtisuk (Youth) Club – Tataskweyak First Nation (Manitoba)	Focuses on youth ages 5 to 14 and attempts to prevent and reduce substance abuse, drug-related crime, and interpersonal violence through after-school and family-based programs.[g]
Do Edàezhe (Dogrib expression for "a person who is capable, skillful, and knowledgeable to survive in the world of the Dene") (Northwest Territories)	A program run in the Catholic schools in Yellowknife that provides youth with community support, mentorship, and the opportunity to participate in a resiliency and leadership program.[h]

[a] N. Pace. 2017, April 4. "Children's Mental Health Program to Expand in Atlantic Canada," *Global News*. http://globalnews.ca/news/3356231/children-mental-health-atlantic-canada.

[b] Public Safety Canada. 2016. "Tyler's Troubled Life: The Story of One Young Man's Paths towards a Life of Crime" [Research report 2016-R005]. Ottawa: Her Majesty the Queen in Right of Canada, p. 12. https://www.publicsafety.gc.ca/cnt/rsrcs/pblctns/2016-r005/2016-r005-en.pdf.

[c] Ibid. p. 13.

[d] Ibid. p. 14.

[e] E. Campanella. 2015, October 25. "CEE Program Connects At-Risk Youth," *Toronto Star*. https://www.thestar.com/news/gta/2015/10/25/cee-program-connects-at-risk-youth.html.

[f] B. DeGusti, L. MacRae, M. Vallée, T. Caputo, and J.P. Hornick. 2009. *Best Practices for Chronic/Persistent Offenders in Canada: Summary Report*. Ottawa: Public Safety Canada. https://www.publicsafety.gc.ca/cnt/rsrcs/pblctns/prstnt-ffndrs/prstnt-ffndrs-eng.pdf.

[g] R. Smandych, M. Dyck, C. La Berge, and J. Koffman. 2016. "Youth Justice in Manitoba: Developments and Issues under the YCJA," in *Implementing and Working with the Youth Criminal Justice Act Across Canada*, edited by M. Alain, R.R. Corrado, and S. Reid, 86–124. Toronto: University of Toronto Press.

[h] D. Lafferty. 2012. "Do Edàezhe: Building Resiliency among Aboriginal Youth," *Pimatisiwin: A Journal of Aboriginal and Indigenous Health, 10*(2), 217–230. http://www.pimatisiwin.com/uploads/vol11/10Lafferty.pdf.

DIFFERENCES BETWEEN THE ADULT AND YOUTH CRIMINAL JUSTICE SYSTEMS

Youth who are arrested have the right to a lawyer and to remain silent and other protections under the *Charter of Rights and Freedoms*. However, the philosophy of the YCJA is that youth should be treated differently than adults. Several of the key differences between the youth and adult systems of criminal justice are highlighted in Table 13.3.

TABLE 13.3

KEY DIFFERENCES BETWEEN THE YOUTH AND ADULT CRIMINAL JUSTICE SYSTEMS

	Youth Justice System	Adult Justice System
Applicable legislation	*Youth Criminal Justice Act*; attempt to avoid youth going to court whenever possible; when a youth is convicted under the *Criminal Code*, the youth court presumes a "diminished moral blameworthiness"	*Criminal Code*; going to court is the usual procedure for adults charged with crimes
Privacy	Privacy of youth protected; names of youth cannot be published unless they receive an adult sentence	Names of adults charged with, and convicted of crimes, can be published
Criminal record	Most youth offenders can avoid having a criminal record	A criminal record is created for most convicted adult offenders
Release from custody	Youths who are released from custody must have supervision in the community	Adult offenders released from custody may not have supervision (e.g., a provincial or territorial offender who serves two-thirds of his or her sentence or any offender who serves his or her entire sentence in custody, with the exception of federal offenders on long-term supervision orders, offenders serving life sentence, and dangerous offenders).
Role of parents/family	Parents must be notified of actions taken against their youth and may play a role in interventions; youth have the right to have parents present during questioning	Parents generally play no role, with the exception of restorative justice initiatives such as circle sentencing where the family of an adult offender may participate in the proceedings, and rare instances in which family members appear at a parole hearing
Probation	Maximum period of probation is two years	Maximum period of probation is three years
Alternatives to court process	Extensive use of alternatives to formal court process	Limited use of alternatives to the formal court process
Time in custody	Maximum period of time a youth can be held in custody is six years	Some offenders may never be released from prison

Source: Government of British Columbia. n.d. "Differences between Youth and Adult Criminal Justice Systems." http://www2.gov.bc.ca/gov/content/justice/criminal-justice/bcs-criminal-justice-system/youth-justice/youth-and-adult-criminal-justice-systems.

THE YOUTH JUSTICE SYSTEM

The youth justice system is illustrated in Figure 13.1. There are four "levels" of the youth justice system, which represent a progression of sanctions and correspond to the severity of the offence and other risk/needs of the young offender. See Figure 13.2.

The *Youth Criminal Justice Act* is federal legislation that provides the framework for the youth justice system. The provinces and territories have the responsibility of implementing the provisions of the Act and provide a continuum of programs and facilities for young offenders, ranging from diversion to custody. This results in variability in terms of the specific programs and services and supervision available across the country.

KEEPING YOUTH OUT OF THE FORMAL YOUTH JUSTICE SYSTEM: EXTRAJUDICIAL MEASURES AND EXTRAJUDICIAL SANCTIONS

> We should be providing offenders with more alternatives than incarceration. I think that what has to be done is that we have to work with our young offenders and our youth a lot earlier. Once a youth has entered an institution, it's going to be very difficult to get that person to change their ways, because once he gets in there, he is going to be conditioned to the situation that is happening. It's a very negative environment. I know in my situation, I had been a youth in a training school. It was being conditioned to the adult person I would be for the longest time, and I would spend 23 years of my life in institutions. If you put that into dollars and

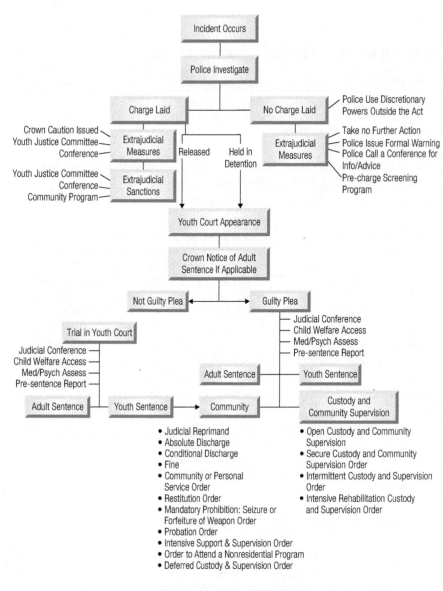

◄ **FIGURE 13.1**

The Youth Justice System

Source: Reprinted from *A Guide to the Youth Criminal Justice Act, 2009.* With permission from LexisNexis Canada, Inc.

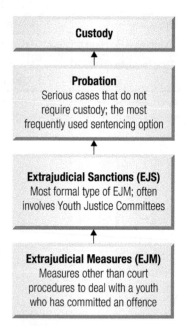

▲ FIGURE 13.2

The Progression of Sanctions in the Youth Justice System

Source: C. Hincks and J. Winterdyk. 2016. "The Youth Justice System: An Alberta Overview," in *Implementing and Working with the Youth Criminal Justice Act across Canada*, edited by M. Alain, R.R. Corrado, and S. Reid, 41–62. Toronto: University of Toronto Press, p. 49. Copyright © 2016 University of Toronto Press. Reprinted with permission of the publisher.

cents, I think it could have been spent a lot better than it was on me. (Ex-offender, personal communication with C.T. Griffiths)

The general intent of the YCJA is to keep as many youth as possible from becoming involved in the formal youth justice system. Two provisions for accomplishing this are **extrajudicial measures (EJM)** and **extrajudicial sanctions (EJS)**.

EXTRAJUDICIAL MEASURES (EJM)

The objective of extrajudicial measures (EJM) is to allow the police and Crown counsel to divert youth from the formal youth court system. Section 6(1) of the YCJA has formalized the practice of police issuing warnings and cautions and referring youth to diversion programs.

Young offenders may be diverted at the pre-charge stage to community organizations whose task is to ensure that they complete specified sanctions in a given time period. Once the young offender has satisfied the requirements as laid out, the police or Crown counsel are notified and charges are not laid for the original offence.

When used at the post-charge stage, youth are diverted to formal community diversion programs. When they have met the requirements of the program, the charges are withdrawn.[17] These sanctions include offering an apology to those impacted by their offence; providing restitution or personal services to the victim(s) of the offence; completing a period of community service; participating in community programs, such as counselling; and/or being subject to a period of community supervision.

A study of Crown counsel decision-making in British Columbia and Saskatchewan found that youth with no previous convictions and those charged with property offences were most likely to be referred to EJM.[18]

As with adults, there is concern that diversion programs may result in net-widening, meaning that low-risk, non-violent youth who would otherwise have received an informal warning from the police are finding themselves caught up in the justice system.[19] This was the finding of a study of the Toronto Police Service Youth Referral Program (TPS-YRP); nearly 90 percent of the participants in this program would have received an informal police caution if the program did not exist.[20] The study also found no evidence that the program had an impact on recidivism when the recidivism rates of the referral group were compared to the recidivism rates of similar youth processed via informal caution or who were processed in court and received post-charge diversion programming.[21]

Youth may also be directed to a specialized court, similar to the problem-solving courts for adult offenders discussed in Chapter 7. Several of these have been established across the country. Within the framework of the YCJA, for example, jurisdictions across the country have developed a variety of programs to assist youth with mental health issues who are involved in the youth justice system. The Youth Mental Health Court program in London, Ontario, for example, assists youths in conflict with the law who have mental health issues, a traumatic brain injury, or a developmental disability.[22]

EXTRAJUDICIAL SANCTIONS (EJS)

Extrajudicial sanctions (EJS) are a more formal type of EJM that can be applied outside of the formal court process. These sanctions can be used in cases involving more serious offences where the Crown believes there is sufficient evidence to prosecute. The youth must accept responsibility for the alleged behaviour and voluntarily agree to participate.

These sanctions are generally used when the police feel that a warning, caution, or referral of the youth are not adequate. The sanctions can include requiring the youth to attending counselling, making restitution to the victim, apologizing to the victim, doing community service, or participating in a restorative justice program such as victim–offender mediation or a healing circle, among others.

An example of a diversion program that accommodates youth as an EJM and EJS is profiled in Youth Justice File 13.1.

YOUTH JUSTICE FILE 13.1

OTTAWA COMMUNITY YOUTH DIVERSION PROGRAM (OCYD)

The OCYD is a pre-charge and post-charge program that diverts youth to the Ottawa Boys and Girls Club; at the pre-charge stage, referrals are made by the police as an extrajudicial measure (EJM); post-charge referrals come from the Crown as an extrajudicial sanction (EJS). An evaluation that compared a group ($N = 170$) of youth who completed the program with a matched group ($N = 208$) of youth who were placed on probation found that the program was successful in reducing reoffending, although the youth who did not complete the OCYD program had higher rates of reconviction than youth in either group.

Source: H.W. Wilson and R.D. Hoge. 2013. "Diverting Our Attention to What Works: Evaluating the Effectiveness of a Youth Diversion Program: A Meta-Analytic Review," *Youth Violence and Juvenile Justice, 11*(4), 313–331.

TABLE 13.4

SPECIALIZED PROBLEM-SOLVING YOUTH COURTS

Aboriginal Youth Court (AYC) (Toronto)	Established in 2012 to encourage the use of alternatives to custody for Indigenous youth, to assist in their rehabilitation, and to engage Indigenous organizations in working with youth in conflict. An evaluation found that the AYC is effective in identifying Indigenous youth to participate in and attend the court; addressing the needs of youth within the framework of the YCJA; and providing a vital service for the youth, their families, and the Indigenous community.[a]
The Toronto Community Youth Court (CYC)	Designed for youths who are charged with an offence and have significant mental health or substance abuse issues. Goals include assisting youth in addressing their issues, facilitating to programs and services, and reducing reoffending. An evaluation involving interviews ($N = 75$) with youth and their parents, judges, Crown, defence lawyers, and persons involved in delivering treatment programs and information on the cases that appeared in the court in 2011 to 2013 found that many of the youth had little information about the court and felt they were not given the choice of whether to attend it; the principle of proportionality in sentencing, as set out in the YCJA, was reflected in the court's decisions; the most common offences that came before the court were property-related; the CYC did not assess the criminogenic needs of the youth; and only about 50 percent of the youth received treatment interventions designed to address the factors associated with their offending.[b]

[a] S. Clark. 2016. *Evaluation of the Aboriginal Youth Court, Toronto.* Toronto: Aboriginal Legal Services. http://www.aboriginallegal.ca/assets/ayc-evaluation-final.pdf.

[b] M. Petersen-Badali, T. Skilling, and K. Davis. 2014. *A Process Evaluation of the Community Youth Court. Final Report for the Department of Justice.* Ottawa: Department of Justice Canada. http://www.justice.gc.ca/eng/rp-pr/cj-jp/yj-jj/pecyc-tcaep/index.html.

SPECIALIZED YOUTH COURTS

Specialized, problem-solving courts are not as pervasive in the youth criminal justice system as in the adult system (see Chapter 7). Two of these courts for youth offenders are highlighted in Table 13.4.

COMMUNITY INVOLVEMENT IN THE YOUTH JUSTICE SYSTEM: YOUTH JUSTICE COMMITTEES AND YOUTH JUSTICE CONFERENCES

A key feature of the YCJA is the involvement of community members and organizations in working with youth who are in conflict with the law. Section 19 of the YCJA contains a provision for convening **youth justice conferences** to discuss the measures that might be taken by a police officer, judge, or other youth justice decision-maker to best address the circumstance of the young offender.

For example, a youth justice conference or a healing circle might be required by a youth court judge to gather information that can inform the judge at sentencing. The conference brings together persons from the community who represent a broad range of backgrounds and experience who provide advice to decision-makers on how best to respond to youth.[23]

Section 18 of the YCJA provides for the creation of **youth justice committees** to assist with youth who are in conflict with the law. Youth justice committees are composed of community volunteers who are involved in providing advice on sentencing, providing guidance to young offenders who have committed less serious offences and are participating in an EJM program.[24]

Youth justice committees also provide support for victims and facilitate victim–offender reconciliation; ensure community support for the young offender through services, short-term mentoring, and community supervision; and coordinate interactions between agencies (e.g., the local child protection agency and the youth criminal justice

Youth justice conference

A group of people who are asked by a decision-maker, such as a judge, to come together to give advice on the case of a young person who is involved in the youth criminal justice system.

Youth justice committees

Community-based committees that sponsor a variety of initiatives for youth in conflict with the law, including extrajudicial measures centred on restorative justice.

▲ A youth justice committee

system). Watch the video of the Calgary Youth Justice Committee of the Calgary Youth Justice Society in the Media Links section at the end of this chapter.

Youth justice committees may be involved in a variety of initiatives, including acting as a youth justice conference, conducting family group conferences, community/neighbourhood accountability panels, victim–offender mediation/reconciliation sessions, multidisciplinary case management conferences, and Indigenous sentencing and healing circles. In addition to providing a creative way in which to address the needs of youth, youth justice committees are cost-effective. For example, the Calgary Youth Justice Society, the agency responsible for operating youth justice committees and that handles 70 percent of extrajudicial youth sanctions for the city of Calgary, produces a 400 percent return on investment with every $1 spent on Y youth justice committees. This results in $4 in savings going back to the community.[25]

There are concerns that youth justice committees are not being utilized to their full potential in many jurisdictions, and in some cases, there has been a decline in the number of committees. In Manitoba, for example, youth justice committees appear to be less active than in previous years, due in part to a lack of referrals from the police and Crown.[26]

YOUTH COURT

The rates of youth charged and cases being heard by Canadian youth courts have been declining over the past decade, due in large measure to the YCJA, which emphasizes extrajudicial measures.[27] Despite this, "administration of justice" offences, such as breaches of curfew, are still being heard in youth court.[28]

There is also a focus in the youth justice system on the speedy resolution of cases. Nearly one-half of all youth court cases are completed within three months or less.[29] Contrast this with the issues that have surrounded case delay for adult offenders, discussed in Chapter 7. There is a recognition that youths are not as mature as adults and that special considerations are required.

Factors that place youth at risk for involvement in delinquent behaviour include a history of antisocial behaviour, parental incarceration, drug consumption, substance abuse, poverty, a negative or disruptive family environment (e.g., involvement in the foster care system), a history of abuse, trauma exposure, delinquent peers, educational difficulties, emotional/behavioural disorders, and gang membership.[30,31]

THE ROLE OF JUSTICES OF THE PEACE (JPS)

The role of justices of the peace (JPs) was discussed in Chapter 7. In the youth justice system, JPs have all of the same authorities, with the exception of accepting pleas, presiding over trials, or adjudicating cases. JPs conduct bail hearings and make decisions on whether a youth should be released.

JUDICIAL INTERIM RELEASE (BAIL)

Sections 28 through 31 of the YCJA set out the provisions for bail for young offenders. Section 29 of the Act states that the pre-trial detention of a youth is not permitted "as a substitute for appropriate child protection, mental health or other social measures." This means, for example, that a homeless youth cannot be kept in pre-trial detention merely because he or she has no place to live or because the youth has mental health issues that require attention but services are not readily available.[32] However, a youth may be kept in pre-trial detention if he or she is charged with a serious offence, the detention of the youth is required to ensure his or her appearance in court, and releasing the youth into the community would not be sufficient to address concerns that the court may have about the youth.[33]

Research on the use of bail for youth has raised concerns similar to those surrounding bail for adults discussed in Chapter 8. This includes the number of conditions attached to release on bail that may set up youth for failure and, in some doing, add to their legal difficulties.[34,35]

A study in Ontario found, for example, that the more conditions that were attached to a youth's release on bail and the longer the youth was subject to the conditions, the higher the rate of youths failing to comply with conditions.[36] It also appears that attaching more conditions to a youth's release on bail does not ensure his or her appearance in court or reduce the risk of reoffending while on release in the community.[37]

Among the justifications for detention of the youth in custody are that the youth has been charged with a serious crime, may not appear in court as required, or detention is required to protect the public. Similar to their adult counterparts, youth in pre-trial detention outnumber those in sentenced custody, a trend for the past decade. The majority of youth in pre-trial detention are released after serving less than a month.[38]

YOUTH COURT CASES

Youth most often find themselves before the court for non-violent offences, including theft, administration of justice offences (e.g., failure to appear, failure to comply with conditions of a court order), common assault, and break and enter.[39]

Figure 13.3 presents the average counts of youth in corrections systems in selected jurisdictions.

LGBTQ YOUTH

Estimates are that while LGBTQ youths represent 5 to 7 percent of the population in the U.S., these youths comprise 13 to 15 percent of youth involved in the youth justice system.[40] Research in the U.S. has also found that LGBTQ youth are more likely than heterosexual youth to be stopped by the police and are twice as likely as their heterosexual peers to have been held in secure detention for non-violent behaviours such as being truant from school, violating the conditions of probation, and prostitution.[41]

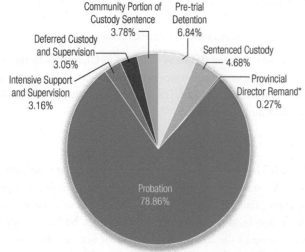

Community Portion of Custody Sentence 3.78%
Pre-trial Detention 6.84%
Deferred Custody and Supervision 3.05%
Sentenced Custody 4.68%
Intensive Support and Supervision 3.16%
Provincial Director Remand* 0.27%
Probation 78.86%

*Youth held in custody following the breach of a community supervision order pursuant to a warrant issued by the provincial director

◄ FIGURE 13.3

Average Counts of Youth in Correctional Services, Selected Jurisdictions, 2015/2016

Source: J. Malakieh. 2017. "Youth Correctional Statistics in Canada, 2015/2016," *Juristat, 37*(1). Statistics Canada Catalogue no. 85-002-X. Ottawa: Minister of Industry, p. 12. http://www.statcan.gc.ca/pub/85-002-x/2017001/article/14702-eng.pdf.

More research needs to be conducted on the experience of LGBTQ research in the youth justice system.

INDIGENOUS YOUTH

Despite the fact that the declining rate of youth correctional populations is positive, a concerning feature is that, similar to their adult counterparts, Indigenous youth continue to be overrepresented in youth correctional populations across Canada, with the greatest disparity experienced by Indigenous young women.

Indigenous youth are overrepresented in the youth justice system, comprising 7 percent of the national population but 33 percent of admissions to youth correctional services. Indigenous women young offenders represent one-third of the admissions to youth correctional services, while comprising 7 percent of the population in those jurisdictions that report on this statistic.[42] In Ontario, the representation of young Indigenous men and women in custody is five times and ten times higher, respectively, than their percentage of the general population.[43] In that province, Indigenous boys between the ages of 12 to 17 comprise 2.9 percent of the population, yet are 15 percent of the male admissions to provincial youth facilities.[44]

The higher rates of Indigenous youth involvement in the youth justice system have been attributed to their life circumstances, which may include poverty, low educational attainment, and exposure to violence and victimization in their home communities, as well as, for some youth, exposure to gangs. It may also be due to differential treatment by police and youth justice system personnel, although this is an area that remains to be examined.[45] The risk profile of Indigenous youth increases their likelihood of engaging in criminal behaviour and becoming involved in the youth justice system.[46] Indigenous young women are particularly at risk of becoming involved in the youth justice system.

One contributing factor to their overrepresentation may be the lack of community programs, resources, and extrajudicial measures in remote, rural communities.[47] Of particular concern is the plight of youth on First Nations reserves. Indigenous youth living on reserves are charged with a criminal offence at a rate more than three times the average rate across the remainder of Canada, and they commit a greater proportion of violent and property crimes. These youth are 11 times more likely to be accused of committing homicide than non-Indigenous youth living off-reserve.[48]

Many of these risk factors rare associated with the impact of colonization, institutional racism, residential schools, and the destruction of Indigenous communities and culture.

The overrepresentation of Indigenous youth in the youth justice system highlights the need to examine whether existing policies and interventions are adequately addressing the risk and protective profiles of Indigenous young offenders.[49] Further, their overrepresentation highlights the need to consider how police, prosecutor, and probation officer decision-making serve to limit the options that youth court judges can consider when sentencing Indigenous offenders under the YCJA.[50] Recall from the discussion in earlier chapters that these same issues surround the overrepresentation of adult Indigenous persons in the criminal justice system.

BLACK YOUTH

Black youth as well are overrepresented in youth custodial populations. In Nova Scotia, for example, African Nova Scotians account for just 2 percent of the general population, yet in 2014–15, they represented 16 percent of incarcerated youth.[51] Black youths are similarly overrepresented in youth custody facilities in Ontario at a rate four times that of their representation in the general population of the province.[52]

SENTENCING YOUNG OFFENDERS

There are two primary objectives of sentencing of young offenders within the framework of the YCJA: (1) the rehabilitation and reintegration of the young offender, and (2) protection of the public. Youth court judges have a variety of sentencing options. A key principle of sentencing is that it is proportional; that is, there should be less serious consequences for less serious offences and more serious consequences for offences that are more serious.[53]

Section 38(2)(d) of the YCJA states that, "all available sanctions other than custody that are reasonable in the circumstances should be considered for all young persons, with particular attention to the circumstances of aboriginal young persons." In addition, youth courts are required by the *Gladue* decision (see Chapter 9) to consider the special circumstances of Indigenous offenders at sentencing.

Youths may be sentenced to open or closed (secure) custody. Youth who are sentenced to open custody facilities often reside in group homes located in the community.

Recently, the courts have also been presented with the argument that the circumstances of offenders from racialized groups should be considered at sentencing. This occurred in the case of *R. v. Gabriel* (2017 NSSC 90), presented in Legal Case 9.3. In what was considered a groundbreaking decision, a youth court judge in Nova Scotia ruled on whether the sentence for a youth defendant who was an African Nova Scotian should be a mitigating factor in determining whether the youth should be sentenced at a youth or an adult. See At Issue 13.1.

Youth can appeal their sentence to a higher court.

AT ISSUE 13.1

SHOULD A YOUTH'S BACKGROUND BE A MITIGATING FACTOR IN SENTENCING YOUNG OFFENDERS? THE CASE OF *R. V. "X"* (2014 NSPC 95)

In April 2013, "X," a 16-year-old boy, shot his 15-year-old cousin "Y" with a hunting rifle at a playground, paralyzing him. The boys were part of a close-knit family and community, and the shooting had a devastating effect on both. "X" was sent to youth court where he was tried and found guilty of attempted murder. Prior to the incident, "X" had become involved in street life and was involved in various criminal activities, including drug trafficking.[a]

The prosecutor argued that "X" should be sentenced as an adult, citing a similar case in which a youth convicted of attempted murder had been sentenced as an adult by a Nova Scotia judge to 14 years in prison. The Crown also presented evidence from a psychological assessment indicating that "X" was at a high risk of committing further crimes.[b]

The defence argued that "X's" African Nova Scotian identity should be a factor in the decision as to whether he should be sentenced as a youth or an adult. A social worker retained by the defence made the following submission to the court: "In our society, racialized status is a condition, a factor, that can reasonably be understood to have influenced a person's behaviour."[c] The social worker further stated that "X's" apparent lack of remorse for the shooting was likely "influenced by race and race models for coping in a criminally-affected community." Discrimination against the Black community in Nova Scotia historically and in contemporary times were cited as contributing factors to "X's" behaviour.

In considering whether to sentence "X" as an adult, the presiding judge had to address the requirements of the YCJA that the goal of the sentence would be to hold "X" accountable for his behaviour, to promote his rehabilitation, while also protecting the community. If "X" were to be sentenced as an adult, he would face a life sentence, as compared to a few years in a youth custody facility should he be sentenced as a youth.

The decision of the judge was to sentence "X" as a youth offender and to send "X" to a youth custody facility for three years. In speaking to this decision, the judge noted that a factor was the history of the racialized community in which "X" was raised and that systemic and background factors should play a role in sentencing decisions in the youth court. Read the court's judgment in *Her Majesty the Queen v. "X"* in the Youth Justice Court of Nova Scotia, available at http://decisions.courts.ns.ca/nsc/nspc/en/item/99584/index.do?r=AAAAAQAMYW5uZSBkZXJyaWNrAAAAAAE.

QUESTIONS

1. Do you agree with the decision of the judge in this case?

2. In your view, should there be limits on the extent to which race and culture should influence the decisions made in youth court?

---

[a] J. Tattrie. 2015, March 9. "The Colour of Justice Part 1: The Crime," *CBC News.* http://www.cbc.ca/news/canada/nova-scotia/colour-of-justice-part-1-the-crime-1.2986746.

[b] J. Tattrie. 2015, March 9. "The Colour of Justice Part 2: The Prosecution," *CBC News.* http://www.cbc.ca/news/canada/nova-scotia/colour-of-justice-part-2-the-prosecution-1.2986755.

[c] J. Tattrie. 2015, March 9. "The Colour of Justice. Part 3: The Defence," *CBC News.* http://www.cbc.ca/news/canada/nova-scotia/colour-of-justice-part-3-the-defence-1.2986750.

NON-CUSTODIAL SENTENCING OPTIONS

The non-custodial sentencing options for youth court judges are set out in Table 13.5. Note that several of the sentencing options are similar to those for adults, set out in Table 9.1 in Chapter 9, although there are also options that are unique to the youth court. As in adult court, certain of the options can be combined; for example, a youth may be required to pay restitution and be subject to a period of supervision on probation.

Particular challenges are faced by youth court judges in sentencing youth with FASD. In Manitoba, concerns have been expressed by defence lawyers that there is not adequate programming for this group of young offenders.[54]

There are also concerns that the *Gladue* provisions have not resulted in a reduction in the numbers of Indigenous youth in the youth justice system. As one justice official in Manitoba stated, "I don't think it's done anything. You can add a *Gladue* component to a sentence … but it doesn't make any difference.… It doesn't speak directly to why kids are in the system."[55]

TABLE 13.5
NON-CUSTODIAL SENTENCING OPTIONS FOR YOUNG OFFENDERS

Sentencing Option	Description
Judicial reprimand	A judge may issue a verbal reprimand to a young offender rather than an actual sentence. This is most often given to first-time offenders convicted of minor offences. These offenders do not receive a criminal record.
Absolute discharge	The youth is found guilty but is released and does not have a criminal record.
Conditional discharge	The youth is found guilty but discharged on the condition that he or she will follow conditions directed by the court. If the youth adheres to the conditions of the order—which may include reporting conditions—no criminal record will result.
Fine	The court can impose a fine not to exceed $1,000, which is to be paid at a time and under conditions the court determines to be appropriate. The judge is required to consider the ability of the youth offender to pay the fine. A youth who is unable to pay it can choose to work off the fine through community service as part of a fine option program.
Restitution	The court may order the youth to make restitution to any other person through money, in kind, or by way of personal services to compensate for a variety of consequences resulting from a criminal offence, including "for loss of or damage to property or for loss of income or support" (YCJA, 42(2)(e)).
Compensation	The youth is ordered to pay the victim for costs incurred as a result of the crime (e.g., the cost of repairs).
Community service order	The court may impose an order for the youth to perform a maximum of 240 hours of community service work. It must be completed within 12 months of the date of the order. This period of free work cannot interfere with the youth's school or normal work hours. Community service orders are commonly included as a condition of probation for young offenders.
Prohibition, seizure, or forfeiture	The sentencing judge may impose prohibitions on the young offender (e.g., the youth is not to possess a firearm and/or ammunition), or seize or require the young offender to forfeit goods obtained via crime.
Probation	This is the most frequently imposed sanction in the youth courts. Around 90 percent of young offenders serving a community supervision sentence are on probation. The maximum term of probation is two years. There are mandatory conditions and often additional ones. Breach of probation is a *Criminal Code* offence.
Non-residential attendance order	A non-residential order is for a period not to exceed 240 hours over a six-month period. The youth is required to attend specific programs to address their needs, such as an alternative school.

Sources: S. J. Bell. 2012. *Young Offenders and Youth Justice: A Century After the Fact* (4th ed.). Toronto: Nelson; J. Malakieh. 2017. "Youth Correctional Statistics in Canada, 2015/2016," *Juristat, 37*(1). Statistics Canada Catalogue no. 85-002-X. Ottawa: Minister of Industry. http://www.statcan.gc.ca/pub/85-002-x/2017001/article/14702-eng.pdf.

YOUTH PROBATION

> They're so young, like they're under the age of 18 and so their lives haven't even started yet ... and they've had things happen to them or experiences that I don't even know as an adult that I could handle, so you see the resilience that a lot of these youth have, and that creates hope for me. (Youth probation officer from Toronto, Ontario)[56]

As in adult corrections, the majority (90 percent) of youth under supervision in the community are on probation. Probation orders include the mandatory requirements that the youth keep the peace and be of good behaviour, and appear before the youth justice court when required by the court to do so. Optional conditions may include attending school, maintaining stable employment, and/or residing with a parent. Approximately half of youth serve one year or less on probation.

Similar to their counterparts in the adult corrections systems, youth probation officers have a variety of tasks to perform: providing supervision to youth probationers; writing pre-sentence reports and attending court; making referrals to community services; and monitoring youth on bail, deferred custody, mandatory supervision, and community service. Probation officers ($N = 20$) in Toronto who were interviewed expressed the importance of a balanced approach to their work with youth, exercising both enforcement and positive, supportive roles to promote accountability and encourage youth to engage in a prosocial lifestyle.[57]

Youth probation officers typically have smaller caseloads than adult probation officers; in British Columbia, for example, they carry average caseloads of 20 probationers. Modes of contact with probationers include office, school, and home visits. These personnel often work with other community agencies. Youth probation officers may also carry specialized probation caseloads, such as youth sex offenders and gang-involved youth.

CASE MANAGEMENT AND RISKS/NEEDS OF YOUTH ON PROBATION

Two important components of youth probation are risk/needs assessment and case management. The probation officer must determine which youth are high-risk/high-needs and require greater supervision and more intensive intervention. Case management refers to how supervision and services will be provided to youth.[58] Many assessment tools and case management strategies are based on the principles of risk, need, and responsivity (RNR).

Youth probation officers hold **integrated case management (ICM) conferences** with young offenders, their parents/guardians, and other support people, such as mental health workers, social workers, and specialists in FASD. The objective of ICM conferences is to establish manageable goals and benchmarks that the youth can achieve while in custody and on probation, as well as after completion of the sentence. When a youth's support network has helped develop and revise the case management plan, everyone is aware of its goals and can identify their role in helping the youth achieve them.

> **Integrated case management (ICM) conferences**
>
> The primary strategy used for case management of young offenders on probation.

CUSTODIAL SENTENCING OPTIONS

Other than the rare instances where youth sentences of less than 90 days may be served intermittently in custody, the maximum length of sentences meted out by youth courts is from two to ten years, depending upon the type of offence that has been committed, the circumstances of the case, and the specific sentencing option.[60]

The custodial sentences for young offenders are set out in Table 13.6.

A judge can send youth to custody only under certain conditions, including if the youth has committed a violent offence and has committed similar violent offences in the past. There are a variety of custodial facilities within which young offenders are housed, ranging from group homes, which are more open and have less restrictions, to secure custody jails.

Within the framework of the YCJA, custodial sentences are generally reserved for youths who have committed serious violent offences, have a record of serious offences, and have proven unable of being supervised effectively in the community.[61] Custody is to be imposed only after all alternatives have been considered and found not to be appropriate. Almost half (46 percent) of youth released from sentenced custody spent less than a month in custody, and 91 percent were released after less than six months.

The YCJA has been successful in reducing the number of youth offenders in custody. The rate of youth incarceration has been dropping in recent years, dropping 27 percent from 2011 through 2016.[62] At the North Slave Young Offender Unit in Yellowknife, for example, the number of youth in custody dropped from 19 in 2005 to 3 in 2015.

TABLE 13.6
CUSTODIAL SENTENCES FOR YOUNG OFFENDERS

Sanction	Description
Intermittent custody	A rarely used sentence wherein a youth is sentenced to custody for no more than 90 days and the sentence may be served intermittently, most often on weekends.
Custody followed by a conditional supervision order	The community supervision period following custody is half as long as the term of custody, and the youth is subject to supervision and conditions. The total term cannot exceed two years for offences, except for those involving imprisonment for life—for which the term cannot exceed three years.
Custody and supervision order	Applies to presumptive offences (e.g., manslaughter, attempted murder). The total term of custody and conditional supervision in the community cannot exceed three years from the date of committal.
Deferred custody and supervision order	The order cannot exceed six months. It excludes cases involving presumptive offences.
Intensive rehabilitative custody and supervision order (IRCS)	The first portion of the sentence is served in intensive rehabilitative custody, the second under conditional supervision in the community. Maximum period of three years from the date of committal. Exception: Youth court judges can impose a ten-year sentence for youth who commit first-degree murder, seven years for youth who commit second-degree murder. Youth spend a maximum of six years in custody for first-degree murder and four years in custody for second-degree murder, serving the remainder of the sentence under conditional supervision in the community.

Source: From John Howard Society of Alberta. 2007. *Youth Criminal Justice Act Handbook.* Edmonton: Author. http://www.johnhoward.ab.ca/pub/old/youthcrim/youth.pdf. Reprinted by permission of John Howard Society of Alberta.

Northwest Territories closed its custody facility for young women offenders in 2011, having averaged fewer than one offender per year.[63] There are exceptions. Yukon in 2015 to 2016 had a youth incarceration rate of 29 per 10,000 youth as compared to an average rate of 5 per 10,000 youth in other provinces and territories.[64]

A youth court judge can also impose an adult sentence on a young offender if he or she is convicted of a serious offence and was at least 14 years old when the offence was committed. This means youth can be subject to mandatory minimum sentences and life imprisonment, among other adult sanctions. (Youth cannot be transferred to adult prisons if they have yet to turn 18.) In 2017, for example, Skylar Prockner, was sentenced as an adult in the Court of Queen's Bench in Regina to life in prison for the stabbing death of his 16-year-old ex-girlfriend. Prockner, now 19, was 16 at the time of the murder. The sentence means that he will not be eligible for parole for 10 years.[65]

YOUTH IN CUSTODY

A relatively small number of young offenders are sentenced to custody. This group of youth tend to have similar profiles. A survey ($N = 114$) of youth in custody in British Columbia found that many of the youth had experienced instability and various types of trauma in their lives, including the loss of a loved one (87 percent) and the loss of a family member or friend to violence (34 percent), suicide (32 percent), and overdose (30 percent). A majority of the youth surveyed had a history of involvement with the youth justice system.

Compared to youth who were not involved in the justice system, youth in custody were more likely to have been in government care, to have gone to bed hungry, and to have mental health, behavioural, and/or addiction issues, as well as to have been physically or sexually abused.[66]

Youth in custody are likely to have experienced problems or trauma in the family home resulting in their removal and placement in youth care. Many lack positive peer, school, and adult attachments in their lives.[67] Youth in custody may be more prone than their non-incarcerated peers to substance abuse, mental health disorders, learning disabilities, and HIV.[68]

Research studies have found that youth in custody are much more likely than youth in the general Canadian population to suffer from conduct disorders, abuse alcohol and drugs, have been diagnosed with depression, or have schizophrenia or FASD.[69] In addition, one in four youth in custody display symptoms of post-traumatic stress disorder (PTSD), as compared to less than 1 percent in the general youth population.

Interviews with young offenders in residential placements in Ontario ($N = 250$; 209 males, 39 young women, 2 no gender recorded) found that 48 percent had a history of involvement with the child welfare system, and of the 129 youth who responded to a question on previous non-custodial, out-of-home placements, 67 percent stated that they had been "in-care" at some point in the past.[70] An important issue is at what point the youth crossed over from the child welfare system to the youth justice system and the factors that were associated with this.[71]

INDIGENOUS YOUTH IN CUSTODY

Despite the overall reduction in the numbers of youth in custody, Indigenous youth (similar to their adult counterparts) continue to be overrepresented in

▼ Burnaby Youth Detention Centre

Arlen Redekop/Vancouver Sun. Material republished with the express permission of Postmedia Network Inc.

A PROFILE OF INDIGENOUS YOUNG WOMEN IN CUSTODY

A study ($N = 500$) of youth in custody in British Columbia found that, among the Indigenous young women

- 97 percent had left home early to live on their own, on the streets, or in foster care;
- 82 percent had been in foster care at some point;
- 80 percent reported childhood trauma, including physical abuse (80 percent), sexual abuse (65 percent), and mental health issues in the family (30 percent);
- 80 percent had been introduced to hard drug use at an early age; and
- Compared to non-Indigenous young women in custody, had spent more time in their lives in custody.

Source: R.R. Corrado and I.M. Cohen. 2002. "A Needs Profile of Serious and/or Violent Aboriginal Youth in Prison," *Forum on Corrections Research, 14*(3), 20–24.

youth correctional populations across Canada, with the greatest disparity experienced by Indigenous young women. See Research File 13.1.

The overrepresentation of Indigenous youth in custodial facilities highlights the need to examine whether existing policies and interventions are adequately addressing the risk and needs profiles of Indigenous young offenders.[72,73]

DOING TIME IN YOUTH CUSTODY FACILITIES

Young offenders in custody experience many of the same challenges and pains of imprisonment as their adult counterparts (discussed in Chapter 11). Youth in custody may be required to deal with bullying, threats, intimidation, and violence. Violence in youth institutions may include bullying, verbal threats, theft, intimidation, physical abuse, predatory aggression, and coercion.[74] Forty-three percent of the youth in custody in one secure facility received no visits from their family or friends while they were in custody, and 13 percent did not have any contact with their family or friends.[75]

Interviews with a sample of youth in custody ($N = 114$) found that 30 percent reported having been bullied or picked on by other youth, while 54 percent indicated having personally bullied or picked on another resident. In addition, 68 percent who had been victims of bullying also reported being a perpetrator.[76] Despite this, 62 percent of the youth always felt safe everywhere in the custody centre. The levels of peer violence appear to be lower in detention and custodial facilities that are more open.[77]

As in adult correctional institutions, youths' fear of victimization and of transgressing the inmate code may undermine treatment efforts.[78] As with their adult counterparts, little is known about the challenges that may be faced by LGBTQ youth in custody.

Youth custody facilities are not immune from disturbances. In March 2017, several young offenders were arrested following what was termed "a rebellion" at a residential youth centre in Sherbrooke, Quebec.[79] Similar to adult corrections, governments have been sued for mistreatment of youth in custody. In 2015, a $125 million lawsuit was filed against the province of Ontario for the alleged mistreatment of youth in Ontario jails.[80] The allegations included placing youth in solitary confinement for up to 15 days and denying youth access to legal counsel.

THE USE OF SOLITARY CONFINEMENT

▼ Solitary confinement cell in a youth facility

AP Photo/Bebeto Matthews, File

"[Secure isolation] turns you into crazy, mad angry people. People [staff] don't listen to you in there." One youth said, "[It] makes us go crazy in here. I have heard kids go crazy—yelling, punching walls until their knuckles bleed cause they can't take it anymore." (a youth's comments on secure isolation in an Ontario youth custody facility)[81]

Similar to the adult corrections system, the use of solitary confinement, most often referred to as "secure isolation," in youth custody facilities is highly controversial. In 2016, the College of Family Physicians of Canada urged governments to abolish its use, noting the significant impact on developing brains and the absence of any evidence that its use was effective.[82]

There is considerable variability across the country in the frequency with which solitary confinement is used for young offenders.[83] The rates are lowest in Atlantic Canada and highest in British Columbia.

A review of the use of secure isolation in Ontario youth custody facilities found that its use overall was declining but that there was variation across facilities, with some using it more than others and for lengthier periods of time. The study also found that, in some instances, youth were being kept in secure isolation beyond 24 hours, although Ontario legislation allows this for youth aged 16 and over. Concerns were also expressed about the impact of secure isolation on youth with mental health issues. The report highlighted the need to ensure that safeguards were in place to ensure that the use of secure isolation was properly monitored and the rights of youth were protected.[84]

TREATMENT PROGRAMS FOR YOUTH IN CUSTODY

The correctional intervention with young offenders begins with an assessment to identify risks and needs and to develop an appropriate correctional plan. Correctional programs can be general, offence-specific, or offender-specific.[85]

Youths in secure custody are provided with a wide range of individual and group programs, although the specific programs that are offered vary among facilities.[86] There are also medical and mental health services.

Education, counselling, and recreation programs are offered to all young offenders: offence-specific programs target certain offenders (e.g., sex offenders); offender-specific programs (e.g., for substance abuse issues) target individual risks and needs. To be effective, qualified staff must deliver custodial programming in an environment characterized by positive staff–youth relationships.[87]

Community-based interventions vary by province, but probation officers everywhere refer young offenders to community services, which range from detox centres to safe houses to psychiatric assessment facilities to educational and employment resources.

To address the trauma that many young offenders have experienced, several jurisdictions have implemented trauma-informed practices and programming into youth custodial centres. Initiating a trauma-informed approach requires agencies to address the effects of trauma on youth given the behaviours youth use to cope with previous trauma. Behaviours may include substance abuse, aggression, and self-injury, among others, and put youth at risk of becoming involved in the youth justice system.[88]

Youth who receive services (e.g., mental health services, vocational services, and the assistance of a caregiver) in custody have been found to have a decreased likelihood of recidivism in the community.[89]

Further, a meta-analysis of 195 studies investigating young offender treatment programs found that youth who participated in *any* form of treatment intervention were less likely to recidivate than youth who did not.[90]

Studies have found that control and punitive approaches focusing on surveillance and deterrence are less effective in reducing recidivism among young offenders than therapeutic approaches that involve skill development, counselling and mentoring, and restorative approaches.[91,92]

Incarcerated young women offenders typically have higher rates of disruptive disorders, major depression, PTSD, separation anxiety, trauma exposure, and comorbid conditions (e.g., depression, substance abuse, anxiety, and suicidality) than incarcerated young male offenders.[93,94]

The unique risk/needs profiles and characteristics of young women highlight the need for gender-specific programming. Evidence suggests, however, that the most effective programs in reducing young offender recidivism—gender-specific or not—are comprehensive, follow the RNR model, and target multiple risk factors.[95] Gender-specific programming may help achieve particular goals, such as empowerment and improved quality of life.[96] Further longitudinal research investigating girls' delinquency is required to develop effective programming for this offender population that reflects their unique socialization and development.

YOUTH–STAFF RELATIONSHIPS

The staff in youth custody facilities play an important role in the incarceration experience for youth. Youth may require emotional support and practical assistance from staff as they adjust to life in the institution. Positive relationships with staff—those based on fairness, respect, and mutual understanding—may alleviate depression, hopelessness, and anxiety among incarcerated young offenders.[97]

Staff can help to create a stable and secure environment where youth do not fear for their personal security. When the rules and boundaries are consistently enforced, positive social interaction can occur between staff and offenders.[98]

Youth who felt there was an adult connected to the custody centre who cared about them were more likely to report better health than those who did not feel that an adult connected to the centre cared. For example, they were more likely to rate their health as good or excellent (91 percent vs. 71 percent), as well as to think this would be their last time in custody (75 percent vs. 53 percent), to have post-secondary plans (64 percent vs. 23 percent), and to have future job aspirations (74 percent vs. 46 percent).[99]

Positive relationships with staff can also affect youth perceptions of whether they will succeed on release. Interviews with serious young offenders found that youth who reported having a release counsellor whose role was to assist them with their preparations for re-entry had lower recidivism rates than those who did not report having this relationship.[100] Further, there is evidence that youth who are involved in making decisions about their release plan are more likely than those who were not involved to know where to access help once they leave custody.[101]

The **Youth Level of Service/Case Management Inventory (YLS/CMI)** is the most extensively used risk/needs measurement tool in youth justice systems.[102] It is based on the RNR principles and is a variant of the Level of Service Inventory (LSI-R) used for adult offenders.[103,104]

Youth probation officers, psychologists, social workers, youth workers, and court workers use this risk/needs assessment tool to assess a youth's risk for general recidivism, to identify the factors that require intervention, and to develop a community supervision plan.[105,106]

Youth Level of Service/Case Management Inventory (YLS/CMI)

The primary risk/need assessment instrument in youth corrections.

THE ROLE OF PARENTS IN THE YOUTH JUSTICE PROCESS

The YCJA provides that the youth's parents should play a role in the justice process and should be encouraged to become involved in addressing the youth's issues and their rehabilitation. Studies that have examined the role of parents in bail hearings and sentencing in your court have found that, while the majority of parents attend the hearings, the information provided by parents did not have a significant impact on the outcomes of the case, with the exception of information provided on supervision and living arrangements at bail hearings.[107] For the most part, parents were bystanders to the court process.[108]

Parents have been found to rarely interact in court with their youth, the youth's lawyer, the Crown, or the judge.[109] Among the suggestions for changing this dynamic has been the creation of the position of "youth justice support worker" who would liaise with the parents, youths, and the justice system.[110]

These findings are due at least in part to the conflicting role of parents in the youth justice system: On one hand, the parents may be viewed as the source of the youth's problems; on the other hand, they are asked to be part of the solution.[111] Illustrative of the former is an exchange between a youth court judge, the youth's father, and the youth, recorded in a youth court in the Toronto area in a case involving a youth who had stolen a car and caused $300 damage:

Judge to Father: Why was this youth out at 12 midnight?

Father: Boys will be boys.

Judge to Father: Yes but I expect parents to be parents.

Father: Your honour I apologize for what my son has done.

Judge to Father: Then keep an eye on him.

Judge to Youth: Your father says boys will be boys. I say grow up.[112]

RESTORATIVE JUSTICE PROGRAMS FOR YOUTH OFFENDERS

Restorative justice initiatives can provide young offenders with the opportunity to make amends with those they have harmed and take responsibility for their behaviour. Victims are given a voice in the process, which promotes their healing, and the community comes together to support the victims and offenders in addressing the harms that have been caused and in achieving peace in the community. Many restorative programs for young offenders are limited to first-time, non-violent offenders, although some programs target more serious offenders.[113]

There are a variety of restorative justice initiatives for youth offenders across the country that are designed to facilitate reparation, reconciliation, and relationship building. These may be particularly beneficial for Indigenous youth offenders, since the programs incorporate elements of traditional Indigenous culture and spirituality. Many of the programs are operated by non-profit organizations.

Several of these initiatives are presented in Table 13.7. Note that for most of the programs, the impact on reoffending is unknown. Research does suggest that restorative justice programs can be effective for less serious offenders, as well as more serious offenders who may be older, have a previous record, and/or have committed property or violent offences.[114,115]

Non-profit organizations are also involved in operating a variety of programs and services for at-risk youth and youth involved in the justice system. The John Howard Society

TABLE 13.7

SELECTED RESTORATIVE JUSTICE PROGRAMS FOR YOUNG OFFENDERS

Initiative	Participants	Approach/Outcome
Calgary Aboriginal Youth Restorative Justice Committee (CAYRJC) (Calgary, Alberta)	Indigenous youth in conflict with the law, their families, the victims and their families, legal system personnel, and the community.	Establish a suitable and meaningful consequence for the criminal behaviour. Participants receive culturally relevant teachings from respected Elders.[a] Impact on reoffending unknown.
Victoria Restorative Justice Society (RJV, Victoria, B.C.)	Referrals from Victoria Police Department and Oak Bay Police, Crown counsel, Victoria Community Corrections, Insurance Corporation of BC, and members of the community. Diversion program deals with pre- or post-charge referrals; youth are held accountable without being legally convicted. Integrative restorative justice program deals with referrals at the pre- or post-sentencing stage; youth have been convicted.	Trained volunteers facilitate community justice conferences, panels, victim–offender mediation, peace-making circles. Programs include a support group for at-risk youth (Girls' Circle). RJV and the Victoria Police Department (VPD) examined the recidivism rates of the individuals ($N = 139$) referred to the program by VPD between 2011 and 2013 and who successfully completed the process. Twenty-seven youth reoffended (recidivism rate = 19.42 percent).[b,c]
Essex County Youth Justice Committee (Windsor, Ontario)	Alternative to formal youth court proceedings for youth aged 12 to 17 who have committed a minor offence; youth who accept responsibility and accountability for their actions.	Offenders, their families, the community volunteers (up to three on the youth justice committee), and the victims (by choice) come together to address the harm caused, victim harm/needs, and community wellness, and how to address the above. Potential sanctions include an apology, donation to charity, volunteer work, and/or attendance at programming or a presentation. Successful completion of sanctions means the police will not lay charges, or the court will withdraw charges.[d] Impact on reoffending unknown.
Island Community Justice Society (Nova Scotia)	Referrals for family group conferences (FGC) and victim–offender mediation (VOM) are accepted at multiple stages of the youth justice process: pre- and post-charge (police and Crown), post-conviction/pre-sentence (judges), and post-sentence (correctional services/victims' services). Referrals for accountability meetings are from police and Crown at the pre- or post-charge stage. For youth aged 12 to 17 in conflict with the law. Pre- and post-sentencing conferences can be requested.	Facilitate FGCs, VOMs, and accountability meetings. Deliver a community service order program. Promote offender accountability to address the harms caused. Provide victims with a voice in the process, and facilitate community support and input. Provide victim and volunteer support services.[e] Impact on reoffending unknown.
Restorative Circles Initiative (RCI; Saskatchewan)	Pre- and post-sentencing conferences can be requested by counsel but most often recommended by judge. Feasibility assessed and then RCI facilitator works with participants (victim, offender, family, and community) to promote understanding of the process and how to contribute meaningfully.	Approximately 30 conferences held per year. Typical purpose of conference is (a) promote victim-offender understanding, and (b) plan for offender's rehabilitation and reintegration in the community. Held in circular courtroom with movable furniture.[f] Impact on reoffending unknown.

[a] Native Counselling Services of Alberta. 2012. *Corrections and Restorative Justice.* Edmonton: Author. http://www.ncsa.ca/online/?page_id=46; Montreal Urban Aboriginal Community Strategy Network. 2012. *The Aboriginal Justice Research Project.* Montreal: Montreal Urban Aboriginal Strategy Network. http://www.crime-prevention-intl.org/uploads/media/Aboriginal_Justice_Research_Project_-_Final_Report.pdf.

[b] Restorative Justice Victoria. 2015. *Restorative Justice Victoria and the Victoria Police Department: Offender Recidivism Study.* Victoria: Author. https://rjvictoria.files.wordpress.com/2011/04/recidivism-results-2015-update.pdf.

[c] S. Warmald. 2011. *Victoria Restorative Justice Society: Annual Review 2010.* Victoria: Restorative Justice Victoria. http://rjvictoria.wordpress.com/about/annual-reports.

[d] Youth Diversion Essex County Diversion Program. n.d. *Youth Justice Committee.* Windsor, ON: Author. http://ecyouthdiversion.ca/programs/youth-justice-committee/.

[e] Island Community Justice Society. n.d. *Restorative Justice: How It Works.* Cape Breton, NS: Author. http://www.islandcommunityjustice.com/howitworks.html.

[f] S. Goldberg. 2011. *Problem-Solving in Canada's Courtrooms: A Guide to Therapeutic Justice.* Ottawa: National Judicial Council. http://www.sasklawcourts.ca/images/documents/Provincial_Court/Problem-Solving%20in%20Canada's%20Courtrooms.pdf.

of Ottawa, for example, provides accommodation and support to homeless youth and youth who have no permanent housing.[116] Also in Ottawa, the Boys and Girls Club of Ottawa operates a diversion program for youth that are referred to it by the police to complete an EJM or by Crown counsel as part of an EJS. Once referred, an assessment is conducted and a case management plan is developed. Youth engage in a variety of activities that include volunteer work, counselling, and job search skills, among others.[117]

RELEASE, RE-ENTRY AND REINTEGRATION OF YOUTH OFFENDERS

Youth offenders released from custody may experience many of the same pains of re-entry as adult offenders re-entering the community on conditional release. A study (N = 114) of youth leaving a custody facility in British Columbia found that while the majority (95 percent) were excited about being released, 31 percent were very nervous about leaving custody, and 11 percent did not want to leave. The majority (87 percent) had a place to live after they left custody, and 76 percent knew where to find assistance in the community.[118] And similar to their adult counterparts, it is important that there be *throughcare*—a seamless transition from the institution to the community in terms of programs and support.

AFTERCARE PROGRAMS

Aftercare programs are designed to address young offenders' unique needs and risks as they re-enter society. They combine community restraint elements with community service strategies to facilitate offender change and increase public safety.[119] Research studies have established the importance of providing young offenders with aftercare programming in community settings and at a lower intensity than the youth received in institutional settings.[120] These programs may be of particular value to older, more mature youth and for those who have committed more serious offences.[121]

THE ROLE OF INFORMAL SOCIAL SUPPORT NETWORKS

Informal social supports, including family and friends, can play a major role in assisting young offenders to re-enter and reintegrate into the community. The youth's peer group can be a source of support and assistance, although also a potential area of risk if the peer group is involved in law-violating behaviour. Young offenders may thus find themselves "walking a fine line" as they limit their contacts with their old social groups so as to avoid trouble, while working to develop a new sense of identity and belonging.[122]

Mentoring can also be a source of support for youths and assist in overcoming the challenges of re-entry, and is often a component of aftercare programming.[123,124] The support of family and program staff can increase the motivation of a young offender to change his or her behaviour and life direction.[125,126] Families are able to provide financial resources, emotional support, encouragement, and, potentially, employment. However, a youth's family may also pose challenges for young offenders, for the environment at home may encourage previous patterns of criminal behaviour.

THE COSTS OF YOUTH JUSTICE

In Chapter 3, it was noted that the criminal justice system is an expensive enterprise, particularly in relation to its effectiveness in preventing and responding to crime and addressing the needs of persons who come into conflict with the law. It is often said

FIGURE 13.4 ▶

The Story of Tyler: The High Costs
of an Offending Pathway

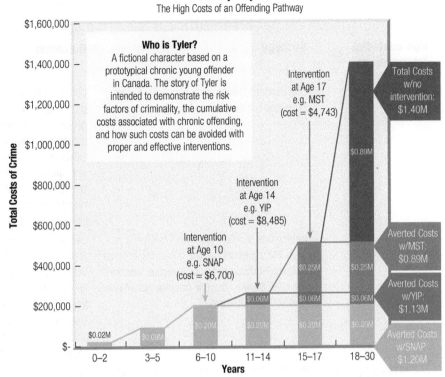

The Story of Tyler:
The High Costs of an Offending Pathway

Source: Public Safety Canada. 2016. "Tyler's Troubled Life: The Story of One Young Man's Paths towards a Life of Crime" [Research report 2016-R005]. Ottawa: Her Majesty the Queen in Right of Canada. https://www.publicsafety.gc.ca/cnt/rsrcs/pblctns/2016-r005/2016-r005-en.pdf. This information was reproduced with the permission of the Minister of Public Safety and Emergency Preparedness Canada, 2017.

that some offenders are "million-dollar persons" for the amount of money that has been spent on processing them through the justice system, including, in some instances, incarceration.

The youth justice system is also costly. Figure 13.4 sets out the costs associated with one offender, "Tyler" (a fictional youth), from an early age into adulthood. Note that these are only "direct" costs—for example, the costs of criminal justice, health care, and social services. Indirect costs, including the pain and suffering of victims, are not included. A key takeaway from Figure 13.4 is that money is being expended on youth but that less costly and more effective interventions are available. In Tyler's case, the SNAP (Stop Now and Plan) program, YIP (Youth Inclusion Program), and MST (multisystemic therapy) are noted as cost-effective interventions at various stages of his childhood and during his young adulthood that may have had a significant impact on his offending pathway.

THE EFFECTIVENESS OF INTERVENTIONS WITH YOUTH OFFENDERS

Materials on the effectiveness of selected interventions are presented in Research File 13.2.

THE EFFECTIVENESS OF SELECTED YOUTH JUSTICE INTERVENTIONS

Non-custodial Interventions	Strategy	Outcomes
Diversion (EJM)	EJM designed to keep youth from being further processed into the youth justice system.	Can be effective in reducing reoffending.[a] Some EJM programs appear to be more effective than others. Evidence of net-widening in some jurisdictions.[b] Certain groups of youth may be more likely to be diverted—one study of a police service in the Greater Toronto Area found that Black youth were more likely to be charged by police and less likely to be cautioned than White youth.[c] Pre-charge interventions based on restorative justice and those that involve family interventions are the most promising.[d]
Boot camps	Intermediate sanction. Short-term residential program. Military model involves demanding exercise routines. Emphasis on labour, discipline, exercise, and drills. Some incorporate cognitive behavioural treatment and aftercare.	Generally, do not have an impact on reoffending unless young offenders are voluntary participants. May increase the likelihood of further crime. Participants in some programs have had higher recidivism rates than those subject to other forms of treatment, including discipline-oriented programs. May improve young offenders' attitudes and impact their adjustment while in the facility. Young offenders view boot camps more favourably than correctional facilities.[e]
Scared Straight programs	Popular in the U.S. Target at-risk youth or youth who have come into conflict with the law, who are taken into correctional institutions for a "sit down" with inmates, who share their stories. Objective is to "scare youth straight," to deter youth from criminal behaviour by showing them the punitive nature of imprisonment.	Programs are ineffective as a general or specific deterrent to future offending, and the program has been found to have a criminogenic effect on youth.[f]
Probation	The most frequently used court intervention. Places youth under supervision in the community, subject to general and, often, specific conditions designed to address their risk and needs.	The effectiveness of probation is enhanced when the principles of RNR are followed (e.g., low-intensity supervision for low-risk young offenders and high-intensity supervision for higher-risk youth).[g]
Open custody and open detention facilities	Provide optimal programming opportunities for youth, prosocial role modelling opportunities, and community reintegration. Middle of the continuum between containment and reintegration.	Evaluation in Ontario found that these facilities can function as transitional programming to facilitate youth reintegration and opportunities for prosocial modelling and relationships between staff and youth.[h] Impact on reoffending unknown.
Intensive rehabilitative custody and supervision (IRCS)	Objectives include appropriate use of courts and correctional institutions for young offenders, as well as proportionality in the youth justice system's response to the offence and offender's level of responsibility. Greater opportunities for social reintegration and rehabilitation.	IRCS has increased the ability of provincial and territorial youth justice systems to provide programming for young serious violent offenders with mental health issues. Each jurisdiction has developed the capacity to administer IRCS sentences.[i] Impact on reoffending unknown.

[a] H.W. Wilson and R.D. Hoge. 2013. "Diverting Our Attention to What Works: Evaluating the Effectiveness of a Youth Diversion Program: A Meta-Analytic Review," *Youth Violence and Juvenile Justice*, 11(4), 313–331.

[b] C.T. Greene. 2011. "Creating Consensus: An Exploration of Two Pre-Charge Diversion Programs in Canada." Unpublished PhD dissertation. Toronto: University of Toronto. https://tspace.library.utoronto.ca/bitstream/1807/29733/11/Greene_Carolyn_T_201106_PhD_Thesis.pdf.

[c] K. Samuels. 2015. "Examining the Utility of Pre-Charge Youth Diversion Programs: A Canadian Context." Unpublished MA thesis. Toronto: University of Ontario Institute of Technology. https://ir.library.dc-uoit.ca/bitstream/10155/539/1/Samuels_Kanika.pdf.

(continued)

d C.S. Schwalbe, R.E. Gearing, M.J. MacKenzie, K.B. Brewer, and R. Ibrahim. 2012. "A Meta-Analysis of Experimental Studies of Diversion Programs for Juvenile Offenders," *Clinical Psychology Review, 32*(1), 26–33.

e B. Meade and B. Steiner. 2010. "The Total Effects of Boot Camps That House Juveniles: A Systematic Review of the Evidence," *Journal of Criminal Justice, 38*(5), 841–853.

f P.M. Klenowski, K.J. Bell, and K.D. Dodson. 2010. "An Empirical Evaluation of Juvenile Awareness Programs in the United States: Can Juveniles Be 'Scared Straight'?" *Journal of Offender Rehabilitation, 49*(4), 254–272.

g D. Luong and S. Wormith. 2011. "Applying Risk/Need Assessment to Probation Practice and Its Impact on the Recidivism of Young Offenders," *Criminal Justice and Behavior, 38*(12), 1177–1199.

h D. Cooke and J. Finlay. 2007. *Open Detention and Open Custody in Ontario.* Toronto: Office of Child and Family Service Advocacy. https://provincialadvocate.on.ca/documents/en/Open%20Custody-OpenDetention%20Review.pdf.

i Department of Justice Canada. 2010. *The Youth Justice Initiative Funding Components Evaluation: Final Report.* Ottawa: Evaluation Division, Office of Strategic Planning and Performance Management. http://www.justice.gc.ca/eng/rp-pr/cp-pm/eval/rep-rap/11/yjifc-vfijj/yjifc-vfijj.pdf.

SUMMARY

The materials in this chapter focused on the Canadian youth justice system. The three legislative acts that have provided the framework for the response to youth in conflict with the law since 1908 were discussed, as were the various programs that are designed to meet the needs of at-risk and justice-system-involved youth. The four levels of the youth justice system were described, each representing an escalation in the sanctions that are applied to young offenders. There are a number of strategies used to keep youth out of the formal justice system and to involve community members in working with youth. The operation of the youth court was discussed, as were the non-custodial and custodial sentencing options available to youth court judges. The experiences of youth in custody and on release in the community were discussed. A number of restorative justice programs for young offenders were identified and discussed.

KEY POINTS REVIEW

1. The legislation that has provided the framework for the youth justice system since 1908 reflects differing philosophies as to the causes and appropriate response to young offenders.

2. Across the country, there are a variety of programs and services operated by the provincial and territorial governments and not-for-profit organizations for at-risk youth and youth involved in the justice system.

3. There are differences between the adult and youth criminal justice systems.

4. The four levels of the sanctions in the youth justice system are extrajudicial measures, extrajudicial sanctions, probation, and custody.

5. Youth justice committees and youth justice conferences are two ways in which the community is involved in the youth justice system.

6. Special challenges may be encountered in the youth justice system by Indigenous, Black, and LGBTQ youth.

7. There are a variety of non-custodial and custodial sentencing options for young offenders.

8. Probation is the most frequently imposed sanction in the youth courts.

9. Young offenders in custody experience many of the same challenges and pains of imprisonment at their adult counterparts, including violence, bullying, the loss of freedom, and high levels of anxiety due to severed family and social ties.

10. Correctional officers play a key role in the incarceration experience for youth; positive relationships with staff members may alleviate depression, hopelessness, and anxiety among incarcerated young offenders.

11. There are issues surrounding the use of solitary confinement for youth in custody.

12. Treatment interventions for young offenders are delivered both in the community and in custodial facilities.

13. Restorative justice programs can provide young offenders with the opportunity to make amends with those they have harmed and to take responsibility for their behaviour.

14. Young offenders released from custody may experience many of the same pains of re-entry as adult offenders.

15. The most effective correctional programs offered to young offenders in community and institutional settings are those that incorporate cognitive-behavioural strategies, education, and vocational skills.

KEY TERM QUESTIONS

1. Compare and contrast the *Juvenile Delinquents Act*, *Young Offenders Act*, and the *Youth Criminal Justice Act*, and note the philosophy and approach of each.

2. Describe the use of **extrajudicial measures (EJM)** and **extrajudicial sanctions (EJS)** in the youth justice system.

3. Describe the role of **youth justice conferences** and **youth justice committees** in the youth justice system.

4. Identify and discuss the purpose of **integrated case management conferences** in the youth probation system and of the **Youth Level of Service/Case Management Inventory (YLS/CMI)**.

CRITICAL THINKING EXERCISES

Critical Thinking Exercise 13.1

"Tyler's Troubled Life: The Story of One Young Man's Path towards a Life of Crime"

An important consideration in the study of young offenders is understanding their offending pathway—that is, the events and situations that contributed to their initial and continuing involvement in offending behaviour and the youth justice system. An examination of a young offender's offending pathway provides insights into what interventions could have been taken to address his or her issues and reduce the likelihood of reoffending. Read "Tyler's Troubled Life: The Story of One Young Man's Path towards a Life of Crime" at https://www.publicsafety.gc.ca/cnt/rsrcs/pblctns/2016-r005/2016-r005-en.pdf.

Your Thoughts?

1. What were the critical turning points in Tyler's life?

2. What are the lessons learned from his case that could be used to reform youth justice policies?

Critical Thinking Exercise 13.2

Programs for At-Risk Youth

Find out about the programs that are offered for at-risk youth in (a) your community and (b) your province or territory.

Your Thoughts?

1. What is the range of programs that are offered?

2. What is the philosophy/approach of the programs?

3. What gaps do there appear to be in the types of programs that are offered?

CLASS/GROUP DISCUSSION EXERCISE

Class/Group Discussion 13.1

Incarcerated Young Offenders in the U.S.

The film *They Call Us Monsters*, available on Netflix, documents the lives of youth offenders in "The Compound," a youth custody facility in Los Angeles. The film focuses on three of the youth who are awaiting trial as adults. After watching the film, access the article "Juan and Jarad Write from Prison" at http://www.pbs.org/independentlens/blog/juan-jarad -they-call-us-monsters-send-update-letter.

Your Thoughts?

1. What issues are raised by the film *They Call Us Monsters*?

2. What options might exist to the current manner in which youth who have committed serious crimes are handled?

MEDIA LINKS

"Homeless Toronto Kid," August 16, 2016, https://www.youtube.com/watch?v =aB6K7Bt9KKQ

Youth Justice System

"Youth Justice Committees—Calgary Youth Justice Society," June 8, 2012, https://www .youtube.com/watch?v=IM0t2tnfJio

"Restorative vs. Retributive Justice in Vermont and New Zealand: A Case Study Comparison," July 3, 2009, www.youtube.com/watch?v=s967kBKEJowandfeature =related

REFERENCES

1. M. Alain and S. Hamel. 2016. "The Situation in Quebec, 'Vive la difference'?" in *Implementing and Working with the Youth Criminal Justice Act across Canada*, edited by M. Alain, R.R. Corrado, and S. Reid, 299–330. Toronto: University of Toronto Press.

2. B. DeGusti, L. MacRae, M. Vallée, T. Caputo, and J.P. Hornick. 2009. *Best Practices for Chronic/Persistent Offenders in Canada: Summary Report*. Ottawa. Public Safety Canada, p. 6. https://www.publicsafety.gc.ca/cnt/ rsrcs/pblctns/prstnt-ffndrs/prstnt-ffndrs-eng.pdf.

3. Ibid., p. 7.

4. Ibid.

5. Ibid., p. 10.

6. United Nations Human Rights Office of the High Commissioner. 2017. Convention on the Rights of the Child. http://www.ohchr.org/EN/ProfessionalInterest/Pages/ CRC.aspx.

7. United Nations Human Rights Office of the High Commissioner. 1989. Convention on the Rights of the Child: Article 2.1. http://www.ohchr.org/EN/ProfessionalInterest/ Pages/CRC.aspx.

8. Ibid., Article 3.1.

9. Society for Children and Youth of BC. 2015. *Realizing Rights—Responding to Needs. Youth with Disabilities in Conflict with the Law in British Columbia. Discussion Paper*. Vancouver: Author, p. 14. http://www.scyofbc.org/wp-content/uploads/2016/05/Youth-Justice-and-Disability-Discussion-Paper.pdf.

10. S.A. Kidd, S. Gaetz, and B. O'Grady. 2017. "The 2015 National Canadian Homeless Youth Survey: Mental Health and Addiction Findings," *Canadian Journal of Psychiatry*, 62(7), 493–500.

11. T.L. Grande, J. Hallman, B. Rutledge, K. Caldwell, B. Upton, L.A. Underwood, . . . M. Rehfuss. 2012. "Examining Mental Health Symptoms in Male and Female Incarcerated Juveniles," *Behavioral Sciences and the Law*, 30(3), 365–369.

12. C.A. Garcia, and J. Lane. 2012. "Dealing with the Fall-Out: Identifying and Addressing the Role that Relationship Strain Plays in the Lives of Girls in the Juvenile Justice System," *Journal of Criminal Justice*, 40(3), 259–267.

13. Society for Children and Youth of BC, *Realizing Rights—Responding to Needs*.

14. Ontario Ministry of Children and Youth Services. n.d. "Success Stories." http://www.children.gov.on.ca/htdocs/English/professionals/oyap/stories.aspx.

15. DeGusti et al., *Best Practices for Chronic/Persistent Offenders in Canada*, p. 9.

16. E. Woollard and J. Chant. 2010. *Realizing Rights—Responding to Needs: Youth with Disabilities in Conflict with the Law. British Columbia Community Consultation*. Vancouver: Society for Children and Youth of BC, p. 6. http://www.scyofbc.org/wp-content/uploads/2016/05/Full-Report-Responding-to-Needs-YWDCWL-Report-on-Community-Consultations.pdf.

17. C.T. Greene. 2011. "Creating Consensus: An Exploration of Two Pre-Charge Diversion Programs in Canada." Unpublished PhD dissertation. Toronto: University of Toronto. https://tspace.library.utoronto.ca/bitstream/1807/29733/11/Greene_Carolyn_T_201106_PhD_Thesis.pdf.

18. S. Moyer and M. Basic. 2004. *Crown Decision-Making Under the Youth Criminal Justice Act*. Ottawa: Department of Justice Canada. http://www.justice.gc.ca/eng/rp-pr/cj-jp/yj-jj/pdf/decision.pdf.

19. Greene, "Creating Consensus: An Exploration of Two Pre-Charge Diversion Programs in Canada."

20. Ibid.

21. Ibid.

22. Centre for Children and Families in the Justice System. n.d. "Youth Mental Health Court Court Worker Program of the Youth Therapeutic Court (YTC)." London, ON: Author. http://www.lfcc.on.ca/wp-content/uploads/2015/04/YTC-Outline.pdf.

23. Department of Justice Canada. 2013. *The Youth Criminal Justice Act: Summary and Background*. Ottawa: Author, p. 6. http://www.justice.gc.ca/eng/cj-jp/yj-jj/tools-outils/pdf/back-hist.pdf.

24. Alberta Justice and Solicitor General. n.d. "Youth Justice Committees—Becoming Involved." https://www.solgps.alberta.ca/programs_and_services/correctional_services/young_offenders/youth_justice_committees/Pages/default.aspx.

25. Calgary Youth Justice Society. 2010. "The Value of a Community—Based Approach to Youth Crime." http://calgaryyouthjustice.ca/what-we-do/measuring-success.

26. R. Smandych, M. Dyck, C. La Berge, and J. Koffman. 2016. "Youth Justice in Manitoba: Developments and Issues Under the YCJA," in *Implementing and Working with the Youth Criminal Justice Act across Canada*, edited by M. Alain, R.R. Corrado, and S. Reid, 86–124. Toronto: University of Toronto Press, p. 102.

27. Z. Miladinovic. 2016. "Youth Court Statistics in Canada, 2014/2015," *Juristat*, 36(1). Statistics Canada Catalogue no. 85-002-X. Ottawa: Minister of Industry. http://www.statcan.gc.ca/pub/85-002-x/2016001/article/14656-eng.pdf.

28. Department of Justice Canada, *The Youth Criminal Justice Act: Summary and Background*, p. 5.

29. Miladinovic, "Youth Court Statistics in Canada, 2014/2015," p. 14.

30. R.R. Corrado and L.F. Freedman. 2011. *Youth At-Risk of Serious and Life-Course Offending*. Ottawa: Public Safety Canada. https://www.publicsafety.gc.ca/cnt/rsrcs/pblctns/lf-crs-ffndng/index-en.aspx.

31. D.M. Day, J.D. Nielsen, A.K. Ward, Y. Sun, J.S. Rosenthal, T. Duchesne, . . . L. Rossman. 2012. "Long-Term Follow-Up of Criminal Activity with Adjudicated Youth in Ontario: Identifying Offence Trajectories and Predictors/Correlates of Trajectory Group Membership," *Canadian Journal of Criminology and Criminal Justice*, 54(4), 377–413.

32. Department of Justice Canada. n.d. "Pre-Trial Detention." http://www.justice.gc.ca/eng/cj-jp/yj-jj/tools-outils/sheets-feuillets/pdf/deten-deten.pdf.

33. Ibid.

34. J.B. Sprott. 2012. "The Persistence of 'Status Offences' in the Youth Justice System," *Canadian Journal of Criminology and Criminal Justice*, 54(3), 309–322.

35. J.B. Sprott and N. Myers. 2011. "Set Up to Fail: The Unintended Consequences of Multiple Bail Conditions," *Canadian Journal of Criminology and Criminal Justice,* 53(4), 404–423.

36. Ibid.

37. J.B. Sprott and J. Sutherland. 2015. "Unintended Consequences of Multiple Bail Conditions for Youth," *Canadian Journal of Criminology and Criminal Justice,* 57(1), 59–81.

38. J. Malakieh. 2017. "Youth Correctional Statistics in Canada, 2015/2016," *Juristat,* 37(1). Statistics Canada Catalogue no. 85-002-X. Ottawa: Minister of Industry. http://www.statcan.gc.ca/pub/85-002-x/2017001/article/14702-eng.pdf.

39. S. Alam. 2015. "Youth Court Statistics in Canada, 2013/2014," *Juristat,* 35(1). Statistics Canada Catalogue no. 85-002-X. Ottawa: Minister of Industry. http://www.statcan.gc.ca/pub/85-002-x/2015001/article/14224-eng.pdf.

40. Development Services Group, Inc. 2014. "LGBTQ Youths in the Juvenile Justice System," *Literature Review.* Washington, DC: Office of Juvenile Justice and Delinquency Prevention. https://www.ojjdp.gov/mpg/litreviews/LGBTQYouthsintheJuvenileJusticeSystem.pdf.

41. K.E.W. Himmelstein and H. Brückner. 2011. "Criminal-Justice and School Sanctions against Nonheterosexual Youth: A National Longitudinal Study," *Pediatrics,* 127(1), 49–57.

42. Malakieh, "Youth Correctional Statistics in Canada, 2015/2016."

43. J. Rankin, P. Winsa, and H. Ng. 2013, March 1. "Unequal Justice: Aboriginal and Black Inmates Disproportionately Fill Ontario Jails," *Toronto Star.* https://www.thestar.com/news/insight/2013/03/01/unequal_justice_aboriginal_and_black_inmates_disproportionately_fill_ontario_jails.html.

44. Ibid.

45. J. Latimer and L.C. Foss. 2004. *A One Day Snapshot of Aboriginal Youth in Custody Across Canada: Phase II.* Ottawa: Department of Justice Canada, Research and Statistics Division, Youth Justice Policy. http://www.justice.gc.ca/eng/rp-pr/cj-jp/yj-jj/yj2-jj2/yj2.pdf.

46. R.R. Corrado, S. Kuehn, and I. Margaritescu. 2014. "Policy Issues Regarding the Over-Representation of Incarcerated Aboriginal Young Offenders in a Canadian Context," *Youth Justice,* 14(1), 40–62.

47. S.J. Bell. 2012. *Young Offenders and Youth Justice: A Century After the Fact* (4th ed.). Toronto: Nelson.

48. National Crime Prevention Centre. 2012. *A Statistical Snapshot of Youth at Risk and Youth Offending in Canada.* Ottawa: Public Safety Canada, p. 9. https://www.publicsafety.gc.ca/cnt/rsrcs/pblctns/ststclsnpsht-yth/ssyr-eng.pdf.

49. R.R. Corrado and A. Markwart. 2016. "Introduction. Successes and Challenges in Implementing the YCJA: A Decade Later," in *Implementing and Working with the Youth Criminal Justice Act across Canada,* edited by M. Alain, R. R. Corrado, and S. Reid, 3–22. Toronto: University of Toronto Press.

50. N. Jackson. 2015. "Aboriginal Youth Overrepresentation in Canadian Correctional Services: Judicial and Non-Judicial Actors and Influence," *Alberta Law Review,* 52(4), 927–947.

51. S. Luck. 2016, May 20. "Black, Indigenous Prisoners Over-Represented in Nova Scotian Jails," *CBC News.* http://www.cbc.ca/news/canada/nova-scotia/black-indigenous-prisoners-nova-scotia-jails-1.3591535.

52. Rankin, Winsa, and Ng, "Unequal Justice: Aboriginal and Black Inmates Disproportionately Fill Ontario Jails."

53. Department of Justice Canada, *The Youth Criminal Justice Act: Summary and Background,* p. 10.

54. Smandych et al., "Youth Justice in Manitoba: Developments and Issues Under the YCJA," p. 111.

55. Ibid., p. 108.

56. J. Umamaheswar. 2012. "Bringing Hope and Change: A Study of Youth Probation Officers in Toronto," *International Journal of Offender Therapy and Comparative Criminology,* 57(9), 1158–1182 at p. 1169.

57. Ibid.

58. D. Luong and S. Wormith. 2011. "Applying Risk/Need Assessment to Probation Practice and Its Impact on the Recidivism of Young Offenders," *Criminal Justice and Behavior,* 38(12), 1177–1199.

59. S. Maroney. 2011. *Through the Glass.* Toronto: Doubleday Canada, p. 245.

60. Department of Justice Canada. 2015. "Sentencing of Young Persons." http://www.justice.gc.ca/eng/cj-jp/yj-jj/tools-outils/sheets-feuillets/syp-dpaa.html.

61. Department of Justice Canada, *The Youth Criminal Justice Act: Summary and Background,* p. 11.

62. Malakieh, "Youth Correctional Statistics in Canada, 2015/2016," p. 12.

63. M. Wiles. 2016, June 8. "Number of Youth at N.W.T. Young Offender Facility Drops to Record Low," *CBC News.* http://www.cbc.ca/news/canada/north/nwt-youth-at-young-offender-facility-drops-1.3621363.

64. Malakieh, "Youth Correctional Statistics in Canada, 2015/2016," p. 13.

65. H. Polischuk. 2017, July 6. "Teen Sentenced as Adult, Given Life in Prison for Murdering 16-Year-Old Ex-Girlfriend," *Toronto Star*. http://www.torontosun.com/2017/07/05/teen-sentenced-as-adult-given-life-in-prison-for-murdering-16-year-old-ex-girlfriend.

66. A. Smith, K. Cox, C. Poon, D. Stewart, and McCreary Centre Society. 2013. *Time Out III: A Profile of BC Youth in Custody*. Vancouver: McCreary Centre Society. http://www.mcs.bc.ca/pdf/Time_Out_III.pdf.

67. B.C. Representative for Children and Youth and B.C. Office of the Provincial Health Officer. 2009. *Kids, Crime, and Care: Health and Well-Being of Children in Care: Youth Justice Experiences and Outcomes*. Victoria: Author. https://www.rcybc.ca/sites/default/files/documents/pdf/reports_publications/kids_crime_and_care.pdf.

68. A.J. Sedlak and K. S. McPherson. 2010. *Youth's Needs and Services: Findings from the Survey of Youth in Residential Placement*. Washington, DC: Office of Juvenile Justice and Delinquency Prevention. https://www.ncjrs.gov/pdffiles1/ojjdp/227728.pdf.

69. Rankin, Winsa, and Ng, "Unequal Justice: Aboriginal and Black Inmates Disproportionately Fill Ontario Jails."

70. 70. D. Cooke and J. Finlay. 2007. *Open Detention and Open Custody in Ontario*. Toronto: Office of Child and Family Service Advocacy, p. 18. https://provincialadvocate.on.ca/documents/en/Open%20Custody-OpenDetention%20Review.pdf.

71. Ibid.

72. Greene, "Creating Consensus: An Exploration of Two Pre-Charge Diversion Programs in Canada."

73. Jackson, "Aboriginal Youth Overrepresentation in Canadian Correctional Services."

74. G. Beck. 1995. "Bullying among Young Offenders in Custody," *Issues in Criminological and Legal Psychology*, 22, 54–70.

75. Smith et al., *Time Out III: A Profile of BC Youth in Custody*, pp. 39, 41, 46.

76. Ibid., p. 39.

77. Cooke and Finlay, *Open Detention and Open Custody in Ontario*, p. 29.

78. A. Kupchik. 2007. "The Correctional Experiences of Youth in Adult and Juvenile Prisons," *Justice Quarterly*, 24(2), 247–270.

79. Canadian Press. 2017, March 22. "Six Teens Arrested after Revolt in Sherbrooke Youth Centre," *CTV News*. http://montreal.ctvnews.ca/six-teens-arrested-after-revolt-in-sherbrooke-youth-centre-1.3335673.

80. K. Dubinski. 2015, November 4. "Ontario Faces $125 Million Claim Over Allegations of Mistreatment of Children and Teens in Youth Jails," *London Free Press*. http://www.lfpress.com/2015/11/04/class-action-lawsuit-launched-against-ontario-for-treatment-in-youth-jails.

81. Office of the Provincial Advocate for Children and Youth of Ontario. 2015. *It's a Matter of Time. Systemic Review of Secure Isolation in Ontario Youth Justice Facilities*. Toronto: Author, p. 44. https://provincialadvocate.on.ca/documents/en/SIU_Report_2015_En.pdf.

82. R. Browne. 2017, June 23. "New Numbers Reveal How Often Solitary Confinement Is Used against Young Offenders in Canada," *Vice News*. https://news.vice.com/story/new-numbers-reveal-how-often-solitary-confinement-is-used-against-young-offenders-in-canada.

83. Ibid.

84. Office of the Provincial Advocate for Children and Youth of Ontario. *It's a Matter of Time*, p. 9.

85. Bell, *Young Offenders and Youth Justice: A Century After the Fact*.

86. C. Hincks and J. Winterdyk. 2016. "The Youth Justice System: An Alberta Overview," in *Implementing and Working with the Youth Criminal Justice Act across Canada*, edited by M. Alain, R.R. Corrado, and S. Reid, 41–62. Toronto: University of Toronto Press.

87. C.T. Lowenkamp, M.D. Makarios, E.J. Latessa, R. Lemke, and P. Smith. 2010. "Community Corrections Facilities for Juvenile Offenders in Ohio: An Examination of Treatment Integrity and Recidivism," *Criminal Justice and Behavior*, 37(6), 695–708.

88. E.M. Espinosa, J.R. Sorensen, and M.A. Lopez. 2013. "Youth Pathways to Placement: The Influence of Gender, Mental Health Need and Trauma on Confinement in the Juvenile Justice System," *Journal of Youth Adolescence*, 42(2), 1824–1836.

89. C.A. Schubert, E.P. Mulvey, T.A. Loughran, and S.H. Losoya. 2012. "Perceptions of Institutional Experience and Community Outcomes for Serious Adolescent Offenders," *Criminal Justice and Behavior*, 39(1), 71–93.

90. J. Latimer, C. Dowden, and K.E. Morton-Bourgon. 2003. *Treating Youth in Conflict with the Law: A New Meta-Analysis*. Ottawa: Department of Justice Canada. http://www.justice.gc.ca/eng/rp-pr/cj-jp/yj-jj/rr03_yj3-rr03_jj3/rr03_yj3.pdf.

91. J.R. Adler, S.K. Edwards, M. Scally, D. Gill, M.J. Puniskis, A. Gekoski, and M.A.H. Horvath. 2016. *What Works in Managing Young People Who Offend? A Summary of the International Evidence*. London, UK: Ministry of Justice.

https://www.gov.uk/government/uploads/system/uploads/attachment_data/file/498493/what-works-in-managing-young-people-who-offend.pdf.

92. M. Evans-Chase and H. Zhou. 2014. "A Systematic Review of the Juvenile Justice Literature: What It Can (and Cannot) Tell Us about What Works with Delinquent Youth," *Crime & Delinquency*, 60(3), 451–470.

93. D.W. Foy, I.K. Ritchie, I. K., and A.H. Conway. 2012. "Trauma Exposure, Posttraumatic Stress, and Comorbidities in Female Adolescent Offenders: Findings and Implications from Recent Studies," *European Journal of Pscyhotraumatology*, 3(1), 1–13.

94. K.M. McCabe, A.E. Lansing, A. Garland, and R. Hough. 2002. "Differences in Psychopathology, Functional Impairment, and Familial Risk Factors among Adjudicated Delinquents," *Journal of American Academy of Child and Adolescent Psychiatry*, 41(7), 860–867.

95. M.A. Zahn, J.C. Day, S.F. Mihalic, and L. Tichavsky. 2009. "Determining What Works for Girls in the Juvenile Justice System: A Summary of Evaluation Evidence," *Crime and Delinquency*, 55(2), 266–293.

96. D. Hubbard and B. Matthews. 2008. "Reconciling the Differences Between the 'Gender-Responsive' and the 'What Works' Literatures to Improve Services for Girls," *Crime and Delinquency*, 54(2), 225–258.

97. Adler et al., *What Works in Managing Young People Who Offend?*

98. C. Cesaroni and M. Peterson-Badali. 2010. "Understanding the Adjustment of Incarcerated Young Offenders: A Canadian Example," *Youth Justice*, 10(2), 107–125.

99. Smith et al., *Time Out III: A Profile of BC Youth in Custody*.

100. Schubert et al., "Perceptions of Institutional Experience and Community Outcomes for Serious Adolescent Offenders."

101. Smith et al., *Time Out III: A Profile of BC Youth in Custody*.

102. R.D. Hoge and D. A. Andrews. 2002. *Youth Level of Service/Case Management Inventory (YLS/CMI)*. Toronto: Multi-Health Systems. https://www.mhs.com/MHS-Publicsafety?prodname=yls-cmi.

103. K. Olver, C. Stockdale, and J.S. Wormith. 2009. "Risk Assessment with Young Offenders: A Meta-Analysis of Three Assessment Measures," *Criminal Justice and Behavior*, 36(4), 329–353.

104. N.A. Vitopoulos, M. Peterson-Badali, and T.A. Skilling. 2012. "The Relationship between Matching Service to Criminogenic Need and Recidivism in Male and Female Youth: Examining the RNR Principles in Practice," *Criminal Justice and Behavior*, 39(8), 1025–1041.

105. L. Brogan, E. Haney-Caron, A. NeMoyer, and D. DeMatteo. 2015. "Applying the Risk-Needs-Responsivity (RNR) Model to Juvenile Justice," *Criminal Justice Review*, 40(3), 277–302.

106. F. Schmidt, S.M. Sinclair, and S. Thomasdóttir. 2016. "Predictive Validity of the Youth Level of Service/Case Management Inventory with Youth Who Have Committed Sexual and Non-Sexual Offenses: The Utility of Professional Override," *Criminal Justice and Behavior*, 43(3), 413-430.

107. K.N. Varma. 2007. "Parental Involvement in Youth Court," *Canadian Journal of Criminology and Criminal Justice*, 49(2), 231–260 at p. 252.

108. M. Peterson-Badali and J. Broeking. 2010. "Parents' Involvement in the Youth Justice System: Rhetoric and Reality," *Canadian Journal of Criminology and Criminal Justice*, 52(1), 1–27 at p. 19.

109. Ibid.

110. Ibid., p. 21.

111. Varma, "Parental Involvement in Youth Court," p. 235.

112. Ibid., p. 248.

113. Canadian Resource Centre for Victims of Crime. 2011. *Restorative Justice in Canada: What Victims Should Know*. Ottawa: Author. http://www.rjlillooet.ca/documents/restjust.pdf.

114. K.J. Bergseth and J.A. Bouffard. 2012. "Examining the Effectiveness of a Restorative Justice Program for Various Types of Juvenile Offenders," *International Journal of Offender Therapy and Comparative Criminology*, 57(9), 1054–1075.

115. K.N. Hipple, J. Gruenewald, and D.F. McGarrell. 2015. "Restorativeness, Procedural Justice, and Defiance as Long-Term Predictors of Reoffending of Participants in Family Group Conferences," *Criminal Justice and Behavior*, 42(11), 1110–1127.

116. John Howard Society of Ottawa. 2017. "Youth Housing." http://johnhoward.on.ca/ottawa/services/housing.

117. Boys and Girls Club of Ottawa. 2017. "Diversion." http://www.bgcottawa.org/child-youth-programs/community-support-programs/diversion.

118. Smith et al., *Time Out III: A Profile of BC Youth in Custody*, p. 50.

119. J.A. Bouffard and K. J. Bergseth, 2008. "The Impact on Reentry Services on Juvenile Offenders' Recidivism," *Youth Violence and Juvenile Justice*, 6(3), 295–318.

120. P.R. Jones and B.R. Wyant. 2007. "Target Juvenile Needs to Reduce Delinquency," *Criminology and Public Policy*, 6(4), 763–771.

121. R.D. Weaver and D. Campbell. 2015. "Fresh Start: A Meta-Analysis of Aftercare Programs for Juvenile Offenders," *Research on Social Work Practice*, 25(2), 201–212.

122. D.J. Martinez and L. S. Abrams. 2013. "Informal Social Support among Returning Young Offenders: A Metasynthesis of the Literature," *International Journal of Offender Therapy and Comparative Criminology*, 57(2),169–190.

123. L.S. Abrams, M.L. Mizel, V. Nguyen, and A. Shlonsky. 2014. "Juvenile Reentry and Aftercare Interventions: Is Mentoring a Promising Direction?" *Journal of Evidence-Based Social Work*, 11(4) 404–422.

124. P. Edwards, C. Jarrett, C. Perkins, D. Beecher, R. Steinbach, and I. Roberts. 2015. *Mediation, Mentoring and Peer Support to Reduce Youth Violence: A Systematic Review*. London, UK: London School of Hygiene & Tropical Medicine. http://whatworks.college.police.uk/About/News/Pages/Mentoring.aspx.

125. Martinez and Abrams, "Informal Social Support among Returning Young Offenders."

126. E.A. Panuccio, J. Christian, D.J. Martinez, and M.L. Sullivan. 2012. "Social Support, Motivation, and the Process of Juvenile Re-Entry: An Exploratory Analysis of Desistance," *Journal of Offender Rehabilitation*, 51(3), 135–160.

© Laurie Justus Pace. Graphics One Design, 2014

RECONSIDERING CRIMINAL JUSTICE

© Laurie Justus Pace. Graphics One Design, 2014

RECONSIDERING CRIMINAL JUSTICE

Chapter 14: Going Forward: Challenges to and Opportunities for Criminal Justice Reform

At the outset of the text, it was noted that the criminal justice system is an integral, high-profile component of Canadian society. It is also very dynamic, and often controversial in its operation. The preceding chapters have explored the various facets of the justice system, including the criminal law, police, courts, and systems of corrections. In addition, materials were presented on the victims of crime, offenders, criminal justice system personnel, and communities, all of whom are stakeholders in the justice system and are impacted by legislation, policies, and other factors that affect its day-to-day operation.

The final chapter of the text sets out several of the more significant challenges that confront the Canadian criminal justice system in the 21st century. It also considers the opportunities that exist to address these challenges. Addressing the challenges and taking opportunities will strengthen the foundations of criminal justice, increase the effectiveness of the responses to criminal offenders, and provide protection for crime victims and communities.

© Laurie Justus Pace, Graphics One Design, 2014

CHAPTER 14
GOING FORWARD:
CHALLENGES TO AND OPPORTUNITIES FOR CRIMINAL JUSTICE REFORM

After reading this chapter, you should be able to

- Identify and discuss some of the challenges that confront the criminal justice system, including the obstacles to change.
- Identify and discuss some of the opportunities that exist to improve the criminal justice system.
- Provide examples of questions that should be asked by informed observers of the criminal justice system.

CHALLENGES FOR THE CRIMINAL JUSTICE SYSTEM

DEVELOPING AND IMPLEMENTING EVIDENCE-BASED LEGISLATION, POLICIES, AND PROGRAMS

> It is apparent ... that empirical evidence does not always inform criminal justice policy.[1]

There is often a disconnect between criminal justice policy and practice and scholarly research. An ongoing challenge in the criminal justice system is ensuring that policies and practice are evidence-based—that is, informed by the findings of evaluation research. This also includes cost-benefit analyses that examine whether the investment of resources produces effective outcomes and improves the efficiency of the justice system.[2]

Unfortunately, these evidence-based practices are often not currently in use. The policies and programs of criminal justice agencies and the decision-making of justice system personnel are rarely evaluated. Most initiatives do not include an evaluation component, and in those relatively few instances in which programs are evaluated, the impact on operational practice may be minimal. It has been argued that the criminal justice system can learn from the business sector that research is strongly related to innovative practices.[3]

The challenges to developing evidence-based practices in the criminal justice system are numerous and include the resistance of policy-makers to new strategies, concerns among politicians that research findings may compromise political agendas, concerns about the costs of new initiatives, and a general fear of the unknown. Even policies and programs whose effectiveness is suspect may be preferable purely because they are known. Changing the status quo may have a significant impact on agencies and their personnel as new priorities and performance measures are established and policies and programs become evidence-driven.[4]

The criminal justice system has been slow to adopt evidence-based strategies and to discard policies and programs that are not effective. The challenge, for Canadians, their governments, and their criminal justice agencies, is to undertake the fundamental structural changes that are required so that the next 50 years of criminal justice do not produce the same outcomes as the present, and so that criminal justice policy and practice do not continue to reel from crisis to crisis.

There are additional challenges in promoting evidence-based practices in the criminal justice system, including the wide discretion exercised by criminal justice professionals and the diverse environments in which they carry out their tasks.[5,6] Attempts to implement evidence-based practices in the criminal justice system have been uneven but are more prevalent in policing and in federal corrections.

A complicating factor is that, generally speaking, research findings do not inform the decisions of governments or criminal justice agencies. A case in point is the crime-control, punitive approach toward crime and offenders taken by the federal Conservative government during the years 2006–2015. Not only were the specific legislation and policies of the government not informed by research, in some instances, such as the expansion of mandatory minimum sentences and the de-funding of Circles of Support and Accountability (COSA) programs, the legislation and policies ran counter to the research evidence. See At Issue 14.1.

PROACTIVE PROBLEM-SOLVING VERSUS REACTIVE SANCTIONING

It is generally agreed that criminal justice agencies and professionals alone cannot prevent and reduce crime, address the needs of crime victims, and ensure effective interventions for offenders. As currently structured, the justice system has a very difficult time providing safety and security for community residents and providing assistance to those persons who are at-risk of committing or recommitting criminal offences.

The levels of crime generally fluctuate independently of the efforts of the criminal justice system, and it is difficult to determine whether an increase in the rates of crime is due to ineffectiveness of the justice system or, conversely, whether a decrease in crime rates is due to effective criminal justice practice.

Of particular concern is the limited ability of the criminal justice system to solve problems rather than simply react to them. Generally, the criminal justice system defines problems according to the law rather than on the basis of how they are experienced by people. This tendency is reflected in the comments of a jury member following a trial in which the accused had been charged with unlawful possession of a firearm and discharging a firearm in a public place:

> At the end of the case, although we found him guilty, we felt we were no nearer to understanding why the man did what he did. He might have been mentally deranged, a drug dealer, an upset father, or high on drugs. We will never know because the case gave us less than 10% of the information that we needed to make a sensible judgment.[7]

Problem-solving courts and various restorative justice approaches offer the potential to address more than criminal behaviour, which may be only a symptom of much deeper issues.

MANAGING TECHNOLOGY

Criminal justice agencies are making increasing use of technology, not only for gathering and managing information but also for control and surveillance. This is often done in the absence of any guidelines or oversight. The introduction of police drones in the absence of any use guidelines (other than those of the aviation authorities) indicates that legislation and policy have not kept pace with the rapid technological changes that are occurring, and this gap may have significant implications for the rights of offenders and citizens.

The challenge is to ensure that the criminal justice system does not come to overly on technology and assume that these types of strategies, in themselves, will ensure public safety. There is also the danger that the increasing use of technology will come at the expense of developing human and helping relationships that have been demonstrated to be a core component of successful criminal justice interventions.

Restorative justice approaches provide the framework for these types of relationships, while the use of technology for surveillance, such as GPS tracking devices, is impersonal and anonymous. It is likely that there will be increasing pressures on governments to employ technology, particularly in monitoring offenders. As this occurs, determining the limits of technology will become even more important.

ADHERING TO THE RULE OF LAW AND RESPECTING THE RIGHTS OF THE ACCUSED AND OFFENDERS

In Chapter 1, the rule of law was identified as a major component of the foundation of criminal justice. To recap, the key principles of the rule of law are that the government and its officials and agents, as well as individuals and private entities, are accountable under the law; laws are clear, publicized, stable, and just; laws are applied evenly and protect fundamental rights, including the security of persons and property; and the process by which the laws are enacted, administered, and enforced is accessible, fair, and efficient.

A continuing challenge for the criminal justice system is to ensure that enforcement of the law and the responses to law-breaking adhere to the rule of law, and that the rights of accused and convicted persons are protected. These goals are crucial to ensuring the legitimacy of the justice system and are fundamental requirements in a democratic society. The materials in this text have revealed that the criminal justice system has often come up short. A common thread in many inquiries is that criminal justice personnel, be they police, judges, or corrections personnel, did not abide by the rule of law.

CONSIDERING ETHICS IN CRIMINAL JUSTICE

Ethics remains an understudied area of Canadian criminal justice, and ethics training for criminal justice professionals is sparse. Yet it is likely that ethical issues will assume even greater importance in the coming years.

Ethical questions abound at all stages of the criminal justice system. Some examples follow.

IN POLICING

- What are the ethics of using deception to secure a confession from a criminal suspect?
- What role do the ethics of individual officers and of their police service play in biased policing?
- How are ethics related to the exercise of discretion by police officers?

IN THE COURTS

- How might ethics be undermined by the practice of plea bargaining?
- How do ethical considerations factor into determinations of punishment for convicted offenders?
- Can an adversarial justice system be an ethical system?

IN CORRECTIONS

- Should incarcerated persons be required to participate in treatment programs?
- Are correctional staff obligated to follow their own ethical code of conduct in making decisions about inmates, regardless of directives from management?
- Should inmate mothers be permitted to have their prison-born babies with them, regardless of whether this reduces the likelihood of their reoffending?

A challenge for the criminal justice system is to ensure that personnel receive ethics training not only at the outset of their careers but on an ongoing basis.

ENSURING ACCOUNTABILITY IN THE CRIMINAL JUSTICE SYSTEM

A recurring theme throughout the text has been the importance of accountability in the criminal justice system. Throughout the book, the discussion has highlighted the various accountability issues that exist at each stage of the criminal justice process and the presence (or not) of structures of oversight.

When criminal justice decision-makers are accountable, it increases the legitimacy of their actions, raises public confidence, and can result in professional commitment to evidence-based policies and practice. Accountability also ensures that accused persons and offenders are accorded their rights, and reduces the likelihood of arbitrary and abusive behaviour toward them. A survey of Canadians (N = 4,200) found that nine of ten persons queried felt that the operation and performance of the criminal justice system should be reviewed on a regular basis.[8]

When accused persons and offenders are abused or dealt with in an arbitrary fashion, or, in extreme cases, wrongfully convicted, it undermines the legitimacy of the entire criminal justice process, reduces public confidence in the justice system, and hinders the effectiveness of the system.

A major challenge is that the majority of civil suits that are brought against the criminal justice system are settled out of court, with no fixing of responsibility or documentation that might provide insights into how such incidents might be avoided in the future.

Although there are a variety of structures of oversight for criminal justice agencies, the findings and recommendations of their investigations are not binding. The federal Office of the Correctional Investigator, for example, has identified numerous problems in the federal corrections system that remain unaddressed. Similarly, provincial and territorial ombudsperson and auditors general may identify systemic issues, but there is no mechanism in place to require agencies to address the issues.

In some instances, auditors general have been denied access to the data required to conduct an audit. This occurred in Saskatchewan where the provincial government denied the provincial auditor access to young offender case management files. This prevented the auditor from conducting an investigation into how the provincial Ministry of Justice provided programs and services to young offenders.[9]

ENSURING THE HEALTH AND WELLNESS OF CRIMINAL JUSTICE PROFESSIONALS

It is only in recent years that attention is being given to the health and wellness of criminal justice personnel. As noted in the preceding chapters, research studies suggest that police officers and correctional officers, among others, may experience high levels of anxiety and stress, as well as post-traumatic stress disorder (PTSD) and its associated symptoms. However, governments and criminal justice agencies have been slow to develop programs and interventions to address mental health issues. The Office of the Auditor General of Canada found, for example, that despite the development of a mental health strategy for RCMP members, many officers did not have access to support services and no evaluation had been conducted of the effectiveness of the interventions that were offered.[10]

ADDRESSING THE NEEDS OF VICTIMS

The criminal justice system has made some progress in recognizing and addressing the needs of crime victims. The *Canadian Victims Bill of Rights* (S.C. 2015, c. 13, s. 2) and provincial and territorial victims' rights legislation are designed to ensure that victims have access to information and services. Despite this, the case of Judge Robin Camp, discussed in Chapter 7, suggests that the "blaming the victim" mentality persists among some criminal justice professionals. General agreement exists that the marginalization and revictimization of crime victims must be addressed; a challenge is how to accomplish this while, at the same time, protecting the accused's right to due process.

A number of high-profile incidents, including inappropriate remarks by judges such as Judge Robin Camp suggests that there is much more work that needs to be done to educate criminal justice professionals in this area. There are increasing calls for mandatory training in victims' rights for all police officers, judges, and Crown prosecutors.[11]

INDIGENOUS PERSONS AND THE CRIMINAL JUSTICE SYSTEM: TIME FOR A RESET?

Despite federal legislation, policy initiatives, and specific programs developed by criminal justice and non-profit agencies and organizations, the number of Indigenous youth and adult offenders in conflict with the law and confined in correctional institutions continues to increase.

In its report, the Truth and Reconciliation Commission (TRC) called upon the provincial, territorial, and federal governments to eliminate the overrepresentation of Indigenous offenders in custody over the next decade and to provide funding to implement and evaluate alternatives to imprisonment that adequately address the root causes of offending.[12] The TRC also called upon governments to reform justice and social services for offenders with fetal alcohol spectrum disorder (FASD), including a focus on providing "community, correctional, and parole resources to maximize the ability of people with FASD to live in the community."[13]

There was also a recommendation that the federal government support the expanded use of healing lodges and Indigenous programming in halfway houses and parole services. The extent to which the federal government will act on these and other recommendations of the TRC is uncertain.

The federal Office of the Correctional Investigator has recommended that Correctional Service Canada (CSC) appoint a deputy commissioner for Indigenous corrections to provide the type of leadership and accountability required to guide the above-noted federal correctional reform.[14]

In the absence of research evaluations, it is difficult to determine the potential for these initiatives to reduce the overrepresentation of Indigenous persons in the criminal justice system and the extent to which the underlying issues that are related to conflict with the law are successfully addressed.[15] There is strong public support for the increased use of community-based alternatives to reduce the numbers of Indigenous persons in the justice system, and this could assist in developing innovative programs.[16]

Research studies have found that Indigenous-centred justice initiatives can increase the involvement of the community and Elders, as well as provide a forum for the use of traditional cultural practices. However, concerns have been raised about the effectiveness of many of these initiatives.[17]

An evaluation of the federal Aboriginal Justice Strategy, which was created to address the high rates of victimization, crime, and incarceration among Indigenous persons found considerable variability in the cultural relevancy and capacity of specific initiatives across the country, a need for police and Crown counsel to be aware of community justice programs in their region, and the need for a more collaborative approach involving Indigenous communities and organizations and justice system personnel.[18] The evaluation also identified the need for greater participation in initiatives by Indigenous communities.

The evaluation also found that Indigenous offenders who participated in culturally relevant, community-based programs had lower levels of reoffending and assisted offenders in making significant changes in their lives.[19]

The findings of the Office of the Auditor General of Canada with respect to Indigenous offenders in federal corrections are illustrative of the problems that have plagued criminal justice initiatives. These included Indigenous inmates' lack of timely access to correctional programming, and that only 20 percent of Indigenous inmates were able to complete their program of treatment prior to being eligible for conditional release.[20] It was also found that CSC did not document how participation in Indigenous-focused treatment programming was related to success upon re-entry into the community.

Research studies have documented the importance of incorporating traditional Indigenous culture and spirituality into treatment interventions, and that programs be delivered by staff with cultural knowledge.[21] The Tupiq program, for example, a sex offender treatment program tailored to accommodate the cultural characteristics of Inuit people, has produced positive outcomes. This bilingual (Inuktitut and English) program uses a holistic approach to assist offenders in identifying and modifying their thought and behaviour patterns.[22]

An ongoing challenge is how to address the needs of Indigenous offenders in rural and northern communities, where there is often a lack of programs and services. There is the potential to make great use of the Internet for counselling and therapy. Research studies have found, for example, that Internet-assisted cognitive-behavioural therapy (ICBT) is effective in addressing a wide range of issues, including depression, anxiety, and stress.[23,24]

A survey (N = 2,001) of persons who did not self-identify as Indigenous found that there was increasing awareness among Canadians of the impact of colonization on Indigenous cultures and communities.[25] The respondents also expressed a strong interest in learning more about Indigenous cultures.[26]

ADDRESSING TRAUMA IN OFFENDERS

The materials presented in this text have revealed that many persons who become involved in the criminal justice system are suffering from trauma as a result of life experiences, including physical, sexual, and emotional abuse during their upbringing and in adulthood. Women offenders, in particular, evidence high rates of trauma.[27] Any efforts to address the underlying reasons why persons come into conflict with the law and to reduce reoffending must consider the role that trauma plays in their lives.[28]

Research studies have found that trauma-informed treatment programs can reduce trauma symptoms, assist in institutional adjustment, and reduce reoffending.[29] While all of the programming for federal women offenders is trauma-informed, the extent to which this approach is used in provincial and territorial institutions for women is unknown. It can be anticipated that women in these facilities suffer from many of the same issues as their federal women counterparts.

Many of the persons who come into conflict with the law have histories of trauma and abuse, which may be exacerbated by their experiences in the criminal justice system. Of particular concern are the experiences of Indigenous persons, Blacks, and other members of racialized groups. The high rates of suicide among inmates and offenders on conditional release suggest that the criminal justice system is not, at present, effectively addressing the needs of persons in its charge. It has been argued that restorative justice approaches offer greater potential for addressing the trauma experienced by offenders than the traditional adversarial system.[30]

REDUCING THE MARGINALITY OF OFFENDERS

Recall that a large number of persons who come into conflict with the law are marginalized with respect to their employment skills, education, and other capacities; may have addictions or mental illnesses; and may have few community supports.

Conflict with the law is often a symptom of much deeper social, economic, and community disorder.

One question is whether the traditional adversarial systems of criminal justice functions to reduce this marginality? The answer is, generally, no. While specific interventions may reduce *reoffending*, there is no conclusive evidence that the *marginality* of offenders (e.g., addiction, poverty, homelessness, mental illness), which may be closely related to their conflict with the law, are successfully addressed long term.

Criminal justice agencies rarely gather data that would allow a determination of the long-term impacts of interventions on persons who come into conflict with the law. There is concern that, for some persons, contact with the criminal justice system may exacerbate their marginality and the likelihood of reoffending.

Expecting that the criminal justice system alone can address these factors is unrealistic. The system can, however, partner with other agencies and organizations. There are numerous examples where collaborative initiatives involving justice professionals working with their counterparts in other agencies and organizations, along with the community, have had success.

ADMINISTERING CRIMINAL JUSTICE IN A DIVERSE SOCIETY

Diversity is a defining characteristic of Canada. A key provision of the *Charter of Rights and Freedoms* is section 15(1), which states, "Every individual is equal before and under the law and has the right to the equal protection and equal benefit of the law without discrimination…." Many of the examples presented throughout this text suggest that the criminal justice system struggles to meet the objectives of this provision.

Little attention has been given to how professionals in the criminal justice system manage when confronted by diversity. Few studies exist on the challenges experienced by Crown counsel, defence lawyers, and the judiciary in processing cases involving Blacks, members of other racialized groups, and persons who are LGBTQ. Nor do we know how effective probation officers and parole officers are in supervising persons who do not speak French or English as a first language.

The potential for Black and other racialized communities to become involved as active partners in creating community-based programs and services to address the needs of victims and offenders has remained unexplored. A recent report on racism and racial profiling noted that ethnic and racialized minorities are underrepresented in public institutions and that governments must take steps to increase the members of these groups in public administration.[31] However, a majority of respondents ($N = 1,000$) to a survey felt that racism could be addressed through education.[32]

Racism and discrimination are also features of Canadian society. The challenge for the criminal justice system is how to address these issues. Among the suggestions are acknowledging that racial profiling exists in the criminal justice system and improving awareness and training of justice system personnel. These efforts are enhanced when Indigenous and persons from racialized groups are consulted and involved in the process.[33]

THE NEED TO REIMAGINE CRIMINAL JUSTICE

A constant refrain from criminal justice agencies and policy-makers is that more resources are required to improve the effectiveness and efficiency of the criminal justice system. This argument has assumed a high profile in the wake of the Supreme Court of Canada (SCC) decision in *R. v. Jordan* (2016 SCC 27), which set strict time limits for the prosecution of summary and indictable offences. This exhortation is often framed in requests for more patrol officers, more prosecutors, and more corrections personnel.

There is no clear evidence, however, that merely adding more resources will improve outcomes for crime victims, offenders, and communities. Much more fundamental changes are required, referred to by scholars as "reimagining criminal justice."[34]

This would involve going "back to the drawing board" to devise more effective strategies for preventing crime and for responding to persons in conflict with the law.

OPPORTUNITIES FOR CRIMINAL JUSTICE REFORM

Where there are challenges, there are also opportunities, and this is no less so in the criminal justice system.

THE ESCALATING COSTS OF CRIMINAL JUSTICE

One of the key trends identified in Chapter 3 is the escalating cost of the criminal justice system. Effort to control costs provides an opportunity for reconsidering traditional policies and practices and to make substantive improvements in the criminal justice process.

Commenting on the then federal Conservative government's "tough on crime" approach, the legendary Canadian criminal defence lawyer, Edward Greenspan, stated, "I have no problem being tough on crime. But we should commit to being smart on crime."[35] The **smart on crime** approach includes a focus on evidence-based assessments of the efficiency and effectiveness of criminal justice policies.[36]

One component of this approach is addressing the issue of **over-criminalization**, which refers to "imposing penalties that have no relation to the gravity of the offence committed or the culpability of the wrong doer" and are therefore excessive and without justification.[37] Over-criminalization also involves the excessive use of the criminal law to address social problems.[38] The risk of over-criminalization is particularly high for persons with mental health and addiction issues as well as persons with FASD and intellectual disabilities.

Initiatives, such as the problem-solving courts and various restorative justice approaches, have emerged out of an effort to reduce the over-criminalization of persons, including those from vulnerable groups.

Reduced resources can also force criminal justice agencies to develop the capacity to monitor how the resources they do have are being used and to assess the impact of their policies and strategies. This change has occurred in many police services where attention is being given to the deployment of patrol and investigative resources.

Smart on crime

An alternative approach to criminal justice reform.

Over-criminalization

The imposition of penalties, often to address social problems, "that have no relation to the gravity of the offence committed" and are therefore excessive and without justification.

EXPANDING EFFECTIVE CRIMINAL JUSTICE INTERVENTIONS AND LEARNING FROM FAILURE

The materials presented in this text reveal that some criminal justice interventions do produce positive outcomes. Specific police strategies have been shown to reduce crime and increase public safety; the work of specialized courts shows promise; and correctional programs and interventions based on the principles of risk, need, and responsivity (RNR) can reduce reoffending. A key component of many successful initiatives is community engagement and the involvement of citizens in addressing crime and social disorder.

In addition to focusing on what works in criminal justice, one observer has called for the creation of a criminal justice clearinghouse that would gather and disseminate detailed information on circumstances in which errors were made in the administration of justice.[39] Criminal justice agencies and personnel would be encouraged to routinely report errors in practice to begin the process of compiling the *lessons learned*.

Some jurisdictions in the U.S. have adopted what has been called the "sentinel event" approach.[40] This provides a process of continuous improvement in the administration of justice, rather than a reactive approach that focuses only on assigning blame when the justice system errs, such as in the case of wrongful convictions. This approach would provide the criminal justice system with a mechanism to identify, and correct, systemic problems that result in conflict between the justice system and racialized groups, hinder the effectiveness of police strategies of crime prevention and crime control, and inhibit the efforts of systems of corrections to address the needs and risks of offenders.

While the research findings presented throughout the text suggest that many of the justice policy and programs are not effective, lack of receptivity continues to restrict innovative practices that may prove to be more effective and efficient. Many of the difficulties that afflict the justice system, such as lengthy delays in resolving cases in the criminal courts, are endemic and long-standing yet remain unaddressed.

DEVELOPING HUMAN AND HELPING RELATIONSHIPS

There are few opportunities in the adversarial system of criminal justice to develop the personal relationships that may assist offenders in addressing their issues and changing life course. The discussion of the problem-solving courts in Chapter 7 revealed that these forums provide an opportunity to develop human and helping relationships that produce positive outcomes. Offenders who appear in these courts ascribe a level of legitimacy to the judges, which assists in reducing the rates of reoffending. This result suggests that helping and human relationships can be equally, if not more, effective than "get tough" approaches to offenders.

In corrections, the success of Circles of Support and Accountability (COSAs), which target high-risk offenders, illustrates the potential for criminal justice professionals, working with community residents, to be involved in reducing reoffending among high-risk offenders. There is a vast, untapped reservoir in the community that, if mobilized and supported, can play a significant role in the criminal justice system.

GIVING VOICE TO AT-RISK AND VULNERABLE GROUPS

A key, and troublesome, feature of the adversarial system of criminal justice is that groups that are at-risk of becoming involved in the system, or who are in conflict with the law, are generally not provided with the opportunity to express their views and to share their perspectives. This is important for prevention efforts as well as during the criminal justice process, and is particularly important for at-risk groups.

Efforts are being made in some jurisdictions to address this shortcoming. In 2013, the Ontario Provincial Advocate for Children and Youth sponsored a forum that brought together 100 youth from 62 northern First Nations communities to share their experiences and to develop an action plan to address issues including the legacy of the residential schools, youth suicide, drugs and alcohol, and identity and culture, among others. The forum was attended by representatives from policing, social services, education, and a number of other provincial ministries.[41]

In 2017, the province of Ontario announced the Black Youth Action Plan, which is designed to provide support programs and services to Black youth and their families, deliver skills development programs to Black youths, and provide support for education.[42]

IMPROVING ASSISTANCE FOR VICTIMS OF CRIME

There is considerable potential to improve the experience of crime victims in the criminal justice system. Participants in a survey of victims of sexual violence in three Canadian cities, for example, offered a number of suggestions as to how the system could improve support for women survivors. These included the following:

- Provide more outreach to survivors (e.g., have an individual approach the survivor to offer help).
- Provide support and information to survivors from an individual who is knowledgeable about sexual violence, such as another survivor.
- Establish more survivor groups where survivors can support one another.
- Where the survivors are women, ensure that the professionals providing support to the survivors are women rather than men.
- Provide more Indigenous counsellors for youth and adults who are fluent in Indigenous languages.
- Allow survivors to work with the same professional throughout the entire criminal justice process to help reduce the number of times survivors have to tell their story to different professionals.[43]

STRENGTHENING RESTORATIVE JUSTICE

In 2016, the province of Nova Scotia became the first jurisdiction to have a province-wide restorative justice program for both youth and adults, and in 2017, the new provincial NDP government announced its intention to expand restorative justice programs in the province.

Despite great potential, the development of restorative justice initiatives across the country has been sporadic. At the same time as Nova Scotia was expanding restorative justice programs, the province of Manitoba defunded the Restorative Resolutions program, one of the longest-running (since 1993) and most successful restorative justice programs in Canada.[44] This coincided with the acknowledgement that provincial jails in Manitoba were overcrowded and a call from a former deputy attorney general for an overhaul of the provincial justice system.

Restorative justice programs seem particularly vulnerable to crime-control approaches to criminal justice, as illustrated by the decision of the federal Conservative government to de-fund Circles of Support and Accountability, despite evaluation research documenting their effectiveness. The funding has since been restored by the federal Liberal government.

There is considerable potential to expand the use of restorative justice approaches. A survey ($N = 1,863$) of Canadians found strong support (80 percent) for requiring the police, prosecutors, judges, and defence counsel to inform persons they come into contact with about restorative justice opportunities.[45] This includes both offenders and victims.

QUESTIONS TO BE ASKED ABOUT THE CRIMINAL JUSTICE SYSTEM

There is no shortage of media coverage of the criminal justice system, nor of pundits and politicians weighing in on the issue of the day. Unfortunately, most of the discussion on criminal justice policy and practice is not centred on core questions that need to be asked. Among those are the following:

- Are criminal justice policies and programs evidence-based and informed by best practices?
- What is the cost-effectiveness of criminal justice policies and practices?
- What are the costs of the "get tough" approach to criminals, including the fiscal costs of building more prison cells and the impact on the ability of offenders to successfully reintegrate back into the community?
- For any one stage of the criminal justice system, would a restorative justice approach be more appropriate or more effective?
- How do politics and ideology affect legislation, policies, and the response to criminal offenders?
- Since research has shown that COSAs are an effective strategy for reducing reoffending among high-risk offenders, why hasn't the program been more widely adopted across Canada?
- What are the conditions that facilitate, and hinder, the implementation and continuity of restorative justice approaches?
- Are the current structures of accountability for personnel in the criminal justice system sufficient to ensure that discretion is being properly exercised and that personnel are held accountable for their actions?
- For Indigenous offenders, why haven't initiatives such as the *Gladue* courts, Indigenous corrections programs, healing lodges, and Indigenous policing programs reduced the levels of Indigenous conflict with the law and the overrepresentation of Indigenous offenders in the criminal justice system?
- It has long been established that offenders returning to the community from prison have a greater chance of success if provided with adequate housing, employment, and social supports. Why are these still absent for most offenders released from confinement?
- To what extent can the religious and cultural practices of newcomers to Canada be accommodated by the law and the justice system?
- How can the needs of at-risk and marginalized youth be addressed to reduce their risk of involvement in the youth justice system?

The discussion in this text has been designed to give you the information required to look critically at the criminal justice system, to ask informed questions, and to pique your curiosity about exploring further this most dynamic dimension of Canadian society. The success of this text will be measured by the extent to which it assisted you, the reader, in achieving some or all of these objectives.

SUMMARY

This chapter has identified and discussed several of the challenges and opportunities faced by the Canadian criminal justice system. The challenges relate to the criminal justice system, victims of crime, offenders, and justice system personnel. The inability of the criminal justice system to problem-solve means that the risk and needs of many offenders remain unaddressed. So too do victims continue to be marginalized in the process. The health and wellness issues of criminal justice personnel have only recently begun to be addressed. As have issues related to racism and discrimination.

These challenges present opportunities to develop innovative approaches to criminal justice in a diverse society, to expand programs that have proven to be effective, and to learn from initiatives that have not produced the expected outcomes. This will require giving voice to at-risk and vulnerable groups, improving assistance to crime victims, emphasizing the development of helping and human relationships, and expanding restorative justice practices. Throughout this process, the fine balance must be maintained between the rights of accused persons and ensuring the safety and security of communities.

KEY POINTS REVIEW

1. The criminal justice system experiences numerous challenges in fulfilling its mandate to protect the community, meet the needs of crime victims, and respond effectively to criminal offenders.

2. The criminal justice system has been slow to adopt evidence-based strategies and to discard policies and programs that are not effective.

3. There are numerous obstacles to the adoption of evidence-based practices that would make the criminal justice system a problem-solving system.

4. The criminal justice system experiences difficulties in problem solving and does not effectively address the marginality of persons who come into conflict with the law.

5. Among the issues that need to be addressed in the criminal justice system are racism and discrimination, the marginality of offenders, and the needs of certain groups of offenders, including Indigenous persons and Blacks, and those of the victims of crime.

6. The diversity of Canadian society presents challenges for the criminal justice system.

7. Ethical issues and dilemmas are endemic to the criminal justice system and require more attention from criminal justice professionals and academic researchers.

8. There are many opportunities for reforming the criminal justice system, including expanding effective criminal justice interventions, learning from failures, developing helping and human relationships, giving voice to at-risk and vulnerable groups, and expanding efforts to assist the victims of crime.

9. There are many questions that an informed observer of the criminal justice system can ask about issues that appear to be systemic and that have, until today, resisted reforms.

KEY TERM QUESTION

1. What is meant by **smart on crime** and **over-criminalization**, and how are these notions related to discussion of criminal justice reforms?

CRITICAL THINKING EXERCISE

Critical Thinking Exercise 14.1

Questions to Be Asked about the Criminal Justice System

In addition to the questions posed at the end of this chapter, can you think of other questions that should be asked?

CLASS/GROUP DISCUSSION EXERCISE

Class/Group Discussion Exercise 14.1

Improving the Criminal Justice System: The Views of Ex-offenders

There is value in hearing the voices of ex-offenders in the discussion of how to improve the criminal justice system to be more effective in preventing and reducing crime. Watch the film "The Road from Crime" at https://www.youtube.com/watch?v=Uzzm9B8n-FA.

Your Thoughts?

1. What lessons can be learned from the film?
2. What role in crime is played by:
   a. The individual
   b. The circumstances in which the individual grew up
3. What does the film suggest about the potential role of the justice system in addressing criminal behaviour?

MEDIA LINK

"Crime and Crime Policy," M.J. Milloy and Erin Gibbs Van Brunschot, December 13, 2013, https://www.youtube.com/watch?v=_hcQqZlUjZQ

REFERENCES

1. J. Vess, A. Day, M. Powell, and J.G. Raffam. 2013. "International Sex Offender Registration Law: Research and Evaluation Issues Based on a Review of Current Scientific Literature," *Police Practice and Research*, 14(3), 205–218.

2. J. Roman. 2013, September. "Cost-Benefit Analysis of Criminal Justice Reforms," *NIJ Journal*, 272, 31–38. https://www.ncjrs.gov/pdffiles1/nij/241929.pdf

3. A. Fox and G. Berman. 2013, July 1. "What Lessons Can Business Teach Criminal Justice? Invest in Research," *Huffington Post* [Blog post]. http://www.huffingtonpost.com/aubrey-fox/what-lessons-can-business_b_3530295.html.

4. M. DeMichele and B. Payne. 2009. *Offender Supervision with Electronic Technology: Community Corrections Resource* (2nd ed.). Washington, DC: U.S. Department of Justice. https://www.appa-net.org/eweb/docs/APPA/pubs/OSET_2.pdf.

5. D.P. Mears. 2007. "Toward Rational and Evidence-Based Crime Policy," *Journal of Criminal Justice*, 35(6), 667–682.

6. D.P. Mears and J.C. Barnes. 2010. "Toward a Systematic Foundation for Identifying Evidence-Based Criminal Justice Sanctions and Their Relative Effectiveness," *Journal of Criminal Justice*, 38(4), 702–710.

7. C.G. Nicholl. 1999. *Community Policing, Community Justice, and Restorative Justice: Exploring the Links for the Delivery of a Balanced Approach to Public Safety.* Washington, DC: Office of Community Oriented Policing

Services, Department of Justice, p. 48. https://ric-zai-inc
.com/Publications/cops-w0033-pub.pdf.

8. Ekos Research Associates. 2017. *National Justice Survey: Canada's Criminal Justice System*. Ottawa: Department of Justice, p. 24. http://epe.lac-bac.gc.ca/100/200/301/pwgsc-tpsgc/por-ef/justice_canada/2017/015-16-e/report.pdf.

9. Provincial Auditor Saskatchewan. 2013. "Chapter 18. Rehabilitation of Young Offenders," in *2013 Annual Report—Volume 1*. Regina: Author. https://auditor.sk.ca/pub/publications/public_reports/2013/Volume_1/2013v1_18_RehabilitationYoungOffenders.pdf.

10. Auditor General of Canada. 2017. "Mental Health Support for Members—Royal Canadian Mounted Police," in *Report 4—2017 Reports of the Auditor General of Canada*. Ottawa: Author. http://www.oag-bvg.gc.ca/internet/English/osh_20170531_e_42309.html.

11. B. Perrin. 2017. *Victim Law: The Law of Victims of Crime in Canada*. Toronto: Carswell.

12. Truth and Reconciliation Commission of Canada. 2015. *Truth and Reconciliation Commission of Canada: Calls to Action*. Winnipeg: Author. http://www.trc.ca/websites/trcinstitution/File/2015/Findings/Calls_to_Action_English2.pdf.

13. Ibid., p. 4.

14. Office of the Correctional Investigator. 2016. *Annual Report of the Office of the Correctional Investigator, 2015–2016*. Ottawa: Author. http://www.oci-bec.gc.ca/cnt/rpt/pdf/annrpt/annrpt20152016-eng.pdf.

15. E. Marchetti and R. Downie. 2014. "Indigenous People and Sentencing Courts in Australia, New Zealand, and Canada," in *Ethnicity, Crime, and Immigration*, edited by S.M. Bucerius and M. Tonry, 360–385. New York: Oxford University Press.

16. Ekos Research Associates, *National Justice Survey: Canada's Criminal Justice System*, p. 55.

17. Marchetti and Downie, "Indigenous People and Sentencing Courts in Australia, New Zealand, and Canada," p. 361.

18. Department of Justice Canada. 2016. *Evaluation of the Aboriginal Justice Strategy*. Ottawa: Author. http://www.justice.gc.ca/eng/rp-pr/cp-pm/eval/rep-rap/2016/ajs-sja/ajs-sja.pdf.

19. Ibid.

20. Auditor General of Canada. 2016. *Report 3—Preparing Indigenous Offenders for Release—Correctional Service of Canada*. Ottawa: Author. http://www.oag-bvg.gc.ca/internet/English/parl_oag_201611_03_e_41832.html.

21. G. Luther, M. Mela, and V.J. Bae. 2013. *Literature Review on Therapeutic Justice and Problem Solving Courts*. Saskatoon: University of Saskatchewan. https://www.usask.ca/cfbsjs/documents/Lit%20Review%20MHC%20Saskatoon%20Academic%20Dec%202013.pdf.

22. Ibid.

23. G. Andrews, P. Cuijpers, M.G. Craske, P. McEvoy, and N. Titov. 2010. "Computer Therapy for the Anxiety and Depressive Disorders Is Effective, Acceptable and Practical Health Care: A Meta-Analysis," *PLoS One*, 5, e13196. https://doaj.org/article/863581772ed24b41ac588fd0c4596c9a.

24. R. Mall. 2017, June 12. "Groundbreaking Online Mental Health Therapy Wins National Competition," *Indo-Canadian Voice*. http://www.voiceonline.com/groundbreaking-national-competition.

25. Environics Institute for Survey Research. 2016. *Public Opinion about Aboriginal Issues in Canada 2016*. Toronto: Author. http://www.environicsinstitute.org/uploads/institute-projects/canadian%20public%20opinion%20on%20aboriginal%20peoples%202016%20-%20final%20report.pdf.

26. Ibid., p. 17.

27. K. Tam and D. Derkzen. 2014. *Exposure to Trauma among Women Offenders: A Review of the Literature*. Ottawa: Correctional Service of Canada. http://publications.gc.ca/collections/collection_2016/scc-csc/PS83-3-333-eng.pdf.

28. M.E. Pearce, A.H. Blair, M. Teegee, S.W. Pan, V. Thomas, H. Zhang, . . . P.M. Spittal. 2015. "The Cedar Project: Historical Trauma and Vulnerability to Sexual Assault among Young Aboriginal Women Who Use Illicit Drugs in Two Canadian Cities," *Violence Against Women, 21*(3), 313–329.

29. Tam and Derkzen, *Exposure to Trauma Among Women Offenders*, p. iii.

30. J. Oudshoorn. 2015. *Trauma-Informed Youth Justice in Canada: A New Framework for a Kinder Future*. Toronto: Canadian Scholars.

31. Commission des droits de la personne et des droits de la jeunesse (Commission on Human Rights and Youth Rights). 2011. *Racial Profiling and Systemic Discrimination of Racialized Youth*. Quebec: Author, p. 16. http://www.cdpdj.qc.ca/publications/Profiling_final_EN.pdf.

32. *The Globe and Mail* and Nanos Research. 2016, May. "Views on Racism in Canada." http://www.nanosresearch.com/sites/default/files/POLNAT-S15-T682.pdf.

33. Ontario Human Rights Commission. 2017. *Under Suspicion: Research and Consultation Report on Racial Profiling in Ontario*. Toronto: Author. http://ohrc.on.ca/en/under-suspicion-research-and-consultation-report-racial-profiling-ontario/1-introduction.

34. C. Klingele, M.S. Scott, and W.J. Dickey. 2010. "Reimagining Criminal Justice," *Wisconsin Law Review, 4*, 953.

35. E. Greenspan. 2012, June. "Tough on Crime, Weak on Evidence," *UCObserver*. http://www.ucobserver.org/features/2012/06/crime.

36. R.A. Fairfax. 2011. "From 'Overcriminalization' to 'Smart on Crime': American Criminal Justice Reform—Legacy and Prospects," *Journal of Law, Economics & Policy*, 7(4), 597–598.

37. USLegal.com. 2014. "Overcriminalization." https://definitions.uslegal.com/o/over-criminalization.

38. E. Luna. 2005. "The Overcriminalization Phenomenon," *American University Law Review*, 54, 703–743. http://digitalcommons.wcl.american.edu/cgi/viewcontent.cgi?article=1707&context=aulr.

39. J.M. Doyle. 2010. "Learning from Error in American Criminal Justice," *Journal of Criminal Law and Criminology*, 100(1), 109–147.

40. Ibid.

41. Ontario Provincial Advocate for Children and Youth. 2013. *Feathers of Hope. A First Nations Youth Action Plan*. Toronto: Author. http://cwrp.ca/sites/default/files/publications/en/Feathers_of_Hope.pdf.

42. Province of Ontario. 2017. "Ontario's Black Youth Action Plan." Toronto: Ministry of Children and Youth Services. https://news.ontario.ca/mcys/en/2017/03/ontarios-black-youth-action-plan.html.

43. M. Lindsay, 2014. A Survey of Survivors of Sexual Violence in Three Canadian Cities, 2014, pp. 23–24. http://www.justice.gc.ca/eng/rp-pr/cj-jp/victim/rr13_19/rr13_19.pdf. Department of Justice Canada, 2014. Reproduced with the permission of the Department of Justice Canada, 2017.

44. K. Annable. 2017, May 30. "Pallister Government to Eliminate 'Ground-Breaking' Restorative Justice Program," *CBC News*. http://www.cbc.ca/news/canada/manitoba/restorative-resolutions-elimated-manitoba-1.4136961.

45. Ekos Research Associates, *National Justice Survey: Canada's Criminal Justice System*, p. 75.

Glossary

Adversarial system A system of justice that is based on two opposing sides—the prosecution and the defence—arguing the guilt or innocence of a person before a judge or jury. (p. 23)

Arbour Report The report of an inquiry into events at the Kingston Prison for Women in April 1994 which documented violations of policy, the rule of law, and institutional regulations, and had a significant impact on the development of women's corrections. (p. 330)

Arrest warrant A document that permits a police officer to arrest a specific person for a specified reason. (p. 121)

Auburn model (for prisons) A system that allowed prisoners to work and eat together during the day and housed in individual cells at night. (p. 315)

Basic qualifications (for police candidates) The minimum requirements for candidates applying for employment in policing. (p. 86)

Beyond a reasonable doubt The standard that must be met to convict a defendant in a criminal case, which requires that the facts presented provide the only logical explanation for the crime. (p. 24)

Bias-free policing The requirement that police officers make decisions on the basis of reasonable suspicion and probable grounds rather than based on stereotypes about race, religion, ethnicity, gender, or other prohibited grounds. (p. 107)

Broken windows approach The view that if minor crimes are left unaddressed in an environment, more serious crime will emerge. (p. 146)

Brown commission An investigation into the operation of the Kingston Penitentiary that condemned the use of corporal punishment against inmates and emphasized the need for rehabilitation. (p. 315)

Canadian Charter of Rights and Freedoms The primary law of the land; guarantees fundamental freedoms, legal rights, and quality rights for all citizens of Canada, including those accused of crimes. (p. 14)

Carceral (institutional) corrections That portion of systems of correction relating to correctional institutions (e.g., inmates, correctional officers, etc.). (p. 285)

Case law Law that is established by previous court decisions and is based upon the rule of precedent. (p. 11)

Case law precedent Law that is established by previous court decisions and based on the rule of precedent. (p. 266)

Case management The process by which the needs and abilities of offenders are matched with correctional programs and services. (p. 340)

Circle sentencing A restorative justice strategy that involves collaboration and consensual decision-making by community residents, the victim, the offender, and justice system personnel to resolve conflicts and sanction offenders. (p. 270)

Circles of Support and Accountability (COSAs) Community-based committees composed of criminal justice personnel and community members that provide mentoring for high-risk sex offenders whose sentences have expired. (p. 387)

Classification The process by which inmates are categorized through the use of various assessment instruments to determine the appropriate security level of the inmate and program placement. (p. 339)

Clearance rates The proportion of the actual incidents known to the police that result in the identification of a suspect, whether or not that suspect is ultimately charged and convicted. (p. 133)

Collateral consequences (of sentencing) The sanctions and prohibitions that are placed on persons convicted of criminal offences (and their families), particularly those offenders who have been incarcerated. (p. 264)

Common law Law that is based on custom, tradition, and practice and is generally unwritten. (p. 10)

Community assessment An evaluation of the feasibility of the release plan, the level of supervision required, and the availability of community resources. (p. 363)

Community notification The practice, usually carried out by police agencies, of making a public announcement that a high-risk offender has taken up residence in an area. (p. 381)

Community policing A philosophy of policing centred on police–community partnerships and problem-solving. (p. 135)

Community-based strategic policing A model of police work that incorporates the key principles of community policing with crime prevention, crime response, and crime attack approaches. (p. 136)

Compstat A strategy designed to increase the effectiveness and efficiency of police services while holding police personnel accountable for achieving crime reduction objectives. (p. 137)

Concurrent sentences Sentences that are amalgamated and served simultaneously. (p. 251)

Conditional release A generic term for the various means of leaving a correctional institution before warrant expiry whereby an offender is subject to conditions that, if breached, could trigger revocation of the release and return to prison; parole is one type of conditional release. (p. 360)

Conditional sentence (of imprisonment) A sentence for offenders who receive a sentence or sentences totalling less than two years whereby the offender serves his or her time in the community under the supervision of a probation officer. (p. 262)

Conflict model The view that crime and punishment reflect the power some groups have to influence the formulation and application of criminal law. (p. 9)

Consecutive sentences Sentences that run separately and are completed one after the other. (p. 251)

Constitution Act, 1867 The legislation setting out the division of responsibilities between the federal and provincial governments. (p. 22)

Continuum of correctional institutions The differences in institutional environments among correctional institutions located at either end of the security spectrum—maximum to minimum. (p. 318)

Contract policing An arrangement whereby the RCMP and provincial police forces provide provincial and municipal policing services. (p. 81)

Core policing Often referred to as quality-of-life policing; involves the police playing a multifaceted role in the community, which includes collaborative partnerships with the community. (p. 76)

Correctional plan A key component of the case management process that determines the offender's initial institution placement, specific training or work opportunities, and preparation for release. (p. 340)

Corrections Structures, policies, and programs to sanction, punish, treat, and supervise in the community and in correctional institutions, persons convicted of criminal offences. (p. 285)

Courtroom workgroup The criminal justice professionals, including the judge, Crown counsel, and defence lawyer, who are present in the criminal court courtroom. (p. 181)

Crime An act or omission that is prohibited by criminal law. (p. 6)

Crime attack strategies Proactive operations by the police to target and apprehend criminal offenders. (p. 148)

Crime control (model of criminal justice) An orientation to criminal justice in which the protection of the community and the apprehension of offenders are paramount. (p. 23)

Crime displacement The relocation—due to effective crime prevention and crime response initiatives—of criminal activity from one locale to another. (p. 134)

Criminal Code Federal legislation that sets out criminal laws, procedures for prosecuting federal offences, and sentences and procedures for the administration of justice. (p. 15)

Criminal injury compensation Financial remuneration paid to crime victims. (p. 232)

Criminal justice system All of the agencies, organizations, and personnel that are involved in the prevention of, and response to, crime; persons charged with criminal offences; and persons convicted of crimes. (p. 22)

Criminal law That body of law that deals with conduct considered so harmful to society as a whole that it is prohibited by statute, prosecuted and punished by the government. (p. 11)

Critical thinking (thorough thinking) In examining an issue, distinguishing between fact and opinion, considering multiple points of view, and being open-minded to all ideas. (p. 5)

Dangerous offender A designation made by the judge after conviction that results in an indeterminate term of imprisonment in a federal correctional institution. (p. 254)

Day parole The authority granted by a parole board that provides an opportunity for inmates to be at large in order to prepare for full release (e.g., for job search) while returning at night to an institution or, more typically, to a community residential facility. (p. 361)

Detention during the period of statutory release A decision by the Parole Board of Canada (after an application by CSC) that a federal inmate be denied statutory release and be detained in the institution until warrant expiry date. (p. 362)

Discretion The power or right to decide or act according to one's own judgment. (p. 27)

Discrimination An action or a decision that treats a person or a group negatively for reasons such as their race, age, or disability. (p. 44)

Diversion Programs that are designed to keep offenders from being processed further into the formal criminal justice system. (p. 289)

Due process (model of criminal justice) An orientation to criminal justice in which the legal rights of individual citizens, including crime suspects, are paramount. (p. 23)

Duty to act fairly The obligation of correctional authorities to ensure that offenders are treated fairly by corrections personnel. (p. 318)

Dynamic risk factors Attributes of the offender that can be altered through intervention, including level of education, employment skills, addiction issues, and cognitive thinking abilities, among others. (p. 340)

Dynamic security A variety of ongoing, meaningful interactions between staff and inmates. (p. 317)

Electronic monitoring A correctional strategy that involves placing an offender under house arrest and then using electronic equipment to ensure that the conditions of supervision are fulfilled. (p. 304)

Ethics The foundation of knowledge that describes right/wrong or better/worse and applies to harm/care and fairness/reciprocity. (p. 28)

Evidence-based practices Policies, strategies, and programs that have been shown by research to be effective in achieving specified objectives. (p. 34)

Extrajudicial measures (EJM; in youth justice) Provide for the police and Crown counsel to divert youth who admit responsibility for less serious offences from the formal youth court system at the pre-charge or post-charge stage. Often involves referral to a community diversion program. (p. 409)

Extrajudicial sanctions (EJS; in youth justice) A more formal type of EJM that can be applied outside of the formal court process for youths involved in more serious offences and can include requiring the youth to attend counselling, make restitution to the victim, apologize to the victim, do community service, or participate in a restorative justice program such as victim–offender mediation or a healing circle, among others. (p. 409)

Full parole   The authority granted by a parole board for an inmate to be at large under supervision in the community for the remainder of his or her sentence. (p. 361)

Gladue **decision**   A decision by the SCC which held that in cases where a term of incarceration would normally be imposed, judges must consider the unique circumstances of Indigenous people. (p. 259)

Gladue report   A report prepared prior to sentencing of Indigenous offenders which sets out historical events and that may be related to the offender's conflict with the law and criminal behaviour. (p. 258)

Hybrid (or elective) offences   Offences that can be proceeded summarily or by indictment—a decision that is always made by the Crown. (p. 202)

Indictable offence   Generally, a more serious criminal offence that may carry maximum prison sentences of 14 years to life; examples include murder, robbery, and aggravated sexual assault. (p. 202)

Information   A written statement sworn by an informant, normally a police officer, alleging that a person has committed a specific criminal offence. (p. 121)

Inmate code   A set of behavioural rules that govern interactions among inmates and with institutional staff. (p. 336)

Inmate subculture   The patterns of interaction and the relationships that exist among inmates confined in correctional institutions. (p. 336)

Institutionalized   Inmates who have become prisonized to such a degree that they are unable to function in the outside, free community. (p. 336)

Integrated case management (ICM) conferences   The primary strategy used for case management of young offenders on probation. (p. 416)

Intelligence-led policing   Policing that is guided by the collection and analysis of information that is used to inform police decision-making at both the tactical and strategic levels. (p. 137)

Intensive probation supervision (ISP)   An intermediate sanction (between the minimal supervision of traditional probation and incarceration) that generally includes reduced caseloads for probation officers, increased surveillance, treatment interventions, and efforts to ensure that probationers are employed. (p. 300)

Intermittent sentence   A sentence that is served on a part-time basis, generally on weekends. (p. 251)

Judicial determination   An order by the sentencing judge that the offender serve one-half of their sentence before being eligible to apply for parole. (p. 252)

Judicial independence   The notion that judges are not subject to pressure and influence and are free to make impartial decisions based solely on fact and law. (p. 187)

Judicial interim release (bail)   The release of a person charged with a criminal offence prior to trial. (p. 207)

Juvenile Delinquents Act **(JDA; 1908)**   Legislation centred on a social welfare approach to youth crime that gave judges considerable discretion to intervene in the lives of young offenders. (p. 404)

Long-term offender   A designation under section 752 or 753 of the *Criminal Code* that requires the offender to spend up to 10 years under supervision following the expiry of his or her sentence. (p. 256)

Maximum-security institutions   Federal correctional institutions with a highly controlled institutional environment. (p. 317)

Medium-security institutions   Federal correctional facilities that have a less highly controlled institutional environment than maximum-security institutions and in which the inmates have more freedom of movement. (p. 317)

Minimum-security institutions   Federal correctional facilities that generally have no perimeter fencing and allow unrestricted inmate movement except at night. (p. 317)

Moral architecture   The term used to describe the design of the first penitentiary in Canada, the intent of which was to reflect themes of order and morality. (p. 315)

Moral entrepreneurs   Individuals, groups, or organizations who seek action against certain groups of people or certain behaviours and bring pressure on legislators to enact criminal statutes. (p. 8)

Mr. Big technique   An investigative strategy designed to secure confessions from crime suspects through the creation of an elaborate scenario. (p. 117)

Need principle   To be effective, correctional interventions must address the criminogenic needs of offenders. (p. 298)

Net-widening   A potential, unanticipated consequence of diversion programs in which persons who would otherwise have been released outright by the police or not charged by Crown counsel are involved in the justice system. (p. 291)

Non-carceral corrections   That portion of systems of correction relating to offenders in non-institutional settings (e.g., parole officers, halfway houses, etc.). (p. 285)

Not criminally responsible on account of mental disorder   A defence that relieves the accused person of criminal responsibility due to a mental disorder. (p. 223)

Occupational stress injuries   Physical and/or mental conditions in police officers caused by their organizational and operational experiences on the job. (p. 91)

One-chance statutory release   A release option whereby offenders who violate the conditions of a statutory release are required to serve the remainder of their sentence in confinement. (p. 363)

Open court principle   The principle that, with certain exceptions, every stage of the court process must be open and accessible to the public. (p. 216)

Operational field training   Instructing the recruit how to apply principles from the training academy in the community. (p. 89)

Optional conditions   Conditions attached to offenders who are supervised in the community that are tailored to their specific risk and needs. (p. 292)

Over-criminalization   The imposition of penalties, often to address social problems, "that have no relation to the gravity of the offence committed" and are therefore excessive and without justification. (p. 446)

Over-policing   A disproportionate police focus on a racialized population or neighbourhood. (p. 107)

Pains of imprisonment   The deprivations experienced by inmates confined in correctional institutions, including the loss of autonomy, privacy, security, and freedom of movement and association. (p. 335)

Pains of probation   The emotional and economic challenges that probationers may experience while under probation supervision in the community. (p. 300)

Pains of re-entry   The difficulties that inmates released from prison encounter as they try to adjust to life in the community. (p. 375)

Pennsylvania model (for prisons) A separate and silent system in which prisoners were completely isolated from one another, eating, working, and sleeping in separate cells. (p. 314)

Plea bargaining An agreement whereby an accused pleads guilty in exchange for the promise of a benefit. (p. 215)

Pluralization of policing The expansion of policing beyond the public police to include parapolice and private security. (p. 70)

Police acts The legislative framework for police service. (p. 74)

Police boards and police commissions Bodies that provide oversight of police. (p. 74)

Policing The activities of any individual or organization acting legally on behalf of public or private organizations or persons to maintain security or social order. (p. 69)

Policing standards Provisions that set out how police services are to be maintained and delivered. (p. 74)

Political policing Secretive police investigative activities and surveillance of persons and groups deemed to be a threat to the stability and status quo of the State. (p. 71)

Post-incarceration syndrome (PICS) A condition of offenders in custody and in the community that is caused by prolonged exposure to the dynamics of life inside correctional institutions. (p. 378)

Post-traumatic stress disorder (PTSD) An extreme form of critical incident stress that includes nightmares, hypervigilance, intrusive thoughts, and other forms of psychological distress. (p. 91)

Precedent A judicial decision that may be used as a standard in subsequent similar cases. (p. 11)

Predictive policing The use of statistical analysis to identify the time and location where criminal activity is likely to occur. (p. 137)

Preferred qualifications (for police candidates) Requirements that increase the competitiveness of applicants seeking employment in policing. (p. 86)

Prejudice The unsubstantiated, negative pre-judgment of individuals or groups, generally on the basis of ethnicity, religion, or race. (p. 44)

Preliminary hearing A hearing to determine if there is sufficient evidence to warrant a criminal trial. (p. 202)

Pretext policing Police stops or searches for a minor reason that are used for more intrusive intervention. (p. 107)

Primary crime prevention programs Programs that identify opportunities for criminal offences and alter those conditions to reduce the likelihood that a crime will be committed. (p. 142)

Principle of accountability The actions of police officers and police services are subject to review and there are formal channels that individuals can use to lodge complaints against the police. (p. 104)

Principle of restraint (in sentencing) Ensures that the sentence that is imposed is a just and appropriate punishment, and nothing more. (p. 247)

Prisonization The process by which inmates become socialized into the norms, values, and culture of the prison. (p. 336)

Probation A sentence imposed on an offender by a criminal court judge that provides for the supervision of the offender in the community by a probation officer, either as an alternative to custody or in conjunction with a period of incarceration in a provincial or territorial correctional institution. (p. 251)

Problem-oriented policing (POP) A tactical strategy based on the idea that the police should address the causes of recurrent crime and disorder. (p. 147)

Problem-solving courts Specialized courts that are designed to divert offenders with special needs from the criminal justice system. (p. 171)

Procedural law The legal processes that protect and enforce the rights set out in substantive law. (p. 10)

Professional model of policing A model of police work that is reactive, incident-driven, and centred on random patrol. (p. 135)

Proportionality (in sentencing) The sentence must be proportionate to the gravity of the offence and to the degree of responsibility of the offender. (p. 247)

Quality-of-life policing Police efforts to improve conditions in an area by targeting disruptive and annoying behaviour. (p. 147)

Racial profiling Any action undertaken for reasons of safety, security or public protection that relies on stereotypes about race, colour, ethnicity, ancestry, religion, or place of origin rather than on reasonable suspicion, to single out an individual for greater scrutiny or different treatment. (p. 45)

Racialization The process by which societies construct races as real, different, and unequal in ways that matter to economic, political and social life. (p. 45)

Racialized persons Persons, other than Indigenous people, who are non-Caucasian in race or non-white in colour. (p. 45)

Racism Prejudice, discrimination, or antagonism directed against someone of a different race based on the belief that one's race is superior. (p. 44)

Radical perspective (of the role of the police) A perspective that views the police as an instrument used by governments and powerful interests to suppress dissent, stifle protest, and help maintain the status quo. (p. 70)

Recidivism rates The number of offenders released from confinement who, once released from prison, are returned to prison. (p. 345)

Recipes for action The actions typically taken by patrol officers in various kinds of encounter situations. (p. 106)

Reintegration The process whereby an inmate is prepared for and released into the community after serving time in prison. (p. 373)

Release plan A plan setting out the residential, educational, and treatment arrangements made for an inmate who is applying for conditional release. (p. 363)

Remand The status of accused persons in custody awaiting trial or sentencing. (p. 210)

Remission/discharge Available to provincial inmates who have served two-thirds of their sentence. (p. 362)

Responsivity principle Correctional interventions should be matched to the learning styles of individual offenders, with particular emphasis on cognitive-behavioural interventions. (p. 298)

Restitution A court-ordered payment that the offender makes to the victim to compensate for loss of or damage to property. (p. 332)

Restorative justice A problem-solving approach to responding to offenders based on the principle that criminal behavior injures victims, communities, and offenders, and that all of these parties should be involved in efforts to address the causes of the behaviour and its consequences. (p. 34)

Re-victimization The negative impact on victims of crime caused by the decisions and actions of criminal justice personnel. (p. 56)

Revocation of conditional release A decision by a releasing authority, such as a parole board, made in connection with an offender whose release has been suspended. (p. 386)

Risk principle Correctional interventions are most effective when matched with the offender's level of risk, and higher-risk offenders benefit from interventions more than medium- and low-risk offenders. (p. 298)

Royal Canadian Mounted Police Act Federal legislation that provides the framework for the operation of the RCMP. (p. 81)

Rule of law The requirement that governments, as well as individuals, be subjected to and abide by the law. (p. 12)

Search warrant A document that permits the police to search a specific location and take items that might be evidence of a crime. (p. 120)

Secondary crime prevention programs Programs that focus on areas that produce crime and disorder. (p. 143)

Security certificates A process whereby non-Canadian citizens who are deemed to be a threat to the security of the country can be held without charge for an indefinite period of time. (p. 211)

Segregation A correctional management strategy that is used for disciplinary or administrative reasons and often involves an inmate being locked in a cell for 23 hours a day; also referred to as *solitary confinement*. (p. 327)

Self-injurious behaviour (SIB) Deliberate self-inflicted bodily harm or disfigurement. (p. 336)

Sentencing disparity Different sentences being meted out for similar offences committed by similar offenders in similar circumstances. (p. 264)

Smart on crime An alternative approach to criminal justice reform. (p. 446)

Social (or argot) roles Roles that inmates assume based on their friendship networks, sentence length, and other factors related to their criminal history and activities in the institution. (p. 337)

Social construction of crime The notion that the legal status of behaviours is not determined by the behaviour itself, but is the result of the social response to the behaviour. (p. 8)

Social contract perspective (on the role of the police) A perspective that considers the police to be a politically neutral force that acts primarily to enforce the law and protect the public. (p. 70)

Stare decisis The principle by which the higher courts set precedents that the lower courts must follow. (p. 11)

State-raised offenders Inmates who have spent the majority of their adult (and perhaps young adult) lives confined in correctional institutions and, as a consequence, may have neither the skills nor ability to function in the outside, free community. (p. 336)

Static risk factors Attributes of the offender that predict the likelihood of recidivism but are not amenable to change, including criminal history, prior convictions, seriousness of prior offences, and performance on previous conditional releases. (p. 340)

Static security Fixed security apparatus in correctional institutions, including fixed security posts wherein correctional officers are assigned to and remain in specific areas, such as a control room or perimeter patrol. (p. 317)

Status degradation ceremonies The processing of offenders into correctional institutions whereby the offender is psychologically and materially stripped of possessions that identify him or her as a member of the "free society." (p. 334)

Statute law Written laws that have been enacted by a legislative body such as the Parliament of Canada. (p. 11)

Statutory release A type of conditional release (made by the CSC and not the PBC) that allows incarcerated federal offenders to be released at the two-thirds point in their sentence and to serve the remaining one-third of their sentence under supervision in the community. (p. 361)

Stay of proceedings An act by the Crown to terminate or suspend court proceedings after they have commenced. (p. 219)

Substantive law Law that sets out the rights and obligations of each person in society; includes the *Criminal Code*. (p. 10)

Summary conviction offence Generally, a less serious criminal offence that is triable before a magistrate or judge and, on conviction, carries a maximum penalty of a fine (not to exceed $5,000) or six months in a provincial correctional facility, or both. (p. 202)

Suspended sentence A sentencing option whereby the judge convicts the accused but technically gives no sentence and instead places the offender on probation, which, if successfully completed, results in no sentence being given. (p. 251)

Suspension of conditional release A process initiated by the supervising parole officer (or in some instances by the parole board) in cases whether the parolee has allegedly failed to abide by the conditions of release. (p. 386)

Task environment The cultural, geographic, and community setting in which the criminal justice system operates and justice personnel make decisions. (p. 28)

Temporary absence A type of conditional release that allows an inmate to participate in community activities, including employment and education, while residing in a minimum-security facility or halfway house. (p. 364)

Tertiary crime prevention programs Programs designed to prevent youth and adults from reoffending. (p. 143)

Therapeutic justice An approach in problem-solving courts that uses the law and the court's authority as change agents to promote the health and well-being of offenders, while ensuring that their legal rights are protected and that justice is done. (p. 171)

Throughcare The notion that there should be continuity between institutional treatment and programs and community-based services for offenders. (p. 343)

Total institutions Correctional institutions, psychiatric hospitals, and other facilities characterized by a highly structured environment in which all movements of the inmates or patients are controlled 24 hours a day by staff. (p. 318)

Typifications Constructs based on a patrol officer's experience that denote what is typical about people and events routinely encountered. (p. 106)

Value consensus model The view that what behaviours are defined as criminal and the punishment imposed on offenders reflect commonly held opinions and limits of tolerance. (p. 9)

Victim impact statement (VIS) Submission to a sentencing court explaining the emotional, physical, and financial impact of the crime. (p. 268)

Warrant expiry date The end of an offender's sentence. (p. 360)

Working personality of the police A set of attitudinal and behavioural attributes that develops as a consequence of the unique role and activities of police officers. (p. 90)

***Young Offenders Act* (YOA; 1984)** Youth legislation that attempted to balance the protection of young offenders' special needs and legal rights and freedoms with the protection of the public, while ensuring young offenders would be held accountable. (p. 404)

***Youth Criminal Justice Act* (YCJA; 2003–present)** The current legislative framework for the youth justice system that applies to young persons aged 12 to 17; one of its key principles is the use of extrajudicial measures for less serious offences to reduce the rates of incarceration of young offenders. (p. 405)

Youth justice committees Community-based committees that sponsor a variety of initiatives for youth in conflict with the law, including extrajudicial measures centred on restorative justice. (p. 410)

Youth justice conference A group of people who are asked by a decision-maker, such as a judge, to come together to give advice on the case of a young person who is involved in the youth criminal justice system. (p. 410)

Youth Level of Service/Case Management Inventory (YLS/CMI) The primary risk/need assessment instrument in youth corrections. (p. 421)

Zero-tolerance policing A crime response strategy centred on the premise that a strict order-maintenance approach by the police will reduce more serious criminal activity. (p. 147)

Index

Specific deterrence, 247

Spousal assault, 26, 50. *See also* Domestic violence

SPVM (Service de police de la Ville de Montréal), 81, 82

SQ (Sûreté du Québec), 81, 82, 83

Square johns, 337

Squealers, 337

SR (Statutory release), 361, 362, 365, 389

St. Leonard's Society, 22, 316, 384, 385

Stan Daniels Healing Centre, 316

Standard of proof, 15

Stare decisis, 11

Starlight tour, 111, 112, 154

Starlight Tour: The Last, Lonely Night of Neil Stonechild, 112

State-raised offenders, 336, 382–383

Static risk factors, 340

Static security, 317, 330–331

Status degradation ceremonies, 334–335

Status restoration ceremonies, 335

Statute law, 11

Statutory conditions of bail, 208

Statutory release (SR), 361, 362, 365, 389

Stay of proceedings, 219

Stelmach, Ed, 256

STICS (Strategic Training Initiative in Community Supervision), 299

Stingray device, 104

Stonechild, Neil, 112

Stop and frisk, 147

Stop Now and Plan (SNAP), 406, 425

Strategic Training Initiative in Community Supervision (STICS), 299

Street checks, 108–111

Structural violence, 52

Substantive law, 10

Suicide, 141, 326, 329, 376

Suicide by cop, 115

Summary conviction offence, 202, 266

Summary trial, 202

Summons, 205

Superior courts, 168, 169, 177–178, 202

Support services, 84

Supreme Court Act, 185

Supreme Court of Canada (SCC), 8, 179–181

    in Canadian legal system, 11

    in criminal court system, 168

    leave to appeal, 179

    police powers, 103–104

Sûreté du Québec (SQ), 81, 82, 83

Surety, 207

Surveillance devices, 104

Surveillance society, 55–56, 71, 143

Suspended sentence, 249, 251, 289

Suspension of conditional release, 386–387

Suzack, Clinton, 391–392

SYBL (Somali Youth Basketball League), 139

Sykes, Gresham, 335

TA (Temporary absence), 361, 364, 389

Tactical-directed patrol, 148, 149

Target hardening, 134

Targeted patrol. *See* Directed patrol

Tasers, 113, 114

Task environment, 28

Tataskweyak First Nation, 406

TAVIS (Toronto Anti-Violence Intervention Strategy), 148–149

Tax Court of Canada, 179

TB (Tuberculosis), 326

TB (Tuberculosis) sanitoriums, 48–50

Team policing, 139

Tear gas, 113

Technical violations of parole, 387

Technology, 440–441

Telewarrant Centre, 122

Temporary absence (TA), 361, 364, 389

Territorial government, 22–23

Territorial jurisdiction, 83

Terrorist activity, 71, 75

Terrorist attacks of September 11, 2001, 71, 75

Tertiary crime prevention programs, 143, 148

Teskey, Leo, 255–256

Therapeutic justice, 171

Thermal-imaging technology (marijuana grow-ops), 103

Thompson, John, 15

Thorough thinking. *See* Critical thinking

Three Ps, 135

Three Rs, 135

Throughcare, 343, 346, 374, 424

Thunder Bay Indian Friendship Centre, 175–176

Time in custody, 422

Todd, Amanda, 141

Toronto Anti-Violence Intervention Strategy (TAVIS), 148–149

Toronto Community Youth Court (CYC), 410

Toronto Gay Pride parade, 157

Toronto Intermittent Centre, 385

Toronto Police, 30

Toronto Police Service, 81, 115, 148

    alleged misconduct, 125

    carding, 108

    composition profile, 87, 88

    Gay pride parades, 157

    hate crimes, 156

    Hate Crimes Unit, 156

    health and wellness programs, 93

    persons with mental illness (PWMI), 151, 152

    racial profiling, 109–110

    recruiting initiatives, 87

    size of, 83

    TAVIS, 148

Toronto Police Service Youth Referral Program (TPS-YRP), 409

Toronto South Detention Centre, 385

Tort law, 10

Total institutions, 318

Tough on crime legislation, 32, 446

TPS-YRP (Toronto Police Service Youth Referral Program), 409

Training academies, 89

Training of police, 88–90

Transgender persons, 51, 338, 385

Trans Mountain Pipeline expansion, 77

TRC (Truth and Reconciliation Commission), 48, 173, 443

Treatment model (for prisons), 315

Treatment programs for youth, 420–421

Trial courts, 177–178

Trial by judge, 217–218

Trial by jury, 217–218. *See also* Prosecution of criminal cases

Trial within a reasonable time, 191, 228

Trials, 219

Trier of fact, 181, 217

Truth and Reconciliation Commission (TRC), 48, 173, 443

Truth in Sentencing Act, 272, 273

Tschetter, Daniel, 368

Tsuu T'ina Nation Peacemaker Court, 175

Tuberculosis (TB), 326

Tuberculosis (TB) sanitoriums, 48–50

Tunnel vision, 234

Tupiq program, 444

Turf policing, 139

Two-for-one credit for time served, 190, 272

Tyendinaga Police Service, 83

Typifications, 106, 107

UN Convention against Torture and Other Cruel, Inhuman or Degrading Treatment or Punishment, 328

UN Convention on the Rights of the Child, 404

Undercover police, 71, 123

Undertaking to appear, 121

"Unfounded" sexual assault, 153–154

United Nations Minimal Standards for Prisoners, 324

United States

    Anonymous, 141

    bail, 207

    bounty hunters, 207

    CCTVs (closed-circuit television cameras), 143

    collateral consequences, 264

    death penalty, 236

    diversion programs, 291

    electronic monitoring (EM), 306